Gender and the Book Trades

# Gender and the Book Trades

*Edited by*

Elise Watson
Jessica Farrell-Jobst

BRILL

LEIDEN | BOSTON

Cover illustration: Virgo Dordracena (Virgin of Dordrecht), printer's device of Hendrik van Esch, woodcut from the title page of Johan van Beverwijck, *Lof der medicine, ofte Genees-konste* [Dordrecht: Hendrik van Esch, 1641]. Image courtesy of the Ghent University Library, BIB.BL.006753/-1.

Library of Congress Cataloging-in-Publication Data

Names: Watson, Elise (Historian), editor. | Farrell-Jobst, Jessica, editor.
Title: Gender and the book trades / edited by Elise Watson, Jessica
    Farrell-Jobst.
Description: Leiden ; Boston : Brill, 2025. | Series: Library of the
    written word, 1874–4834 ; volume 128 | Includes index.
Identifiers: LCCN 2024040255 (print) | LCCN 2024040256 (ebook) | ISBN
    9789004701649 (hardback ; acid-free paper) | ISBN 9789004701656 (ebook)
Subjects: LCSH: Book industries and trade—History. | Book industries and
    trade—Case studies. | Women in the book industries and trade—History.
    | Women in the book industries and trade—Case studies. | LCGFT: Case
    studies. | Essays.
Classification: LCC Z280 .G46 2025 (print) | LCC Z280 (ebook) | DDC
    381/.45002081—dc23/eng/20240918
LC record available at https://lccn.loc.gov/2024040255
LC ebook record available at https://lccn.loc.gov/2024040256

Typeface for the Latin, Greek, and Cyrillic scripts: "Brill". See and download: brill.com/brill-typeface.

ISSN 1874-4834
ISBN 978-90-04-70164-9 (hardback)
ISBN 978-90-04-70165-6 (e-book)
DOI 10.1163/9789004701656

# Contents

**PART 3**
*Editorial Interventions*

**PART 4**
*The Bookshop and the Marketplace*

**PART 5**
*Shaping Collections: Gender and Value*

**PART 8**
*Towards Inclusive Histories*

# Figures and Tables

## Figures

## Tables

# Notes on Contributors

*Rebecca Baumann*
is the Head of Curatorial Services and Curator of Modern Books at the Lilly
Library, the rare book and manuscript library of Indiana University. They
are also Adjunct Associate Professor in the Department of Information and
Library Science at IU, teaching courses in Rare Book Librarianship, Rare Book
Curatorship, and the History of the Book, 1450 to the Present. They are the
curator of the 2018 exhibition *Frankenstein 200: The Birth, Life and Resurrection
of Mary Shelley's Monster* and author of the accompanying catalog, published
by Indiana University Press. Their interest in pulp and paperback publishing
has led to articles in *Fine Books & Collections* and *Dangerous Visions and New
Worlds: Radical Science Fiction* (PM Press, 2021).

*Montserrat Cachero*
has a degree in Economics from the University of Seville and a doctorate in
History from the European University Institute. She was distinguished academic visitor at Queens' College (University of Cambridge) in 2005 and visiting fellow at the Center for History and Economics (Harvard University) in
2016. She has been teaching Economic History at Pablo de Olavide University
since 2004 as part of the Economics department where she received her tenure track in 2012. She is an expert in 16th century Atlantic Trade focusing
on conflicts and institutions for contract enforcement. Since 2015 has been
involved in the Social Network Analysis and its use as a methodological tool
for historians. She has published several articles on both the theoretical side
and its application in specialised journals. She has headed a research project
about early modern credit markets and their role in trade financing, funded
by the European Commission (EDRF). In 2023 she edited, jointly with Natalia
Maillard Álvarez, the volumes *Book markets in Mediterranean Europe and Latin
America* (Palgrave) and *Instituciones, imprenta y mercados de libros en Europa y
América* (University of Seville Press).

*Verônica Calsoni Lima*
teaches Early Modern History at the Federal University of Triangulo Mineiro
(UFTM) in Minas Gerais, Brazil. Her PhD in Social History from the University
of São Paulo (2023) focuses on an underground network of authors, booksellers, and bookbinders known as the 'Confederate Stationers' and their clandestine production and dissemination of non-conformist and anti-monarchist
books, tracts, pamphlets, and broadsides during the English Revolution and

the Restoration of Charles II in the seventeenth century. She holds a master's (2016) and a bachelor's degree (2012) in History from the Federal University of Sao Paulo. She was awarded grants and scholarships to study and research projects in Brazil, Portugal, the United States, and the United Kingdom. Verônica was also a Visiting Research Fellow at Goldsmiths College, University of London (2014–2015 and 2018–2019), at Chetham's Library, Manchester (2018–2019), and Houghton Library, Harvard (2024). Additionally, she integrates h_moderna (the Brazilian Network of Studies in Early Modern History) and participates in three research groups: 'Metamorphose: Materiality and Interpretation of Early Modern Manuscripts and Printed Texts' (University of Brasilia), 'Early Modern Iberian History Study Group' (University of Sao Paulo), and 'Power and Religion in the Early Modern Period' (Federal University of Sao Paulo).

### Matthew Chambers

is visiting research fellow at the University of Reading and honorary lecturer at University College London. He has written on literary networks and publishing history in *Modernism, Periodicals, and Cultural Poetics* (Palgrave 2015) and in *London and the Modernist Bookshop* (Cambridge 2020), and has articles which have appeared in *Modernism/modernity*, *Transatlantica*, and the *Journal of British and Irish Innovative Poetry*. His most recent research, part of a two-year grant funded by the Excellence Initiative (University of Warsaw), looks to build out from his last monograph to explore the social, political, and literary roles bookshops played in the early decades of the twentieth century. He is a member of the Centre for Book Cultures and Publishing (University of Reading) and the Bookselling Research Network. He is also editor of the peer-reviewed journal *The New Americanist* (Edinburgh University Press), which is planning a special issue on Print Cultures and Bookishness in Contemporary Life (2024).

### Kanupriya Dhingra

is an Assistant Professor and Assistant Dean at the Jindal School of Languages and Literature, O.P. Jindal Global University (India). She researches the History of the Book and Print Cultures, with a focus on Delhi (India), from an ethnographic perspective. Kanupriya's recent monograph, *Old Delhi's Parallel Book Bazaar* (Cambridge University Press, 2024), is based on her doctoral research at SOAS (University of London), supported by the Felix Scholarship Fund. She has written extensively about her research for journals, magazines, and digital news publications such as *Comparative Critical Studies* (Edinburgh University Press), *The Caravan*, *Scroll*, and *Himāl SouthAsian*. She is also contributing a chapter to the fourth volume of the *Book History in India* series, edited by

Abhijit Gupta and Swapan Chakravorty. Kanupriya has been invited to deliver talks the parallel book markets and the *nayi-jaisi* books of Old Delhi at the University of Oxford, The British Library, The Books and Prints Initiative and The Institute of Historical Research, Jadavpur University, Ambedkar University, Jamia Millia Islamia, University of Delhi, among others. Apart from her interest in 'the book', Kanupriya's research engages with oral history, urban studies, interdisciplinary spatial studies, and the theories of the everyday. Kanupriya is deeply interested in Hindi, Punjabi, and Urdu poetry, especially that of Amrita Pritam, and continues to research and translate it. Her creative writing and translations have appeared in *Indian Literature* (A *Sahitya Akademi* imprint), *Scroll, Indian Writers Forum, Guftgu, Aainanagar,* and *Antiserious.* Her translations of two short stories, by Premchand (Hindi) and Nasira Sharma (Urdu), into English, have appeared in edited volumes published by Niyogi Books (2022) and Oxford University Press (2022), respectively. In July 2023, she was awarded the Charles Wallace India Trust Grant for *Bristol Translates,* an international Summer School for translation, in recognition of her contributions to the field.

### Nora Epstein

is the Instruction and Outreach Librarian at the Newberry Library and a Postdoctoral Fellow with Yale University's Paul Mellon Centre for Studies in British Art. She received her PhD from the University of St Andrews in 2021. Her thesis centred on the copying and reuse of Tudor devotional illustrations and introduced the framework of 'Visual Commonplacing' as a way to appreciate repeating images in early modern print as a function of memory culture. She holds a master's of library and information science from the University of Illinois and a master's in book history from the University of St Andrews. In 2022 she was awarded fellowships from the Folger Shakespeare Library and the Bibliographical Society of America.

### Natalia Fantetti

has recently completed her PhD on women's contributions to the medieval manuscript trade ca. 1900–1945 as part of the CULTIVATE MSS team at the Institute of English Studies, School of Advanced Study. Her thesis situated better-known women involved with manuscripts and rare books within wider trade networks and brought to light the work of relatively forgotten names such as Anne Nill and Alice Millard. As a medieval-modernist, her work seeks to draw links between the two periods and how they may inform each other. She holds a BA in English and an MA in Modern Literature and Culture, both from

King's College London. Her findings during a Turing Scheme Fellowship at the University of Pennsylvania resulted in an Annotation published in *Manuscript Studies* in 2023. She has also contributed to the newly published volume, *The Pre-Modern Manuscript Trade and its Consequences, ca. 1890–1945.*

### Jessica Farrell-Jobst

is an early modern scholar who recently completed her doctoral research at the University of St Andrews. Her thesis examined the multifaceted ways women participated in the book trades in Nuremberg during the sixteenth and seventeenth centuries. Her previous work has explored ideas about gender and familial dynamics that shaped women's work in print shops and book businesses in the early modern period. Her upcoming research will explore governmental support of local print trades, civic authorities as publishers, and the variety in printing practices and processes in early modern Germany.

### Agnes Gehbald

is a Lecturer in Modern History at the University of Bern. Her research interests include the study of printing and book history, the Viceroyalty of Peru, and transatlantic history. In 2020, she completed her PhD in Latin American History at the University of Cologne. Before, she was a short-term fellow at the John Carter Brown Library at Brown University (2018) and a visiting PhD student at the Centre of Latin American Studies at the University of Cambridge (2019–2020). Her first monograph, *A Colonial Book Market: Peruvian Print Culture in the Age of Enlightenment* (Cambridge University Press, 2023), reveals how books permeated late colonial society on a broad scale and how they figured as objects in the inventories of diverse individuals, both women and men, who, in previous centuries, had been far less likely to possess them.

### Rabia Gregory

is Associate Professor of the History of Christianity at the University of Missouri and the author of *Marrying Jesus in Medieval and Early Modern Northern Europe: Popular culture and Religious Reform* (Ashgate/Routledge 2016). She has published articles on Christian material culture, gender, and the relationship between religion, new media, and medieval culture in contemporary video games. In addition to preparing a critical introduction, biography, and facing-page edition and translation of the poetry of Anna Bijns (1493–1575), she is currently undertaking research to explain how the introduction of affordable paper to western Europe changed how Christians understood their religion.

*Laura Guinot Ferri*

is a postdoctoral researcher (APOSTD 2022) from the University of Valencia and the University of Bologna since September 2023. She has been a member of the Project CIRGEN: *Circulating Gender in the Global Enlightenment. Ideas, Networks, Agencies* (ERC2017-AdG 787015) (University of Valencia) between 2019 and 2023. She obtained her PhD in 2019 with a research focus on the intersection between women's studies, history of medicine and the history of religious practices. She is the author of *Mujeres y santidad: sanadoras por mediación divina. Un estudio desde la microhistoria (siglos XVII y XVIII)* (Comares, 2021) (Women and sainthood: healers by divine mediation. A microhistorical case study (17th and 18th centuries)). She has also focused on the circulation of books "for women" in the Hispanic world and in the contrast between imagined female readerships and actual readers, as well as in the role of women as cultural mediators. On this topic she has co-edited with Carolina Blutrach the special issue *Agencia y mediación cultural en femenino: bibliotecas, correspondencia y redes transnacionales en los siglos XVII y XVIII (Arenal. Revista de Historia de las Mujeres* 2022) (Female Agency and Cultural Mediation: Libraries, Correspondence and Transnational Networks in the 17th and 18th centuries), and co-edited with Mónica Bolufer and Carolina Blutrach the book *Gender and Cultural Mediation in the Long Eighteenth Century. Women across Borders* (Palgrave Macmillan, 2024).

*Elizabeth Le Roux*

is an Associate Professor in the Department of Information Science at the University of Pretoria, where she coordinates the Publishing Studies programme. She is co-editor of the journal *Book History*, and her research focuses on the history of publishing and book cultures in South Africa and Africa more broadly. She is author of *Publishing Against Apartheid: A case study of Ravan Press* (Cambridge University Press Elements, 2020), *A Survey of South African Crime Fiction* (with Sam Naidu, UKZN Press, 2017), and *A Social History of the University Presses in Apartheid South Africa* (Brill, 2016). She is also closely associated with industry-driven research, for the Publishers' Association of South Africa, the South African Cultural Observatory, and the Department of Sport, Arts and Culture. Before becoming a full-time academic, she worked in the scholarly publishing industry in South Africa.

*Sarah Lubelski*

is an independent scholar whose work focuses on equity, diversity, and inclusion within the creative industries. Her postdoctoral work, which was supported by the Social Sciences and Humanities Research Council of Canada, explored gender bias and the gendering of publishing work and publishing organisations throughout the nineteenth and twentieth centuries. Her doctoral thesis, titled 'A Gentlewoman's Profession: The Emergence of Feminized Publishing at Richard Bentley and Son, 1858–1898,' was the recipient of the 2020 iSchools Doctoral Dissertation Award. She has published in the journals Archivaria, Book History, and Publishing History.

### Natalia Maillard Álvarez

has a degree in Geography and History and holds a PhD in History (2007) from the University of Seville. She was Visiting Fellow (2009) and Marie Curie Fellow (2010–2012) at the European University Institute in Florence, and EURIAS fellow at the Collegium de Lyon (2015–2016). Since 2012 she has been associated with the Department Geography, History and Philosophy at the University Pablo de Olavide, first as lecturer and postdoc fellow and, since 2022 as associate professor of early modern history. Her research field is book history, especially the history of the book trade and the history of readers in the Hispanic Monarchy during the 16th and 17th centuries. She has edited the volume *Books in the Catholic World during the Early Modern Period* (Brill, 2014) and was principal investigator (PI) of the research project "International Book Trade Networks in the Hispanic Monarchy, 1501–1648", funded by the Spanish Government. Currently she is leading a new research project with Montserrat Cachero on the networks, agents, and financial architecture of the early modern book markets (PID2022-137793NB-100).

### Charley Matthews

is completing their AHRC-funded PhD in English Literature at the University of Edinburgh. Their thesis is in the field of Book History, exploring queer and trans reading practices in nineteenth-century Britain. They examine the diaries, letters, and book reviews of Anne Lister, David Lyndsay, Geraldine Jewsbury, Frances Power Cobbe, and others, to recover how these queer readers interacted with restrictive nineteenth-century discourses about women's reading. Charley has published on Anne Lister's reading habits in the *Journal of Lesbian Studies* (2022) and in *Reception: Texts, Readers, Audiences, History* (2023). They have presented to international audiences at conferences, including at the Institute of English Studies' *Queer Bibliography* (2023) and at *SHARP: Moving Texts* (2021). Charley teaches undergraduate English Literature courses at the University of Edinburgh, and is training as a professional indexer. Their research interests also include the development of the anthology, narratology in the nineteenth-century novel, and digital humanities methods.

*Susan McElrath*

is the current Head of Public Services at the Bancroft Library at the University of California, Berkeley, where she manages circulation, duplication, exhibits, interlibrary loan, reference, research, and stacks maintenance. During her tenure as University Archivist at American University, she developed expertise in digitization, web harvesting, and preservation. She has worked in archives, libraries, and museums for over thirty years in a variety of capacities, including instruction, acquisitions, archival description and processing, and reference. She has served in leadership positions in the Mid-Atlantic Regional Archives Conference and the Society of American Archivists. She holds an M.A. in American History and an M.L.S from the University of Maryland. An extension of her interest in women, work, and society, her current research project is a prosopographical study of the San Francisco Bindery Women's Union. She has also written/spoken on African American women's history, archives management, and digitization.

*Kirk Melnikoff*

is Professor of English at the University of North Carolina at Charlotte where he teaches courses in Book History, Shakespeare and his contemporaries in performance, and Early Modern British Literature. He is the author of *Elizabethan Publishing and the Makings of Literary Culture* (U Toronto P, 2018) and has edited four collections of essays, most recently, with Roslyn L. Knutson, *Christopher Marlowe, Theatrical Commerce, and the Book Trade* (Cambridge UP, 2018). He has also recently published editions of *James IV* and *Selimus*. He is currently jointly putting together a volume of transcribed early modern book-trade wills for Manchester UP, working on an edition of *Edward II* for *The Oxford Marlowe: The Collected Works*, jointly editing the *Oxford Handbook of Christopher Marlowe*, and finishing a monograph on early modern London bookselling and bookshops.

*Malcolm Noble*

is an historian who received his PhD from the University of Edinburgh in Economic and Social History. He has worked on print in a range of settings including eighteenth-century street literature and chapbooks, debates on nineteen-century political reform, twentieth century corporate catalogues and magazines, and zines in the twenty-first century. In February 2024 he co-organized a symposium 'Queer Bibliography: Tools, Methods, Practices, Approaches', at the Institute of English Studies, School of Advanced Study, University of London with Sarah Pyke, and together they are guest editing a special number of *Papers of the Bibliographical Society of America* as well as an edited collection of papers from the symposium. Malcolm's interests in queer bibliography are framed around affect, emotional labour, and touch, as well as broader approaches to bibliography.

### Kate Ozment

is Team Leader of the Digital Scholarship group in Kelvin Smith Library at Case Western Reserve University. She is co-editor of the *Women in Book History Bibliography*, which was awarded honourable mention for an archive or digital project from the Modern Language Association in 2019. She has published on feminist bibliography and women's engagement with books in *Textual Cultures, Digital Humanities Quarterly*, and *Eighteenth-Century Studies* and has held research fellowships from the Newberry, Folger, Smith College Special Collections, Princeton Rare Books, and Houghton Library. Her Cambridge University Press Element, titled *The Hroswitha Club and the Impact of Women Book Collectors*, was published in 2023 and is a historical recovery project focused on the most influential group of women book collectors in the United States. Currently, she is working with the *Women's Print History Project* team to input data on women's contributions to print production in England from 1700 to 1750, focusing specifically on the firm run by Anne Dodd and its connections to other women-run bookselling businesses.

### Joanna Rozendaal

is an antiquarian bookseller. She is also working on her PhD *Female book ownership in the eighteenth-century Dutch Republic. Buying books, building libraries*, at Radboud University (Nijmegen, The Netherlands). By drawing on the data from the MEDIATE-database and bookseller's archives, Joanna aims to gain more insight in eighteenth-century Dutch female book ownership, women's access to knowledge and their participation in the cultural field.

### Kandice Sharren

is an Assistant Professor of English at the University of Saskatchewan, as well as the lead editor of the Women's Print History Project. Most recently, her writing has appeared in Women's Writing, *Huntington Library Quarterly, Eighteenth-Century Studies, Review of English Studies*, and *English Studies in Canada*.

### Valentina Sonzini

researcher in History of Printing at the University of Florence, SAGAS Department (Italy); member of the board of JLIS.it (open access review in Library Science); member of the Scientific Committee of Bibliothecae.it (open access review in Bibliography, Library Science, History of Printing, History of Books); member of the Scientific Committee of the Summer School La Digital Library: evoluzione, strutture, progetti-The digital Library: evolution, structures, projects (University of Bologna). Her research activity concerns the fields of Library Science, History of Books, History of Printing, Gender studies, Decolonization and Post colonization studies. She has focused her studies on the project Repertorio delle tipografe in Italia dal Cinquecento al Settecento-A Repository of Italian Women Printers from the XVI to the XVIII Century, which is now available for consultation on Wikidata. Thanks to an institutional protocol between the University of Florence e the Marucelliana Library (Florence, Italy), in the latest months she has been involved in a new project concerning the Mare Magnum, one of the biggest manuscript bibliographic repositories in the world.

### Elise Watson

is a postdoctoral researcher with the Universal Short Title Catalogue Project at the University of St Andrews, where she works on early modern France and the Low Countries. Her PhD, completed in 2022, documented the clandestine Catholic book trade in the Dutch Republic, examining how the availability of print shaped minority religious experience. She has been published in *Studies in Church History* (2021), Brill's Library of the Written Word series (2021 and 2022), and the *Jaarboek voor Nederlandse boekgeschiedenis* (2022). She is also the Managing Editor of Brill's Book History Online database.

### Joëlle Weis

is a research associate at the Trier Center for Digital Humanities, where she heads the research area Digital Literary and Cultural Studies. Until 2021 she was a post-doctoral researcher for the Marbach-Weimar-Wolfenbüttel research association, working on the project 'Weltwissen. Das kosmopolitische Sammlungsinteresse des frühneuzeitlichen Adels'. Together with her colleagues, she investigated the private collections of members of the princely family of Brunswick-Wolfenbüttel from the seventeenth and eighteenth century. She obtained her Ph.D. in History in 2019 at the Universities of Vienna and Luxembourg with a dissertation on the scholarly practices of the historian Johann Friedrich Schannat (1683–1739) and his correspondence network. From 2010 to 2014, she was a researcher with the Viennese project 'Monastic Enlightenment and the Benedictine Republic of Letters' involved in the edition of the correspondence of the brothers Pez. Her research focuses on (digital) methods of collection research, book and library history, and the history of scholarship in the early modern period.

### Helen Williams

is Associate Professor of English Literature at Northumbria University. She has published widely on eighteenth-century literature and book history, being the author of *Laurence Sterne and the Eighteenth-Century Book* (Cambridge University Press, 2021), the co-editor of John Cleland's *Memoirs of a Woman of Pleasure* (Broadview, 2018), and the co-director of the Cambridge Digital Library dataset, *Laurence Sterne and Sterneana* (2019). Her most recent work is on women and the book trade in the long eighteenth century. She is currently undertaking a British Academy Innovation Fellowship in collaboration with the Archive of the Worshipful Company of Stationers and Newspaper Makers entitled *Communicating Women's Work in the Historical Archive*. Through sharing evidence of women's labour in the book trades with public audiences, the project aims to improve the visibility of diverse heritage in one of the UK's major livery companies and to foster more inclusive research and archival practices within academia and the wider archives community.

### Alexandra E. Wingate

is a book historian studying early modern Spain and is a PhD candidate in Information Science at Indiana University Bloomington. She holds an MA in the History of the Book from the University of London's Institute of English Studies, a Master of Library Science from Indiana University Bloomington, and a BA in Hispanic Studies and Linguistics from the College of William and Mary. She has researched both booksellers and private libraries in early modern Navarre, Spain using inventories and other archival sources, and her dissertation research seeks to uncover the practices of Navarrese booksellers and the specific books they sold. More broadly, she is interested in how quantitative methods, mixed methods, and GIS can expand our approach to book history; the use of digital humanities in book history; and the intersection between book history and information science. She is also the Bibliography Editor for the Chymistry of Isaac Newton Project tracing Newton's citations in his manuscripts, and she produces bibliographies on book historical topics as the Bibliographer for SHARP News.

### Georgianna Ziegler

is the Louis B. Thalheimer Associate Librarian and Head of Reference Emerita at the Folger Shakespeare Library. She has published widely on early modern women in literature and art, including the manuscripts of Esther Inglis as early "artists books", and has curated major exhibitions at the Folger including: *Elizabeth I: Then and Now* (with catalogue); and *Shakespeare's Sisters: Voices of English and European Women Writers 1500–1700*. She has written blog posts for the Folger's *Collation*, and for *Female Book Ownership* and *Art Herstory*. Her most recent publications are essays on early women as book owners, in *Women's Labour and the History of the Book in Early Modern England* (2020), ed. Valerie Wayne; and Esther Inglis's self-portraits in *Renaissance Quarterly* (2023). She has written the entries on Esther Inglis for the *New Biographical Dictionary of Scottish Women* (2018) and the Routledge *Encyclopedia of the Renaissance World*. Currently she is finishing a book-length biography of Inglis, as well as maintaining the website https://estheringlis.com.

# CHAPTER 1

# Gender as an Inclusive Model for Book History

*Elise Watson, Jessica Farrell-Jobst and Nora Epstein*

This volume starts from a place of inclusion and collaboration. The chapters that follow began as part of the twelfth annual St Andrews Book History Conference in June 2021 of the same name. Through four packed online days, more than 300 participants and attendees from six continents and eighteen time zones explored the unexpected connections between gender and book history across time and space. The content was equally vast in scope, from papers discussing gendered depictions of saints in incunabula to gendered perceptions of bookshelves in the backgrounds of virtual events. This conference and volume also belong to the microgeneration of works born out of the early days of the COVID-19 pandemic. With our conference's original 2020 date postponed, the organisers quickly realised that a transition to a fully digital conference brought new challenges, but also opened the door to wider participation by those who would not normally be able to travel to Scotland. Suddenly, global restrictions removed our own restrictions. Rather than trying to create a digital facsimile of an in-person conference, we embraced this situation by asking how we could incorporate and reflect this lack of boundaries to amplify this unanticipated inclusivity.

What emerged from this process was unexpected and remarkable. The conversations that took place within highly structured panel discussions, Special Collections sessions, and lunchtime conversations on the accessibility and shareability of data began to converge and coalesce around a set of central questions and methodologies that all forty-two papers seemed to address. As the event progressed, participants commented on the feeling that we were developing a shared language to talk about gender and book history that was different from what they had experienced previously, and the analysis carried out in our conversations felt entirely new. While we recognised and built on the critical foundation of women's book history, for the first time we began to talk about what gender might look like as a methodology for book historians. We moved from lamenting the archival silences we all faced as gender historians to excitement around archival presence and embodiment. The mood in the (virtual) room was a unified one: if we only look for these sources in archives and libraries, we agreed, we will find them.

© KONINKLIJKE BRILL BV, LEIDEN, 2025 | DOI:10.1163/9789004701656_002

At the same time, this work felt deeply personal. In several panels, we discussed how research on gender was messy and circumstantial, yet at the same time it was enumerative and data-driven. We acknowledged the emotional investment that accompanied recovery studies in archives and libraries, especially for female scholars, queer and trans scholars, and scholars of colour. We discussed Achille Mbembe's claim that the conceptual archive is 'a tactile universe because the document can be touched, a visual universe because it can be seen, a cognitive universe because it can be read and decoded', alongside Saidiya Hartman's characterisation of her work 'straining against the limits of the archive'.[1] We shared our dissatisfaction with the limits of current scholarship: how few studies have discussed masculinity on its own terms, as separate from the default mode of life and book production, or how queer bibliography is only beginning to emerge as its own field.

As a result, once we began to work on this volume as editors we felt the responsibility not only to make these ideas discoverable through the work of these participants, but to try and reproduce some of the electrifying syntheses these collaborations created. Based on the diversity of the contributions, we had a limited ability to shape the content, instead intervening merely to respond and integrate the themes that emerged. The one issue on which we found ourselves repeatedly insisting, was for each author to make clear how they used gender as a methodology, rather than a subject. We encouraged contributors to move beyond providing lists of female names or noting the presence of exceptional, individual early modern women in the book trades, and cultivate more comprehensive analyses of how bookmaking itself was a gendered practice.

At the core of this volume, rather than a central thesis that united the claims of its contributors, we discovered a call to action. With this work, we propose that it is time to consider seriously what an inclusive history of the book looks like. Instead of examining individual women in the book world, as studies of gender and book history have traditionally done, it is time to move towards a model that radically emphasises inclusion and collaboration within communities, families, in reading practices, and on the floor of the print shop. In studies of the book trade, we need to start from a place of presence rather than absence, assuming that these interactions were happening in all sites of bookwork rather than just the ones that name it. Equally, we want to de-emphasise

---

1   Achille Mbembe, 'The Power of the Archive and Its Limits', in Carolyn Hamilton, Verne Harris, Jane Taylor, Michele Pickover, Graeme Reid, and Razia Saleh (eds.) *Refiguring the Archives* (Dordrecht: Springer, 2002), pp. 19–26, at 20; Saidiya Hartman, 'Venus in Two Acts', *Small Axe: A Caribbean Journal of Criticism*, 26 (2008), pp. 1–14, at 11.

practices that focus on exceptional women or individuals abstracted from the whole. Rather than another volume about women and print, this chapter is a manifesto and this volume a prototype of the value of this critical methodology, and a new understanding of book production as fundamentally collaborative. The twenty-five chapters that comprise this book cover a wide chronological and geographical spread. We want to make the point, strongly, that these pieces do not speak only to their own contexts, but collectively build to something larger. These chapters demonstrate the benefits of inclusive thinking, and their very existence testifies to the importance of gender as a methodology in book history.

This is also evident in the title of this volume, which very intentionally pluralises the word 'Trades'. We did not want to collect works that only focus on bookmaking or ownership but sought to find representations of all the ways people interacted with book culture. Our notion of 'Book Trades' parallels the term recently suggested by Whitney Trettien of 'bookwork'. In her work, Trettien employs 'bookwork' as a framework for studying the book as an 'assembled product of knowledge and itself an engine of knowledge production; it crystallizes ideas through historically contingent processes of labor and disperses them back into the world as particles for others to gather.'[2] In this volume, the reader will find insights into gendered practices of bookmaking, bookselling, reading, patronising, and collecting. This wide approach reveals entangled and multifaceted identities and underscores the importance of taking a holistic approach to book history.

The editors and authors of this work firmly reject any notions of a restrictive gender binary. Gender, broadly considered, has always been a part of book history, although this has often been implicit rather than explicit. Paper mills, print shops, bookstores and libraries have always been gendered spaces. From Empress Wu Zetian, who popularised woodblock printing in seventh-century Tang Dynasty China, to the gender nonconforming bookseller John de Verdion in eighteenth-century London, books themselves and their movements have been sites of gendered interaction.[3] However, most studies of gender and book

2 Whitney Trettien, *Cut/Copy/Paste: Fragments from the History of Bookwork* (Minnesota: Minnesota University Press, 2021), pp. 21–22.
3 Under the reign of Wu Zetian (634–705 AD), the most powerful female ruler in the history of China, woodblock printing was invented and spread widely. This story of Wu Zetian is most popularly told in T.H. Barrett, *The Woman Who Discovered Printing* (New Haven, CT: Yale University Press, 2008). See also links between gender, textile work and woodblock printing in this period in T.H. Barrett, 'Woodblock dyeing and printing technology in China, c. 700 A.D.: the innovations of Ms. Liu, and other evidence', *Bulletin of the School of Oriental and African Studies*, 64 (2001), pp. 240–247. Mentions of De Verdion in secondary literature

history have been within the domain of women's history. Although this volume is made possible by and hopes to add to research on women's labour, its aims are more broad. While gender history grew out of women's history, it has moved beyond studies of individual 'women worthies' to a more inclusive model that looks at gender as a tool of analysis, rather than an essentialist category, and how gender was one of many defining identities for bookworkers. Certainly, a large portion of the authors of this volume contributed works focusing on a single woman, groups of women, or how womanhood functioned within book practice. However, also included here are studies of masculinity and maleness, a historically ignored, but incredibly promising, subject in book history. Many chapters also shift focus from named authority on a title page to communities of often unnamed bookmakers and gendered spaces. In this way our volume's approach is very differently to recent volumes dedicated to women and print history. By rejecting this binary and focusing on gender as an inclusive model, we can start to see broad truths that are difficult to uncover in more myopic studies.

Like our conference, this resulting volume does not exclude contributions based on geography. Chapters also come from many periods in the history of the book. At first glance, investigations into book stalls in modern-day Delhi and early modern printing in the colonial Viceroyalty of Peru may not seem to have much in common. However, by exploring these subjects collaboratively, we start to develop a picture of how the book conforms to and confronts gendered spaces. Several of the chapters open dialogues with corresponding frameworks including intersectionality and critical race theory, with the understanding that these methodologies have their own important contexts and histories. This book is structured around commonalities that are independent of time and place. The distant juxtapositions that compose this volume emphasise universal connections while also opening space to detail specific and unique stories.

This inclusive methodology has implications not only for book history but for critical bibliography, in particular the need to acknowledge the complexity and imperfection that accompanies inclusion and presence. The image on the cover of this volume is a printer's device from the 1643 edition of Johannes van Beverwijck's *Van de wtnementheyt des vrouwelicken Geslachts* (On the

---

almost exclusively refer to him by his birth name and gender assigned at birth. As he resolutely rejected both of these during his life, we have not followed this example. See for example Graham Jefcoate, *Deutsche Drucker und Buchhändler in London 1680–1811: Strukturen und Bedeutung des deutschen Anteils am englischen Buchhandel* (Berlin: De Gruyter, 2015), p. 91; Nicola McLelland, 'The history of language learning and teaching in Britain', *The Language Learning Journal*, 46 (2018), p. 8.

Excellence of the Female Sex), utilised by Dordrecht publisher Hendrik van Esch. It depicts the *Virgo Dordracena*, the Virgin of Dordrecht. In one hand she holds a quill pen, and in the other she holds up her skirt, under which books are tumbling out around her. Underneath, the Latin motto 'libros non liberos pariens' makes a bold claim for female education: give birth to books, not babies.[4] While motherhood and bookmaking are both generative acts, the early modern world created strict binaries around gendered roles. Although this image and the work to which it is affixed advocate for women's education, the motto carved into its banderole sends a very specific message: the relationship between these two roles is an 'or', not an 'and'. This image usefully represents the tension between idealised and real depictions of gendered roles. What is lost in the strict black and white of the woodcut composition is the lived realities of bookmakers: that women, regardless of sexual activity, have always been active bookmakers, and that, in some periods, their ability to have children was an essential aspect of establishing publishing dynasties. This is exemplified by the Virgin, the only woman in the early modern imagination who was able to preserve both her sexual purity and her sacred role of motherhood as the virgin mother of Christ. Rather than the perfected ideal, as this woodcut represents, our volume proposes the need to look at what is real and present in archives and libraries, in all of its fascinating disarray. The creation of books is always a gendered and embodied practice, and by focusing on the unattainable ideal, we obscure a complex and imperfect reality.

Similarly, in traditional bibliographic description, copies are collected in order to detail the 'ideal copy' of an edition. The bibliographic principle of recovering the 'ideal copy' is explained as a description of the book at its most perfect state, not as it survives today but as it was intended by the printer or publisher.[5] This description of the ideal copy is constructed by hypothesising based on the evidence in lacking or 'aberrant' copies.[6] Foundational bibliographer Fredson Bowers further prescribes that 'No individual copy, unless it corresponds to the form of the ideal copy arrived at by analysis, is worth presentation ... by this principle one avoids the sin of offering a description only

---

4   'De boekenmaagd van Dordrecht', *Oud-Dordrecht*, 39 (2021), pp. 249–251; Cornelia Niekus Moore, '"Not by Nature but by Custom": Johan van Beverwijck's *Van de wtnementheyt des vrouwelicken Geslachts*', *The Sixteenth Century Journal*, 25 (1994), pp. 633–651.

5   Philip Gaskell, *A New Introduction to Bibliography* (Oxford: Clarendon Press, 1979), p. 321, see also p. 315.

6   Ibid; Fredson Bowers, *Principles of Bibliographic Description* (New Castle, DE: Oak Knoll Press, 1994), p. 115.

of an imperfect state'.[7] While speculating about the ideal copy has practical bibliographic applications, especially in pre-digital research, it is fundamentally engaged with aggregating and assimilating diversity in order to make a speculative generalisation. Many of the assumptions and binaries directly challenged in this volume were constructed in the same manner, by privileging an assumed model over a variant because of perceived imperfections. As critical bibliographers, we seek to unbind ourselves from the gendered assumptions inherent in past bibliographical inquiry and find value in the imperfect, rather than focusing on what is lacking or how it might conform to rigid expectations.

With the diversity of these contributions, we hope to address an important misconception in book history: that stories around gender are undiscoverable due to a lack of evidence or archival silences around them. The twenty-five chapters of this volume, covering the majority of the globe and five hundred years of history, show that there is no lack of evidence for those who are looking for it. In fact, we want to not only speak into these archival silences but ground them in practical application. We argue for the importance of printing as an action, carried out by family networks and communities, rather than an isolated action by an individual. By emphasising these networks, recognising gendered labour and addressing archival silences, we can develop not only innovative scholarship but pedagogy that recognises the importance of gender in the book trades. We propose a shift in the discussion of gender and book history from the absence of women in the historical record to the presence of gender as a category of analysis. Utilising concepts of radical inclusion and archival presence in book history, while broadening our chronological and geographical scope, breaks this mould.

1        Moving beyond Women and the Book

All books, in the handpress period as well as today, owe their existence to previous works and networks of bookmakers. This book is no different. It relies on the foundation laid by scholars of women's history and book history alongside feminist bibliographers and the founders of inclusive bibliography. Because of this, it is also naturally interdisciplinary. Book history is itself a composite of diverse disciplines, including history, literary and textual studies, digital

---

7   Alexandra Gillespie, 'Introduction: Bibliography and Early Tudor Texts', *Huntington Library Quarterly*, 67 (2004), pp. 164–165. Sarah Werner, 'Feminist Bibliographical Praxis', lecture given for the London Rare Book School and Institute of English Studies, University of London, June 29, 2022. YouTube: <https://www.youtube.com/watch?v=UX4EmH8f9ko>, minute 24.

humanities, and library and information science. These disciplines have not all approached gender with the same level of rigour. To account for this oversight, our introduction will analyse and describe the relationship between gender and print culture from two primary perspectives, the historical and the bibliographical. Within book history, gender studies grew out of women's history, focusing on the perceived absence of women in the historical record, aiming to restore them through recovery history and studies of women's agency. Within bibliography, successions of critical bibliographers have pioneered approaches to feminist and inclusive bibliography that utilise feminist theory as a transformative tool for the systematic study of textual artefacts.

This study, as most book historical studies do, owes its underpinnings to the indispensable work of Robert Darnton. In 1982, Darnton's 'What is the History of Books?' presented the idea of the communication circuit, which describes the book trade as a network of activity, driven by individuals and interpersonal interactions.[8] This perspective highlights historical agents over the books themselves, giving greater emphasis to the social impact of print and book production. In this way, Darnton repopulated the book trade with people, each with their own motivations, roles and understandings of books. Individuals become conduits through whom economic, social, judicial and cultural factors directly shape the functions and operations of the book trade. One central aspect affecting these figures is gender. In a 2007 revisiting of his landmark article, Darnton mentioned that his work had previously disregarded the impact of gender on his circuit, suggesting that

> My diagram hardly did justice to the complexities, but it brought out the way the parts were linked, and I think it conveyed something of the nature of book history as it was experienced by the men (and also many women—la veuve Desaint in Paris, Mme La Noue in Versailles, la veuve Charmet in Besançon) who made it happen.[9]

While the addition allows a place for women in his circuit, even the structure of the sentence still frames women as auxiliary points rather than integral and consistent: the clause is in parentheses, and lists only three French women as examples. In response to this piece, a fundamental change in attitude towards women, gender and book history came with Helen Smith's *'Grossly Material Things': Women and Book Production in Early Modern England*, published in

---

8   Robert Darnton, 'What is the History of Books?', *Daedalus*, 111 (1982), pp. 65–83.

9   Robert Darnton, '"What is the History of Books?" Revisited', *Modern Intellectual History*, 4 (2007), pp. 495–508.

2012. Smith problematised the communication circuit's lack of consideration for questions of gender. This revolutionary work not only argued for the frequent participation of women in the making of books, but even questioned scholars' ability to gender books. Smith argued that collaboration between genders was a customary, even conventional, method for textual production.[10] Smith's work marked a change in direction when considering gender and book production. First, her book spoke to the gradual change felt in the field of gender studies and gender history that emphasises women's actions and activities despite the formal limitations and inherent social inequalities they faced. Secondly her work was one of the first to move from looking at women to looking at gender. In her book, Smith suggested that the page is an interface for the cooperation and exchange between genders. Moreover, by focusing on exchange and cooperation, Smith's study took into account how expressions of masculinity functioned in textual production. Rather than a circuit as proposed by Darnton, Smith painted a vivid picture of a more complicated web that can more thoroughly describe gendered interactions. This work began to break down rigid categories not only of gender but of book production more broadly.

In 2014, Michelle Levy followed this question with her article 'Do Women have a Book History?', referencing Joan Kelly's field-defining 1977 article 'Did Women Have a Renaissance?'. In her examination of women of the book world during the Romantic period, Levy stressed the gendered nature of both book historical scholarship and of the history of book production. Critiquing Darnton's circuit structure as too rigid, Levy suggested that 'whereas men have occupied all positions along the circuit at all times, women have rarely done so', due to their unequal economic and social status.[11] As a result, women have been primarily represented as authors and readers, and vastly underrepresented in roles relating to the production of books. This disparity has meant that gender has received considerable attention in literary studies, while remaining relatively absent in discussion of the labour itself. When represented in historical works, most were concerned with unearthing individual women, rather than examining how gender affected their participation in the book world.[12]

---

10    Helen Smith, *'Grossly Material Things': Women and Book Production in Early Modern England* (Oxford: Oxford University Press, 2012), pp. 4–8.

11    Michelle Levy, 'Do Women have a Book History?', *Studies in Romanticism*, 53 (2014), pp. 297–317, quote at p. 298; Joan Kelly, 'Did Women Have a Renaissance?', in Renate Bridenthai and Clandia Koonz (eds.), *Becoming Visible: Women in European History* (Boston: Houghton Mifflin, 1977), pp. 137–164.

12    Important earlier examples of this work include Paula McDowell, *The Women of Grub Street: Press, Politics, and Gender in the London Literary Marketplace 1678–1730* (Oxford:

Since 2017, in part thanks to the publication of *Grossly Material Things*, scholarship on the subject of women, gender and books has, wonderfully, exploded with interest. Doctoral theses, articles, exhibitions, edited volumes and research projects have been dedicated towards the study of women as producers of books, unpacking gendered assumptions and developing new methodologies.[13] In 2018 the University of Birmingham's Centre for Printing History and Culture hosted a conference on 'Women in Print' which eventually led to the publication of Valerie Wayne's edited volume, *Women's Labour and*

Oxford University Press, 1998); Maureen Bell, 'Women Writing, Women Written', in J. Barnard and D.F McKenzie (eds.) *A History of the Book in Britain IV* (Cambridge: Cambridge University Press, 2002), pp. 431–451; Deborah Parker, 'Women in the Book Trade in Italy, 1475–1620', *Renaissance Quarterly*, 49 (1996), pp. 509–641; Martha Driver, '"By me Elysabeth Pykeryng": women and book production in the early Tudor period', in Emma J. Cayley and Susan Powell (eds.) *Manuscripts and Printed Books in Europe 1350–1550: Packaging, Presentation and Consumption* (Liverpool: Liverpool University Press, 2013), pp. 115–119; Susan Broomhall, *Women and the Book Trade in Sixteenth-Century France* (Surrey: Ashgate, 2002); Leslie Howsam, 'Women in Publishing and the Book Trades in Britain, 1830–1914', *Leipziger Jahrbuch zur Buchgeschichte*, 6 (1996), pp. 67–79; Beatrice Beech, 'Charlotte Guillard: A Sixteenth-Century Business Women', *Renaissance Quarterly*, 36 (1983); Paul G. Hoftijzer, 'Women in the Early-Modern Dutch Book Trade', in Suzan van Dijk et al. (eds.), *Writing the History of Women's Writing: Towards an International Approach* (Amsterdam: Royal Netherlands Academy of Arts, 2001), pp. 211–22; Albrecht Classen, 'Frauen als Buchdruckerinnen im deutschen Sprachrum des 16. Und 17 Jahrhundert', *Gutenberg-Jahrbuch*, 75 (2000), pp. 181–195.

13    Heleen Wyffels, 'Women and Work in Early Modern Printing Houses. Family Forms in Antwerp, Douai, and Leuven (1500–1700)', PhD Thesis: KU Leuven (2021); Cait Coker, 'Liminal Ladies: Reconstructing the Place of Women in Seventeenth-Century English Book Production', PhD Thesis: Texas A&M University (2019); Saskia Limbach, 'Life and Production of Magdalena Morhart. A Successful Business Woman in Sixteenth-Century Germany', *Gutenberg-Jahrbuch*, 94 (2019), pp. 151–172; Saskia Limbach, '"Darzu mancher Mann sich viel zu schwach unnd zu wenig Befinden wu [e] rde", Buchdruckerinnen und ihre Tätigkeiten im Alten Reich, ca. 1550–1700', *Zeitschrift für Historische Forschung*, 49 (2022), pp. 399–440; Saskia Limbach, '"Doing Men's Work". Katharina Rebart, Her Life and Her Activities in Context', in Arthur der Weduwen and Malcolm Walsby (eds.) *The Book World of Early Modern Europe* (Leiden: Brill, 2022), pp. 51–60; Claire Battershill, *Women and Letterpress Printing 1920–2020: Gendered Impressions* (Cambridge: Cambridge University Press, 2022); The Grolier Club, *Five Hundred Years of Women's Work: The Lisa Unger Baskin Collection* (December 10, 2019–February 8, 2020); Georg Peabody Library Exhibit Gallery, 'Women of the Book: The Spiritual Lives of Early Modern Women, 1450–1800)'; Betty A. Schellenberg and Michelle Levy (eds.), 'Women in Book History, 1660–1830', *Huntington Library Quarterly*, 84 (2021); Artemis Alexiou and Rose Roberto (eds.), *Women in Print 1: Design and Identities* (Bristol: Peter Lang, 2022); Caroline Archer-Parre, Christine Moog and John Hinks (eds.), *Women in Print 2: Production, Distribution and Consumption* (Bristol: Peter Lang, 2022). Remi Jimenes, *Charlotte Guillard: Une femme imprimeur à la Renaissance* (Tours: Presses universitaires Francois-Rabelais, 2017).

*the History of the Book in Early Modern England*.[14] Wayne's volume sets a prec-
edent for this work, gathering a collection of chapters dedicated to the study
of women's labour in early modern England. However impactful this book has
been to the field, this volume's contribution differs in two fundamental ways.
First, while Wayne's contributors focus solely on women as a social category,
our approach has stressed the indeterminacy of 'woman', suggesting that the
focus is not on the mere existence of a woman, or 'finding women' necessarily,
but that the process enlightens more about the operations and conceptions
about gender more generally. In this line of thought we have selected the word
gender carefully, as not to restrict our scholarship to the essentialist category of
woman. Moreover, unlike Wayne's anthology, our volume opens the discussion
to a wider global and temporal context, drawing similarities in the operations
and experiences of gender from a global community and across centuries. The
abundant connections between vastly differing places and times have illustrated the persistence of a gendered social reality.

In searching for explanations for the lack of women in book history and
their role in book production, early feminist historians landed upon the concept of agency. In the twentieth century, scholars used the idea of agency to
demonstrate that some women defied patriarchal systems to attain political,
social and economic power in misogynist societies.[15] However, to imply that
humans, particularly women, have or lack agency brings into question the
ability of any individual's ability to act autonomously within the confines of
social and institutional expectations. In the end, gender historians grappling
with this conundrum have suggested that agency is a process of negotiation
between the agent and the larger social structures in society. Recently, Martha
Howell, Deborah Simonton and Anne Montenach have examined the concept
and problems with the idea of female agency, suggesting that it refers instead
to responding to or resisting the patriarchal realities of their time and place.[16]
For Howell in particular, female agency arises when women negotiate, by
both circumnavigating or confronting patriarchal norms, and are able to do

---

14    Valerie Wayne (ed.), *Women's Labour and the History of the Book in Early Modern England*
      (London: Bloomsbury Publishing, 2020).

15    See Merry Wiesner-Hanks' recent overview of this discourse: Merry E. Wiesner-Hanks,
      'Introduction', in Merry Wiesner-Hanks (ed.) *Challenging Women's Agency and Activism in
      Early Modernity* (Amsterdam: Amsterdam University Press, 2021), pp. 9–24.

16    Martha Howell, 'The Problem of Women's Agency in Late Medieval and Early Modern
      Europe', in Sarah Joan Moran and Amanda Pipkin (eds.) *Women and Gender in the Early
      Modern Low Countries* (Leiden: Brill, 2019), pp. 21–31; Anne Montenach and Deborah
      Simonton, 'Introduction', in Anne Montenach and Deborah Simonton (eds.), *Female
      Agency in the Urban Economy: Gender in European Towns, 1640–1830* (Abingdon: Taylor &
      Francis Group, 2013), pp. 1–14.

so due to the inherent instability of patriarchal constructs.[17] The contradictions, absences, and inconsistencies in patriarchal ideology, which is fundamentally fabricated on fallacy, make it illogical, nonsensical and often absurd. However, the amorphous structure of the patriarchy has also allowed space for negotiation.[18] The search for agency has also augmented the dichotomy between prescriptive and descriptive sources, where one side represents social attitudes and ideals, constructed by a particular set of values, and the other records the daily interactions, exchanges and decisions of individuals, which has been termed as 'practise studies'. Merry Wiesner-Hanks's recent volume *Challenging Women's Agency and Activism in Early Modernity* addressed the multifaceted ways women enacted agency. In her introduction, Wiesner reiterated the arguments of Lynn Thomas and Joan Wallach Scott, who have criticised the way that female agency has become the conclusion of too many studies, an 'uncontroversial conclusion applicable to nearly every situation'.[19] In line with this critique, Wiesner's volume explored how historical agents understood and enacted agency. This volume likewise strives to go beyond simply arguing whether women had agency or not, and instead investigate the gendered realities with which all agents contended.

Our work, then, takes the direction of Joan Wallach Scott, asking whether gender is a useful category of analysis for book history. Scott's influential arguments moved the conversation from 'women's history' to 'gender history', suggesting the fluidity and changing nature of gendered categories. Moreover, this move helps break down the isolation of women's history from history, and critically analyse the multiple ways gender was constructed, understood and lived in history.[20] Since 2017, it has been encouraging to see the absence of women in histories of book production has received increasing attention, as book historians have searched for evidence of women as printers, booksellers, illustrators, bookbinders and publishers, fleshing the production circuit out with more and more women. However, adding names to a list of contributors is only half of the first step. While some researchers have taken this consideration further by thinking about how the production and circulation of books impacted constructions of gender, new studies require a further breakdown of existing categories of identity in order to find diverse and inclusive participation in the book world. This involves not only deconstructing the binary of

---

17    Howell, 'The Problem of Women's Agency', pp. 24–25.

18    Ibid. p. 29.

19    Wiesner-Hanks, 'Introduction', p. 11.

20    Joan W. Scott, 'Gender: A Useful Category of Historical Analysis', *The American Historical Review*, 91 (1986), pp. 1053–1075; Joan Wallach Scott, 'Gender: Still a Useful Category for Analysis?', *DIOGENES*, 225 (2010), pp. 7–14.

male and female and embracing studies of gender nonconformity but broadening our definition of bookmaker to include the physical and intellectual
labour of those who sorted rags for paper, carried out uncredited editing and
translation work, and worked in illustration and with textiles. Although we can
never name all the agents who participated in the book trade, regardless of
gender, we can shift how we envision the practice.

An important ally in this shift is the field of feminist bibliography, which
seeks to integrate and restore female and gender nonconforming bookworkers
into bibliographies where they remain uncredited. While women's and gender
history have important intersections with feminist bibliography, they come
from different source bases and methodologies, requiring an interdisciplinary
focus to integrate them. In 1998, Leslie Howsam took the first important step
towards acknowledging women systematically in bibliography with her piece
'In my View: Women and Book History', published in the quarterly newsletter
of the Society for the History of Authorship, Reading and Publishing (SHARP
News). In it, she argued for a more nuanced approach to gender and books,
one moving away from excavating women from the bedrock of history to one
that considers gender in a more multifaceted and nuanced way. Whereas the
former approach ends up framing women's participation as 'atypical' or as
'outstanding anomalies in a cultural field dominated by men', the latter allows
scholars to understand books as a gendered product, created in a gendered
process.[21] Using Jane Marcus' feminist art theory, Howsam argued for the utility of feminism to book history, suggesting the need for a feminist approach to
the book as object or feminist analysis for literature. Both, she suggested, rely
on the core feminist principles of being anti-establishment, anti-conventional,
and above all inclusive.[22] While Howsam was writing generally about gender
and book history, because of her focus on the materiality of the book and its
relationship with gender, bibliographers have taken up her call for feminist
book history most emphatically.

Of course, this focus on breaking rules and traditions seems at first to sit
at odds with the principles and practise of bibliography, the practice of listing and describing books systematically. Yet as the work of Sarah Werner and
Kate Ozment in developing a methodology for a feminist bibliography has
shown, bibliography can improve with the applications of feminist theory and
ideals. Werner, who in 2018 coined the idea of feminist printing history, postulated that previous scholarship on gender and history had largely focused

---

21    Leslie Howsam, 'In My View: Women and Book History', SHARP News, 7 (1998), pp. 1–2.
22    Ibid.

on recovery work, reintegrating women into the larger historical narrative.[23] However, Werner argues that a more useful feminist understanding of printing history would consider a structural and process-based account of printing. Werner asks, 'what is a feminist history of printing and what do we lose by thinking of it primarily as the history of women printing?'[24] Werner is not criticising recovery work, nor suggesting it was unimportant, but rather is pushing the boundaries of how scholars approached print history. Werner calls for greater inclusivity and intersectionality in the history and practices of bibliography, saying 'a true feminist printing history needs to bring more people into our field.' Both Howsam and Werner highlight that at the centre of feminist theory, and its applicability to bibliography, is inclusivity. Another pioneer of feminist bibliography, for both its theory and practise, is Kate Ozment (see chapter 24). With Cait Coker, Ozment developed the Women in Book History Bibliography, an online database of secondary sources in women's writing and labour.[25] From this project Ozment has developed a rationale for feminist bibliography, which she defines as a remediation of bibliographic history to better categorise and analyse women's texts and labour.[26] Providing the tools and underlying methodology for feminist scholars, her work helps break down categories, challenges traditional beliefs and confronts the constructed values in bibliography that have excluded individuals and activity as irrelevant. Ozment's feminist bibliography crucially revises the way scholars conceptualise and study the material book, transforming the masculine narrative of book history's origins and roots.[27]

Feminist bibliography, or feminist print history to use Werner's term, stresses the transformative nature of feminist theory, a body of scholarship that at its core rejects tradition, officiality and exclusivity. Applying such an attitude to bibliography as a field, and as a tool for book history, not only opens new avenues of discussion but also becomes an agent for historical representation. The discussion of feminist bibliography also addresses larger themes central to our work as book historians, including archival silences and the importance of family and community.

---

23 Sarah Werner, 'Working Towards a Feminist Printing History', *Printing History*, 27/28 (2020), pp. 11–25.

24 Werner, 'Working Towards a Feminist Printing History', p. 21.

25 <http://www.womensbookhistory.org/>; see also Cait Coker and Kate Ozment, 'Building the Women in Book History Bibliography, or Digital Enumerative Bibliography as Preservation of Feminist Labor', *Digital Humanities Quarterly*, 13 (2019).

26 Kate Ozment, 'Rationale for Feminist Bibliography', *Textual Cultures*, 12 (2020), p. 151.

27 Ozment, 'Rationale', p. 165.

## 2      Commonalities

This volume's twenty-five chapters seek to emphasise three major themes: problematising archival absences, new emphases on family and community networks of bookworkers, and the transformative potential of new approaches such as studies of masculinity and queer bibliography. First, the scholarship of feminist bibliography has also heavily relied on and highlighted the work on archival absence and critique presented in critical race theory. Similar to bibliographic practices, archives are not neutral. Methods of archival appraisal enshrine, reflect, and project systems of value, and all too often, archival administration has limited institutional access. Both are composed of societal constructions of race, class, imperialism, gender and sexuality. As Saidiya Hartman and others have explored for the context of Caribbean histories and black women's life writing, archives are colonial and racist conduits; in the selective process of collection and preservation archives represent the dominant culture or regime.[28] In this way archival practices have engaged in intentional erasure. With archives being representative of the dominant culture, gender becomes an avenue of erasure. It is commonly held that women are hard to find in the archives, and this 'common knowledge' has been understood as representative, or read as proof, that women did not, or could not participate in history. However, given the revelations from critical race theory, and novel arguments from feminist historians, this view is insufficient. Historians have a responsibility to explain their rationales or interpretive choices when they come up against archival absences and historical gaps, and not fill them with gendered assumptions.

Several chapters in this volume address this silence explicitly, and demonstrate how careful archival research can provide a qualitative approach to filling these gaps. In their chapter, Rebecca Baumann draws an explicit line between women's presence on the cover of twentieth-century paperbacks and how the labour of women in the publishing industry has been erased. They address this erasure with painstaking biographical research. In particular, this research models how books are made by 'communities of makers' (p. 112),

---

28   Many thanks to Dr Claire Battershill for this recommendation. Hartman, 'Venus in Two Acts'; Jocelyn Fenton Stitt, *Dreams of Archives Unfolded: Absence ad Caribbean Life Writing* (New Brunswick, NJ: Rutgers University Press, 2021); Rachael Scarborough King, 'Critical Pedagogy and Feminist Scholarship in the Archives', *Huntington Library Quarterly*, 84 (2021), pp. 189–201. Furthermore, Gracen Brilmyer has recently looked at the archives as preserver and promoter of ableist narratives, see Gracen Brilmyer, 'Archival assemblages: applying disability studies' political/relational model to archival description', *Archives and Museum Informatics*, 18 (2018), pp. 1–24.

including trans women and women with disabilities, whose stories are far less likely to be told. In the same way, Elizabeth Le Roux uncovers how histories of African publishing are beginning to recognise women's contributions utilising oral histories and news. These exemplary approaches to filling archival gaps in studies of modern publishing demonstrate how historians can recover marginalised voices.

Susan McElrath's meticulous examination of the record books of the all-female bookbinding union in San Francisco presents a new perspective on women's labour history from a source that is not only understudied but entirely anonymous, describing family and class networks in the early twentieth century. Similarly, J.C. Rozendaal's work in the Luchtmans bookseller's vast archives reveals previously unknown patterns of female collecting and book ownership in eighteenth-century Leiden. Using catalogues and provenance research, Joëlle Weis reconstructs Elisabeth Sophie Marie of Brunswick-Wolfenbüttel's donated collection that no longer exists intact within the Herzog August Library, and is able to discover a vast amount about her life and collecting habits as a result. All of these qualitative methods directly address the erasure of these figures in their time and in modern book history.

Along with these qualitative approaches to archival research, quantitative research can also reveal broader trends. This work is being pioneered not only in short-title catalogues such as the Universal Short Title Catalogue and its new gendered metadata practices, but innovative data projects such as the Women's Print History Project and the Black Bibliography Project that utilise principles of inclusive bibliography.[29] In this volume, big data makes it possible to reveal broader trends related to gender within the book world. Kate Ozment and Kandice Sharren utilise thousands of records from the Women's Print History Project dataset and the framework of intersectionality to analyse identity-based language related to gender, race and social standing. The chapter by Natalia Maillard Álvarez and Montserrat Cachero demonstrates the efficacy of network analysis and data visualisation in demonstrating gendered family

---

29  Women's Print History Project <https://womensprinthistoryproject.com>. See in particular the 'Project Methodology' section <https://womensprinthistoryproject.com/blog/page/12>, and Kandice Sharren, Kate Ozment and Michelle Levy, 'Gendering Digital Bibliography with the Women's Print History Project', *Eighteenth-Century Studies*, 54 (2021), pp. 887–908. See also the Black Bibliography Project <https://blackbibliog.org/>; Brenna Bychowski and Melissa Barton, 'Modeling Black Literature: Behind the Screen with the Black Bibliography Project', in Raymond Pun, Melissa Cardenas-Dow and Kenya S. Flash (eds.), *Ethnic Studies in Academic and Research Libraries* (Chicago, IL: Association of College & Research Libraries, 2021), pp. 217–231; Jacqueline Goldsby and Meredith L. McGill, 'What is "Black" about Black Bibliography?', *The Papers of the Bibliographical Society of America*, 116 (2022), pp. 161–189.

and professional relationships in the Iberian Atlantic. Alongside these projects, the work of Kirk Melnikoff and the Book Trade Probate team show how
early modern women's wills can reveal the unrecognised work of Stationers'
Company widows, both when their husbands were living and after they died.

Widowhood was just one of the family-centred distinctions that defined
women's role in print culture, especially in periods when family and workshop
structures vastly overlapped. As such, the second major theme of this volume
is family and community networks. Like Smith, this volume aims to dissect
the Darnton model and repopulate it with not only men, but women and children, making the book production circuit one not about business but about
family relations, in any time and in any place. Marriages and kin constituted
the next generation of workers and underpinned the business relationships
of the trade, and this meant that whole families and communities were part
of the bookmaking process. This was true both of printing and distribution.
As Jessica Farrell-Jobst's chapter demonstrates, book production relied on the
family, and in particular the family name. While a name on the book may be
interpreted as male, book families continuously accounted for the interests
of their female members in the larger business of books. Similarly, Verônica
Calsoni Lima proves that in Restoration England, the business relationship
between husband and wife was essential to maintaining the business and
continuing the work of clandestine publishing. In fact, it even afforded these
women unique opportunities. Elise Watson's chapter shows that communities
of Catholic women in the Dutch Republic were able to work within the clandestine book trade as distributors due to their gender, which protected them
from the critiques of magistrates.

Family networks necessarily require a discussion of legal boundaries and
official and class structure. Agnes Gehbald's chapter examines how property
structure and inheritance determined whether widows could obtain printing
privileges and continue to maintain and lease equipment in the Viceroyalty
of Peru. Similarly, Laura Guinot Ferri shows how book circulation and inheritance could be calculated decisions within a noble family, based on who was
allowed to read prohibited books and to what privileges noblewomen had
access. Social status and class were some of the most essential signifiers of
identity along with gender, and essential elements of the book trades such as
guild membership, imprints on title pages, tax records and property ownership were determined by who was permitted to participate in certain activities. However, as the multifaceted elements of this volume show, these official
markers can obscure the multifaceted labours and participants involved in
print work.

Status mattered not only for how gendered roles functioned, but also
how society perceived femininity and gender nonconformity. In her chapter,

Alexandra Wingate discusses the moral expectations placed upon female readers in seventeenth-century Navarre, and how this limited not only their canon of literature but also the value they placed on the books themselves. Similarly, Rabia Gregory examines image and paratext in early printed prayer manuals, determining how gender and piety were perceived in print. While piety itself was gendered, and women had less access to certain kinds of monastic community, men could be exemplars of feminine piety, and the sixteenth century saw the downplaying of gender-specific aspects of piety overall.

Beyond families, communities were spaces for gendered interaction. Sometimes, these were all-female spaces: in her chapter, Valentina Sonzini discusses how women's monasteries in Italy had their own systems of organisation and autonomy when it came to library curation. Conversely, these interactions sometimes entail women in exclusively male spaces: Kanupriya Dhingra's ethnographic research in the modern Daryaganj Sunday Book Market in Old Delhi demonstrates how female booksellers are excluded from the community of vendors due to gendered understandings of agency and duty. Matthew Chambers shows how Sylvia Beach and Adrienne Monnier carefully and intentionally fashioned their own bookselling spaces as modern literary salons, which led to their establishment as respectable institutions according to their male contemporaries.

As Chambers demonstrates, communities could also be intellectual, and demonstrate gendered intellectual labour. Charley Matthews and Helen Williams demonstrate two closely related examples of this in their subsequent chapters: Matthews deftly shows how Mary Hays' reading, editing and anthologising work in the early nineteenth century created community and challenged traditional narratives of book production, and Williams tells the remarkable story of Constantia Grierson, a printer and polymath whose poetry was reprinted long beyond her lifetime in eighteenth-century literary spheres. Finally, Georgianna Ziegler stretches the boundaries of gender and book history by describing the interplay of print, manuscript, embroidery and lacemaking as bookwork in the life of the Franco-Scottish artist Esther Inglis. Ziegler's work demonstrates the need to discover an innovative approach to finding gender in archives and relying on family, community and intellectual networks as a model for understanding gender.

## 3     A Call to Action

With so much varied and multifaceted work that brings together gender and book history, it is time to move past ignoring or making assumptions about archival silences and towards developing both interpretive frameworks and innovative pedagogies that address them. Part of this is recognising the extent to which the discipline of book history has made assumptions about the masculine default, and paving the way for fruitful future studies of masculinity in the book trades. This pressing need is especially apparent when we scrutinise how many foundational bibliographies implicitly assumed that an anonymous or abbreviated name stood for a male subject. As Sarah Lubelski reminds us in her chapter, the publisher was not a neutral figure but in fact a highly gendered one, with a series of social expectations based on masculinity and class. Book collecting, book work and professional identities were masculinised, to the extent that female printers almost universally adopted identities of their own that relied on proximity to a male professional such as 'widow of' and 'heir of'. Inclusion of these viewpoints begin an important conversation about how scholarship has previously addressed gender history, where the majority of studies focus on either women or femininity, and scholars engaged into this work are largely female or non-binary. As Natalia Fantetti demonstrates in her discussion of Wilfrid Michael Voynich, putting constructions of masculinity and femininity in explicit contrast and comparison with each other can yield fascinating results, particularly in their relationship to the public. It is this innovative work that moves from women's history into a broader and more inclusive gender history.

Finally, as the radical pedagogy introduced by Malcolm Noble's final chapter instructs us, understanding gender changes our relationship to the book itself. Queer bibliography, in its dimensions of addressing both gender and sexuality, disrupts and destabilises hierarchies of male and female, normative and marginal binaries. Recovering the meanings that books as objects and repositories of knowledge had for their readers is an essential aspect of gendered book history. Noble proposes a radical re-understanding of the systems that underpin the study of print, including catalogues, similar to how Kate Ozment and Kandice Sharren demonstrate the power of inclusive metadata to identify trends in feminised authorship identity in their preceding chapter. However, Noble also proposes an explicitly pedagogical element, pioneering an affective, fluid approach to bibliography itself. The intersectional approaches offered by rethinking strategies of reading and book interaction exemplify how thinking critically about gender can fundamentally change book history and bibliography as fields.

It would be impossible, and ill-advised, for one person to write a history of all genders in all book trades. As such, this book presents case studies of how gender shaped the long history of the book, in service of a new methodology that starts from the assumption of archival presence and a base of inclusive and collaborative thinking. We caution readers not to approach these case studies as singular and extraordinary examples, but as proof of the rich stories that can be found when researchers attend to book history with an inclusive gender framework. Like a bibliography itself, this volume collects individual examples of surviving stories, not in order to provide something as comprehensive as the original, but rather to discover something larger. *Gender and the Book Trades* demonstrates that we can learn more by studying the fragmented evidence on its own terms than trying to rationalise them within some constructed ideal. As such, the following chapters should not be seen as exceptional, but evidential. The stories presented in this volume are proof that in gender and book history there is no pervasive norm, only the presumptive norm.

# PART 1

## *Familiar Networks*

∴

# CHAPTER 2

# Women in the Family Business: the Case for Nuremberg's Endter Printing Dynasty

*Jessica Farrell-Jobst*

On 7 March, 1917, Reverend William James Couper presented a paper to the Historical and Philological Section of the Royal Society of Philosophy of Glasgow, where he began with this statement, '[w]omen have never taken a prominent part in the business of printing and publishing.'[1] A century later, the historiography on gender and the book trades proves the contrary. Although profoundly archaic and fallacious, this statement describes printing and publishing as little more than a labour-driven activity, rather framing these activities as a business. Despite Reverend Couper's sentiments, it is in the development and management of the business of books that women were most active. This paper argues that due to the familial nature of the book trade, women were continually included in, inherited and benefitted from book and trading companies. In particular, my research on the activities of the Endter family, a publishing powerhouse in Nuremberg, demonstrates conclusively that early modern women acted as partners, shareholders, and owners to family-based book companies.

The Endter family established a book company that lasted for over a century, printing books under the Endter name until 1746 and operating as booksellers far into the eighteenth century.[2] Starting in bookbinding operations in the sixteenth century, the company expanded by the mid-seventeenth century to include printing, publishing, long-distance trading and papermaking.[3] Several members of this industrious family worked for the Nuremberg city council as council printers and booksellers, printing official decrees and documents or procuring literary material for the council, and several were appointed to the

---

1   W.J. Couper, 'Mrs. Anderson and the royal prerogative in printing', *Proceedings of the Royal Philosophical Society of Glasgow*, 48 (1917), p. 79.

2   Michael Diefenbacher and Wiltrud Fischer-Pache (eds.), *Das Nürnberger Buchgewerbe, Buch- und Zeitungsdrucker, Verleger und Druckhändler vom 16. Bis zum 18. Jahrhundert* (Nuremberg: Das Stadtarchivs Nürnberg, 2003), p. 679. Hereafter abbreviated as DNB.

3   Lore Sporan-Krempel, 'Zur Genealogie der Familie Endter in Nürnberg', *Archiv für Geschichte des Buchwesens*, 8 (1967), pp. 505–532.

© KONINKLIJKE BRILL BV, LEIDEN, 2025 | DOI:10.1163/9789004701656_003

*Große Rat* (Great Council) of Nuremberg.[4] Despite the importance of this company to the history of the book trade (it has been estimated recently that the Endter family produced 50% of the annual output in Nuremberg, dominating the city's book industry), the wives, mothers and daughters of the family remain overlooked in the historiography.[5] Their invisibility in the subsequent scholarship mirrors the invisibility they suffered in their familial companies, invisibility which was produced by the changing nature of the book trade of the seventeenth century and reproduced by traditional bibliographic practises.

In the sixteenth century, when imprint data was more likely to be an accurate record of the maker, the names of women printers and publishers were found on the books they produced. Printers like Kunigunde Hergotin and Katherine Gerlachin represented their proprietorship and management of the print shop by emblazing their full names on the front pages or colophons of the products they made.[6] For historians, the activities of these individuals are easier to trace. Yet, as the seventeenth century progressed, the Nuremberg book trade became increasingly dominated by book companies and the idea of an individual as producer no longer held credence. Instead, family names were often used like company monikers, representing larger operations that could comprise multiple trades, interests and parties. For the Endter family, the name on the imprint data often represented only a portion of those involved in the company. Moreover, the names on the imprint data of the surviving books published with the name Endter are all male. This tactic hides the women who participated in the familial business, who shared in the business as members of that family. Furthermore, this invisibility is exacerbated by traditional bibliographic practises, which has habitually considered imprint data at face value, attributing books to the individuals named. Relying on just the name in the imprint has cemented the notion of the individual as producer, obscuring the reality that all genders participated in the book trade. Where imprint data is no longer reliable, or even misrepresentational, historians must supplement their research with accounting and business records to find the efforts and labour of women.

---

4   A collection of 'Buchdrucker Zettel', or receipts and invoices, in the *Stadtrechnungsbelege* of the Staatsarchiv Nurnberg attest that multiple members of the Endter family were frequently hired by the Nuremberg city council to print official government decrees and mandate throughout the seventeenth century, see Jessica Farrell-Jobst, 'Women as Book Producers: The Case of Nuremberg', PhD Thesis: University of St Andrews, 2021, pp. 58–65.

5   Hans-Otto Keunecke, 'Buchverlag, Buchdruck und Buchhandel in Nürnberg 1640 bis 1650', in Dirk Niefanger and Werner Wilhelm Schnabel (eds.), *Johann Klaj (um 1616–1656). Akteur—Werk—Umfeld* (Berlin: De Gruyter, 2020), p. 221.

6   See USTC 700740 or USTC 631834 for examples.

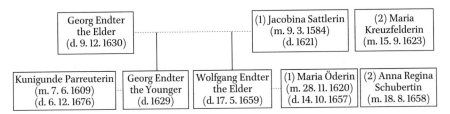

FIGURE 2.1   George Endter the Elder's Sons

## 1      Partners: Wives

The most recognised way women entered into the book trades was through marriage. In the sixteenth century, the women who gained proprietorship of a print business often did so through inheritance as a widow (although in Nuremberg there are cases of women working in tandem with men on their own products). In the role of wife, early modern women often acted as partners in the domestic economy.[7] The early modern home was a site of production and work, involving the family unit in various tasks and for artisans and merchants, shops and offices were often in their homes. The sixteenth century printing office and bookshop was regularly placed inside the home of the master printer.[8] When the place of production was a part of the domestic environment, the boundaries between shop and home became reasonably porous. Marriage customs in Nuremberg followed the *Gutergesellschaft* practice, where a couple brought their belongings, wealth and property into a community of goods.[9] Moreover, in Nuremberg residential property purchased by a married couple was in the name of both spouses, and either spouse needed the permission of the other to sell or transfer it. Georg Endter the Elder, the patriarch of the Endter dynasty, alludes to this set up in a marriage contract drawn up for the marriage of his son, Wolfgang Endter to Maria Öderin in 1620. The contract specified what each person brought to the marriage, as well as a special gift Georg and his wife Jacobina (née Sattlerin) passed on to their son.[10] On the

---

7   Martha C. Howell, *Women, Production, and Patriarchy in Late Medieval Cities* (Chicago, IL: The University of Chicago Press, 1986), pp. 9–43.

8   Cait Coker, 'Gendered spheres: theorizing space in the English printing house', *The Seventeenth Century*, 33 (2018), pp. 323–336.

9   Merry Wiesner, 'Frail, weak, and helpless: women's legal position in theory and reality', in Merry E. Wiesner, *Gender Church, and State in Early Modern Germany* (Harlow: Addison Wesley Longman limited, 1999), pp. 86–87.

10  *DNB*, pp. 225–226 (Nr. 1370).

occasion of his marriage, Georg and 'in the Name of his wife, Frau Jacobina' bestowed on their son a print shop with its equipment and tools. The gift was specifically from Georg and Jacobina, as both were the owners of the property, having purchased the print shop with its equipment and tools in 1602 from renowned printer and bookseller Catherine Dietrichin. The sale contract specifies that Catherine sold this print shop to 'the honourable Georg Endter and Jacobina, his wife', identifying her as partner to the property.[11]

Despite occupying the legal framework to act as a business partner, it is difficult to get a tangible idea of how much a wife participated in the familial business. We know that Jacobina was active in supporting the business. In 1600, Jacobina sent a supplication to the city council of Nuremberg requesting an appeal to the council of Regensburg regarding the arrest of three of her barrels with goods by one of their citizens.[12] Likewise, when Wolfgang's (later known as Wolfgang the Elder) first wife Maria died in 1657, a funeral oration was printed in which her contributions to the business were mentioned. In it, we are told that for her husband she was 'an indefatigable helper, a diligent nurse of his body, a highly sensible councillor and representative of his large and difficult trade'.[13] All laudatory exaggerations aside, it would seem that Wolfgang had relied on his wife to represent or direct the business in his absence. In at least one case, Maria was required to give a report in her husband's stead to the city council regarding a payment to a creditor.[14]

However, inheritance had a way of moving goods and property out of a family lineage. In the *Gutergesellschaft* arrangement, in the event of one spouse's death, the other received total authority over the community of goods. This inheritance scheme let multiple women enter into the trade independently by inheriting an established print business, gaining control over the shop, equipment, and capital. In the event of remarriage, property, businesses and other assets were transferred into a new community of goods with the new partner. This is a common story for sixteenth-century Nuremberg, where a printer's widow inherits the shop, remarries, and the new husband takes over the shop operating under a new name. The seventeenth century changed this process by implementing legal devices like the marriage contract in order to stabilise linear inheritance. In the marriage contract between Wolfgang Endter and Maria Öder, it was stipulated that both parties were responsible for the conjugal fund,

---

11      *DNB*, p. 129 (Nr. 829).
12      *DNB*, p. 129 (Nr. 828).
13      *DNB*, pp. 258–259 (Nr. 1623).
14      *DNB*, p. 235 (Nr. 1447).

and both were to make a financial contribution.[15] Maria brought 300 *Gulden* and the groom gifted 500 florins.[16] The contract lays down that the surviving spouse would retain the right to the original contribution, plus, for Maria, any gifts made to her from her husband during their marriage, and for Wolfgang, his 'einshandguter' (one-hand goods) that were 'brought, and in other ways won and gained', including the print shop that was ceded to him by his parents.[17] With this clause, Wolfgang's parents were protecting linear familial inheritance by excluding Wolfgang's new wife from any right to inherit the shop and equipment. Clearly, for Georg and Jacobina, it was important that the shop and business should remain within the Endter family.

Maria died in 1657, and Wolfgang married his second wife, Anna Regina Schubertin, shortly thereafter in 1658, for which he drew up another marital contract. As with the contact for his first marriage, Wolfgang was similarly careful to prevent Anna from inheriting the company he clearly intended to leave for his sons from the previous marriage. The contract specified that upon his death, his wife-to-be would not inherit any of the profit of his company.[18] She was granted a sum of 3,000 *Gulden* as compensation and, later, it appears that Wolfgang's heirs granted her a further 9,000 *Gulden* and the marriage bed as an inheritance from her short marriage to their father.[19] Wolfgang also excluded his daughter, Dorothea Maria, from inheriting any of his company's assets, while his two eldest sons, Wolfgang the Younger and Johann Andreas, were bequeathed a trading company, and his two youngest, Christoph and Paul, received their father's paper mills and remaining paper stock. Despite the appearance of dismissing his daughter's and wives' inheritance, Wolfgang did not necessarily neglect these women's rights to property and wealth. Wolfgang and Maria purchased several residential properties whilst wed, all of which were purchased in both their names.[20] Furthermore, Wolfgang left his daughter an equal portion of a house sale, giving each of his five children 10,000 *Gulden*.[21] The difference is the separation from company property and private property, a concept which was less clear a century earlier. As we will see with later examples, excluding wives and daughters from company inheritance did not necessarily derive from notions about women

---

15    *DNB*, pp. 225–226 (Nr. 1370).
16    Records used Florins and Gulder interchangeably; I have rendered it as stated in the contract.
17    'zugebrachten und in andere weg eroberte', *DNB*, pp. 225–226 (Nr. 1370).
18    *DNB*, p. 259 (Nr. 1624).
19    *DNB*, p. 261 (Nr. 1628).
20    *DNB*, p. 227 (1382); *DNB*, p. 252 (Nr. 1577); *DNB*, pp. 253–254 (Nr. 1588).
21    *DNB*, p. 268 (Nr. 1648).

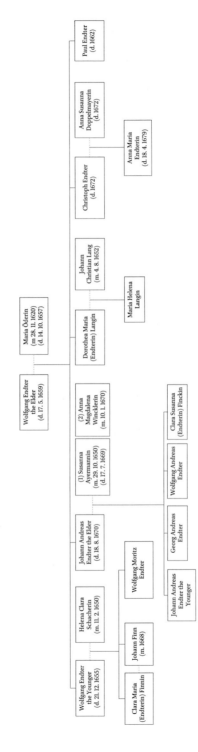

FIGURE 2.2  Wolfgang Endter the Elder's Children and Grandchildren

and work or women in business, but rather an attempt to preserve the family name with the business. In fact, despite Wolfgang's exclusion of his daughter from the company, he advocated for his granddaughter's right to a portion of her father's book company.

## 2     Shareholders: Sisters

Wolfgang the Elder's son, Wolfgang the Younger, predeceased his father in 1655, leaving his wife and two young children to inherit his estate. After receiving a trading company from his parents in 1651, Wolfgang the Younger and Johann Andreas purchased the print shop of Jeremias Dümler in 1653, whereupon they were immediately entered into the city's record of offices (the *Ämterbüchlein*) in 1654.[22] Both were entered under the *Buchführer* (Bookseller) category twice, alongside one another, as 'Johann Andreas Endter und Wolff Endter Jun.' and 'Wolff Endter jun. und Johann Andreas Endter', cementing their partnership.[23] In 1655, Wolfgang was also entered into the *Buchdrucker* (Printer) category of the workbook, suggesting that the printing department was delegated to him.[24] However the imprints stated both brothers' names on the title page, often reading 'Nürnberg/ Bey Wolffgang den jungern und Johann Andreas Endter' (Nuremberg/ By Wolfgang the Younger and Johann Andreas Endter).[25] The imprint remained unchanged until 1659, when Wolfgang's heirs were included, even though Wolfgang had died four years earlier.[26] The change in imprint reflected a change in the business, as on 9 December 1658 Johann Andreas had merged a trading company with his niece and nephew, seven-year-old Clara Maria and five-year-old Wolfgang Moritz.[27] In the revised testament of Johann's father, Wolfgang the Elder wished for his 'eldest son's children' to remain in the company for 'a number of years', according to their 'newly established trading company'.[28] Later in the same will, Wolfgang referred to his grandchildren as Johann Andrea's 'shareholders'.

The original document uses the word *Kinder* (children) rather than *Sohn* or *Sohnlein* (son or sons), making it clear that both Wolfgang Moritz and

---

22   Christoph Reske, *Die Buckdrucker des 16. Und 17. Jahrhunderts im deutschen Sprachgebiet* (Wiesbaden: Harrassowitz, 2015), p. 799.

23   *DNB*, p. 639.

24   *DNB*, p. 637.

25   See VD17 39:119893B.

26   See VD17 39:118321K.

27   *DNB*, pp. 259–260 (Nr. 1625).

28   'neu aufgerichteten handelscompganie', Ibid.

Clara Maria were to be considered shareholders of the trading company. This arrangement guaranteed the children's inheritance and also effectively relinquished control of the business solely to Johannes Andreas. The timing of this merger may have been a response to the impending remarriage of Wolfgang the Younger's widow, which took place in 1659. This remarriage would have potentially disassociated the firm from the Endter name. The merging of the company excluded her from any control over her late husband's business. It is unlikely that Wolfgang or Clara participated meaningfully in the company until much later, yet establishing both children as shareholders guaranteed their future association with the business and a portion of the profits when they reached adulthood. Despite this, it was their uncle, Johann Andreas (later Johann Andreas the Elder) who was left to run the company.

Johann Andreas Endter ran the company until his death in 1670, when his children took over. From Wolfgang the Younger's death until even after Johann Andreas' own death, the imprint used on company publications was 'Johann Andreas Endter and Wolfgang Endter the Younger's heirs.' In 1674 the imprint changed to reflect a change in directorship. The imprint now read 'by Wolfgang Moritz Endter and Johann Andreas Endter's Heirs', indicating not only Wolfgang Moritz's maturity but also the inheritance of Johann Andreas' children, Johann Andreas the Younger, Georg Andreas, Wolf Andreas and Clara Susanna. The imprint remained the same until 1679 when Johann Andreas' 'heirs' was changed to 'sons'. This small adjustment reflected the sale of company shares by Clara Susanna and her husband, Dr Johann Martin Finck in August 1679.[29] The change in imprint impacts not only how we conceive of the business but also how the Endter family wanted to portray it. From 1674 when the 'heirs' imprint was first used, if not 1670 when Johann Andreas Endter the Elder died, until 1679, we must consider Clara Susanna as an integral part of the family company. It was clearly important to the family who chose to use the gender-neutral term *heirs* when she was a part of the business, only to change it after her shares were sold.

In these two instances women were purposefully included in their family business, receiving equal shares of the company, yet their involvement was not reflected in the imprint data. Instead, the imprint refers to deceased males by name and an unspecified collective. It is only revealed that this collective is heterogeneous when we look at the wills and contracts of the business. Although both Clara Maria and Clara Susanna sold their shares to their male relatives, they were not only bequeathed a portion, but older family members actively protected their right to that inheritance. The reasoning behind these sales is

---

29    *DNB*, p. 146 (Nr. 940).

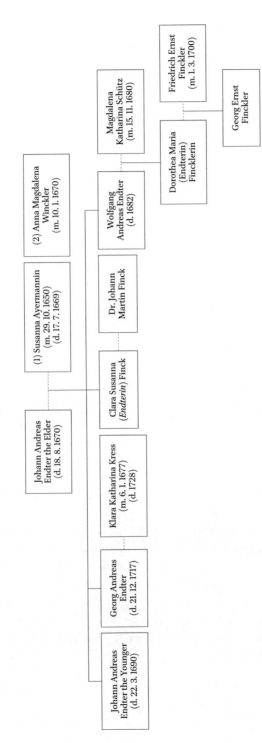

FIGURE 2.3 Johann Andreas Endter the Elder's Children and Grandchildren

provided in several later cases where, instead of inheritance split between brothers and sisters, the business fell upon the shoulders of a single woman.


## 3        Figureheads: Daughters

Wolfgang the Elder, who had amassed a large operation upon his death, had four sons to take over such a large trade. Where Wolfgang the Younger and Johann Andreas had received a book trading company, Wolfgang the elder's youngest sons, Christoph and Paul Endter, also went into the book business, having received paper stock and at least one of Wolfgang's paper mills. Paul Endter died at a relatively young age, leaving his estate to Christoph. In 1664 Christoph purchased a print shop, joining his elder brothers in the production and publication of books. However, Christoph Endter died in 1672, shortly after his wife Anna Susanna, née Doppelmayerin, had passed, leaving his company, which was now an amalgamation of Paul's paper mills and his book company, to his only daughter, Anna Maria Endterin. Although Christoph Endter left his daughter the company and print shop in his will, he also included a list of mandatory stipulations.[30] Firstly, if Anna Maria should die before she married, then the company would be given to the sons of his deceased brothers, Wolf Moritz and Johann Andreas the Younger, Georg Andreas, and Wolfgang Andreas. After achieving maturity, if Anna Maria wished to sell the company, her cousins would have the first right to buy. Furthermore, she would have to sell the company (presumably to her cousins), if she reached adulthood and married. Christoph explained his reasoning for these somewhat odd stipulations. He claimed that his wish was for his company and print office to flourish and retain the 'Endterischen' name.[31] The association between the name Endter and the book trade had been well established through his grandfather, father, uncle, cousins and brothers for at least the previous 50 years. Almost every male kin was involved in the trade and the name was found on many books. It is little wonder that Christoph would be keen to have continued this tradition. But if his only daughter inherited the business and subsequently married, her husband could potentially head the business under his own name, or under her married name, breaking this dynasty. On the other hand, Anna Maria's father was not willing to write her out of this heritage and Anna Maria remained sole inheritor.

---

30     *DNB*, pp. 126–127 (Nr. 814).
31     Ibid.

Although the seven-year-old was technically owner, management was split between the shop's *Faktor* and Anna Maria's paternal uncles. Although *Faktors* managed the print output and her guardians decided both personal and professional matters, the legal inheritor, Anna Maria, was regarded as the rightful owner. In a legal case, where the *Faktor* was accused of using a false place of publication, thus defying both imperial and Nuremberg's censorship laws, the city council interceded on behalf of the Endter family. In their letters, the council recognises Anna Maria as legal owner, stating that the imperial privileges in question were for Anna Maria Endterin. The imperial rescript referred to the 'impressorium' for the 'daughter of Christoph Endter', which would cover a period of nine years.[32] Therefore the renewed privilege was issued for Anna Maria, rather than Wolfgang Moritz, the *Faktor*, or any of Johann Andrea's sons. Furthermore, in the council's communication about the case, they do not refer to the *Faktor* or guardian by name but regularly frame their relationship to 'Christoph Endter's Daughter' or to the 'Endterin'.[33] Despite her gender, and even her young age, Anna Maria remained the legal heir of Christoph Endter and therefore at least the ceremonial head of Christoph Endter's *Buchhandel* (Book Company). In this way we can understand Anna Maria as a ceremonial, but real, figurehead of the company. Although, at such a young age, she could not fully participate in the management of the company, her family and local authorities not only considered her the rightful heir but protected her right to the business.

Unfortunately, Anna Maria died in 1679, at the age of 14. Following Christoph's will, Johann Andrea's sons and Wolfgang Moritz inherited his shop and company, fulfilling their uncle's wishes that the company be associated with the Endter name.[34] Anna Maria Endterin's premature death leaves us with many questions as to how she would have dealt with her inheritance. Would she have continued the business as sole proprietor? Would she marry and sell her shares? It is impossible to tell, but what is interesting is that she legally had that choice.

In another instance, the family company, now consisting of Christoph Endter's book company, was left to another underage girl. By 1683, Wolfgang Moritz and the three sons of Johann Andreas Endter divided their company

---

32    *DNB*, pp. 123–124 (Nr. 800).

33    'Intercessions-Schreiben fur die Vormunder der Christof Endterischen Tochter', *DNB*, p. 124 (Nr. 802); 'Ausserdem soll den Vormundern und Druckereifaktoren der Endterin das Rescript vorgelesen', *DNB*, p. 124 (Nr. 801).

34    At Anna Maria's death the company left to her was a significant enterprise, see Lore Sprohan-Krempel and Theodore Wohnhaas, 'Das Inventar der Christoph Endterischen Buchhandlung anno 1679', *Archiv fur Geschichte Buchwesens*, 18 (1977), pp. 1557–1572.

into two separate ventures.[35] The company, now known as Johann Andreas Endter's *Seligen Sohnes* (blessed sons), was composed of Johann Andreas the Younger, Georg Andreas Endter and Wolfgang Andreas Endter. However, Wolfgang Andreas Endter died in 1682, leaving his share of the company to his only daughter, Dorothea Maria Endterin. Unlike the earlier case of Anna Maria Endterin, Dorothea Maria reached an age of maturity. Furthermore, unlike the inheritance of Anna Maria, which stipulated that she would sell her company if she married, Dorothea Maria's inheritance was clearly not conditional, as she remained a shareholder well after marriage, eventually passing the company to her son. Before this, however, her share of the company increased. In 1690 her eldest uncle, Johann Andreas the Younger died, having left his only niece with one-third of his remaining share in the company, from which she would receive a portion of the capital (20,000 *Gulden*).[36] Georg Andreas, now the only brother alive, continued to act as director of the company until 1717 when he passed away. Upon his death, his widow, Klara Katherina, née Kress, inherited his shares in the company. She immediately established a contract with her niece's son, guaranteeing Dorothea Maria's inheritance.[37] Klara acted as administrator of the company until 1728 when she, too, died, leaving the whole company to Dorothea Maria's son. Before her death, the office continued to print and trade books, using her husband's chosen imprint 'Johann Andreas Endter' despite the majority of the company now being owned by two women.[38] Here again we see an instance of the imprint referring to a deceased male and his offspring. However, by 1717, where the imprint indicates a group of Endter males, the surviving contracts reveal that the business was partially owned by a woman.

## 4        Conclusion

The family dynamics and business decisions of the Endter book company this study reveals conflict with some prior assumptions about the early modern book trade. First, such cases suggest that, while useful, imprint data is flawed, and we need to address that more systematically.[39] We can see several times in the history of the Endter family that the imprint data is less a record of

---

35    There is a closing balance sheet and inventory from 1683 showing that Wolf Moritz had ceased operations with Johann Andreas Endter's Sons, DNB, p. 277 (Nr. 1699).

36    DNB, pp. 149–150 (Nr. 952).

37    DNB, p. 165 (Nr. 1024).

38    VD18 10099093.

39    Eist, Isabelle. "'Printed by—': Imprints and Firms in the WPHP', *The Women's Print History Project* (10-07-2023): <https://womensprinthistoryproject.com/blog/post/122>.

labour and producers but company branding demonstrating that imprints are complicated paratexts. In fact, the name on the imprint is often hiding a whole network of people, many of whom were women. Imprint data that seems singular and male at first glance actually contains a variety of agents and genders. Even in cases where the imprint data more accurately represents the master printer, the use and structure of this data continues to hide the multiple parties involved in a book's creation. Therefore, it is necessary that scholars reconstruct their understanding of early modern book production from a model of individuals moving books through the stages of production towards a network of communities, many of whom are unnamed or recorded for posterity.[40] An inclusive framework, or methodology, asks us to work from this understanding that there were individuals whose contributions to a process have gone unnoticed, undocumented, and undervalued. Moreover, the idea of community contributions, or community labour, facilitates the reintroduction of women's labour back into the discourse. Even when archival documents, colophons and guild records present a male-dominant field, focusing on the larger network that these individuals operated within can provide a more complicated and representative picture.

Second, the move from individual to community changes our conception of women's work. Whereas the historiography on women's work generally postulates a model of decline, in which women's participation in the workforce waned, the case study of the Endter family suggests that like previously, women's work continued in the framework of the ultimate community, that of the family.[41] Moreover, women's involvement in this work changed with the

---

40    Printer compendiums and bibliographies likewise should highlight the community aspect of book production, highlighting family connection and business development over individuals. As it is, these sources, on which scholars rely for vital information, currently under-represent women's involvement at best, or, frame them as assistive. Farrell-Jobst, 'Women as Book Producers', pp. 3–4.

41    The initial scholarship on women's work painted a very bleak picture for working women in the early modern period, and tremendous scholars like Merry Wiesner, Judith Bennet and Natalia Zemon Davis (working from the narrative of Alice Clarke) argued there were declining opportunities for women to work in response to guilds and incorporation. See Merry Wiesner, *Working Women in Renaissance Germany* (New Brunswick, NJ: Rutgers University Press, 1986); Natalie Zemon Davis, 'Women in the Crafts in Sixteenth Century Lyon', *Feminist Studies*, 8 (1982), pp. 57, 66–67; Judith Bennett, *Beer, Ale and Brewsters: Women's Work in a Changing World, 1300–1600* (Oxford: Oxford University Press, 1999). Carol L. Loats and Clare Crowston were early critics of this argument, suggesting a more nuanced situation: Carol L. Loats, 'Gender, Guilds, and Work Identity: Perspectives from Sixteenth-Century Paris', *French Historical Studies*, 20 (1997), pp. 15–30; Clare Crowston, 'Women, Gender, and Guilds in Early Modern Europe: An Overview of Recent Research', *International Review of Social History*, 53 (2008), pp. 19–44. More recently, studies examining women's work have developed thanks to projects like the *Gender and Work* group

changing nature of the book trade itself. Print offices, book shops and work-spaces moved away from the domestic environment. Bookwomen, who had once inherited the business as widow and partner of the household produc-tion unit, became a part of a larger familial operation. Furthermore, imprint data was used as a branding device to further a familial empire. All these changes increasingly hid women's involvement. In the interest of continuing family identity, through the fraternal organisation of the firm, women initially seem absent. However, going through business contracts and wills shows that book families consistently included and protected their wives', sisters', nieces' and daughters' rights to be a part of the business. In this way, women acted as partners, shareholders and figure heads of the family business.

Lastly, the evidence from the present chapter asks us to question our ability to gender books, or gender more broadly, based on 'creator' or named individu-als in its production, whether that be the author, printer, editor, or publisher. As Helen Smith argued for early modern authorship, printing, publishing and book trading (selling) was also a place where exchanges and interactions between multiple genders constituted much of the book trade.[42] It is some-times difficult to witness the multitudes of participants from the evidence we have left, requiring us to broaden our understanding of 'individual creator' to an idea of community, or networks, whose interests, labour and objectives fur-thered and sustained book production. These communities consist of many individuals of many genders, and women's interests were taken into account. Thus, we can vehemently reject Reverend Couper's sentiments that women were never prominent in the book business and advocate instead that not only have women always participated, but were prominent in their labour, their communities and their families.

---

at Uppsala Universitet, whose work on the Verb-Oriented Model goes beyond officiality and job titles to look at the verb recorded in the records to determine the variance and consistency of women's work. Maria Ågren, 'Making Her Turn Around: The Verb-Oriented Method, the Two Supporter Model, and the Focus on Practise', *Early Modern Women: An Interdisciplinary Journal*, 13 (2018), pp. 144–152; Rosemarie Riebanz, Erik Lindberg, Jonas Lidström and Maria Ågren, 'Making Verbs count: the research project 'Gender and Work' and its methodology', *Scandinavian Economic History Review*, 59 (2011), pp. 271–293; Jonas Lindstrom Rosemarie Riebranz, Goran Ryden, 'The Diversity of Work', in Maria Ågren (ed.), *Making a Living, Making a Difference: Gender and Work in Early Modern European Society* (Oxford: Oxford University Press, 2017), pp. 24–56.

42     Helen Smith, *'Grossly Material Things': Women and Book Production in Early Modern England* (Oxford: Oxford University Press, 2012), pp. 4–8.

# CHAPTER 3

# Knitting Ties in a Global Trade Network: the Maldonado Women and the Book Business in the Sixteenth-Century Iberian Atlantic

*Natalia Maillard Álvarez and Montserrat Cachero*

The Spanish printing industry had an early start and, from the onset, it witnessed the rapid emergence of printing shops all over the Iberian Peninsula.[1] The first known book to be printed in Castille, the *Sinodal de Aguilafuente*, was published in Segovia (North Castille) in 1472, by the German printer Juan Parix, and over the following few years printing shops are attested in Barcelona, Valencia, Seville, and Zaragoza, among other cities.[2] Most of the first printers to arrive on the Iberian Peninsula in the fifteenth century were Germans.[3] This trend continued during the sixteenth century, when foreign printers, not only from Germany, but also from Italy, France and Flanders, were attracted to Spain by higher salaries and a more flexible legal framework for printing activities.[4]

Despite this, the printers based on the Iberian Peninsula could not compete with the publisher-booksellers at the core centres of the European printing industry, such as Venice or Lyon, and always played a peripheral role in the international book market. In the words of Angela Nuovo, '[a]s production grew and the market expanded, the need to find buyers meant that the laws

---

1　This study was undertaken within the framework of projects 'Las redes internacionales del comercio de libros en la Monarquía Hispánica.1501–1648' (reference HAR2017-82362-P), funded by the Spanish Government, and 'La revolución de los precios y el negocio del crédito en Sevilla ¿Una burbuja en el siglo XVI?' (reference UPO-1261964), funded by the European Regional Development Fund (FEDER). Julián Martín Abad, *Los primeros tiempos de la imprenta en España* (Madrid: Laberinto, 2003).

2　Fermín de los Reyes, *El Sinodal de Aguilafuente y la primera imprenta española* (Segovia: Ayuntamiento de Aguilafuente, 2017); *La imprenta incunable, el nuevo arte maravilloso de escribir* (Madrid: CSIC, 2015), pp. 39–40.

3　Konrad Haebler, *Impresores primitivos de España y Portugal* (Madrid: Ollero y Ramos, 2005), p. 23.

4　Clive Griffin, *Oficiales de imprenta, herejía e Inquisición en la España del siglo XVI* (Madrid: Ollero y Ramos, 2009), pp. 113–133. Griffin points out that the general lack of printers' guilds in Spain stimulated the arrival of foreign workers, who were able to find jobs even before finishing their training.

---

© KONINKLIJKE BRILL BV, LEIDEN, 2025 | DOI:10.1163/9789004701656_004

of commerce came to govern printing. In particular, entrepreneurial hege-
mony passed from the printer to the publisher-bookseller'.[5] The superiority of
the final products offered by some European publishing firms, together with
their access to financial networks and their commercial dynamism allowed
them to achieve a prominent role in that market, due to the development of
international distribution networks. These networks facilitated the connection between production centres and distant markets, reaching 'a transnational reading community dispersed around all of Europe', and, soon after, the
Americas.[6] Spanish printers focused mainly on a local audience, while international or high-quality books progressively became imported commodities.[7]
This was also promoted by the monarchy's policy of granting tax exemptions
for imported books, and the scarcity of printing privileges for domestic products.[8] To supply the Iberian market, from the early sixteenth century, European
companies (mostly Italian, French, and later Flemish) sent their agents to the

5   Angela Nuovo, *The Book Trade in the Italian* Renaissance (Leiden: Brill, 2013), p. 47. For a gen-
     eral study of the geography of the European book market, see Andrew Pettegree, 'Centre and
     Periphery in the European Book World', *Transactions of the Royal Historical Society*, 18 (2008),
     pp. 101–128. A detailed analysis about the reasons behind the weakness of the Spanish print-
     ing industry can be found in Jaime Moll Roqueta, 'El impresor y el librero en el Siglo de Oro',
     in Francisco Asín (ed.), *El mundo del libro Antiguo* (Madrid: Editorial Complutense, 1996),
     pp. 27–41; P. Berger et al., *Histoire du livre et de l'édition dans les pays ibériques. La dépendance*
     (Bordeaux: Presses Universitaires de Bordeaux, 1986).
6   Andrew Pettegree and Shanti Graheli, 'How to Lose Money in the Business of Books:
     Commercial Strategies in the First Age of Print', in Shanti Graheli (ed.), *Buying and Selling.
     The Business of Books in Early Modern Europe* (Leiden: Brill, 2019), p. 10. Pettegree and Graheli
     suggest that these firms, created by powerful families, followed a cartel-like business model
     inspired by early modern bankers. See also James Raven, 'Distribution: The Transmission of
     Books in Europe and its Colonies', in Joseph. P. MacDermott and Peter Burke (eds.), *The Book
     Worlds of East Asia and Europe, 1450–1850* (Hong Kong: Hong Kong University Press, 2015),
     pp. 235–240.
7   Alexandre Wilkinson, 'The Printed Book on the Iberian Peninsula, 1500–1540', in Malcolm
     Walsby and Graeme Kemp (eds.), *The Book Triumphant. Print in Transition in the Sixteenth
     and Seventeenth Centuries* (Leiden: Brill, 2011), p. 91. See also Klaus Wagner, 'Les libraires esp-
     agnols au XVIe siècle', in *L'Europe et le livre. Résaux et pratiques du négoce de librairie XVIe–
     XIXe siècles* (París: Klincksieck, 1996), pp. 31–42.
8   For the tax exemption policy, initiated by the Catholic monarchs in 1480, see Fermín de los
     Reyes, *El libro en España y América. Legislación y censura. Siglos XV–XVIII*, vol. 2 (Madrid:
     Arco/Libros, 2007), pp. 771–772. Regarding printing privileges, although at the beginning of
     the sixteenth century some were granted to a few powerful Spanish typographers with the
     aim of controlling the book production, this policy was generally abandoned in the 1520s,
     leaving an open market that the European firms were eager to attend to, see José L. Gonzalo,
     'Los impresores ante el Consejo Real: el problema de la licencia y del privilegio (1502–1540)',
     *Dos pinceladas sobre mercaderes de libros en el siglo XVI* (Badajoz: Unión de Bibliófilos
     Extremeños, 2009), pp. 119–184.

Iberian Peninsula. This was, for instance, the case with the Venetian Giunti, or the Lioness Portonariis, of which more will be said later.[9]

At the same time, a global demand for books emerged as the colonisation process unfolded in the Americas.[10] The commercial flow between Spain and the Americas was controlled by the *Casa de la Contratación* (House of Trade), the headquarters of which were in Seville. The book market, however, had its own special regulation, which went through different stages. After a first period during which colonisation was restricted to the Caribbean, where the circulation of books was limited, the creation of the viceroyalties of New Spain (1535) and Peru (1542) boosted the Atlantic book trade. For New Spain, the Crown adopted at first a privilege-based policy. In 1539, Juan Cromberger, a Seville-based printer, was granted an exclusive privilege to supply books and primers to New Spain and to print books in the viceroyalty, while the rest of Spanish America remained a free market.[11] This policy was reversed in 1550, and thereafter books were treated, from the commercial point of view, like any other commodity. However, fear of the dissemination of heretical ideas in the Americas, especially after the Reformation, led the authorities to tighten their ideological control over books, and from the second half of the sixteenth century books had to be authorised by the Spanish Inquisition and declared at the *Casa de la Contratación* before their dispatch.[12]

## 1 Family and Business

It was common for foreign merchants and artisans in early modern Spain to marry native women to consolidate their social and economic status.

---

9 Giovanni di Giunti, known in Spain as Juan de Junta, arrived at Salamanca in 1514, to act as his uncle, Luc'Antonio di Giunti's, agent. William Pettas, *A History and Bibliography of the Giunti (Junta) printing family in Spain. 1514–1628* (New Castle, DE: Oak Knoll Press, 2004).

10 Irving A. Leonard, *Books of the Brave: Being an Account of Books and of Men in the Spanish Conquest and Settlement of the Sixteenth-Century New World* (Berkeley, CA: University of California Press, 1992).

11 Clive Griffin, *Los Cromberger. La historia de una imprenta del siglo XVI en Sevilla y Méjico* (Madrid: Ediciones de Cultura Hispánica, 1991).

12 Unfortunately, we do not have complete series of the books shipped to the Americas until the 1580s. But the Archivo General de Indias (AGI) holds a great volume of information about the Atlantic book business. See Carlos A. González Sánchez, *Los mundos del libro. Medios de difusión de la cultura occidental en las Indias de los siglos XVI y XVII* (Sevilla: Universidad de Sevilla, 1999); Pedro Rueda Ramírez, *Negocio e intercambio cultural: El comercio de libros con América en la Carrera de Indias. Siglo XVII* (Sevilla: Diputación de Sevilla, 2005).

According to the Castilian legal system, these marital alliances offered them the possibility to become *vecinos* (citizens) or *naturales* (native), facilitating their business practice.[13] This policy was particularly relevant for those who wished to participate in the Atlantic trade, since the law barred non-Castilians from taking part in this market.[14]

Foreign printers and booksellers also followed this strategy, including Jusquín Lecarón, one of the many foreign booksellers who went to Spain to make his fortune there.[15] His origins are obscure; he might have been born in France or in Flanders.[16] What is certain is that he was established in Salamanca

---

13   Tamar Herzog, *Defining Nations. Immigrants and Citizens in Early Modern Spain and Spanish America* (New Haven, CT: Yale University Press, 2003). According to Herzog, 'belonging to a local community or the community of the kingdom in the early modern period was a process' (p. 5). One of the most important conditions to be recognised as *vecino* in Spain and Spanish America was to be head of a household (p. 25) and, therefore, marriage was an essential part of that process.

14   José M. Díaz Blanco and Natalia Maillard-Álvarez, '¿Una intimidad supeditada a la ley? Las estrategias matrimoniales de los cargadores a Indias extranjeros en Sevilla (siglos XVI–XVII)', *Nuevo Mundo. Mundos Nuevos* <https://doi.org/10.4000/nuevomundo.28453> (accessed on 10 October 2021).

15   Often they chose to marry Spanish women who already had links with their trade, such as daughters or widows of other printers and booksellers. The examples abound in the fifteenth and sixteenth centuries: the German printer Fadrique Biel de Basilea married Isabel de la Fuente, and their daughter, Isabel de Basilea, would later marry the Florentine book merchant Juan de Junta; the French Benito Boyer married Beatriz Delgado del Canto, daughter of the bookseller Mateo del Canto; the Turinese Antonio Ricardo (first printer in Peru), married Catalina Aguda, daughter of a bookseller and widow of a printer. See Sandra Establés Susán, *Diccionario de mujeres impresoras y libreras de España e Iberoamérica entre los siglos XV y XVIII* (Zaragoza: Prensas de la Universidad de Zaragoza, 2018), pp. 278, 241,176. Intermarriage between families that were involved in the book business was also common in Europe: Pettegree and Grahelli, 'How to Lose Money in the Business of Books', p. 16.

16   His surname seems French, but evidence in the will of the German gunner and 'stamp printer', Nicolás Alemán, signed in Seville in 1507, suggests a Flemish origin. According to the will, Alemán's brother-in-law was Jusquín, a bookseller in Salamanca. Although no surname is provided, the only known bookseller with that name at that time in Salamanca was Jusquín Lecarón. If this affiliation is correct, Jusquin's sister was called Juana de Flandes (i.e. from Flanders), and their mother Margarita de Flandes, strongly suggesting the family's Flemish origins. Interestingly, Jacobo Cromberger, whose son married one of Jusquín's daughters, was appointed by Nicolás as executor of his will, see Juan L. Carriazo Rubio and Natalia Maillard Álvarez, 'Un artillero e impresor de estampas alemán en la Sevilla del Descubrimiento', in Juan L. Carriazo (ed.), *El triunfo de la pólvora. Artillería y fortificaciones a finales de la Edad Media* (Huelva: Uhu.es Publicaciones, 2020), pp. 499–536.

from at least 1505.[17] Situated in North Castille, Salamanca had a flourishing printing industry by the fifteenth century; having one of the largest university in Europe, the demand for books in the city was pretty much guaranteed, especially regarding professional books and university texts, which progressively became imported from abroad.[18] The increasing demand and the city's proximity to Medina del Campo, the main hub for international books in the Iberian Peninsula during the sixteenth century, attracted the agents of many publishing houses.[19] In Salamanca, Jusquín Lecaron married the Spaniard Juana Maldonado before 1507.[20] In the colophon of the first book printed in Medina del Campo he is presented as 'vecino' of Salamanca.[21] Jusquín and Juana's marriage was prolific; he died before 1530, leaving his wife with seven young children: three boys (Martín, Juan, and Mateo) and four girls (Catalina, Ana, Beatriz, and Brígida).

At the time, the transmission of family names was not yet a consolidated custom in Castile. As a rule, women did not take their husbands' family names and siblings did not always share surnames. In the case of Jusquín and Juana's children, for instance, the boys took their father's name, while the girls retained the name Maldonado. Regarding property rights, the general rule in the Iberian Peninsula was for all heirs to receive equal shares of the will, so widows and daughters had an 'ample claim to their husband's and parents' states'.[22] Although widows had greater freedom to act autonomously, as they

---

17    In this year, his name features in some documents concerning house rentals, held in the Cathedral archives. Vicente Bécares Botas, 'Los agentes del libro incunable salmantino (1483–1510)', *Titivillus*, 2 (2016), pp. 81–105.

18    For the printing industry in Salamanca, see Lorenzo Ruiz Fidalgo, *La imprenta en Salamanca. 1501–1600* (Madrid: Arco/Libros, 1994); Richard L. Kagan, *Universidad y sociedad en la España moderna* (Madrid: Tecnos, 1981), p. 242; Vicente Bécares Botas, *La compañía de libreros de Salamanca. 1530–1534* (Salamanca: SEMIR, 2003), p. 9; *Guía documental del mundo del libro salmantino del siglo XVI* (Salamanca: Instituto Castellano y Leonés de la Lengua, 2006); Marta de la Mano, *Mercaderes e impresores de libros en la Salamanca del siglo XVI* (Salamanca: Universidad de Salamanca, 1998).

19    Medina del Campo has been described as a major warehouse for books ('gran almacén de libros'), most of which came from abroad; Anastasio Rojo, 'El negocio del libro en Medina del Campo. Siglos XVI y XVII', *Investigaciones históricas. Época moderna y contemporánea*, 7 (1987), pp. 17–26.

20    Bécares Botas, *Guía documental del mundo del libro salmantino*, p. 98.

21    The book, entitled *Valerio de las historias escolásticas*, by Diego Rodríguez de Almela, was printed by Nicolás Gazini de Piemonte in 1511. Alexander Wilkinson (ed), *Iberian Books. Books Published in Spanish or Portuguese or on the Iberian Peninsula before 1601* (Leiden: Brill, 2010), p. 629.

22    Jutta Gisela Sperling and Shona Kelly Wray (eds.), *Across the Religious Divide. Women, Property, and Law in the Wider Mediterranean, ca. 1300–1800* (New York, NY: Routledge, 2010), p. 7.

became the head of their households and had to protect the rights of their underage children, the participation of married women in different businesses was also common in Castile, and it is not rare to find them selling and buying property or joining a commercial company, usually with their husband's licence.[23]

## 2      The Maldonado Women

The first generation of the Maldonado women (sometimes referred to in the documents as Maldonada), is represented by the previously mentioned Juana Maldonado. We do not have any information about her life before she married Jusquín Lecarón, nor do we have any evidence of her involvement in her husband's commercial activities while he was still alive. However, after his death (before 1530), the young widow assumed the responsibility of managing the family business, being the only woman among the earliest partners of the *Compañía de Libreros de Salamanca*.[24]

The *Compañía de Libreros de Salamanca* was created on 7 January 1530 to satisfy the growing demand for international books.[25] The original company contract was signed by a group of twelve Salamanca and Medina del Campo-based booksellers and printers, most of which were foreigners. The duration of the partnership was four years, and its aim was to distribute books from Lyon and Venice in the Iberian Peninsula. Very soon the *Compañía de Libreros* took over the market, displacing smaller competitors and, consequently, the company was denounced to the Royal Council for monopolising the book trade.[26] Despite the frequent complaints, the company remained active until 1534 with great success.

The company's partners include some of the most important printers and book merchants in the Iberian Peninsula during the sixteenth century. Among the foreigners, Juan de Junta from Venice, Alejandro de Canovas from

---

23      Mary Elizabeth Perry, *Gender and Disorder in Early Modern Seville* (Princeton, NJ: Princeton University Press, 1990), pp. 14–15.

24      Bécares Botas, *La compañía de libreros de Salamanca*; Mano, *Mercaderes e impresores de libros en la Salamanca*.

25      Mano, *Mercaderes e impresores de libros*, pp. 121–139.

26      Only a month after its foundation, Sancho de Salaya doctor in law, informed the local council that 'the booksellers from the company had certain agreement or monopoly to increase book prices at the expense of the city, the doctors and the students living here' (*los libreros que residen en el tal Estudio tienen hecha cierta liga e monipodio e concierto entre sí para encarecer los libros y venderlos en más de lo que valen en perjuicio de la dicha ciudad, doctors y estudiantes de ella*), Bécares Botas, *La compañía de libreros de Salamanca*, p. 11.

Burgundy, Lorenzo Liondedei from Pesaro, Bernardino Castronovo from Milan, and Gaspar Trechsel and Lorenzo de Anticeno both from Lyon. The Spaniards Cristóbal de Pascua, Blas de Vergara, and Alonso de Ribas were also part of the Company. Initially, the list included a single woman, Juana de Maldonado, who acted alongside her son, Martín Lecarón.[27] Two other women were to join the company later: Ana Maldonado and Úrsula Martínez.[28]

During the early modern age, participation in a company was determined by the initial investment of each partner. In this case, the investment was divided into different concepts: the books provided by each partner, transport costs and binding costs. The only exception was Gaspar Treschel, who invested 375,000 maravedis (i.e., 1,000 ducats), the highest share of all. Overall, Juana Maldonado contributed with the third largest investment; 62,680 maravedis, which accounts for 12% of the total (excluding Treschel). She was only behind Gaspar de Ruiseñolis (198,510 maravedis) and Juan de Junta and Alejandro de Cánova's joint contribution (69,425 maravedis).

The success of the *Compañía de Libreros* can be explained by its global structure; with it headquarter in Salamanca, branches in Lyon and Venice, and storehouses in Medina del Campo and Salamanca, the company started to channel an important proportion of the international books on offer in the Iberian market. According to the company's ledgers, the society registered over 870 titles, and nearly 5,000 volumes.[29]

---

27　Although her son was a full partner, having previously worked alongside his father, Juana signed on her own behalf.

28　Ana Maldonado, married to the Milanese bookseller Bernardino de Castronovo, joined the *Compañía* after her husband passed away, ca. 1533. Mano, *Mercaderes e impresores*, pp. 111–113. Despite the shared surname, we did not find any evidence to confirm that Ana Maldonado was related to Juana, Establés, *Diccionario de mujeres impresoras y libreras*, p. 349. Nevertheless, it is worth pointing out that some early documents link Jusquin Lecaron with Bernardino de Castronovo, Bécares Botas, 'Los agentes del libro incunable'. Bernardino and Ana's daughter, Lorenza Maldonado, married the Italian book merchant Guillermo de Millis. Úrsula Martínez (or Martín), was the widow of the bookseller Pedro de Pascua, and remarried with Juan Lecarón, Juana and Jusquín's son. A son from her first marriage, Cristóbal de Pascua, also joined the company in his own name and on his mother's behalf, Bécares Botas, *La compañía de libreros de Salamanca*, p. 14.

29　The Spanish *Compañía* was, no doubt, inspired by the *Grande Compagnie des librai-res de Lyon*, in which the Lyonnaise branch of the Giunti and the Portonariis also took part, and a similar joint venture founded in Venice in 1507 for printing law books, again with the participation of the Giunti, Jeanne-Marie Durau-Lapeyssonie, 'Recherches sur les grandes compagnies de libraires lyonnais au XVIᵉ siècle', *Nouvelles études lyonnaises* (Genève-Paris: Droz, 1969), pp. 5–63; Nuovo, *The Book Trade in the Italian Renaissance*. pp. 55–56. In fact, Marta de la Mano suggests that the *Compañía de Libreros de Salamanca* was created on the initiative of Juan de Junta to forward his family interests, Mano, *Mercaderes e impresores de libros*, p. 182. However, a key difference between the three

The descendants of Juana continued with the family tradition and were frequently involved in the book business. Her three sons had careers as book merchants in Spain and the Americas, while Juana's daughters and granddaughters often married book professionals from different cities; like the matriarch, they often married foreigners. Their marriage policy played a central role in the crystallisation of a close-knit network, which included some of the most prominent publishing houses in operation across the Spanish Empire. Two dynasties benefited particularly from this policy; the Crombergers of Seville, and the Portonariis of Salamanca.

Seville was the largest city in Castile, and a hub for the production and distribution of books.[30] In 1503, Seville was officially designated as the sole port for the Atlantic trade, and a few years later the city became the point of departure and arrival of the fleet. Besides this, Seville was the point where global trading routes linking the Mediterranean, North European, and American markets converged. The city was a bottleneck for global trade and a particularly attractive location for international companies, and this was Brígida's, one of Juana's daughters, destination.[31] In approximately 1524, Brígida moved to Seville to marry Juan Cromberger, the eldest son of Jacobo Cromberger, a German printer who arrived in Castile in the late fifteenth century and ran a flourishing printing shop in Seville. Jacobo was one of the first book professionals to trade with the Americas, first through different agents and, after 1525, on his own behalf in virtue of a special licence granted by the emperor.[32]

---

companies is that the Spanish society focused on distribution, while the other two were mainly concerned with production.

30   Several works have addressed the Sevilian printing industry and book market, Arcadio Castillejo Benavente, *La imprenta en Sevilla en el siglo XVI. 1521–1600* (Sevilla: Universidad de Sevilla, 2019); Carmen Álvarez, *La impresión y comercio de libros en la Sevilla del Quinientos* (Sevilla: Universidad de Sevilla, 2007); Carlos A. González Sánchez and Natalia Maillard Álvarez, *Orbe tipográfico. El mercado del libro en la Sevilla de la segunda mitad del siglo XVI* (Gijón: Trea, 2003).

31   Many studies are devoted to this subject, from classics such as Robert S. Smith, 'Seville and the Atlantic: Cycles in the Spanish Colonial Trade', *The Journal of Economic History*, 22 (1962), pp. 253–259; James D. Tracy, *The Rise of the Merchant Empires. Long-Distance Trade in the Early Modern World, 1350–1750* (Cambridge: Cambridge University Press, 1990); Horst Pietschmann (ed.), *Atlantic history: history of the Atlantic system, 1580–1830* (Göttingen: Vandenhoeck and Ruprecht, 2002); Natalia Maillard Álvarez and Clive Griffin, 'Doña Brígida Maldonado, la Familia Cromberger, y la imprenta sevillana', in M. Garone and A. Corbeto (eds.), *Muses de la Impremta. La dona i les arts del llibre. Segles XVI–XIX* (Barcelona: Associació de Bibliòfils de Barcelona, 2009), pp. 99–128.

32   Griffin, *Los Cromberger*, 94–96.

In the same year, Jacobo transferred the printing office to his son Juan, who became the most prominent printer in the Iberian Peninsula.

Brigida's husband was already Spanish-born, so he enjoyed all the advantages of *vecinos*. He was allowed to trade in the Americas, and he did so, expanding the business that his father had begun. In fact, as noted, Juan Cromberger was the grantee of a monopoly to sell and print books in Mexico, awarded in 1539. Juan already enjoyed a privileged position within the book market, his marriage reinforced the commercial bonds between both families. Indeed, we know that the Lecaron were buying books from Jacobo Cromberger, and in 1528, Brígida's mother-in-law (Comincia de Blanquis) and her children granted the power of attorney to Jusquín Lecarón and his son Martín, to collect a debt owed to the recently deceased Jacobo.[33]

Juan passed away in 1540, leaving Brígida with nine underage children. According to Clive Griffin, after becoming widowed Brigida signed notarial records as *la desdichada* (the unfortunate) or *la triste* (the sad).[34] The oldest son, Jácome, was still too young to take over the printing office that had been left to him, and his name did not start appearing in book colophons until the end of 1545. Did Brígida manage the printing office during the intervening five years? It is difficult to say for certain, because there is no direct evidence, such as the use of her name in colophons or any printing contract signed by her, but everything else points in this direction. If Brígida controlled the printing office or delegated it to male relatives or employees is unclear, but different documents refer to her as *ymprimidora* (i.e., printer) and book merchant, particularly between 1540 and 1545. During that period, the Crombergers' office produced around 60 high-quality editions, signed off as *La imprenta de Juan Cromberger que Dios aya* ('In the workshop of Juan Cromberger, God accepts in His Glory') and similar formulas.[35] The titles chosen also suggest that the business went into decline after 1546, when the workshop, under his son Jácome, began producing only lower-quality editions of existing titles.

At the same time, Brígida controlled other family businesses, not only in Spain, but also in the Americas. In April 1542, she sold the Sevillian bookseller Pedro Ximénez a shipment of books worth more than one hundred golden

---

33  Maillard Álvarez and Griffin, 'Doña Brígida Maldonado'. pp. 100–10; Joaquín Hazañas y la Rúa, *La imprenta en Sevilla: noticias inéditas de sus impresores desde la introducción del arte tipográfico en esta ciudad hasta el siglo XIX*, vol.1 (Seville, 1945–49), p. 155.

34  Griffin, *Los Cromberger*, p. 106.

35  Such as 'In the house of Juan Cromberger' or 'In the house of Cromberger'.

ducats, a considerable sum at the time.[36] That same year, Brígida negotiated the extension of the monopoly for selling and printing books in New Spain with the Spanish Crown, proroguing it until the mid-sixteenth century.[37] She was also involved in financial transactions with her brother-in-law, the famous merchant Lázaro de Nuremberg, who was very active in the American trade, and in 1545 she appointed her brother, Mateo Lecarón, as her representative in Mexico.[38]

When Brígida's son Jacome came of age in 1545, she passed on the family workshop to him, but still remained active, although focusing on different pursuits. For instance, she was involved with the wine market, producing and exporting Spanish wines, and with the Mexican mining industry. She was eighty years old when she passed away in 1590; she never stopped working and closing deals, as a wine sale signed on 13 April 1590 attests.[39]

In order to understand her professional activity, we have applied Social Network Analysis (SNA) to the information yielded by notarial records, leading to a graph in which nodes represent individuals involved in Brígida's commercial transactions and lines illustrate their commercial relationships (Fig. 3.1). The nodes are sized according to their degree, a common metric in SNA, accounting for the number of direct links for every actor in the network, which in this case represent contracts. As such, the largest nodes represent the most active agents in the network.[40]

This graph is a so-called ego network, which revolves around a central node, or ego (in this case Brígida Maldonado), to reconstruct her interactions with other individuals. In this case, most of the connections link the central, and largest, node, Brígida Maldonado, with its most direct connections. The star shape of the network is typical of ego networks, in which the central node

---

36    Carmen Álvarez Márquez, *Impresores, libreros y mercaderes de libros en la Sevilla del Quinientos. vol. I. Impresores* (Zaragoza: Libros Pórtico, 2009), p. 157.

37    Griffin, *Los Cromberger*, p. 165. In 1550, once the Mexican workshop was no longer the property of the Cromberger, Juan Pablos, the new owner (a former employee of the Crombergers) signed a power of attorney to collect some debts from Brígida, Gestoso y Pérez, *Noticias inéditas de impresores sevillanos* (Seville: Imp. & Lit. Gómez Hnos., 1924), pp. 115–116.

38    About the professional activities of Lázaro de Nuremberg, see Enrique Otte, *Las perlas del Caribe: Nueva Cádiz de Cubagua* (Caracas: Fundación John Boulton, 1977); Juan Friede, *Los Welser en la conquista de Venezuela* (Caracas: Edime Ediciones, 1971). On Mateo Lecarón, see Griffin, *Los Cromberger*, pp. 105–106.

39    Maillard Álvarez and Griffin, 'Doña Brígida Maldonado'. p. 106.

40    Software Gephi 0.9.2 was used to produce the graph and calculate the metrics. About SNA's potential for book history, see John Hinks and Catherine Feely (eds.), *Historical Networks in the Book Trade* (London: Routledge, 2017).

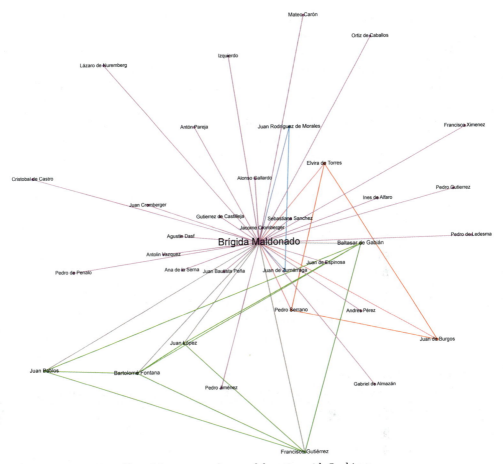

FIGURE 3.1 Brígida Maldonado's ego network; own elaboration with Gephi 0.9

controls most of the information that circulates through it. In this case Brígida holds a privileged position because she is directly connected with all the nodes in the network. This is a result of the criteria used to collect the evidence. The contracts in which Brígida features were selected from on a pre-existing database, adding the information provided by her will and codicil.[41]

In addition, four groups or clusters can be identified in the graph. The clusters are groups of nodes that share close mutual connections. The members of these clusters, each of which is assigned a different colour, were involved

---

41 The database stores almost 2,000 contracts signed by book professionals, or persons in some way related to the book trade, in Seville, Salamanca, and Mexico City between 1501 and 1635.

in various transactions with Brígida. The 'green' group is the largest cluster in the graph; it is formed by the Mexican printer Juan Pablos, his brother-in-law Francisco Gutiérrez, and the Italian merchants Baltasar de Gabián and Bartolomé Fontana. The contract, signed in Mexico City in 1550, involved a very complex transaction. Before 1550, Francisco Gutiérrez travelled to Seville as Juan Pablos's representative to hire different journeymen-printers for his workshop in Mexico. In the course of this mission, Francisco Gutiérrez contracted a loan on behalf of his brother-in-law with Baltasar Gabiano and his partner Bartolomé Fontana. From Mexico City, Juan Pablos granted a power of attorney to the luthier Juan Lopez, the purpose of which was twofold; first, to keep an eye on Francisco Gutiérrez and, second, to collect a considerable sum of money from Brígida Maldonado. The source of the money was from a ship cargo split between Brígida and Juan Pablos, which sank near the Caribbean; Brígida had received the whole of the associated insurance payment, and the printer was now demanding his part from Mexico. This is a perfect example of the complexity of transatlantic commercial transactions during the early modern era and the active role played by women like Brígida.[42]

We can establish some aspects of Brígida's activities just by searching information about transactions included in the blue cluster. In this case, Brígida granted powers of attorney to Juan Rodríguez de Morales, a clergyman who was about to sail for Mexico City. With this notarial act, the widow of Juan Cromberger could monitor the work performance of Mateo Lecarón, her representative in Mexico. She also added an extra legal formality to the act, requiring approbation from Juan de Zumárraga, Bishop of Mexico.[43] The orange cluster illustrates the role of Brígida as broker for the distribution of books in Andalusia. In 1560, Brígida granted power of attorney to the Sevillian printer Pedro Serrano, to collect a debt from the bookseller Juan de Burgos and his wife, Elvira de Torres, neighbours of Jerez de la Frontera.[44]

Brígida was exceptional, but she was not an exception. Women were involved as printers and booksellers from soon after the arrival of the printing press to Spain. However, it is uncommon to find evidence of single or married women

---

42    Álvarez Márquez, *Impresores, libreros y mercaderes de libros*. vol. 1. pp. 106–107.

43    Diego Fernández Martín, 'obligación de pago' and 'licencia', 3 January 1547, Catálogo de Protocolos del Archivo General de Notarías de la Ciudad de México, Fondo Siglo XVI. Online. Ivonne Mijares (ed.), Seminario de Documentación e Historia Novohispana, México, UNAM-Instituto de Investigaciones Históricas, 2014 <http://cpagncmxvi.histori cas.unam.mx/catalogo.jsp> (accessed on 12 October 2021). Zumárraga was a key figure in Juan Cromberger's business activities in New Spain. Griffin, *Los Cromberger*, pp. 123.

44    Archivo Histórico Provincial de Sevilla (AHPSe), Leg. 13506, fol. 264r–v. the fact that the debtor's wife's name features in the contract is yet further evidence of the agency that Castilian women could achieve in their husbands' commercial activities.

working at the workshop, and even when they were widowed, they often kept their husbands' names in colophons, among other reasons to keep a recognisable commercial brand.[45] Although they often remained in the background, we know that women actively participated in the book business.[46] Sandra Establés has found evidence that 62 women in Spain and four more in Mexico City were involved actively in the publishing trade in the sixteenth century.[47]

## 3      Family Strategy and Networks

Social Network Analysis tools also allow us to reconstruct the network woven by the Maldonado women, visualising not only their business, like in Brígida's case, but also their family ties. By placing them into the network they helped to build, we can test their relevance in the book industry within the Iberian world in a period in which the book market was becoming global. The results of the analysis reveal a certain degree of specialisation in the marriage market, displaying the endogenous practices that dominated the book sector during the period under consideration.

The following graph reflects the information collected in various archives and secondary sources. We could refer to it as a 'family graph', which we believe stands as a useful alternative to classic family trees (Fig. 3.2). Here the nodes are the Maldonado women, their spouses, and their descendants. The links that connect the nodes capture family interactions, summarised in three categories: wives-husbands, parents-children, and siblings. One of the issues, on which our contribution focuses, is the impact of the marriage policies followed by the Maldonado women on the book world in Spain. Therefore, we have highlighted the links between spouses, which are represented in the graph with a thicker line. One of the advantages of this approach is to bring together different family groups and generations, displaying their links, alliances, and strategies in a single image.

The architecture of the graph makes for a better understanding of the role played by the family Lecarón-Maldonado, especially the women, in connecting two printing dynasties (Cromberger and Portonariis) and two markets (Salamanca and Seville). The strategic nature of this alliance was especially

45    María del Mar Fernández Vega, 'Jerónima de Gales. Una impresora valenciana del siglo XVI', in *La memoria de los libros. La memoria de los libros. Estudios sobre la historia del escrito y de la lectura en Europa y América, vol. I* (Salamanca: IHLL, 2004), pp. 405–434.

46    Alejandra Ulla Lorenzo, '¿Viudas de mercaderes o verdaderas mercaderas? Mujer y comercio de libros en los siglos XVI y XVII', *Hipógrifo*, 1 (2018), pp. 321–340.

47    Establés, *Diccinario de mujeres impresoras y libreras*, pp. 31–33.

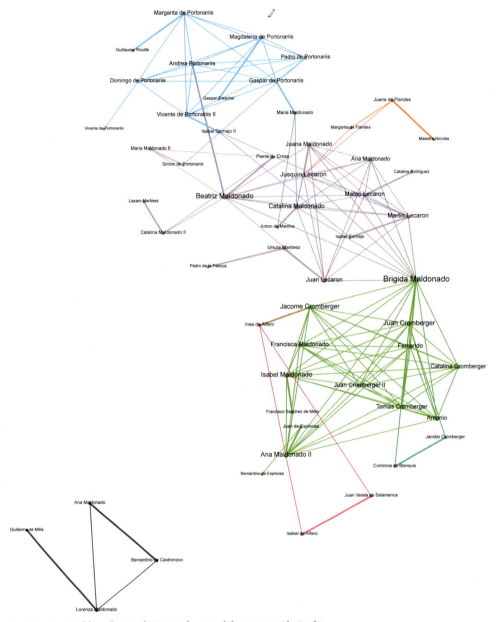

FIGURE 3.2  Maldonado Family Network; own elaboration with Gephi 0.9

clear at a time in which the Crombergers were the only firm allowed to trade books with New Spain.

   In the graph, the Portonariis form a separate cluster (blue), which is mainly linked to the Maldonado through four marriages (Andrea-Beatriz Maldonado, Gaspar-María Maldonado I, Vicente-Isabel Cornejo II, and Simón-María

Maldonado 11). The Portonariis, originally from Trino (North Italy), settled in Lyon in the early sixteenth century, facilitating the connection between the Italian, French, and Spanish markets through that city.[48] In order to do so, like many other European publishing firms, they sent their relatives as agents to important business hubs. The first Portonariis moving from Trino to Lyon were Vincent I and his brother, Domenico. While Vincent remained in Lyon, Domenico travelled to Spain to expand the scope of their commercial activities. In the following years, Domenico's sons (Andrea, Vicente, Gaspar, and Pedro), acted as the family company's agents in Spain, while also developing their own businesses. The Portonariis followed a cunning marriage policy, which allowed them to consolidate the position of their different family branches. Domenico's two daughters, stayed in Lyon, where Margarita married the famous printer Guillaume Rouille, and Magdalena the book merchant Gaspar Treschel, who, as noted, acted as liaison between the *Compañía de Libreros de Salamanca* and the *Grand Compangnie des Libraires de Lyon*. Their brothers in Spain followed a similar strategy, as reflected in the graph. Indeed, the alliance between the Portonariis and the Maldonados was to last for at least two generations.

A key figure in this whole picture is Beatriz Maldonado, Brígida's sister, who, as shown by the graph, married twice, connecting with the Portonariis network on both occasions. She first married Pierres de Cros (or Ducros), a French book merchant, in Salamanca, who represented the Portonariis business in 1531, together with Guillermo de Millis.[49] When her first husband passed away, Beatriz married Andrea de Portonariis, Vincent I's nephew. Obviously, the Portonariis were aware of the comparative value of keeping close bonds with the Maldonado. Andrea de Portonariis was greatly successful; his professional career in the Iberian Peninsula reached its peak when he was appointed *Tipógrafo Real* (Royal Printer).[50] Despite her illiteracy, Beatriz was not simply a pawn for marriage plans. In 1565 she participated in the negotiation of a contract signed by her husband to print different books by Fray Luis de Granada, one of the most successful Spanish writers of the sixteenth century.[51] Once her husband passed away, she hired solicitors to represent her in court.[52]

Before his marriage in 1574 to María de Maldonado, granddaughter of Juana and niece of Brígida and Beatriz, Andrea's brother (and therefore Beatriz's brother-in-law), Gaspar Portonariis, travelled between France and Spain. He

---

48    Maria Cristina Misiti, 'Una porta aperta sull'Europa: i de Portonariis tra Trino, Venezia e Lione. Ricerche preliminari per l'avvio degli annali', *Il Bibliotecario*, 3 (2008), pp. 55–91.

49    Bécares Botas, *Guía documental del mundo del libro salmantino*, p. 109.

50    Juan Delgado Casado, *Diccionario de impresores españoles (siglos xv–xvii)*, vol. II (Madrid: Arco Libros, 1996), pp. 551–553.

51    Archivo Histórico Provincial de Salamanca, Leg. 3876, ff. 5–12.

52    Archivo Histórico Provincial de Salamanca, Leg. 4859, f. 764.

was also fairly active in the American market, having important commercial connections with Peru.[53] Another sibling, Vicente Portonariis II, married Isabel Cornejo, as illustrated in the graph. Despite her name, Isabel was also Juana's granddaughter. She was the child of Martín Le Caron and Isabel Cornejo (remarkably, the girl again inherited her mother's surname) and, like her aunts, she did not play a secondary role in the family business. In 1585, Isabel Cornejo (already a widow) bought nine bales of books in Medina del Campo, and that same year she wrote a letter to her husband's partner in Mexico City, the book merchant Juan Treviño, stating 'I shall try to serve your in everything that you request, and I shall endeavour to keep the deal ... I shall even adapt the book prices'.[54] In the same document Isabel portraits an extraordinary understanding of her husband's economic affairs.

The fourth Portonariis brother, Pedro, followed a different path and did not marry into the Le Caron-Maldonado family. His son Simón, however, married María de Maldonado, daughter of Beatriz and her first husband, Pierre de Cros. Furthermore, Simon's stepdaughter, also named Beatriz Maldonado, married the book merchant Antonio Sajete.[55]

As a group, the Crombergers and the Portonariis deployed different strategies. While the latter prioritised marriage within the profession, the former tended to choose spouses from the Sevillian elite, in the hope of raising their social status.[56] The graph clearly illustrates these different strategies, reflected in the number of thicker lines, which, as noted, represent marriages inside the book market.

---

53   Vicente Bécares Botas, 'Le testament de Gaspard de Portonariis (1591)', *Revue Française d'histoire du livre*, 122–125 (2004), pp. 107–120.

54   Regarding the bales of books acquired in Medina del Campo, see Cristóbal Pérez Pastor, *La imprenta en Medina del Campo* (Madrid: Sucesores de Rivadeneyra, 1895), p. 451. Isabel's letter to Treviño can be found in Francisco Fernández del Castillo, *Libros y libreros en el siglo XVI* (Mexico City: FCE, 1982), p. 299. About Juan de Treviño, see Natalia Maillard Álvarez, '*One man's bookshop*: Juan de Treviño y el comercio de libros global en el siglo XVI', *Revista Complutense de Historia de América*, 45 (2019), pp. 49–67.

55   Beatriz was the offspring of María and her first husband Sebastián de Ledesma. In 1580 Antonio Sagete paid back the dowry of his deceased wife to his parents-in-law (Archivo Histórico Provincial de Salamanca, Leg. Leg. 3193, f. 219). Afterwards, he moved to Seville, where he continued dealing in books and married Úrsula Maldonado, widow of another bookseller (Archivo Histórico Provincial de Sevilla, Leg. Leg.3512, ff. 668r–669r).

56   Of the six children of Brígida and Juan that came of age, only two married within the profession; Ana's spouse was Juan de Espinosa, a powerful book merchant from Medina del Campo, while the older son, Jácome, who inherited the printing workshop, married Inés de Alfaro, daughter of a Sevillian printer. Catalina, Isabel and Tomás married into important families of the Sevillian commercial elite and even into the aristocracy, while Francisca became a nun in one of the city's oldest convents. See Griffin and Maillard, 'Doña Brígida Maldonado'.

We have, however, chosen to include only one marriage alliance outside of the book profession in our graph: that of Isabel Maldonado (Brígida's daughter) and Francisco Sánchez de Melo. We have done so to emphasise an additional strategy followed by these families to expand or secure their commercial networks, one of spiritual parenting. Around 1560, Pedro de Portonariis arrived in Seville to manage his brother's business concerns there and in the Americas. Pedro's brother's marital bonds facilitated Pedro's initial success in Seville, having been awarded the status of *vecino* after only a year and opening a bookshop at the core of the city's commercial area. But, although Pedro married an outsider from the book market, he chose Isabel Maldonado and Francisco Sánchez de Melo as godparents for his first child.

## 4 Conclusions

Traditional historiography has shown little interest in these women. In most of the cases they have been relegated to a secondary role, as wife or mothers. Nevertheless, a close analysis of the notarial records presents a different picture. As we have seen with the Maldonado family, women administered the family estate, closed commercial agreements, appointed agents to collect debts in different markets, controlled cargoes, signed all sort of notarial deeds, oversaw customers, operated in the financial market, sent letters of exchange and promissory notes, and even brought actions before the courts. Furthermore, marriage, baptisms, and partnerships with these women helped knot the ties of commercial networks, which allowed books to circulate not only in Europe, but also in the Atlantic. Their voices may not sound as loud as that of their husbands in the documents, but we have proved that they were deeply involved in the early modern book world.

### Acknowledgement

*To Clive Griffin, in gratitude for his teaching*

# CHAPTER 4

# Women in the Workshop: Property Structure, Print Culture, and Female Management in Colonial Peru

*Agnes Gehbald*

Printing was a business dominated by men in the early modern period especially so in colonial Peru in South America. While it would be hard to imagine a woman working as a press(wo)man, as a puller or a beater in the workshop, they were not absent from the printing trade. The Peruvian capital of Lima supplied the whole continent with locally produced reading material that was all signed by male printing masters. No woman's name can be found in any surviving colonial Peruvian imprints from the first publication in 1584 until 1821, with the beginning of the Independence era. Despite this lack of representation, widows, daughters, granddaughters, and nieces assisted in the trade or administered the business in the name of the family. Focusing on archival evidence of women reveals their various activities in printing affairs, as the following survey of women in the workshops in colonial Peru demonstrates. This chapter aims to open new approaches for the study of printing practices and workshop culture, beyond the publishers' names in imprints.

From the 1960s on, feminist historiographies have emphasised the historical constructions of gender by studying women's experiences.[1] Despite methodological innovations, women as historic agents are still overlooked, in particular in the male-dominated business of printing, and especially in the rigidly hierarchical Viceroyalty of Peru. An exception to this is the pioneering work of Ella Dunbar Temple, who has explored the role of women as authors and readers in colonial Peru.[2] In addition to these female authors and readers in

---

1 For the history of women in Peru, see Carmen Meza Ingar and Teodoro Hampe Martínez (eds.), *La mujer en la historia del Perú, siglo XV al XX* (Lima: Fondo Editorial del Congreso del Perú, 2007); Claudia Rosas Lauro (ed.), *Género y mujeres en la historia del Perú: del hogar al espacio público* (Lima: Fondo Editorial Pontificia Universidad Católica del Perú, 2019). On the role of women in the book trades in Latin America, see Marina Garone Gravier (ed.), *Las mujeres y los estudios del libro y la edición en Iberoamérica: panorama histórico y enfoques interdisciplinarios* (Bogotá / México / Santiago: Universidad de los Andes; Universidad Autónoma Metropolitana; Universidad de Santiago de Chile 2023).

2 Ella Dunbar Temple, 'Curso de la literatura femenina a través del período colonial en el Perú', *Revista*, 3 (1939), pp. 25–56.

the colonial book market, women also contributed to the making of books. To date, there is no study that examines their activity in the printing workshops in Peru, whereas for other parts of the Spanish Empire, this has been analysed in a number of recent studies. Women there, often in their role as widows, presided over workshops, a fact that is reflected in the publication data.[3] Due to the lack of representation in Peruvian imprints, little is known about the various tasks of women in the printing workshops of Lima.

Studying the role of gender in the workshop contributes to a better under-standing of the trade and re-frames the working environment, so far character-ised as an exclusively male one. With its long typographic tradition, starting in 1584, colonial Lima represents a particularly interesting site to examine gen-der roles in the printing workshop. Characterised by a hierarchical system of inclusion and exclusion, the social structure not only depended on notions of lineage—or ethnicity and race, in subsequent terminology—but also on gender, which again, was socially constructed. Following the colonial Spanish ideology of honour and the threat of illegitimate children, women lived under different conditions than men. According to Susan Migden Socolow, women in colonial Spanish America were defined, above all, by their sex and only then by their race and class.[4] By tradition, men presided over the printing trade in the Viceroyalty, but women stepped in whenever any action was required, especially in the absence of men, which happened frequently. To explain their situation, the women of the following case studies referred to the laws, in

---

3 For a general overview of printing activities by women see, Marina Garone Gravier, 'La mujer y la imprenta en las colonias españolas de América: México, Guatemala y Perú', in Marina Grone Gravier and Albert Corbeto (eds.), *Muses de la imprenta. La dona i la imprenta en el món del llibre antic* (Barcelona: Museo Diocensano de Barcelona y Asociación de Bibliófilos de Barcelona, 2009); Sandra Establés Susán, *Diccionario de mujeres impresoras y libreras* (Zaragoza: Prensas de la Universidad de Zaragoza, 2018). For New Spain, see Marina Garone Gravier, 'Herederas de la letra: mujeres y tipografía en la Nueva España', in Guadalupe Fernández López (ed.), *Casa de la primera imprenta de América. X aniversario* (México: Universidad Autónoma Metropolitana, 2004); '¿Ornamentos tipográficos? las mujeres en el mundo del libro antiguo: algunas noticias bibliográficas', in Idalia García Aguilar and Pedro J. Rueda Ramírez (eds.), *Leer en tiempos de la Colonia: imprenta, bibliotecas y lectores en la Nueva España* (México: UNAM, 2010); *Las otras letras, mujeres impresoras en la Biblioteca Palafoxiana: memorias* (Puebla: Secretaría de Cultura del Estado de Puebla, 2009); Sara Poot-Herrera, 'El siglo de las viudas: impresoras y mercadoras de libros en el XVII novohispano', *Destiempos*, 3 (2008), pp. 300–316. For Spain, see Sandra Establés Susán, 'Las mujeres y la imprenta manual en España (siglos XV–XVIII): una aproximación a la actividad profesional femenina', *Titivillus*, 3 (2017), pp. 15–23.

4 Susan Migden Socolow, *The Women of Colonial Latin America* (Cambridge: Cambridge University Press, 2015), p. 1.

particular the Leyes de Velleyano and Leyes de Toro, which at the same time protected and limited the female scope of action.

Though it is difficult to trace and locate female activity in colonial workshops, archival documents including printing contracts, last wills, and court proceedings provide proof of the variety of tasks and their contributions throughout the period. These sources reveal how women associated with workshops through family ties helped in the business in Lima by fighting for printing privileges, signing contracts, or insisting on the right to sell workshop equipment of the family. Their names are not recognised and mainly uncharted, yet isolated instances provide insight into the various modes of female work in colonial print production when women, under certain circumstances, acquired agency to contribute to print culture. Investigating the hidden stories of women in the workshops of the Viceroyalty of Peru helps to understand gendered business practices common in the trade.

## 1    Property Structure

The business of books in colonial Spanish America was shaped by lineage and gender. While a printer's career was possible for a man, customarily of Spanish or foreign origin or for a *criollo*, who was born on American territory with Spanish forefathers, women were not supposed to engage in the business. In a small number of exceptions, however, they assisted or even managed a family company. In his classical overview of workshops, first published in 1904, the bibliographer José Toribio Medina includes various names of women. In a short paragraph about the peculiar features of printing in Peru, he describes the women in the trade as 'capitalist' owners, mainly without any relationship to printing. He highlights their independent role without any association in a printers' guild while only some of them had family relationships that associated them with workshops.[5] Apart from these instances, the bibliography remains largely silent about the participation of women in the printing trade in Spanish America. According to Marina Garone Gravier, this gap in research can be explained first by traditional approaches to the topic, secondly by the range of sources that have been studied, and thirdly by the lack of knowledge about the social and legal situation of women in the past.[6] Contemporary

5    José Toribio Medina, 'La imprenta en Lima', *Historia de la imprenta* (Santiago de Chile: Universo, 1958), p. 483.
6    Garone Gravier, 'Ornamentos tipográficos', pp. 168–170.

assumptions about work and gender impeded a physical collaboration between men and women in the printing workshop. However, managing a workshop was a different matter. Through administrative roles, women—most of them with the Spanish title of 'Doña', indicator of an upper-class status in the Viceroyalty—contributed to the printing trade in colonial Lima.

Property structure, along with generally held assumptions about the gendered division of labour, inhibited women from being master printers as they would have to take on a role presiding over a printing workshop and the male employees. In general, the leadership was in the hands of men, as was the execution of the craft of printing. Women of the upper classes did not work, at least not in public, yet in the absence of husbands, they often had to assume economic activities.[7] For example in textile production, which transformed to a primarily female activity after the Spanish conquest, Peruvian women worked full-time.[8] Yet, they did not work customarily as printers. In printing workshops, only men were formally trained, worked as journeymen, and could pursue a career as a printing master. In addition to them, women of the family contributed as unpaid helpers, knew about the trade, and in decisive moments, were necessary for the survival of the family's businesses. Women continued with the workshop in the name of the family at critical times when the husband or father had died. Furthermore, it can be assumed that through the general physical proximity of workshops and living spaces, all members of the family must have been familiar with the trade. While there is only little evidence about such tasks and the probable informal training in a family's shop, Natalie Zemon Davis has shown how daughters of a printing master assisted with hanging up printed paper to dry in early modern France.[9] While almost nothing is known about the family relationships of printing masters in the case of colonial Peru, the following examples shed light on the property situation of workshops in Lima.

Unlike the engagement of women in printing shops elsewhere, women in colonial Peru and in other places on the continent, such as La Plata, did not assume a similar role in the trade. In both places, the printing press was historically associated with the religious orders, thus constituting a space dominated

7    Migden Socolow, *The Women*, pp. 120–123.
8    Karen B. Graubart, 'Weaving and the Construction of a Gender Division of Labor in Early Colonial Peru', *Journal American Indian Quarterly*, 24 (2000), pp. 537–561.
9    Natalie Zemon Davis, 'Women in the Crafts in Sixteenth-Century Lyon', *Feminist Studies*, 8 (1982), pp. 46–80, 53. On the recovery of women's labour history in the printing house, see Cait Coker, 'Gendered Spheres: Theorizing Space in the English Printing House', *The Seventeenth Century*, 33 (2018), pp. 323–336.

by male printers.[10] Supply difficulties in a colonial site such as Peru, located on the Pacific coast of South America, meant that manufacturing materials, such as paper, types, and printing tools were scarce. Basic equipment and accessories had to be imported regularly from Spain or other sites in Europe. To overcome this shortage, tools on site were inherited, exchanged, and rented by the printers in the city. Most often, printers in Lima did not own the press and the equipment, but they worked in a hired workshop. The first printer, Antonio Ricardo, had brought a press with him to Peru.[11] In the following decades, however, often monasteries owned the workshop. In this way, and in line with the general need for religious printing, the orders maintained control over the printing equipment, leasing tools and accessories to different printers.

In the Viceroyalty of Peru, it was the monasteries that maintained the printing utensils rather than family dynasties. This structural feature of renting workshops formed a general phenomenon throughout the colonial period. In 1628, the monastery of Santo Domingo rented its two printing presses to Jerónimo de Contreras, who was allowed to establish his workshop on the premises of the monastery according to the contract. Together with the monastery, he would form a printing 'company' for three years; the master printer had to publish the Dominican texts (which were not to exceed one sheet) for free, and he would receive a daily meal from the monastery.[12] In 1796, the Mercedarians made a contract with Martín Valdivieso y Torrejón regarding the equipment of a printing workshop, including seven sets of type together with two printing presses and further tools, for a period of five years.[13] These typical arrangements, where individuals only rented spaces and equipment for a period of time rather than owning property, resulted in fluctuating employment and limited the familial continuation of printing businesses that we see in print workshops elsewhere. The organisational difference partially explains the comparatively less visible position of printers' widows in Peru to other centres of print. Women lacked the position to run a business except when they

---

10      Garone Gravier, 'Ornamentos tipográficos', p. 200.

11      Antonio Rodríguez Buckingham, 'The Establishment, Production, and Equipment of the First Printing Press in South America', *Harvard Library Bulletin*, 26 (1978), pp. 342–354.

12      Compañía entre el impresor Jerónimo de Contreras y el convento de Santo Domingo, para regentar la imprenta propiedad de este último, 15 December 1628, transcribed in Pedro Guibovich Pérez, *Imprimir en Lima durante la colonia: historia y documentos, 1584–1750* (Madrid: Iberoamericana; Vervuert, 2019), pp. 182–185.

13      Escritura de arrendamiento de la imprenta de los padres Mercedarios a don Martín Valdivieso y Torrejón, 16 September 1796. The inventory is transcribed in the Apendice XXVII in Carlos A. Romero, *Adiciones a 'La imprenta en Lima' de José Toribio Medina* (Lima: IRA, 2009), pp. 491–492. See document 24 in Guillermo Lohmann Villena, 'Documentos para la historia de la imprenta en Lima (1584–1796)', *Revista del Archivo General de la Nación*, 6 (1984), pp. 101–143, 140–143.

were taking over family property. In that case, if the workshop was owned and operated by the family, women participated in the workshop, taking on various tasks in the absence of men.

## 2      Print Culture

In the historiography of print culture in regions such as Peru, the analysis of gendered practices remains largely absent. Due do the paucity of information in the sources, scholarly examinations of print culture have traditionally neglected the diverse roles of individuals in printing workshops, particularly when these roles were transient or temporary. While 'print culture' serves as an umbrella term to describe the technological innovation and the changes to a particular society, it also describes the social relationships and activities of printing and distribution that situate print culture.[14] A study based on the relationships in a printing workshop focuses on the different actors related to a workshop. Journeymen constituted a major part of the presswork with their mechanical exercises as puller and beater. However, as craftsmen, often of humble origin, they remain largely shadowy figures in the history of printing.[15] Women did not physically work in a workshop, as this was not deemed appropriate for their sex but rather managed the business. Despite their weak standing in the property structure and the succession of workshops, the women of the owner's family often helped in the management to keep a workshop running.

Although not a single woman's name appears in any colonial Peruvian imprint, their participation was often indispensable when they carried out the administrative duties. In most cases, their work remains 'invisible' and their historic voice 'silent', but archival sources give proof of their work and responsibilities. An early example in Peru is Leonor de León, who was involved in a printing contract in 1642, three years after her husband Jerónimo

---

14     For an overview of the debates around the term and its different meanings, see Harold Love, 'Early Modern Print Culture: Assessing the Models', *Parergon*, 20 (2003), pp. 45–64. For the larger context in the Viceroyalty, see Agnes Gehbald, *A Colonial Book Market: Peruvian Print Culture in the Age of Enlightenment* (Cambridge: Cambridge University Press, 2023).

15     An exception to this is the research by Clive Griffin, *Journeymen-Printers, Heresy, and the Inquisition in Sixteenth-Century Spain* (Oxford: Oxford University Press, 2005). For a study of the journeymen in early New Spain, see Griffin, 'La formación profesional de los operarios de los primeros talleres tipográficos novohispanos', in Idalia García Aguilar and Pedro Rueda Ramírez (eds.), *El libro en circulación en la América colonial: producción, circuitos de distribución y conformación de bibliotecas en los siglos XVI al XVIII* (México: Quivira, 2014), pp. 23–34.

de Contreras had passed away. In this contract, she described herself as a 'printer of books' (*ynpresora de libros; ynpresora* being the feminine version of *impresor*, or printer). She led the negotiations and would receive money from the Dominicans, who ordered 250 Marian prayer books.[16] In the imprint of the *Tratado breve del dvlcissimo nombre de Maria*, however, it was not her name but her son's that appeared in the print 'Impresso en Lima por Josef de Contreras'.[17] Whereas her contractual partners, who were male, signed the treaty, Leonor de León did not add her signature, as she was not able to write.

Literacy was low, and more so for women of the time, as in many other places across the world. This reality, however, did not exclude them from participation in a workshop. In 1761, a century after Leonor de León, the signature of another woman, Doña Manuela Quesada, appeared in a contract on the management of a printing workshop.[18] In this case, a witness signed his name instead of the illiterate widow for the conclusion of a contract. While literacy was a necessary skill in the workshop for many tasks, such as typesetting and proofreading, the management could be carried out without any knowledge of writing. Women assumed the necessary responsibilities, because family had brought them to this position, without an apprenticeship or earlier career in the craft and whether or not they knew how to read and write.

Regarding the 'capitalist' character of female workshop owners, as in the description of Medina, many women (mostly in their role as widows) had to manage enterprises in precarious conditions.[19] In their economic pursuits, they supervised production and managed the workshop. It was not uncommon in the printing trade in colonial Lima for projects to go bankrupt. Like male masters, women who managed a workshop also were responsible for acquiring sufficient capital and pursuing economic profit. Magdalena Sotil presided over the workshop on Calle de la Barranca from 1747, and the printing master in her service, Francisco Sobrino y Bardos, published regularly until 1755.[20] Yet in 1774, she regulated the legacy of the workshop, describing the situation as 'of much poverty', referring to her physical and economic state.

---

16    Contrato suscrito por Leonor de León, viuda de Jerónimo de Contreras, 15 February 1642, cited as number 10, in Guillermo Lohmann Villena, 'Más documentos para la historia de la imprenta en Lima', *Revista del Archivo General de la Nación*, 12 (1995), pp. 77–98, 78. Compare the transcription of document 34 in Guibovich Pérez, *Imprimir en Lima*, pp. 222–225.

17    José Toribio Medina, *La imprenta en Lima (1584–1824)*, vol. I (Santiago de Chile: Impreso y grabado en casa del Autor, 1904), p. 335.

18    Compañía entre doña Manuela Quesada y Don Mateo Antonio de Bonilla para explotar una imprenta, 12 December 1761, transcribed in document 23 in Lohmann Villena, 'Documentos', pp. 137–140.

19    Medina, 'La imprenta en Lima', p. 483.

20    Ibid., 465.

She did not bequeath the workshop to one of her sons from different husbands, but to her daughter, Luisa Peralta, who already owned half of the workshop from her father's inheritance.[21] Following in the footsteps of her mother, Doña Luisa Peralta managed and fought for her rights to print, even engaging in the illegal production of invitation cards, called *convites*, that were used, above all, for upper class get-togethers, without a licence as required for the small popular books.[22] Against the privilege system in force, she stood up for the 'freedom of the craft'. From at least 1775 onward, Luisa Peralta served as proprietor of the press on Calle de Juan de Medina, which must have moved from the place in Barranca, where her mother had owned the workshop.[23] Women, from Leonor de León to Luisa Peralta, shaped the print culture by assisting in the trade and managing workshops.

## 3      Female Management

Women proved their managerial skills when it came to defending the *familia*. If there was no male heir, it was left to the widow or the daughters to maintain the printing business. The family relationship between husband and wife, or father and daughter, turned these cases into a professional legacy. According to a printer's will in 1659, Doña Francisca Gutiérrez inherited the workshop of her husband, Julián Santos de Saldaña, who had worked as the owner of the printing workshop with close connections to the Augustinians. In his last will, he declared that neither the printing press (*emprenta*) nor his books (*librería*) were to be sold but should remain with his wife, and that a certain Blas Fernández de Quebedo had to continue to work for her. In case that a sale would become necessary, she had to be favoured for her good services.[24] This

---

21      Testamento Magdalena Sotil. Archivo General de la Nación, Lima, Peru (AGN). Prot. 579, siglo XVIII, Pedro Lumbreras, 1774. This document of 5 March 1774, unknown to Medina, describes the sequence of the two women.

22      Autos seguidos por Don Luis de Asurza, en 1775, contra Francisco Mayorga y doña Luisa Peralta, sobre el descubrimiento de imprentas clandestinas. Incluye unos autos seguidos sobre el mismo asunto por Don Tomás Arandilla, mayordomo de la Real Casa de Niños Expósitos. Archivo de la Beneficencia (BENE), Lima, Peru . Huérfanos, I.25, 1778.

23      Expedientes e instancias de partes. Archivo General de Indias (AGI), Seville, Spain. Lima, 1013, 1811–1812. Diligencia, 3 March 1758.

24      For a transcription of the will of her husband Julián Santos de Saldaña of 18 September 1659, see document 50 in Guibovich Pérez, *Imprimir en Lima*, pp. 263–269. Since 1638, Santos de Saldaña had been publishing in Lima, favoured by the Viceroy with the privilege of *cartillas* in 1652, José Toribio Medina, *Historia de la imprenta en los antiguos dominios españoles de América y Oceanía*, vol. 1 (Santiago de Chile: Fondo Histórico y Bibliográfico José Toribio Medina, 1958), pp. 456–458. Real cédula por la que se concede a Julián Santos de

short reference in his will proves her long standing connection to the work-shop, as well as the confidence he had in his wife to maintain the business.

When a printer died, it was necessary to organise the succession of the workshop and to arrange the printing privileges. Women provided some conti-nuity in this thread. In 1679, most likely the same Francisca Gutiérrez Caballero fought to maintain the privilege of her deceased husband, the printer Juan de Quevedo y Zarate. The first imprints with his name are from the early 1660s, which confirms that Juan de Quevedo was the second husband of Francisca Gutiérrez, possibly working on the same press as her first husband, Julián Santos de Saldaña, had before him. After the death of her second husband, Doña Francisca insisted on the privilege to print primers, a genre in much demand for teaching literacy and a steady income for the printing workshop. As the former holder of the privilege had died, another printer applied for the privilege, yet the widow protested, claiming that it was her right to con-tinue with the printing—as her husband Juan de Quevedo had done—for the remaining days of her life.[25] It was not uncommon for widows to 'remain in the trade' by remarrying another printer. This might have provided her with some continuity and also assured the survival of the business, as the equip-ment and contacts could stay in the family.[26] Although no publication activity in the name of Francisca Gutiérrez is known, the archival files prove that the widow tried to continue in the tradition of her printer husbands.

It was customary for widows to fight for the printing privileges and for the right to maintain and lease the equipment. Every time a printer died, solicita-tions and often litigations followed about the privileges. In general, the exclu-sive rights to print certain genres were granted to a person and not to a specific workshop. This could create difficult situations for a family business. Similar to the case of Francisca Gutiérrez, the unnamed widow of the printer Agustín Ramos, inherited the privilege for the printing of official decrees and edicts in 1787.[27] In this case, the woman was not even named in the document but

---

Saldaña privilegio para la impression de cartillas, 23 September 1652, Medina, *Historia de la imprenta*, p. 526.

25    Against her requests, the Viceroy decided to grant the privilege to Manuel de los Olivos in 1681, presumably after an agreement had been found, the widow rescinded. 'Diligencias actuadas en Madrid por Manuel de los Olivos, mercader de libros, a fin de obtener el privilegio para la impression de cartillas en Lima, 1681–1688', transcribed in document 13 in Medina, *Historia de la imprenta*, p. 528. For the printer's biography, see Medina, *Historia de la imprenta*, p. 458.

26    For patterns of marriage in the printing trade and professional advancement, see Davis, 'Women in the Crafts', p. 58; Robert Darnton, *Pirating and Publishing: The Book Trade in the Age of Enlightenment* (Oxford: Oxford University Press, 2021), pp. 45, 51.

27    Carta n° 142 del virrey Joaquín de la Pezuela, a Martín de Garay Perales, secretario de Hacienda. AGI. Lima, 757.18, 1817.

only referred to by her family connection. Against aspiring applicants, printers' widows repeatedly tried to retain privileges that assured steady revenues for a workshop in the often risky business of book production. If the press belonged to the family, this meant an economic asset for the widow, at least if the workshop was in good shape. In 1761, the aforementioned Manuela Quesada managed to establish a company with a printer for a partially destroyed workshop. She was not even the owner of the workshop but negotiated as a tutor on behalf of her granddaughter Doña Antonia.[28] In 1821, another widow, María del Carmen Vallejo, spoke up for a quick sale of a press, which was encumbered with a mortgage by Bernardino Ruiz, before the workshop was going to lose all its value.[29] Apart from these brief mentions and citations, little else is known about their lives. While the widows took action in order to monetise the workshop rapidly, defend printing property, and the rights to certain printing privileges, a few women were described as owner-managers of a workshop.

Whereas all male owners presided over a workshop as a single person in colonial Lima, in at least these two cases, women collaborated in the management. While the before-mentioned cases demonstrate how women negotiated, defended, and commissioned work provisionally in case of a vacancy in the male succession, others appear as workshop owners. In 1734, Doña Francisca de Contreras was described as the 'owner' (*dueña*) of the press in Calle de Valladolid. A few lines below in the same document, another woman, María Granados, was mentioned as 'owner of the same press' (*dueña asimismo de dicha imprenta*).[30] Apparently, they managed the workshop on Calle de Valladolid, which was called 'Imprenta Real' for the royal privilege, together for at least two years. In another document, Doña Francisca's niece, Andrea Contreras, daughter of the printer Jerónimo de Contreras, also appears as a contract partner. While the women administered the workshop, the printer

---

28  Compañía entre doña Manuela Quesada y Don Mateo Antonio de Bonilla para explotar una imprenta, 12 December 1761, transcribed in document 23 in Lohmann Villena, 'Documentos', pp. 137–140. Ten years before, in 1751, another printer called Juan Balero worked on the press on Calle de las Mantas, already managed by Manuela Quesada, Medina, 'La imprenta en Lima', p. 465.

29  Borrador de la solicitud de María del Carmen Vallejo, viuda de Francisco Uville, en los autos que sigue con la testamentaría de Bernardino Ruiz sobre que el secuestro de la imprenta hipotecada se realice en caso de haber dinero o especies de enajenación. AGN. VS-RA, 1.398, 1821.

30  Carta nº 98 del virrey José Fernando de Abascal, al ministro de Gracia y Justicia. AGI. Lima, 739, N.54, 1809, 364. Francisca Contreras was most probably the sister of Jerónimo de Contreras, the second one with this name in the Limeño printer dynasty of the Contreras y Alvarado.

Félix de Saldaña y Flores physically worked on their press.[31] Repeatedly, when women owned a workshop in Lima, they did so in partnership with others. In addition to the Contreras–Granados partnership, the sisters María and Paula Meléndez formed another company for the press on Calle de Palacio, in which Agustín de Orue printed for them.[32] Following the description of Medina, they were the nieces of a canon of the Cathedral in Lima, Doctor Don José Meléndez, who had imported a press from Madrid in 1711.[33] While almost nothing else is known about the two sisters, family relations had probably brought them into the printing trades. Even though some women were at times able to own and run a workshop, and in several cases guaranteed the continuity of a workshop, they have not yet occupied a prominent position in the history of printing.[34]

As the examination of the property structure reveals, printing workshops in colonial Peru were only occasionally family property. Often the printers did not own the equipment needed to print but leased it from monasteries and ecclesiastical institutions. This helps to explain the largely invisible role of women in the workshops in the Viceroyalty. Moreover, gendered operations determined a certain division of labour with women segregated to a business' various managerial tasks, those of administrative nature. Women managed printing privileges, assets, and equipment, acted as negotiating partners, and continued with a family's printing business. Some of them remained in the trade by marrying printers, while others led a workshop in partnership with other women. These women contributed behind the scenes to the growing printing production that shaped the print culture. Whereas the names in Peruvian imprints show exclusively male masters during colonial times until 1821, studying the role of women in the workshop reveals the variety of female agents. Often these women were family members, like wives and widows, daughters, granddaughters, and nieces who made a living from the printing trade too. Only in 1822 did Mónica Sierra, the last female printer of the Viceroyalty, finally print her name on the publications of her press on Calle de San Jacinto in Lima. Like many of her predecessors, nothing is known about her life, except for the printing products as a result of her work.[35]

---

31    Medina, 'La imprenta en Lima', pp. 461–462; Rubén Vargas Ugarte, *Impresos peruanos* (*1584–1650*), vol. vii (Lima: Tipográfica Peruana, 1953), p. xxxviii.

32    Carta n° 98 del virrey José Fernando de Abascal, al ministro de Gracia y Justicia, 364v.

33    Medina, 'La imprenta en Lima', p. 462.

34    As they did not work physically on the press, Pedro Guibovich Pérez does not mention any woman in his figure of printers in colonial Lima, Guibovich Pérez, *Imprimir en Lima*, p. 59.

35    Medina, 'La imprenta en Lima', p. 466; Graciela Araujo Espinoza, 'Adiciones a La imprenta en Lima (1584–1824)', *Fénix* 8 (1952), pp. 467–704, p. 654.

# PART 2

## *Publishing Gender*

∴

# CHAPTER 5

# 'Best Left to Men': Women and Publishing Histories in Africa

*Elizabeth Le Roux*

Asenath Bole Odaga, founder of Lake Publishers in Kenya in 1983, described her struggle as a woman in publishing: she was confronted by male colleagues who suggested that publishing was 'best left to men'. She recalled in an interview that they suggested it might be more appropriate if she were to set up a restaurant instead of a publishing house—a more acceptable space for a woman, being associated with food rather than ideas.[1] Obituaries of Odaga emphasise her role as the first East African woman to start a publishing house and also underscore her toughness in overcoming obstacles and making her way in a male-dominated world. In tributes, she is described in gendered terms, which are also very specific to the African location: as a 'literary lioness' and 'the queen of folklore in Africa'.[2]

Contrast this depiction with that of a different African publisher: the South African publisher Jonathan Ball, who started an eponymous publishing house in the 1970s and died in April 2021. In obituaries, he is described as 'larger than life', a 'shrewd businessman' and 'a bon vivant publisher in the classic mould, whose favourite pastime was holding court at a well-appointed table'. He is also described as a publisher who broke all moulds in his industry, always working, in his words, 'at the frontier.'[3] Another obituary paid tribute to his personal characteristics as a 'brilliant businessman and savvy negotiator':

---

1  Quoted in Hans M. Zell, 'Women in African Publishing and the Book Trade: A Series of Profiles', *African Book Publishing Record*, 47 (2021), p. 3.

2  'Literary Lioness Asenath Bole Odaga closes her chapter at 83', *Business Daily*, 4 December 2014 <https://www.businessdailyafrica.com/bd/lifestyle/society/literary-lioness-asenath-bole -odaga-closes-her-chapter-at-83-2074508>; 'A tribute to Asenath Bole Odaga: The queen of folklore', *The Nation*, 5 December 2014 <https://nation.africa/kenya/life-and-style/weekend /a-tribute-to-asenath-bole-odaga-the-queen-of-folklore-1049184>.

3  Ben Williams, 'Jonathan Ball (1951–2021): A disruptor who transformed South Africa's publishing industry', *Daily Maverick*, 6 April 2021 <https://www.dailymaverick.co.za/article /2021-04-06-jonathan-ball-1951-2021-a-disruptor-who-transformed-south-africas-publishing -industry/>.

He was also huge fun, a large man who celebrated the traditional publishing lunch—and, on trips to London, dinner the same evening too. He was excellent company at Frankfurt and in London, and a famously hospitable host to visiting publishers and authors in South Africa. He could be bombastic, but he had a marvellous sense of humour and was held in the highest respect and affection by all the international authors and publishers who worked with him.[4]

A similar description can be found of many male publishers. For example, the non-fiction publisher Howard Timmins was described in his obituary as having 'a remarkable flair for publishing and ... an acute sales sense'.[5] His friend Johan Simon, a bookseller, described him as an enthusiastic gambler, gambling on books, cards and horses, who lived to excess, smoked too much and drove his Jaguar sportscar recklessly.[6]

The often flamboyant, eccentric male founders of publishing imprints are probably most associated in the public mind with publishing—they are depicted as having business skills that enable them to take calculated risks, but also as having the personality and passion that enable them to be successful. They are uncompromising and confident, and both charming and difficult to work with. These traits, which emphasise the publishers' individuality as the source of their success, are associated with masculine stereotypes. Publishing has thus been constructed as a masculine enterprise, even as the industry has become increasingly dominated by women. This positioning of male leaders is not specific to publishing, as studies have shown in other contexts that businessmen are usually framed in terms of masculine characteristics, such as decisiveness, assertiveness, and flair and individuality.[7] In contrast, as Eikhof, Summers and Carter have shown, women in business are often depicted as 'less purposeful, professional and successful' than their male counterparts, and as being driven by personal concerns rather than broader social or business motivations.[8] They are described less in terms of individual flair, and more of

---

4   Andrew Franklin and Eugene Ashton, 'Obituary: Jonathan Ball', *The Bookseller*, 16 April 2021.

5   'Death of Howard Timmins', *Rand Daily Mail*, 10 September 1984.

6   Herman Oosthuizen, 'Johan Simon, prins onder boekhandelaars', *Die Volksblad*, 13 November 1996.

7   See D. Ruth Eikhof, J. Summers and S. Carter, '"Women doing their own thing": media representations of female entrepreneurship', *International Journal of Entrepreneurial Behavior & Research*, 19 (2013), pp. 547–64; Maria Hameed Khan, 'Analysing media framing of women in contemporary Australian business leadership', PhD Thesis: (Queensland University of Technology, 2020).

8   Eikhof, Summers and Carter, 'Women doing their own thing', p. 548.

perseverance. Reference is commonly made to their husbands and role in their household.[9] Descriptions of men—and also occasionally women—in publishing may also use gendered terms such as 'midwife' or 'mother', in an example of traditionally feminine identities being co-opted.[10]

These trends can be seen both when looking at the representation of women in the present day, and when looking back at the lives and descriptions of historical women publishers. Increasingly, historical studies of women in publishing are painting a much more complex picture of the role, personalities and impact of such women. Significantly, such research has highlighted the methodological and practical difficulties of identifying women in publishing history.[11] However, very little research thus far has examined the depiction of women publishers in African countries.

Part of the reason is that publishing is relatively recent in most parts of Africa. Although manuscript writing dates back many centuries, printing in Africa is mostly the result of missionary or colonial endeavours on the continent, and book publishing can largely be traced to the twentieth century, even the post-colonial period for indigenous publishers.[12] Reading and writing—and thus involvement in print culture—was largely confined to a literary elite until the spread of education in the post-independence period. Publishing remained dominated by the colonial centres of London and Paris (and still is dominated by multinationals). Studies of publishing history in this region tend to focus on the men who formed literary networks, established printing or publishing businesses, and distributed books through the book trade—men like Chinua Achebe and his work on the Heinemann African Writers Series, Henry Chakava in Kenya, or Walter Bgoya in Tanzania.[13] However, unlike the 'vast network of

---

9     Odaga is described as believing in women's empowerment 'without belittling any hus-
      band', see Abnea Ndago-Kabira,' Asenath Odaga: Matriarch who bequeathed us rich
      literature and sense of belonging', *The Standard*, 2015; online <https://www.standard
      media.co.ke/entertainment/arts-and-culture/article/2000143792/asenath-odaga-mat
      riach-who-bequeathed-us-rich-literature-and-sense-of-belonging>.

10    N.B. Pascal, 'The editor: in search of a metaphor', *Publishing Research Quarterly*, 7 (1995),
      pp. 169–88.

11    See, the work being done by Cait Coker and Kate Ozment, 'Building the Women in Book
      History Bibliography, or Digital Enumerative Bibliography as Preservation of Feminist
      Labor', *Digital Humanities Quarterly*, 13 (2019).

12    See, for instance, Hans M. Zell, 'Publishing in Africa', in Philip G. Altbach & Edith S
      Hoshino (eds.), *International Book Publishing: An Encyclopaedia* (New York, NY: Garland
      Publishing, 1995), pp. 366–372.

13    These studies are an important contribution to African publishing history, but they sel-
      dom include female publishers. For example, Nourdin Bejjit, 'The Publishing of African
      literature: Chinua Achebe, Ngugi wa Thiong'o and the Heinemann African Writers
      Series 1962–1988', PhD Thesis (The Open University, 2009); Kiarie Kamau and Kirimi

women printers and publishers in Britain' that has been identified, and knowledge of women's diverse roles as printers, publishers, booksellers and authors in other countries, in the African context we find only scant mention of the role of women in print production.[14] Women publishers in African countries are still seen as a deviation from the 'norm', male publishers, and so they are also repeatedly described in terms of their scarcity, to the extent that they are called the 'first' even when they are clearly not. The implication is that the previous 'firsts' have been forgotten or are less visible.

## 1    Framing the African Woman Publisher

One limitation of research to date is that much of what is written about 'women in publishing' is actually about women writers and especially writers of literary fiction. Moreover, what we have available on women publishers is largely anecdotes and personal profiles, with little archival research or attempts to place them within a larger publishing landscape, or to engage with broader debates in cultural or book history. For example, a study by Urvashi Butalia and Ritu Menon aimed 'to map a history of feminist or women's publishing in what is known as the Third or Southern World', although their work largely described the contemporary—not historical—challenges which women publishers face in developing countries, including some African countries.[15] Another of the profiles available is a collection of personal essays by ten African women publishers from Ghana, Kenya, Namibia, Nigeria, Senegal, South Africa, Uganda, and Zimbabwe.[16] A similar series of profiles was published by Hans Zell in 2020, including publishers from nine countries such as Flora Nwapa (who is better known as an author) and the aforementioned Asenath Bole Odaga.[17] Notably, the descriptions in these profiles include indicators of priority ('first', 'pioneer'):

Mitambo (eds.), *Coming of Age: Essays in Honour of Dr Henry Chakava at 70* (Nairobi: East African Educational Publishers, 2016).

14    Paula McDowell, 'Women and the business of print', in Vivien Jones (ed.), *Women and Literature in Britain, 1700–1800* (Cambridge: Cambridge University Press, 2000), p. 135; see also Michelle Levy, 'Women and print culture, 1750–1830', in J.M. Labbe (ed.), *The History of British Women's Writing, 1750–1830* (London: Palgrave Macmillan, 2010), pp. 29–46.

15    Urvashi Butalia and Rita Menon, *Making a Difference: Feminist Publishing in the South* (Chestnut Hill, MA: Bellagio Publishing Network, 1995).

16    Mary Jay and Susan Kelly, *Courage and Consequence: Women Publishing in Africa* (Oxford: African Books Collective, 2002).

17    Zell, 'Women in African Publishing'.

To encourage more women's writing, and discussion of women's issues in society, Flora Nwapa set up Tana Press in Enugu in 1974, and the Flora Nwapa Company in 1977, and which is generally credited to be the first publishing house and printing press in Africa founded and run by a woman.[18]

Similarly, a collection of essays by the publisher Nana Ayebia Clarke pays tribute to other African women publishers, including Flora Nwapa, Efua Sutherland, Margaret Busby, and Buchi Emecheta. She argues that they inspired a new generation of African women writers and publishers: 'In so doing, they opened up spaces and spearheaded what would become the beginning of a literary revolution in writing about female challenges and experiences, and publishing their narratives on the continent in publishing houses owned by them at a time when African women writers and publishers were unheard of'.[19] Rebecca Clarke has also written about the contemporary challenges women publishers face, including lack of finance, shortages of technical skills, widespread occupational gender discrimination, the problems of stereotyping writing by women, and accessing mainstream markets.[20]

These works provide rich anecdotal evidence of the emergence of a generation of women publishers, with new initiatives being launched such as FemRite in Uganda and the PublisHer network, a networking community that seeks to empower women in publishing and promote gender balance in the worldwide book business: 'African woman publishers are beating down a path while building a literary establishment that is inclusive and diverse'.[21] However, we have little evidence-based understanding of how these women publishers fit into a larger history of women in print culture, or of publishing history more generally. This has led to almost every new women's publishing initiative being labelled as the 'first'.

An ahistorical understanding is likely to continue without more detailed research into the role of women in publishing history. Although book publishing appears to have been more male-dominated, there is evidence of women's

---

18  Ibid., p. 26.

19  Nana Ayebia Clarke, 'Pioneering African Women Publishers: Publishing as Cultural Activism', Washington DC: ALA Conference, 2018.

20  Rebecca Clarke, 'Women Publishers in Africa and the North', in Cassandra Veney and Paul Zeleza (eds), *Women in African Studies Scholarly Publishing* (Trenton: Africa World Press, 2001), pp. 45–64.

21  Emeka Joseph Nwankwo, 'How Women Are Changing the Face of African Publishing', *LitHub* (2020). For more on FemRite, see <https://www.femriteug.org/> and on PublisHer, see <https://womeninpublishing.org/>.

involvement in newspapers, magazines and other periodicals, as well as books, throughout the twentieth century. For instance, Audrey Gadzekpo's work on women in the media in Ghana is a notable exception to the ahistorical trend. She has shown that, 'despite women's absence in secondary texts on the history of Ghanaian newspapers, there was considerable female presence in both the operations and discourses of the very vibrant nationalistic press throughout much of the colonial period'.[22] This was largely, as she reveals through detailed archival work, in gendered spaces such as women's columns. Another piece is Patricia Mwazvita Madondo's study of women in textbook publishing management in Zimbabwe.[23] The exploratory nature of this research is reflected in the brevity of most studies—just a few pages, based on surveys or interviews—as well as their sporadic nature, based on a personal interest from a researcher rather than a sustained investigation (apart from Gadzekpo's exemplary studies). There is space for a broader consolidated research network, with a specific focus on African women in publishing.

There thus remains a gap when it comes to describing the historical role of women publishers in Africa, and my own research to date has shown that it is difficult even to identify such publishers, let alone write them back into the publishing history of this region. This raises questions of method and historiography: How do we identify women's involvement in the African book trades? What sources can be tapped for the data, beyond interviews and personal recollections?

## 2       Women as Editors in South Africa

In South Africa, some initial work has been done to identify women in publishing history. But it remains difficult to answer fairly basic questions, such as: How many women were involved, and at what times? What were their typical jobs? Where can we find evidence of their work? The first stop for any research on printing in South Africa is the comprehensive bibliographies compiled by Sidney Mendelssohn in 1910 and 1925, followed by Fransie Rossouw's index of

---

22      Audrey Gadzekpo, 'The Hidden History of Women in Ghanaian Print Culture', in Oyeronke Oyewumi (ed.), *African Gender Studies* (Basingstoke: Palgrave Macmillan, 2005), pp. 279–295.
23      Patricia Mwazvita Mudondo, 'Women in Textbook Publishing Management. The Zimbabwe Experiences', in Tembeka Mbobo, Joyce Siwani and Charlotte Witbooi (eds.), *Proceedings of the First Annual National Conference on Women in Writing*, (Kwa-Zuma: Centre for Cultural and Artistic Expression, 2000), pp. 63–66.

South African printers and publishers.[24] In the bibliographies, which cover the period between 1800 and 1925, we find multiple references to women as writers and illustrators, but no details linking women to publishing houses.[25] Rossouw's more recent index listing printers, booksellers and publishers in the country, contains only a single possible lead: a 'Miss Allardyce', working as a selling agent in 1893. She is included in the *Argus Annual* of 1893 and 1894, in a list of stationers in Kimberley, but apart from that brief mention no more information could be located.[26] The other main sources regarding printing and freedom of the press in the nineteenth century hardly mention women at all. For instance, while Anna Smith's survey of the spread of printing mentions only men, L.J. Picton's work on the history of printing notes that Hubertus Elffers (1858–1931) established the Rustica Press in 1902 and 'excited considerable comment by employing women compositors'.[27] These tantalising instances support what we know must be true: that women were involved in the book trade in the nineteenth and twentieth century, and further archival digging could unearth more names. One of the difficulties in fleshing out these scattered references has been that few publisher, printer or even, in some cases, newspaper archives have been digitised, and those that have been may be difficult to access, focus only on literary figures and especially authors, and are often incomplete.

Journalism, newspapers and periodicals appear to be the most fruitful source, at present, for information on women in the book trades, perhaps in part because more research has been undertaken on newspaper and media history than on publishing history.[28] In the gendered sphere of women's magazines, particularly those aimed at an Afrikaans audience, it seems that a good number of the editors were women from the early twentieth century. For example, while the women's magazine *Die Huisgenoot* (The Home Companion) was

24    Fransie Rossouw, *South African Printers and Publishers, 1795–1925* (Cape Town: South African Library, 1987).

25    Sydney Mendelssohn, *A South African Bibliography to the Year 1925, Being a Revision and Continuation of Sidney Mendelssohn's South African Bibliography 1910* (London: Mansell, 1979).

26    *Argus Annual* (1894), p. 761.

27    Anna Smith, *The Spread of Printing. Eastern Hemisphere. South Africa* (Amsterdam: Van Gendt & Co, 1971); A.C.G. Lloyd, 'The birth of printing in South Africa', *The Library*, 5 (1914), pp. 31–43; L.H. Meurant, *Sixty Years Ago* (Cape Town: Saul Solomon, 1886); L.J. Picton, 'Nicprint 50: Being some account of the history of the printing, packaging and newspaper industry of South Africa', MA Thesis (University of Cape Town, 1969), p. 47.

28    In particular, Lizette Rabe has laid the foundations for further study of gender in the South African media, Lizette Rabe, 'Women voices in the media of the Afrikaans language community: an historical perspective', *Communitas*, 9 (2004), pp. 31–46.

established in 1916 and overseen by men at the Nasionale Pers, the smaller *Die Boerevrou* (The Afrikaner Housewife, 1919–1931) was run by owner-editor Mabel Malherbe. Perhaps because of her prominence as a politician—Malherbe was the first woman mayor in South Africa (1931–32) and one of the first elected to Parliament (1933–38)—more research has been carried out on her career than on most other women in the book trades in South Africa. While almost all popular or media sources refer to her role as Pretoria's first woman mayor, scholarly attention has focused on analysis of the magazine she established and ran, and to a limited extent on the reading group, the Hollands-Afrikaanse Leesunie, she founded in 1912.[29] Malherbe, who came from a celebrated English family in the Cape, married Kenne Malherbe, a lawyer who sometimes referred to himself as Mr Mabel Malherbe—a joke, but also an indication of how unusual Mabel was, at a time when many married women were referred to by their husbands' names.

Malherbe's father was a journalist, which may explain her interest in starting a magazine herself. She explained her motivation as follows, in the first issue of *Die Boerevrouw* in 1919:

> *Die Boerevrouw* is a monthly magazine for the Afrikaans woman. We are tired of always getting one or maybe two pages devoted to our interests in a far corner of magazines (with the children's section)![30]

Like the readership, the team working at *Die Boerevrouw* was also largely female, including Malherbe's cousin Marguerite Pienaar who oversaw the administration and correspondence. According to Kruger, neither Malherbe nor Pienaar worked for a salary.[31] M.E.R. (Maria Elizabeth Rothmann) was a regular contributor and editor, who would later become a celebrated author in South Africa. She is sometimes seen as the first woman Afrikaans journalist, and certainly one of the first to get a Bachelor of Arts degree. As both owner

---

29    For example: see, Janette van Rensburg and Fransjohan Pretorius, 'Die ontstaan, bestuur en ontvangs van *Die Boerevrou*, die eerste Afrikaanse vrouetydskrif', *South African Journal of Cultural History*, 26 (2012), pp. 171–189; Lou-Marie Kruger, 'Gender, community and identity: Women and Afrikaner nationalism in the Volksmoeder discourse of Die Boerevrou (1919–1931)', MS Thesis (University of Cape Town, 1991).

30    *'Die Boerevrouw is 'n Maandblad vir die Afrikaanse vrou. One is nou moeg daarvan om altijd in 'n uithoekje van tijdskrifte (bij die kinder afdeling) een, of miskien twee bladsije to krij wat aan ons belange gewij is!'* Quoted in Van Rensburg and Pretorius, 'Die ontstaan, bestuur en ontvangs van *Die Boerevrou*'.

31    Kruger, 'Gender, community and identity', p. 174.

and publisher, Malherbe played a significant role in determining the editorial direction of the magazine, and more broadly in shaping Afrikaans literary heritage in the early twentieth century. For example, she was one of the first to publish one of South Africa's best-known poets, Eugène Marais (also a cousin), and sketches by the artist Pierneef. The close link between gender and nationalist ideology has been explored in various studies of Afrikaner women, but to my knowledge the ways in which literary, cultural and political networks contributed to the emergence of women print culture has not been examined.[32]

Unlike the male publishers I refer to at the beginning of this essay, Mabel Malherbe was not described as a dashing risk-taker. Rather, media reports and tributes depict her as dedicated, as 'a woman of tremendous integrity' and appreciated for her 'tact and charm, and her well-balanced mind'.[33] Her dedication and attention to detail are often referenced; for instance, M.E.R. described Malherbe as being 'closely concerned with the quality of what she published: it had to be impeccable'.[34] M.E.R. added an affectionate pen portrait of Malherbe at work:

> I can still picture her sitting at her desk with the month's pieces in front of her, busy setting up the dummy—articles, 'Coffee Table' letters, stories, poems, illustrations, decorations, inserts. I see her handling every piece, every fragment and crumb with the pleasure of a young mother dressing her only little girl and tying ribbons in her hair.[35]

This description adds a trope that is commonly found in describing women in business: motherhood. Malherbe was the mother of two children, and this role is carried over into descriptions of her as 'the mother of Afrikaans women's

---

32    Van Rensburg and Pretorius, 'Die ontstaan, bestuur en ontvangs'; Kruger, *Gender, community and identity*; Louise Vincent, 'Bread and honour: White working class women and Afrikaner nationalism in the 1930s', *Journal of Southern African Studies*, 26 (2000), pp. 61–78.

33    Kruger, *Gender, community and identity*, p. viii; 'Women in the Capital', *Rand Daily Mail*, 17 March 1933, p. 8.

34    *'Sy was keurig besorg oor die kwaliteit van wat sy gegee het: dit moet onbesproke wees'*. Quoted in Lizette Rabe, 'Ontstaan en ontwikkeling van Sarie Marais as massatydskrif vir die Afrikaanse vrou', PhD Thesis (University of Stellenbosch, 1985), p. 20.

35    *'Ek sien haar nou nog by haar lessenaar sit met die maand se stukke voor haar, besig om die 'dummy' op te stel—artikels, 'Koffietafel-briewe', stories, versies, illustrasies, dekorasies, bladvullings. Ek sie haar elke stuk, elke brokkie en krummel met die genoeë hanteer waarmee 'n jong moeder haar enigste dogtertjie aantrek en linte in die hare bind'*, quoted in Rabe, *Ontstaan en ontwikkeling*, p. 42.

magazines', and of the Afrikaans Reading Group as being her 'baby'.[36] She herself spoke of her magazine as her child:

> It was (if I may express it in this way) my own creation, and I poured all my ideas and ideals into it; it was a living being which grew under my hands and which I could steer in the direction I wanted.[37]

While Malherbe is one of the most prominent examples of women in the media, other names can also be mentioned. A contemporary of Malherbe's is Minnie Donovan, the first editor of *Die Huisvrou* (The Housewife), a conservative Christian magazine for women, from 1922 to 1927. Under Donovan, *Die Huisvrou* was considered exceptionally conservative, as it provided tips on how to be a 'proper housewife', while firmly opposing women getting the vote and working outside of the home.[38] In spite of publicly opposing women's right to vote and work, Donovan edited the magazine herself for six years, and wrote articles in her husband's satirical journal, *The Cape*, under the pseudonym 'M'. *Die Huisvrou*, which continued until 1976, also encouraged the publication of women authors, such as Louise Latsky (the first woman to be awarded a doctorate at Stellenbosch University) and later Audrey Blignault. Another example is Rykie van Reenen, who was appointed as the second professional woman journalist on the Cape daily *Die Burger* in 1945, and has been called 'undoubtedly the most outstanding Afrikaans journalist of the [twentieth] century'.[39] Van Reenen was described as the 'wedge' that cracked open the 'brute rock of male domination' from which a new generation of women could enter the profession.[40] She thus opened the way for further women editors, such as Jane Raphaely, who launched *Fairlady*, the first local English-language women's magazine, in 1964.

It is not only in white women's magazines that the role of women has started to be identified—the intersections between gender and race, and

---

36    Van Rensburg and Pretorius, 'Die ontstaan, bestuur en ontvang'; 'Reading group is now 50 years old', *Rand Daily Mail*, 15 March 1962, p. 9.

37    '*Dit was (as ek dit so mag uitdruk) my eie skepping, en daarin het ek uitgestort al my gedagtes en ideale; dit was iets lewendigs wat onder my hand gegroei het en wat ek kon stuur in die rigting wat ek wou*', Mabel Malherbe, 'Ek sien haar win', *Sarie*, 6 July 1949.

38    Amy Rommelspacher, 'Food, nutrition and the Afrikaans housewife in *Die Huisvrou*, 1922–1945', *Historia*, 65 (2020), pp. 38–60. Interestingly, the first cover features a mother and her two children reading in the home.

39    Giliomee, quoted in Lizette Rabe, *Rykie van Reenen: 'n Lewe met woorde* (Cape Town: Tafelberg, 2011). This is one of the only full-length biographies of a woman in media or the book trades in South Africa.

40    Rabe, *Rykie van Reenen*.

legislated racial stratification, add a level of complexity to the South African situation. Black authorship, printing and publishing has, like white publishing, been construed as male-dominated. For example, Tim Couzens has shown that pseudonyms were sometimes used to obscure the identity and gender of contributors—to the extent that the 'editress' of the women's pages in some magazines was in fact a man:

> the editress of the women's pages of *The Bantu World* was, in the late Thirties, Rolfes Dhlomo, undoubtedly male in all other respects! Indeed, as is predictable, the newspapers were largely male controlled. A picture of the 15-strong staff of *Umteteli wa Bantu* in 1930, for instance features an all-male cast.[41]

Very little research has focused specifically on the role of black women as publishers. In one example, Nicolette Ferreira has shown that, from the 1960s, black women were involved in running women's magazines:

> At both *Grace* and *The Townships Housewife*, the staff for the most part comprised of black women. *Grace* was, moreover, presented as the brainchild of Mrs Esther K. Nyembezi, with the January 1965 issue stating that 'whilst working among her own people, [Mrs Nyembezi] realised the need for a magazine for women by women' ... Patience Khumalo edited *The Townships Housewife*, along with a white compiling editor, Patricia Fitzgerald.[42]

These brief portraits of women in periodicals history appear only to scrape the surface of a full picture of gendered roles in the media in South Africa. They raise as many questions as they answer, about the different political alignments of the women and their periodicals, the editorial philosophies and the audiences. Matters of ownership, social position and status would also impact the role of these women and the kinds of social, cultural and financial capital they could access—further complicated in the case of black women. At present, the jigsaw puzzle pieces do not fit together (and many are still missing!), and so the impact of these women on each other, on the development of the media overall, and on women in other kinds of publishing, has not yet been

41    Tim Couzens, 'History of the Black Press in South Africa 1836–1960' (The University of the Witwatersrand: Wits Institute for Social and Economic Research Seminar, 1984), p. 35.

42    Nicolette Ferreira, '*Grace* and *The Townships Housewife*: Excavating black South African women's magazines from the 1960s', *Agenda*, 25 (2011), pp. 59–68.

examined. As scholars (especially women) produce more research on key figures in media and periodical history, this creates an impetus for connections to be made.


## 3        Women in Book Publishing: Two Case Studies

Book publishing appears to have been even more male-dominated, on the basis of the key sources tracing the development of printing and publishing in South Africa.[43] They tell a well-trodden story of men, many of them immigrants, moving to South Africa and founding mission presses and later publishing houses in their own names. The founding and development of culturally significant publishers like Nasionale Pers have been examined, but it is true to say that, apart from memoirs and brief tributes, even the histories of important publishers such as J.L. van Schaik, Thomas Maskew Miller, Ad Donker, A.A. Balkema, and Howard Timmins, have not been researched in much depth.[44] With little systematic research of the men at the helm, even less attention has been given to the women who were often active behind the scenes and even partners in the business. In this section, I will examine two broad case studies of the role of women as publishers in South Africa: the university presses and the oppositional publishers.

South Africa has around 26 public universities, but only four university presses, the oldest of which was established in 1922, at Wits University. The university presses were all established by male scholars, in a time before many women were able to obtain degrees. They were run by men, and they largely published the work of male scholars. However, the archives are filled with the work of women, most of whom are referred to by their married names.[45] Many of these were appointed on a temporary basis: Mrs S.E.H. Logie was the first woman to be hired at Witwatersrand University Press (WUP), in 1947. For a temporary assistant, the scope of her duties was wide-ranging, including administrative and editorial tasks such as correspondence and filing, sales, preparing copy for press, proof-reading and advertising. Logie remained with the Press for just two years, a common pattern at that time as married women would have to resign when they became pregnant, due to discriminatory laws.

---

43    See Lloyd, *The Birth of Printing*; Smith, *The Spread of Printing*.

44    For example, Wessel de Kock, *The House of Juta: Pioneer Publisher, 1853–1903* (Cape Town: Juta, 2007); C.F.J. Muller, *Sonop in die Suide: Geboorte en Groei van die Nasionale Pers, 1915–1948* (Cape Town: Nasionale Boekhandel, 1990).

45    This section is based on Elizabeth le Roux, *A social history of the university presses in apartheid South Africa: Between complicity and resistance* (Leiden: Brill, 2016).

She was replaced by Mrs M.A. Hutchings, who would become an institution at WUP, remaining from 1950 until her retirement in 1969. Hutchings was also on a temporary contract, until in 1954, a Treasury ruling permitted cost-of-living allowances for married women for the first time, after which she was appointed permanently to the position of Publications Officer. In 1953, the University appointed Elizabeth Hartmann to the position of Acting Librarian, and thus by default to the position of Publications Officer. She was the first woman to be appointed University Librarian in South Africa. The coupling of library duties and publishing was a common trend at the university presses, especially for women in these roles. At the University of Natal Press, for instance, Margery ('Mobbs') Moberly was temporarily released from some of her Library duties around 1969—in just two hours a day, she was expected to undertake all editorial tasks, as well as continue her work in launching the University Archives, supported by only a Press Secretary (a position filled by Mrs Cook and later Mrs Cockcroft). The part-time set-up was intended to be temporary, but it took a number of years before Moberly was appointed as full-time manager.

Other women worked their way up from administrative positions, and never quite managed to escape the secretarial associations. As one example, Nora ('Nan') Wilson joined WUP as a bookkeeper in 1967 and later became manager of the press in all but name, until 1984, when she was finally formally titled Head of the Press. She worked closely with Professor Desmond Cole, who was Chairman of the advisory Publications Committee rather than a hand-on manager, but his contribution to the Press is more celebrated than her own: 'As Chairman, Editor of *African Studies* and of the Bantu Treasury Series, Professor Cole made many personal sacrifices to build the Press into an organisation which is respected throughout the academic world.'[46] Indeed, although Wilson saw the Press through a very difficult period in the 1970s, when it was losing money and struggling from a lack of institutional support, she is remembered more as a competent administrator than a far-sighted publishing manager.[47]

Later women directors of the university presses were admired for their professionalism and skills—indeed, 'professionalism' is the most commonly used term when describing them. When Eve Horwitz (later Gray) joined WUP in 1988, her qualifications were emphasised: she had recently obtained her MA in English, and was working as a lecturer. In addition, she had experience in editing and publishing in Europe. These credentials may explain why her position was upgraded to that of Publisher. Similarly, Moberly's post was also renamed

---

46    Witwatersrand University Press Annual Report, S83/240, 1982: 350.
47    These are largely comments from colleagues. See archival records such as 'Review of WUP', 1987 (S87/415), pp. 2–3; and several interviews conducted for my PhD research.

as Publisher, after some years in her dual Library/Press position. An obituary notes the shift in terminology, in rather patronising terms:

> Initially termed the manager of the University of Natal Press, she was eventually awarded *the rather grand title of Publisher* to the University and built up the press from a shaky start as a somewhat amateur and part-time operation to a highly professional institution, internationally respected for the quality of its scholarly publications.[48]

Moberly was also a scholar in her own right, with a commitment to the local history of the province of Natal (now Kwa-Zulu Natal). While some remember her research and her 'relentless energy and enthusiasm', at least one colleague has downplayed her work, suggesting that, 'It was crucial research and writing but I suspect was also a way of evading conflict with the censors and playing it safe.'[49] Thus, descriptions of Moberly do vary according to the source. Some recall her as 'a most stimulating colleague, and her endless fountain of ideas will be a source greatly missed. So too will be her editorial expertise as a professional publisher', while others noted her perfectionism, highly autocratic decision-making and sometimes sharp tongue.[50] One obituary also noted that she was unmarried. The terms in which Moberly is described thus range from her energy and ideas, to her professionalism and efficiency.

Similarly, Phoebe van der Walt had worked in educational and trade publishing before joining the University of South Africa (Unisa) Press as Deputy Director in the 1970s. Like those mentioned before, she had to leave her job when she fell pregnant. After her return to Unisa, Van der Walt was appointed Director of the Press—and the first woman to head a department at Unisa—in 1989. Like Moberly, she micro-managed the activities and output of the Press and was known for her firm managerial style. This may be seen in the record books, in which every item is signed off by the Director, as well as instances where Van der Walt involved herself in editing individual papers and designing covers for journals. She researched various potential innovations for the Press and the broader Production Department, such as print-on-demand, and incorporated lessons learned at a professional publishing course at Stanford

---

48   Jack Frost, 'Obituary: Margery (Mobbs) Moberly (1938–2008)', *Natalia*, 38 (2008), p. 82; emphasis added.

49   Obituary, *The Witness*, 19 June 2008; Unnamed colleague quoted in Le Roux, *A social history*, p. 198.

50   'Editorial', *Natalia*, 20 (1990), p. 5; Frost, 'Obituary', p. 82; Unnamed colleagues interviewed for Le Roux, *A social history*.

University. She also had academic inclinations, writing several papers on distance education and the role of the Press.

Two phrases stand out in descriptions of Van der Walt, and are telling for the ways in which they prioritise the gender of the publisher. The first comes from an interview with her in a journal focusing on teaching and learning, *Progressio*: the interviewer, a fellow academic at Unisa, called her 'the dainty iron lady'.[51] This phrase couples a reference to Van der Walt's small stature and femininity with a comparison to the strength and authoritarianism of Margaret Thatcher. The description, intended for a local audience in Afrikaans, is interesting because it reinforces the now common trope of autocratic leadership, which suggests a woman leader feeling the need to downplay her femininity, at the same time as it stresses a stereotype. The second is also from a profile, for the internal newsletter *Unisa Link*, which begins with a complimentary description of Van der Walt's publishing prowess:

> She's one of South Africa's leading publishers, having taken the then Department of Publishing Services from near closure in 1989 to the respected position now held in the publishing world by Unisa Press. ... She's also a hard-headed business woman: since 1990, when Unisa Press stopped receiving Council grants to fund its operations, she's managed to build up a reserve fund of R5,2 million, *and she hasn't done it by publishing Mills and Boons*.[52]

At first, the portrait is of a professional, a 'hard-headed business woman', but any authority built up by that description is quickly diluted by the reference to the popular romance genre (incidentally, mostly enjoyed by women readers). It is hard to imagine a profile of the male director of a university press including such a trivialising description. The representation of the women who ran the university press thus centres largely on their professionalism and dedication to their work, even as it downplays their individual contributions as managers. It also implicitly critiques their stern, even schoolmarmish, managerial styles.

## 4        Oppositional Publishers

The second case study concerns the activist publishers, who opposed the apartheid state and its censorship regime. They were run by men who took

51    A.I. le Roux, 'Progressio gesels met Phoebe van der Walt', *Progressio*, 13 (1991), pp. 11–15.
52    'Women transformed and transforming', *Unisa Link* (2003), p. 1; emphasis added.

a firm political stance and created important literary networks.[53] One person who had a very important influence on these networks was the writer (and later Nobel Prize-winner) Nadine Gordimer. She served on the boards of various publishers, encouraged writers, and produced local editions of several of her own literary works—a position of patronage. However, like other trade publishers, these are also closely associated with the men who established and ran them, and the role of women is far more behind the scenes. For instance, the anti-apartheid publisher David Philip set up a publishing house in 1972 with his wife, Marie, and she was an active partner throughout until the couple retired together in the 1990s. However, she modestly claims to have been happy to have only his name heading up the business; a case illustrating the contention that 'the existence of the man effectively blocks out any record of activity by the woman'.[54] At first, I theorised that the inclusion of wives, friends and other women in subordinate roles, often for little pay, could be related to these publishers being activists rather than publishers—anti-apartheid activism has been criticised for being heavily male-dominated and even constructed as a masculine form of protest.[55] However, it is becoming clear that this is a pattern in other sectors of publishing as well, with work 'behind the scenes' being invisible and devalued.

Ravan Press was established in 1972, and its name is made up of the names of its three founders—Peter Randall, Danie van Zyl and Beyers Naude. Randall was the director, and his level of micro-management led him to be nicknamed—not kindly—as *Baas* Randall.[56] But, in spite of interest being focused on the founders, women were an integral part of the operations at Ravan from the beginning: from 1974, the writer Rose Zwi was appointed as an editor, Pat Schwartz as proofreader, and Glenda Webster as accountant. Designers included Jackie Bosman and Merle Stoltenkamp, and Gillian Berkowitz managed the marketing and distribution. Their names appear liberally in the archival records, but their contribution has been almost invisible. This position did not change much when Peter Randall was banned by the apartheid state and Mike Kirkwood became director of the press. His larger-than-life personality

53    Elizabeth le Roux, *Publishing against apartheid South Africa: A case study of Ravan Press* (Cambridge: Cambridge University Press Elements, 2020).

54    Marie Philip, *Books that Matter* (Cape Town: David Philip Publishers, 2014); Maureen Bell quoted in McDowell, 'Women and the business of print', p. 145.

55    Pumla Dineo Gqola, 'In search of female s/staffriders: Authority, gender and audience, 1978–1982', *Current Writing*, 13 (2001), pp. 31–41.

56    This section is based on Elizabeth le Roux, *Publishing against Apartheid South Africa: A case study of Ravan Press* (Cambridge: Cambridge University Press, Elements in Publishing and Culture, 2020).

has certainly served to obscure the contribution of most other members of staff, both men and women. According to interviews and archival evidence, he was both charming and abrasive, extremely encouraging of authors, but also slapdash in correspondence and record-keeping, and fiercely idealistic. His wife, Marilyn, also played an important part at Ravan Press, but before I interviewed her for my research on Ravan, her role had not been recognised. Marilyn gave up a promising career in teaching to move to Johannesburg when Mike was appointed at Ravan; she then turned down a potential new position to work at the Press—initially for no salary. In her words:

> So Mike came home and I told him [about the teaching position], and he said, 'You know, I have been thinking. I need someone to help me at Ravan Press. I can't afford to pay anyone a salary. I need you there to work for me.' For nothing. We were both fired up—this was for the Struggle. So, it didn't occur to me to think, how are we going to manage?[57]

Marilyn was instrumental in improving the marketing and distribution at Ravan, and she also had an influence on what was published. She accepted the manuscript that launched a series, Books for the Children of Africa, and which launched the career of Marguerite Poland, a prizewinning author. Yet, in interviews at the time Poland tended to talk about her relationship with Mike: 'I am also very lucky that I have such a superb editor in Mike Kirkwood of Ravan Press.'[58] As part of her marketing duties, Marilyn was also closely involved in book launches, and her description of one event gives a feel for her practicality as a woman in publishing:

> We had one [event] at Wits in some big place, and we had no idea how many people were going to come. And suddenly there were 200 people there, and they'd brought things to read and to listen, and they didn't have food. Ravan Press didn't have money; PEN didn't have money. Rose [Zwi] and I went out, and with our own money in our purse bought a whole lot of brown bread and margarine and tomatoes and Oros. We made tomato sandwiches that we dished out, so there was something.[59]

Marilyn remained at Ravan until her marriage split up, and shortly afterwards Mike left the company as well. She later became a successful PR agent for

---

57      Marilyn (Kirkwood) Honikman, Interview with author, 23 May 2016.

58      'Appeal gives rise to skill', *Eastern Province Herald*, 24 May 1982.

59      Honikman, interview.

various publishers, and trained newspaper publishers in sales and marketing. But, in addition to Marilyn, there were a variety of other women behind
the scenes, including in-house typesetters such as Merle Stoltenkamp, Anne
Robertson and Dorothy Wheeler (who also managed the administration).
Former students of Mike's, such as Biddy Crewe and Joyce Ozynski, worked
on design. Peter Randall's wife, Isobel, a successful author of schoolbooks,
was brought in to work on the growing children's and educational list from
1982. Jessie Duarte—until recently a senior member of the African National
Congress—was appointed as a bookkeeper in 1984, and much of her role was
placating authors who had not received regular royalties accounts and strug-
gled to get responses out of Mike. Another political activist was typesetter
Esther Maleka, who was detained in 1987 under the Emergency regulations.
None of these is regularly mentioned in studies or memoirs of Ravan Press;
only the high-profile directors and authors are mentioned.

In fact, Ravan did have a female director, when Monica Seeber took over
the position in 1995, shortly before a buyout by Hodder & Stoughton. She
later became involved in authors' rights, and especially negotiating copyright.
Seeber passed away in 2022, and her obituaries and tributes are warm, emphasising friendship and kindness. While most refer to her commitment and
contribution to South African publishing, few mention her role as director of
Ravan Press or her later involvement in other publishing programmes.[60]

Many, though by no means all, of the women discussed so far have been
white, usually middle class. Black women were even further behind the scenes,
often in lower-level positions. Thus, black women as publishers or managers
were almost unheard of. In the 1980s, there was a real pioneer in black women's
publishing and in oppositional publishing: Dinah Lefakane. In 1988, she left
the black-owned oppositional publisher Skotaville to found Seriti sa Sechaba
('dignity of the nation') with the aim of promoting women writers.[61] Ellen
Kuzwayo wrote in the foreword to one of the first of their books, *Women from
South Africa*, that Seriti sa Sechaba made it possible for 'these few women' to
write about issues which concerned them directly, and that the new publisher
'wiped out that feeling of defeat and of being left out of the game' for black

60   For example, <https://www.anfasa.org.za/anfasa-mourns-the-passing-of-monica-seeber/;
     https://internationalauthors.org/news/monica-seeber-obituary/>; <https://ifrro.org/page
     /article-detail/remembering-monica-seeber/>.

61   Joan Pinkvoss, 'Seriti sa Sechaba: Black women publishing in South Africa', *The Feminist
     Bookstore News*, 11, (November 1988).

women authors.[62] The publishing house was not long-lived, due to financial difficulties, but also, it seems due to Lefakane's position as an outsider:

> Seriti sa Sechaba, the women's publishing company run by Dinah Lefakane, has had extreme difficulty getting funding and attracting writers which, Lefakane suggests, has to do with the fact that the company is not politically aligned. In 1989 she was asked at a political meeting where she got 'the mandate' to open a publishing house.[63]

This quote shows that Lefakane experienced many of the same challenges as Odaga in Kenya, feeling unwelcome in a male-dominated environment. She was able to overcome these challenges in the context of late apartheid South Africa. Seriti sa Sechaba was revived by Christine Qunta in 2013, but current media references seldom mention the earlier iteration.[64] This is an interesting trend, because it ignores the possibility of developing a tradition or lineage of women in publishing, and especially black women. In terms of black women's publishing, every new black woman publisher is referred to as being 'the first': Qunta's revived Seriti sa Sechaba; Thabiso Mahlape's Blackbird Books; Rose Francis's African Perspectives. The media sources I have located all refer to Francis as a former model when discussing her career as a publisher from 2005, and include a glamorous photograph of her.[65] The intention is not to downplay her success as a publisher, but the focus on 'beauty and brains' does devalue her work.[66]

## 5    Conclusion

The evidence points to the ongoing involvement of women in publishing and the book trades in South Africa. Women in publishing are often active behind

---

62    Kuzwayo, in Seageng Tsikang and Dinah Lefakane, *Women in South Africa: From the Heart* (Johannesburg: Seriti sa Sechaba, 1988), pp. 2–3.

63    Dorothy Driver, 'Appendix II: South Africa', *Journal of Commonwealth Literature* (1991), p. 169.

64    As part of my ongoing research into anti-apartheid publishing, I plan to examine both Skotaville and Seriti sa Sechaba in more detail, and I hope to be able to highlight the position of Lefakane in so doing.

65    Avantika Seeth, 'Too few Rose Francises in mostly white-male books industry', *City Press*, 7 June 2016; Edward Tsumele, 'Sticking to real quality', *Sowetan*, 26 April 2012.

66    This is a common strategy, as Barbara Reskin shows: 'Culture, commerce, and gender: The feminization of book editing', in Barbara Reskin and P.A. Roos (eds.), *Job queues, gender queues* (Philadelphia: Temple University Press, 1990), pp. 93–110.

the scenes and traces of their activity can be found, at least piecemeal, in the archival records. The case studies of women as magazine editors, scholarly publishers and oppositional publishers outlined here reveal a rich, and largely unexplored, area of publishing history.

What, then, does it mean to say that publishing is 'best left to men'? Even as the industry has become increasingly staffed by women, publishing has been constructed as a masculine enterprise. Differences in how men and women are framed as publishers suggest that women are accepted in *support* roles, but that the role of the eccentric, innovative, bon vivant *publisher* is seen as the preserve of men. Women might be worker bees, but men are visionaries and leaders. To move away from this 'big man' paradigm, research needs to employ more innovative methodologies and access a wider range of sources. With incomplete record keeping, oral histories and interviews may be one of the best means of accessing a more comprehensive picture of the operations of publishing companies in South Africa.

# CHAPTER 6

# Beneath the Bright Covers: Women in Twentieth-Century Paperback Publishing

*Rebecca Baumann*

There is something inherently appealing and even comforting about the mid-century pulp paperback. In one sense they are inherently ephemeral, often printed on the cheapest paper available, acidic and yellowing, spines cracked, covers chipped, bookmarked by receipts and train tickets and punctuated with readers' notes, hastily jotted down phone numbers, doodles, or exclamations of love. In another sense, they *beg* to be collected and preserved, defying their seeming destiny to return to the pulp mill. They are colour coded, numbered, and emblazoned with logos: the iconic 'dignified but flippant' Penguin, Gertie the Kangaroo of Pocket Books, Avon's head of Shakespeare, Bantam's rooster, Fawcett's gold medal—all designed to encourage brand loyalty.[1] They are the perfect consumer good. They fit in your pocket, bag, or purse and can be taken anywhere—companionate and comforting. They are cheap; the price of paperbacks has historically hewn closely to the cost of minimum wage, allowing anyone to buy an unabridged book with one hour of labour.[2]

And then of course there are the bright covers, often valued far more by paperback collectors than the contents beneath. The pulp artists of the twentieth century painted strange worlds of science fiction, the monstrosities of horror, the dastardly deeds of crime, the scorching passion of romance, and, in a wide array of genres, beautiful, scantily-clad women. Mid-century paperbacks are perhaps best known and collected for what is often called 'Good Girl Art' (or GGA), which Richard A. Lupoff defines as '[a] cover illustration depicting an attractive young woman, usually in skimpy or form-fitting clothing, and designed for erotic stimulation. The term does not apply to the morality of

---

[1] The assertion that Allen Lane wanted a 'dignified but flippant' logo has been part of the Penguin lore since its inception, and the phrase appears on many Penguin promotional products that tell the company's story and inside the covers of many Penguin books. The Penguin as logo was suggested by Lane's secretary Joan Coles and drawn by artist Edward Young. 'Celebrating Sir Allen Lane's life and legacy', *Penguin UK Blog*. <https://www.penguin .co.uk/articles/company-article/celebrating-sir-allen-lanes-life-and-legacy>.

[2] Richard A. Lupoff, *The great American paperback* (Portland: Collectors Press, 2001), p. 37.

the 'good girl,' who is often a gun moll, tough cookie or wicked temptress.'[3] As a queer nonbinary person, the sometimes-aggressive heterosexuality of paperback art is humorous, baffling, strange, and alluring to me—these covers are the Rosetta Stone to the world whose shoulders we stand upon uneasily. These books embody the hopes, fears, anxieties, and lusts of our grandparents and great-grandparents, the generations who shaped us and against whom we often rebel.

The history of the twentieth-century paperback is often told as a litany of male names: Allen Lane founded Penguin; Robert de Graaf founded Pocket; Ian Ballantine founded Signet, then Bantam, then Ballantine; George T. Delacorte founded Dell; Aaron A. Wyn founded Ace, and so on. The only comprehensive history of the paperback remains Kenneth C. Davis' *Two Bit Culture: The Paperbacking of America* (1984). According to the press release which Houghton Mifflin issued for the book, Grant was 'a freelance writer (and former bookseller) who has specialised in covering the book world for the past six years. He is a regular contributor to the publishing industry's principal journal, *Publisher's Weekly*.' The opening copy on the two-page press kit (a document sent to news outlets to promote the book) promises the following:

> When publisher Robert de Graff launched Pocket Books in June 1939, he fired the first shot in the Paperback Revolution, a cultural phenomenon that profoundly shaped American society, literature, and education. By making books affordable and accessible to the whole population, the Paperback Revolution democratised reading in America and made cultural heroes of such writers as Erskine Caldwell, J.D. Salinger, Joseph Heller, Betty Friedan, and—of course—Dr. Spock.[4]

This promotional material is reflective of the book as a whole: it is a popular history focused on explaining an American phenomenon, with little regard to paperbacks' British and European precedents. Davis presents paperbacks as a revolutionary, heroic American phenomenon, led by great men such as Robert de Graff. He promotes the American myths of the self-made man and of teleological, inevitable democratisation of reading. He also wants to redeem the reputation of the American paperback: 'To many people, the paperback book has always been little more than second-rate trash. Literary flotsam. Schlock

---

3  Lupoff, *The great American paperback*, p. 318.
4  Houghton Mifflin. Press kit for Kenneth C. Davis, *Two-bit culture. The paperbacking of America* (Boston: Houghton Mifflin, 1984).

turned out to appease a gluttonous mass appetite for sex and sensationalism.'[5] While Davis acknowledges that there is some truth behind these assumptions, he also wants to show the ways in which cheap books for everyone are a social good, leading to increased literacy and exposure to complex literary and cultural texts as well as 'schlock.'

Davis's argument and methodology are quite personal, a trend which continues in much of the writing that has been done about paperback publishing. He opens his history with an intense self-examination of the ways that paperbacks have affected his life: his introduction to Shakespeare in a Pocket Book collection; his 'first sexual education from Terry Southern and Mason Hoffenberg and their wild story of a girl's sexual adventures' (*Candy*, originally published by the Olympia Press in 1958 and subsequently published in numerous American paperback editions); his first questioning of the myths of American greatness in books like Upton Sinclair's *The Jungle* and Dalton Trumbo's *Johnny Got His Gun*.[6] Perhaps it is the companionate, intimate format of the paperback itself that encourages authors to centre their own experiences when writing about them. Perhaps it is because the range of material is simply so vast that the only place to start is with what one knows. Davis's personal involvement in his subject extends to his connections with the book world as a bookseller and writer for *Publisher's Weekly*, the major American trade publication dealing with the twentieth-century publishing world. His main sources of information for the book are interviews with people in the publishing industry. There is no full list of interviewees or dates of interviews, and while the interviews are sometimes quoted in the text, a great deal of information is uncited. Davis is enmeshed in the world of paperback publishing, which is both an asset and a drawback, as many of his biases remain unexamined, especially when it comes to gender. He expounds on the greatness of publisher Ian Ballantine, 'the man who was there when the idea for this book was hatched' but refers to Betty Ballantine (Ian's publishing equal in every regard, as we shall see) only as 'his dear wife'.[7] His list of 'Fifty Paperbacks that Changed America' includes only nine authored by women.

While he acknowledges the importance of the feminist revolution, when he discusses the publication of Betty Friedan's *The Feminine Mystique*, his only source of information is male editor Don Fine, 'who was responsible for the

---

5   Kenneth C. Davis, *Two-bit culture. The paperbacking of America* (Boston: Houghton Mifflin, 1984), p. xi.
6   Ibid., p. xiii.
7   Ibid., p. xv.

acquisition of rights, although at the urging of several female colleagues.'[8] When powerful Dell Publishing editor (and later president) Helen Honig Meyer is mentioned, it is as an 'asset' to Dell founder George T. Delacorte.[9] It is unclear whether Davis's treatment of women in the publishing industry is malicious erasure or simply benign neglect—or a complex mixture of both. It is the bias of an author, who, at the end of his Introduction, thanks his wife Joann 'for her collaboration, guidance, assistance, suggestions, support, typing, and most of all, patience when the going got rough.'[10] This same view of the wife—providing support, collaboration, and (of course) *typing* is very similar to the way that women were perceived in the paperback publishing industry. Although they often rose to positions of power, they were still expected to clean up messes, perform secretarial labour, and provide all the amenities (including sexual ones) of a wife. As something of an 'insider' in the paperback industry, it is no surprise that Davis's history is deeply biased, but it is also clear that his history cannot stand as the only comprehensive source on the American paperback revolution.

Other histories of the paperback reflect the perspective of the collector. Three that are often cited and that contain a great deal of useful information alongside inevitable bias are *The Book of Paperbacks* by Piet Schreuders (1981), *Under Cover: An Illustrated History of American Mass Market Paperbacks* by Thomas L. Bonn (1982), and *The Great American Paperback: An Illustrated Tribute to Legends of the Book* by Richard A. Lupoff (2001). Schreuders was a graphic designer and paperback collector. He was close friends with Thomas L. Bonn, a librarian, collector, and editor of *Paperback Quarterly: Journal of Mass-Market Paperback History*, and they worked on their books in tandem, sharing resources from their collections. Richard A. Lupoff was a science fiction and mystery writer who also collected paperbacks. These three books have much in common; they are focused very heavily on matters of interest to paperback collectors, the majority of whom have historically been white men. And while paperback collectors in reality are far from homogenous, all three authors seem to have little sense that anyone other than someone with a background similar to their own might want a history of the paperback industry. They all heavily promote the 'great man' litany of paperback founding fathers, with only casual asides to women in the industry. All three books are also focused almost entirely on cover art, as this has traditionally been the primary point of interest for collectors. Because the cover artists of these books

---

8      Ibid., p. 304.

9      Ibid., p. 94.

10     Ibid., p. xvi.

were nearly exclusively male, this focus adds to the already-present tendency to neglect women's contributions to the paperback industry. When women are mentioned, they are not given the same biographical examination or importance that men are; for example, all three books cite Ruth Belew as the artist of most of the Dell mapback back-cover illustrations, but none provide any detail other than her name. And yet all three books spend time lavishly discussing and dissecting the various poses, gazes, and seductive looks of the 'girls' who compose the 'good girl art' of the covers. It is as if the only space in the history of paperback publishing for women is the space on the bright covers.

This is not to say that there are not women who collect paperbacks—there are—but their voices are more likely to be found in zines or online forums than in mainstream publications. Miriam Linna, drummer and founding member of The Cramps, has one of the largest private collections of paperbacks and has published numerous zines (including *Smut Peddlar* and *Bad Seed*) and co-edited *Sin-A-Rama: Sex Paperbacks of the Sixties*. Donna Kossey edited the zine *Book Happy* from 1997 to 2002 and ran a website which helped and encouraged collectors of strange and bizarre books find their quarries in the early days of the internet. In 2014, Paula Rabinowitz published *American Pulp: How Paperbacks Brought Modernism to Main Street*, which is perhaps the best scholarly work on the history of paperbacks to date. Rabinowitz is far more attentive to the role of women in the paperback industry, and she does not forget, diminish, or dismiss female editors and publishers in the way that her male predecessors did. However, her study is primarily focused on readership and reception, still leaving a gap in the literature when it comes to the biographies and stories of the women who produced this kind of book.

The purpose of this paper is to acknowledge that gap and briefly to introduce readers to just a few of the women who made important contributions to the twentieth century paperback industry as well as suggest that the entire industry itself was contingent on the labour of women whose names have not been recorded or celebrated. This is by no means intended to be a comprehensive history of women in the paperback industry, but it is intended to challenge the dominant narrative of the industry offered by Kenneth C. Davis and others. All these writers are in agreement that the advent of mass market publishing was a 'revolution' and to a large extent democratised reading. But the culmination of five centuries of printing in the dream of putting the printed word into the hands of anyone with twenty-five cents was not simply the work of publishing titans like Allen Lane and Robert de Graff. There were also countless women editing, writing, and performing the kinds of invisible labour that men shunned. Feminist book history, at its core, is shifting the way we see books—not as the products of individuals but *always* as the continuing work of many hands—decentring the names on the colophon and title page and widening our view to see the many lives whose labour went into making books and whose time and intellect were engaged with reading, discussing, collecting, and preserving them.

Below I will detail five women in the paperback industry who have had a major impact on the ways that paperbacks are conceived and published, followed by brief mention of numerous others who are lesser known. I begin with women representing the two traditional paths of women into the publishing industry: secretary and wife. Women like Penguin's Eunice Frost and Dell's Helen Honig Meyer began as secretaries and worked up through the ranks, a path that typically led to male colleagues seeing powerful women as shrews or bitches. Betty Ballantine, who founded a paperback empire beside her husband, escaped the fate of being named a bitch and instead was considered a mother—clearly another male-defined role. Following these archetypes, I discuss Rona Jaffe and the 'Girls of Publishing' detailed in a 1966 *Cosmopolitan* article. These women represent a shift to some level of acceptance of women in the industry, though they are still expected to be attractive as much as intelligent and are persistently framed as 'girls' rather than women. Finally, in a section of 'Briefly Mentioned' women, I discuss women about whom little information is available. Some of these women are queer, disabled, or women of colour, identities which have caused them to be further marginalised. Others worked with types of books such as smut and romance that are not considered worthy of literary attention. From the frosty boss to the motherly helpmeet, from the peppy career girl to the completely neglected, these women deserve to be brought forth from beneath the bright covers of the books they helped to create. I want the history of the paperback and of mid-century publishing to be rewritten.

## 1      Eunice Frost (1914–1998)

While the scope of this paper is primarily the American paperback industry of the twentieth century, it is impossible to avoid a discussion of Penguin. Although there are many precedents to the Penguin paperback, including Tauchnitz, Albatross, Boni Books, pulps, dime novels, and cheap publications going well back into the nineteenth century, Penguin is very often taken as the 'beginning' of paperback history. It was reading about the history of Penguin in *Penguin Special: The Life and Times of Allen Lane* by Jeremy Lewis (2005) that, more than anything, inspired me to start looking for women in paperback publishing. The book is, as the title suggests, entirely centred on Allen Lane and contributes to the 'great man' model of publishing history, centring narratives on powerful and charismatic male individuals who founded firms and drove the industry, rather than looking at the field as a community of countless contributors. Lewis, himself a veteran of the British publishing industry, describes the world of publishing that Lane entered as 'masculine and middle-aged; its denizens sported fiery tweeds or chalk-striped suits, were keen members of the Garrick or the Savile, scribbled memos and did their suns on the backs of envelopes, and were firm believers in the long alcoholic lunch.' He goes on:

> Much of the hard work was done by a combination of old-fashioned clerking types, well-heeled public schoolboys with vague literary ambitions, and—most invaluable of all—a steady supply of middle-aged spinsters, all of whom were wretchedly underpaid, devoted their lives to the firm, and every evening lugged home baskets brimming with typescripts or proofs.[11]

Lane himself was supported throughout his career by powerful women, including his mother, whose surname he took in order to be allowed to join his uncle's publishing business, and titans of literature like his close friend Agatha Christie. But the world of 'wretchedly underpaid,' devoted, overworked women propping up the male titans of the publishing industry became the model for much of twentieth century publishing.

The most powerful woman at Penguin—one of the few women who gets mentioned in histories of the paperback at all—was Eunice Frost, who started at the company as Lane's secretary in 1937, became an editor, and eventually director of the company. The introduction to Frost in Lewis' history of Penguin reveals a deep vein of misogyny running through this work:

> Like her slightly older contemporary, the even more formidable Norah Smallwood of Chatto & Windus, Eunice Frost was one of the first women to rise to the top (or near the top) of what had always been an exclusively male preserve: this in itself was enough to make her both pushy and prickly, and the fact that both women had started at the bottom of their respective firms, as secretaries, and neither had been to university or received that much in the way of 'higher education,' made them still more sensitive to slights, and more aware than necessary of their own intellectual and literary shortcomings. Both were feared and sometimes detested

---

11    Jeremy Lewis, *Penguin special. The life and times of Allen Lane* (New York: Penguin, 2005), p. 3.

by those who worked for them in junior capacities—one embattled secretary summed up Eunice as 'plain horrible'—and both were addicted to large and eye-catching hats; but whereas Mrs. Smallwood managed, through force of personality, to cling on to power at Chatto until well into her seventies, Eunice Frost was only in her early forties when—neurotic, bronchitic and increasingly out of touch with changes in the publishing and literary world—she was edged out of Penguin to spend the rest of her life in exile in Lewes, grumbling about the sad falling-off of the firm, bombarding former colleagues with letters and interminable phone calls, and nursing that sense of grievance that is all too liable to affect those who have entrusted their all to a firm or institution.[12]

Lewis takes as an inevitability that women in power will be 'pushy and prickly.' He faults them for having a chip on their shoulders about not receiving a higher education rather than pointing toward the barriers that prevented them from receiving that education or towards male colleagues who treated them with disrespect because they lacked those credentials. He refers to Frost only by her first name, uses the words of a subordinate woman as weapons against her, mocks her fashion choices, and attributes her ousting to neuroses rather than sexism. The story of a woman who devotes her life to her job, only to be despised by her colleagues for gaining authority in a male-dominated field, is one that is sadly still all too familiar.

Frost went from being 'the fourth, last and unwanted child of parents who should never have had children at all' to being the most powerful woman in the publishing industry.[13] When artist Rodrigo Moynihan was commissioned to paint a portrait of the Penguin editors, he placed Frost in the centre in a white dress, a stark contrast to the old boys' club surrounding her.[14] Lane himself acknowledged that she was second in influence only to him: 'Although he exploited her ruthlessly in terms of both her workload and her pay, Lane valued her very highly.'[15] Although many assumed that she only worked with fiction—considered a lesser area because it dealt only with reprints—Frost was active in many arms of Penguin, including Pelican and King Penguins, and frequently dealt directly with authors.

---

12    Ibid., p. 123.
13    Ibid., p. 124.
14    Louise Butterworth, 'A touch of Frost', *What was lost is found*, 18 March 2020 <https://www.whatwaslostisfound.co.uk/a-touch-of-frost/>.
15    Lewis, *Penguin*, pp. 125–6.

And yet she is often remembered more for her hats than her editorial work (the story of the cartwheel hat she wore when she first interviewed with Lane has been endlessly reprinted). A 2010 article in *The Telegraph* repeats many of Lewis' stories and portrays Frost as an important and hardworking editor but also as a neurotic scold.[16] Even her obituaries are peppered with insults, calling her a 'dragon' (*The Times*)[17] and quoting a colleague who said she had a 'scatty, dotty air' (*The Independent*).[18] Clearly, Frost was a complex figure, with a polarising personality and many quirks of character that made her both beloved and despised. In the web of anecdotes, remembrances, and references to her remaining in print it is impossible to untangle her true self from the threads of misogyny, resentment, misunderstanding, and bias woven into her legacy.

Frost is perhaps best understood by looking at her own words, in an essay she wrote for *The Penguin Collector* (issue 41, 1993):

> How did I become a literary midwife? Because there was no one else to hold the baby at the time. Somehow I was expected to take on all kinds of reading, negotiating with authors, agents, and publishers in addition to general office administration. I remember that in my very first week, instead of being told what to do, I was expected to do the extraordinary.
>
> Allen said 'do you like reading?' and pushed a whole pile of books across his desk. And that's how I learned you had to carry the baby home with you every night.[19]

It is interesting that Frost reframes the work of the publishing industry explicitly as woman's work—as labour in the sense of childbearing and midwifery. The image of the underpaid secretary hauling a slush pile home with her is one that emblematises the role of women in the paperback publishing industry, as we will see in our discussion of Rona Jaffe. 'I was expected to do the extraordinary' is a line that could no doubt be said of any of the women discussed in this essay.

---

16   Gaby Wood, 'A touch of Frost. The story of Penguin's secret editor', *The Telegraph*, 5 August 2010. <https://www.telegraph.co.uk/culture/books/7926458/A-touch-of-Frost-the-story-of-Penguins-secret-editor.html#>.

17   Eunice Frost obituary, *The Times*, London, 26 August 1998.

18   Isabel Quigly, 'Obituary: Eunice Frost', *The Independent*, 23 October 2011. <https://www.independent.co.uk/arts-entertainment/obituary-eunice-frost-1172443.html>.

19   Quoted in Rebecca E. Lyson, 'Thanks for Penguin: Women, invisible labour and publishing in the mid-twentieth century', in Juliana Dresvina (ed.), *Thanks for typing. Remembering forgotten women in history* (London: Bloomsbury, 2021), p. 52.

## 2      Lee Wright (1904–1986)

Lee Wright is representative of many women in the early and mid-twentieth-century publishing business in that her name is sprinkled throughout the histories, but she is never discussed as a full person—only a glancing reference to a woman who prompted something of more interest to the expected male audience of paperback histories. In this case, the 'something' was the introduction of the mystery genre into the Pocket Books line. Like Frost, she began her career as a secretary, in this case to Richard Simon, co-founder of Simon & Schuster.

Pocket Books, the first American paperback imprint, was founded by Robert de Graff, with financial backing from Richard Simon and Max Schuster. The line debuted in 1938 with an unabridged reprint of Pearl S. Buck's *The Good Earth*. After a successful test print run, de Graff began creating a list of ten books to serve as the brand's debut. The goal was to offer a wide range of titles and see what sold. Among the offerings were bestsellers such as *Bambi* and *Lost Horizon*, classics such as *Five Great Tragedies of Shakespeare* and *Wuthering Heights*, and even a self-help book, *Wake Up and Live!* by Dorothea Brande, which was the initial bestseller of the ten. The only work of what we would now call 'genre fiction' was *The Murder of Roger Ackroyd* by Agatha Christie.

According to Richard D. Lupoff, it was long thought in the industry that the mystery was only included at the urging of Lee Wright, a prominent and successful editor of detective fiction at Simon & Schuster who had launched the popular Inner Sanctum series of mystery novels. De Graff later claimed credit for it himself (perhaps speaking truthfully or perhaps taking away his female colleague's accomplishment) but allowed Lee to retain an important place in the history. In a 1972 interview, he claimed that Lee's intervention came after the Christie title did not sell well—only seventh or eighth on the list of ten. De Graff recalled: '[Lee] came to me and said 'Why don't you do more mysteries?' I told her about the sales of *The Murder of Roger Ackroyd* ... She said, 'Well, you know the trouble is, you don't do them fast enough ... You should do two or three of these a month and you'll find they will go quickly ...' I respected her opinion, and from then on we did two-three a month, and boy, they went. The sales were terrific.'[20] She later brought Earle Stanley Gardner to Pocket Books, and reprints of the Perry Mason novels became among the publisher's most reliable bestsellers.[21]

---

20      Lupoff, *Great*, p. 32.
21      Davis, *Two-bit*, p. 91.

Lee's career was stunning, as is evidenced by her brief obituary in *Publisher's Weekly*.[22] Among other accomplishments, she corresponded with the burlesque performer Gypsy Rose Lee and convinced her to write a bestselling mystery *The G-String Murders* (and Wright defended Lee's authorship when others suspected a ghost-writer), published Ira Levin's bestseller *Rosemary's Baby*, and brought in Alfred Hitchcock as a 'brand' for Simon & Schuster and Pocket. She also edited numerous Pocket anthologies, including *The Pocket Book of Great Detectives* and *A Butcher's Dozen of Wicked Women*. Although she is only remembered glancingly in the histories, it is clear that American detective fiction owes a great deal to her work.

3     Betty Ballantine (neé Elizabeth Norah Jones, 1919–2019)

If Eunice Frost and Lee Wright represent one of the major entry points of women into the publishing world—that of secretary—Betty Ballantine represents another—that of wife. Because she is almost always written about as part of a married team, very little of the subtle contempt that is heaped upon many female editors falls on her. However, it is difficult to separate her legacy from her husband's, and only after her recent death and subsequent obituaries did I begin to get a sense of Betty as separate from the powerhouse team of Betty and Ian Ballantine.

To give a sense of the inequality with which she has been treated in the histories of paperback publishing, we need only look at the index of Davis's *Two-Bit Culture*. Betty is mentioned only on two pages: she is the 'eighteen-year-old bride' who helped Ian set up his first shop and noted as 'an indispensable and widely admired editor.'[23] Ian, meanwhile, has thirty-six entries, most of them spanning multiple pages. As the founder of three of the biggest paperback houses in American history (American Penguin, Bantam, and Ballantine), he is treated as one of the 'great men' of paperback history—a founding father so to speak. And yet, when Ian and Betty co-wrote a short history of their business in *The New York Times* in 1989, they referred to themselves as 'the only surviving founding father and mother of the paperback revolution' and only use the pronoun 'we' to discuss all their work over the course of five decades

---

22    'Lee Wright', *Publisher's Weekly*, December 26, 1986, p. 20. <https://www.threeinvestiga torsbooks.com/LeeWrightEditor.html>.

23    Davis, *Two-bit*, p. 54, 330.

in publishing.[24] And yet, later researchers and journalists have left Betty out of the Ballantine story.

When Betty Ballantine died in 2019, Katharine Q. Seelye's obituary in *The New York Times* made an effort to separate Betty's achievements from Ian's, though there is still little sense of her role in the business. She is portrayed primarily as a nurturing editor, and it is interesting that, when applied to Betty, editorship takes on feminine characteristics. This is something we see in other writing about the Ballantines, even though in other contexts, editorship is considered a masculine profession and secretary as a woman's role. But when women do it, they become midwives or nurturers. Seelye writes:

> While Ian Ballantine, who died in 1995, was the better known of the publishing duo, Betty Ballantine, who was British, quietly devoted herself to the editorial side. She nurtured authors, edited manuscripts and helped promote certain genres—westerns, mysteries, romance novels and, perhaps most significant, science fiction and fantasy.
> Her love for that genre, and her knowledge of it, helped put it on the map.
> 'She birthed the science fiction novel,' said Tad Wise, a nephew of Ms. Ballantine's by marriage.[25]

Betty is 'quiet,' 'nurturing,' and cast as a mother of science fiction. Betty Ballantine's role in science fiction publishing deserves much more attention. She brought radical New Wave authors like Samuel R. Delany and Joanna Russ to the imprint. In a 2002 interview with Locus magazine, she said,

> We really, truly wanted and did publish books that mattered. And science fiction matters, because it's of the mind, it predicts, it thinks, it says, 'Look at what's happening here. If that's what's happening here and now, what's it going to look like ten years from now, 50 years from now, or 2,000 years from now?' It's a form of magic. Not abracadabra or wizardry. It is the minds of humankind that make this magic.[26]

---

24    Ian and Betty Ballantine, 'Paperbacks from the two-bit beginning', *The New York Times*, 30 April 1989, p. 46.

25    Katherine Q. Seelye, 'Betty Ballantine, who helped introduce paperbacks, dies at 99', *The New York Times*, 15 February 2019. <https://www.nytimes.com/2019/02/15/obitua ries/betty-ballantine-dead.html>.

26    'Betty Ballantine: Publishing Pioneer', *Locus Magazine*, November 2002. <https://www .locusmag.com/2002/Issue11/Ballantine.html>.

In the same interview, Betty also characterises herself as a mother—but also as many other things:

> To me, the essence of editing lies in helping the author say what he wants to say in the way he wants to say it. Sounds simple. But often they don't know what they want to say, they're struggling—so you become psychologist, as well as mother, banker, lawyer: a whole gamut of relationships. And certainly, and always, the author's champion within the house: I mean you are on their side, no matter what.[27]

Betty was also instrumental in getting one of the cornerstones of science fiction and fantasy published in an authorised paperback edition. She relates the story of a 'switchboard operator, a very nice person by the name of Mary', who encouraged her to bring J.R.R. Tolkien's *The Hobbit* to Ballantine Books.[28] Though their initial offer to Houghton Mifflin was rejected, once Houghton discovered that Ace was publishing pirated paperback editions of Tolkien, they eagerly worked with Betty and Ian to bring out authorised paperback editions under the Ballantine imprint. The story of Mary the switchboard operator also hints at the huge number of unnamed women who influenced the paperback industry: the female readers whose tastes dictated the market. A similar story of one woman reader whose taste had massive impact is that of Ace editor Jerry Gross's mother, whose undying love of Daphne du Maurier's *Rebecca* led Gross to launch an entirely new genre—that of the Gothic romance—that dominated a large corner of the publishing market throughout the 1960s and 70s.[29]

Betty Ballantine's story is told most fully in Al Silverman's *The Time of Their Lives: The Golden Age of Great American Publishers, Their Editors and Authors* (2008). Silverman's section on the paperback revolution (approximately the last fourth of the book) is by far the best published history to date in terms of taking women's contributions in the industry into account, though he often still slips into judging women based on their appearance, sex lives, and connections to powerful men. Largely using her own words, Silverman (himself an editor at the Book-of-the-Month Club and Viking/Penguin) portrays Betty Ballantine as a bookish but adventurous young woman who married a friend of her cousin at age eighteen (Ian himself was only twenty-one) and was immediately swept onto a ship with crates of Penguin paperbacks, swept to America

---

27    'Betty Ballantine: Publishing Pioneer'.

28    Al Silverman, *The time of their lives: The golden age of great American publishers, their editors and authors* (New York: Truman Talley Books, 2008), p. 391.

29    Silverman, *The time*, pp. 439–41.

to begin as a secretary-wife and swiftly become a true equal in decades of successful publishing ventures. Silverman also details the later years of the Ballantines' work; once big conglomerates began buying up publishers in the 1970s, they were forced to sell and continued to work as consultants for larger firms, a common story in the paperback publishing industry.

### 4      Helen Honig Meyer (1907–2003)

Along with Betty Ballantine, Helen Honig Meyer, 'the doyenne of Dell,' was probably the most powerful woman in mid-century American paperback publishing.[30] Meyer entered the publishing world at age sixteen, joining Dell when they only had seven employees, after working as an adjustment clerk handling complaints at Select Distributing. She interviewed with George Delacorte, the founder of Dell and soon became his 'right-hand man'. As is typical in paperback history, she is treated only briefly (on one page) by Kenneth C. Davis, who notes that she was 'described as 'shrewd' by some and 'a man-eater' by one male colleague.' Although Davis notes that Meyer had to operate in a 'man's world'—in one instance she was not allowed to enter a negotiation session because a client would not allow women in the room—he still chooses to repeat the sexist assessment of 'one male colleague' rather than offering any serious discussion of Meyer's negotiation of the male publishing world.[31]

Al Silverman's discussion of Meyer is more fulsome and fairer, neither glossing over the bigotry she faced nor trying to paint her as an unproblematic female saint among male sinners. He relates her meeting with Richard Baron, who was selling his Dial Press to Dell:

> 'I hear you're a playboy,' Ms. Meyer said to Baron.
> 'I hear you're a bitch,' he replied.
> The truth was that, indeed, Richard Baron did like women, and Helen Meyer—the first female to become head of a book publishing house—did sometimes bare her teeth.[32]

---

30      William H. Lyles, *Putting Dell on the map. A history of the Dell paperbacks* (Westport: Greenwood Press, 1983), p. 4.

31      Davis, *Two-bit*, p. 94.

32      Silverman, *The time*, p. 409.

Various interviewees speak of the ways in which Meyer opened doors for women in publishing, both by her mere presence but also proactively in getting jobs for young women seeking to break into the industry. She could be a harsh boss—one employee recalls Friday afternoon 'purges' in which employees would be let go at the end of the day, but they also note that 'This [was] a woman who asks no more of herself than anybody else.'[33]

Meyer rose from being a secretary to being the first woman to head a major American publishing house; she was President and Chief Executive of Dell from the early 1950s through 1976, when Delacorte sold Dell to Doubleday (and continued as President through 1979 and then as a consultant into the 1980s). She was not only active in Dell's paperback and hardback lines but took a leadership role in Dell's comic book publishing arm. She was successful in gaining more licenced characters (including Disney) for the imprint, published the first comic series (*Lobo*) with an African American lead character, testified in Congress against psychiatrist Frederic Wertham's crusade against comic books' alleged immorality, and resisted the subsequent Comics Code Authority, which led the industry to censor itself.[34] She created the slogan 'Dell Comics are good comics' to avoid using the Comic Code Authority stamp of approval.[35] In the literary realm she signed authors including Kurt Vonnegut, Jr., James Baldwin, James Clavell, Danielle Steele, and Belva Plain. Silverman's interviewees recount an array of stories about her, from her romance with her husband, to her austerity in refusing to give Christmas bonuses, to her refusal to pay more for a Robert Ludlum book than an Ira Levin book, to one employee who was embarrassed to be sexually attracted to an older woman. Although it is a wonderful array of stories, we still see only fragments of how this powerful 'empress' and 'dragon lady' was perceived by others—never in her own words.[36] Delacorte's assessment of hiring women in the publishing industry was one of pure expedience: 'I'm a great believer in hiring women ... If you hire a capable man and your competitors know about it, they'll start propositioning him. Women are more loyal.'[37]

---

33   Ibid.
34   Randy Duncan and Matthew J. Smith, *Icons of the American comic book. From Captain America to Wonder Woman*, vol. 1 (Westport: Greenwood Press, 2013), pp. 199–200.
35   Wolfgang Saxon, 'Helen Honig Meyer, who led Dell publishing, dies at 95', *The New York Times*, 24 April 2003. <https://www.nytimes.com/2003/04/24/business/helen-honig-meyer-who-led-dell-publishing-dies-at-95.html>.
36   Silverman, *The time*, pp. 408–15.
37   Saxon, 'Helen'.

## 5      Rona Jaffe (1931–2005)

Rona Jaffe is by far the most well-known person on this list because she was an author in her own right. While much work has been done in the past fifty-plus years to recover and promote women's writing, far less has been done to bring the women who published those books to the fore. The truth is that if you want to learn about women in the paperback publishing industry, the best place to start is not in histories of the paperback but in Rona Jaffe's fictionalised account of her years as an associate editor at Fawcett, *The Best of Everything*, published in 1958. Al Silverman calls Jaffe 'an attractive, saucy woman, who was very smart and took to fooling around with the higher-ranked Fawcett players.'[38]

In his gossipy memoirs of the publishing world, Simon & Schuster editor-in-chief Michael Korda discusses the importance of Jaffe's novel as 'the very prototype of the hot 'woman's novel' that would eventually reach its climax with Jacqueline Susann's *Valley of the Dolls*.'[39] It is also, along with Helen Gurley Brown's *Sex and the Single Girl*, the model for the HBO series *Sex and the City*, as well as a major influence on the television show *Mad Men*. Korda further elaborates on the novel's landmark status by noting that the movie rights (it was filmed with Joan Crawford in 1959) were bought before the manuscript had been edited, the film company was involved in the marketing of the book, and an unprecedented amount of money and care was spent on the dust jacket, which was a photograph of Jaffe herself, standing in New York City, surrounded by skyscrapers and looking hopeful (arguably the jacket influenced the opening credits of *The Mary Tyler Moore Show* as well). The copy reads 'Rona Jaffe, a native New Yorker, is 26 years old and a graduate of Radcliffe College. *The Best of Everything* is her first novel. She is the girl on the front of the jacket.' Korda writes, '*The Best of Everything* was to usher in the new era in which the author's potential for glamour, real or faked, mattered almost as much as the writing.'[40]

Most importantly, Jaffe's novel exposes the sexism of the paperback industry—and the fact that the great enterprise of 'books for everyone' is built on the labour of underpaid secretaries toting home a slush pile to wade through on their 'off' hours. As Frost said, 'I learned you had to carry the baby home with you every night.' In the novel, a fatuous male editor, Mr. Shalimar, tells green 'country girl' April, newly come to the big city to be a secretary, '[i]t's

38   Silverman, *The time*, p. 459.
39   Michael Korda, *Another life. A memoir of other people* (New York: Random House, 1999), p. 51.
40   Ibid., p. 52.

our books, with our sexy covers, and our low cost, and our mass distribution that are teaching America to read. Let people who don't know anything say Derby Books are trash. They'll see.'[41]

Along with the constant lecherous advances of Shalimar, whose generous offers of allowing girls to take home manuscripts to read for extra work and editorial experience always comes with a hand creeping up the knee, the girls also must deal with the acidic and bitter Amanda Farrow. She is the firm's top female editor, a role enlarged for the film so that it could feature Joan Crawford, who perfectly embodies every sexist stereotype ascribed to women like Eunice Frost. She missed her chances at marriage, is stuck in a fruitless affair with a male colleague, and she shamelessly abuses the young pretty women under her control. Jaffe's obituary notes, "[u]nlike her rather passive fictional characters, however, the tough-talking Ms. Jaffe was professionally ambitious and openly spoke of her desire to be a success. After graduating from the Dalton School at 15 and Radcliffe College four years later, she became a file clerk at Fawcett, eventually becoming an associate editor before leaving to write 'The Best of Everything.'"[42] Jaffe went on to write fifteen further novels, many of them bestsellers. Her legacy has somewhat been overshadowed by the fact that one of her books played into the 'Satanic panic' surrounding the tabletop game Dungeons & Dragons, something that has not made her popular with fans of that franchise or with fantasy fans in general. Although *The Best of Everything* provides insight into the paperback publishing world of the 1950s, there is still a great deal of research that needs to be done to fill in the large gap between that fictional world—tailored to become a blockbuster film—and Jaffe's real-life experience as a paperback editor.

## 6    The 'Girls' of Publishing

Jaffe's bestselling novel brought new public interest to women in the publishing industry beyond the world of fiction. In its November 1966 issue, *Cosmopolitan* published an article on 'Girls in the Publishing Business' by Rex Reed, now better known as a film critic. Just one year earlier, in 1965, Helen Gurley Brown, herself a powerhouse of the publishing industry, had taken over editorship of the magazine and radically reinvented it, gearing its content toward modern

---

41    Rona Jaffe, *The Best of Everything* (New York: Penguin, 2005), p. 28.
42    Mitchell Owens, 'Rona Jaffe, author of popular novels, is dead at 74', *The New York Times*, 31 December 2005. <https://www.nytimes.com/2005/12/31/arts/rona-jaffe-author-of-popular-novels-is-dead-at-74.html>.

(mostly single) career women who were culturally and sexually adventurous. The article on women in publishing is a perfect fit for mid-60s *Cosmopolitan*, calling out to its readers and showing them the kind of woman they too could be if they subscribed to the *Cosmopolitan* lifestyle, every bit as aspirational and ultimately unrealistic as the *Playboy* lifestyle pitched to the men who Cosmo girls were expected to date. This article signifies a shift in the industry's perception of women, suggesting that they are no longer the exceptions that Frost, Lee, Ballantine, Meyer, and others were perceived to be; there was a place for women in the publishing world, albeit a closely circumscribed one.

Although the article is not focused only on paperback publishing but on the larger industry, the article neatly encapsulates the dazzling aura this career had for young women—as well as the sexist assumptions about how such women achieved their positions. The article begins:

> It was the pretty, young secretary's first job in the big New York publishing house. The salary was low and she was only a member of the office typing pool. But her eyes were shining and her hopes were high. 'It's the most exciting business I know—it's got the most attractive, brainiest men and the biggest opportunities for a girl to go places in a short amount of time!'[43]

This opening sets the breezy tone for the piece; it is all about opportunities for women to shine intellectually, work hard, and to interact with (and perhaps marry) 'the brainiest men.' It is a rare and useful primary source for this time period in that we get to hear the women themselves—though their quotes are of course chosen and edited by the male author of the piece.

Reed also embellishes the interviews with breathless prose regarding the women's wardrobes and personal qualities. Leslie Elliott is 'peppery-voiced' and 'looks like a member of the Long Island horsy set.' Carolyn Amussen 'looks more like a fashion illustrator or a woman's panel show moderator than a hardworking girl in publishing,' Hester Mundis is 'a creamy, wide-eyed blonde,' and Letty Cottin Pogrebin looks like she 'just stepped off of a motor scooter.'[44] While the article focuses on the women's glamorous lives, sparkling parties (including Pogrebin's press party that she planned to take place ringside at a boxing match), smart wardrobes, creative challenges, and sympathetic husbands (Pogrebin's husband is 'comfortable with his masculinity' and prefers 'a partner who is a complement and not a servant'), many of the

---

43    Rex Reed, 'Girls in the publishing business', *Cosmopolitan*, November 1966, p. 96.
44    Ibid., pp. 98–100.

quotes from the women themselves emphasise the brutally hard work they have done to achieve their positions. Leslie Elliott, a subsidiary rights editor for The Macmillan Company, says 'Corny as it sounds, there are no menial tasks in publishing. Girls who think their IQs are too high to sharpen pencils will never make it. Even if it's not your job to replenish the paper towels in the washroom, do it anyway. The way to get ahead is by doing your own work and half of other people's—if they're dumb enough to let you.'[45] We learn that Harper did not have a woman editor in the book department until World War II and that there was no ladies' room on the editorial floor at Scribner's.

As fascinating as this article is—and anyone studying the mid-twentieth-century publishing industry would do well to track it down—most of the women profiled worked in other parts of the publishing industry, not in paperbacks. Ines de Torres was in charge of Latin American fiction at Scribner's; Carolyn Amussen was an Assistant Editor at Houghton Mifflin; Letty Cottin Pogrebin was the director of publicity at Bernard Geis, a small progressive publisher; and Leslie Elliott was a subsidiary rights editor at Macmillan. Only Hester Mundis, at the time of the article's publication, worked in paperback publishing, as a copywriter at Dell. It is clear in the article that paperbacks are the low end of the field. Amussen discusses her early days trying to break into the field when she 'tried her hand at producing second-rate paperbacks'. She recalls, 'It was awful. Tammy-type books [referring to the plucky heroine of a series of books by Cid Ricketts Sumner, penname of Bertha Louise Ricketts], detective mysteries and a few lurid sex stories. I was just about ready to give up when I heard about an opening at Houghton Mifflin. After all the searching, I ended up again as a secretary.'[46] The framing of this article—to its credit—emphasises the intellectual fulfilment that these college-educated women receive from their careers, and the assumption behind Amussen's statement is that 'second-rate paperbacks' are not the part of the industry where that kind of fulfilment can be found.

Hester Mundis is the only woman interviewed who currently worked in paperbacks, though they were certainly not 'second rate' ones. Dell was a pioneer in paperback publishing, one of the first companies to aggressively pioneer the concept of 'paperback originals'—that is, books that were not reprints of hardback books but were published for the first time in paperback. The Dell 'First Editions' helped to begin the long process of breaking the stigma of publishing in the paperback format, with important titles such as Kurt Vonnegut, Jr.'s *The Sirens of Titan*, Jim Thompson's *The Nothing Man*, and Jack Finney's

---

45    Ibid., p. 100.
46    Ibid., p. 98.

*The Body Snatchers*. Paperback royalties were a lower rate (about four to six percent rather than ten percent) than hardback royalties, and paperbacks sold at a much lower price; however, they sold in exponentially higher quantities, so the authors brave enough to attempt the paperback original format often ended up seeing higher profits.[47] The editor in chief of the Dell First Editions line, Arlene Donovan, was one of the women responsible for bringing Betty Friedan's *The Feminine Mystique* to paperback publication, which is what led to it being the cultural bombshell it was. She and others 'bulldozed' editor Don Fine into considering it. He told Kenneth C. Davis, "I was away, and when I came back, there were memos on my desk from every woman in the office, '[t]his is the book we've been waiting for. You've got to buy it.'"[48] Because paperback publishers were not as prestigious as hardcover publishers, they were more likely to hire women, and many women in publishing got their start in paperbacks.[49] And as the story told by Fine and Davis shows, male editors were more likely to listen to them. Before Dell, Mundis notes that she worked in the same office that had inspired Rona Jaffe to write *The Best of Everything*. This was Fawcett, which published Gold Medal paperbacks (also known for their originals), though Mundis does not name it. 'All the stories were true,' she says, '[it] was like stepping right into that novel. All the office romances, after hours cocktails with the boss, *everything*. But it was glamorous!'[50]

At Dell, Mundis's job involved buying books to be published in paperback, writing cover copy, attending parties with Norman Mailer, 'negotiating for books on Bob Dylan, the rock 'n' roll craze, LSD and Vietnam,' and much more. She talks about seeing movie previews and deciding what movies need a book tie-in. 'We assign a writer to do a paperback of the movie if it's never been a book before, splash Doris Day's picture on the cover—presto!—instant novel.'[51] This practice was made famous by Genevieve Young, editor at Harper several years later when she commissioned Erich Segal to write a novel version of his screenplay for *Love Story* (1970) and worked closely with him in crafting the structure of the text, convincing him that the heroine's death needed to be revealed on the first page.[52] Young, one of the few Asian-American women to work in the publishing industry in any capacity, is photographed for the

---

47    Lupoff, *Great*, p. 132.

48    Davis, *Two-bit*, p. 304.

49    Patricia Bradley, *Mass Media and the Shaping of American Feminism, 1963–1975* (Jackson: University Press of Mississippi, 2003), p. 23.

50    Reed, 'Girls', p. 100.

51    Ibid., p. 100.

52    Hillel Italie, 'Genevieve Young, editor who helped shape 'Love Story' and other books, dies at 89', *The Washington Post*, 18 February 2021. <https://www.washingtonpost.com

*Cosmopolitan* article but not profiled at the same level as the other five women. She is quoted at the beginning of the article as 'an editor who interviews girls for jobs,' saying:

> It may be a male-oriented field, but that makes it ideal for women. For talented girls who want to do something with their lives, publishing gives them a chance to compete in a man's world. It helps to have a husband on the side to *feed* you while you climb. ... If your hair's not purple and you don't wear open-toed sneakers to work, you can get a job. All that jazz about hats and gloves and chic hairdos is a lot of nonsense. You have to be prepared to do a bit of everything, but you'll meet the most attractive men in the world.[53]

Young's husband 'on the side' was photographer and filmmaker Gordon Parks. As an Asian-American woman in an interracial marriage (Parks was Black), Young's powerful position in the world of publishing was remarkable for her time. And yet when she died in 2020, her survivors could not get anyone interested in reporting on her death and had to pay to place a death notice in the *New York Times* (a belated obituary was published in *The Washington Post* a year later).[54]

The advice given by Young at the beginning of 'Girls in the Publishing Business' is taken to heart in the interview with Mundis. She is prepared to do 'a bit of everything.' As do several of the interviewees, she emphasises that a girl in publishing cannot turn up her nose at secretarial work: 'If you're a good secretary in a good house, you'll get moved up. The whole publishing business is like a close-knit family. There's a lot of promoting from within, breeding from your own kind. It's a very small clique—but once you're in, you've got the key to everything.' It is hard not to feel a certain amount of dissonance when reading this article because many of the perks expounded by the women sound rather dystopian to current sensibilities. Mundis also embodies Young's advice to marry intelligently, having married a freelance writer who also worked in publishing: 'I'm not guaranteeing matrimony,' she says, 'but a job in publishing is a wonderful way for girls ... to meet some of the most attractive men in New York. They're not all after your body, either, and if they are, they use enormous subtlety, instead of the go out and grab 'em approach. A publishing executive

/local/obituaries/genevieve-young-editor-who-helped-shape-love-story-and-other-books
-dies-at-89/2021/02/18/a607fbd8-720a-11eb-b8a9-b9467510f0fe_story.html>.

53  Reed, 'Girls', pp. 97–8.
54  Italie, 'Genevieve'.

makes a girl feel desired for her brains. The approach is very cool. 'Did you read Norman Mailer's new book?' he'll say. 'Yes.' Then, 'Let's discuss it' as the hand rests lightly on your arm.'[55]

The *Cosmopolitan* article is, overall, aspirational and glosses over the negative aspects of the industry or reframes them as positives. At the end, Reed encourages girls reading it to hop on a plane to New York, no doubt excited about the prospects of sexual harassment (albeit for their *brains*, not just their figures) that await them in the glittering skyscrapers that house the big publishing houses.

## 7      Briefly Mentioned

The following are women about whom I know little (yet) but who deserve more attention and research from future scholars. The women discussed so far, with the exception of Genevieve Young, are all white, heterosexual (as far as we know), cisgender, and non-disabled. However, women of all kinds found their way into the paperback industry; unfortunately, their stories are even less documented than the more prominent women discussed above.

### 7.1      *Frances Ferris (or Deegan) Yerxa Hamling (1917–2019)*
Hamling was involved in science fiction and sleaze publication via her second husband, William Hamling. As Frances Yerxa (while married to Leroy Yerxa) she wrote scientific nonfiction in sci-fi magazines. After Yerxa passed away, she married Hamling, who brought her on as managing editor of one of his science fiction magazines, *Imagination*. Hamling went on to publish *Rogue* (a men's magazine that was a competitor with *Playboy*) and found Greenleaf Classics, which came to be one of the great sleaze empires of the midcentury, publishing thousands of smut titles between 1959 and 1973. According to science fiction publisher Earl Kemp, William and Frances worked on *Rogue* side by side, sitting at matching desks in their basement, all while raising six children, four from Frances' marriage to Yerxa. Frances provided much of the funding, editorial work, and office work that made Greenleaf possible.[56] She is perhaps the founding mother of sleaze, but very little has been written about her. There is some confusion on Hamling's maiden name. She is cited in countless science fiction publications as Frances Deegan Yerxa Hamling, but her grave says Frances Ferris Yerxa Hamling.

---

55      Reed, 'Girls', p. 100.
56      Earl Kemp. *eI*, vol. 2, no. 6, December 2003. <https://efanzines.com/EK/eI11/index.htm>.

## 7.2    Elaine Williams (neé Elaine H. Cumming, 1932–1963)

Williams is best known for the lesbian pulps novels she wrote under the pseudonym Sloan (or Sloane) Britain, which are highly desirable on the collector's market. In 1949, she became an editor at Midwood, a publisher specialising in erotic and sleazy novels, often written by more famous writers using pseudonyms. There, she acquired and edited novels by such famous writers as Lawrence Block, Donald Westlake, and Robert Silverberg. The first year she published her first novel, First Person—Third Sex, which, like most of her work, detailed the 'twilight' world of lesbian love, often ending in heartbreak. One novel, These Curious Pleasures (Midwood, 1961) even uses her own pseudonym for the main character (suggesting it may be semi-autobiographical) and parodying Midwood publisher Harry Broadman.[57]

One can only imagine the complexities of life as a queer woman writing lesbian fiction and working as an editor at a sleaze publishing firm. She was married to Earnest E. Williams and had four children. She was killed (and her husband injured) in a car crash; newspaper accounts differ on who was driving, but the publishing industry lore is that Williams killed herself.[58] There is little evidence to support this other than, it seems, the assumption that she was a lesbian married to a man and consequently could not bear to live. Most of what has been written about her is speculation and gossip.

## 7.3    Vivian Stephens (1932–Present)

Vivian Stephens is one of the better known and best documented names on this list—but she is only known within the genre of romance, which is often kept separate from or ignored in conversations about the paperback publishing industry. Male-authors histories tend to dismiss it or leave it out entirely. Stephens is also one of the most prominent Black women in a field to this day completely dominated by white names.

Stephens is an editor, literary agent, and the founder of Romance Writers of America (RWA). At Dell, she created and edited the Candlelight Ecstasy line in 1980. This was the first line of category romance to waive the requirement that heroines be virginal, a change which revolutionised the genre and helped open the door to open expressions of female sexual desire in romance fiction and popular culture.[59]

---

57    Michael Hemmingson, 'The curious case of Sloane Britain', Those sexy vintage sleaze books. A blog about vintage softcore paperbacks, November 17, 2009. <https://vintagesleazepaperbacks.wordpress.com/2009/11/17/the-curious-case-of-sloane-britain/>.

58    Joanne Passet, Indomitable. The life of Barbara Grier (Bella Books, 2006), p. 117.

59    Mimi Swartz, 'Vivian Stephens helped turn romance writing into a billion dollar industry. Then she got pushed out,' Texas Monthly, September 2020. <https://www.texasmonthly

The RWA was thrown into turmoil in 2019 when years of allegations of racism, gatekeeping, and problems with inclusivity came to a head in a Twitter battle that spilled into the real world and ended in the cancellation of the Association's annual awards. Many participants pointed to the fact that the organisation was founded by a Black woman and yet the genre community is still dominated by white voices.

### 7.4    Judy-Lynne del Rey (1943–1986)

Judy-Lynne del Rey is often discussed, like Betty Ballantine, as half of a famous husband-and-wife team. However, Judy-Lynne only married Lester del Rey long after she had already worked her way up the publishing ladder. In fact, she brought Lester to Ballantine to help revitalise the science fiction line which Betty had worked on previously. She is best known for obtaining the publishing rights to the *Star Wars* franchise. Judy-Lynne was born with Achondroplasia, the most common form of dwarfism. Author Isaac Asimov included a chapter about her in his autobiography. In a passage that might best be described as disgustingly honest, he admits that '[w]hen I first saw her [at a science fiction convention], I winced and turned away,' a statement that gives us some idea of what kinds of bigotry she must have encountered on a daily basis, and what she had to overcome to work with the ruling guard of while male writers that Asimov represents. He pats himself on the back for quickly learning to overlook her disability: 'And then a strange thing happened. I was not talking to Judy-Lynn long before I forgot that she was a dwarf. Her luminous intelligence (I can think of no more appropriate adjective) totally obscured her physical appearance.'[60] Despite his easy condescension, Asimov's tribute to Del Rey is well worth reading, especially for the details of the extravagant practical jokes that she liked to play on the somewhat gullible and uptight author. She would provoke Asimov by deliberately misspelling his name, creating fake bad reviews to send him into a rage, and creating an elaborate ruse in which she pretended she had been fired and replaced by a younger, prettier model. Once Asimov was hooked on flirting with the replacement via correspondence, she revealed herself: 'So, Asimov! How quickly you forget all about me and take up with my replacement!'[61] She directly inspired several of Asimov's stories

---

.com/arts-entertainment/vivian-stephens-helped-turn-romance-writing-into-billion -dollar-industry/>.

60    Isaac Asimov, *I, Asimov. A memoir* (New York: Random House, 2009), p. 320.
61    Ibid., p. 321.

(including 'Feminine Intuition' and 'The Bicentennial Man') and 'had more different ways of calling [a man] an idiot than you could possibly imagine.'[62]

## 7.5 Nancy Coffey (1947–Present)

Nancy Coffey was the editor at Avon responsible for the publisher creating and cornering the market on a new genre: the bodice ripper. All sources I have found on Coffey make sure to include the fact that she was a fourth-grade teacher before she came to editing; it seems the contrast between a mild schoolteacher and a powerful editor of erotic fiction was a titillating one. Coffey's innovation was prompted by Avon's search (under Director Peter Mayer) for more titles to publish as paperback originals, bypassing the expensive rights for hardback bestsellers. Coffey pulled a manuscript from the slush pile called *The Flame and the Flower* by Kathleen Woodiwiss, 'a small-town Minnesota housewife. It had already been turned down by 10 hardcover houses, some on the grounds that it was too long to be commercially practicable.'[63] Coffey found that the story gripped her from the first page and smelled a potential bargain for the publishing firm. She bought the rights for $1,500 and a four percent royalty. It was published, with only minor edits, in 1974 and immediately became a major bestseller, with over two million copies sold by 1977.[64]

*The Flame and the Flower* launched a new evolution of the romance genre that came to be known as the bodice ripper. These were historical romances with more on-page sexual content than their predecessors:

Coffey doesn't like it when the word 'erotic' is applied to her romances. She acknowledges that they're definitely not descendants of 'Jane Eyre,' as the Gothics are. Nor are they first-kiss-on-the-last-page stories like the Harlequin Romances, formula yarns that differ only as to exotic setting. Nor are they bare outlines for stories, which Coffey believes Barbara Cartland's are. They are the fantasies of typical modern women—their authors—acted out in glamorous periods of the past, with just the amount of sexual detail 1977 women crave.[65]

Although early bodice rippers such as *The Flame and the Flower* now seem terrifically problematic due to their reliance on rape and sexual assault as a way to allow women to be sexually active without themselves initiating sex, the genre has evolved and changes and is still incredibly popular.

---

62   Ibid., p. 324.
63   Ray Walters, 'Paperback talk', *The New York Times*, 7 August 1977 <https://www.nytimes
     .com/1977/08/07/archives/paperback-talk-paperback-talk.html>.
64   Silverman, *The time*, p. 399; Walters, 'Paperback.'
65   Walters, 'Paperback.'

### 7.6    *Jean Marie Stine (1945–Present)*

Jean Marie Stine is the only trans woman I have found (so far) working in the paperback publishing industry, though there are no doubt others. I have previously written about the radical science fiction pornography novels she wrote for the 1968–9 short-lived publishing firm Essex House under the name Hank Stine and in that research learned that she later became an editor, working, among other places, for Leisure, a horror publisher of the 1980s.[66]

## 8    Conclusions

I will end with one final piece of trivia about Eunice Frost that seems especially poignant: the famous penguin logo, chosen because it was 'dignified and flippant,' has a name. The penguin's name is 'Frostie,' the office sobriquet for Eunice Frost.[67] In the history of the paperback, women are objectified—as cute logos (Frostie the Penguin, Gertrude the Kangaroo) and as the alluring ladies featured in Good Girl Art, the focus on which in paperback collecting has feminised the book as object and created an untrue assumption of a male consumer, reader, collector.

I hope that future studies of the paperback will pay more attention to the women who were taking book babies home and getting little credit for their nurturing. There needs to be a shift from a focus on male founders and male cover artists to a wider focus that includes editorial practices, secretarial work, and readership. Some avenues of future research include digging into publisher archives, reading trade publications (which are collected by very few institutions), finding fan publications, and conducting interviews with living women publishers, editors, writers, and readers. The history of paperback publishing must be rewritten not only to include women, nonbinary, and queer individuals but to cultivate an understanding that these books are not the projects of great individuals but—like most books—of communities of makers.

---

66    'Jean Marie Stine', *FuturesPast editions. Off-trail science fiction, fantasy & horror.* <https://
       futurespasteditions.com/?page_id=723>.
67    Quigly, 'Obituary'.

# CHAPTER 7

# A 'Gentlemen's Profession': the Historical Masculinisation of British Publishing

*Sarah Lubelski*

'Fred Warburg is tall, dark and striking. He wears fine British tweeds and uses a cigarette holder' reads the front flap of *An Occupation for Gentlemen*, Warburg's 1960 memoir of his life and publishing career. 'He went to Westminster, a public (British) school and to Oxford. His manner is grave, even sardonic. He has a reputation as a wit'.[1] This less-than-subtle conflation of the ideal English gentleman—handsome, well-dressed and well-educated, witty (or clubbable), and intelligent, among other traits—with the figure of the English publisher reflects the cultural construction of publishing as a 'gentlemen's profession' throughout the nineteenth and twentieth centuries. The phrase, which speaks to the gender and class hierarchies that have governed the industry, has been utilised by scholars, journalists, and publishing professionals alike to call attention to the gender disparity at work within the field.

Pointing to publishing's historical identity as a 'gentlemen's profession' has become a starting point from which to investigate women's marginalisation within this professional landscape, setting the backdrop of male dominance and control against which women have attempted to build their careers. According to Eileen Cadman, Gail Chester, and Agnes Pivot, the image of the gentleman publisher as a wealthy, male figure and head of a family-controlled publishing house established publishing as the domain of elite men, limiting participation and professional development.[2] As part of their oral history project, the organisation Women in Publishing (WiP) includes a thematic section called 'A Gentleman's Profession', which shows how the 'old boy networks' that have dominated the industry worked to exclude and subordinate women professionals.[3] Despite the ubiquity of the term 'gentlemen's profession', or the notion of the gentleman publisher, however, scholars have yet to investigate

---

1 Frederic Warburg, *An Occupation for Gentlemen* (Boston: Houghton Mifflin, 1960).

2 Eileen Cadman, Gail Chester, and Agnes Pivot, *Rolling Our Own: Women as Printers, Publishers and Distributors* (London: Minority Press Group, 1981), p. 17.

3 'A Gentleman's Profession', *Women in Publishing: An Oral History*, Women in Publishing (2021) <https://www.womeninpublishinghistory.org.uk/content/category/themes/a-gentlemans-profession> (accessed 21 April, 2021).

the socio-cultural history of this concept. Drawing on cultural materials from nineteenth and twentieth centuries Britain, such as periodicals, memoirs, interviews, and essays, this chapter analyses depictions of publishers and editors, mainstream publishing firms, and the industry itself, to show how the profession and practice of publishing was constructed as an upper-class masculinised space through gender ideology and gendered notions of power and hierarchy, education and intellectual tradition, cultural influence and national identity.

This view of the publishing industry as a masculinised space stands in contrast to depictions of the contemporary industry, and publishing work itself, as feminised. Giles Clark and Angus Phillips observe that by the 1980s, badly paid women comprised the majority of the mass-market publishing workforce, managed by far better-paid men.[4] This numerical trend has continued into the twenty-first century. A 2020 UK Publishers' Association study on diversity in the publishing workforce found that 64% of the 14,076 study participants identify as cis women.[5] Simultaneously, publishing has been qualitatively feminised. Publishing work is not only characterised as caring, but is also economically devalued, which are common features of feminised professions. Descriptions of the emotional work of supporting authors through the publishing process, for example, serve to emphasise the feminised nature of publishing, aligning the industry with pursuits such as nursing and teaching. Such caring work—long associated with and undertaken by women—is typically both poorly paid and precarious. In the past decades, the field of feminist book history has brought new attention to the impact of gender on the book trade, from literary production to the marketplace, and put women's experiences at the forefront.[6] This examination of the history of the masculinisation of publishing serves as part of this feminist body of scholarship by exposing the gendered hierarchies that are woven into the industry's organisational structure and illuminating the gender bias that has challenged women in publishing, even as they have become numerically dominant within the industry.

---

4   Giles Clark and Angus Phillips, *Inside Book Publishing* (New York and London: Routledge, 2014), pp. 29–30.

5   'Diversity Survey of the Publishing Workforce 2020', *Publishers Association*, 11 February 2021 <https://www.publishers.org.uk/publications/diversity-survey-of-the-publishing-workforce -2020/>.

6   For example, see Michelle Levy, 'Do Women Have a Book History?', *Studies in Romanticism*, 53 (2014), pp. 297–317; Simone Murray, *Mixed Media: Feminist Presses and Publishing Politics* (London: Pluto, 2004); Kate Ozment, 'Rationale for Feminist Bibliography', *Textual Cultures*, 13 (2020) pp. 149–178; Beth Palmer, *Women's Authorship and Editorship in Victorian Culture: Sensational Strategies* (Oxford University Press, 2011); Trysh Travis, 'The Women in Print Movement: History and Implications', *Book History*, 11 (2008), pp. 275–300.

## 1    Constructing the Gentleman Publisher

The utilisation of the phrase 'gentlemen's profession' in relation to the publishing industry is more than a reference to the fact that historically, the majority of publishers and publishing employees were men. Rather, it contextualises the publishing industry, and its workers, within systems of power and marginalisation based on factors such as gender, class, and race. Sonam Peldon et al. note that from an etymological standpoint, the word 'gentleman' is a reference to a man above the class of yeoman who owned property and were not engaged in business or a profession.[7] While upper-class men could engage in professional activities, such pursuits were undertaken under the pretence of purpose and intellectual growth rather than the need for an income. The phrase 'gentlemen's profession', then, is inherently contradictory, given it refers to upper-class men working in the commercial realm for profit. In practice, however, the word 'gentleman' has been used more broadly to infer masculinity and status. His was a 'powerful class construction', explain Peldon et al., which was more tied to his privileged status above 'cultural, ethnic, and gender difference' rather than actual wealth. Certainly, what A. James Hammerton refers to as the 'well-known phenomenon of family impoverishment or genteel poverty' in the nineteenth century indicates that class was considered inherited and fixed, regardless of financial status.[8] Characteristics such as good breeding, courtesy, honour, and chivalry, which were seen as markers of upper-class masculinity, did not always coincide with affluence.[9] Stephen Harrison notes that the Victorian English gentleman was not only defined by factors such as 'moderation, clubabbility, leisured gentility, patriotism, and (even) religion', but also a cultivated intellect and high-culture taste.[10] The use of the term 'gentlemen's profession' in relation to publishing work, then, situated publishing within what Harrison calls the 'male and homosocial Victorian elite'.

This notion of the Victorian gentleman was increasingly intertwined with the figure of the editor and publisher, whose gender, class, and racial identity justified the positions they occupied within the literary realm. Beth Palmer notes that the mid-to late-nineteenth century editor was expected to exhibit

---

7    Sonam Peldon et al., 'Ladies, Gentlemen and Guys: The Gender Politics of Politeness', *Social Sciences*, 56 (2019), p. 3.

8    A. James Hammerton, *Emigrant Gentlewomen: Genteel Poverty and Female Emigration, 1830–1914* (London: Croom Helm Ltd., 1979), p. 21.

9    Peldon et al., 'Ladies, Gentlemen and Guys', p. 4.

10   Stephen Harrison, 'Horace and the Construction of the English Victorian Gentleman', *HELIOS*, 34 (2007), p. 207.

manly and upper-class virtues such clubbability, integrity, taste, and prestige.[11] An article in *Chambers's Journal* on the responsibilities of editors reinforces this point, claiming that the periodical editor was a position of 'power and influence'. Furthermore, the article notes that the office of the editor was an 'attractive' career for a man who was well-educated and 'imbued with the fire of genius'.[12] An account of a banquet celebrating Edwin Brett, editor and publisher of several magazines for boys, relays that Brett was recognised as a 'kindly-hearted, generous, honest English gentleman', who has served his country as an 'apostle of good literature'.[13] Like their colleagues working in the periodical press, publishers were described as figures of good breeding, education, and manner—all characteristics that appeared to imbue them with literary authority and taste. An article on the firm of Rivington lauds 'each generation' of the publishing family for their honour, respectability, and achievement in the realms of political leadership, religion, and literary ability.[14]

Such accounts of editors and publishers are evidence of the effort to redefine publishing and its role in Britain's social and cultural landscape. The rebranding of publishing as a 'gentleman's profession' created distance from its trade-based roots. It was not until the nineteenth century that publishing emerged in a modern sense, explains John Feather, noting that publishing, printing and bookselling were often undertaken as a cohesive role, with the same person managing the financing, manufacturing, and distribution of a given work.[15] According to James Raven, the separation of these functions accelerated dramatically throughout the eighteenth century, eventually evolving into distinct positions within the industrial book trade.[16] While nineteenth-century printers retained their identities as tradesmen, undertaking the physical labour necessary to materialise intellectual work, publishing was increasingly located within the professional realm. Rather than deny their trade-based past, Victorian publishers instead foregrounded the industry's evolution from its lower-class origins. Publishers' biographies and firm histories frequently positioned the transition from printing or bookselling to publishing

11    Palmer, *Women's Authorship and Editorship*, p. 5.

12    'Newspaper Editors and Their Work', *Chambers's Journal*, 16 September 1882, pp. 585–587.

13    'Complimentary Banquet and Presentation to Mr. Edwin John Brett', *The Boy's Comic Journal*, 1892, p. 30.

14    'A London Publishing House', *National Observer*, 25 August 1894, p. 380.

15    John Feather, *A History of British Publishing*, 2nd Ed. (London: Routledge, 2006), p. 4.

16    James Raven, *The Business of Books: Booksellers and the English Book Trade* (New Haven and London: Yale University Press, 2007), p. 328.

as evidence of a publisher's social and cultural worth, meaning that the role of the publisher depended on performing gender as well as class.

Musing on 'how far the position of publishers has changed since the days when they were but exalted booksellers', the author of the 1894 article on Rivington praises 'older and more famous firms' for being 'proud of their evolution from the trade of selling books to the profession of publishing them'.[17] Within the article, the firm's advancement from a printshop and seller of religious tracts to preeminent theological publisher is connected to their rise in social status. As Rivington became better known, the writer observes, the publishers not only became 'friends of the dignitaries of the Established church', but were also themselves 'influential office-holders in the Worshipful Company of Stationers of the City of London'.[18] An article on the history of Blackwood in *Chambers's Journal* similarly recounts William Blackwood's advancement from mere bookseller to influential publisher, whose position and power in the literary realm was attributed to his literary instinct and knowledge.[19] While Blackwood was not 'born with a silver spoon in his mouth', the author notes, his 'keen interest in the contents of the books' and 'thorough knowledge of his craft' prepared him for 'something still higher' than bookselling; namely, the 'liberal profession' of publishing. His abilities and 'genuine' interest in 'considerations of a loftier order' not only brought Blackwood professional success, but also guaranteed his access to higher social and intellectual circles.[20] This performance of gentility extended to lower-level employees. In Charles Morgan's account of Macmillan's acquisition of Bentley and Son in 1898, he notes that Bentley's former employees arrived for work at their new firm 'in the top-hats and formal dress which were the custom of Bentley's employees'.[21] This use of consumer goods, including clothing, by non-aristocratic people to align themselves with the English gentility is a process that Daniel R. Smith identifies as 'gent-rification'.[22]

---

17  'A London Publishing House', p. 380. Rivington was established by Charles Rivington in 1711.

18  'A London Publishing House', p. 380.

19  'Blackwoods: The History of a Publishing House', *Chambers's Journal*, 27 November 1897, p. 753.

20  'Blackwoods', p. 754.

21  Charles Morgan, *The House of Macmillan, 1843–1943* (London: Macmillan & Co. Ltd., 1943), p. 184.

22  Daniel R. Smith, 'The Gent-rification of English Masculinities: Class, Race, and Nation in Contemporary Consumption', *Social Identities*, 20 (2014), p. 393.

## 2      Dynasty and Empire

The rising social status of publishers and publishing organisations is reflected in the mythology that surrounded the histories of mainstream firms. While many were no older than the century itself, publishing organisations were presented as patriarchal dynasties rather than commercial entities, often through language associated with the English gentry, which created the impression of tradition and prestige. Eminent mainstream firms were described not as companies, but 'houses', led by families who were the architects of Britain's cultural history. A series of articles called 'Histories of Publishing Houses' in the *Critic*, which ran from 1860 to 1861, exemplifies this representation of publishing firms and their families. Taken as a series, these articles identify a ruling elite of the literary world, who not only governed the book trade, but also defined the literary character of the nation. Each article functions as a 'chapter' of the history of a mainstream firm, such as Bentley, Blackwood, Longman, Macmillan, and Murray, which intertwines the firm's own history with that of the United Kingdom, and builds each firm's cultural and familial legacy. In an article on Blackwood, for example, the firm is located within the literary history of the city of Edinburgh, placed alongside notable figures such as bookseller and publisher Alexander Donaldson and poet Robert Burns.[23] An article on the history of Longman, titled 'After the Founder', describes the firm in dynastic terms:

> Thomas Longman ... was succeeded by Thomas his nephew. ... He walked steadily in the footsteps of his uncle; he completed the superstructure which the founder had reared, and left his successor the business which he had inherited, ripe for the expansion which the nineteenth century was to bestow on it.[24]

The language utilised in this article, including terms such as 'succession', 'inheritance', and 'bestow', lends an air of nobility to the publishing firm, whose leadership is described as a natural right, and whose success is almost divinely preordained by being 'bestowed' rather than as the result of commercial acumen. Importantly, the second Thomas is also seen to be deserving of his place at the firm's helm due to his bloodline and gentlemanly characteristics rather than his commercial instincts. The author of the article assures readers that

---

23    'Histories of Publishing Houses. No. III.—The House of Blackwood', *The Critic*, 7 July 1860, pp. 6–9.
24    'Histories of Publishing Houses. No. II.—The House of Longman', *The Critic*, 7 April 1860, p. 431.

the second Thomas was a man of 'exemplary character', respected for his 'benevolence' and 'integrity'.

The understanding of the publisher as a preeminent social and cultural figure extended far beyond this series. The article on Rivington referred to the late-nineteenth century as the 'age of apotheosis of publishers' with their 'house in the country' and 'palace[s] in Paternoster Row', language which projects an image of publishers as rulers of the cultural realm.[25] A crucial element of this reverence for publishers was their presumed contribution to the British literary tradition, which was a cornerstone of the country's identity, prestige, and power on a national and international stage. An 1821 article in *Edinburgh Magazine* equates the contributions made to the nation by great literature with that of an army.[26] The author writes,

> a piece of finished contribution, in which every sentence, every word, nay every letter, performs its duty gives great delight to the mind ... by presenting an image of perfect beauty. It is like a great army, levied for the defense of the peculiar endearments of our society.

Such a work allows the reader to 'rejoice' in their country's 'stately ranks, its graceful evolutions, its magnificent impact', he adds. This notion of dynasty has been woven into publishing history scholarship. In his work on the 'publishing dynasty' of John Murray, for example, Humphrey Carpenter recounts the history of the firm through the lives of seven successive John Murrays who occupied a 'fabled' and 'ancestral' home at 50 Albemarle Street in London from the eighteenth to the twenty-first century.[27] The founder of the firm, Carpenter notes, was historically described like a 'character in a novel', who was 'decent and honourable, with a gentility that conceals romantic depths' and an 'ancestry' which tied him to the British military elite—a narrative which shaped the social position of the first John Murry and his successors.[28]

The integration of military imagery in histories of literature and literary figures shows the extent to which literary production was part of the narrative of nation-building. British literature was not only a point of internal pride, but also acted as a vehicle for spreading British culture throughout the empire. Scholars such as Priya Joshi and Alexis Weedon note that the dissemination

25    'A London Publishing House', p. 380.

26    'Literary Labour, Popularity, and Merit', *Edinburgh Magazine and Literary Miscellany*, August 1821, p. 108.

27    Humphrey Carpenter, *The Seven Lives of John Murray: The Story of a Publishing Dynasty* (London: John Murray, 2008), p. xi.

28    Carpenter, *John Murray*, p. 5.

of British literature furthered the imperial project, acting as a tool for shaping the culture, opinions, education, and morals of readers worldwide.[29] Morgan's preface to his history of the firm of Macmillan reinforces this point. He refers to his work as a 'salute' to the firm 'as their ship continues ... her long voyage across the world'.[30] Morgan further refers to the publishing house's international branches in New York, Toronto, Melbourne, Bombay, Calcutta and Madras as the fruit of Macmillan's seeds spread across the globe.[31] His clarification that all offices were 'still in the effective ownership of the British Macmillans' and his comparison of the opportunities, which lay in 'trade' and 'art' to 'soldering', identify the global expansion of British publishing as an extension of cultural control over dominions, i.e. an assertion of empire.

Authors have served as the public face of this literary tradition as it has been ingrained within the nation and spread across the globe. Figures such as Geoffrey Chaucer, Edmund Spenser, William Shakespeare, Jonathan Swift, Alexander Pope, William Wordsworth, Walter Scott, George Byron, Thomas Carlyle, Alfred Tennyson and Robert Browning—whose names are etched into the dome atop the British Museum reading room—were the rulers of the country's literary sphere. Ruth Hoberman argues that the names chosen for deification in this space serve as the physical manifestation of 'a model of cultural achievement clearly gendered as male', contributing to a portrait of British cultural and intellectual history that wholly belonged to upper-class men.[32] If authors were the exalted figureheads of this space, however, publishers were in essence its kingmakers, who worked in the shadows to control ascendance in the literary realm. Publishers' gatekeeping was not always portrayed in a positive light. Throughout the nineteenth century, many authors publicly denounced publishers as capital owners who profited off the creative work of the subjugated author. Historian and novelist Walter Besant's characterisation of the relationship between authors and publishers exemplifies this line of thinking. Besant observes that within the literary landscape, literary property belonged 'as a right, exclusively and naturally, to publishers', while 'authors—the producers of literary property—were still considered as

---

29    See Priya Joshi, 'Culture and Consumption: Fiction, the Reading Public, and the British
       Novel in Colonial India', *Book History*, 1 (1998), pp. 201–206; Alexis Weedon, *Victorian
       Publishing: The Economics of Book Production for a Mass Market, 1836–1916* (Aldershot:
       Ashgate, 2003), pp. 32–44.
30    Morgan, *House of Macmillan*, p. vii.
31    Morgan, *House of Macmillan*, pp. 4–5.
32    Ruth Hoberman, 'Women in the British Museum Reading Room During the Late
       Nineteenth and Early Twentieth Centuries: From Quasi to Counterpublic', *Feminist
       Studies*, 28 (2002), p. 507. The reading room was opened in 1857.

publishers' hacks'.[33] This rendered the writer a 'workman without rights' who was dependent on his masters, he argues,

> the publisher considers nothing but the getting of the property into his own hands, on his own terms; the author, helpless and ignorant, yet suspicious and resentful, yields up his property as meekly as a cow yields up her milk. ... No worker in the world ... [is] more cruelly sweated.[34]

Though written from a place of personal interest, Besant's writings show the extent to which writers considered themselves manufacturers, whose labour was exploited by greedy publishers. Indeed, Thomas Carlyle's 1829 essay 'Signs of the Times', and George Gissing's late-nineteenth-century novel *New Grub Street*, which focuses on literary production, similarly lament the increasingly mechanised nature of literary production, and the subjugation of authors within the publishing industry.[35]

In different contexts, however, publishers were revered as governors of the literary realm. An article on a bibliographical volume of Macmillan's publications from 1843 to 1891 highlights the firm's central role in fostering Britain's great literature, noting that the firm's publications list includes 'no small proportion of the most illustrious names of the present day', representing 'the best thought and intellectual work of our century'.[36] Far more than an uninvolved manufacturer or capitalist, Macmillan was credited with defining the literary landscape. To send a manuscript to Macmillan, the unnamed author adds, is to apply to be part of this 'first-class club':

> In this catalogue ... are some names (and these not the least eminent) of men who would never have produced a book, never have won fame, if it had not been for the help they received from the publisher. And when we speak of help we make no reference to mere assistance in money ... We mean direct intellectual assistance, the kind of guidance by which a man is led to do his own special work in life ... It is one part of the publisher's business—if he knows it aright—to discover the men who are

33    Walter Besant, 'The First Society of British Authors (1848)', in *Essays and Historiettes* (London: Chatto and Windus, 1903), p. 290.

34    Walter Besant, 'Literature as a Career', in *Essays and Historiettes*, p. 314.

35    See Thomas Carlyle, 'Signs of the Times', in *Critical and Miscellaneous Essays: Collected and Published by Thomas Carlyle*, vol. II (London: James Fraser, 1840), pp. 266–284; George Gissing, *New Grub Street*, ed. John Goode (Oxford: Oxford University Press, 1993).

36    'A Great Publishing House', *The Speaker*, 5 September 1891, p. 285.

really fitted to become the friends and leaders of the reading world, and
to draw them into the vocation for which Nature has designed them.

This passage highlights the perception of publishers as the true architects of
Britain's literary canon and legacy, whose tireless work served to uphold the
more visible 'leaders' (i.e. authors). It was not only high-brow publishers who
had a role to play in this literary landscape. Although mass-market publishers could not be credited for engendering the literary elite, they were praised
for their contribution to popular culture and the education of the masses. An
article on Charles Knight defines the firm as a publishing house of the 'material
age' that produces 'food for the mind'.[37] Such 'purveyors of cheap literature',
the author argues, have 'shed the light of wholesome knowledge into the dark
corners of society'. Their work is similarly described in the masculinised language of nation building, with the author noting that publishers of popular
works were leading an 'intellectual revolution', which would ultimately allow
the workingman to rise and take part in the governance of the country. Their
publishing work, which is described as a 'battle', is proclaimed a mass triumph
for the influence that it has over the British public.

## 3      The Emergence of the Professional Gentleman

That publishing is positioned more as a calling than a trade within these
sources—an altruistic activity or service rather than a pragmatic material
pursuit—reinforces its gentlemanly character. Although gentlemen traditionally derived income passively, particularly through land ownership, it
became increasingly normalised for upper-class men to undertake work in
the public realm. Indeed, publishing was not the only profession which was
defined as appropriate for 'gentlemen.' Throughout the eighteenth and nineteenth centuries, the category and definition of 'profession' expanded beyond
the three learned professions of medicine, law and theology. Moreover, as
Penelope J. Corfield observes, the previous category of 'occupation', which
had encompassed all manners of work, was further broken down. The professions became 'a sector of employment' which stood in contrast to "industrial
'crafts' and commercial 'trades'" as well as 'casualized unskilled services, which
lacked the connotations of specialist knowledge, linked with long training and

---

37     'Histories of the Publishing Houses. No. IV. The House of Charles Knight', *The Critic*,
        18 May 1861, p. 624.

professional dedication,' she explains.[38] Examples of occupations newly styled as professions included architecture, dentistry, engineering, optometry, and accountancy.

Such professions were commonly described as 'gentlemen's professions', which was an indication of the shifting relationship between the notion of gentility and paid work. As scholars such as Leonore Davidoff, Catherine Hall, and John Tosh observe, the emerging distinction between the public and private spheres in the nineteenth century normalised the notion of men working outside of the home—and indeed posited men's ability to maintain this distinction as an essential aspect of their masculine duty. Davidoff and Hall note that from 1831 onwards, the British census focused on adult men as providers, and recognised nine occupational categories—a shift from the previous tactic of designating families as either agricultural or trade-based units.[39] Beyond evidencing emerging trends in home finances, the new format of the census reflects socio-cultural notions of masculine and feminine roles. By the mid-nineteenth century, Tosh writes, men were called upon to be adventurers and 'captains of industry', whose accomplishments in the public space and status among their men peers were central to their masculinity.[40] This was true for middle-and upper-class men alike. An 1868 article in *Chambers's Journal* encourages gentlemen to consider a variety of emerging professions for their sons' futures. Calling the learned professions 'overdone', the author notes that 'the attainment of wealth and social eminence through commercial pursuits and colonial enterprise is acquiring a significant prominence', and particularly recommends the civil service for young men.[41] The idea that professional work was suited to the life of a gentleman became accepted truth. Although English gentlemen must still be formally educated and financially comfortable, as Edward A. Baugh writes in an article on music as a gentleman's profession, this class of men could choose any number of pursuits.[42] Gentlemen could be 'in the Church, the Army, the learned profession, and nowadays, perhaps, the higher walks of commerce', he claims, adding that the 'finest men' can be found within all professional spaces, including the military, civil service, and creative

---

38   Penelope J. Corfield, *Power and the Professions in Britain, 1700–1850* (New York and London: Routledge, 1995), p. 19.

39   Leonore Davidoff and Catherine Hall, *Family Fortunes: Men and Women of the English Middle Class, 1780–1850* (University of Chicago Press, 1987), p. 230.

40   John Tosh, *A Man's Place: Masculinity and the Middle-Class Home in Victorian England* (Yale University Press, 1999), pp. 3–11.

41   'What to do with my Sons!', *Chambers's Journal*, 30 May 1868, p. 342.

42   Edward A. Baugh, 'The Gentlemen in Music', *Monthly Musical Record*, 1 November 1901, p. 371.

worlds. Baugh further assures readers that this is not a threat to class status: 'These men, however stirring may be their life, never lose the tone which their family connection and education have given them … It is a well-mannered, courteous class'.

While these new professional opportunities opened doors for men of privilege, however, they did not offer broad social and economic mobility. Like the learned professions before them, emerging professions erected barriers to entry (i.e. educational requirements, licensing or association memberships) to create the impression of specialised knowledge, a process known as occupational closure.[43] This is one of the methods by which the professions became intertwined with gentility. As Davidoff observes, the education and training associated with readying boys for the working world was an expensive endeavour.[44] An 1899 article titled 'Professions for Boys' bears witness to this practice.[45] 'The picture of the British parent with a son of fifteen to launch into life is a rather pathetic one', the unnamed author attests, continuing,

> He is confronted by innumerable wicket-gates, each of them guarded by a gentleman in a cap and gown holding a packet of examination papers, and by another gentleman, no less terrifying and important, jingling a still hungry bag of sovereigns.[46]

This article, which details the specialised requirements for various professions, highlights the gatekeeping taking place within the professional realm that undeniably limited entrance by gender, class, and race. Even professions that did not have official barriers, such as degrees, examinations, or licences, constructed social and educational prerequisites to entering their field. Like authors, publishers were motivated to manufacture a masculinised, upper-class identity for their profession to establish its authority and prestige. While many nineteenth-century publishers hailed from middle-class families and initially trained as booksellers or printers, they connected their professional practice to the masculinised worlds of intellectual achievement and education, social clubs, and professional associations to signal that theirs was an elite pursuit.

---

43    Corfield, *Power and the Professions*, pp. 209–210, 244–245.
44    Leonore Davidoff, *Thicker Than Water: Siblings and Their Relations, 1780–1920* (Oxford: Oxford University Press, 2012), p. 103.
45    'Professions for Boys', *The Academy Educational Supplement*, 16 September 1899, p. 281.
46    Ibid.

Publishing has never had a formal barrier to entry with regards to education or accreditation.[47] The absence of a formal educational requirement, however, did not hinder the impression that publishers and editors were the product of a liberal education, which included a deep understanding of literature, philosophy, politics, the sciences, and the arts, as well as natural genius and literary ability. George Bentley's 1883 collection of essays, *After Business: Papers Written in the Intervals of Work* exemplifies the construction of publishers as intellectuals. In the essay 'What the Firelight Fell On', for example, Bentley reflects on time spent in his friend Lawrence's library, and aligns himself with the 'men of genius' whose works rest on the shelves. Calling the 'grand writers' contained within the library his companions, he explains that he is,

> on terms of equality with them, and there is a republican sort of citizenship between you. Montaigne prattles with his wise prattle, Molière with the inexhaustible runnings of his wit, old Pepys takes you to the Duke of York's playhouse to see the *Ungrateful Lovers*, Evelyn steers you decently through the gay court of Charles; or if your mood be more serious, the terrible earnestness of Carlyle reveals the meanings of the French Revolution to you.[48]

In this essay, and throughout the publication, Bentley communicates that although his business serves the commercial marketplace, he personally belongs to the intellectual and literary elite.[49] The publication places Bentley and his peers in a higher class of men than the general reading public they serve, and establishes a liberal education as a prerequisite for his line of work.

In the twentieth century, it became more common for publishers to have a top-tier education, which endowed them with both the cultural knowledge and the social network necessary to obtain a position in publishing. Warburg's

---

47    Today there are several degree programs in publishing, however, obtaining a degree in publishing is not a requirement for a job in the field.

48    George Bentley, 'What the Firelight Fell On', in *After Business: Papers Written in the Intervals of Work* (London: privately printed, 1883), pp. 41–42.

49    It is possible that this essay was inspired by a letter written by Niccolò Machiavelli, which would therefore represent George's attempt to further align himself with men of genius. In a letter to Francesco Vettori, Machiavelli writes that at the end of the day, he enters into his study, 'tak[ing] off the days' clothing, covered with mud and dust,' and once appropriately dressed, he communes with 'ancient men.' His interaction with them is described as 'food which only is mine and which I was born for.' Machiavelli to Francesco Vettori, December 10, 1513, in Allan Gilbert (ed. And Trans.), *The Letters of Machiavelli: A Selection of his Letters* (New York: Capricorn Books, 1961), p. 142. I would like to thank Alan Galey for this reference.

account of the beginnings of his own career emphasises both the importance of an Oxbridge education and the opportunities afforded by membership to the right social sphere. Describing his interviewer at George Routledge & Sons Ltd., Warburg writes that William Stallybrass was a 'product of the Victorian age', pointing to Stallybrass's dedication to the 'advancement of reading, the enhancement of scholarship, ... the practice of bibliography' and enlightened thought as evidence.[50] For his part, Warburg credited his own institutional and familial connections, his classical education (which gave him 'no doubts about [his] ability to be a publisher'), and his 'reasonable humility', for his success at the interview.[51] Similarly, Cambridge graduate and former Longman employee, Tim Rix, describes his path to entry into the 'gentlemanly school of publishing' as being facilitated by the contacts he acquired through his elite education. Recalling that his interview included questions about where he had gone to school and his role in the Navy rather than 'silly questions like, did I like books', Rix referred to the 'paternalistic' and nepotistic nature of Longman as an 'upside', indicating that it was his educational and military pedigree rather than his aptitude for publishing that enabled his career.[52]

A similarly informal yet significant element of a publishing career was membership to a gentlemen's club that catered to men in literature and the arts. As Marissa Joseph explains, nineteenth-century English gentlemen's clubs were both 'social forces' and 'cultural influencers', which helped to create an elite class of men.[53] Nineteenth-century histories of gentlemen's clubs trace the practice to antiquity—including a group of 'Greek gentlemen' called The Sixty who met in a temple, and 'social gatherings of Roman gentlemen', where 'clubbability' was equated with wit—which situated their own practice within the social traditions of upper-class men.[54] Clubs had grown 'grander and more ostentatious with the progress of civilization', writes a journalist in *All the Year Round*, who notes that club houses were like palaces 'where the soul is dazzled with gilding'.[55] The club house was a place where gentlemen could dine, read, host meetings, smoke, and engage in other social, intellectual, and professional

---

50    Warburg, *An Occupation for Gentlemen*, p. 81.
51    Warburg, *An Occupation for Gentlemen*, p. 82. Stallybrass's son served as Vice Chancellor at Oxford University, Warburg's alma mater, and Walburg's brother-in-law, A.L. Schlesinger, worked for Routledge.
52    Qtd. in Sue Bradly (ed.), *The British Book Trade: An Oral History* (London: The British Library, 2008), pp. 18–20.
53    Marissa Joseph, 'Members Only: The Victorian Gentlemen's Club as a Space for Doing Business 1843–1900', *Management and Organizational History*, 14 (2019), p. 124.
54    'On Some Clubs, and Their Ends', *Temple Bar*, March 1872, p. 469.
55    'Clubs and Club-Men', *All the Year Round*, 26 September 1866, p. 283.

activities. A subset of clubs in nineteenth-century London were associated with the literary set, including the Athenaeum, the Garrick, and the Savile, and several articles point to the literary roots of club life, including references to the Mermaid Club, where the 'most illustrious poets and scholars' of the sixteenth century met, and the Apollo Club, which was headed by the playwright Ben Jonson.[56]

Joseph notes that nineteenth-century clubs 'were important facilitators for doing business in the British publishing industry', with men of letters utilising these spaces for networking and deal-making.[57] Accounts of these clubs often showcased famous members to establish prestige, and reports on events were similar to society pages or celebrity gossip columns. Referring to the Garrick club as a space where artists and patrons could meet on 'equal terms', Percy Fitzgerald highlights the social and productive nature of the organisation:

> What fun! What characters! How many of the 'good things' on circulation were engendered at the Garrick; which is natural enough when we think that Theodore Hook, Barham, Thackeray, Poole, and many of that choice kidney were about.[58]

The article also includes a ballad written about the club and attributed to Richard Barnham, which revels in the 'gossip and grub' of the club, including the conversations had, food eaten, drink consumed, and entertainment enjoyed.[59] In addition to penning this ballad, Barham published a profile of the club's most notable members, including publishers Richard Bentley, Thomas Longman, and John Murray.[60] Of course, who was excluded from club life was just as significant as who was included. A letter from author Marie Corelli to George Bentley highlights the professional hit taken by literary professionals—notably women—who were denied membership. On 30 April 1890, for example, Corelli writes to Bentley: 'Rudyard Kipling is a young mushroom growing on the roots of the Savile Club, and this is why he is elevated into a sudden 'Genius'—though of genius he has none', she complains.[61] Here, Corelli calls attention to the ways in which undeserving

---

56  'Club-Men', p. 284.
57  Joseph, 'Members Only', p. 123.
58  Percy Fitzgerald, 'The Garrick Club', *The New Century Review*, November 1899, p. 350.
59  Fitzgerald, 'The Garrick Club', pp. 350–351.
60  Richard Barham, 'Some Former Members of the Garrick Club', *The Bookman*, October 1894, pp. 13–14.
61  Qtd. in Annette R. Federico, *Idol of Suburbia: Marie Corelli and Late-Victorian Literary Culture* (Charlottesville: University of Virginia Press, 2000), p. 63.

men were elevated by these patriarchal clubs. Her critique would have been particularly pointed given Bentley's own association with the Garrick Club.

Beyond these ostensibly social spaces, publishers were starting to create and operate official organisations, which cemented their identity as a professional body. The *Publishers Circular*, a trade publication, which began in 1837, focused on topics and issues of interest to publishing professionals, such as the state of manufacturing as it related to book production, expanding markets for different types of books, and social events. London publishers were known to collectively invest in business ventures that benefited their industry, including Edward Petherick's Colonial Booksellers' Agency.[62] Annual dinners held at the Stationer's Hall, which was the historical home of London printers, publishers, and booksellers, brought together professionals from across the literary realm to make connections and discuss the state of the book trade. Printed seating charts for these events speak not only to their formality, but also showcase the same parameters of inclusion and exclusion as club membership—namely, only middle-and upper-class men were invited to attend.[63] These examples were seemingly precursors to the establishment of the United Kingdom's Publishers Association in 1896, which addressed three main concerns: copyright, the netbook agreement, and author-publisher relations.[64] Although predominantly administrative, the Association was characterised as an elite organisation overseen by prestigious literary figures. In an article on the Association in the *Athenaeum*, F. Francis Barry claims that the 'common society' served the 'interests' and 'the reputation of publishers as a whole'.[65] Comparing the Association to other professional bodies, such as the Incorporated Law Society, Barry envisions the Publishers Association as an organisation that handled all concerns regarding the industry and its practitioners, and emphasises the inherent trustworthiness of the organisation based on the nature of its membership: 'it should be made clear to all that the members of the Publishers' Association are men at once honourable and honest, always above the least suspicion of unfair dealing', he concludes.

This language—encompassing the assumption of honour and respectability, which was due to English gentlemen—explicitly places publishers in

---

62    See Alison Rukavina, 'A Victorian Amazon.com: Edward Petherick and his Colonial Booksellers' Agency', *Book History* 13 (2010), p. 108.

63    The Richard Bentley and Son Papers at University of California Los Angeles (UCLA) contains a number of seating charts for the Booksellers' Association Trade Dinner from the 1880s. See Box 3, Richard Bentley and Son Papers, UCLA.

64    'Our History', *Publishers Association* <https://www.publishers.org.uk/about-us/> (accessed 12 May 2021).

65    F. Francis Barry, 'The Publishers' Association', *The Athenaeum*, 9 May 1896, p. 621.

the upper echelons of society, where their authority is beyond question and their behaviour above reproach. Evidence suggests that publishers commonly utilised their position as gentlemen to claim the upper hand within professional relationships, particularly when it came to women or lesser-known authors. In correspondence between George Bentley and a poet identified as Miss Vaughan, who had accused the publisher of 'covert discourtesy and ridicule,' Bentley haughtily retorts that he had spoken to her as a 'gentleman to any lady'.[66] On another occasion, when an author identified as Miss Bewicke ventured to express opinions on the publication of her own works, Bentley informs her that 'when Ladies 'insist' they lose the advantage which is always yielded by gentlemen to their 'Wish', adding that he would 'decline to yield to a command'.[67] By invoking social rather than professional roles, Bentley reminds Vaughan and Bewicke of the hierarchy that governed their relations. Their challenges to the publisher's behaviour or decisions were dismissed out-of-hand based on his presumed gentlemanly authority and superiority.

## 4 Gender Politics and Power

The understanding and characterization of publishing as a gentlemen's activity and profession emerged throughout the nineteenth century and persisted well into the twentieth century. As Warburg's memoir attests, the strategic branding of publishers as manly, upper-class figures—liberally educated and intellectual, socially and culturally refined, honourable, and distinguished in both behaviour and appearance—was both widely adopted and enduring. This image of the publisher, combined with romanticised notions of nineteenth-century publishing houses as patriarchal and aristocratic institutions, whose work shaped the nation's cultural identity, dovetailed with an unprecedented expansion of the professional world beyond the traditional professions of law, medicine, and the clergy. A number of occupations—including publishing—were reborn as professions, whose prestige made them suitable pursuits for members of the upper-class and a vehicle of upwards mobility for middle-class men, as evidenced by articles that described various professions as 'gentlemen's professions'. This history of publishing as a masculinised, upper-class space provides essential context for investigations into women's participation in the industry. The social and cultural elevation of publishing

---

66   George Bentley to Miss Vaughan, 13 December 1878, MS 46644, Bentley Papers, British Library (BL).

67   George Bentley to Miss Bewicke, 7 July 1874, MS 46643, BL.

practice, and its location in the intellectual and professional spheres, excluded women and members of other marginalised groups. The weaving of gendered hierarchies into the industry's organisational structure ultimately created what Sylvia Walby has identified as a public patriarchy—a system whereby women are collectively separated from power, wealth, and influence within the working world.[68]

Indeed, questions surrounding power and influence within the publishing industry (e.g. who holds power, how is influence gained, used and maintained) ultimately serve to highlight the fact that presence is not synonymous with power. In other words, entering the industry, and gaining social, cultural, and economic authority within the industry, are not mutually inclusive processes. Crucially, the cultural history of publishing defines the environment that women publishing professionals still operate within today, even as women have proliferated throughout the industry. As Fiona Colgan and Frances Tomlinson report, in the same year (1988) where women made up 60 percent of the British publishing workforce overall, they were underrepresented in managerial positions, making up 40% of management and only 22 percent of company directorships. In comparison, men were only 40% of the industry overall, but occupied 60% of managerial roles and 78% of directorships. Essentially, this meant that women in publishing were low in the professional hierarchy, with many filling junior positions.[69] These statistics reflect the lived experiences of publishing professionals as it relates to gender politics and power. Despite author Stephen Birmingham's assertion in a 1971 *Cosmopolitan* article that women were 'finally beginning to make some inroads into what was once literally a man's world,' his observation that women in publishing in the mid-twentieth century were 'tweedy, deep-thinking, practically pipe smoking little wren[s]' is itself an example of the gender-based discrimination that women faced.[70] Birmingham's own interviewee, Nan Talese of Random House referred to women as 'a 'beleaguered race' in publishing': 'I'd certainly earn more if I were a man', she explains. 'The minute a woman applies for a job in this business ... the first question they ask is 'How long do you plan to stay?' They don't ask a man that—though plenty of men hop from job to job'.

Beyond a notable pay gap between men and women employees, it was the power inequalities that stood out, reflects Clare Baker, who worked as a sales

---

68    Sylvia Walby, *Theorizing Patriarchy* (Oxford: Basil Blackwell, 1989), p. 20.

69    Fiona Colgan and Frances Tomlinson, 'Women in Book Publishing—A 'Feminized' Sector?', in *Women in Organisations: Challenging Gender Politics*, eds. Sue Ledwith and Fiona Colgan (Basingstoke: Macmillan Business, 1996), pp. 44–48.

70    Stephen Birmingham, 'The Publishing Business: Still a Gentleman's Game?', *Cosmopolitan*, April 1971, p. 162.

representative for Routledge, Keagan Paul, and Cambridge University Press throughout the 1980s and 1990s. 'It was very much about the glass ceiling', she explains in an interview for the WiP's Oral History Project:

> because there were so many women in publishing why weren't we running the industry? We were more interested in the power aspect than the salary aspect ... it was certainly more about who gets promoted and why, and who goes on to run the company.[71]

Such disparities in power reflect long-held assumptions about the nature of femininity and women's resulting inability to operate rationally in the world of business. For example, Tommy Joy, once the President of the Booksellers' Association, notes that while women were capable employees, they were also ill-suited for leadership positions: 'I was very much a feminist ... I always thought women could do the job', he says. But 'I did sometimes wonder how far they were the best at the top, because they can act emotionally, which would cloud their judgement'.[72] Ironically, he goes on to note that women's emotions would prevent them from promoting appropriately, because promotions should be based on who can 'do the job' and not a manager's personal impressions of the employee.

The challenges that faced women in publishing in the twentieth century are hardly out of date. As Philip Jones observes in an article published in 2015, 'women tend to ... dominate the trade—from recent Booker winners, to best-selling commercial fiction, to agenting, to publishing, and finally (perhaps crucially) to readers ... It is more of a wonder, therefore, that all of the chief executives running our major trade publishing businesses are men'.[73] According to an article that appeared in *Publishers Weekly* in 2017, 51% of management roles are filled by men in an industry where 80% of the workforce is comprised of women.[74] The top positions, it seems, continue to elude the disproportionately women-dominated workforce that drives the industry. Additionally, women

---

71    Clare Baker, 'Clare Baker Discusses the Glass Ceiling and "Twice as Many, Half as Powerful"', 3 September 2018, in *Women in Publishing*, audio, 1:01 <http://www.womeninpublishing history.org.uk/content/interviewees/clare-baker/6-clare-baker-discusses-glass-ceiling-twice-many-half-powerful> (accessed 7 November 2018).

72    Qtd. in Bradley, *The British Book Trade*, p. 125.

73    Philip Jones, 'Generation xx', *Bookseller*, 13 February 2015 <https://www.thebookseller .com/blogs/generation-xx>.

74    Rachel Deahl, John Maher, and Jim Milliot, 'The Women of Publishing Say #MeToo', *Publishers Weekly*, 20 October 2017 <https://www.publishersweekly.com/pw/by-topic /industry-news/publisher-news/article/75175-sexual-harassment-is-a-problem-in-pub lishing.html>.

have been subject to more precarious employment conditions than their men peers. Colgan and Tomlinson observe that women's jobs are less stable during times of corporate restructuring and economic downturn.[75] In 1993, after a period of industry decline, they found that women represented only 53 % of the workforce, indicating that 'women working in publishing have been disproportionately affected' by the effort to create 'leaner' corporate structures. As Penny Mountain, former deputy editor of the *Bookseller* explains it, bad economic conditions drive publishing firms to put their companies in what they see as stable hands—'and those hands are seen as male.'[76] Such reflections on the gender bias, which is engrained within the publishing field and mediates women's movement within it, highlights the abiding impact of nineteenth-and twentieth-century efforts to define British publishing as a gentlemanly endeavour. If class and masculinity combined conferred value upon the publishing industry—encompassing publishing institutions, practices, and professionals—its quantitative and qualitative feminisation throughout the late-twentieth and twenty-first centuries have conversely coincided with a loss in cultural and economic capital for the industry, including its practitioners and output. The history of British publishing as a 'gentleman's profession', then, not only speaks to the branding of the industry as publishing industrialised and emerged as a corporate entity, but also underscores the gender politics that continue to shape publishing practice in the contemporary literary landscape.

---

75    Colgan and Tomlinson, 'Women in Publishing', pp. 48–51.
76    Qtd. in Harriet Marsden, 'A Gentleman's Profession? The Women Fighting for Gender Equality in Publishing', *Independent*, 6 April 2018 <https://www.independent.co.uk/arts -entertainment/books/features/women-publishing-gender-pay-gap-wage-british-library -hachette-penguin-random-house-a8285516.html>.

# PART 3

## *Editorial Interventions*

∴

# CHAPTER 8

# Mary Hays' *Female Biography* (1803), the Anthology, and Reading as Gendered Labour in the Early Nineteenth Century Book Trades

*Charley Matthews*

Feminist historiographers have identified the need for a 'major reconceptualization of labo[u]r history' in order to dismantle patriarchal historiographies.[1] Book historians such as Sarah Werner and Kate Ozment have begun this work within book history scholarship, considering how to establish a Feminist bibliographic practice.[2] This chapter argues for the importance of studying the history of reading in order to reconceptualise book trade labour and establish an inclusive book history discipline.

The marginal reader is an elusive figure for the historian of reading. I use 'marginal' here to indicate those historical agents who are pushed to the edges of book historical discourse, such as women and gender-nonconforming people, Black and minority ethnic people, disabled people and many others whose reading has been deprioritised in academic spaces. Women remain underrepresented in accounts of historical reading practices, despite indications that women's labour as publishers' readers and periodical reviewers significantly influenced nineteenth-century publication histories.[3] It is in the scribbled margins of history books that we perhaps find the most illuminating records, and this chapter will suggest how we might map this female book historical labour by examining a literary form often treated as marginal: the anthology.

---

1   Joan Wallach Scott, *Gender and the Politics of History* (New York City, NY: Columbia University Press, 1999), p. 53.

2   Sarah Werner, 'Working Toward a Feminist Printing History', *Printing History*, 27/28 (2020); and Kate Ozment, 'Rationale for Feminist Bibliography', *Textual Cultures*, 12 (2020), pp. 149–178.

3   See, for instance, work on Geraldine Jewsbury's influence on publishing cultures via both these roles. Jeanne Rosenmayer Fahnestock, 'Geraldine Jewsbury: The Power of the Publisher's Reader', *Nineteenth-Century Fiction*, 28 (1973), pp. 253–272; Monica Correa Fryckstedt, *Geraldine Jewsbury's* Athenaeum *Reviews: A Mirror of Mid-Victorian Attitudes to Fiction* (Uppsala: Acta Universitatis Upsaliensis, 1986).

The anthology is both the material evidence of this reading labour, and an indicator of how its own readers were expected to interact with text. The first section of this chapter maps the gendered history of the anthology and explores why the form is so useful to the historian of reading. The second section examines a case study in detail, arguing that the anthologising practices of Mary Hays (1759–1843) involved interventional reading practices that proactively influenced the early nineteenth-century London book trade, and encouraged the dissemination of knowledge across economic and class boundaries. The final section uses close textual analysis of Hays's *Female Biography* (1803) to suggest how these interventional reading practices functioned in her daily labour, and how they may have influenced her contemporary readers' interactions with the print cultures in which they were immersed.

## 1       Anthologies and Their History

Anthologies and anthologising practices are one relatively untapped source for examining women's reading labour. Leah Price has demonstrated the usefulness of researching anthologies in her study of the influence of anthologising practices on the development of the novel.[4] Her findings suggest that the bibliographic and intellectual influence of anthologies was far-reaching during this period. Price points out that anthologies 'determine not simply who gets published or what gets read, but who reads, and how,' effectually creating readerly communities and demographics by anticipating readers' tastes and textual interactions.[5] Likewise, William St Clair's foundational study of Romantic-period reading argues for the significance of the early nineteenth-century 'flood of verse and prose anthologies,' as their 'cultural effects on the reading of the Romantic period were to be immense.'[6] However, St Clair replicates nineteenth-century gendered assumptions about anthologies. When discussing the gift anthologies of the 1820s that became popular with the invention of marbled paper bindings, he states:

> I do not know if a time came when fathers, husbands, brothers or the printed-book industry began consciously to discourage women from

---

4  Leah Price, *The Anthology and The Rise of the Novel: From Richardson to George Eliot* (Cambridge: Cambridge University Press, 2000), pp. 11.
5  Price, *Anthology*, pp. 3.
6  William St Clair, *The Reading Nation in the Romantic Period* (Cambridge: Cambridge University Press, 2004), pp. 72.

keeping private manuscript commonplace books. But in the 1820s, we see the arrival of a new type of printed book.[7]

St Clair presents anthology reading as a passive form of consumption done uncritically and mainly by women. These statements assume a gendered binary between masculine production and feminine consumption, between masculine knowledge dissemination and feminine empty vessels waiting to be filled. This logic places men as the exclusive agents of history, even in the personal reading lives of women, and therefore as the cause of related developments in the book trade. He also presents a linear, binary narrative in which print replaces manuscript. Commonplace books are treated as evidence of passive reading, rather than active intervention into texts, and the printed anthology as a means to feed pre-digested knowledge to women.

However, David Allan has demonstrated that the printed anthology did not replace the commonplace book, but continued co-extensively.[8] Mark Towsey also complicates St Clair's gendered narrative in his study of a network of socially elite Scottish women who engaged in collective commonplacing practices and exchanged knowledge by circulating both manuscript excerpts and printed anthologies.[9] Towsey uses this example to demonstrate the fluidity of the divide between print and manuscript, but the case study is also telling about these women's active engagement in the transmission of texts. They copied out sections for one another, summarised texts before sending the full printed work, and swapped favourite volumes of texts out of order—visibly without the guiding hand of their 'fathers, husbands, and brothers.'[10] Considering the slippery division between anthologising and commonplacing, it is unsurprising that many women went on to compile anthologies during the early nineteenth century, and examining these published works may give us insight into the reading and working lives of these women. In compiling and editing, an anthologiser combines reading labour with writing labour, which challenges the artificial binary between production and consumption, as acts of reading are mobilised to produce new printed texts.

Although St Clair points out the 'immense' 'cultural effects' of early nineteenth-century anthologies, he does not go into detail about what these

---

7       St Clair, *Reading Nation*, pp. 229.
8       David Allan, *Commonplace Books and Reading in Georgian England* (Cambridge: Cambridge University Press, 2010), pp. 27.
9       Mark Towsey, "'I can't resist sending you the book": Private Libraries, Elite Women, and Shared Reading Practices in Georgian Britain', *Library & Information History*, 29 (2013), pp. 210–222.
10      Ibid.

effects are, which is perhaps because he does not consider them to be positive effects, or because they are effects that only touched marginal readers and which he therefore considers non-teleological to the history of the book trades or to nineteenth-century literary developments. But for the historian of mass reading practices, anthologies are revealing precisely because they were so abundant, which means that the surviving copies may suggest ways in which knowledge was disseminated en masse. For instance, the eighteenth and nineteenth centuries witnessed a key but often-overlooked trend in history writing: the biographical anthology, such as Pierre Bayle's famous and densely footnoted *Dictionary Historical and Critical* (1734). In the first half of the nineteenth century, a sub-genre emerged and became popular: anthologies focusing on women's lives, a genre that forms the basis of this paper's claims. There is no settled term for this category of works. They have productively been labelled 'collective biographies,' 'multibiography,' and 'biographical dictionaries,' but what they hold in common is their emphasis on women's social lives and the articulation of feminine character.[11] These texts were often in dialogue with other contemporary debates about femininity, particularly with the contentious topic of female education, and with the conduct books that were popular in the reactionary decades following the French revolution. These women-only anthologies were very often compiled and edited by women, and so can help us to trace the critical reading practices of their writers, as well as understanding them as models for other women's reading, as exemplars of the educatory practice advocated by some didactic works.

Many of these works are more accurately called 'collections' by modern definitions, as the text is often written by a single author. However, I choose to use the term anthologies to draw attention to the magpie nature of these texts; due to the exclusion of women from access to primary documentation housed behind the institutional barriers of the archive or the university, many of these works draw heavily on pre-existing histories and anthologies, collecting others' work in paraphrase or quotation. But this does not mean that they are simply derivative; the labour of reading, editing, re-shaping, and juxtaposition of texts that went into their creation shaped how these material objects functioned as transmitters of historical knowledge and value systems. Traditional book historiography and literary criticism have sometimes overlooked the analytical and

---

11      Sibyl Oldfield, *Collective Biography of Women in Britain, 1550–1900: A Select Annotated Bibliography* (London: Mansell, 1999), p. xii; Alison Booth, 'The Lessons of Medusa: Anna Jameson and Collective Biographies of Women', *Victorian Studies*, 42 (1999), p. 265; Helga Schwalm, 'Embedded Biographies in Interaction: Brief Lives in Dictionaries and Encyclopedias', ISECS Congress, 19 July 2019, University of Edinburgh.

even radical interventions made by these authors into their compiled texts, instead privileging the earliest version of a printed text.[12]

Considered in this light, these historical anthologies become overlooked sites of historiographical resistance to hegemonic history writing and an emerging body of scholarship understands women's authoring of women-centred biographical anthologies as an 'aggregate model of resistance to historical canons.'[13] Women's reading of history genres remains under-represented in the scholarly landscape of the history of reading, partly because women's history writing was itself under-represented in twentieth-century narratives of Romantic-era historiography. The eighteenth and nineteenth centuries witnessed an increasing division between 'professional' and 'amateur' history writing, which became tied to codes of masculine and feminine behaviour. The enclosure of 'professional' history research within institutions that excluded women, such as the university library and archive, created a gendered hierarchy of value within forms of historical writing, and 'claims of universality were accompanied by the elevation of men and the concomitant devaluation of women.'[14] Despite this, 'thousands of women pursued their calling as amateurs,' using whatever tools were at their disposal to imagine women's lives in past centuries, often in the form of biography.[15] Due to this association with women and amateurism, biographical writing remains 'the least studied and understood of the major literary genres.'[16] Literary representations that denigrate women's leisured reading have combined with the 'devaluation' of women's amateur history writing to encourage an ongoing critical vacuum around Romantic-era women reading and writing historical genres. Yet biography is a key feature in the history of reading, as 'readers come back and back to biography, ceaselessly seeking to understand the way human beings lived.'[17]

---

12    This preoccupation is rooted in early bibliography's debates around copy-texts and authenticity. See, for instance, W.W. Greg's foundational 'The Rationale of Copy-Text', in J.C. Maxwell (ed.) *Collected Papers* (Oxford: Clarendon, 1966), pp. 374–392. These assumptions have been challenged by the emergence of reader-response criticism and reception theory. See, for instance David Bleich's assertion of the subjective paradigm, which treats each reading experience as a text in itself; David Bleich, *Subjective Criticism* (Baltimore: Johns Hopkins University Press, 2019).

13    Booth, 'The Lessons of Medusa', p. 260.

14    Bonnie G. Smith, *The Gender of History: Men, Women, and Historical Practice* (Cambridge: Harvard University Press, 1998), pp. 4, 6.

15    Ibid.

16    Paula R. Backscheider, *Reflections on Biography* (Oxford: Oxford University Press, 1999), p. xiv.

17    Backscheider, *Reflections*, p. xii.

## 2      Mary Hays' Female Biography

Mary Hays' anthology *Female Biography* (1803) provides an illuminating study of how anthologising practices challenge traditional gendered models of Romantic-era reading and book production. Hays came from a Rational Dissenting family, and early in her adult life developed correspondences with various dissenting ministers, particularly Baptist minister Robert Robinson (1735–90) and Unitarian Joseph Priestley (1733–1804), who encouraged intellectual development and learning as part of a dutiful spiritual life. Like her friend Mary Wollstonecraft, Hays was a self-consciously 'revolutionary Feminist' and devoted promoter of women's education, and in her anthologising practices, Hays sought to model the educatory practice imagined by Wollstonecraft.[18]

Hays wrote unapologetically for a female readership, stating in her preface that 'my pen has been taken up in the cause, and for the benefit, of my own sex.'[19] She argues that women, 'unsophisticated by the pedantry of the schools, read not for dry information, to load their memories with uninteresting facts, or to make a vain display of erudition,' and therefore 'require pleasure to be mingled with instruction.'[20] The terms 'pedantry' and 'vain display of erudition' mirror accusations often levied at learned women during the period, from the ongoing anxiety about women acquiring superficial manners in order to attract men, and the double standard this logic entails. Hays turns this accusation towards masculine institutional spaces (the 'schools'), subverting the reader's expectation that has been preconditioned by feminine conduct books and thus inverting the value judgements that normally favoured men's reading practices. For Hays, 'narrative' reading, in contrast to scholarship, is an 'alternative, and not necessarily a lesser literacy.'[21]

Hays spent three years researching and writing this collection, drawing on a variety of sources, including monograph history and other biographical dictionaries written by men.[22] Hays cited the original French edition of Bayle's *Dictionnaire Historique et Critique* (1697) as both source and model in her

---

18    Andrew McInnes, 'Feminism in the Footnotes: Wollstonecraft's Ghost in Mary Hays' Female Biography', *Life Writing*, 8 (2011), pp. 273–285, at 273.

19    Mary Hays, *Female Biography; Or, Memoirs of Illustrious and Celebrated Women of all ages and countries. Alphabetically arranged in six volumes* (London: Richard Phillips, 71 St. Paul's Church-yard, 1803), vol. I, p. iii.

20    Hays, *Female Biography*, vol. I, p. iv.

21    Sarah Peterson Pittock, 'Mary Hays's *Female Biography*: Feminist Remix', *Women's Writing*, 25 (2018) p. 229.

22    Gary Kelly, *Women, Writing, and Revolution, 1790–1827* (Oxford: Oxford University Press, 1993), p. 237.

preface, and George Ballard's *Memoirs of Several Ladies* (1752) also features heavily. Hays would mostly have borrowed these books from the personal collections of her dissenting minister friends, and from private libraries around London.[23] She reworked this material, but also did primary research, such as interviewing a surviving family member for the entry on eighteenth-century historian Catharine Macaulay, a tactic Spongberg calls an 'innovative use of oral history,' and quoting verbatim from letters.[24] Hays scholar Sarah Peterson Pittock argues that her work in 'recontextualizing and repurposing' previously published material 'models critical literacy' for the female autodidact, encouraging them to think analytically about her sources.[25] For instance, in her entry on 'Philippa,' (wife of Edward III) she cites Hume's *History of England* as her major source, but is deeply sceptical of his main anecdote, in which Philippa saves the lives of the townspeople of Calais through 'tears and supplications' to her husband. Hays argues that this characterisation is 'romantic and ill-founded. It accords but little with the temper of the times ... Many extraordinary women appeared with lustre at this period, which was the reign of gallantry and chivalry.'[26] Hays relocates the site of 'gallantry' as female, typically critical of 'what she considered excessive displays of femininity in her subjects,' and her re-assessment of Hume's story models 'critical literacy' for her readers, encouraging them to participate intellectually in the creation of printed history.[27]

Importantly, Hays includes basic citations in the form of short lists of her sources at the end of entries. She is not consistent in this practice, but her specific use of citations also forms part of her model of critical literacy. The establishment of scholarly citation use is a slippery historical moment, difficult to pin to a specific moment in history. As Anthony Grafton points out, it has been assumed that the appearance of footnotes and related citational apparatus 'separates historical modernity from tradition,' but closer study makes this assertion 'less secure' because there were varied and conflicting practices used by writers from classical times until the early twentieth century.[28] This is particularly true of the biographical dictionary; as Helga Schwalm recently argued,

---

23    Gina Luria Walker, 'General Introduction', in Gina Luria Walker (ed.), *Memoirs of Women Writers* (London: Pickering & Chatto, 2014), vol. 5, p. xvii; Mary Spongberg, 'Appendix 2: The Sources of *Female Biography*', in Gina Luria Walker (ed.), *Memoirs of Women Writers* (Pickering & Chatto, 2014), vol. 10, p. 539.

24    Spongberg, 'Appendix', p. 542.

25    Pittock, 'Mary Hays', p. 220.

26    Hays, *Female Biography*, vol. 6, pp. 58–59.

27    Spongberg, 'Appendix', p. 541.

28    Anthony Grafton, *The Footnote: A Curious History* (London: Faber, 1997), pp. 24–25.

the form expanded and contracted its use of footnotes multiple times during the eighteenth century.[29] This is partly in response to the eighteenth-century shift from intensive (focused, linear) reading to extensive (ephemeral, inter-referential) reading as 'texts began to be treated as commodities.'[30] *The Biographia Brittanica* (1747–1766), for instance, proliferates with intertextual and evaluative footnotes and marginal notes, sometimes so many to a page that only a few lines of original text remain, so that 'the weight of peritexts threatens to explode the centrality of the original text,' and the reader is sent on a 'paper chase' through the volumes.[31] In response, *The Beauties of Biography* (1777) was subtitled 'In which all superfluous matter is avoided, and everything interesting, entertaining, or curious carefully preserved,' and eliminated footnotes. The peritexts are condensed into a single narrative, attempting to re-establish intensive reading and 'create a spirit of emulation.'[32] In this context, by including brief citations at the end of narrative entries, Hays carefully balances the historiographical need to cite, with an unencumbered narrative style that allows immersive, emulative reading. Her anticipated women readers are offered a choice of reading style—intensive or extensive—as Hays' formal choices make reading for narrative pleasure or moral instruction and to follow a 'paper chase' equally possible. Just as her critical literacy model encourages active participation, her citation practices permit slippage between styles of reading history at a moment of change in both dominant reading practices and the social enclosure of professional history research.

Bibliographic form also plays a key role in Hays' print project. In the early 1800s, Hays' publisher Richard Phillips was known for being a radical publisher with revolutionary sympathies, frequently writing anti-government periodical contributions, and prosecuted in 1793 for disseminating Thomas Paine's *Rights of Man*, so it is perhaps unsurprising that Hays chose him to publish her 'revolutionary feminism.'[33] Some of Hays' literary friends were nervous about her decision to publish with the Republican Phillips, voicing the ongoing anxiety around mass literacy. When she was still a year away from publishing, Henry Crabb Robinson cautioned her in a letter, 'Is he increasing in

---

29   Schwalm, 'Embedded Biographies'.

30   Robert Darnton, 'What is the History of Books?', in Michelle Levy and Tom Mole (eds.), *The Broadview Reader in Book History* (Peterborough: Broadview, 2015), p. 246.

31   Schwalm, 'Embedded Biographies'.

32   *The Beauties of Biography* (London: Printed for G. Kearsley, 1777), title page.

33   Thomas Seccombe, 'Phillips, Sir Richard (1767–1840)', revised by M. Clare Loughlin-Chow, *Oxford Dictionary of National Biography* (Oxford University Press, 3 January 2008) <www.oxforddnb.com> (accessed 13 June 2019).

respectability? ... I confess I feel ashamed to have any thing [sic] to do with him.'[34] Aside from publishing the successful *Monthly Magazine*, Phillips' biographer argues his main importance was 'as a purveyor of cheap miscellaneous literature designed for popular instruction.'[35] Hays and Phillips were neighbours, so she likely understood or even directed the material packaging of her work.[36] The six volumes of *Female Biography* were printed in duodecimo, each volume easily read in one hand, a significant departure from previous biographical dictionaries. Ballard's *Memoirs*, for instance, was printed in a large quarto format, with lots of white space and luxury features, such as decorative page breaks and excerpts set in contrasting type. Hays' contemporary rival, Matilda Betham's *A biographical dictionary of the celebrated women of every age and country* (1804), was printed in a thick, single-volume octavo, with a full-page frontispiece by respected engraver James Hopwood. These high-end productions established the works as exclusive sites of knowledge, destined for the aristocratic or upper-middle-class library, unlike the small and plain volumes of *Female Biography*. Materially, the work more closely resembles the cheap didactic fiction of writers like Hannah More and Mary Pilkington than the weighty tomes of her sober historical sources. This suggests Hays wished to covertly extend historical knowledge to women from the lower-income middle classes like herself, packaging the text to mimic the conservative didactic literature considered suitable for lower-income women.

The price matched this intended readership. The work was advertised in Phillips' *Monthly Magazine* as a set of 'six large volumes' for '1l 11s 6d.'[37] According to Richard Altick, the average price for a single duodecimo volume at the time was around six shillings, which places the combined price for the set at slightly less than the average price for that format. To put this into context in the book trade, Scott's early poem *Lays of the Minstrel* (1805), sold over 15,000 copies over three years, and cost £1 5s for the single volume. Standard entry fees to subscription libraries grew from three to five pounds in the 1780s to around twenty in the 1820s.[38] The six volumes of Hays' work were not as cheap as pamphlets and tracts, but an example of history writing made specifically affordable to the kind of lower-income middle-class readers that used these libraries.

---

34  Henry Crabb Robinson, letter to Mary Hays, 26 January 1802 <www.maryhayslifewriting
    scorrespondence.com> (Accessed 13 June 2019).

35  Seccombe, 'Phillips, Sir Richard'.

36  Robinson, fn. 1.

37  'List of New Publications in November', *Monthly Magazine, or, British Register*, 14, no. 94
    (December 1802) pp. 446–450, at pp. 446. Proquest Historical Periodicals.

38  Richard D. Altick, *The English Common Reader: A Social History of the Mass Reading Public,
    1800–1900* (Columbus, OH: Ohio State University Press, 1998), pp. 260–262.

Hays makes clear that she understood the impact of printed anthologies on reorganising and prioritising knowledge. In the preface to her later anthology, *Memoirs of Queens* (1821), she writes, 'the invention of printing, the consequent diffusion of literature and extension of education, necessarily leads to a new order of things.'[39] A contemporary reader may have been sensitive to the phrasing 'new order of things' during decades that saw protests and reforms across the country. For Hays, middle-class women's reading is not only privately useful for developing domestic sensibilities, but a rebellious act with social consequences. This disdain for normative hierarchies is reflected in the textual organisation of *Female Biography*; Hays stands out as the first to organise a women's history anthology alphabetically.[40] Where most anthologies of the period formed a guided course of study, the dictionary form forces the female autodidactic reader's active participation in the text through choice. Alphabetisation imposes a visibly arbitrary organisational structure on the collection, destabilising any notion of hierarchy within the subjects, and encouraging referential and non-linear reading patterns. The reader must choose the 'new order of things' for herself.

Hays' project in *Female Biography* is to create a 'virtual academy,' a kind of forum in which women could speak to one another across history; many biographical entries emphasised women's intellectual achievements, citing their works and allowing this work to speak for its original author.[41] This also meant including entries that 'extended existing definitions of female worth.'[42] Previous compendia of women's lives largely focused on particular themes, usually a particular feminine virtue; piety was an especially popular one, as it conveniently also demonstrated codes of reserved femininity that complemented the conduct books of conservative writers such as Fordyce, whilst justifying reading through the trope of scriptural study.[43] Hays, in contrast, includes the pious and impious, the rebel and the monarch. As we will see in the final section, Hays shifts her narrative tone from moralistic to literary critical, making it very difficult to draw a code of conduct or ethical framework from her collected examples of womanhood. The primary common factor is instead an emphasis on women who read and write, rooted in the Wollstonecraftian impulse to promote women's voices in the public intellectual sphere. French

---

39   Mary Hays, *Memoirs of Queens, illustrious and celebrated* (London: T. and J. Allman, 1821), p. vii.
40   Mathilda Betham may have called her version a 'dictionary', but it is not actually alphabetical.
41   Spongberg, 'Appendix', p. 538.
42   Pittock, 'Mary Hays', p. 229.
43   Spongberg, 'Appendix', p. 538.

Revolutionary writer Manon Roland and Republican historian Catherine Macaulay, for example, both receive lengthy and carefully researched entries. Both these women enjoyed literary celebrity in the eighteenth and early nineteenth centuries, Roland as *salonnière* and political commentator and Macaulay as writer of narrative history. Both also lived controversial lives, Madame Roland as Jacobin activist, and Macaulay by scandalously marrying a much younger man.

These types of morally complex figures caused problems for some reviewers. Lucy Aikin, a fellow Dissenter and otherwise relatively sympathetic reader of Hays' work, wrote in a letter to a friend:

> Though Miss Hayes [sic] has wisely addressed herself to the ladies alone, I am afraid the gentlemen will peep at her book and repeat with tenfold energy that women have no business with anything but nursing children and mending stockings ... A general biography is something like a great London rout, everybody is there, good, bad and indifferent, visitable and not visitable, so that a squeamish lady scarcely knows whom she may venture to speak to.[44]

Although Aikin is critical of the inclusion of certain women, it is striking that she writes about the anthology (or 'general biography') using an image of physical space ('a great London rout'), as a forum in which socially diverse characters could meet. Reading is bound up with the social standing and respectability of the text's subject matter and voice. Hays understands the anthology as a socio-intellectual forum or coterie in which the reader is 'visited' by the subjects, revealed by her emphasis on women's voices through quoting from her subjects' works. For instance, revolutionary writer Manon Roland's 210-page entry is mostly formed of verbatim quotations from her memoirs and letters, edited and shaped into a clear narrative entry. The 'amateur' form of the biographical dictionary, as well as her explicit address to women, materially camouflages the radical voice being quoted.

## 3    Case Study: Mary Astell and Narratological Innovation

A revealing case study that supports this view of Hays' print project as a socially-extended 'visitable' space is Hays' entry on Mary Astell. Mary Astell

---

44    Lucy Aikin, *Memoirs, miscellanies and letters of Lucy Aikin*, Philip Hemery Le Breton (ed.) (London: Longman, Roberts and Green, 1864), p. 126.

(1666–1731) was an essayist who argued that charges of vanity and superficiality laid against women were due to women's lack of education.[45] In her ground-breaking treatise, *A Serious Proposal to the Ladies* (1694), Astell advocated the establishment of a female-only secular seminary where unmarried women could retire from the 'hurry and noise of the world' and develop their critical faculties on a basis of intellectual equality with one another.[46] Hays lists Astell's publications and their printed signature format, suggesting again that awareness of knowledge as materially produced and marking Astell's own words as valuable.[47] For the entry on Astell, Hays drew heavily on George Ballard's *Memoirs of Several Ladies* (1752), a collective biography that presents examples of what the author considers ideal and pious feminine lives. Hays rewrites Ballard's narrative along with occasional details from original research.[48] Hays's entry is much shorter than Ballard's, because he includes lengthy quotations from other writers that lay various judgments on Astell's skills as a writer and her feminine conduct, whereas Hays excises these passages and retains sections from Astell's own writing, letting her words speak across the intervening century without Ballard's mediating para-texts written mainly by men.

This stripping away of the mediating voice becomes part of the text's granular narratological construction. Harnessing methodologies pioneered by recent historians of reading can reveal subtle ways in which Hays interacts with her audience's reading practices through narratological innovation. Elspeth Jajdelska has modelled an analytical technique that relates narrative style to historical reading practices. In *Silent Reading and the Birth of the Narrator*, she documents an eighteenth-century shift from reading aloud to silent reading as the dominant reading practice in Britain. By examining the ways in which novels were abridged, she shows how this shift in reading practices shaped prose style. Many writers increased punctuation use, in order to introduce pauses in reading pace to allow the silent reader to make sense of the text, pauses that were previously supplied for the listening audience by the intonation of the storyteller reading aloud. She also documents the introduction of an

---

45    Mary Astell, *A Serious Proposal to the Ladies* (1694), ed. Sharon L. Jansen (Steilacoom: Saltar's Point Press, 2014), p. 58.

46    Astell, *Proposal*, p. 62.

47    As in, whether a book is printed in folio, quarto, octavo etc. This is partly an indication of the quality and likely cost of a book, as folios were generally much bigger and pricier than quartos or octavos.

48    For instance, she references Astell's year studying at the Royal Observatory in Greenwich, not included in Ballard's account. Hays' source for this remains unknown (*Memoirs of Women Writers*, p. 446, note to p. 216).

'anchor'—a narrator from a stable point in time and space outside the events of the narrative. This 'anchor' takes the place of a real-life vocal storyteller and provides a consistent spatial point of reference from which to comprehend the changing scene, helping the reader make sense of the narrative by easing spatial and temporal transitions.[49]

Analysis of Hays' narrative techniques using Jajdelska's methodology reveals that her writing style encourages the reader to understand her anthology space as an imagined Astellian intellectual seminary. Hays interacts phenomenologically with reading practices of the period by encoding a spoken interpretation of the anthology into her prose style, re-arranging sentence structure in order to conjure the voices of her subjects. For example, when describing why Astell chose to write her treatise on women's education, Ballard wrote:

> The learning and knowledge which she had gained, together with her great benevolence and generosity of temper, taught her to observe and lament the loss of it in those of her own sex: the want of which, as she justly observed, was the principal cause of their plunging themselves into so many follies and inconveniences.[50]

Hays reworked this idea as:

> From having experienced in the study of letters a fruitful source of independent pleasure, she became solicitous to impart to her sex the satisfaction she enjoyed, to raise the general character of women, and to rescue them from ignorance and frivolity. In a defective education, she was persuaded, was to be found the true cause of those frailties and follies absurdly attributed to sex.[51]

The content change is clear: whilst for Ballard 'follies and inconsistencies' are bound up with femininity, Hays sees them as a product of a 'defective education.' But she also complexly reworks the narrative, reframing the educational aim from Astell's perspective. In line with Jajdelska's observations, the thought is broken into two sentences to help the reader more fluently follow the sense. But more importantly, the subordinate phrase 'as she justly observed' becomes

---

49    Elspeth Jajdelska, *Silent Reading and the Birth of the Narrator* (Toronto: University of Toronto Press, 2007), pp. 47–48, 181, 184.

50    George Ballard, *Memoirs of Several Ladies of Great Britain* (London: Printed by W. Jackson, for the author, 1752), pp. 445–446.

51    Hays, *Female Biography*, vol. 1, p. 214.

'she was persuaded.' A phrase that Ballard uses to insert his own judgment on Astell's writing becomes an overt intervention from a seemingly neutral narrator who remains outside the action or intentionality of an otherwise subjective sentence. This grammatical sleight-of-hand creates a seemingly objective but sympathetic 'anchor' (the unknown narrator) from which the reader understands Astell's story, and leads the reader through Astell's thought process, rather than the anthologist's. This prompts the reader to hear the surrounding sentences in the imagined voice of Mary Astell. 'To raise the general character of women, and to rescue them from ignorance and frivolity' is a mimetic embedding of Astell's voice and critical judgements into the third-person prose of the entry.

This technique presages the free indirect discourse that was pioneered by Jane Austen and became so important to nineteenth century novels. Gina Luria Walker has demonstrated that Austen had access to a copy of *Female Biography* at her sister-in-law's house, where she often stayed when writing.[52] Austen may have been influenced by Hays' narrative experiments when honing her own novelistic style. Austen's style 'imagines author and reader, not as master and slave (or vice versa), nor as connate twins ... but as related,' because the voice of the narrator mimics her characters in a way that might be done when speaking to an intimate friend.[53] Likewise, Hays' embedded mimesis of her subjects' voices constructs a friendly relationship between narrator and reader, unlike the hierarchical relationship created in Ballard's anthology-as-moral-didacticism. The reader is invited to participate in intellectual history on a basis of equality between reader and narrator, a narrative framing that may have been appealing to writerly women like Austen. Similarly, life-writing scholar Felicity James notes that Mary Heywood Gaskell owned a copy of *Female Biography* and often remembered Hays as biographer in her letters. Perhaps Gaskell's more famous relative, Elizabeth Gaskell, borrowed the 'immediacy and boldness of Hay's biographical and autobiographical practices' for *The Life of Charlotte Brontë* (1857).[54]

*Female Biography* resembles a print manifestation of Astell's all-women intellectual space, prioritising not just female lives but female voices. Unlike Ballard's visibly male-authored 'memoirs' that survey women from history critically, Hays harnesses the narratological possibilities afforded by changing

---

52    Walker, 'General Introduction', p. xiv.

53    Bharat Tandon, *Jane Austen and the Morality of Conversation* (Anthem, 2003), p. 25.

54    Felicity James, 'Writing Female Biography: Mary Hays and the Life Writing of Religious Dissent', in Daniel Cook and Amy Culley (eds.), *Women's Life Writing: gender, Genre and Authorship* (London: Palgrave, 2012), p. 132.

reading practices in order to create an Astellian space in which women can speak to one another and produce knowledge through intellectual exchange. This model is reliant on the heterogeneous potential of the 'self-effacing' anthology, which produces an ostensibly neutral space for contrasting women to speak for themselves.[55] Hays' model of reading as productive and requiring active, socially disruptive participation is transgressive to conservative nineteenth-century models of passive women's reading. She even challenges Wollstonecraft's 'vocabularies of duty and discipline' to create 'affectionate wives and rational mothers,' as she shifts focus away from women's participation in a male-dominated society, and towards a gynocentric, egalitarian space that was imagined by Astell a century earlier.[56]

## 4    Conclusions

Hays's anthologising practices were not a form of passive consumption, as assumed by St Clair, but an active intervention into the early nineteenth-century book trade by covertly making radical histories available to lower-income women, and responding to and shaping readerly practices by means of narratological innovation and by following 'revolutionary' bibliographic choices. Her collaboration with her publisher represents just one example of how conceptualising book trade labour through the lens of the history of reading could shift our understanding of print culture's economic, social, and literary processes. Treating the anthology as evidence of these kinds of interventions can produce striking insights into book trade histories, particularly when reconsidering assumed binaries between reading and writing, print and manuscript, active labour and leisure activity, and production and consumption. By considering reading as labour, we uncover a rich seam for reassessing women's contributions to the book trade.

---

55    Price, *Anthology*, p. 3.
56    Vivien Jones, 'Wollstonecraft and the literature of advice and instruction', in Claudia L. Johnson (ed.) *The Cambridge Companion to Mary Wollstonecraft*, (Cambridge: Cambridge University Press, 2002), p. 138; Mary Wollstonecraft, *A Vindication of the Rights of Woman* (1792), Miriam Brody (ed.) (London: Penguin, 2004), p. 11.

# CHAPTER 9

# Constantia Grierson's Ghost and the Problem of Posthumous Print

*Helen Williams*

## 1 Introduction

Constantia Grierson was a polymath, a 'great genius', to borrow the words of her friend, the poet Mary Barber.[1] She was a woman openly participating in three distinct sectors of the male-dominated public sphere of eighteenth-century Ireland: classical scholarship, poetry, and the book trade, as a printer and corrector of the press. To be a female printer in this period, like being a female scholar and poet, was to transcend the usual gender boundaries.[2] Grierson's printing house expertise combined with her poetry and textual editing meant that, for contemporary commentators, she exemplified a singular kind of womanhood characterised by a combination of unsurpassed virtue and industry. As Paul Hiffernan would write in *The Hiberniad* (1754), Constantia Grierson was 'an extraordinary Phaenomenon'.[3]

Grierson's gendered family legacy has been explored by Lisa Marie Griffith, who demonstrates her role in retaining the family's near 140-year tenure as King's Printer in Ireland. As she remarks, in subsequent generations, 'the intellectual legacy of Constantia was called upon to prove respectability'.[4] This essay echoes Griffith's concern with the uses of Grierson's reputation but looks beyond its impact on the family's upward mobility. Rather than focus on how the poetry—or rather the idea of poetry—helped the Grierson family curate a book trade brand of quality literary heritage, I explore how the instability of the Grierson canon emerges as a result of two of the standard means by which female manuscript poets tended to end up in print: exploitation by

---

1  I would like to thank the Interlibrary Loans team at Northumbria University for their assistance in this project, as well as the librarians of Pennsylvania, Kansas and Emory Universities for supplying digital images in an extraordinarily efficient and generous manner. Mary Barber, *Poems on Several Occasions* (London: Rivington, 1734), p. xxix.
2  Lisa Marie Griffith: 'Mobilising Office, Education and Gender in Eighteenth-Century Ireland: The Case of the Griersons', *Eighteenth-Century Ireland*, 22 (2007), p. 76, n. 73.
3  Paul Hiffernan, *The Hiberniad* (Dublin, 1754), p. 31.
4  Griffith, 'Mobilising Office,' pp. 64–65.

a bookseller and friends' and families' desires to create a monument to the deceased author.[5] Some indication of Grierson's somewhat paradoxical standing as obscure genius is demonstrated by the fact that this is the first piece of scholarship—article, chapter, or book—to treat Grierson as its main focus. Here, I argue that the inherently gendered Grierson brand—the idea of the female printer-poet—has shaped and misshaped her poetry and our understanding of her (place within the) literary canon.

## 2    A Literary Legacy

Grierson was born Constantia Crawley into a poor, illiterate Irish-speaking Catholic family in County Kilkenny in 1705.[6] Without any formal schooling, with the help of the parish priest, she learned history, literature, philosophy and mathematics. She then moved to Dublin to be apprenticed to the first man-midwife in Ireland, Jan Van Lewen, the father of budding poet Laetitia Van Lewen, soon to be Laetitia Pilkington. In Dublin, she befriended Pilkington, joined the literary circle of Jonathan Swift, and became celebrated for her poetic talents. She was one of the 'Senatus Consultum' which, according to Pilkington, revised Mary Barber's poetry for the press, a group including Matthew Pilkington, Swift, and Mary and Patrick Delany. Fluent in Latin, Greek and Hebrew as well as modern languages, in the 1720s Grierson worked as proofreader and editor at the press of George Grierson in return for access to his impressive library. When George Grierson's first wife died in 1726, he and Constantia married. By this stage she had already begun producing classical scholarship, having published her edition of Virgil in 1724, which would be followed by editions of Terence (1727) and Tacitus (1730), all of which became central to the standard eighteenth-century schoolboy's education on both sides of the Irish sea.[7]

---

5  Margaret J.M. Ezell, 'Posthumous Publications of Women's Manuscripts and the History of Authorship', in Nathan Tinker and George Justice (eds.), *Early Modern Women writers and the Circulation of Ideas* (Cambridge: Cambridge University Press, 2002), pp. 126–27.

6  Laetitia Pilkington, *Memoirs of Laetitia Pilkington*, A.C. Elias Jr. (ed) (Athens, GA: University of Georgia Press, 1997), vol. I, p. 17; Edith Hall and Henry Stead, *A People's History of Classics: Class and Greco-Roman Antiquity in Britain and Ireland 1689 To 1939* (London: Routledge, 2020), p. 234.

7  For example, Joseph Stock selected Grierson's as the most accurate text for his 1787 edition of Tacitus: *C. Cornelii Taciti opera ad fidem editionis Parisinæ Gab. Brotier ... illustravit Josephus Stock*, 4 vols (Dublin, 1787–88), p. 4552.

Alongside Grierson's role as a professional printer, textual editor and compositor, she wrote poetry. We know of only two poems that she published in print in her lifetime, a Latin epigraph to the son of John Carteret, Lord Lieutenant of Ireland, and an anonymous pamphlet in defence of her friend Patrick Delany, the popular Irish priest, against the implication—by Swift and others—that he was sycophantic towards Carteret. She circulated her poetry in manuscript within her coterie, and it would only appear under her name in print posthumously in Barber's *Poems on Several Occasions* (1735) and the notorious *Memoirs of Mrs. Laetitia Pilkington* (1748).[8]

Eighteenth-century women writers working across print and manuscript have suffered from a misperception that they were, firstly, exceptional in their focus on manuscript production and, secondly, that those writings were 'subordinate and preliminary' to their printed works.[9] Grierson's careers as both printer and poet make her a perfect case for destabilising those perceptions, demonstrating the ongoing symbiosis of two worlds: the eighteenth-century book trade and manuscript circulation. Recent work by Betty Schellenberg and Margaret Ezell has sought to correct the assumption that women producing manuscript verse were simply 'cultural victims who lacked the nerve, will, or means' to print.[10] Grierson did not want any of those things, though she did carefully curate the materials that made it into print. Grierson was, in a sense, a perfect paradox which summed up the delicate line toed by female poets in this period. She was a poet who had retained her feminine respectability by largely restricting her works to manuscript circulation. But she was also a partner to her husband in the book trade, contributing to the family business as printer, typesetter and editor. This printed work and the scholarship she produced was, like her poetry, unsigned, and through its wide circulation brought a respectable renown to the 'George Grierson' brand and came to be recognised as her own work. Thus Grierson had a reputation as the ideal learned woman: the anonymous scholar who appeared in print intended for the scholarly edification of the masses, and manuscript poet circulating poetry which signalled her taste and elegance for the private amusement of friends.

Grierson composed and disseminated her poetry within a manuscript world, or what Margaret Ezell has called 'a nonprint literary culture', independent of

---

8      A. C. Elias, 'A Manuscript Book of Constantia Grierson's', *Swift Studies: The Annual of the Ehrenpreis Center*, 2 (1987), pp. 33–56.

9      Betty Schellenberg, *Literary Coteries and the Making of Modern Print Culture: 1740–1790* (Cambridge: Cambridge University Press, 2016), p. 5.

10     Ezell, 'Posthumous Publications', pp. 121–36, 124.

the conventions and constraints of commercial print.[11] Much of it is addressed to friends, arising from her participation first in the circle around Delany and then, through him, that of Swift. As Betty Schellenberg points out, literary coteries provided intermediation points between print and manuscript, including participants who straddled both cultures.[12] The institution of the coterie helped organise literary production long into the eighteenth century, fostering 'a culture in which the media of script and print, with their distinctive practices and priorities, were nevertheless in close conversation, sometimes interdependent, sometimes mutually antagonistic, but between them offering a rich array of options for literary expression, exchange, and preservation'.[13] Schellenberg makes clear that this was a gendered system: for eighteenth-century women writers, 'systems of scribal exchange were used to construct and underwrite cultural power and how that power was used, often to enhance print productions'.[14] All but two of Grierson's poems—or poems reputed to have been written by her—would appear in print posthumously, published by her friends and family in a bid to further their own careers.

Grierson's work has been most often considered for what it tells us about Swift rather than for its own inherent value, though scholarship by Paula Backsheider, Margaret Ann Doody, and Catherine Ingrassia has been important in bringing the work of Swift's 'triumfeminate' to contemporary readers.[15] But in her own lifetime and in the decades that followed Grierson was recognised as a talented poet. *The Grubstreet Calvacade* (1727), an anonymous ballad, satirically targets Grierson's poetic reputation during her lifetime by reminding

11    Margaret J.M. Ezell, *Social Authorship and the Advent of Print* (Baltimore, MD: Johns Hopkins University Press, 1999), pp. 22, 24.

12    Schellenberg, *Literary Coteries*, p. 3.

13    Schellenberg, *Literary Coteries*, p. 2. See also Moyra Haslett, *From Pope to Burney, 1714–1779* (Basingstoke: Palgrave, 2003), pp. 12–13.

14    Schellenberg, *Literary Coteries*, p. 15.

15    Bernard Tucker, '"Our Chief Poetess": Mary Barber and Swift's Circle', *The Canadian Journal of Irish Studies*, 19 (1993), pp. 31–44; Paula Backsheider, 'Inverting the Image of Swift's "Triumfeminate"', *Journal for Early Modern Cultural Studies*, 4 (2004), pp. 37–71; Paula R. Backsheider, *Eighteenth-Century Women Poets and Their Poetry: Inventing Agency, Inventing Genre* (Baltimore, MD: Johns Hopkins University Press, 2008), p. xx; 209; 386; Margaret Ann Doody, 'Swift among the Women', *Pope, Swift, and Their Circle*, special issue of *The Yearbook of English Studies*, 18 (1998), pp. 68–92; Bernard Tucker, '"Swift's 'Female Senate": Three Forgotten Poets', *Irish Studies Review*, 2.7 (1994), pp. 7–10; Catherine Ingrassia, '"Who Praises Women Does the Muses Praise": Mary Barber, Laetitia Pilkington, and Constantia Grierson's Poetic Tributes', in Laura L. Runge and Jessica Cook (eds.), *The Circuit of Apollo: Eighteenth-Century Women's Tributes to Women* (Charlottesville, VA: University of Virginia Press, 2019), pp. 87–103.

us of her medical apprenticeship, suggesting that she was at this point 'no less famous for her Poetical Productions, than for her Skill in Midwifery'.[16] Emerging at a time when only one of Grierson's poems had appeared in print, the satire suggests how far manuscript publishing was central to Grierson's poetic practice and to her literary reputation. Grierson herself identified as a skilled poet capable of capturing life in art, as indicated by the afterlife for her son that she crafts in the poem 'Unhappy Child to Early Sorrows Born', who 'With other infants shan't forgotten Ly | But by the Muse snatch'd fro' the dismal herse | Still Live In thy unhappy Mother's Verse'.[17] However, her poetry is currently out of print, and scholars tackling Grierson's oeuvre are faced with ambiguity and misrepresentation.[18]

## 3    The Politics of Printing Barber's *Poems*

The first printed appearance of poetry signed by Grierson was three years after her death, in 1735, in Mary Barber's *Poems on Several Occasions*. Though its title-page announces a 1734 publication date, multiple factors, primarily Barber's health, had delayed its appearance.[19] It was a plea for survival. Barber was in her fifties, suffering from debilitating gout and asthma, and aiming to survive though her own means since her marriage to a 'ne'er-do-well' merchant.[20] As Adam Budd has shown, Barber's impressive subscription list did not translate into a handsome return.[21] Beyond its initial appearance, the quarto volume of Barber's poetry still needed to appeal to subscribers, in a bid to encourage them to relinquish their promised money for the volume, and to sell it more widely.

Barber's project of making her volume more saleable included both anthologising poetry by other admired poets and including in her preface a

16    *The Grubstreet Cavalcade, or, The Hungry Poets Petition, Humbly Dedicated to a certain Great Man* (Dublin: Waters, 1727).

17    Constantia Grierson, 'The Miscellaneous Poems of Constantia Grierson', Kislak Center for Special Collections, Rare Books and Manuscripts, University of Pennsylvania Libraries, MS. Codex 1825, ff. 6r–7r.

18    The most recent edition of her work is Bernard Tucker, (ed.), *The Poetry of Laetitia Pilkington (1712–1750) and Constantia Grierson (1706–1733)*, Studies in British Literature 20 (Lewiston: NY: Edwin Mellen, 1996). She also appears in Roger Lonsdale, ed., *Eighteenth-Century Women* Poets (Oxford: Oxford University Press, 1989), pp. 91–93.

19    Sarah Prescott, *Women, Authorship and Literary Culture, 1690–1740* (Basingstoke: Palgrave, 2003), p. 131.

20    Elias, *Memoirs*, vol. 2., p. 392.

21    Adam Budd, '"Merit in Distress": The Troubled Success of Mary Barber', *Review of English Studies*, 53 (2002), pp. 204–227.

commendatory verse by her well-respected friend, Grierson. Christopher
Fanning has described Grierson's as one of several 'voices' of Barber.[22] Grierson
and Barber made a compelling duet. Barber's trade background, being the
wife of a woollen-draper, meant that with Grierson she shared a rare position
as a female working class poet. Barber recognised an appetite for more public knowledge about her friend, providing in the opening pages of her work
the first biography of Grierson. Much of it is dedicated to how, together, the
Griersons were awarded the royal patent of King's Printer in Ireland, giving
them the sole licence to publish Bibles and official government documentation. The patent was the first in Ireland to name a woman, explicitly citing
Constantia Grierson's work as a primary motivation for its award:

> Petitioner Constantia hath, in a more particular Manner, applied herself
> to the Correcting of the Press which she has performed to the general
> Satisfaction; insomuch, that the Editions corrected by her are held in
> great Esteem in Great Britain, Holland, and elsewhere, and the Art of
> Printing through her Care and Assistance, has been brought to greater
> Perfection than has been hitherto in this Kingdom.[23]

Barber's memoir would be much reprinted, and Grierson became, according
to one early twentieth-century commentator, a 'heroine of bookselling' and
a 'romantic figure in the printing trade', with her mastery of print technology
popularised by Barber:[24]

> I persuade my self that this short Account of so extraordinary a Woman,
> of whom much more might have been said, will not be disagreeable to
> my Readers; nor can I omit mentioning what I think is greatly to the Lord
> CARTERET's honour, that when He was Lord Lieutenant of Ireland, He
> obtained a Patent for Mr. Grierson her Husband to be the King's Printer,
> and to distinguish and reward her uncommon Merit, had her life inserted
> in it.[25]

---

22   Christopher Fanning, 'The Voices of the Dependent Poet: The Case of Mary Barber',
     *Women's Writing*, 8.1 (2001), pp. 81–98: esp. p. 81; p. 85.
23   *Journals of the House of Commons, of the Kingdom of Ireland*, 21 vols (Dublin, 1796–1802),
     3: 631. Quoted in James W. Phillips, *Printing and Bookselling in Dublin, 1670–1800: A
     Bibliographical Enquiry* (Dublin: Irish Academic Press, 1998), p. 66; Mary Pollard, 'Control
     of the Press in Ireland through the King's Printer's Patent 1600–1800,' *Irish Booklore*, 4
     (1980): pp. 92–93; Mary Pollard, *A Dictionary of Members of the Dublin Book Trade 1550–
     1800* (London: Bibliographical Society, 2000), pp. xviii–xix.
24   Anon., *British Books*, 83 (1906), p. 218.
25   Mary Barber, *Poems on Several Occasions* (London: Rivington, 1734), p. xxx.

Barber closed her preface with the commendatory poem 'To Mrs. Mary Barber, under the Name of SAPPHIRA: Occasion'd by the Encouragement She Met with in England, to Publish Her Poems by Subscription'. In this verse, Grierson praises Barber's poetry as innovative and the poet as modest. By including Grierson's work, Barber brings to her own printed volume some praise of herself as a writer and the reflected glory of being associated with Grierson, all while centring her own affiliation with a literary circle that included both Grierson and the celebrated Dean Swift.

Grierson's poem in Barber's preface tackles the subject of British charity in supporting her friend through subscription publication:

> THESE Works, which Modesty conceal'd in Night,
> Your Candor, gen'rous BRITONS, brings to Light;
> Born, by your Arms, for Liberty's Defence;
> Born, by your Taste, the Arbiters of Sense:
> Long may your Taste, and long your Empire stand,
> To Honour, Wit, and Worth, from every Land.[26]

In his influential anthology of women writers, *Memoirs of Several Ladies of Great Britain* (1752), George Ballard reads the poem straight, as one that praises English subscribers: 'Mrs Barber having made a tour hither, and meeting with very great encouragement for printing her poems by subscription: Mrs. Grierson expressed her sense of the generosity of the English, and Mrs. Barber's merit'.[27] But upon a closer reading, Grierson makes us question whether Barber's entry into public life via publication is being praised here, asking us to reflect on the conditions which have caused Barber to drop her veil of modesty. Grierson's alignment of candour with arms and defence politicises the Irish poet's resort to the English book trade. Grierson couches as colonisation the charitable work that she sees British consumers doing by subscribing to Barber's poetry, militaristically bringing the dark other into the Light. Suggesting that this amounts to cultural appropriation, Grierson argues that the taste and sense of British readers are as much a construct as the British Empire, about which we would be naïve to assume she is serious or unsatirical when she wishes it longevity.

---

26    Constantia Grierson, 'To Mrs. Mary Barber, under the Name of SAPPHIRA: Occasion'd by the Encouragement She Met with in England, to Publish Her Poems by Subscription', in *Poems on Several Occasions*, pp. xlv–xlviii, lxiii.

27    George Ballard's *Memoirs of Several Ladies of Great Britain, who have Been Celebrated for their Writings or Skill in the Learned Languages Arts and Sciences* (Oxford: for the Author, 1752), pp. 463–64.

Grierson, like Barber, is well aware at this time of economic pressures coming from London that she argues elsewhere are choking Irish trade. In 'To the
Honourable Mrs Percival, on her desisting from the Bermudan Project,' also
anthologised by Barber, albeit much deeper within the 382-page volume,
Grierson states 'Our Gold may flow to *Albion* with each Tide', considering the
numbers Irish who choose to live in London as traitors, 'Who sacrifice their
Country to their Pride'.[28] In an unpublished poem from her manuscript volume,
sometimes entitled 'Irelands Complaint', Grierson's politics are unambiguous:

Let Britain now insult no more
Nor taunt us with her boundless store
What tho her senators may boast
What mighty sums their honours cost
Yet how does that her wealth display
When—will those sums repay
But we who squander mony here
And for our boroughs pay so dear
To sit in empty pomp and show
Without the powr of ay or no
When after all our cost and pains
None either place or pension gains
More wealth or virtue sure possess
Must have more gold or prize it less.[29]

The poem opens with a reference to harvest failures in Ireland in the early
decades of the 1700s, while England sat 'with her boundless store', taunting and
insulting the Irish as they suffered from a series of famines. Grierson juxtaposes
the wealth of English politicians, who 'boast | What mighty sums their honours
cost' with the boroughs, systems of local government in Ireland whereby the
aristocratic elite ruled small areas. She thereby exposes the corruption at the
heart of the English honours system, suggesting that such sums are likely to be
repaid through preferential treatment of the English (or at least the English

28   Grierson, 'To the Honourable Mrs *Percival,* on her desisting from the *Bermudan* Project', in
     *Poems on Several Occasions*, p. 139, line 23; p. 139, line 14.
29   Constantia Grierson, [Untitled,] in 'Miscellaneous by Mrs. Constantia Grierson',
     Miscellaneous Poems of Constantia Grierson, University of Pennsylvania MS Codex 1825,
     32r-33r.14r. Not in D.R. Foxon, *English Verse, 1701–1750: A Catalogue of Separately Printed
     Poems with Notes on Contemporary Collected Editions*, 2 vols (London: Cambridge UP,
     1975).

ruling classes), while Irish citizens suffer taxation without political representation: 'Without the powr of ay or no | When after all our cost and pains | None either place or pension gains'.

In Grierson's commonplace book, 'Irelands Complaint' appears only eight pages before that which deals with Barber's subscription project. The manuscript suggests a very different political worldview to that presented by Barber's printed volume. 'Irelands Complaint' was not kept private. It was circulated in manuscript at least among the circle that included Edward and Lady Henrietta Harley (1694–1755), as it appears with minor revisions within Harley Manuscript 7318, composed in the 1730s, and in the Portland Collection in the hand of Henrietta, with the first line 'Let Albion now insult no more'.[30] Members of Grierson's coterie networks, which included Barber, the Harleys, Swift, Laetitia Pilkington, and the Delanys, and perhaps, too, readers beyond those networks, would have been conscious of Grierson's capacity for cutting Irish satire.

The version of the poem that Barber prints for a primarily English readership is ambiguous in its critique of empire. The version extant in Grierson's manuscript notebook reveals that Barber's printed version omits a long stanza critical of Anglo-Irish relations:

> Nor shall your Favours to Saphira shown
> Be by your Sons unhonor'd or unknown
> For tho long fam'd for Science & for Arms
> For Wisdom's Glory & for Beauty's Charms
> Not all the mighty actions you have done
> The Realms you've humbled & the fields you won
> The dred your fleets convey to every Coast
> The Arts you've found & Heroes you can boast
> Shall more your worth to future times declare
> Than your regard to this illustrious fair
> This does your taste refin'd & Virtue show
> Wile they from these can but your Grandure know.[31]

---

30    Harl. MS. 7318, fol. 77v (p. 22): described as 'A folio miscellany of poems chiefly on affairs of state, in a single neat hand, i + 131 leaves, in half black morocco gilt. c.1730s'. Elias, 'A Manuscript Book', pp. 33–56'; Portland Collection, University of Nottingham Special Collections, Pw V 1099.

31    Constantia Grierson, 'To Saphira on the Respect her Works in England', in 'Miscellaneous by Mrs. Constantia Grierson', Miscellaneous Poems of Constantia Grierson, University of Pennsylvania MS Codex 1825, 32r–33r.

These 'missing' lines suggest that grandeur might be indicated by a history of military conquest and colonisation, but only by subscribing to Barber's poetry can the Britons' 'taste refin'd and Virtue show'. And yet, because so many lines are devoted to describing how England humbles its realms, conveying dread to every coast, Grierson reminds her readers of both hers and Barber's Irishness, thereby aligning Barber's subscribers with colonial plunderers ('arts you've found'). Grierson critiques the socio-political context that has led to her friend's supplication to their richer neighbours. Grierson, after all, was a leading figure in a national print trade which must have been incapable of recompensing her friend to the degree to which subscription publishing from London donors could. This is not to say that Barber was unaware of Grierson's political intent. Indeed, some of Barber's own poetry is deeply critical of the treatment of Ireland and the Irish by the English. But Barber was certainly conscious of the politics of her intended readership. While it remains unclear whether Barber's publication of the poem constitutes abridgement, censorship, or simply an alternative version of Grierson's poem, its new context in the preface of Barber's London-printed text means that its original meaning is skewed almost beyond recognition, and this adaptation of the poem conveniently aids its appeal to—or at least mutes the satire that targets—Barber's ostensibly English readership.

In Barber's *Poems*, the preface prints Grierson's biography and poem so closely as to underline and perpetuate in the public imagination an image of Grierson's poetic genius as integrally combined with her work as a female printer. Barber's emphasis on Grierson's role in the printing patent highlights the key role of the Lord Lieutenant of Ireland: 'It was truly worthy a Nobleman so eminent for Learning and great Abilities, to distinguish those Excellencies wheresoever He found them': in other words, particularly in women.[32] Barber implicitly challenged her readers to emulate this model of nobility, encouraging them to show their 'Learning and great Abilities' by (financially) distinguishing poets like herself for their 'Excellencies' as Carteret had done. But this was also an important rhetorical move which resulted in Grierson's legacy as a poet being inherently shaped by her practice as a female printer. Giving so much space to the patent and the poet's book trade achievements underlined Grierson's exceptional status as a woman poet who also printed.

---

32   Ibid.

4      Grierson's Ghost in the *Gentleman's Magazine*

Grierson's poem praising Barber's subscription project would also be printed
in the *Gentleman's Magazine* for August 1735, just two months after the printing of Barber's volume in June 1735, when Barber was on the verge of bankruptcy.[33] The periodical press, and especially the *Gentleman's Magazine*, 'propelled'
the popularity of poetry in this period, which often functioned as advertising
material as well as art. As George Justice demonstrates, even 'minimal direct
quotation' could make a poet's reputation.[34] But rather than include a short
quotation from Barber, the magazine publishes an entire poem by Grierson in
praise of her works. The title is modified to market Barber's project: 'To Mrs.
Mary Barber, under the Name of Sapphira: Occasion'd by the encouragement
she met with in England, to publish her poems by subscription, *which are
now printed*' [italics mine]. The posthumous appearance of Grierson's poem
in the magazine, which is described as having been composed in Dublin on
5 January 1732, has the unsettling effect of bringing back Grierson from the
dead to comment upon the occasion of her friend's volumes being in print.
It is difficult to imagine who might have conceived of this project other than
Barber herself. Moreover, it was a gendered strategy. The reprinting of a poem
by Grierson, an occasional poet, on the occasion of the publication of a volume of poems by Barber, another occasional poet, spoke out for the longevity
and flexibility of a form long maligned because of its association with female
writers.

Grierson's presence in the *Gentleman's Magazine* seemed to catch the attention of its readership, as the following instalment suggests:

> Many of our Readers being very inquisitive concerning the ingenious
> Ladies who do Honour to this *Magazine* by their poetical Performances,
> we hope some Time or other to be enabled to satisfy their Curiosity; mean
> while we shall oblige them with Mrs *Grierson*'s Character, as we find it in
> Mrs *Barber*'s Preface to her Poems.

Barber's memoir of Grierson follows, which, as in the original, underlines 'her
known Friendship to me', while revealing that she holds a number of Grierson's

---

33      Budd, '"Merit in Distress"', p. 214.
34      George Justice, 'Poetry, Popular Culture, and the Literary Marketplace', in Christine
        Gerrard (ed.), *A Companion to Eighteenth-Century Poetry* (Malden, MA: Blackwell, 2006),
        pp. 97–110.

manuscripts, which 'she made me promise, a little before her Death, to publish' on the occasion of her own volume reaching print.[35] Barber thereby casts herself as the preserver of the Grierson canon. The publication of Grierson's poem swelled her printed posterity even if it served primarily as a means of raising money for her struggling friend.

The ghost of Grierson appeared one last time in the *Gentleman's Magazine* for November 1735. She congratulates Barber on her poetic accomplishments, opening with a series of lines about Barber's talents and character:

> To Mrs Mary Barber, on Reading her Poem[s] lately publish'd
> > *'Tis not to wound, but to instruct she writes.*
> Mrs Grierson, to the Author, See p. 492.
>
> Let wanton lovers in an amorous way,
> *Cloe*'s or *Flavia*'s boasted charms display;
> With nobler passion, to no fair confin'd,
> I sing th' enchanting beauties of the mind.
> Such thine *Sapphira*—fraught with arrows keen,
> Which pierce the soul, and wound, thy self unseen.

Though this seems to be the only version of the poem that survives, we can infer that two impositions have been made to Grierson's original.[36] The epigraph is taken from 'To Mrs. Mary Barber, under the Name of Sapphira: Occasion'd by the Encouragement She met with in England, to publish her Poems by Subscription', the poem which fronts Barber's collection. It is added by someone other than Grierson, intended to direct us to the 'other' poem in praise of Barber on p. 492 of the *Gentleman's Magazine*, in turn taken from the preface to Barber's works.

The title, 'To Mrs Mary Barber, on reading her Poem 'lately publish'd', is also a posthumous addition. The superscript 's' after 'Poem' hints at the fact that it is impossible for the verse to have been composed upon the appearance in print of Barber's collection, since Grierson was dead at the time of its publication. Rather, this is a poem which seems to have been written upon an earlier instance of a work of Barber's appearing in print. The internal evidence suggests that, despite its new title, Grierson's poem was composed as a response to 'The Prodigy':

---

35  *Gentleman's Magazine*, 5 (1735), p. 550.

36  The poem does not appear in Carl Lennart Carlson's *The First Magazine: A History of the Gentleman's Magazine* (Providence, RI, 1938).

The *PRODIGY's a lesson for that clan,
Who, like Xantippe, plague unhappy man.
Oh! May your friendly zeal, devoid of pain,
Correct that foible, and disciples gain.
For Philomel, we're told in antient story,
Losing her tongue acquir'd immortal glory.
Let Caelia titter, Fulvia vent her spite,
You've prov'd that Females can with judgment write.[37]

With the asterisk, the editor directs the reader to the page upon which Barber's poem, 'The Prodigy', is printed within the *Gentleman's Magazine*. There, it immediately follows Grierson's biography, meaning that readers are encouraged to read the poem as addressed to the friend with whom they have just become better acquainted, especially as Barber refers to herself as 'Sapphira' within it ('O Jove, for what crime is *Sapphira* thus curst?'), Grierson's nom de plume for Barber.[38] 'The Prodigy' had been reprinted in *Poems on Several Occasions*, but had first been published as a broadside in Dublin in around 1726, as 'The prodigy: or, the silent woman, in a letter from a lady in town to a friend in the country'.[39] It is a comic poem about a female poet, cast as the stereotypical prattler, who is silenced by a toothache. Barber's 'Prodigy' and Grierson's 'To Mrs Mary Barber, on reading her Poem⁵ lately publish'd' are evidently companion pieces. We can therefore date Grierson's verse as composed in or around 1726, rather than from beyond the grave in 1735, as implied by the magazine.

It is difficult to imagine that anyone would have had access to Grierson's poem at this stage other than its addressee, Mary Barber. Certainly no one would have had as much to gain from its publication at this moment. Its title—carefully constructed to advertise Barber's latest project—is an obvious attempt at book marketing. Barber's inclusion in her volume and her insertion in the *Gentleman's Magazine* of her friend's life and works raised her own profile while establishing for Grierson a literary legacy inseparable from her identity as a woman printer. As a woman of the Irish peasantry who had thrived by her intellectual abilities while continuing to work, Grierson became enshrined as a female icon of working class learning both in and beyond Barber's work.

---

37   *Gentleman's Magazine*, 5 (1732), p. 732.
38   *Gentleman's Magazine*, 5 (1735), p. 550.
39   Mary Barber, *The Prodigy: or, the Silent Woman, in a Letter from a Lady in Town to a Friend in the Country* (Dublin: printed by E.S., [1726?]).

Grierson's gendered identity as a female printer who was also a poet was mediated and perpetuated by Barber's print interventions, which were widely repeated and recirculated, in the *Gentleman's Magazine*, as well as in another periodical, *The Present State of the Republick of Letters*, which printed Barber's biography of Grierson alongside Grierson's epigraph to Mrs. Percival on Hutcheson's *Treatise on Beauty and Order*.[40] Being a manuscript inscription, this article must have been composed either by Percival herself or, what is more likely, Barber. Barber's account of Grierson was reprinted verbatim in several influential publications celebrating the achievements of the period's women, such as *Beauty's Triumph: or, the Superiority of the Fair Sex Invincibly Proved* (1751), George Ballard's *Memoirs of Several Ladies of Great Britain* (1752), and *Biographium fæmineum. The Female Worthies: or, Memoirs of the most Illustrious Ladies* (1766). It was also used in broader canon-making projects such as those by Paul Hiffernan in *The Hiberniad* (1754) and Robert Shiells and Theophilus Cibber in *The Lives of the Poets of Great Britain and Ireland* (1753). Barber's account of Grierson, in turn, had an impact upon the ways in which her legacy was shaped by others, including Grierson's descendants.

## 5    Grierson Rides the Franchises, Posthumously

Since the 1790s there has been a desire to attribute to Grierson one of two broadside poems concerning the art of printing, each printed posthumously on a moving press in Dublin during a three yearly celebration called 'riding the franchises'. Neither has been completely accepted nor removed from the Grierson canon, but the motivation for attribution stems from Grierson's posthumous reputation as a woman printer.

Dublin had 24 guilds that processed around the bounds of the city every three years, on Lord Mayor's Day in August. The Corporation of Cutlers, Painters and Stationers usually brought with them a printing press mounted upon a cart, from which souvenir broadsides were printed. This was a spectacular event that was increasingly attracting an international audience of tourists and was widely reported in the Irish and English press, as in this 1752 report:[41]

> The Corporation of Cutlers Painters, and Stationers, had two Men cloathed in Buff Leather, bearing Shields on their Arms, a Vulcan dressed in a fine Suit of Steel Armour; and a large Carriage on which was erected

---

40    *The Present State of the Republick of Letters*, 15 (1728–36), pp. 310–313.
41    Pollard, *Dictionary*, pp. xviii–xix; *Dublin Courier*, 24 July 1761.

a Scaffold, drawn by six fine Horses, on which there was printing Tipes in a Case, and a very neat Printing-Press; there was also a Painter drawing a Venus and an Adonis; and Printers setting the Letters, and printing off many Sheets, with the following Poem, which was distributed to the Populace and gave them great Satisfaction.[42]

During the riding of the franchises in 1728, a year when Grierson was actively writing poetry and working in the Grierson print firm, the corporation produced for onlookers 'A Poem on the Art of Printing, Which was wrought at the PRINTING MACHINE carry'd before the Corporation of Stationers, Cutlers and Painters'. It is headed with an epigram from Horace's *Ars Poetica*: 'Sic honour et nomen divinis vatibus ast; Carminibus venit—' ('and so honour and fame fell to bards and their songs, as divine').[43] This was an epigraph that Swift himself had included in his *Letter of Advice to a Young Poet: Together with a Proposal for the Encouragement of Poetry in this Kingdom* (1721). The broadside poem concerns Grierson's favourite themes of 'Th'immortal Labours of Old Greece and Rome' and the arts as gifts from God:

Hail Sacred Art! thou Gift of Heaven, design'd
T'impart the Charms of Wisdom to Mankind,
To call forth Learning from the Realms of Night,
And bid bright Knowledge rise to Publick Sight.

Th'immortal Labours of Old Greece and Rome,
By Thee secur'd from Fate, shall ever bloom,
To farthest Times their lasting Charms display,
Nor worn by Age, nor subject to Decay.[44]

This is a poem which has been attributed to Grierson without source. The poem was first associated with Grierson in 1952, by James Phillips.[45] Sarah

---

42   *Dublin Journal*, 4 August 1752.

43   Horace, *Satires. Epistles. The Art of Poetry*, trans. by H. Rushton Fairclough, Loeb Classical Library 194 (Cambridge, MA: Harvard University Press, 1926), p. 422. The Loeb edition translates the passage as 'The first poets were inspired teachers'. This quotation from Horace is also the epigraph to Swift's *A Letter of Advice to a Young Poet* (Dublin: Boreham, 1721). The franchise broadside also includes 'Verses added to the Former by another Hand', beginning 'Say, Cadmus, by what ray divine inspir'd', by James Sterling. For further context, see Pollard, *Dictionary*, who argues that the poem is 'possibly by Constantia Grierson' p. xix.

44   'A Poem on the Art of Printing' (Dublin, 1728). British Library.

45   Phillips, *Printing and Bookselling*, p. 16. See also Vincent Kinane, *A Brief History of Printing and Publishing in Ireland* (Dublin: National Print Museum, 2002), p. 14.

Peterson Pittock argues that the poem 'defends the authority, relevance, and beauties of classical literature, and, obliquely, her own efforts to maintain it', i.e. through her printing of new editions of classical texts.[46] There seems to be no more compelling evidence for the attribution to Grierson than the convenience of its date and content, with the poem's final stanzas asking whether it was Johann Fust or Laurens Janszoon Coster who first invented printing ('Then let Them Both the Common Prize receive | And *Fust* and *Coster*'s Name for ever Live'). In fact, it seems that Phillips only attributed the poem to Grierson on the basis that she was rumoured to have written such another broadside poem, which begins 'Hail Mystick Art!', first published in 1764. On the basis of the posthumous date of publication, Phillips argued that the poem beginning 'Hail Sacred Art!' must be Grierson's instead, having been printed during her lifetime.

The 1764 poem was similarly printed on a moving press during the riding of the franchises. It is much more frequently attributed to Grierson than the earlier one, though it appeared 32 years after her death. The poem is addressed to the 'Mystick Art' which collapses distance and brings all of the world to the reader:

> Hail Mystick Art! which Men, like Angels, taught,
> To speak to Eyes, and paint unbody'd Thought!
> Though Deaf, and Dumb; blest Skill, reliev'd by THEE,
> We make one Sense perform the Task of Three.
> We see, we hear, we touch the Head and Heart,
> And take, or give, what each but yields in part.
> With the hard Laws of Distance we dispence,
> And, without Sound, apart, commune in Sense;
> View, though confin'd; nay, rule this Earthly Ball,
> And travel o'er the wide expanded ALL.[47]

Though printing is never mentioned in the body of the poem itself, the final couplet could be considered to obliquely refer to printing's contribution to the physicality of the book: 'Arts, Hist'ry, Laws, we purchase with a Look, | And keep, like FATE, all Nature in a BOOK'. The poem reappeared—usually unattributed—in newspapers throughout the second half of the eighteenth

---

46  Sarah Peterson Pittock, 'Constantia Grierson (1705?–1732)', in Frans De Bruyn (ed.), *Eighteenth-Century British Literary Scholars and Critics* (Detroit, MI: Gale, 2010), pp. 105–112: p. 109.

47  *The Art of Printing. A Poem* (Dublin: Printed before the worshipful Company of Stationers, &c. the 7th of August, 1764, being the day of perambulating the Franchises, Mears, Limits, and Bounds of that City). British Library.

century and was used anonymously on a nineteenth-century trade card, presumably for a printer, held by the Metropolitan Museum of Art, New York.[48]

This poem was first associated with Grierson in a copperplate print of the 1790s published by her step-grandson, George Grierson II, King's Printer between 1784–1821.[49] It refrains from giving the poem a formal title, instead introducing the poem discursively: 'Having been favoured with the following beautiful lines on the ART of PRINTING, written by Mrs. Constantia Grierson, we here present them to the Public'.[50] The poem is printed above the family coat of arms. The piece survives in single sheets, as collected by Jane and Anna Maria Porter, and was also included as an illustration in *A View from Ancient and Modern Dublin* by John Ferrar (1796). The name 'George Grierson' appears below the crest on the single sheets, but not in the version serving as Ferrar's illustration. The repetition of the surname on the broadside underlines the effect of the family crest, which is to promote the business as one with family heritage, proud of Constantia's achievements.

Elias finds 'nothing in either proposed poem to confirm or rule out an attribution to Mrs Grierson, although the somewhat more fervent and other-worldly tone of the 1764/1796 text sounds more like her'. He considers Grierson II careless and unscholarly about his family history.[51] But there are scraps of supporting evidence that survive from the eighteenth and nineteenth centuries. Perhaps most compelling is the claim that a poem by Rev. Thomas Birch, Grierson's contemporary (beginning 'Long had mankind with darkness been oppressed') was inspired by 'Hail Mystick Art', because, as Charles Henry Wilson maintained, Birch 'esteemed the worth and talents of Mrs. Grierson'.[52] In *Illustrious Irishwomen* (1877), Elizabeth Owens Blackburne asserted, without source, that Grierson addressed this particular poem to George Grierson just before they were married.[53]

---

48    'The Art of Printing: A Poem' [trade card], accession number 26.28.173, The Metropolitan Museum of Art, New York.

49    Constantia's widower George Grierson went on to marry Jane Blow. George Grierson II was the son of Hugh Boulter Grierson, the eldest son of that marriage.

50    'A printed poem, 'Hail Mystic Art! Which Men like Angels taught, / To speak to Eyes, ...' [by?] George Grierson' [one leaf], Porter Family Collection, box 41, folder 14, item 29, Phillipps number 14678, Spencer Research Library, University of Kansas.

51    Elias, 'A Manuscript Book', pp. 33–35 n. 2.

52    Charles Henry Wilson (ed.), *Brookiana*, 2 vols. (London: Phillips, 1804), vol. 2, p. 128.

53    Elizabeth Owens Blackburne (1877), *Illustrious Irishwomen: Being Memoirs of Some of the Most Noted Irishwomen from the Earliest Ages to the Present Century* (Cambridge: Cambridge University Press, 2010), vol. 2, p. 24.

Complications emerge, as Phillips has pointed out, when we consider the franchise expenses for that year. Phillips notes that the unnamed author of this poem was paid 8s 11/2d in the master's account of franchise expenses for that year.[54] Mary Pollard takes that as sufficient evidence for de-attribution.[55] However, when we consider that more poetry by Grierson was printed after her death than during her lifetime, it becomes feasible that Grierson's estate, or the holder of this particular manuscript poem, may have been paid a sort of copyright fee.

Perhaps the most celebrated reader of 'Hail Mystick art' would be Phillis Wheatley. Sometime before 1773 Wheatley copied 'The Art of Printing' ('Hail Mystick Art') into her commonplace book, alongside two others, all of which she would reference as having been sourced from the *Massachusetts Spy*. The *Massachusetts Spy* was a newspaper that had been established in 1770 and which had advertised her own *Elegiac Poem, on the Death of that Celebrated Divine, and Eminent Servant of Jesus Christ, the Reverend and Learned George Whitefield* (1770).[56] In Wheatley's manuscript, the poem is presented under a slightly, but significantly, different title: 'The Art of Printing or Writing, a Poem'. Rereading the poem with this title reveals that its content more perfectly represents the act of poetic rather than printerly composition. The poem would reappear under the title of 'On the Art of Writing' in Joseph Longman's *Sentences, Divine, Moral, and Historical; in Prose and Verse* in 1786, indicating the verses' praise of poetic composition in the broadest sense.[57]

Elizabeth Eisenstein suggests that the mystical component of the poem 'is activated by reading books, not by producing or marketing them. One might assume, wrongly, that the poem reflected a learned lady's distance from the prosaic actualities of printing and book-selling'. Eisenstein suggests that this poem 'reflected a venerable printing house tradition, one that went back to the earliest days of the wooden handpress, when humanities editors and correctors drew on classical mythology to compose their encomiums'.[58] But the

---

54  Records of the Guild of St. Luke, or Corporation of Cutlers, Painters, Stainers and Stationers, MS 12,130, 1763/4, National Library of Ireland; Phillips, *Printing and Bookselling*.

55  Pollard, *Dictionary*, p. xix.

56  'The Art of Printing or Writing a Poem', in 'Joining Copies,' small copybook, Phillis Wheatley collection, 1757–1773, Manuscript Collection No. 796, box 1 folder 1, p. 11, Stuart A. Rose Manuscript, Archives, and Rare Book Library, Emory University. *Massachusetts Spy*, 11 October 1770.

57  Joseph Longman, *Sentences, Divine, Moral, and Historical; in Prose and Verse* (Salisbury: Easton, 1786), p. 357.

58  Elizabeth Eisenstein, *Divine Art, Infernal Machine: The Reception of Printing in the West from First Impressions to the Sense of an Ending* (Philadelphia, PA: University of Pennsylvania Press, 2011), pp. 99–100.

couplet 'Dead Letters, thus with Living Notions fraught, | Prove to the Soul the Telescopes of Thought', in particular, is best suited to a discussion of how poetry brings life to dead letters, making little sense in the context of print. And if the common Augustan metaphor of printing's capacity to render life immortal seems to be captured in the poem, it could equally refer to the act of making Literature, rather than printed books specifically:

> To Mortal Life a deathless Witness give;
> And bid all Deeds and Titles last, and live,
> In scanty Life, ETERNITY we taste;
> View the First Ages, and inform the Last.

The poem's content, and Wheatley's title for it, makes us wonder whether an original manuscript may have been adapted for its guild context of 1762. George Grierson II's copperplate broadside, which implies access to the original manuscript through his assertion of its provenance within his family, certainly avoids providing it with a title. Moreover, the copperplate visually presents the poem as if it is a manuscript—rather than replicating its appearance as it emerged from the moving press—in a cursive hand, reflecting the remediation of a manuscript poem through print. Wheatley and Eisenstein's readings show us that the poem is about much more than just printing, but also concerns meaning in books and the art of writing poetry more generally. The slippage in the poem between (manuscript) poetic creativity and its potentially superimposed title indicating printing practice reflects the duality in Grierson's legacy across her roles as manuscript poet and printer, and the ways in which the latter has shaped and misshaped the former.

Grierson's manuscript commonplace book includes thirteen poems. She accords titles to only six.[59] George Grierson II's discursive introduction to the poem beginning 'Hail Mystick Art', without a formal title, brings home the fact that its appearance in 1764 as the 'Art of Printing' had been conveniently in keeping with the tradition of broadsides printed on the moving press during the procession of the guilds. Moreover, Grierson's posthumous appearance in the *Gentleman's Magazine* teaches us nothing if not how far titles could be posthumously adapted to meet new requirements. If Grierson did write one of the poems that was printed on a moving press, as with the rest of her printed verse, it was most likely a posthumous publication which served first to meet short-term business needs, in this case, the immediate requirements of the

---

59    Harl. MS. 7318.

guild and, then, the longer-term reputation of her descendants in the print trade. While not completely solving the crux, the attribution debate around the two poems on the art of printing can be nuanced by remembering Grierson's preference for manuscript publication of her poetry during her lifetime whilst also underlining how far her poetic legacy has been posthumously interwoven with her role as a woman printer.

# 6    Conclusion

During her lifetime, Grierson succeeded in maintaining two distinct and deeply gendered roles, on the one hand, as a well-respected manuscript poet and, on the other, as a leading figure in a print trade to which she rarely publicly contributed poetry. After her death, Mary Barber united these roles in a printed legacy which presented her friend as a female genius. The publication of Grierson's poetry in Barber's volume, and then in the *Gentleman's Magazine*, acted as promotional material for Barber's *Poems on Several Occasions* but also widely popularised an image of Grierson as printer-poet, an image which would become useful to Grierson's descendants in the print trade. Both Barber and George Grierson II drew upon Grierson's dual reputation as manuscript poet and printer, publishing her poetry in print to promote their own respective bookselling endeavours. Barber's posthumous publication of Grierson's poetry has encouraged scholars to make attributions to her based on her legacy as a female printer-poet while obscuring the degree to which her signed work is deeply critical of Anglo-Irish relations and printed in contexts curated to appeal to a wealthy English readership. In other words, two poems apparently about printing may or may not be by Grierson, and the work which is certainly is, on Barber's subscription publishing project, does not yet represent the poem as she wrote it. Grierson's friend Mary Barber and her descendant Grierson II manipulated her success as a female printer to enhance the reputations of their own printed works, creating a canon of Grierson's poetry which is by no means stable. The story of Grierson's ghost underlines how far her labour as a printing woman became central to the shaping and misshaping of her poetic canon.

# PART 4

## *The Bookshop and the Marketplace*

∴

# CHAPTER 10

# The Bookshop Salon: Sylvia Beach, Adrienne Monnier, and Gendered Forms of Bookselling in Interwar Paris

*Matthew Chambers*

Sylvia Beach and Adrienne Monnier are familiar figures in the histories of literary modernism, and there has been no shortage of description and analysis on their romantic relationship, their respective bookshops in Paris, and how they ran them. Where attention has been more generally paid to their literary networking skills, the bookshops themselves have received less attention. Beach's Shakespeare and Company and Monnier's La Maison des Amis des Livres have commonly been regarded as unique social spaces with innovative commercial practices. They are similar to other modernist bookshops in the United States and the United Kingdom in their functions as distributors of modernist literature and as sites of literary networking, however, where they may differ from most of the shops of their kind lies in their intent and self-presentation. This chapter, although primarily focused on Beach and her shop, addresses how both Beach and Monnier established their own spaces within the literary and commercial milieu of interwar Paris, and analyses how these cultural institutions have come to be memorialised as gendered hybrid spaces between 'bookshop' and 'salon.' As women business owners in an almost exclusively male domain, Beach and Monnier successfully fashioned a place within the commercial market by rendering what were ostensibly public spaces into semipublic ones, through an effacement of the mechanics of their trade. By presenting their businesses as social networking spaces first and foremost, rather than as places of commerce, while successfully deflecting attention away from questions about their relative unique place in the trade as women, Monnier and Beach used dominant gender roles to their advantage. In order to demonstrate this, I will first review how Beach set up and ran her business, how her efforts to foreground the social nature of the shop led to the business's characterisation as a 'bookshop salon,' and finally, how Beach's memorialisation of her bookshop framed this gendered characterisation of the bookshop as a salon for posterity.

Beach and Monnier entered bookselling at a time when it was uncommon for women to own businesses in Paris outside of some family connection or through inheritance, even though both of their families supported their ventures. Monnier opened up her shop in 1915 with compensation her father had received after getting injured on the job. Monnier benefited from less (male) competition in Paris because of the requirements and hazards of the war.[1] Beach, unlike Monnier, came from a moderately wealthy family, and was in a position to ask her mother for \$3,000 in startup money in 1919.[2] An even greater challenge, which Beach touches on, would have been the willingness of Parisian landlords to rent business space to foreigners—a challenge Monnier was prepared to help Beach overcome.[3] While the details of Beach and Monnier's personal relationship have mostly been hidden from view, we do know they were extremely close from the moment they met to the end of Monnier's life in 1955, and their professional relationship began in 1919 when Beach was in need of a French citizen to provide a reference so she might rent shop space.

Beach had no book trade experience when she opened her shop and she faced some business realities straight away. Paris was awash in bookshops, book stalls, and other forms of print circulation, and there was a new mass literary culture and an expansive national network of bookshops in France, so that by the end of the 1910s, the book trade was flourishing.[4] But this meant there was space in the market for a new venture specialising in contemporary, and even foreign, literature. Beach's shop, both at the initial 8 rue Dupuytren and subsequent 12 rue de l'Odeon addresses placed her near the Sorbonne and plenty of student foot traffic, even as she faced competition in the English language book trade at the time. In 1919, Brentano's in New York City and W.H. Smith in the United Kingdom both had branches in Paris, and the English language

---

1   Richard McDougall, 'Introduction' in *The very rich hours of Adrienne Monnier* (Lincoln: University of Nebraska Press, 1996), pp. 12–13.

2   Just over \$50,000.00 in 2022 when adjusted for inflation; *U.S. Bureau of Labor Statistics online*. <https://www.bls.gov/data/inflation_calculator.htm> (accessed 26 July 2022).

3   Richard Ford, *Published in Paris. American and British writers, printers, and publishers in Paris, 1920–1939* (London: Garnstone Press, 1975), pp. 8–9; Sylvia Beach, *Shakespeare and Company* (New York: Harcourt, Brace and Company, 1959), pp. 16–7.

4   For the development of a national reading culture and the growth and dynamics of bookshops in mid-to-late nineteenth-century France, see Martyn Lyons, *Reading culture and writing practices in nineteenth-century France* (Toronto: University of Toronto Press, 2008), pp. 43–62. On the success of Hachette's, the French counterpart to British railway book stall vendor W.H. Smith's, in the late nineteenth-century, see Eileen S. DeMarco, *Reading and riding. Hachette's railroad bookstore network in nineteenth-century France* (Bethlehem: Lehigh University Press, 2006).

book supplier Galignani Library had been in business since 1800. Despite such competition, the bookshop did attract customers in its early months. Beach attributed her initial success to a word-of-mouth campaign among expats, and certainly her association with James Joyce after she published his *Ulysses* in 1922 greatly boosted the shop's visibility.[5] Yet, Beach was also not averse to promoting her business. She instituted a lending library, a common feature in early twentieth-century bookshops in the United Kingdom, and held that aspect of the business up as the cornerstone of the shop's operations. I write elsewhere how smaller booksellers would attempt to draw business by featuring a lending library, and Beach shared these booksellers' general disregard for profit from the lending library subscriptions, often letting favoured patrons, like Ernest Hemingway, walk away with books for no charge.[6] Numerous stories attest to Beach's fondness for some of her 'company'. She was particularly close to Hemingway and Joyce, and from the many accounts of Beach we can see glimpses of how she must have been as a 'personality,' especially from a few late interviews she gave, which are readily available online.

Beach's interpersonal skills are also evident in her correspondence, and as it will be further explored later, illustrates a canny knack for crossing a gendered divide between commercial and private spheres. A letter she wrote to a representative at Chatto & Windus in 1920 captures how she put her energy, enthusiasm, and networking ability towards successfully managing a business. In it, she makes reference to a lunch she had with Harold Raymond (her addressee) on her trip to London the previous year to purchase her initial stock for the store,

---

5  For one version of how this unfolded, see Noel Fitch Riley, *Sylvia Beach and the Lost Generation. A history of literary Paris in the twenties and thirties* (New York: W.W. Norton & Company, 1985), pp. 42–64.

6  Matthew Chambers, *London and the modernist bookshop* (Cambridge: Cambridge UP, 2020), pp. 30–32. Ernest Hemingway's account of meeting Beach in *A Moveable Feast*, for example, heavily emphasises his pleasant surprise at being able to walk home with so many books, Ernest Hemingway, *A moveable feast* (London: Arrow Books, 1994), pp. 20–22. The usual takeaway from these tales is that Beach carried a disregard for her business's profitability, but a different Hemingway anecdote suggests something else. As the story goes, Hemingway walked into the shop when Beach was away and the clerk working that day attempted to charge him for the books he wished to take. He left in a rage and when Beach discovered what had happened chastised the clerk, saying, 'Brentano's would pay Hemingway if he came to their shop!' Beach understood her competition and what it did and did not offer. What Shakespeare and Company could offer was the promise of an opportunity to join in literary greatness. If the cost of doing business, and generating business, was some of her stock, then that was what was required, Mary McAuliffe, *Paris on the brink. The 1930s Paris of Jean Renoir, Salvador Dali, Simone de Beauvoir, Andre Gide, Sylvia Beach, Leon Blum, and their friends* (Lanham, MD: Rowman and Littlefield, 2018), p. 237.

My bookshop has been going very well indeed and is great fun. You must run over to Paris and see it soon. There is a signboard with Shakespeare on it 'n' everything' as they say in the song.

I should like to open an account with Chatto & Windus. I have one at a number of publishers and at Lloyd's Bank, London.[7]

She then proceeds to list all her references: Harold Monro, Edward Shanks, Harriet Weaver, Elkin Mathews, Valery Larbaud, Andre Gide, Jules Romains, Luc Durtain, Léon-Paul Fargue, Paul Valery, and James Joyce. After briefly sharing her struggles of the past year and crediting Monnier's help, she closes the letter with 'I hope all this doesn't bore you too much. Ever since last year I have been intending to write you all about everything as you were kind enough to interest yourself in my plans'.[8] In the letter, Beach deftly shifts back and forth between the personal and the professional—hooking Harold Raymond with a pleasant memory to ask after a business matter, name-dropping several people someone in his position would surely know, and reminding him of his previously expressed interest in her business. Her ability to use the personal to succeed at the professional became one of the hallmarks of Shakespeare and Company. Moreover, based on surviving correspondence, her rhetorical strategy with publishers tended to work in her favour. Following her aforementioned stop at Elkin Mathews, publisher to W.B. Yeats, Ezra Pound, and others, in addition to operating as a bookseller, she began a business relationship with him, which ran throughout the 1920s. Mathews wrote in response to a comment Beach made about her visit to his shop,

You must not on any account think I was impatient, and you may be sure I smiled when you said something about being more prompt in payment for future orders—as it would be quite unnecessary, you are promptness itself and if I had the same confidence in most of my clients as I have in *you*, I shouldn't have anything to worry about![9]

Mathews' enthusiastic and warm response to Beach certainly was not unique. In a letter sending a catalogue of books, Grant Richards also expressed his interest in the bookshop: 'I am much interested in your venture and in what you tell

---

7   Letter from Sylvia Beach to Harold Raymond (13 October 1920). CW 2/12. Chatto & Windus letters file 1915–25: Ba-Bo. Records of Chatto & Windus Ltd. University of Reading Special Collections.

8   Letter from Beach to Raymond (13 October 1920).

9   Letter from Elkin Mathews to Sylvia Beach (5 February 1920). Box 60, folder 4. Sylvia Beach Papers, 1872–1999. Princeton University Library.

me in your letter, and when I go to Paris, as I hope to do next month, I shall give myself the pleasure of calling to see you'.[10] It is clear from the tone of these letters that Beach excelled at establishing solid relationships with publishers in rapid fashion, as both these letters date from the first months the shop was open. She was then able to exercise this skill in arranging trade accounts with dozens of publishers, mostly based in London. For example, an examination of the acquisitions made during the years 1928–1929, a two-year period where Shakespeare and Company was at the peak of its prosperity, reveals that Beach ordered just over 5,000 books.[11] About 70% of those acquisitions were from twelve publishers (e.g., Chatto & Windus, Hogarth Press, Heinemann), and 87% of the total were acquired from UK publishers. Averaging about seven copies arriving per day, Beach's business would have been greatly occupied with these publishers. Indeed, the full stretch of Beach's business management—including receiving book travellers, poring over catalogues, placing orders, receiving packages through customs, documenting incoming stock, shelving and presenting new arrivals, dealing with special orders, managing her staff, fulfilling invoices, returning damaged or unsold stock, and negotiating net prices and outstanding accounts—all point to someone fully enmeshed in the work of running a bookshop, even as she was able to present the bookshop to the public as the social space it is best remembered as.

Beach's ability to successfully operate a commercial space was neither overvalued at the time nor emphasised often in literary scholarship since. Rather, the sociability of the shop space, akin to a literary salon or club, especially with the large number of modernist writers who stopped in, has been Shakespeare and Company's legacy. There is a long history of literary salons in Paris—semipublic spaces where women and men could meet on more or less equal terms to discuss events or publications of the day—and as I discuss below, the labelling of Beach and Monnier's shops as 'bookshop salons' underscored the gendering of their spaces as a step removed from the masculine, public spheres of commerce. As Emma Sterry has recently emphasised, literary salons continued in the interwar years as essential networking sites:

> The literary salon, a staple of bohemian culture, played a vital role in forming and maintaining networks between highbrow writers, especially

---

10    Letter from Grant Richards to Sylvia Beach (13 December 1919). Box 60, folder 5. Sylvia Beach Papers, 1872–1999. Princeton University Library.

11    This does not include the various periodicals she stocked, nor the copies of *Ulysses* she was still printing and selling, nor most of anything acquired locally from wholesalers or in trade from customers.

for women associated with literary modernism. Salons had emerged in France back in the seventeenth century, but gender roles were more rigidly prescribed in the *belle époque* where, as Shari Benstock has argued, it was 'women's duty to enhance the discourse of men'.[12]

Benstock, writing on Beach and Monnier, and their respective bookshops, describes them both as salons in the more traditional sense she outlined and in a more transformative sense of a 'small salon' where people were not only treated to readings, conversation, and drinks in the shops, but also in their apartment where Monnier would cook and entertain guests. Benstock concludes that 'these women made no distinction between their professional and personal lives; their public and private interests were integrated to such a degree that it was difficult even for them to say how their professional alliance was different from their personal and intimate friendship'.[13]

We know Adrienne Monnier had much to do with Beach's approach to Shakespeare and Company. Monnier's bookshop Les Maisons des Amis des Livres had for years before Shakespeare and Company functioned as a kind of salon for Parisian writers, including Paul Valery, Andre Gide, and Andre Breton. While Monnier had helped establish Beach at an address in Paris, her contribution to Shakespeare and Company runs deeper than the practicalities—she helped Beach see an idea of what a bookshop could be beyond a place of commerce. In a short piece published to promote her own bookshop, Monnier wrote of the bookshop as a 'true magic chamber':

---

12    The possible influence of Barney's salon on Monnier and Beach is outside the scope of this writing, but as Sterry goes on to note, Benstock emphasised its transformative impact in Paris, Emma Sterry, *The single woman, modernity, and literary culture. Women's fiction from the 1920s to the 1940s* (Houndsmills, UK: Palgrave Macmillan, 2017), pp. 100–101. The possible influence of Barney's salon on Monnier and Beach is outside the scope of this writing, but as Sterry goes on to note, Benstock emphasised its transformative impact in Paris. Benstock has credited Natalie Barney's salon in Paris with reimagining women's roles in salon culture. Barney often arranged women-only meetings, offering 'a semi-private space' for women to be open about their sexuality. At a time when popular representations of lesbians depicted them as marginal figures, the prominent lesbian writers of the 1920s Left Bank—including Gertrude Stein, Djuna Barnes, and Barney herself—could express both their sexuality and creativity in the refigured space of the literary salon. (Sterry, p. 101)

13    Sheri Benstock, *Women of the Left Bank. Paris, 1900–1940* (Austin: University of Texas Press, 1986), pp. 197–8.

> We think, first of all, that the faith we put into selling books can be put
> into all daily acts; one can carry on no matter what business, no matter
> what profession, with a satisfaction that at certain moments has a real
> lyricism.[14]

Monnier pitches an idea of bookshopping as experiential, not merely transactional. Crossing the threshold into a bookshop ('a place of transition between street and house'), the customer enters a 'third place'.[15] Elizabeth F. Evans, writing on the 'new public women' and the 'threshold' between public and private spheres in turn of the century London, argued that '[e]nclosed places of commerce and sociability frequently provided a middle ground between the restrictions and securities of private domestic space and the dangers of wholly public byways'.[16] The bookshop created a semipublic space where women and men could meet outside the norms and confines of domestic and public spheres. The sociability of Monnier's bookshop did not displace the commerce of the business, but simply was part of the packaging for the public. Shakespeare and Company, in turn, took this idea to make Beach's shop an essential literary centre in interwar Paris. If the name of Monnier's shop—La Maison des Amis des Livres, or The House of the Friends of Books—emphasised a community of readers and collectors, Beach's Shakespeare and Company held out the promise of joining an elevated literary community. Joyce, Hemingway, and other famous writers could shop for free because other 'ordinary' people would come and pay for the association. The shops, in effect, operated as open-door salons, significantly differing from the more exclusionary historical model, inviting both women and men to join the company, regardless of their background.

The sociable nature of the shops was not lost on their contemporaries. The two bookshops have not only been retrospectively viewed as literary salons, but were given those labels on at least two occasions in publications in 1919 and 1930. Sisley Huddleston, a patron of both shops and an early reviewer of

---

14    Adrienne Monnier, 'La Maison des Amis des Livres' in Richard McDougall (trans. And
      ed.), *The very rich hours of Adrienne Monnier* (Lincoln: University of Nebraska Press,
      1996), pp. 69–70. For further commentary on this piece and on the relationship between
      Monnier and Beach see Joanne Winning, '"Ezra through the open door". The parties of
      Natalie Barney, Adrienne Monnier and Sylvia Beach as lesbian modernist cultural pro-
      duction' in Kate McLoughlin (ed.) *The modernist party* (Edinburgh: Edinburgh University
      Press, 2013), pp. 127–146; Andrew Thacker, '"A true magic chamber". The public face of the
      modernist bookshop', *Modernist cultures*, 11(2016), pp. 429–451.
15    Ray Oldenburg, *The great good place. Cafes, coffee shops, bookstores, bars, hair salons, and
      other hangouts at the heart of a community* (New York: Hachette Books, 1999).
16    Elizabeth F. Evans, *Threshold modernism. New public women and the literary spaces of
      imperial London* (Cambridge: Cambridge University Press, 2019), p. 11.

the Shakespeare and Company edition of *Ulysses*, wrote in great detail about how Monnier's shop functioned as a salon:

> Imagine a lending library, a bookselling establishment, and a literary parlour rolled into one. You drop in casually; there is a smiling greeting for you from the pleasant hostess who presides over this drawing-room with the ever-open door; you chat about the latest publications, with which she is, of course, *au courant*, and upon the merits of which she possesses a cultivated judgement; you handle the volumes which line the walls, browsing to your heart's content, and you select your purchases or your borrowings with the freedom of a man who is in his private library. That alone makes the little institution a welcome haven from the turmoil of the Paris *rues*; but what is infinitely more is that it is, at all hours of the day, a rendezvous and the haphazard meeting-place of people like yourself who are interested in literature or who are endeavouring to make literature.[17]

Huddleston's description of Monnier's shop closely recalls Evans' definition of the threshold (especially his concern over the 'turmoil of the Paris *rues*'), and the entire characterisation hinges on how much he emphasises the domesticity of what is effectively a commercial space. It emphasises the characteristics of a traditional feminine-coded space for what can be non-typical for a bourgeois gender order. In other words, what makes Les Maisons des Amis des Livres successful as a business is precisely that it asks you to forget it is one.[18] Huddleston also wrote on Beach, and indeed, she was regularly profiled throughout the 1920s. A 1930 *Publishers' Weekly* piece sought to situate her and Shakespeare and Company as representative of a preferred model of bookselling. In 'The Bookshop as a Salon', Robert Ulric Godsoe lamented the rise of commercialised bookshop spaces, but also worried, in his terms, about the enthusiasms of uninitiated and idealistic women arriving from the Midwest to open a shop in a city. Referring to Beach as 'the distinct compromise type of bookseller', he expands on this label defining what works at her bookshop:

---

17    Sisley Huddleston, 'The bookshop salon', *Today*, December 1919, pp. 149–50.
18    Huddleston closes by considering the relation of the bookshop salon to the commercial market, arguing that '[i]nsofar as the traffic in books can be saved from the vulgarisation of mere money-making, it is so saved in the Bookshop Salon; the machinery of trade is cleverly hidden; one has the impression that literature does not depend upon financial calculations', Huddleston, 'The bookshop salon', p. 152.

[S]he has, and perhaps this is the point above all which should be stressed, with consummate skill concealed the commercial mechanism from the eyes of her public. That is the point around which the entire discussion must revolve. It is the contention of this earnest advocate that someone will open an ambitious bookstore, preferably in a metropolitan area, on strictly intimate lines, foster the growth of its salon with the same calm assiduity which Miss Beach has brought to her work. Buy, sell, handle personnel and advertising with the same acumen as that displayed by our most mercantile bookmen, and yet, throughout the process manage to conceal from the public every semblance of mechanical process.[19]

As with Huddleston, Godsoe frames the bookshop as straddling a gendered divide of the masculine public sphere (commercial market) and feminine private sphere (salon). As an intimate space, the bookshop itself, in its idealised form, functions as a semipublic space—if a shop is well-structured, in Godsoe's terms, the customer momentarily forgets the commercial side of the space and becomes a guest hosted in a salon.[20] The lending library functions as an extension of this dynamic: commerce is muted, books become a loan among friends—the 'company'. The lending library function of these businesses speaks to Beach's and Monnier's relationship to their books and their social function. Sheila Liming has referred to women's libraries of the period as 'technologies of self-making', and we can read how strongly her shop reflected her own interests, tastes, and intellectual development. Gisèle Freund reported that Monnier told her 'she had become a bookseller in order to read the books she had been unable to buy for herself'.[21] Thus, the bookshops were a public expression of their private interests; their 'self-making' was not an isolated practice but something to be shared with a coterie of like-minded friends.

A late indicator in Beach's life of how the bookshop served as a form of self-making can be seen in her processing of the memories and surviving documents of all her years running the shop. Melanie Micir has recently argued

---

19   Robert Ulric Godsoe, 'The bookshop as a salon', *The Publishers' Weekly*, 28 June 1930, pp. 3096–7.

20   Godsoe's argument, in fact, reflects what John Xiros Cooper has to referred to as modernist market society's thriving "on the anomalous and aberrant, especially in the practicalities of creating wealth ... [and the] growing pervasiveness of the market-form and its disruptive effects on the settledness of a particular order brings into play the continuously renewable necessity that allows the creative person to make it new, i.e. hypothesise systemic breakdown and, from it, propose and profit from the 'upwelling of the incalculable,'" John Xiros Cooper, *Modernism and the culture of market society* (Cambridge: Cambridge University Press, 2004), p. 164.

21   Gisèle Freund, *Gisèle Freund. Photographer* (New York: Harry N. Abrams Inc., 1985), p. 66.

that Beach's form of self-presentation, especially when it came to her late life archival curation and memoir writing served as a deliberate type of memorialisation: '[t]hese intimate biographical practices, which document the trace of desire between women with very different relations to avowal and orientation, feminism and lesbianism, and the work of partnership in private and professional life, are driven by an implicitly pedagogical, future-oriented impulse.'[22] Indeed, following Monnier's death in 1955, Beach was even more acutely aware of the pressure to leave behind an archive to represent their stories. Micir points to an unpublished page from the manuscript of Beach's memoir of the bookshop where Beach wonders at her purpose after Monnier:

> Sometimes you wish you had left with her as she suggested—she knew what living without her was going to be like. She knew everything—Adrienne.
> But leaving my jobs unfinished, I seemed to feel it important to tidy up before going—why were years not enough to clear away rubbish—why and how and when and where did it accumulate? Been playing around all my life.[23]

Even after her Shakespeare and Company had long since closed, Beach was intent on presenting the memory of the shop within terms she designed. Micir has argued that Beach's last years were preoccupied with the 'cultivation and demonstration of an archival consciousness'.[24] She continues:

> [Beach's] 'official period'—she was (a) writing a memoir, (b) 'cataloguing' her massive archive of literary material, and (c) curating a major cultural exhibit filled with artifacts from her personal collection ... I suggest that we must understand these activities as interrelated modes of turning years of personal witness into public testimony and commentary. This is the act of collection, of curation—rather than creation and innovation—as modernist artistic work.[25]

Where I may differ from Micir is in terms of time frame; Beach was always cultivating an idea of what Shakespeare and Company was, right from the outset.

---

22    Melanie Micir, *The passion projects. Modernist women, intimate archives, unfinished lives* (Princeton: Princeton University Press, 2019), p. 7.
23    Ibid., p. 84.
24    Ibid, p. 86.
25    Ibid., p. 87.

The 'official period' was simply an extension and rolling up of that exercise. If Shakespeare and Company was an experiential space in Monnier's terms, then archiving the memory of the bookshop was more than 'turning years of personal witness into public testimony and commentary'. It was a final form of public outreach and networking, drawing us—the future participants in the memory of Shakespeare and Company—into an idea of the bookshop as a communal space.

Beach and Monnier successfully navigated a male-dominated book trade and ran commercially viable establishments for over two decades. It took an economic depression and a world war to shutter their shops, and even then Beach carried on with her subscription library when she could. Their shops remained well-regarded throughout their existence, and a second iteration of Shakespeare and Company (with different owners and named in the 1960s in honour of Sylvia Beach) flourishes to this day in Paris. Their success hinged on emphasising those elements it shared with traditional literary salons—a kind of semipublic sociality with a broad networking reach. Their ability to quickly recognise this dynamic and create cultural institutions, which operated on the threshold between the private and public, remains their most significant contribution to the interwar book trade and literary modernist networks.

# CHAPTER 11

# Boundary Work in the Bazaar: the Women Booksellers of Daryaganj Sunday Book Market

*Kanupriya Dhingra*

Daryaganj Sunday Book Market, popularly known as *Daryaganj Sunday Patri Kitab Bazaar*, is an informal weekly bazaar (market) for used and pirated books in Old Delhi. Recently relocated to a gated compound called Mahila Haat on Asaf Ali Road, the market survived for more than fifty years with books stacked on the sidewalks of Netaji Subhash Road and Asaf Ali Road (Fig. 11.1).[1] Since its inception, the vendors of this market have relied on both vertical bonds of kinship and horizontal bonds of friendship to enable a dense locality-specific social network. The civic administrative units that supervise the city area in agreement with the central/national bodies of governance have formed laws and regulations that sanction a vendor their place in the local and professional community. In addition, the vendors have made their own internal definitions, or 'boundaries', based on what they see as the 'traditional' or the norm.[2] In this article, I explore the explicitly acknowledged and implicitly assumed ways in which gender has played a role in the history of Daryaganj Sunday Book

---

1 In less than four weeks of starting my fieldwork in Daryaganj Sunday Patri Kitab Bazaar, it was lifted off the streets. Based on a Delhi High Court order dated 3 July 2019, the North Delhi Municipal Corporation mandated that the street market be removed, quoting 'traffic concerns'. Netaji Subhash Road, which housed a part of Daryaganj Sunday book bazaar, was declared a non-vending zone. For more information on the relocation, the protests held by the booksellers, its effect on the vendors, the change in the social, visual, and cultural landscape of the Book Bazaar, and what I call the 'death of a book bazaar', see: Dhingra, 'The Death of a Book Bazaar', *Himal Southasian*, 05 February 2020 <https://www.himalmag.com/the-death-of-a-book-bazaar-daryaganj/>; Dhingra, 'Will Delhi Soon Have a Daryaganj-Used-Books-Market-Shaped Hole?', *Scroll.in*, 03 August 2019 <https://scroll.in/article/932656/will-delhi-soon-have-a-daryaganj-used-books-market-shaped-hole>; Dhingra, 'Delhi's Daryaganj Book Bazaar Has a New, Sanitised Home, Which Has Benefits as Well as Drawbacks', *Scroll.in*, 28 September 2019 <https://scroll.in/article/938776/delhis-daryaganj-book-bazaar-has-a-new-sanitised-home-which-has-benefits-as-well-as-drawbacks>; Dhingra, 'Delhi's Daryaganj Second Hand Books Market: Going, going ... but not quite gone yet?', *Scroll.in*, 24 August 2019 <https://scroll.in/article/934936/delhis-daryaganj-second-hand-books-market-going-going-but-not-quite-gone-yet>.

2 Thomas F. Gieryn, 'Boundary-Work and the Demarcation of Science from Non-Science: Strains and Interests in Professional Ideologies of Scientists', *American Sociological Review*, 48(1985), pp. 781–95.

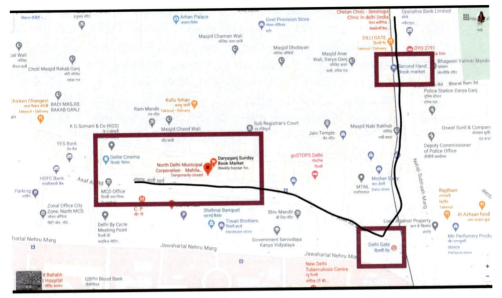

FIGURE 11.1  Present-day map of Daryaganj (and Daryaganj Sunday Book Market)

Market. With the help of my ethnographic research in the bazaar, I examine the external boundaries created by the civic authorities and the internal boundaries constructed and sustained by the vendors at the bazaar, which altogether result into the 'housewifization' of women as 'inauthentic' members of this community.

## 1    *'Ek Alag Experience'*: Shared Rhetoric of Belonging[3]

The book vendors at the Patri Kitab Bazaar demarcate their community from other street vendors and street hawkers. They associated *garv* (pride) and *shauq* (pleasure, interest, hobby) with their business—these were the terms they would use frequently in the interviews. Often, they would talk about their *lagaav* (attachment) to the *patri* (footpath/pavement) and the business of selling books. While narrating their stories, they often found ways to differentiate their bazaar from other weekly or permanent street markets in Delhi, emphasising the sale of books as its distinguishing factor. Selling books on the *patri* is not the same as selling everyday consumer goods found in most local weekly markets or LWMS (in official parlance), they implied.

---

3    'A unique experience'.

There are formal and informal ways in which bookselling at Daryaganj Patri Kitab Bazaar and its community of vendors can be defined. The formal ways include a written indication of business to the civic authorities and registering oneself as a street vendor, so that one can comply with state and central policies such as the Protection of Livelihood and Regulation of Street Vending Act, which came into effect in 2014. This Act protects the rights of urban street vendors and provides regulations for street vending activities. The vendors must safeguard these proofs of their registration. Before 2011, the street vendors received a gulabi parchi or a pink squatting receipt every Sunday from the Municipal Corporation of Delhi (Figure 11.2). This parchi was an acknowledgement of the fee they paid to the civic authorities to occupy the streets. In 2011, the sale of books on the streets of Daryaganj was legalised through the Tehbazaari system. Tehbazaari is a license for the grantee to squat at a notified site on a pavement to conduct business. (Fig. 11.2). From September 2019 onwards, after the relocation of the bazaar to Mahila Haat, the vendors have another *parchi* (replacing the previous pink slip) that declares that they have paid their share of rent for that specific Sunday. Another significant official document is a list of vendors that was generated as an appendix to officiate the 'Darya Ganj Patri Sunday Book Bazaar Welfare Association' under the Societies Registration Act of XXI of 1860 (Fig. 11.3). The official documents also provide, as it were, a written recognition of a vendor's attachment to the place where they have carried their professions—a document that shows their official timeline at the *patri* as a vendor of books (or other goods). Whenever asked to verify or even describe their association with the bazaar, whether it is by the civic authorities or by keen

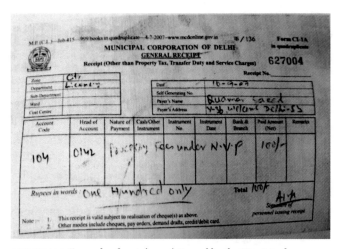

FIGURE 11.2  Example of a *pink parchi* issued by the Municipal
Corporation of Delhi

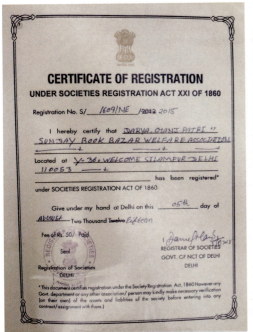

FIGURE 11.3 Two official documents produced by the vendors of Daryaganj

photojournalists and ethnographers of the bazaar, these documents become a convenient way of declaring such attachment (Fig. 11.3).

However, these documents are not entirely reliable in determining who is 'officially' a vendor at the Patri Kitab Bazaar. Suvrata Chowdhary, in his systematic study of the Local Weekly Markets (LWMs) in Delhi, has the following to say about how an official database is *supposed to* be maintained by officials from the Municipal Corporation of Delhi (MCD) that accounts for the number of and other details about the vendors:

> The Municipal Corporation of Delhi does not distinguish between weekly markets and individual street vendors and hawkers. There is a provision in the scheme which states that a centralised database of the registrations of traders and vendors must be maintained and full details like name, address, photograph etc. along with their locations. The information would be accessible at all Zones to avoid delicacy. A public notice inviting applications from squatters/hawkers who are squatting/hawking without authorisation in MCD's jurisdiction and from unemployed persons who are desiring to make their livelihood by squatting/vending in accordance with the eligibility conditions would be advertised by the

Central Licensing and Enforcement Cell, MCD in leading newspapers and shall also be displayed on the MCD website. The aforementioned provision of the scheme has only written importance. The MCD does not maintain a systematic record of registered vendors let alone of prospective applicants.[4]

Continuing from Chowdhary's remarks on the inconsistencies in the official system that records the number, types, and degree of formality of street vendors, especially those in the local weekly markets, there are comparable ambiguities that are found in Daryaganj Patri Kitab Bazaar. Ideally, the MCD should have a systematic record of those selling books at Daryaganj, since the booksellers here come under the authority of the said civic body. The North Delhi Municipal Corporation or NDMC (a subset of MCD) maintains an 'official' list of the vendors of Daryaganj. This official list of vendors at Daryaganj book market includes 258 names, with their names, date of birth, address, and contact details. Each vendor also has a certificate authorising them to set up a stall on the designated pavements at Daryaganj. However, there were never as many vendors sitting on the *patri* at once. On any given Sunday there were only ever approximately a hundred vendors. This was because some of the vendors, although registered individually, belong to a single family, and run their stalls together. For example, at least ten members of the immediate and extended family of Satish Aggarwal are present individually on the official list. However, they set up their stalls in sets of at least three. This allows members of one family to establish extended stalls beyond the officially sanctioned space of 6 feet by 4 feet. By registering multiple members of the family, it is also easy for one person to replace another in case of a medical emergency, or any other reason. Hence, while there are formal means to define and regulate this community of vendors, the vendors are largely able to run their stalls according to their own preferences, escaping the bylaws that regulate their presence on the streets and their business.

## 2      Who Is a Vendor at Daryaganj?

Traditional vendors have kept the bazaar running for years through resiliently building corpuses of reliable knowledge unique to the bookselling business at Daryaganj Patri Kitab Bazaar. Their knowledge and presence at the bazaar

---

4   Suvrata Chowdhary, 'The Local Weekly Markets of Delhi: Operating in the Formal 'Space' and Informal Economy', *E-journal of the Indian Sociological Society*, 1(2017), pp. 781–95.

continue to shape the bazaar, even as hundreds of other booksellers have joined them over the course of the last fifty years. However, for both new and traditional vendors, what does it mean to 'grow' in this business? One, there are newer ways of selling books because stocks and buyer's demands keep changing. Secondly, the way informal business is conducted keeps changing. For instance, regulations by civic authorities are updated every few years. Or, how the booksellers at Daryaganj bazaar had to update their stock and adjust their prices to make up for the loss during the protests held between July and September—or whenever in the past there has been a period of no sale when the bazaar on the streets were shut down caused by national holidays, civil unrest, and so on.[5] For the traditional vendors, their previous knowledge helped them. For new vendors, this was a space for experiment. In this way, it was the easiest for the newest vendors at the bazaar, that of pirated books (or what the vendors call duplicate/ 'D' books), to accommodate to the new space since they did not have to update their stock—their stock portions and profit margins are decided by middlemen who are not present at the bazaar.[6] In fact, some traditional vendors told me that they were now inclined to sell 'D' books to make up for the loss that they had incurred, given that the profit margin is guaranteed.

'It is our hobby, as well as, a means to earn our livelihoods', said Asharfi Lal Verma about his business of selling books on the *patri*.[7] In another meeting, later,

---

5  The market is closed around national holidays, such as Republic Day, observed on 26 January. In the year 2018, the Patri Kitab Bazaar observed its longest break so far, which made the general public speculate that the market is not going to revive, given several debates that have happened in the past over the legality of its presence on the streets, see; Sanghmitra Jethwani, 'Shut for Three Weeks, Daryaganj Book Market Might Never Reopen', DNA, 18 January 2018 <https://www.dnaindia.com/delhi/report-shut-for-3-weeks-daryaganj-book -market-might-never-reopen-2576371>; 'Daryaganj Book Market Remains Shut for the Fifth Week in a Row', *Hindustan Times*, 28 January 2018 <Daryaganj book market remains shut for the fifth week in a row | Latest News Delhi—Hindustan Times>; 'Delhi's Daryaganj Book Market Reopen After Five Weeks', *Indian Express*, 4 February 2018 <Delhi's Daryaganj book market shuts down: This is not the first time | Lifestyle News, The Indian Express>. Further, Delhi's recent episodes of smog during the winters (2016 onwards) affected the Patri Kitab Bazaar only so much with visitors still finding their way there, donned with masks; unlike during monsoon when the footfall decreases quite evidently. The booksellers also do not station their book stall if it is raining. As the market shifted to Mahila Haat in September 2019, the sellers found it rather challenging to manage, there being no shade, unlike on the streets where the market was previously located.

6  To read more on the 'D-books' circuit, see Kanupriya Dhingra, 'The 'D-Books' of Daryaganj Sunday Book Market', *Comparative Critical Studies*, 18 (2021), pp 309–26.

7  '*Hobby bhi hai, roti bhi hai*': Asharfi Lal Verma (bookseller at Daryaganj Sunday Book Bazaar) in discussion with the author, July 2019.

he exclaimed: 'See, there are some jobs that you enjoy doing; I could have done my business in a shop or I could have done a job. But this is a distinct experience altogether'.[8] Asharfi Lal has spent more than twenty years as a vendor at the Patri Kitab Bazaar. He used to assist with the sale of books in a bookshop else-where in Delhi before he became a street vendor in Daryaganj. Ramesh Ojha, who sells a similar stock of books in a rented shop on Netaji Subhash Road, made this enthusiastic and slightly exaggerated claim: 'According to me, there is no better profession than that of selling books in this bazaar. There is a lot of 'enjoy' [enjoyment] in this profession. You do not care about the time you have spent sorting books; you can go hungry and thirsty, it is so much fun, *oho*!'[9] Like Ojha, most of the vendors I talked to who belonged to the traditional and study circuits spoke about the pleasure they derive from sorting and acquiring books, that is, by putting their knowledge to work. Sorting books is, in fact, key to bookselling at the Patri Kitab Bazaar. Books of Daryaganj are drawn from various sources such as paper markets, discarded stocks from public, private, and individual libraries, and remaining stocks from publishers. Booksellers derive pleasure and enjoyment from creating value out of books derived from these parallel sources. Their pleasure is linked to how they perform and choose to specialise in this business. This contrasts with 'detached' vendors, a term I use for those who, in my conversations with them, did not exhibit a sense of *lagaav* (attachment) with the book business at Daryaganj. Such 'detached' vendors are also those who have suffered from a greater sense of instability in this business. Despite the instability and lack of profits, these 'detached' ven-dors have been part of this community for a long time, which shows that there is space for both specialised and non-specialised sellers. As much as longevity is not a marker of their aptitude for bookselling, it also does not guarantee attachment to bookselling as their profession.

Related stories followed from almost all the vendors I interviewed. One common thread, however, was each vendor describing how selling books at Daryaganj is what Asharfi Lal calls *alag* (unique): just as the market is officially regarded to be a specialised weekly bazaar compared to other Local Weekly

---

8  *'Dekhiye, kuch kaam karne mein maza aata hai; agar hum chahte to dukan ya naukri bhi kar sakte the. Lekin ismein ek alag experience hota hai.'*: Asharfi Lal Verma (bookseller at Daryaganj Sunday Book Bazaar) in discussion with the author, September 2019.

9  *'Mere hisaab se is bazaar mein kitaab bechne ke kaam se achha kaam koi hai hi nahin. Ismein "enjoy" hai. Aap jab kitaab chhantne lagte hain to time ka pata nahin chalta, bhookh-pyaas nahin lagti, itna maza aata hai, oho!'* Ramesh Ojha, (bookseller at Daryaganj Sunday Book Bazaar) in discussion with the author, December 2019.

Markets.[10] The vendors, too, believe that their profession is specialised and more sophisticated than it may appear because of its location and operation on a *patri* in Old Delhi. A shared rhetoric of belonging also implies the creation of unofficial internal boundaries.

In other words, given this keen sense of community, the traditional vendors have also created informal ways of exclusion by deciding who *should* be a part of the community, and who must not be identified as such. Such exclusion is rhetorical and implied, and attests that there is a boundary that most booksellers have drawn around the ways to belong to this community. Such 'boundary work' implies various practices of self-differentiation, wherein some members of a professional community will claim to be more authentic than others.[11] One major indicator of this unexpressed officiality is gender. In this light, I will now look at the women book vendors of Daryaganj.

### 3    Women as 'Non'-Vendors: the Case of Lata Devi and Vimla Wadhwa

Out of the 258 vendors mentioned in the official list of vendors, only eight are women. These women work at the market only *in lieu of* their husbands, sons, or fathers-in-law, except for Lata Devi and Vimla Wadhwa. During the period of my fieldwork between June 2019 and February 2020, both Lata and Vimla were present regularly at their respective stalls. Lata's stall was that of used books, and Vimla sold out-of-syllabus children's books such as books on alphabets, simple mathematics, colouring books, and so on.[12] That is, both their stocks of books belonged to two major circuits that operated in the bazaar.[13]

---

10    Daryaganj Sunday Patri Kitab Bazaar has been distinguished from the other Local Weekly Markets that are set up periodically 'by the poor for the poor' across various locations in Delhi—also referred to in the Street Vendor's Act 2014 as LWMs. In the Act, the book bazaar is recorded as a *specialised* weekly market, as against any other local weekly market, since it bears the sale of a special good, i.e. books, across the breadth of the street market. Other local weekly markets sell diverse commodity goods such as clothes, footwear, kitchen utensils, sports equipment, everyday hygiene essentials, and so on, all available in the same market.

11    Gieryn, 'Boundary-Work and the Demarcation of Science from Non-Science', pp. 781–95.

12    There are two kinds of books available for school and college going students at the Patri Kitab Bazaar: (a) syllabus books, and (b) out-of-syllabus books. The latter includes books that are not a part of the formal curriculum of the schools/ colleges/ universities but are considered helpful as supplementary learning aids.

13    There are three major circuits of books that I have identified at the bazaar: (a) traditional circuit of used books, (b) study material circuit which includes syllabus and out-of-syllabus books (it is a subset of the first circuit), and (c) 'D' books circuit, or the circuit of pirated books.

How the women did the business or performed their role of a bookseller was no different than any other regular, male seller at the Patri Kitab Bazaar; they set up the stalls by spreading their stock across the given floorspace, negotiated with the buyers, sat and ate around their stalls over the course of each Sunday, and even made major and minor business decisions. Lata was, in fact, an elected member of the now dismantled Darya Ganj Patri Sunday Book Bazaar Welfare Association and held the position of Treasurer. More likely, she was merely a cursory representative of her gender, as mandated by the by-laws of the Association.[14] However, despite their visibly active role, their identity as a vendor was not 'authorised' by the male vendors.

Since the very first Sunday of my fieldwork and throughout the protests held by the vendors between July and September 2019, and even after the relocation, I met Lata Devi every Sunday, and we often chatted more about the book market's situation than her life as a bookseller. A woman in her late fifties, she preferred staying in one place and not moving around the stall or the streets; she blamed her age for her aching back and knees. Lata expressed her refusal to identify herself as a bookseller as such; each time she would talk about her engagement with the market, she repeated this sentence, '[t]his business can only be run by men. How do you think women will manage handling such heavy stacks of books?'.[15] Since her husband passed away some thirty years ago, she has manned the bookstall, while her son, Shekhar, took their book business beyond the streets of Daryaganj; Shekhar deals with the middlemen and outsources the stock of second-hand books to other countries. At the stall, Lata negotiated with the customers who visited the stall, since Shekhar was rarely present at the site of business. Yet, instead of Lata, Shekhar was the one who the rest of the booksellers engaged with—from informal discussions over *chai* (tea) about the business to buying books from him to sell in their stalls. He is one of the younger vendors but is known among the booksellers as someone who has gained extensive knowledge about the business. Since Lata (and Shekhar) sold second-hand English novels, they were both what I understand as traditional vendors of the Patri Kitab Bazaar. Yet, it was Shekhar who was publicly acknowledged (by the vendors) as one by the booksellers, not Lata.

When I met Vimla Wadhwa, who was in her early forties, she was grieving for her husband. Her husband died of a heart attack in May 2019. 'He had the attack

---

14   The by-laws suggest that there must be at least one woman in the core committee of members in the new location of the bazaar.

15   'Ye aadmi logon ke hi bas ka kaam hai. Itni bhaari-bhaari kitabein auratein kaise uthyengi, aap hi batao?': Lata Devi (bookseller at Daryaganj Sunday Book Bazaar) in discussion with the author, July 2019.

on a Sunday evening, after having spent the day on the *patri*, selling books', said a vendor, and several vendors quoted the same incident to me, suggesting how essential his relation was to the book market. When I met her in 2019, first at the *patri* and later inside Mahila Haat, Vimla's son Dev had just started to assist her and was quickly learning the tricks of the business to take over whenever it was suitable. Vimla felt the need to find other means of employment because she could not identify as a bookseller. Similar to the case of Lata and Shekhar, the vendors would often only communicate with Dev rather than with Vimla about issues and opportunities related to the Patri Bazaar, say, issues related to the relocation or the arrival of new stock. Since Dev is only sixteen and is relatively younger and much more inexperienced than Shekhar, the vendors took it upon themselves to train him as a forthcoming vendor from the new generation, but one who would sell books at the bazaar in the traditional sense. This included knowledge such as what books to gather, building contacts that may be relevant for his business and how to negotiate with the customer and the middlemen. However, Vimla seemed familiar with the tricks of the trade when I met her. At their stall, they sold newly acquired out-of-syllabus supplementary course material for children such as colouring books, books on alphabets and numbers, and some comics. Her husband's old assistant was responsible for selling the stock of old novels that he had accumulated. In this sense, Vimla had created her own specialised stall, borrowing from the knowledge corpus created by the traditional vendors. While Dev was still learning, she already knew what would sell, and how to fetch profits. Vimla had taken over the business overnight since there was no other way available to them to survive. They lived in a rented house, and the book business paid all their bills. Vimla was active during the protests that were held between July–September 2019, demonstrating her resilience by fighting for their book-business to continue on the streets, but a few weeks after the relocation was made official by the North Delhi Municipal Corporation, she decided to move to Mahila Haat. She told me that she had to find some way to feed her family of two. While she too, like Lata, waited for Dev to gradually take over the business, she was looking for a more 'stable' job, since the book business inside Mahila Haat had been quite erratic. She was an active vendor, much like Lata, or any other male vendor. However, the two months when the Patri Kitab Bazaar was lifted off the streets had demotivated her due to the lack of stability in the book-business at Mahila Haat. Trusting her skills as a businesswoman, she decided to sell homemade chocolates as a side business. Selling chocolates would also limit her interaction with a male-dominated space and would not require her to depend on the men who apparently ran the book business. However, since her experience and acquired training and knowledge was in bookselling and in a bazaar-like space, she realised she could not apply it to another commodity at large. This, in turn, testifies that this space and this commodity is specialised and requires specific modes of training, and the execution of that training into the business. Learning how to sell chocolates, or, in other words, becoming a vendor for chocolates, demanded a different skill-set and knowledge, one which she assumed was also suited to her life as a 'woman'-entrepreneur.

Daryaganj Sunday Book Market's new location at Mahila Haat (literally, A Market By Women) is part of an initiative by the Delhi wing of the Self Employed Women's Association (SEWA), a trade union that organises female workers in the informal sector. The motivation behind the project was to establish safe spaces for female street vendors, who face a multitude of problems owing to the nature of their work such as lack of safety and a major lack of footfall as well. However, the efficacy of establishing an exclusive market run only by women also turned out to be a failed experiment, where its economic viability also turned out to be a failed experiment, where its economic viability had not been thoroughly thought through, making the proposition novel and noble, but not profitable. It is ironic that now, at a site set up exclusively for women, there is a bazaar where the majority of vendors are men and their traditional organisation is thoroughly patriarchal in character.[16]

## 4    'Housewifization': *'yeh aadmi logon ka kaam hai'*[17]

Maria Mies, a Marxist feminist scholar renowned for her theory of capitalist-patriarchy, which recognises third world women and difference, explains how women's work often makes up the 'shadow economy'—there is a substantial lack of data vis-à-vis their contribution to the informal economy. Mies calls this phenomenon the 'housewifization' of labour, which allows for women's

---

16    "Haat", in Hindi, refers to a quasi-permanent marketplace. In North India, a haat is usually a weekly market. Mahila Haat, as the name suggests, was an initiative by the North Delhi Municipal Corporation to set up a place for women artisans to showcase their skills. The Mahila Haat at Asaf Ali Road was marketed as the first of its kind to be set up in Delhi in 2011, but no such *haats* were set up after it. See: (a) Establishment of the first 'Mahila Haat' in Delh, Hamari Jamatia, 'Women only: MCD's Mahila Haat to open in April', *Indian Express*, 18 February 2011 <http://archive.indianexpress.com/news/women-only-mcd-s-mahila-haat-to -open-in-april/751594/>; (b) The Haat to be utilised for purposes other than the original, as North Delhi Municipal Corporation became cash-trapped over time, Vibha Sharma, 'Mahila Haat, Ramlila Ground may host weddings, private parties soon', *Hindustan Times*, 20 January 2017 <https://www.hindustantimes.com/delhi/mahila-haat-ramlila-ground-may-host-wed dings-private-parties-soon/story-BT5uB4TWk4iP3w8CpkMAzJ.html>.

17    The subtitle translates to 'this work belongs to men'.

labour to be gauged as house work or subsistence work instead of contributing to the production of capital. This is apparent in Lata and Vimla's case as well, where they have internalised such housewifization.

In a conventional sense, Lata and Vimla's case is that of devalorisation of work that women do outside their homes. Lata and Vimla are the only two women vendors who run independent bookstalls in the Patri Kitab Bazaar—both because their husbands have passed away and their sons cannot stay at the stall regularly. Yet, during my interviews with them, both suggested that they are merely 'assisting' with the book selling business. Both considered the business unsafe for women in terms of procurement of books, selling books in a visibly male space, and manning the stall. In fact, Vimla's father-in-law and other male booksellers would visit their stall often, every Sunday, to check if they were safe and comfortable. In a way, this ostensibly charitable manoeuvre asserted men's continued presence at the stall. The crowded streets of Old Delhi are exposed to a heterogenous crowd, prone to theft and petty crimes. The majority of the vendors are men. Managing stocks of books from the godowns to their stall involved other men—rickshaw pullers and other labourers. Even while they actively engage in the profession of selling books, Lata and Vimla see themselves as belonging to the space of the house and not the outside world of street vending—it was only out of necessity, and only until Dev could take over, that Vimla was willing to work. Even Lata expressed that this was one way for her to 'pass' (spend) her time, and nothing beyond that. In a way, this restriction is also cultural, where women are tied to the boundaries of housework, and not worldly affairs such as running a business. Consider the case of 35-year-old Kiran. 'My husband is a heart patient. He used to sell books in this bazaar, near Delite cinema. In 2018, when he fell really sick, it got difficult for us to manage our finances, I decided to come and sell books here. He is not happy with the fact that I come out of the house to work', she says.[18] He would rather she stays inside. Kiran cannot, and should not (according to her husband), *replace* him at the bazaar, and as the bread-winner of the family. In this sense, Kiran is defying the unofficial internal boundaries created by the male members of the bazaar.

Daryaganj Patri Kitab Bazaar is visibly a male-dominated space—professionally and socially. The only two regular women vendors could never

---

18    'Mere pati dil ke mariz hain. Wo is bazaar mein kitab bechte the, Delite ke baaju mein. 2018 mein jab wo bahot beemar hue tab humare paas paise jamana mushkil ho gaya. Tab maine socha, main yahaan kitabein bechungi. Wo is baat se khush to nahin hain, ke main baahar aakar kaam karti hoon.': Kiran (bookseller at Daryaganj Sunday Book Bazaar) in discussion with the author, September 2019.

associate themselves with the space. It is, however, common to see women vending on the streets across Delhi. For instance, at a rather famous street market in Central Delhi, popularly known as Janpath Gujarati Market, it is mostly women who sell Gujarati artefacts, jewellery, upholstery, and bags. Although, in the adjacent second-hand cloth market, it is again men who are vending on the streets, as is the case with Sarojini market, another, bigger market for export apparels. Janpath Gujarati Market is set in a different lane, and in turn, becomes an exclusive space for women to sell their goods. Even where the market merges with the nearby market for export clothes, which again is a male-dominated space, women vendors are often seen sitting together. In contrast, Daryaganj Patri Kitab Bazaar is larger in size and scale, the commodity being sold is different, and it is also situated in a more conservative part of the city. Hence, even if it is not obviously stated that the space is unsafe for women or is exclusively male-dominated, it is not only assumed but also shown. The civic authorities speculated and argued that the bounded architecture and outlook of Mahila Haat would be a 'safer' space for women to pursue book vending. There were certainly more female members and vendors seen inside the Haat, but most of them were sitting along with their husbands, brothers, or other male family members. One of the reasons for an increase in this number was also that the vendors needed extra hands in setting up their stalls inside the new site. Since it was already an expensive arrangement compared to the streets, family members, especially women, became suitable unpaid labour. However, it would be premature to claim that the conventional boundary that the vendors have created will loosen with the change in space.

Two other women vendors, Meenu and Divya Aggarwal, are also worth mentioning here. Both are members of the extended Aggarwal family, as is Vimla. Meenu began coming to the market to participate in the 2019 protests along with her daughter Divya. During the protest, Divya informed me that, due to some family feud, the Aggarwal brothers were fighting for their individual stalls and not as a unit, which is why both mother and daughter had come to support her father.[19] Divya worked in the sales department of a jewellery shop and had to leave the protest site for work every Sunday. Her mother was present throughout the duration of the protest. Both Meenu and her daughter Divya are registered in the official list of vendors. However, while remaining absent from the bazaar in its day-to-day activities, these two vendors could 'replace' the routine vendors—members of their family—as the community was experiencing a significant moment of change. Through their show of resilience, Divya and

---

19      Divya Aggarwal (daughter of a bookseller at Daryaganj Sunday Book Bazaar) in discussion
        with the author, August 2019.

Meenu were in fact expected to participate in the protest as authentic parts of the bazaar. This does not, however, make them an authentic part of this community, since their presence and activity are intermittent and limited, and like Lata and Vimla, they would not have been accepted as authentic or traditional vendors. Women booksellers found it difficult to claim the space of the bazaar as their own—they did not find pride nor pleasure enough to state it.

5      Conclusion: a Space for Women

In India, only agriculture seems to absorb a significant number of women workers. Often, this is because as men find more profitable non-agricultural occupations, women are often 'left behind' in rural areas, especially when access to non-agricultural work entails male migration. Those who come to the city do find street vending as an agreeable option for women who need to earn their living, given the low cost of entry. That being said, it is true that the female participation in the informal sector is majorly due to economic compulsion rather than any change in the working ethos of the society. Furthermore, according to the National Sample Survey Office (NSSO), almost 82% of India's workforce is employed in the unorganised sector.[20] The National Commission of Women highlights that 94% of the total female workforce is in the unorganised sector.[21] Therefore, it is natural that there exists a correlation between the vulnerable segments of society and the underprivileged. Women street vendors sell their goods mostly on the pavement or streets, unlike men who use push-carts. They also earn less than their male counterparts. The Ministry of Urban Employment and Poverty Alleviation quotes that the average income for men of the sector is seventy rupees, while the average earning for women is approximately fifty rupees on a daily basis.[22]

Hence, in this essay, by examining how ideological views coincide with economic systems, I ask why it is that women vendors are not defined as, and do

---

20    The National Commission for Enterprises in the Unorganised Sector, in their *Report on Conditions of Work and Promotion of Livelihoods in the Unorganised Sector*, the term 'unorganised sector' in the Indian context as '... consisting of all unincorporated private enterprises owned by individuals or households engaged in the sale or production of goods and services operated on a proprietary or partnership basis and with less than ten total workers'; 'Life of Women Street Vendors: Protection of Livelihood and Need for Regulation', BW *Business World*, 24 December 2018 <https://www.businessworld.in/article/Life-Of-Women-Street-Vendors-Protection-Of-Livelihood-And-Need-For-Regulation /24-12-2018-165482/>.

21    'Life of Women Street Vendors', BW *Business World*.

22    Ibid.

not define themselves as a member of the community of vendors at Daryaganj Sunday Book Market. The booksellers, especially those who I have recognised as the 'traditional' vendors, have prescribed boundaries as to who can authentically enter the profession that they have specialised over the years. The organisation of the community of vendors at the Patri Kitab Bazaar shows a persistence of older family forms and structures within which individuals, and women in particular, must continue to engage. The women vendors at the bazaar accommodate their agency and autonomy within the existing constraints of duty and obligations, both social and familial.[23] Lata and Vimla are not creating any new forms of specialisation or adding to the knowledge corpus. Instead, they choose to act within the traditional norms that the male vendors have created and continue to create. Considering the way gender is construed in the book market, the female vendors are subjected to internalised and imposed devalorisation of their labour. Their housewifization has prevented the female vendors at Daryaganj from forming their independent identity as 'proper' vendors of Daryaganj Patri Kitab Bazaar, which, this article notes, will require as much internal renegotiation as mere formal, policy changes. Their place in the history of the book is yet to be located.

---

23    Sanjay Srivastava, *Passionate Modernity: Sexuality, Class, and Consumption in India* (Routledge, 2007), p. 274.

# CHAPTER 12

# The Bookseller and the Lady: the Literary Ambitions of Anna de Sterke (1755–1831) and Her Dealings with Bookseller Luchtmans

*J.C. Rozendaal*

Anna van der Aar de Sterke, daughter of a wealthy Leiden-based lawyer, was eighteen years old when she first visited Luchtmans' bookstore on her own on 24 January 1774.[1] Luchtmans, situated in the centre of Leiden in the direct vicinity of Leiden University, was one of the foremost publisher-booksellers of its day. During this visit, Anna de Sterke bought a copy of Hendrik Matthijsz. Lussing's *Gezangen over de geboorte, het lijden, de opstanding, de hemelvaard van den Heiland* (Songs on the birth, suffering, resurrection and ascension of the Saviour), a music book written to improve domestic, religious singing.[2] Lussing, a Dutch Reformed pastor, would later win silver honorary medals for his entries in two poetry contests organised by literary society *Kunst Wordt Door Arbeid Verkregen* (*KWDAV*; Art is obtained through craft).[3]

This first purchase, and especially its indirect link to a literary society, would go on to characterise Anna de Sterke's later acquisitions. But what exactly do the book acquisitions of van der Aar de Sterke tell us about her and her literary aspirations? What did this young woman, who would years later establish the first known all-female literary society in the Dutch Republic, buy exactly?[4] And how did she get the idea to simply walk into a bookstore of high standing, in a time when, usually, the head of the family would be responsible for all book purchases? This essay will offer a glimpse into the dealings of an eighteenth-century Dutch bookstore, and how and why some women were accepted into its circle of clients. It will also demonstrate how closely

---

1  Leiden Municipal Archives, Arch.1004 Baptisms Pieterskerk 1741–1769, inv. 229, dd. 26-02-1755.

2  H. Lussing, *Gezangen over de geboorte, het lijden, de opstanding, de hemelvaard van den Heiland* [...] *nevens een nieuwjaarszang* (Amsterdam: H. Vieroot,wed. Loveringh, Allart 1774).

3  In 1778 and 1780, for his poems *De Voortreffelijkheid van den Christelijken Godsdienst* (The excellence of the Christian faith) and *Gods wijsheid in zijne werken* (God's wisdom in his works) respectively. P.G. Witsen Geysbeek, *Biographisch anthologisch en critisch woordenboek der Nederduitsche dichters* (6 vols., Amsterdam: Schleijer, 1821–1827) vol. IV, pp. 259–260.

4  This all-female literary society was discovered early 2021 by Leiden University student Evi Dijcks. *NRC/Handelsblad*, 15 February 2021.

© KONINKLIJKE BRILL BV, LEIDEN, 2025 | DOI:10.1163/9789004701656_013

connected a woman's book acquisitions might be to her personality, and how book acquisitions can tell us more about a woman's interests and activities.

Evidently one has to know what is ordinary in order to identify the extraordinary. Scholars such as José de Kruif, Jeroen Blaak, Han Brouwer, Joost Kloek and Wijnand Mijnhardt have laid the groundwork for a comprehensive overview of early modern Dutch book ownership.[5] But because of their focus on general book ownership, the nuances of female book ownership get overshadowed somewhat. Moreover, by focussing on gender as an analytic category and on common ground of female book ownership, the uniqueness of each particular collection may be overlooked. The common dismissal of female book ownership as 'mainly literary' or comprising primarily devotional works does not do justice to either the acquisitions themselves, nor to their owner. The emphasis on common denominators obscures the heterogeneity and the uniqueness of women's book purchases. And only in the *specific* do we find that the books on women's bookshelves actually reflect their personal agendas and aspirations. Their book purchases require a 'close reading'; not of texts, but of the contents and context of the purchases themselves. Only then can a woman's acquisitions shed light on herself and the personal and literary circles in which she moved.[6]

Basing myself on the information drawn from the Luchtmans bookseller's archives, I will use Anna van der Aar de Sterke's book acquisitions as a case study to show how an individual woman's book purchases can reveal her unique personality. The client books in the Luchtmans archives are an abundant source for book historical and cultural research in the early modern Dutch Republic. These immensely rich archives cover the entire period from 1697 to 1848, and are one of the very few extant publishers' archives from the eighteenth century that have been preserved in their entirety—in eleven metres of archival material, now digitised by the University of Amsterdam.[7] Arend Smilde has made a first attempt at using these vast archives methodically, but no others

---

5   José de Kruif, *Liefhebbers en gewoontelezers. Leescultuur in Den Haag in de achttiende eeuw* (Zutphen: Walburg, 1999); Jeroen Blaak, *Geletterde levens. Dagelijks lezen en schrijven in de vroegmoderne tijd in Nederland 1624–1770* (Hilversum: Verloren, 2004); H. Brouwer, *Lezen en Schrijven in de Provincie; de boeken van Zwolse boekverkopers 1777–1849* (Leiden: Primavera Pers, 1995); J.J. Kloek, W.W. Mijnhardt, *Leescultuur in Middelburg aan het begin van de Negentiende Eeuw* (Middelburg: Zeeuwse Bibliotheek, 1988).

6   For more on how books and libraries could strengthen women's reputations and firmly position them within a network of peers, see Rindert Jagersma and Joanna Rozendaal, 'Female Book Ownership in the Eighteenth-Century Dutch Republic. The Book Collection of Paper-Cutting Artist Joanna Koerten (1650–1715)', *Quaerendo*, 50 (2020), pp. 109–140.

7   Archive of the Luchtmans firm, UBA354. Allard Pierson—the Collections of the University of Amsterdam.

have yet studied their contents systematically.[8] This essay will demonstrate the value of these client books for research on female book ownership. I will start characterising the Luchtmans firm before moving to van der Aar de Sterke, and offer some thoughts on the practicalities of female book acquisition in the Dutch Republic.[9]

Situated on the central Rapenburg canal, the Leiden-based firm of Luchtmans specialised in academic texts—especially concentrating on classical, eastern philology—from the onset.[10] They covered almost all aspects of the academic book trade: their publishing house was renowned, their bookshop welcomed the most astute scholars, and they partook in the lively second-hand book trade among university professors by organising auctions and by selling and buying used books. The variety and sheer volume of the stock in their bookshop was astonishing.[11] More popular, less scholarly books were obtained from colleagues within the Dutch Republic. Like many other early modern booksellers, the Luchtmans firm made sure their stock remained up-to-date and varied by taking works of other publishers on commission, by trading their own publications with those of other publishing houses, and by acquiring second-hand books from private individuals.[12] Their extensive European network ensured a steady influx of the most interesting titles; their book sale catalogues often offered thousands of works for sale, including incunables and other hard-to-find antiquarian books.[13] In keeping with this focus on the academic market, they carefully presented themselves as a scholarly publishing house and bookstore. This image was further strengthened when in 1730, they became Leiden's official city and university printer.[14] Arend Smilde even states that 'non-academically schooled clients were a rarity at Luchtmans', and indeed, the overwhelming majority of clients at Luchtmans were highly

8    Arend Smilde, *Lezend Leiden bij boekhandel Luchtmans, 1801–1812* (Utrecht, 1986).

9    The results presented here are the preliminary conclusions of a larger doctoral dissertation on female book ownership in the eighteenth-century Dutch Republic, based on the Luchtmans archives on the one hand, and private library auction catalogues on the other.

10   Arend Smilde, 'Lezers bij Luchtmans', *Negentiende eeuw*, 14 (1990), pp. 149–150, 152.

11   Smilde, 'Lezers bij Luchtmans', pp. 149–150.

12   Hannie van Goinga, 'The long life of the book: public book auctions in Leiden 1725–1805 and the second-hand book trade', *Quaerendo*, 24 (1994), p. 244.

13   Sytze van der Veen, 'De Leidse boekhandelaars Luchtmans: gedegen verlichting, 1683–1848', *Mededelingen van de Stichting Jacob Campo Weyerman*, 31 (2008), pp. 18–31, pp. 27–28.

14   I.H. van Eeghen, 'De uitgeverij Luchtmans en enkele andere uitgeverijen uit de 18de eeuw', *Documentatieblad werkgroep Achttiende eeuw*, 34/35 (1977), p. 6.

educated, and primarily male.[15] Nonetheless, over 175 different female clients were present in the Luchtmans' archives, accounting for the acquisition of around 3,500 volumes.[16]

This female presence in relatively large numbers makes it possible to start teasing out commonalities in female book buying habits in the eighteenth-century Dutch Republic on the one hand, and identify what is most specific to individual book acquisitions on the other. Hitherto scholars had to resort mainly to single case studies to come closer to the individual eighteenth-century Dutch female book owner, but without knowledge of the common, it is difficult to tease out the exceptional. With a source like the Luchtmans archives it becomes feasible to enrich case studies with a more general analysis, surpassing at least to some extent the level of the micro-history, while simultaneously filling some gaps of more general studies.[17] Furthermore, when we compare and combine the findings in the Luchtmans archives with other sources that describe female book ownership, such as the auction catalogues of female owned libraries incorporated in the *MEDIATE* database (*Measuring Enlightenment: Disseminating Ideas, Authors, and Texts in Europe, 1665–1830*), the risk of statistical bias will diminish and broader patterns in early modern female book ownership start to become visible.[18]

Many of the women who became patrons of Luchtmans were widows of scholars, men who had been clients of Luchtmans themselves during their lifetime.[19] Other women who frequented the Luchtmans bookshop include those who were tied to the Luchtmans firm by familial bonds, members of the aristocracy such as the countess of Gronsveld and the baroness of Alkemade, and a few 'independent' women, who at first sight do not seem to have been

---

15    'Een niet-academisch gevormde klant was uitzondering bij Luchtmans'. Smilde, 'Lezers bij Luchtmans', p. 152. My impression is that less than 5% of the Luchtmans clientele was female.

16    The actual number of different women may even be a bit higher: the method of describing buyers in the account books sometimes makes it difficult to distinguish between different buyers with the same name.

17    José de Kruif's *Liefhebbers en gewoontelezers* is an example of a larger-scale research based on probate inventories (see note 5 for other examples).

18    Alicia C. Montoya, Micha Hulsbosch, Helwi Blom, Evelien Chayes, Anna de Wilde, Rindert Jagersma, Juliette Reboul, and Joanna Rozendaal, *MEDIATE* database, 2022— (ongoing), <https://test.mediate-database.cls.ru.nl/>.

19    The widow of Professor Pieter Burman is an example, client in 1741; as are the widow of Van den Honert (client from 1763 until 1778) and the widow Snakenburg (1755–1758).

introduced to the Luchtmans firm by their husbands.[20] However, upon closer examination it emerges that even these 'independent' women had been in contact with Luchtmans via a male mediator or guardian before they opened an account at the store themselves. Anna van der Aar de Sterke made her first visit to Luchtmans in 1774, after her father had been an irregular client there for years. The account ledgers indicate that he had frequented the store since October 1768.

The earliest veiled mention of Anna de Sterke dates from 24 October 1770, when her father commissioned Luchtmans to buy 'tracts for the miss, at the auction of Hasebroek, quarto, no. 14' (Uijt de auctie bij Hasebroek, quarto, nr. 14: Tractaten voor de Juffr.).[21] A few years later, his daughter was mentioned again: on 9 June 1773 Theodorus bought three books by the popular religious-literary author Dirk Smits, and the seller notes that these books were 'for his noble daughter' (voor zijn ed. Dogter).[22] The ledgers do not tell us why it is made explicit that these books were for her specifically. Women's purchases are generally invisible in the archives of booksellers, as accounts would be listed under the name of the head of the family.[23] Here, and in a few other cases as well, the bookseller makes clear that the books were bought for someone else.[24] Such a note almost seems to have been an introduction, a first meeting

---

20    The countess of Gronsveld (1775–1777) and the baroness of Alkemade are examples of the former, while cousin Catharina Segwaart, mother-in-law Musschenbroek, and cousin Anna Teijken were directly related to the Luchtmans family.

21    I have not been able to link this reference with certainty to a known auction. Leiden-based bookseller Johannes Hasebroek did organise an auction on the 15th of October that year; another possible contender is the auction organised by Abraham Kallewier on 24 October 1770. Kallewier and Hasebroek had collaborated before, on 25 September 1758—when the books of Gerardus Ruyter were auctioned off. See Hannie van Goinga, Bibliopolis: <https://www.bibliopolis.nl/veilingen/search/database/REPVEIL+DBSC+VERZCAT/ auctioneer/Hasebroek/date/1770/sort/auctioneer/maximumRecords/1>; for Kallewier: <https://www.bibliopolis.nl/veilingen/search/database/REPVEIL+DBSC+VERZCAT/auc tioneer/Kallewier/date/1770/sort/auctioneer/maximumRecords/1>. (Both accessed 18 January 2021).

22    Archive of the Luchtmans firm, UBA354. Allard Pierson—the Collections of the University of Amsterdam, (hereafter: Luchtmans Archives Online), <https://dpc2.uba.uva.nl /archives/viewer/view.php?id=UBAinv354.479>, p. 458.

23    Jeroen Blaak, *Literacy in Everyday Life. Reading and Writing in Early Modern Dutch Diaries*, (Leiden: Brill, 2009), p. 313.

24    See for example the widow Romswinkel, who bought books for 'haar Ed. Zoone Pieter' (her son Pieter) on the fifth of May in 1757. On 21 February 1758, Pieter van Romswinkel enters the account books himself. Luchtmans Archives Online, <https://dpc2.uba.uva .nl/archives/viewer/view.php?id=UBAinv354.477>, p. 45. Other examples are the widow Clignet, who visited the bookstore together with her son in April 1757 (her son would come in unaccompanied in August 1764), idem, p. 68; and the widow Peene, who bought

between Luchtmans and the hitherto unknown secondary buyer, perhaps to establish an acquaintance that would later allow the secondary buyer to open an account for themselves.

Anna de Sterke herself appeared independently half a year later, and she would be buying books on her own for a few years to come. As the daughter of Theodorus van der Aar de Sterke, Lord of Esselickerwoude and Jacobswoude, and Lady Esther Johanna Wasteau, she had the means and opportunity to buy books regularly.[25] Anna disappeared from the Luchtmans archives not long after her marriage to Maximiliaan van 's-Gravesande on 27 July 1775 and their subsequent move to Delft.[26] She visited Luchtmans for the last time on 18 June 1776. Anna was accompanied by her father, and possibly her grandmother as well. They all bought a set of editions that were to be bound in a volume described as the 'Centenary', probably a book celebrating the second centenary of Leiden University.[27]

I have looked closely at the 64 books Anna de Sterke bought in these two years, and at first sight her purchases suggest that she bought a large number of religious books, and a modest amount of literary works, sometimes with a Christian connotation, thus fitting well into the general categorisation of early modern female book ownership. But a closer look reveals there seems to be a strong link between her book purchases and her later literary aspirations. To find out how special or meaningful these purchases actually were, one has to identify the general trends in female book purchasing. To that end, I have looked at the book acquisitions of 145 different women who bought books at Luchtmans.[28] Up to now I have identified 2,768 instances of these women either buying books or having books bound at Luchtmans. The earliest acquisition dated from 22 February 1702, when a Ms. van de Nieburg bought *Rudimenta Latina*, a schoolbook for learning Latin. The last purchase was made by Elizabeth van der Stel in 1781: the *Maatschappij der Landbouw* (Society of

---

books for Mr. A.S. and Pieter Peene in July 1759 (A.S. or Abraham would appear solo in June 1760; Pieter only started to buy his own books in May 1761). Luchtmans Archives Online, <https://dpc2.uba.uva.nl/archives/viewer/view.php?id=UBAinv354.478>, p. 194 for Pieter, p. 178 for Mr. A.S. (= Abraham).

25    Leiden Municipal Archives, Arch. 1004 NH Notice of Marriage 1575–1795, inv. 40, leaf QQ-188, dd. 18-05-1754.

26    Leiden Municipal Archives, Arch. 1004, NH Notice of Marriage 1575–1795, inv. 44, leaf VV-135, dd. 27-07-1775.

27    Luchtmans Archives Online, <https://archives.uba.uva.nl/repositories/2/resources/480>, p. 196.

28    I.e., women with different surnames. Only when I could differentiate with absolute certainty between different women with the same last name (e.g. because their first names were mentioned) did I count them as two individuals.

Agriculture).[29] As these two cases already show, female book purchases turn out to be extremely varied.

The fact that Anna regularly bought religious works is not remarkable in itself. But a more thorough examination reveals that even some of De Sterke's devotional acquisitions demonstrate the uniqueness of her taste. On one occasion, in March 1774, she bought James Fordyce's *Sermons to Young Women* (in Dutch translation: *De vriend der jonge juffrouwen*). While that title would fit well into commonplace generalisations regarding gender and book culture, whereby female readers supposedly demonstrated a marked preference for devotional literature, Anna van der Aar de Sterke was the only woman who bought this title at Luchtmans. Naturally, bibles, catechisms and psalms were bought by other women as well—they head the best-selling list—but the number of copies bought by de Sterke is unequalled (sixteen copies of the same psalm book, ten catechisms, nine identical bibles, and a further two psalm books and seven bibles). She had all these religious works bound in 'Russian' leather with copper fastenings; sturdy, high-quality bindings.[30] The number of copies she bought, and the manner in which de Sterke had them bound suggest she intended them as gifts. Whether she intended these as end-of-year gifts for friends, family, staff or other acquaintances is not clear.

TABLE 12.1   Authors women bought most frequently at Luchtmans (1702–1783)

| Author | Number of women buying the books | Number of different titles bought |
| --- | --- | --- |
| Joan van den Honert (theologian) | 16 | 33 |
| Gerardus Joh. Vossius (scholar) | 10 | c. 10 |
| Cicero | 8 | 3 |
| Mattheus Gargon (clergyman) | 7 | 6 |

29   Ad 1: this probably refers to a schoolbook, possibly *Linguae Latinae rudimenta* [...] *in usum scholae Amstelodamensis*, (Amsterdam: Janssonius van Waesberghe, 1701. Most recent edition up until then). Ad 2: this may refer to the *Verhandelingen uitgegeeven door de Maatschappy ter bevordering van den landbouw, te Amsterdam*, (Amsterdam: Guerin, 1780–1781).

30   These bindings cost over one guilder a piece, more than the psalm books themselves cost.

TABLE 12.1   Authors women bought most frequently at Luchtmans (1702–1783) *(cont.)*

| Author | Number of women buying the books | Number of different titles bought |
| --- | --- | --- |
| Hieronymus van Alphen (poet, ao. poetry for children) | 6 | 4 |
| Pierre Marin (linguist) | 6 | 4 |
| James Hervey (clergyman) | 5 | 7 |
| Johannes Lulofs (theologian, professor) | 5 | 2 |
| Ovid | 5 | 2 |

TABLE 12.2   Works women bought most frequently at Luchtmans (1702–1783)

| Short-title | Number of women buying the title | Contents |
| --- | --- | --- |
| *Bijbel* (unspecified) | 61 | Bible |
| Psalmboek (unspecified) | 25 | Psalms |
| *Boekzaal der geleerde wereld* | 16 | Scholarly and religious periodical |
| *Catechismus* (unspecified) | 14 | Catechism |
| *Rudimenta latina* | 6 | Latin schoolbook |
| Passieboek (unspecified) | 5 | On the Passion of Christ |
| *Staat der Nederlanden* | 5 | Published in instalments, history and current description of The Netherlands |
| *Vaderlandse Historie* | 5 | History of The Netherlands |
| *Grammatica contracta* | 5 | Latin schoolbook |
| *Grammatica graeca* | 5 | Greek schoolbook |
| Cato, *Disticha* | 5 | Moral proverbs (also used in Latin schools) |
| Aesop, *Fabulae* | 4 | Fables (also used in Latin schools) |
| Avondmaalsboek | 4 | Sacrament book |

TABLE 12.2    Works women bought most frequently at Luchtmans (1702–1783) (*cont.*)

| Short-title | Number of women buying the title | Contents |
| --- | --- | --- |
| Calmet, *Woordenboek van den gantschen H. Bybel* | 4 | Biblical encyclopaedia |
| Erasmus, *Colloquia* | 4 | Dialogues (also used in Latin schools) |
| Gaubius, Redevoering | 4 | Celebrating the lustrum of the Leiden University |
| Snakenburg, *Poezie* | 4 | Poetry |
| *Vaderlandse Letteroefeningen* | 4 | Literary, cultural periodical |

Apart from the obligatory acquisitions of bibles, psalm books, catechisms and the like, it is difficult to find a common denominator in female book purchases in the account books. Schoolbooks for learning Latin, and more rarely Greek, books that were on the curriculum of the Latin schools, appear often in women's accounts, although academic literature written in Latin does not appear as often as on men's balances.[31] Women's purchases are very religious, but also literary, and sometimes practical in nature. Other than that, there are few similarities between the book purchases of the different female customers at Luchtmans (Tables 12.1 and 12.2). The work of the best-selling author and theologian Joan van den Honert (1693–1758) appeared in the accounts of 16 of the 175 women. A very limited number of books or periodicals were regularly purchased by many different women, like the literary periodical *Boekzaal van Europa* (1692–1863; the Library of Europe). Not counting the unspecified editions of devotional texts, the *Boekzaal* appears most frequently, in the accounts of 16 different women. This periodical was founded to introduce a general public to the latest scientific discoveries of the age.[32] These findings suggest that

---

31    It seems probable that these books were bought for school-going sons. Ernst Jan Kuiper, *De Hollandse "Schoolordre" van 1625* (Groningen: Wolters, 1958).

32    Continued under the titles: *Boekzaal der geleerde wereld / De republiek der geleerden* (1715–1863, Library of the learned world / The republic of scholars), periodical, bought by: widow Block, Elizabeth van Deutekom, widow Hollebeek, widow Do. Hubert, Ms. Jacobi, widow Professor la Mort, ms. Rijcke, widow Alderman Trigland, widow Ulrichus Velingius. Other, less frequently appearing examples are: *De algemene historie* (A universal history), book: widow J.H. Bakker, widow Pompe van Meerdervoort, widow Schultens; *De*

women book buyers, like men, were interested in the scientific and literary developments of their day, and they took the opportunity to inform themselves when they could.[33]

The following figures indicate that Anna de Sterke may not have been especially interested in current affairs, or that she obtained her news through different channels (Tables 12.3 and 12.4). But her purchases are as distinctive for her as those of other women often are for them. The majority of her acquisitions are unique, in the sense that they were bought by no other woman (see Table 12.3). Furthermore, four of the books that were bought by Anna de Sterke as well as by others, were bought by a certain widow Wasteau. The similarities in taste suggest a link between both women, and indeed, further research showed that the widow Wasteau was probably Anna de Sterke's grandmother Anna Caauw. The widow Wasteau first appears in July 1769, and in that same year, Luchtmans brought to auction the library of a late Jan Wasteau, lawyer. Anna de Sterke's grandfather, a lawyer, went by the same name. The fact that both Anna, her father Theodorus, and this widow Wasteau all bought the plates that accompanied the 'Centenary' on the same day in 1776, further corroborates the idea of a family relationship.[34] This example shows not just how personal book acquisitions were or could be, but also how seemingly random similarities between book acquisitions can help uncover the identity of otherwise almost entirely anonymous women.[35]

---

  *philosooph* (The philosopher), periodical: widow Block, ms. C.A. Bodel, ms. J.D. Sandra; the *Bibliothèque des Sciences et des beaux-arts*, published in instalments: Ms. Rucker, widow Hollebeek; *Staat der Nederlanden* (The present-day State of the Netherlands), book: widow Bazijn, widow Pompe van der Meerdervoort, widow Trigland, widow Vromans.

33 However, here, it is important to remember that the source may have influenced the results: it is likely that results would differ significantly when looking at acquisitions at a less academically-inclined bookseller, such as the Van Benthems in Middelburg, a provincial bookstore with an important regional function (see J.J. Kloek, W.W. Mijnhardt, 'Bij Van Benthem geboekt. Een reconstructie van het Middelburgse koperspubliek in 1808', in W. van den Berg, J. Stouten (eds.), *Het woord aan de lezer. Zeven literatuurhistorische verkenningen.* (Groningen: Wolters-Noordhoff, 1987), pp. 142–165). Moreover, the real best sellers—certain songbooks, pamphlets, or plays—may forever remain hidden because they were sold by hawkers and peddlers, about whose dealings we still know painfully little.

34 They also visited Luchtmans on the same day in December 1774.

35 I highly suspect a link between the misses Schop and the widow Bassée as well, and for the same reasons: both bought Joselijn's *Wegwijzer naar Gods heiligdom* (Guide to Gods Sanctuary) on 2 July 1739, and both returned on 21 July 1739 to buy Johan van den Honert's *Brief aan Watteville, voorstander der herrnhutsche broederen* (Letter to Watteville, proponent of the Morovian brethren). However, these books appeared in the year they were bought, so I cannot rule out the possibility that they just bought the books as soon as they became available.

Anna de Sterke's book purchases distinctively reflected her literary interests: her acquisitions are remarkably literary in nature. While the works she bought were generally written by male authors, two books were written by women (Table 12.3 and Fig. 12.4). De Sterke did not pick the most popular female authors for her gender: Jacoba Petronella Winckelman with her *Stichtelijke Gedichten* (Devout poetry), and Catharina Brakonnier-de Wilde, each appearing with five different titles. Their works were bought by four different women—but not by de Sterke. The pedagogical works of Marie Le Prince de Beaumont, appearing in three different accounts, follow, but again, de Sterke never bought her books. Anna de Sterke did buy the theatrical work of Lucretia van Merken, cowritten by her husband Nicolaas van Winter, as did one other woman. But most striking is perhaps, that Anna van der Aar de Sterke was the only woman who bought a work authored by Agatha Deken: 'Bosch & A. Deken. Poems in quarto. 3 guilders and 12 stuivers' (Bosch & A. Deken. Gedigten in 4. 3.12).[36] Before Agatha Deken partnered up with Elizabeth Wolff-Bekker and they became the Republic's most famous female writing duo, Deken wrote this work together with her friend Maria Bosch. No other woman bought this book at Luchtmans. In fact, even later in the century and in the beginning of the nineteenth century, no works of Bosch, Deken or Bekker were bought by any woman.

TABLE 12.3   Books bought only by Anna de Sterke at Luchtmans

| Date of acquisition | Title | Date of publication / notes |
| --- | --- | --- |
| 24 October 1770 | From the auction of Hasebroek, in Quarto, No. 14, Tractaten | (Bought by her father, for the young lady) |
| 9 June 1773 | **Smits**, *Rottestroom* (collection of poetry) | (Bought by her father, for his noble daughter) |
| 9 June 1773 | **Smits**, *Israëls Baälfegorsdienst* (a biblical epic) | (Bought by her father, for his noble daughter) |
| 9 June 1773 | **Smits**, *Nagelaten gedichten* (Posthumous poetry) | (Bought by her father, for his noble daughter) |

---

36    Luchtmans Archives Online, <https://dpc2.uba.uva.nl/archives/viewer/view.php?id=UBA inv354.480>, p. 196.

TABLE 12.3   Books bought only by Anna de Sterke at Luchtmans (*cont.*)

| Date of acquisition | Title | Date of publication / notes |
|---|---|---|
| 3 February 1774 | [Fordyce] *Vriend der Jonge Juffrouwen* (Sermons, litt.: 'Young ladies' friend') | [latest edition: 1767] |
| 3 February 1774 | Steenwijk, *Gideon in zes zangen* (Gideon, in six songs—a biblical epic) | [latest edition: 1748. Published in 1774: Klaudius Civilis, in zestien zangen.] |
| 19 April 1774 | Le Roy, [*De waarheid der heilige*] *godgeleertheid* (The truth of the holy divinity) | [latest edition: 1762] |
| 27 August 1774 | de Timmerman, *Nagelaten gedichten* (Posthumous poetry) | [published] by Bohemer [1774] |
| 10 December 1774 | ***Mengeldichten** van het kunstgenootschap Prodesse canendo* (Miscellaneous poetry by literary society Prodesse Canendo) | [1774]* |
| 29 December 1774 | Willemsen, *Hertsterking* [= *Hertsterkte in Jehova*?] (Strength of the heart in God) | [1775?] |
| 7 January 1775 | Gellert, *Brieven* (Letters) | [published] by Meijer [1774] |
| 27 March 1775 | Bosch & Deken, *Stichtelyke Gedichten* (Edifying poetry) | [1775] |
| 21 November 1775 | **Leuter**, *Kruiskerk* [*of spiegel van gewetensdwang*] (Cross church) | [1776] |
| 29 December 1775 | [**Bakker**], *Leven van Wagenaar* (Life of Wagenaar | [1776] |

* On 30 December 1773 the widow Wasteau bought *Zoografia*, by the same society.
Boldfaced: works authored by men affiliated to literary societies

TABLE 12.4 Books bought at Luchtmans by Anna de Sterke and other women

| Date of acquisition | Title | Other buyers |
| --- | --- | --- |
| 24 January 1774 | **Lussing**, *Gezangen [over de geboorte, het lijden, de opstanding]* (Songs on the birth, suffering, and resurrection of Christ) | Bought by 1 other, both in January 1774 ** |
| 10 September 1774 | Van Winter & van Merken, *Tooneelpoëzy* (Theatrical poetry) | 1 other |
| 14 October 1774 | Psalmen (Psalms) | 25 others [unspecified eds.] |
| 14 October 1774 | Catechismus (Catechism) | 14 others [unspecified eds.] ** |
| 22 October / 3 December 1774 | Bijbel (Bible) | 61 others [unspecified eds.] |
| 10 December 1774 | *Hedendaagsche Vaderlandsche Letteroefeningen* (Current Dutch Literary Exercises) | 3 others [2: crossed out] |
| 27 December 1774 | **Lucas Pater**, *Poezij* (Poetry) | 1 other ** |
| 31 December 1774 | Gellert, *Fabelen en vertelsels* (Fables and Stories) | |
| 19 June 1775 | Gaubius, *Redevoering [Feestrede by den heuglyken aanvang der derde eeuwe van Hollands hooge schole, te Leyden?]* (Oration, on the Anniversary of Leiden University?) | 4 others, 4 of 5 bought in the second half of June ** |

** The widow Wasteau was one of the other buyers

Most visible in de Sterke's account is her focus on authors that were affiliated with literary societies, a predilection that fits less readily in inherited narratives about women's reading. Some of the very first books Anna obtained from Luchtmans already foreshadow the nature of her later acquisitions and her interest in these literary societies. De Sterke's father bought her three literary works by Dirk Smits, member of the literary society *Natura et Arte*, and one of its most talented writers.[37] Her later independent purchases confirm the presumption that Anna de Sterke favoured works written by members of literary societies. I already noted in the introduction that Hendrik Lussing, author of the first book that De Sterke bought at Luchtmans herself, would win the second prize in a writing competition organised by literary society *KWDAV*. Lucas Pater, whose poetry Anna bought in December 1774, also had strong ties to a number of literary societies of his day. Modern-day scholar Marleen de Vries even dubs him an 'authority in many a literary society'.[38] And when de Sterke bought *Het leeven van Jan Wagenaar* (the life of Jan Wagenaar), she took home the biography of a member of the prestigious *Maatschappij der Nederlandse Letterkunde* (Society of Dutch Literature).[39] Lastly, Pieter Leuter, the author of *Kruiskerk* (Cross Church), was the head of the society *Studium Scientiarum Genetrix*, and a member of both *Kunstliefde Spaart Geen Vlijt* (*KSGV;* Love of art spares no industry) and *KWDAV*.[40] About half of all de Sterke's purchases that could be identified with certainty, were written by members of various literary societies.

Anna's preference for the works of men associated with literary societies was not coincidental. A book that Anna de Sterke bought in the autumn of 1774 clarifies this preference: she bought *Mengeldichten van het kunstgenootschap, onder de zinspreuk: Prodesse canendo* (Miscellaneous poetry by the artistic society operating under the motto Prodesse Canendo). In this publication Anna is mentioned on the list of recent members—she had become a member earlier that year.[41] By then, Anna had already been approached by *KSGV* to become an honorary member. Founded in 1766, this literary society was the first in the Dutch Republic to allow women to become honorary members. Female honorary members were not supposed to partake in the society's meetings, but they were allowed to submit their work, and could enter writing competitions

---

37  'The best writings in the works that this society published from time to time, are written by Smits.' (translation mine). P.J. Blok & P.C. Molhuysen, *Nieuw Nederlandsch biografisch woordenboek*, (10 vols., Leiden: Sijthoff, 1911–1937), vol. III. p. 1187.

38  Marleen de Vries, *Beschaven! Letterkundige genootschappen in Nederland, 1750–1800* (Nijmegen: Vantilt, 2001), p. 71.

39  De Vries, *Beschaven!*, p. 234.

40  K. ter Laan, *Letterkundig woordenboek voor Noord en Zuid* (Den Haag: Van Goor, 1952), p. 305. Anna de Sterke would become a member of *Studium Scientiarum Genetrix* as well, in 1778. Rietje van Vliet, 'Veemgerecht, De Marsyas-bende van Frans van Lelyveld', *Mededelingen van de Stichting Jacob Campo Weyerman*, 32 (2009), pp. 123–124.

41  *Mengeldichten van het kunstgenootschap, onder de zinspreuk: Prodesse canendo* (Rotterdam: Bennet, Haken, 1774), p. xi.

that the societies organised.[42] Shortly after accepting her membership of *KSGV*, she must have been invited to join *Prodesse Canendo*, and in May of the same year an invitation by *KWDAV* followed, which she accepted as well. At the latter society, Anna de Sterke was the first female member. The following woman to join was female dramatist Cornelia de Lannoy, who was invited to join four years later.[43]

It seems remarkable that such a young woman, virtually unknown to us today, was at the forefront of some of the most important cultural changes of her time. Just as literary societies started to open their doors to women, Anna van der Aar de Sterke found herself in de midst of these changes. Her literary star rose quickly, as she was accepted into three literary societies in the same year, being the first female member ever in one of them, and in the years to come, at least one other literary society invited her to join.[44] As was discovered just recently, her memberships were a prelude to her establishing a literary society of her own, exclusively for women, in 1782, *Die Erg Denkt Vaart Erg in 't Hart* (a free adaptation of *'Honi soit qui mal y pense'*).[45] This was a remarkable event, for this was the first and only all-female literary society recorded to date in the eighteenth-century United Provinces.

Anna van der Aar de Sterke's book purchases were thus closely related to her literary interests and her membership of several literary societies. Her acquisitions could very well have been used as a sort of preparatory material, a model or an example to base her own 'societal' writings on, or to get further acquainted with her fellow society members, whom she had met, at least on paper, in the months before her purchases. But however she may have used her books, it is clear that her book purchases surpass the dominant categorisations of female book ownership, and reflect her personal ambitions more than anything. Most of the time we look for what women have in common, but the variety I have presented in this paper transcends these general conclusions, and

---

42 Pim van Oostrum, 'Honneurs aux dames? J.C. de Lannoy en de heren van KSGV', *De Nieuwe Taalgids*, 88 (1995), pp. 311–312. Dutch writer Cornelia de Lannoy was the first woman to join this society in 1772. Van Oostrum, 'Honneurs aux dames?', pp. 307–308.

43 Van Oostrum, 'Honneurs aux dames?', p. 311.

44 *Studium scientiarum genitrix*. In their *Dichtoeffeningen van het Kunstlievende genootschap, onder de spreuk Studium scientiarium genitrix*, (Literary exercises of the literary society operating under the motto Studium scientiarium genitrix. Leiden/Rotterdam: Hoogeveen, Vis, Manheer, 1780), she is named as one of the honorary members. The only other woman on mentioned here is Anna Cornelia Perrenot, née Mollerus (member of *KSGV* as well). p. xvii, xxi.

45 News of this discovery by Dutch student Evi Dijcks was broadcasted in February 2021. Publication forthcoming.

rather tells us more about women as individuals. It illustrates that the books women bought reflect who they were as an individual and how these women equipped themselves to navigate successfully the domain of their choice; thereby further challenging the treatment of woman as a monolithic category. In De Sterke's case, it has shed light on her prolific life as a member and later founder of a literary society of her own.

# PART 5

## *Shaping Collections: Gender and Value*

∵

# CHAPTER 13

# 'No entiende en el Balor de los libros': the Value of Books for Women Owners in Seventeenth-Century Navarre

*Alexandra E. Wingate*

In April 1693, María Josepha de Soraburu declared via her lawyer to Pamplona's diocesan tribunal that she was 'A poor woman who does not understand the value of books'.[1] One might think this indicates she was illiterate and simply had no use for books, but in fact, it was a strategic, gendered way of expressing the lack of monetary value she perceived in a certain set of books. The books in question were a portion of the bookseller Lorenzo Coroneu's stock left after his death in July 1684. Nine years later in 1693, his executor was attempting to repay Coroneu's debt to Soraburu using those books; however, María Josepha de Soraburu felt the books were worthless and refused them as payment.[2]

Soraburu's case is just one of many complex interactions early modern women in Navarre had with books. Women read, owned, inherited, loaned, and printed books, not to mention litigated rights over their creation, received them as payment, or, as in the case of Soraburu, refused them as payment. In these interactions, the myriad values that these women perceived in books emerges. In this study, I analyse these values through the lens of 'affordances', a term first coined by ecological psychologist James J. Gibson which denotes the potential uses of an object based on its perceivable physical characteristics and who is using it.[3] I adapt this term to include tangible and intangible traits of books, which afford various values to the women interacting with them. Through eight seventeenth-century Navarrese women who appear in the inventories, wills, and court cases preserved at the Archivo General de Navarra (AGN) and the Archivo Diocesano de Pamplona (ADP), I argue that the expectations of gender constrained socially acceptable choices as they related to books when their primary assumed affordance was reading, giving

---

1    'una pobre mujer que no entiende en el Balor de los libros', Archivo Diocesano de Pamplona, C/1436 N. 2, ff. 642$^r$–642$^v$.
2    ADP, C/1436 N. 2, ff. 52$^v$, 497$^r$, 641$^r$.
3    James J. Gibson, *The ecological approach to visual perception*, Classic edition (New York: Psychology Press, 2015; originally published by Taylor & Francis 1986), pp. 223–225.

women in particular reduced access to books. Books with a primary reading affordance also afforded opportunities for devotional practice and demonstration of wealth and prestige. Conversely, gender seems to have had very little limiting effect on women's interactions with books when the object's primary affordance was economic.[4]

## 1      Affordances

Before delving into the case studies, I will expand on my use of the term 'affordance.' James J. Gibson theorises in his study of visual perception that individual animals and humans directly perceive what characteristics objects have and what uses or values (affordances) those objects offer (afford) that individual animal.[5] Knappett, building on later works that revise Gibson's original concept, identifies three important elements of affordances—relationality, transparency, and sociality—which are helpful when considering the potential affordances of books. Relationality establishes the interdependence between the specific agent, object, and situation in determining an affordance.[6] For example, the same book might be readable by one person and not another because one cannot read the language in which the book is printed. A large-print book or audiobook affords readability to those with print disabilities, while a codex with smaller text does not.[7] For reading at a children's story hour, a phonebook does not afford the children entertainment, but a child could

4   In writing this paper, I thank Dr. Alice Wickenden and Joe Saunders for their suggestions and conversations while proposing the paper for the USTC conference. Profs. Jorge Terukina, Lu Ann Homza, Francie Cate, Noel Blanco Mourelle, and the Institute of English Studies provided immense support and suggestions when this research existed as parts of my undergraduate and masters theses. Prof. Carmen Sanchis Sinisterra's comments were invaluable while revising this work. I also thank Peio Monteano Sorbet of the AGN and doña Teresa Alzugaray of the ADP for all their support while I researched at their institutions. Finally, this paper is deeply indebted to the work of don José Luis Sales Tirapu, the former archivist of the ADP who created the ADP's catalogue, and to the staff contributing to the AGN's Archivo Abierto. Without either of these, it would be difficult to locate the cases relevant to this research.
5   Gibson, *The ecological approach*, pp. 223–225.
6   Carl Knappett, 'The affordances of things: a post-Gibsonian perspective on the relationality of mind and matter' in Elizabeth DeMarrais, Chris Gosden, and Colin Renfrew (eds.) *Rethinking materiality: the engagement of mind with the material world* (Cambridge: McDonald Institute for Archaeological Research, 2004), p. 46.
7   National Network for Equitable Library Services, 'About NNELS' (n.d.), <https://nnels .ca/about>. Thank you to Ellen Forget for sharing this citation and her expertise on print disabilities.

be boosted in their chair with it to see. Transparency refers to discerning an affordance from an object's physical form in Gibson's original formulation, but Knappett points out that cultural knowledge is often necessary to make an object's affordances visible.[8] Cultural knowledge is key to certain affordances discussed in the case studies, especially since every book is so entwined with the culture in which it appears.[9] Sociality means that a situation may contain a set of objects but more than one agent, and these agents may agree, disagree, and arbitrate about the affordances of the objects.[10] This too is useful to consider since some case studies involve multiple agents interacting with the same books.

Gibson and Knappett focus on the physical characteristics which determine affordances, and physical characteristics are certainly important in discussing the affordances of books—after all, book historians are keenly interested in the book as a material object. Affordances for books, however, must also consider intangible characteristics. The genre or subject matter, whether it is a banned book, its reputation or popularity with readers, the language of the book, and the intellectual content (text, music, illustrations, etc.) all contribute to the affordances of the book. In the case studies that follow, the intangible and physical characteristics of books, cultural knowledge, and relations between agents, objects, and situations within the broader context of seventeenth-century Navarre all play a role in the affordances that emerge.

## 2        Reading Affordances

The first five cases analysed involve women and their books where the assumed primary affordance is reading. I use 'assumed' because these books had multiple affordances, such as devotional use or the ostentation of prestige, and these other affordances could have been as or more important than reading. The assumption these were books that might be read by women brings with it expectations of ideal behaviour based on gender, which restricted what books women were supposed to read and how they procured books. The following women mostly matched moral conventions in terms of the types of books they read, whereby these books could afford them evidence of being virtuous women—a socially useful affordance. At the same time, they appear to have

---

8    Knappett, 'The affordance of things', p. 46.
9    Leslie Howsam, 'The study of book history' in Leslie Howsam (ed.), *The Cambridge Companion to the History of the Book* (Cambridge: Cambridge University Press, 2015), p. 4.
10   Knappett, 'The affordance of things', p. 47.

had different levels of freedom to choose their books, likely affected by their marriage statuses, and some were able to acquire books without the mediation of a masculine relative as was generally recommended by male moral philosophers.

Spanish and Navarrese women read and owned books in a context where the discourse surrounding women's reading was geared towards restriction. Moralistic works, such as Juan Luis Vives' *De institutione feminae christianae* (1523) or Juan de la Cerda's *Vida política de todos los estados de mugeres* (1599), which discussed the behaviour of 'virtuous' women stated that reading could be a useful tool in a woman's development of virtue. Others, like Fray Luis de León in his *La perfecta casada* (1583), saw reading as a threat since it allowed young women to read 'dangerous' *libros de caballerías* (romantic works of chivalry).[11]

If women did read, these authors argued that they should only read books devoted to developing virtue and morals. Women were considered physically, intellectually, morally, and spiritually inferior to men, and therefore less adept at achieving virtue.[12] This drove a division between ideal feminine and masculine reading matter, which is visible in Juan Luis Vives' work:

> It is reasonable that the man be equipped with the knowledge of many and varied subjects, which will be of profit to himself and to the state ... I wish the woman to be totally given over to that part of philosophy that has assumed as its task the formation and improvement of morals.[13]

Men, being considered more virtuous and participating in a wider variety of 'important' activities, were entitled to read many types of books, while women had to make up for their supposed inherent lack of virtue with religious and moral works.[14]

It is significant, however, that both men and women could be judged on the appropriateness of their reading. Juan Álvarez de Toledo y Monroy, count

---

11  Luis de León, *La perfecta casada* (Salamanca: En casa de Juan Fernandez, 1583), p. 28 (USTC 339465); Juan Luis Vives, *The education of a Christian woman a sixteenth-century manual*, Charles Fantazzi (trans.) (Chicago: University of Chicago Press, 2000), pp. 59, 65; Juan de la Cerda, *Vida política de todos los estados de mugeres* (Alcalá de Henares: en casa de Juan Gracian, 1599), f. 12$^v$ (USTC 335621).

12  Nieves Baranda, 'Las lecturas femeninas', in Jean-François Botrel et al. (eds.), *Historia de la edición y de la lectura en España, 1472–1914* (Madrid: Fundación Germán Sánchez Ruipérez, 2003), p. 159; Susan Migden Socolow, *The women of colonial Latin America* (Cambridge: Cambridge University Press, 2000), pp. 6–7.

13  Vives, *The education*, pp. 71–2.

14  Ibid., p. 71; Cerda, *Vida política*, f. 42$^r$.

of Oropesa, used a written survey to assess suitors to wed his daughter and become heir to the title. One of his questions enquired what books potential suitors tended to read. Essentially, one's books were an important way to judge character—important enough to factor into finding an heir.[15] Books thus afforded the opportunity to build or maintain one's reputation, and women had a narrower acceptable selection with which to do so. It appears Spanish women's libraries generally matched these guidelines since most or all of the books tended to be religious in nature.[16]

The other major restriction of books based on gender was the lack of unmediated access to choose one's own books. It was not considered appropriate for women to choose their own path in reading because of their supposed lack of virtue and reason. Vives counsels that women should seek the advice of educated men when choosing books versus relying on their own judgement. Specifically, he says that a woman

> must not rashly follow her own judgement, lest with her slight initiation into learning and the study of letters she mistake false for true, harmful for salutary, foolish and senseless for serious and commendable.[17]

This same logic was applied to the general Spanish population (efficaciously or not) through pre-publication censorship by the Crown and post-publication censorship of the Inquisition.[18] Men with sufficient education and need could access banned books through licences, but this in principle limited books to a 'learned' and 'virtuous' male elite.[19] Pedro Cátedra and Anastasio Rojo in their study of women's libraries and reading in sixteenth-century Spain note that single women and nuns generally did not directly choose books from a bookstore

---

15    Fernando Bouza, *Communication, knowledge, and memory in early modern Spain*, Sonia López and Michael Agnew (trans.) (Philadelphia: University of Pennsylvania Press, 2004), pp. 41–42; Alexandra Wingate, '"A qué manera de libros y letras es inclinado": las bibliotecas privadas de Navarra en los siglos XVI y XVII', (Unpublished BA Thesis, College of William and Mary, 2018), <https://scholarworks.wm.edu/honorstheses/1241>, pp. 1–2. This undergraduate thesis addresses the construction of identity through books for clergy and legal professionals in addition to women.
16    Anastasio Rojo Vega, 'El libro religioso en las bibliotecas privadas vallisoletana del siglo XVI', in Pedro Cátedra and María Luisa López-Vidriero (eds.), *El libro antiguo español IV: coleccionismo y bibliotecas* (Salamanca: Universidad de Salamanca, 1998), pp. 464–65; Baranda, 'Las lecturas femeninas', p. 185.
17    Vives, *The education*, p. 78.
18    Bouza, *Communication*, p. 44.
19    Virgilio Pinto Crespo, *Inquisición y control ideológico en la España del siglo XVI* (Madrid: Taurus, 1983), p. 145.

themselves, though they might express what books they wanted to a male family member. Spiritual advisors and confessors had a hand in guiding the content of women's libraries. For example, Cristóbal López, a Jesuit, guided the acquisitions of doña Ana Manrique, countess of Puñonrostro. Alternatively, more independent women like widows could enter bookstores directly.[20] This practice of male mediation when women acquired books appears to have been practised elsewhere and later in Europe since Joanna Rozendaal in this volume notes that it was usual for the head of the household to go to booksellers on behalf of the whole family, while for the most part women directly acquiring books themselves were widows. In the cases that follow, widowhood appears to have similarly given Navarrese women more freedom of direct choice.

The biographical details of the five women readers—Antonia García Jiménez (d. seventeenth century), Mariana Vicenta de Echeverri (d. 1684), María de Ceniceros (d. 1644), sor María de la Purificación (d. seventeenth century) and Ana de Sarasa (d. 1629)—are scarce. They mostly come from the wills and other legal documents accompanying the court cases in which they appear, and their backgrounds facilitated the acquisition of literacy and books. They were mostly urban women: María de Ceniceros and Ana lived in Pamplona, and Mariana Vicenta resided at least partially in San Sebastián.[21] Sor María's location was likely Pamplona since she obviously lived in a convent relatively close to Gazólaz due to her friendship with its priest, and Gazólaz is less than eight kilometres from Pamplona. Antonia's location at the time of the events studied here is similarly unknown, but her uncle from whom she received her books lived in Pamplona.[22] That urban women appear as readers in archival documents is unsurprising since they were closer to a greater selection of books and more likely to be literate. Sara Nalle's study of seventeenth-century literacy reveals estimated literacy rates of 3% to 28% for women overall and as high as 57% for urban women.[23] The women also tended to be elites of

---

20    Pedro Cátedra and Anastasio Rojo, *Bibliotecas y lecturas de mujeres siglo XVI* (Salamanca: Instituto de Historia del Libro y de la Lectura, 2004), pp. 98–9. However, even with this guiding masculine force in women's reading, it appears men still supplied their female relatives with 'dangerous' texts since both Vives and Cerda complain about men giving these works to their wives and daughters, Vives, *The education*, pp. 74, 76; Cerda, *Vida política*, f. 42[r].

21    ADP, C/618 N. 10, f. 73[r]; ADP, C/849 N. 27, f. 54[r]; C/1456 N. 10, f. 60[v]. Mariana Vicenta de Echeverri seems to be more Basque than Navarrese since she lived in San Sebastián, but as her case ended up in the court of the diocese of Pamplona, and her library includes books on Navarre, I have included her in this analysis.

22    AGN, n. 89984, f. 45[v].

23    Sara T. Nalle, 'Literacy and culture in early modern Castile', *Past & Present*, 125 (1989), p. 68.

society, which similarly increased their chances of literacy and their ability to own books, though Sara Nalle finds that lower class readers owned books more often than expected by many historians.[24] Mariana Vicenta was the countess of Villalcázar and marchioness of Villarrubia.[25] María de Ceniceros and Antonia García Jiménez were both related to legal professionals. Ana de Sarasa was possibly minor nobility, since she is addressed as 'doña' in documents and the inventory of her goods has a specific section for silver, including a large plate described as having her coat of arms.[26]

Complete knowledge about each woman's book collection is similarly elusive. While Mariana Vicenta de Echeverri and Ana de Sarasa's post-mortem inventories of their books have an average or better amount of description (title, sometimes author and format for each book), some books cannot be identified to the work from their descriptions, and few can be identified to the edition (26% and 14%, respectively).[27] These two also have the largest collections in the corpus. The 634 volumes in Mariana Vicenta's inventory likely represent decades of collecting by her relatives, making it not just her library, but that of her noble family. Ana de Sarasa's collection is much more modest with 28 volumes. María de Ceniceros' books are less well described since the inventory of her goods (including books) describes 24 books in just four entries, where 21 books are grouped in one entry and simply described as small, medium, and large books in Spanish.[28] With inventories, it must also be remembered that more ephemeral items that would help clarify reading habits were not usually inventoried.[29] For Antonia García Jiménez and sor María de la Purificación, the picture of their collections are seriously incomplete because the books associated with them are bequests of two or three books and described in the inventory of Antonia's uncle and the will of sor María's friend Miguel Lanzarot

24  Nalle, 'Literacy and culture', pp. 77–79.

25  José Alonso del Val, 'Juan Echeverri y Rober (1609–1662), Capitán General y Almirante de las reales flotas de Indias', *Itsas Memoria. Revista de estudios marítimos del País Vasco*, 6 (2009), p. 730.

26  Archivo Diocesano de Pamplona, C/849 N. 27, f. 54$^r$.

27  Archivo Diocesano de Pamplona, C/1456 N. 10, ff. 86$^v$–99$^r$; ADP, C/849 N. 27, ff. 57$^r$–57$^v$. To identify editions, I consulted bibliographies like the USTC and Iberian Books as well as catalogue records on WorldCat or for specific libraries to conduct a process of elimination in terms of editions. As such, an undescribed or non-surviving edition could alter the validity of my identifications.

28  Archivo Diocesano de Pamplona, C/618 N. 10, ff. 77$^r$, 78$^r$, 82$^v$, 84$^v$.

29  Victor Infantes, 'Las ausencias en los inventarios de libros y de bibliotecas', *Bulletin Hispanique*, 99 (1997), p. 288.

de Gazólaz.[30] The full size and composition of their collections at any point in their lives is unknown.

The first woman analysed is Antonia García Jiménez, the niece and heiress of Martín Jiménez, the *relator* for the Corte Mayor of Navarre and in 1603 when Martín died, it appears she was unmarried.[31] Upon Martín's death, his goods were inventoried, including his 61 books.[32] The inventory lists '*Item* La Carolea in a small volume and another book of the examples of saints which were taken for the heiress'.[33] From this description, it is possible to infer that a religious book on the lives of saints and *La Carolea* by Jerónimo Sempere, an epic poem about Charles v, were taken for Antonia.[34] Unfortunately, the passive voice wording of 'taken for the heiress' obscures whether she took them or another took them for her.

Regardless, that these two books were taken indicates recognition of their affordances for reading and for the development of virtue. Here, these affordances do not derive from the books' physical qualities but rather their intangible qualities (language and subject matter), as well as the cultural knowledge of what was appropriate for an unmarried young woman. They are two of the few vernacular and non-legal works present, and the decision to take *La Carolea*, a work of epic poetry, might particularly demonstrate an interest in reading since it is slightly different from the moralist-recommended moral and religious works. The other books would have been out of reach in terms of language (Latin) and subject matter (Roman law). Selecting *La Carolea* and a devotional work based on a potential affordance of reselling them seems improbable since the folio-sized legal tomes in Jiménez's collection were likely worth more. The selection of the book of saints fits perfectly into the

---

30    Archivo General de Navarra, n. 89984, f. 46ᵛ; Archivo Diocesano de Pamplona, C/698, f. 15ᵛ.

31    AGN, n. 89984, ff. 27ᵛ, 44ʳ–44ᵛ, 46ᵛ. She was married by 22 October 1606, when she signed her own will in anticipation of the dangers of childbirth (Archivo General de Navarra, Caja 18909, Pamplona, Ulibarri, 1606, n. 37). The *relator* was a person appointed to give a report or summary on cases for each tribunal. See the second definition of 'relator' in Real Academia Española. 'Diccionario de Autoridades (1726–1739).' Diccionario de Autoridades, n.d. <https://apps2.rae.es/DA.html>. (Accessed 1 July 2022).

32    AGN, n. 89984, ff. 45ᵛ–46ᵛ. A full transcription of Martín Jiménez's book inventory is located on *Bibliotecas privadas de Navarra* <https://sites.google.com/view/bibliotecasnavarras/owners/legal-professionals/martin-jimenez>.

33    AGN, n. 89984, f. 46ᵛ. 'Ytten la carolea en un cuerpo pequeño y otro libro de exemplo de santos los quales se lleva para la heredera'.

34    Another possibility could be *Primera parte de la Carolea* by Juan Ochoa de la Salde (Lisboa: Marcos Borges y Antonio Ribeiro y Antonio Álvares, 1585) (USTC 337880), but that is in folio. The 'cuerpo pequeño' described in the entry fits much better with the first or second part of Sempere's edition, both printed in octavo in Valencia by Juan de Arcos in 1560 (USTC 341728 and 341729, respectively).

recommended reading for women, especially younger women, meaning that Antonia or someone else, possibly her mother, perceived that it would afford her the 'opportunity' to grow in virtue and have a material demonstration of practising said virtue. *La Carolea* is a more ambiguous choice in regard to virtue since it is neither religious nor moral philosophy, but its author puts it in the category of history, not the more 'dangerous' *libros de caballerías*.[35]

The second library is that of Mariana Vicenta de Echeverri. Her 634-volume library represented the needs and wishes of successive generations of her noble family in addition to her own.[36] As a result, the contents of the library are much more varied than the other collections analysed here. As seen in Table 13.1, the majority deal with religion and history, but books about government and politics, military matters, maps, and navigation are also prominent due to her male relatives' involvement in maritime trade and the Spanish navy.[37]

TABLE 13.1    Number of volumes divided by subject in
Mariana Vicenta de Echeverri's library[a]

| Subject | Volumes |
| --- | --- |
| Religion | 177 |
| History | 152 |
| Government/Politics | 42 |
| Didactic | 25 |
| Poetry | 20 |
| Military | 18 |
| Heraldry and Genealogy | 17 |
| Literature | 17 |
| Astronomy/Astrology | 14 |
| Maps | 14 |
| Philosophy | 13 |
| Nautical/Navigation | 11 |

35    Jerónimo Sempere, *Primera parte de la Carolea*, (Valencia: Juan de Arcos, 1560) (USTC 341728), f. 2v; Wingate, 'A qué manera' pp. 157–158.

36    ADP, C/1456 N. 10, ff. 86ᵛ–99ʳ. A full book inventory is located on *Bibliotecas privadas de Navarra* <https://sites.google.com/view/bibliotecasnavarras/owners/women/mariana -vicenta-de-echeverri>. The earliest datable book in the library has a publication year of 1526: *De la vida y milagros de san Julian* (Alcalá de Henares: Miguel de Eguia) (USTC 343541).

37    Val, 'Juan Echeverri y Rober', p. 729.

TABLE 13.1   Number of volumes divided by subject (*cont.*)

| Subject | Volumes |
| --- | --- |
| Cosmography | 10 |
| Emblems | 9 |
| Language | 7 |
| Natural Philosophy/Science | 5 |
| Law | 4 |
| Agriculture | 3 |
| Art/Architecture | 3 |
| Medicine | 3 |
| Mathematics | 2 |
| Rhetoric | 2 |
| Economics | 1 |
| Epistolary | 1 |
| Hunting | 1 |
| Travel | 1 |
| Uncategorised | 88 |

a   The number of volumes will add up to slightly more than
    634 since some volumes have been assigned more than
    one subject.

It is not clear whether Mariana Vicenta read outside the recommended religious books and moral philosophy, and it may have been expedient to read more widely as the countess during her marriage (1665–1675) when her husband was at sea and during her widowhood (1675–1684) to maintain her affairs.[38] However, the volumes that can be dated to her marriage and widowhood show her interest in books, and therefore their affordance to her as objects to be read. They also generally fit moral philosophers' guidelines and general reading patterns of early modern women. That she adhered to religious and moral philosophy during her widowhood—her greatest period of autonomy—may indicate her genuine interest in the subjects, but they would have had the additional affordance of constructing virtue, which could also have guided her choices. Of those from her marriage, five are religious, one is

---

38   Val, 'Juan Echeverri y Rober', p. 727.

literature, and one is a history of Navarre.[39] The three from her widowhood are all moral and religious.[40] These are likely not the only books acquired during those periods, but they are the only ones that were almost definitely acquired then since for each there is only one surviving edition that matches the description given in the inventory entry based on consultation of available bibliographies.[41]

Additionally, Mariana Vicenta de Echeverri's library afforded her and her family an opportunity to flaunt their familial prestige and wealth. This affordance derives from the conjunction of these books as a physical unit as opposed to the intellectual content between the covers. Drawing from Victor Infantes' categorisation of private libraries, this library is clearly a 'biblioteca museo' since it reaches Infantes' threshold of 300 books.[42] In this category, a library indicates the wealth of its owners, particularly in conjunction with a household whose riches are expressed in other material goods. Echeverri's library fits this characteristic too, since her post-mortem inventory lists two folios worth of silver, two and a half folios of jewels, and 62 paintings, in addition to 15 more paintings and two shields with the family's arms contained specifically within the library.[43] No matter the importance of the books' affordance as reading materials to the countess, her library had value as a testament to the power, wealth, and virtue of her ancestors.

María de Ceniceros was an upper-class widow and a third order Franciscan in Pamplona.[44] The arrangement of her much smaller collection of 25 books in her household at her death and the description of their physical and intangible characteristics indicate that María had a close relationship with her books, and that their affordances to her were as reading material, devotional use, and prestige.[45] The majority of her books were kept in a pine chest along with a large quantity of fabric. They are simply described in the inventory of her goods in terms of language and size as 'twenty-one small and large and

39    See entries 6, 35, 93, 452, 495, and 541 of Echeverri's inventory <https://sites.google.com/view/bibliotecasnavarras/owners/women/mariana-vicenta-de-echeverri>.

40    See entries 335, 351, and 400 <https://sites.google.com/view/bibliotecasnavarras/owners/women/mariana-vicenta-de-echeverri>.

41    Again, an undescribed or non-surviving edition could alter the validity of my identifications. See note 25.

42    Infantes, 'Las ausencias', p. 284.

43    ADP, C/1456 N. 10, ff. 72r, 73r–77r.

44    ADP, C/618 N. 10, f. 5r.

45    A full book inventory is located on *Bibliotecas privadas de Navarra* <https://sites.google.com/view/bibliotecasnavarras/owners/women/maria-de-ceniceros>.

medium books in Castilian, all different works'.[46] A few books, however, specifically two books of hours, a small book in Castilian, and a book on confession
by one Fray Antonio, were spread around other desks and chests.[47]

The separation and placement of these books in more elaborate containers
away from those in the pine chest with fabric suggest they had greater value to
her or were used frequently enough that they were kept in a more functional
location. For example, the small book in Castilian and the book by Fray Antonio
were kept in a large inlaid or marquetry desk with several practical items and
clothing, such as two sets of balances for gold and silver, a bowl, worn women's
silk stockings, letters, and spindles for spinning yarn.[48] This is a veritable miscellany of items from the perspective of reading the inventory almost four hundred years later, but the fact that these two books are segregated from the main
body of her collection indicates a different set of affordances.

As with Mariana Vicenta de Echeverri's whole library, the physical properties of María de Ceniceros' most lavishly described and decorated book, a book
of hours with gold or gilt clasps and boards, attests to its affordance for exhib-
iting wealth and prestige.[49] A book of hours with gold decoration reflects her
higher status in society as the wife of the licenciado Juan de Aragón, a lawyer
for the Audiencias Reales. Other personal goods, such as her gold jewellery, 24
paintings (all religious scenes), and a bequest to one of the king's chaplains
in her will also evidence her higher social status.[50] The ornate six-drawer oil
painted desk in which the book was kept further reflected the luxury of the
book within.[51]

The desk also contained a box with St. Jerome painted on the lid with a copper sheet (lámina) painted with an image of the baptism of Christ inside it,
three reliquaries, and a rosary, and the book's proximity to these objects points
to a devotional affordance.[52] The devotional affordances of all these items
reinforce each other since while she was praying from the book, she might

---

46    ADP, C/618 N. 10, ff. 82ʳ–82ᵛ. 'veynte y un libros pequeños y grandes y medianos de
      romançe todos de diferentes tomos'.
47    ADP, C/618 N. 10, ff. 77ʳ, 78ʳ, 84ᵛ.
48    ADP, C/618 N. 10, ff. 84ᵛ.
49    ADP, C/618 N. 10, f. 77ʳ. 'unas oras de nuestra señora con sus manillas y cubiertas doradas'.
50    ADP, C/618, N. 10, ff. 8ʳ, 74ʳ–75ʳ, 82ᵛ–83ᵛ.
51    ADP, C/618 N. 10, f. 75ᵛ; Lucy Razzal, Boxes and books in early modern England: Materiality,
      metaphor, containment (Cambridge: Cambridge University Press, 2021), pp. 34–35.
52    ADP, C/618 N. 10, ff. 75ᵛ–77ʳ. The desk appears to be quite capacious and varied in its con-
      tents. Other fascinating items in this desk include two silk bags embroidered with gold,
      silver, and pearls and three yards of colored braid in the same drawer as the book of hours,
      as well as new women's silk stockings, other embroidered items, new men's gloves, a gilt
      bronze alarm clock, 48 buttons, an illuminated cardboard sheet (pasta), a large cardboard

contemplate the images on the box and *lámina* or hold her rosary. These items had the additional affordance of outwardly supporting her pious identity as a third order Franciscan. It seems likely that the rest of her undescribed books would be similarly religious and follow 'ideal' female reading behaviour, but out of interest versus affectation.

Interpreting all her books as having the basic affordance of reading material is supported through her more transparent connection with the collection—these books were clearly hers because they were kept apart from her husband's, and she had full control over the collection at her death since she died a widow. With married women and widows, it is often difficult to discern which books in a collection were the wife's, which were the husband's, or if there is any distinction at all.[53] However, in the case of María de Ceniceros, there is clear separation between her books and her husband's, unlike between Mariana Vicenta and her family. Juan de Aragón died around 1631 judging from the fact that Ceniceros had an inventory made of his books in 1631, and these books (but not hers) were sold at some point to the licenciado don Lucas de Ybuluzqueta.[54] Aragón's books were also inventoried separately from Ceniceros' in the same 1644 inventory of Ceniceros' goods discussed above, which seems to indicate they were in a different section of the house from her books in the chest and desks. His books are also always referred to in the court proceedings as a separate conceptual unit using the word '*librería*'.[55] The lack of description in the inventory entries makes it impossible to date any of her books to her marriage or widowhood, but she still either kept or acquired these books for her use during her widowhood. Additionally, the fact that María de Ceniceros could write—as indicated by her two *libros de memoria* (commonplace books)—means she could have annotated her books or noted passages into her commonplace books and more deeply engaged with her reading material.[56]

Our fourth women reader, Ana de Sarasa appears to be the primary director of her own library's acquisitions. A significant portion of her books can be dated to her widowhood when she would have had the most control over her

---

sheet with an image of Rome, two rocks that look like bezoars, more rocks, and eight large silver spoons and four small silver spoons in the other drawers of the desk (ff. 76$^r$–77$^v$).

53    María Carmen Álvarez Márquez, 'Mujeres lectores en el siglo VI en Sevilla', *Historia Instituciones Documentos*, 31 (2004), pp. 19–20.

54    ADP, C/618 N. 10, ff. 190$^r$–190$^v$.

55    ADP, C/618 N. 10, ff. 90$^v$–97$^v$. An inventory of Aragón's books is located on *Bibliotecas privadas de Navarra* <https://sites.google.com/view/bibliotecasnavarras/owners/legal-professionals/juan-de-aragon>.

56    ADP, C/618 N. 10, ff. 84$^r$, 89$^r$.

book purchases. Out of her 28 books, almost half were published after 1587, the approximate date of her husband Fausto de Echalaz's death.[57] Only five books can be identified to their exact edition and all were published after 1587, and eight more books exclusively have editions after 1587 (and obviously at least one before 1629).[58] She essentially had 42 years of widowhood to buy books without male mediation, and she took advantage of this fact.

Her choices of books indicate that she was interested in books that would afford her religious edification and signal her virtue as a widow. Additionally, she acquired books that afforded practical use in daily life due to their content. At her death, her library contained 20 religious books (several devotional and lives of saints), three law books, one of moral philosophy, one of epic poetry, a chant book, a cookbook, and one book of unidentified genre.[59] The cookbook and 12 religious texts appear to date to her widowhood.

Last among our women readers is a nun named sor María de la Purificación.[60] The evidence for sor María's book ownership, interest in books as affording reading, and unusual opportunity to choose books appears in the 1625 will of don Miguel Lanzarot de Gazólaz, presbyter of the parish of Gazólaz. In his bequest to her, don Miguel shows that both he and sor María are readers, and sor María is given the freedom to pick whatever books she wants. He dictates to the scribe taking down his will: 'Also, leave two books to sor María of the Purification ... the ones that she would like most, with which should be restored her volume of fray Luis de Granada'.[61] One suspects they were very well acquainted and friendly with each other since he remembers to mention that her book should be returned to her in his will and offers her the gift of two books of her choice. Loaned books and this final bequest indicate a shared understanding and valuing of books' affordance for reading, but the freedom

---

57    The folios I have transcribed from ADP, C/849 N. 27 record a marriage contract between the two dated 31 October 1584 (fol. 63$^r$), but not a death date for Echalaz. Searching the finding aid descriptions in the AGN's Archivo Abierto <http://www.navarra.es/home_es /Temas/Turismo+ocio+y+cultura/Archivos/Programas/Archivo+Abierto/>, Fausto de Echalaz was a defendant in a case running from 31 January 1586 to 20 May 1586 (n. 175909), but in a case ending on 24 October 1587, Ana de Sarasa is listed as the widow of Echalaz. Any cases mentioning Sarasa post-1587 in the Archivo Abierto describe her as his widow.

58    As with Mariana Vicenta de Echeverri, the identifications of editions are based on the fact that for each book there was only one surviving plausible edition matching the inventory entry description.

59    ADP, C/849 N. 27, ff. 57$^r$–57$^v$. A full book inventory is located on *Bibliotecas privadas de Navarra* <https://sites.google.com/view/bibliotecasnavarras/owners/women/ana-de -sarasa>.

60    There is no indication of her order or congregation in the will where she is mentioned.

61    'Itten deja dos libros a sor maria de la Purificación ... los que mas ella gustare con que restituya su tome de fray luis de granada', ADP, C/698 N. 5, ff. 12$^r$, 15$^v$.

in the request is even more significant. Don Miguel states that she should choose what she wants and specifically according to *her* tastes. Nuns did not usually enter bookstores themselves, and here she receives a chance to 'shop' in his library.[62] One might expect for him to gift two specific books to her, but he wants her to have whichever books she would most value. Furthermore, she is the only one allowed to take books from the library at his death since he requests that all the rest be sold except for the breviary, which should be returned to Juan de Arazuri, parish priest of Cizur Mayor.[63] While his collection is mostly religious in nature and certainly not controversial for a nun, she would have had the freedom of choice among the books without mediation, thereby contravening restrictions on book acquisition prescribed to women.

## 3    Economic Affordances of the Book

While there were many stated restrictions on women's interactions when books were considered reading objects, this does not appear to be the case when economic affordance was at the fore. Women made an impact in the book trade: they were printers, publishers, booksellers, and barterers of books. As Javier Ruiz Astiz has pointed out, 24.5% of the entries in Juan Delgado Casado's *Diccionario de impresores españoles (siglos XV–XVII)* mention women, and Sandra Estables Susán's *Diccionario de mujeres impresoras y libreras de España e Iberoamérica entre los siglos XV y XVIII* has 415 entries for fifteenth- to eighteenth-century female printers and booksellers.[64] Alejandra Ulla Lorenzo has published on the varying and sometimes principal roles women took in the book trade.[65] Of the women discussed here, Isabel de Labayen exemplifies the presence of women in the professional book trade, but two others, Josepha Pardo and María Josepha de Soraburu, demonstrate the involvement of women in an unofficial book trade via the bartering of books.

These three women, all from Pamplona and belonging to lower classes than the previously discussed women readers, handled books that would have been out of bounds for most women readers either because of their language or

---

62    Cátedra and Rojo, *Bibliotecas y lecturas*, pp. 98–99.

63    ADP, C/698 N. 5, f. 20ʳ.

64    Javier Ruiz Astiz, 'Isabel de Labayen: impresora y editora en la Pamplona del siglo XVII', *Bibliotecológica*, 35 (2021), p. 104.

65    Alejandra Ulla Lorenzo, 'Women and the Iberian book trade, 1472–1650', in Alexander Samuel Wilkinson and Alejandra Ulla Lorenzo (eds.), *A maturing market: The Iberian book world in the first half of the seventeenth century* (Leiden: Brill, 2017), pp. 67–83; Alejandra Ulla Lorenzo, '¿Viudas de mercaderes o verdaderas mercaderas? Mujer y comercio de libros en los siglos XVI y XVII', *Hipogrifo*, Special Issue 1 (2018), pp. 321–340.

subject matter. It seems that if women were in a situation where the primary affordance under consideration was the potential monetary value revealed during the production, sale, or bartering of books, there was no gender-based restriction on women interacting with or owning these books.

Isabel de Labayen was a printer in Pamplona active from about 1643 to 1672. Her father, Martín de Labayen, was also a printer, and she and her first husband, Diego Zabala, inherited the business in 1643 when they married. Widowed in 1655, Isabel married another printer, Gaspar Martínez of Huesca. They had a very difficult relationship, and in 1666 he stole books and equipment from the business to fund himself. She sued for separation from him and for his imprisonment because of his abuse, threats, and robbery of goods from her business.[66]

Two years later in a 1668 court case, Labayen claimed that since 1666 when her second husband left, she had been missing 1,500 copies of the *Arte* of Antonio de Nebrija and another 1,500 copies of Nebrija's *Libro quarto* (both works of Latin grammar). She contended that she discovered Juan de Enciso and Juan Micón binding large quantities of these texts provided by bookseller Lorenzo Coroneu on 14 August 1668.[67] She sued them to recover what she saw as stolen property and to defend a privilege she claimed gave Gaspar Martínez (and therefore her) exclusive rights to print and sell these titles in Navarre.[68]

Labayen's suit against these men substantiates that the affordance of these books and privilege was economic, specifically the ability to provide a livelihood. These objects have enough monetary value and represent enough potentially lost revenue that she felt she needed to go to court. In the case, Lorenzo Coroneu explains that at least 200 of the copies he possessed were sold to him by Labayen because she was in financial need after Gaspar left her. Martín de Ylarregui, Coroneu's lawyer, claims Coroneu generously bought these 200 copies at one *real* each to help Labayen and her son in their time of need, stating that:

---

66    Javier Itúrbide Díaz, *Los libros de un reino: historia de la edición en Navarra (1490–1841), Diccionario de impresores y libreros en Navarra (1490–1841), Anexo CD* (Pamplona: Gobierno de Navarra, 2015), pp. 322–23; Ruiz Astiz, 'Isabel de Labayen', p. 106.

67    Archivo General de Navarra, n. 165001, f. 7ʳ. Javier Ruiz Astiz also discusses this case in 'Isabel de Labayen: impresora y editora en la Pamplona del siglo XVII', *Bibliotecológica*, 35 (2021), pp. 101–125.

68    AGN, n. 165001, f. 7ʳ. For more examples of women in the book trade as plaintiffs or defendants, see Alejandra Ulla Lorenzo and Alba de la Cruz Redondo, 'Women and conflict in the Iberian book trade, 1472–1700', in Alexander Samuel Wilkinson and Graeme Kemp (eds.), *Negotiating conflict and controversy in the early modern book world* (Leiden: Brill, 2019), pp. 129–141.

[T]he opposing party finding themselves in need asked my client to buy up to 200 *Artes* bound in paper from them, and because of their stated need he bought them at one *real* each to aid them as the witnesses will testify.[69]

The others came to him as part of a complicated bill of exchange, for which he was the guarantor between Gaspar Martínez and Paulo Lorento.[70] José Martínez, the secretary of the Consejo Real points out that the privilege she cites was only for two years and just for selling the *Arte* and *Libro quarto*.[71] Assuming that the privilege was granted before Martínez's flight, the privilege would have expired in 1668, possibly leaving Coroneu in the clear, but likely not since Labayen is suing him.

Most importantly, however, her gender was not an impediment to the defence of her rights or the production and sale of books. At no point is it suggested that she should not be printing these Latin grammar books as a woman or that she should not sue. In fact, she strategically wields her gender, calling herself in an appeal to the court in her own hand 'a poor woman'.[72] It paints her as the weaker, aggrieved party via 'affected modesty' to express her gendered subordination and emphasise the dominant position of the tribunal.[73] Labayen litigated other cases against other members of the book trade, her husband, and even her own son to defend her business without restriction in regards to gender.[74]

Josepha Pardo by contrast was not a professional bookseller, but her proficient selection of books as payment in kind from her uncle's executors demonstrates some level of experience with the trade, as well as a familiarity with legal, theological, and medical texts that would have been unusual and transgressive if their principal affordance for her was as reading material. However, since the affordance of these books tacitly negotiated by her and the executors was economic, there were no restrictions on her choices due to her gender.

After the 1684 death of the aforementioned Lorenzo Coroneu, her uncle by marriage, the diocesan tribunal of Pamplona recognised Pardo as a creditor to

---

69  'las partes contrarias biendose con necesidad pidieron a mi parte que les comprasse asta ducientos artes en papel y por socorrerles la necesidad que de presentavan se los compro a real cada uno como lo diran los testigos', AGN, n. 165001, f. 13$^r$.

70  AGN, n. 165001, ff. 13$^{r-v}$.

71  Javier Ruiz Astiz, 'Litigantes ante los tribunales reales de Navarra: impresores y libreros durante los siglos XVI y XVII', *Titivillus*, 1 (2015), p. 338.

72  AGN, n. 165001, f. 16$^r$. 'por ser yo una pobre mujer'.

73  Josefina Ludmer, 'Tretas del débil', in Patricia Elena González and Eliana Ortega (eds.), *La sartén por el mango* (Río Piedras, Puerto Rico: Ediciones Huracán, 1985), pp. 48–49.

74  Ruiz Astiz, 'Isabel de Labayen', pp. 108–114.

Coroneu's goods. Her uncle was not strictly in debt to her, but she was owed 200 *ducados* as ordered in the will of Coroneu's wife and her aunt, Juana María de Burlada, plus 113 *ducados* of the goods of her grandparents (Juana María's parents).[75] Records the executors submitted to the court indicate that as part of her payment, Pardo accepted 943 *reales* worth of books, which accounts for almost a third of what was owed to her.[76]

The case does not explicitly mention her working in Coroneu's bookshop, but considering the strategic nature of her choices, it seems she acquired some knowledge of the trade, such as what books attracted which customers and maybe even a bibliographic knowledge of Latin. The books she selected are not books that she likely would have read herself; instead, they are large, more expensive books, generally written in Latin, that she could sell to the professional classes. In other words, she chose books that had the dual affordance of potential future profit and payment for money owed to her. Further, neither the male executors nor the officials of the diocesan tribunal took issue with her selecting for payment what would have been controversial choices for a woman to read.

Among the 115 volumes chosen by Pardo from the 2,487 volumes Coroneu left behind, at least 69 are in Latin, 16 are bilingual Latin-Spanish primers, and nine are in Spanish. The rest are likely in Spanish or Latin, though 18 volumes listed in Pardo's selection cannot be connected with entries in the main inventory made directly after Coroneu's death (see Table 13.2). About half are folios and quartos (see Table 13.3), and they are within the medium to expensive range of Coroneu's stock (compare Tables 13.4 and 13.5). Tables 13.6 and 13.7 show religion and law as the genres most represented in Pardo's selection. These tendencies in terms of language, format, and subject point towards clergy and legal professional customers. Pardo's targeting of the legal market and clergy is unsurprising considering that these were Coroneu's primary customers.[77] In addition, the last column in Table 13.5 shows that she has a marked interest in medical books since her acquisitions account for almost half of Coroneu's stock. It seems likely then that she intended to sell to a third market: medical professionals. While she may not have been known as a *librera*, she clearly had some of the skills and planned to use them.

---

75   ADP, C/1436 N. 2, f. 497ʳ.

76   ADP, C/1436 N. 2, f. 619ᵛ. There are 11 Navarrese reales and 11 Castilian reales in 1 ducado, 1 Navarrese *real* equals 36 *maravedis*, and 1 Castilian *real* is 34 *maravedis*.

77   Alexandra Wingate, "'Prosigue la librería': Understanding late seventeenth-century Navarrese book culture through Lorenzo Coroneu's Bookstore', Unpublished MA Dissertation (University of London, 2019), p. 36.

TABLE 13.2    Language comparison between Coroneu's entire inventory and Pardo's selection[a]

| Language | Coroneu | | Pardo | | |
|---|---|---|---|---|---|
| | Volumes | Percentage of total | Volumes | Percentage of total | Percentage of Coroneu |
| Italian | 11 | 0.44% | | | |
| Italian? | 1 | 0.04% | | | |
| Latin | 1079 | 43.39% | 69 | 60.00% | 6.39% |
| Latin? | 113 | 4.54% | 3 | 2.61% | 2.65% |
| Latin, Greek | 6 | 0.24% | | | |
| Latin, Hebrew | 1 | 0.04% | | | |
| Latin, Spanish | 506 | 20.35% | 16 | 13.91% | 3.16% |
| Portuguese | 4 | 0.16% | | | |
| Spanish | 391 | 15.72% | 9 | 7.83% | 2.30% |
| Spanish? | 375 | 15.08% | | | |
| Book not matched to Coroneu 1684 inventory | – | – | 18 | 15.65% | |
| Total | 2,487 | 100.00% | 115 | 100.00% | 4.62% |

a    Languages with a question mark after them indicate that the books in that row are likely to be in that language, but it is not known for certain.

TABLE 13.3    Format comparison between Coroneu's entire inventory and Pardo's selection

| Format | Coroneu | | Pardo | | |
|---|---|---|---|---|---|
| | Volumes | Percentage of total | Volumes | Percentage of total | Percentage of Coroneu |
| Folio | 791 | 31.80% | 36 | 31.30% | 4.55% |
| Quarto | 316 | 12.70% | 25 | 21.74% | 7.91% |
| Octavo | 289 | 11.62% | 9 | 7.83% | 3.11% |
| 12mo | 61 | 2.45% | | | |
| 16mo | 36 | 1.45% | 1 | 0.87% | 2.78% |
| 24mo | 13 | 0.52% | | | |
| 32mo | 18 | 0.72% | | | |
| Unknown format | 963 | 38.72% | 26 | 22.61% | 2.70% |
| Book not matched to Coroneu 1684 inventory | – | – | 18 | 15.65% | – |
| Total | 2,487 | 100.00% | 115 | 100.00% | 4.62% |

TABLE 13.4 Pardo's purchases in volumes grouped by format and price paid[a]

| Format | Grand Total | <1 real | 1 real | 2–2.99 reals | 3 reales | 4 reales |
|---|---|---|---|---|---|---|
| Folio | 36 | | | 3 | 2 | |
| Quarto | 25 | | 1 | 4 | 2 | |
| Octavo | 9 | | | 5 | 1 | |
| 16mo | 1 | | | 1 | | |
| Format not stated in 1684 inventory | 26 | 20 | | 6 | | |
| Book not matched to Coroneu 1684 inventory | 18 | | | | 2 | |
| Grand Total | 115 | 20 | 1 | 19 | 7 | 1 |

a The price paid by Pardo is slightly different from the price appraised in the original 1684 inventory for certain books. I have chosen to show the price paid versus the price appraised for Pardo's selection because the data from the 18 books not matched to original inventory can then be included.

TABLE 13.5 Coroneu's entire inventory in volumes grouped by format and price

| Format | Grand Total | No price appraised | <1 real | 1 real | 2–2.99 reals | 3 reales | 4 reales |
|---|---|---|---|---|---|---|---|
| Folio | 791 | | 9 | 7 | 269 | 28 | |
| Quarto | 316 | 1 | 1 | 40 | 101 | 73 | |
| Octavo | 289 | | | 81 | 161 | 12 | |
| 12mo | 61 | | | 2 | 11 | 7 | |
| 16mo | 36 | | | 11 | 10 | 5 | |
| 24mo | 13 | | | 8 | 4 | | |
| 32mo | 18 | | | | 18 | | |
| Format not stated in 1684 inventory | 963 | 1 | 901 | 22 | 10 | 7 | |
| Grand Total | 2,487 | 2 | 911 | 171 | 584 | 132 | |

| es | 6–10 reales | 11–15 reales | 15.1–20 reales | 20.1–25 reales |
|---|---|---|---|---|
| 2 | 14 | 4 | 6 | |
| | 2 | 2 | 9 | |
| 1 | 1 | | | |
| | 4 | 1 | 2 | 8 |
| 3 | 21 | 7 | 17 | 8 |

| es | 6–10 reales | 11–15 reales | 15.1–20 reales | 25.1–40 reales | 20.1–25 reales | >40 reales |
|---|---|---|---|---|---|---|
| 9 | 180 | 88 | 63 | 5 | 31 | |
| | 29 | 18 | | | | |
| 2 | 18 | | | 4 | | 1 |
| 3 | 16 | 1 | | | | |
| | 8 | | | | | |
| 2 | 12 | 3 | 3 | | | |
| 16 | 263 | 110 | 66 | 9 | 31 | 1 |

TABLE 13.6    Genre comparison between Coroneu's entire inventory and Pardo's selection

| Genre | Coroneu | | Pardo | | |
| | Volumes | Percentage of total | Volumes | Percentage of total | Percentage of Coroneu |
| --- | --- | --- | --- | --- | --- |
| Agriculture | 2 | 0.08% | | | |
| Architecture | 1 | 0.04% | | | |
| Astronomy/Astrology/ Math | 9 | 0.36% | | | |
| Drama | 4 | 0.16% | | | |
| Emblems | 3 | 0.12% | | | |
| Epistolary | 3 | 0.12% | | | |
| Government/Politics | 5 | 0.20% | 1 | 0.87% | 20.00% |
| History | 76 | 3.06% | 6 | 5.22% | 7.89% |
| Language | 523 | 21.03% | 16 | 13.91% | 3.06% |
| Law | 755 | 30.36% | 21 | 18.26% | 2.78% |
| Literature | 11 | 0.44% | | | |
| Logic/Dialectic | 5 | 0.20% | 1 | 0.87% | 20.00% |
| Medicine | 26 | 1.05% | 12 | 10.43% | 46.15% |
| Military | 6 | 0.24% | | | |
| Morals | 5 | 0.20% | | | |
| Music | 2 | 0.08% | | | |
| News | 1 | 0.04% | | | |
| Philosophy/Proverbs | 25 | 1.01% | | | |
| Poetry | 20 | 0.80% | | | |
| Reference | 4 | 0.16% | | | |
| Religious | 914 | 36.75% | 30 | 26.09% | 3.28% |
| Rhetoric | 14 | 0.56% | | | |
| Science | 13 | 0.52% | 1 | 0.87% | 7.69% |
| Unknown genre | 75 | 3.02% | 9 | 7.83% | 12.00% |
| Book not matched to Coroneu 1684 inventory | – | – | 18 | 15.65% | |
| Total | 2,487 | 100.00% | 115 | 100.00% | 4.62% |

TABLE 13.7    Pardo's purchases in volumes grouped by format and genre

| Genre | Grand Total | Book not matched to Coroneu 1684 inventory | Folio | Quarto | Octavo | 16mo | Format not stated in 1684 inventory |
|---|---|---|---|---|---|---|---|
| Book not matched to Coroneu 1684 inventory | 18 | 18 | | 1 | | | |
| Government/ Politics | 1 | | | 1 | | | |
| History | 6 | | 1 | | | | 5 |
| Language | 16 | | | | | | 16 |
| Law | 21 | | 16 | 4 | 1 | | |
| Logic/ Dialectic | 1 | | 1 | | | | |
| Medicine | 12 | | 4 | 3 | 4 | 1 | |
| Religious | 30 | | 13 | 8 | 4 | | 5 |
| Science | 1 | | 1 | | | | |
| Unknown genre | 9 | | | 9 | | | |
| Grand Total | 115 | 18 | 36 | 25 | 9 | 1 | 26 |

## 4      False Economic Affordances

Finally, we return to María Josepha de Soraburu who like Josepha Pardo was a creditor of Coroneu and was offered books as repayment, but she did not find the same affordances of repayment of debt and potential future profit in Coroneu's stock after his death. In fact, Soraburu framed monetary value as a false affordance, meaning it was erroneous and not actually present, against the assertions of the executor.[78] It is worth noting that these are again books that would have been deemed inappropriate for female readers because Coroneu's stock was mostly legal and theological texts in Latin, but a priest and diocesan tribunal were begging her to take them.[79] The primary affordance

---

78    William W. Gaver, 'Technology affordances', *CHI '91: Proceedings of the SIGCHI Conference on Human Factors in Computing Systems*, (1991), p. 80.

79    Wingate, 'Prosigue la librería', pp. 23, 27.

under consideration by all parties was economic though, so there were no gender-based restrictions.

On 13 April 1693, Coroneu's executor, the priest Pedro de Peralta, asked the court to force Soraburu to choose among Coroneu's books and goods to fulfil Coroneu's debt to her, saying she had ignored his summons multiple times previously.[80] On 23 April, her lawyer wrote to the court that 'she is a poor woman who does not understand the value of books', and that they cannot force her to take them.[81] Further, he states that the remaining books were 'old and incomplete' (mui biejos y descabalados) and that they should be put up for final sale in order to pay Soraburu in money, 'since it isn't reasonable to pay her in books that she can't sell'.[82]

This statement simultaneously positions Soraburu as weak and in need of protection from being swindled in her repayment and as an assertive, economically savvy woman who knows her rights and what she is due. Her use of 'poor woman' is a gendered rhetorical strategy using 'affected modesty' to gain sympathy employed similarly to Labayen.[83] This position is followed by a strong statement that she cannot be forced into taking the books.

She understood perfectly well the monetary value of books since she used their physical characteristics—old and incomplete—to evidence her claim that the vendable affordance of these books was false. Further, she might have been able to assess the books' vendability based on their content because she could read well enough to understand a written edict of the diocesan tribunal.[84] As the last creditor in the case, she received the final pickings of books, which when originally appraised in 1684 were already quite old (Coroneu ran a used bookstore) and even less appealing nine years later.[85] Josepha Pardo was a higher-ranked creditor than Soraburu and, therefore, made her apparently satisfactory selection before the dregs were offered to Soraburu. This example shows the relationality of affordances: the same objects, different agents, and slightly different situations make for different affordances. Further, Coroneu's original debt of 393 reales to her was for 'merchandise from her shop', meaning she was a merchant.[86] She did not have the same level of experience with

80    ADP, C/1436 N. 2, ff. 641r–641v.
81    'es una pobre mujer que no entiende en el Balor de los libros', ADP, C/1436 N. 2, ff. 642r–642v.
82    'pues no sera razon se le pague en libros que no pueda Bender', ADP, C/1436 N. 2, ff. 642r.
83    Josefina Ludmer, 'Tretas del débil', pp. 48–49.
84    The specific wording is '... haviendo leydo [el auto] por si misma y comprendido su contenimiento ...', ADP, C/1436 N. 2, f. 643v.
85    Wingate, 'Prosigue la librería', p. 51.
86    'mercaderia de su tienda', ADP, C/1436 N. 2, f. 497r.

books as Pardo and Labayen, but she had experience with valuing, buying, and selling goods. Had Soraburu agreed with their affordance as acceptable barter items, she would have accepted them as payment. Instead, she uses her gender and the tangible attributes of the books to contest an affordance.

## 5    Conclusion

A lingering question remains: did Soraburu ever get paid? It appears that for the next three years, there was a continued back-and-forth exchange between Peralta, the diocesan tribunal's prosecutors, Soraburu, and her lawyer. Peralta and the prosecutors wanted her to take the goods, but Soraburu continued to resist. While a judgement issued by the tribunal the same day as Soraburu's above statement said that she needed to choose goods within three days or she had to give up any right to being paid back, two years later on 12 March 1695 the prosecutor asked that Peralta be allowed to hold another public auction of Coroneu's goods and that any remaining creditors (aka Soraburu) should pick goods as payment before the auction.[87] The next document recorded in the case is from Soraburu's lawyer one year later on 8 March 1696 stating the goods and books were finally sold and Soraburu was just waiting to be paid.[88] Finally, on 24 March 1696, the prosecutor wrote to the court that all creditors had been satisfied, and we can infer Soraburu got her money.[89] Soraburu maintained for three years that Coroneu's books had no economic affordance in opposition to the executors, and in the end, she received payment in a form with actual value to her.

These eight women's circumstances demonstrate a myriad of affordances that Navarrese women assigned to and refused to assign to books. Books facilitated devotional practices and the display of personal and familial prestige, but the most crucial affordances were books' ability to be read or to be sold because of the effect they had on women's choices. Isabel de Labayen, Josepha Pardo, and María Josepha de Soraburu could manage books as they pleased since they and the male agents they dealt with cared about the books' economic affordance to the exclusion of reading despite the fact that all three women could read. Those same books would not have been destined for women readers because of their likely lack of Latin literacy and because the content was generally deemed inappropriate for women. Women were supposed to focus

---

87    ADP, C/1436 N. 2, ff. 645$^r$–645$^v$.
88    ADP, C/1436 N. 2, ff. 646$^r$–646$^v$.
89    ADP, C/1436 N. 2, ff. 648$^r$–648$^v$.

their attention on religion and morals to combat their supposed lack of virtue, and unless they were widows, their access to bookstores to acquire books was likely mediated by men. In the book collections here, women appear to have followed this virtuous criteria in their collecting, but they would have done so either out of interest or because the acquisition of these books could help construct a virtuous identity. The characteristics of the individuals themselves (gender and class), the tangible and intangible features of the books, and each situation combine to reveal patterns of affordances in early modern Navarre. Expanding beyond these eight women and to other times and places will bring forward more affordances for examination which will in turn bring more nuance to our incomplete picture of women and the book.

# CHAPTER 14

# The 'Librara', a Female Librarian in Seventeenth-Century Genoese Nunneries

*Valentina Sonzini*

The purpose of this article is to discuss the relatively unknown figure of the *librara*, a kind of ante-litteram librarian present in the Italian female monastic communities after the Tridentine Reforms. The research has focused on the analysis of some printed rules and constitutions related to some orders of nuns operating in Genoa during the XVII century. The Monastic Rule Codes define the practices pertaining to the nuns' life, and some of these rules illustrate the existence of a role for nuns specifically dedicated to the management and preservation of the books in the monasteries.

Beyond the issues that remain unresolved at the end of the research, what clearly emerges is that the librarian was a kind of professional chosen from among the other nuns, with specific skills in the management of bibliographic material. The discovery recognises a new agency for nuns that, while respecting the directions that came from superiors and confessors, nevertheless gave some leeway and autonomy in the acquisition of bibliographic materials and, as we shall see in one case, even in financially supporting the printing of their own Rules.

Five main points will be discussed: first, some light will be shed on the case of the Humiliati Nuns of Saint Martha and the publication of their Rules by Vittorio Baldini thus proving the agency of nuns also in relation to printing; in the second and third section of the article, an attempt will be made in order to outline the organisation of libraries operated by nuns, confirming the validity of the aforementioned thesis through other printed Rules and Constitutions; finally, the fourth and fifth sections will address the introduction of the figures of the *librara* (the librarian) and *scrittora* (the nun dedicated to the monastery archive).

## 1 The Nuns of Saint Martha in Genoa and the Printer Vittorio Baldini

In 1612 in Ferrara, Vittorio Baldini, Printer to the Duke, printed the *Constitutioni delle rr. Madri del monastero di s. Marta di Genoua, cauate dalla Regola del p. s. Benedetto, sotto la quale militano* [Constitution of the Mothers of the Monastery of Saint Martha in Genoa derived from the Rule of Saint Benedict They Militate Under].[1] The publication, as the full title suggests, was warmly endorsed and supported by cardinal archbishop Orazio Spinola (1537–1616) and printed on behalf of the nuns themselves (the title page reads 'upon request of the above-mentioned Mothers').[2] The 48-page quarto booklet bears a woodcut depicting Spinola's coat of arms on its title page. His presence on such occasions was justified by his Genoese birth and his close ties with the nunnery, as well as his position as papal legate in Ferrara.[3] Therefore, we can make sense of the involvement of Ferrara printer Vittorio Baldini in connection with the role played by the cardinal in the city's context.[4] Baldini had been active as a printer in Estes since 1575, holding a partial monopoly on printing work for the dukes and ecclesiastical authorities in the city, which he retained until 1618, the year of his death. Besides the *Constitutioni*, Baldini printed ten other books including a quarto decree in 1612.[5] These were usually short and inexpensive publications, with the exception of the *Synodi Ferrariensis*

---

1   *Constitutioni delle rr. Madri del monastero di s. Marta di Genova* (Ferrara, per Vittorio Baldini, 1612) USTC 4022543 (SBN BVEE073272). It is legitimate to ask oneself why the nuns of Santa Marta, as well as other female monastic orders, had decided to print their own Rules, documentary material related to the internal management of the order and of limited interest to the external public. The reasons, not only of a strictly editorial nature, can be found first of all in the need to codify the Rule through printing, thus defining it in an incontrovertible way (i.e., giving rise to a sort of *princeps* of the work). In addition, probably, the print runs—which did not fall below one hundred and fifty to two hundred copies—were justified by the provision of standard documentary materials for submission to the novices and nuns. Furthermore, there is the will to promote their institution: in fact, in the seventeenth century, the application of the Tridentine decrees is ironclad and there is a permanent shift to seclusion to the extent that women are pushed toward alternative and less strict forms of religiosity (I thank Isabella Gagliardi for clarifications on this matter).

2   "ad instanza delle sopradette Madri"; Orazio Spinola is not Agostino Spinola as erroneously mentioned in the SBN-Servizio Bibliotecario Nazionale. For some of his biographical details see: <https://cardinals.fiu.edu/bios1606.htm#Spinola>.

3   Orazio Spinola is "the expert and prestigious (one of the three that went from being Ferrara's vice-delegates to being cardinals, and the only one that immediately went from being a vice-delegate to being a legate)" in 1606, Andrea Gardi, 'La vicelegazione di Ferrara, tappa di una carriera prelatizia' in Giampaolo Borghello and Vincenzo Orioles (ed.), *Per Roberto Gusmani 1. Linguaggi, culture, letterature 2. Linguistica storica e teorica. Studi in ricordo* (Udine: Forum, 2012) p. 290.

4   In 1598 Ferrara had passed from Este domination to that of the Pope following the Devolution, which occurred due to the lack of direct heirs of Alfonso II.

5   Data obtained through the consultation of SBN-Servizio Bibliotecario Nazionale (last consultation May 10, 2021).

*constitutiones* and the rarely found *Sacramentale Genuensis Ecclesiae*, the latter also commissioned by Cardinal Spinola.[6]

As the Duchy's devolution unfolded, Baldini acted as Chamber Printer at the service of the newly established power. It is not unlikely that the nuns' commission was part of a broader political plot conceived by the Legate, and that the relationship between the printer and Spinola favoured the Ferrara environment rather than the Genoese one, where in that very same period Giuseppe Pavoni practised the art of typography.[7]

The protagonists of the publication are the Humiliati Nuns of Saint Martha in Genoa who, in 1498, had moved to the monastery of Saint Germano all'Acquasola (their previous nunnery was located in piazza dell'Annunziata).[8] In 1518, with the extinction of the male branch, the nuns abandoned the rule of the Humiliati and joined the Benedictine congregation of Cassino. The Congregation's presence in Genoa came to an end in 1798 with its expulsion sanctioned by the government of the Ligurian Democratic Republic.[9]

The books owned by these Benedictine nuns are documented in three lists compiled in the year 1600 by the Congregation of the Index, now contained in manuscripts Vat. lat. 11266 and Vat. lat. 11286, and allow us to find out more about the texts that the Congregation deemed unsuitable for the nunnery of Saint Martha.[10] They include a list of about thirty books, some of which are incunabula, and none of which were printed in Genoa. The lists mention a Bible printed in 1546 as well as an undated Gospel, both in vernacular Italian.

---

6    For example see USTC: 4022442 (SBN: BVEE068750); USTC: 4040043 (SBN: LI2E000019).

7    About Pavoni see Graziano Ruffini, *Sotto il segno del Pavone: annali di Giuseppe Pavoni e dei suoi eredi, 1598–1642* (Milano: Angeli, 1994). Spinola's name can be found in Pavoni's publications only in the 1611 Genoese edition of the *Decisione d'vn caso, e con esso d'alcuni altri dubii in materia di cambii. Del p. d. Antonio di S. Saluatore* (USTC 4029566; SBN LO1E042115), in which the archbishop appears on the title page that reads "D'ordine dell'Illustriss. & Reuerendissimo Sig. Cardinal Spinola" [upon request of the very illustrious and most reverend Cardinal Spinola]. It is unclear why the nuns relied on Vittorio Baldini and not on Giuseppe Pavoni for the publication of their Rules. It can be assumed that the edition was entirely financed by the Cardinal and that, given his Ferrara relations with Baldini, he had preferred to turn to the Este typography rather than to the Genoese one.

8    Once the old church of Saint Martha had been demolished, the church of the Annunciata del Vastato was built on its ruins (1520–1530); for more details see T.M. Maiolino and C. Varaldo, *Liguria monastica* (Cesena: Badia di Santa Maria del Monte, 1979), pp. 133–134.

9    Archivio di Stato di Torino (AST) Monache di diversi paesi, Genova, Monache di Santa Marta, mazzo 8, fasc. 15.

10   *Le biblioteche degli ordini regolari in Italia alla fine del XVI secolo* <https://rici.vatlib.it /site/index> (last consultation September 23, 2021). Many thanks to Giovanni Petrocelli for reporting.

They bear witness to the fact that after the Council of Trent the spread of religious works in the vernacular had been highly restricted.[11] The publication of the *Constitutioni* is especially interesting in this circumstance because it highlights the relationship between the nuns and the world of books: they were at the same time clients, publishers, and subsequently librarians and readers, too. It was anything but unusual for Italian nuns to entrust local printers with works of spiritual improvement, or, just like in this case, the Rules of their order. Gabriella Zarri reminds us that 'it is not unlikely in the early 16th century for nuns to commission printed texts or manuscripts', and nuns could either purchase books directly, or have books purchased on their behalf (as well as books being transferred to nunneries in the dowers of novices).[12]

## 2     The Organisation of Nuns' Libraries

The *Constitutioni* calls attention to a known fact, that the sisters were educated and capable of reading, recommending nuns to not simply read the page but to fully understand the words and put them into practice.[13] More importantly, the *Constitutioni* also indicates that nuns were able to manage the small-scale bibliographical collections in their possession. Indeed, this text also proves that the nunnery included a space specifically meant for books. Though at this point in time it was probably not an actual library yet, and the sisters were not granted direct access to its contents or the rules to run it. References to

---

11    On the censorship and reading of the bible and other religious texts by nuns, see Gigliola Fragnito, 'Censura ecclesiastica e identità spirituale e culturale femminile', in *Mélanges de l'École française de Rome. Italie et Méditerranée*, vol. 115 (2003). *Représentation et identité en Italie et en Europe (xve–xixe siècle)*, pp. 287–313.

12    "non mancano nei primi decenni del Cinquecento monache che commissionano testi a stampa o manoscritti", Gabriella Zarri, 'Le monache e i libri nel secolo xvi: produzione, letture, uso' in *Libri e biblioteche: le letture dei frati mendicanti tra Rinascimento ed Età moderna* (Spoleto: Fondazione Centro italiano di studi sull'alto Medioevo, 2019), p. 369. The cost of an edition commissioned by the monastery was certainly noted in the cash register (receipts and expenditures), but, at the present time, it has not been possible to recover any document that attests to such disbursements; See, the case of the Florentine bookseller Pietro Morosi, who between 1588 and 1607, wrote down in his account book the credit transactions with some female convents of the city, Paul F. Gehl, 'Libri per donne. Le monache clienti del libraio fiorentino Piero Morosi (1588–1607)', in Gabriella Zarri (ed.), *Donna, disciplina, creanza cristiana dal xv al xvii secolo. Studi e testi a stampa* (Roma, Edizioni di storia e letteratura, 1996), pp. 67–84.

13    "che non douete contentarui di tenerle ftampate fopra di quefta carta per leggerle folamente, ma douete inoltre indurui (come volea Mofe foffero trattate le fue parole) a portarle ligate in mezzo delle mani, per porle in efecutione" (c. A2r–v).

the presence of books inside the convent can be found in the third part of the publication. Chapter XII is actually centred around an *ante-litteram* librarian, the so-called *librara*. We know that she managed the volumes acquired by the nunnery, supervised their conservation and oversaw the loans to the sisters. Her role is specific although no particular aptitude is mentioned as the basis of a nun's destination to this function. It is not clear if she was chosen on the grounds of her educational background, or on the basis of a personal inclination, or whether it was a role played in turn by the sisters. Whatever the reasons behind the designation of one nun rather than another, in her functions, the *librara* was expected to place the editions in alphabetical order (though it is not clear whether such order was by title or by author), to register the loans, to keep the books intact and possibly repaired. In this vein, not only was the *librara*'s role aligned with librarianship, but also with the conservation and preservation of the materials.

We can only guess what kind of books were housed in the library. Perhaps music books, since it was known, at least at the end of the sixteenth century, that it was printed in Saint Martha.[14] Likely materials meant to support the religious formation of nuns and lay-sisters alike were also acquired, including hagiographic and mystical production, as well as spiritual and confessional rules.[15] The volumes were likely also used by convent girls, who were sent to nunneries by their families to ensure they would get basic education (estimates show that at the end of the seventeenth-century the convent of Saint Martha was home to 71 women, 56 of which were nuns, the remaining 15 lay-sisters).[16]

## 3    Ordering the Books: the Library and Librarian in Monasteries

As of today, no light has been shed on the arrangement of the books the nunnery owned and the spaces where they were kept. We could guess that at some time in the early 1600s the chests were replaced with shelves that might have

---

14    Although it should not seem strange to us that the music was kept and distributed by a specific nun, the "cantora", specifically designated to undertake such tasks, and that sometimes and in certain cases, she was also designated "librara", G. Zarri, *Le monache e i libri nel secolo XVI*, p. 374; M. Rosi, *Le monache nella vita genovese*, p. 105.

15    G. Zarri, *Le monache e i libri nel secolo XVI*, p. 371.

16    Documents suggest that in the 1660s the convent girls were especially numerous at Saint Martha, see M. Rosi, 'Le monache nella vita genovese dal secolo XV al XVII' in *Atti della Società ligure di Storia Patria* (ASLSP), 27 (1895), p. 91; Giuseppe Felloni e Valeria Polonio, 'Un sondaggio per le comunità religiose a Genova in età moderna' in *Studi e Documenti di Storia Ligure in onore di don Luigi Alfonso per il suo 85° genetliaco* Atti della Società ligure di storia patria, Nuova Serie—Vol. XXXVI (CX) Fasc. II 1996, p. 166.

occupied a precise place in the convent, like a study room or possibly even the cell *librara* herself. It is clear that, once registered, the books became part of the nunnery's belongings:

> in obedience to the vow of poverty the nuns were not supposed to own books; we know, however, that they could be granted the use of them, and the numerous late-sixteenth century library inventories witness that in the cells of several nuns a more or less significant number of books were to be found. After all, it is also known that a certain number of books were required in the monastic endowment. Thus, professed nuns had to bring all the prescribed texts to the monastery, although they had to give up their possession in favour of the convent.[17]

The nuns of Saint Martha were not the only ones in Genoa to have a rule that contained references to a librarian. Indeed, printed material bears witness to at least another contemporary example, the *Regole et auisi per le officiali del monastero della Annontiata* [Rules and notices for the sisters of the Annunciata monastery].[18] This book is an octavo edition, printed locally in Genoa by Giuseppe Pavoni in 1624. In the first part of the booklet, the *Regole*, on page 59 (c. D7), a specific chapter is dedicated to the 'Rules dedicated to the *Librara*, that is to say who is in charge of spiritual books'.[19] The designated nun would 'take care of all the nunnery's spiritual books and will have them all noted down on a booklet'. The rules propose that the *Librara* '[leave] enough space for each alphabetical letter, as much as necessary to mark down all of the books that, time after time, will be taken into the nunnery', further suggesting that acquired materials should be registered in alphabetical order.[20] A constant book supply was guaranteed by the novices, who were evidently required to bring bibliographic material with them upon entering the nunnery ('every novice will take books that will be marked down on a register and become the nunnery's property').[21] Contrary to what is stated in the *Constitutioni*, that mention the *librara*'s role but not the spaces where the volumes were kept, the *Regole* informs us that the books were

---

17    G. Zarri, *Le monache e i libri nel secolo XVI*, p. 370.

18    *Regole et avisi per le officiali del monastero della Annontiata* (Genova, per Giuseppe Pavoni, 1624) USTC 4042752 (SBN LIGE006324). Rare edition marked in SBN as available only at the Biblioteca Universitaria in Genoa (last consultation September 23, 2021).

19    "Regole della Librara, ò Perfetta de i libri spirituali".

20    "lasciando per ogni lettera tante carte, quanto basterà per notare in esse, tutti quelli, che di tempo in tempo saranno portati in casa".

21    "haurà cura di ricordare alla Madre, ch'ogni Nouitia, che verrà, ne porti qualch'vno, massime de quelli, che si noteranno a basso".

housed in a specific room, claiming that the prefect will store them in a locked room tidily stacked on different bookshelves, kept clean from dust and with their title written on the outside, so it will be easier to find them'.[22]

The designated nun was also supposed to mark, 'in neat handwriting, on the first page of each book, the name of the Monastery,' thus branding these books as property of the monastery.[23] Moreover, the *librara/prefetta* would also provide reading materials for the meals and would ensure that the nuns kept only one book in their cell at a time. The Mother Superior likewise had a role in library and book supervision. She was responsible for checking over bibliographic materials, granting book loans to the sisters and for overseeing and authorising the registration of new books, making sure that 'no book contrary to the Rule is introduced'.[24]

## 4    The *Librara*

The *librara* is again found in Chapter XII of the *Constitutioni per le Madri dell'Ordine della Santissima Annunciata* [Constitution for the Mothers of the Most Holy Annunciation] published in 1643 by Farroni in Genoa.[25] In addition to specifying that the nuns could not keep more than one volume in their cell, the author of these rules also clarifies that, 'it [was] necessary to put one nun in charge of storing books in one place, and of keeping track of all the nunnery's books in alphabetical order, so she immediately would know where to find them'.[26] Again, the text does not specify whether the alphabetical order is to be attributed following the name of the author or the title of the work. Most likely, as was also the case for booksellers' catalogues, the choice between the author's name/surname or the title would be made depending on how the work was more commonly identified. Moreover, in the notes on inventory, the *Constitutioni per le Madri* also suggests that the *librara* should perform a custodian role, stating that 'she would be responsible for the maintenance and

---

22  "Li conserverà [la prefetta] tutti in vna camera sotto chiare, bene ordinati tra loro in diverse scansie, netti dalla polvere, & con li suoi titoli scritti di fuora, accio sijno facili a ritrovarsi".

23  "con buona lettera ... sulla prima carta di ciascuno, il nome del Monastero".

24  "veda che non s'introducano libri proibiti nella sua Regola".

25  *Constitutioni per le Madri dell'Ordine della Santissima Annunciata* (Genova, per Giovanni Maria Farroni, 1643) USTC 4017690 (SBN UTOE674403).

26  "necessario sarà deputar una, che abbia cura di mantenere li libri in luogo commune, la quale tenga nota di tutti li libri, che sono in casa per ordine d'alfabeto acciocche ... ella sappia subito ritrouarlo".

conservation of the artefacts' and that she should 'make sure to keep them clean from dust and safe from any other dreadful accident'.[27]

In addition to any book possibly borrowed from the convent library, the nuns were permitted to keep 'the writings or the books containing our rules, the instructions on prayer and on extirpating vices and acquiring virtues' in their cell.[28] It is probable that these materials were owned by the nun herself and did not become part of the convent's book endowment. How the community handled these volumes once the owner had passed away can only be guessed: they either returned to the family of the owner, or they became part of the monastery's collection and were then made available to novices and lay sisters. However, there are no certain references concerning the management of these books to be found in the rules of the individual orders or in the documentation of the monasteries. In the notes on the inventory it is also written that the *librara* 'will also keep track of the books she will lend, so she will be able to get them back from the sisters who borrowed them once they are done reading'.[29] The figure of the *librara* according to the *Constitutioni* of 1643 was to be included among the minor officials and was elected by the most powerful members of the monastery: the Mother Prioress, the Vice Prioress, and the 'Discrete' (the Mother Prioress' advisors). She would remain in office for a time ranging from one to three years, and her appointment was basically unquestionable. At the discretion of the Mother Superior, she could possibly be joined by another nun as an assistant.

5       The *Librara* and the *Scittora*

The obligation for nuns to have a small number of books at their personal disposal is also highlighted in the *Regula Saluatoris vulgo nuncupata de Sancta Birgitta* [The Rule of the Saviour Commonly Known as Saint Birgitta's] published in Genoa by Benedetto Celle in 1668.[30] In the third chapter, which features 'delle celle, e de letti' (Of the Cells and of the Beds), it is clearly stated that the endowment of each nun can include 'two spiritual books other than the

---

27   "terrà anche nota delli libri ch'ella presterà; accioche quando quelle Sorelle, a quali s'eran prestati l'haueranno letti, gli sappia ricuperare"; "procurerà di tenerli guardati dalla polvere, e da tutti gl'altri sinistri accidenti".

28   "i scritti, o libri contenenti le nostre regole, le instruttioni sopra l'orazione, & sopra l'estirpatione de Vitij, & acquisti della virtù".

29   "terrà anche nota delli libri ch'ella presterà; accioche quando quelle Sorelle, a quali s'eran prestati l'haueranno letti, gli sappia ricuperare".

30   SBN BVEE073352.

Constitutions and the Rule. Once read they have to be replaced by two others with the Mother's approval and according to the confessor's advice' (the latter were evidently owned by the single nun, and therefore the question about their destination once the owner passed away arises again).[31]

Although these rules again provide no direct reference to a room in which the books for the education and continued training of the nuns were kept, chapter ten makes reference to a sort of archive, a closed space where the accounting books and the documentation pertaining to the structure were stored,

> The public documents belonging to the monastery will not be kept in [the librara's] room, but will be stored away in a special place, or a closet, locked with two keys ... the books recording all of the nuns, the moment they entered the monastery, their age and so on will also be kept in the same place. The same goes for their profession of vows and death, as it is appropriate to have sound knowledge of this, and to preserve memory.[32]

The archive, defined as such, is also mentioned in Chapter xii 'Dell'Officio della Scrittora' of the *Constitutioni delle RR. monache del monastero di Sant'Antonio di Padova in Carignano* (Constitutions of the Nuns of the Monastery of Saint Anthony of Padua in Carignano) published in Genoa by Benedetto Guasco in 1656.[33] In fact, it mentions the figure of the *Scrittora* who 'will have a room named Archive in which there will be specifically made cabinets where the public writings concerning the monastery will be tidily stored away and separate from one another, so it will be easy to find them. This room, the so-called Archive, will always be locked'.[34] The books kept in the archive had on the one hand the purpose of recording incoming and outgoing institutional correspondence, on the other hand to report the name, surname and date of entry of the nuns into the community. Another book was used to record 'the

---

31  "due libri spirituali; li quali letti, se ne prenderanno due altri, con licenza della Madre, e consiglio del confessore, oltre le Constitutioni, e la Regola", ch. I1v–I2r.

32  "Le scritture pubbliche, spettanti al monasterio, non le terrà in sua Camera, ma si conserveranno in vna stanza particolare, ouero armario, chiuso con due chiavi ... Nello stesso luogo si conserueranno quelli libri, nella quali saranno notate tutte le Monache; il tempo di ingresso loro, età, &c. Così anche la Professione, passaggio all'altra vita: essendo conueniente d'hauere di tutto questo, distinto ragguaglio, e conseruarne la memoria".

33  SBN BVEE073466.

34  "hauerà vna stanza, che si chiamerà Archiuio, dentro la quale, e ne gli armarij perciò fatti, riporrà le scritture publiche del Monastero ordinatamente, e con distinzione, acciò si possano con facilità trouare. Questa stanza, o vogliamo dire Archiuio, starà sempre serrato".

chapter's actions, the election of the Abbess and the other officials'.[35] Finally, the licences granted by the Superior were recorded in a further register. This Archive also served as a room dedicated to personal writing, as it housed paper, ink and inkwells.

Besides the *scrittora*, the Carignano nuns also had a *librara*. Her role and duties are detailed in the twenty-first chapter. Compared to the rules previously analysed, the *Constitutioni* clearly specified that the nun in charge of the books was required to keep them in a room designated for this purpose by the abbess. The text also adds some references to library management, '[the *librara*] will keep track of all of the nunnery's books, marking them down in alphabetical order in a register. She will keep them tidily stored away and marked with some sign that will make it easy to find them'.[36] It is the first time that in the rules there is a direct reference to the placement of the volumes, to be identified through conventional signs probably chosen by the librarian or borrowed from internal procedures. The chapter also reiterates the importance of the conservation of bibliographic materials. In fact it emphasises that the assistant 'will regularly check on the books, keep them clean from dust and when the volumes will be showing signs of wear she will communicate it to the Abbess, so they will be rebound or fixed according to necessity'.[37] Seemingly this duty was not maintained by a single sister, but rather the nuns alternated, as paragraph IV mentions that 'once her assignment will be over, she will hand in to her successor the register where all the books lent to the sisters have been marked down, she will say who borrowed them, so it will be easy to retrieve them'.[38] The role of the *librara* therefore participated, even among the nuns of Carignano, in the management of the volumes and in the supervision of the readings of the nuns that were diligently recorded in a specific register, a small-scale reflection of the control that the sisters experienced at all levels of their monastic life.

From the analysis of these rule books taken into consideration, the first thing that emerges is that in some female monastic orders there was a figure

35    "le attioni capitolari, come le elettioni dell'Abbadessa, e delle altre Officiali, e le accettazioni delle figlie all'habito, & alla professione".

36    "questa [la *librara*] hauerà la nota in vn libro, fatto per Alfabeto, di tutti i libri, che sono in casa, li quali conseruerà ordinatamente compartiti e notati con qualche segno, nella stanza, che l'Abbassa assegnerà, acciò possa richiesta facilmente trouarli".

37    "visiterà spesso detti libri, e li custodirà dalla poluere, e quando per essere stati assai adoprati, haueranno patito, n'auuiserà l'Abbadessa, acciò li faccia rilegare, ò altrimenti accomodare, secondo, che sarà bisogno".

38    "nel finire dell'officio consegnerà alla Successora il libro, nel quale stanno tutti notati, e quelli, che hauerà dati alle Sorelle, dirà appresso di chi sono, acciò a suo tempo si possa ricuperare".

responsible for the organisation and management of the bibliographic material kept in the monasteries. The printed *Rules* codify the presence of a figure that had not heretofore emerged in the analyses of Italian nuns' reading habits and education. Although the sources considered are exclusively in print and no archival documents were dealt with, the information obtained highlights the post-Tridentine desire to organise and supervise the bibliographic material present in the monasteries, in fact already perceiving the need for a figure with specific skills to take care of it.

## 6     Conclusions

Beyond the issues that remain unresolved, what clearly emerges is that the librarian was a kind of professional chosen from among the other nuns, with specific skills in the management of bibliographic material. In fact, it is a role that we do not always find among the 'officers' elected and designated within the convent walls. In the case of the Augustinian nuns of Saint Sylvester in Genoa, the *Regola, e constitutioni della monache di S. Siluestro delle pouere dell'Ordine di santo Agostino di Genoua* [The Rule and Constitutions of the Nuns of Saint Silvester of the Poor of the Order of Saint Augustine in Genoa] makes no reference either to a librarian, or to an endowment of volumes for study and prayer.[39] This *Regola*, published in Genoa by Pavoni in 1604, limits itself to providing indications on the daily management of the community, perhaps proving the fact that an institutionalisation of bibliographic management was not present in all orders. However, the role of the *librara* is progressively documented and with an increasingly detailed job description probably expressing the will, on the part of the mother superior but, ultimately, of the ecclesiastical bodies to which the convents were subordinate, to control and direct the readings of the nuns, as a long wave of post-Tridentine reforms.[40]

The questions that arise following the analysis of the above mentioned texts are of an exquisitely librarian nature: in fact, if on the one hand the documentation relating to the book endowments of Italian nuns is rather well known and analysed, on the other hand, the figure of the *librara* and the nuns' role as publishers are lesser known, and so are the management systems of the volumes owned by the female monasteries. The contribution presented here

---

39    *Regola, e constitutioni della monache di S. Silvestro* (Genova, appresso Giuseppe Pavoni, 1604) USTC 4030687 (SBN BVEE067839).

40    The assumption would need further investigation based on an extensive census of women's monastic rules published during the period in question in the Italian Peninsula.

mainly aims at introducing a more precise cognitive investigation, while offering a limited sample of materials relating to the Genoese seventeenth-century environment. What is evident, however, is that the *librara* was assigned tasks that were not specifically detailed, but only grossly outlined. She was a partly blurred figure, with little autonomy and who operated without specific regulations; her work probably involved a small range of materials anyway (even if the quantity of banned volumes reported for the convent of Saint Martha suggests that the collection exceeded a hundred), managed rather according to a logic of common sense than explicit internal rules dictated by a library practice that was, if not consolidated, at least roughly outlined. Such lack of specific regulations probably gave her some discretion, not so much in purchases, but in the management of materials and the granting of loans. What emerges is the figure of a woman who learned by doing, who is guided by intuition and common sense, who probably also learns from those who preceded her, treasures established practices, but also invents new ones. Far from shaping themselves as pale reflections of a hierarchical system that left no space for women's existence, the *librara* tells a story of autonomy that once again places women at the centre of their personal experience and not on the margins of male decision-making or governance.

# CHAPTER 15

# Between Piety and Scholarship: the Bible Collection of Elisabeth Sophie Marie of Brunswick-Wolfenbüttel

*Joëlle Weis*

After the death of her husband in 1735, Elisabeth Sophie Marie of Brunswick-Wolfenbüttel (1683–1767) started a much-admired collection of Bibles, which was to become one of the largest in the Holy Roman Empire at that time. She set up her 1,200 Bibles in her city palace in Brunswick until 1764, when the now 80-year-old dowager Duchess decided to donate her substantial collection to the Ducal Library in Wolfenbüttel. However, the endowment was not considered an unconditional gift; Elisabeth Sophie Marie set clear terms. Duke Carl I (1713–1780) reported to his Chancellor, Georg Septimus Andreas von Praun (1701–1786) that while organising her library ('Bücher Saal'), Elisabeth Sophie Marie resolved to gift her Bible collection complete with her mahogany bookshelves to the Wolfenbüttel library, but with the condition that they remained in a separate cabinet flanked by her portrait. Additionally, she wanted an inscription stating that the collection was kept for her 'everlasting memory'.[1] Even though the valuable donation came with logistical problems, as there was not enough space in the library, Duke Carl I gladly accepted. While her books constitute a significant contribution to the collection, only a few visitors know about it.

The story of the donation is only a footnote in the Herzog August Library's (HAB) history. Still, it contains important clues about the relationship between the collector and the collection, which has been neglected in the scarce research on Elisabeth Sophie Marie.

---

1  Wolfenbüttel, Herzog August Bibliothek, BA II, 205, fol. 2, *Letter from Duke Carl I. to Georg Septimus Andreas von Praun* (26.09.1764): "[...] bey geschehener Aufräumung ihres Bücher Saales resolviret, die Ihnen zugehörige kostbare und zahlreiche Bibel Samlung, mit Inbegrif der Repositorien welche von Mahoni Holtz sind, der großen Bibliothek in Wolfenbüttel zu schenken; jedoch mit der Bedingung, daß solche in ein apartes Cabinet verwahret, über den Eingang deßselben deero portrait, und unter solches die inscription, 'daß diese Sammlung von Ihnen der Bibliothec zum immerwährenden Andenken verehret worden' gesetzet werden solle". I want to thank Stephan Bialas-Pophanken for pointing me to this letter.

© KONINKLIJKE BRILL BV, LEIDEN, 2025 | DOI:10.1163/9789004701656_016

While in the past years, women's book ownership and reading practices in the Early Modern period has gained more attention, especially in English speaking countries, most German collections remain unexplored, even though there is a lot of evidence on women's libraries.[2] In the British case, research has focused especially on the reading of the Bible and a number of studies have revealed the reading and writing practices of women, as well as their involvement in religious activities.[3] This research is absent for German speaking countries, which is why I want to take the discovery of the letter from Carl I to his Chancellor as an opportunity to reflect on the Duchess's agency as a collector of old books and Bibles.

After a brief introduction to Elisabeth Sophie Marie, I will focus on her collecting and cataloguing practices and her role as a promoter of scholarship. In the third part, I will examine the general efforts currently undertaken in researching the many personal collections that entered the Wolfenbüttel library in the eighteenth century, leading to greater visibility of almost forgotten contributions, especially by the Duchesses and the non-ruling Princes.

## 1      Elisabeth Sophie Marie

We do not know many details of Elisabeth Sophie Marie's biography. She was the daughter of Rudolf Friedrich (1645–1688), Duke of Schleswig-Holstein-Sonderburg-Norburg, and Bibiana von Promnitz (1649–1685).[4] After her parents' early death, she was brought up at her custodian's court in Wolfenbüttel,

---

2    Edith Snook, *Women, Reading, and the Cultural Politics of Early Modern England* (Aldershot: Ashgate, 2005); Leah Knight etc. (eds.), *Women's Bookscapes in Early Modern Britain: Reading, Ownership, Circulation* (Ann Arbor: University of Michigan Press, 2018). For case studies on female book ownership beyond the English speaking world see, Anne J. Cruz and Rosilie Hernández (eds.), *Women's Literacy in Early Modern Spain and the New World* (Aldershot: Ashgate, 2011); Anne-Marie Legaré (ed.), *Livres et lectures de femmes en Europe entre moyen âge et renaissance* (Turnhout: Brepols 2007).

3    See most prominently Kate Narveson, *Bible Readers and Lay Writers in Early Modern England: Gender and Self-Definition in an Emergent Writing Culture* (Aldershot: Ashgate, 2012); Femke Molekamp, *Women and the Bible in Early Modern England: Religious Reading and Writing* (Oxford: Oxford University Press, 2013).

4    On Elisabeth Sophie Marie, see Maria Munding and Heimo Reinitzer, 'Elisabeth Sophie Marie', in Dieter Lohmeyer (ed.), *Biographisches Lexikon für Schleswig-Holstein und Lübeck*, 11 (Neumünster: Wachholtz, 2000), pp. 91–94; Christina Hillmann-Apmann, 'Elisabeth Sophie Marie', in Horst Rüdiger Jarck (ed.), *Braunschweigisches Biographisches Lexikon. 8. bis 18. Jahrhundert* (Braunschweig: Appelhans, 2006), p. 199.

which meant that books and scholarship closely surrounded her for most of her childhood.[5] In 1701, she married Adolf August, heir to the throne of Schleswig-Holstein-Sonderburg-Plön, who died in 1704. She took over as regent for her infant son. Only two years later, the little Leopold August died at four years old. Elisabeth Sophie Marie lost all her official duties at court and retreated to her widow's seat in Ahrensbök. Her late husband's cousin, and new ruling Duke, considered her a financial burden and left her with no substantial securities.[6] Elisabeth's marriage to her much older cousin and godfather, August Wilhelm of Brunswick-Wolfenbüttel, in 1710 at least afforded her some financial stability. It was August's third marriage, but the Wolfenbüttel family's hopes to produce an heir through this alliance remained unfulfilled. The marriage was childless, and after Wilhelm August's death in 1731, the members of a junior branch of the family became the new rulers.[7] But Elisabeth Sophie Marie had learned from her previous marriage and had herself particularly well secured in her marriage contract. She procured the donation of substantial lands and the so-called Grauer Hof, a city palace in Brunswick, where she lived until she died in 1767, surviving her husband for 36 years.[8]

As a widow, Elisabeth Sophie Marie, who already owned a substantial private library, started to collect Bibles, which resulted in one of the most significant Bible collections in Europe.[9] By the end of her life, Elisabeth's Bible collection consisted of approximately 1,200 Bibles. She had a keen interest in editions of the Luther Bible and their translations, but owned many other exceptional pieces, such as 47 Polyglot Bibles, two Malaysian Bibles and a variety of rare manuscripts. Until 1764, she kept them at her residence in Brunswick before she decided to donate them to the Wolfenbüttel library. Today, Elisabeth Sophie Marie's Bibles still make up the most important part of the Herzog August Library's own Bible holdings. The non-biblical books in

---

5  Both the ruling Duke Rudolf August (1627–1704) as well as his younger brother and co-regent, Anton Ulrich (1633–1714) were appointed as her legal guardians. Anton Ulrich was married to Elisabeth Sophie Marie's aunt, Elisabeth Juliane of Holstein-Norburg (1634–1704).

6  For details on her situation as a widow in Ahrenbök and marriage plans, see Niedersächsisches Landesarchiv (NLA), Wolfenbüttel, 1 Alt 22 Nr. 284, *Einige eigenhändige Schreiben des Herzogs Anton Ulrich*, fol. 27.

7  On the history of the principality Brunswick-Wolfenbüttel, see Horst-Rüdiger Jarck and Gerhard Schildt (eds.), *Braunschweigische Landesgeschichte. Jahrtausendrückblick einer Region* (Braunschweig: Appelhans, 2000).

8  See NLA, Wolfenbüttel, 1 Alt 23 Nr. 292, *Eigenhändiger Aufsatz des Erbprinzen August Wilhelm, betitelt: "Die Raisons so mich zu die Ehe der Herzogin von Arensbök gebracht"*.

9  On the Bible collection in general, see Werner Arnold, 'Die Bibelsammlung', in Paul Raabe (ed.), *Herzog August Bibliothek Wolfenbüttel* (Braunschweig: Westermann, 1978), pp. 42–49.

her library, which consisted of over 3,000 volumes, came to Wolfenbüttel only after her death.[10]

## 2    Elisabeth Sophie Marie: a Book Collector

The sheer numbers show that acquisition of books must have been an integral part of Elisabeth's everyday life. It is incomprehensible how little scholarly attention she has received as a collector so far. In the general history of the HAB, the Duchess is acknowledged only (and barely) as an essential contributor to the general holdings, and even though recent research has hinted towards her collection activities, no extensive study exists on the contents or the emergence of the collections.[11] Scarce source material is partly at fault for this scholarly neglect, which in itself is a sign of how women's papers were not considered worthy for conservation, greatly contributing to the gender bias in historical research today.[12] Over time, both of Elisabeth's collections were integrated into the Wolfenbüttel holdings and the provenance simply forgotten. For decades, no one bothered to have a closer look at the books, even though the traces of her activities are omnipresent in the HAB's holdings. Her bookplate (Fig. 15.1), which she used systematically, can be found in hundreds of books in the so-called 'Mittlere Aufstellung' (a mixed section containing books that were acquired between 1705 and 1950), and the current Bible collection is full of Elisabeth's original Bibles. It is evident that she was proud of her collection and marked ownership with self-confidence. The Duchess's regular use of bookplates allows us to clearly identify her volumes, which is not always self-evident, especially in the case of women's libraries, since their private belongings are usually not well documented.[13]

---

10    The partial reconstruction of the non-biblical library is published under <https://bib liotheksrekonstruktion.hab.de/esm> (accessed 24 October 2022). Statistical data on the Bible collection is currently being prepared in the project "Weltwissen. Das kosmpolitische Sammlungsinteresse des frühneuzeitlichen Adels" at the HAB.

11    The most recent research includes, Ulrike Gleixner, 'Lutherbildnisse im Dienst fürstlicher Selbstdarstellung', in Hole Rößler (ed.), *Luthermania. Ansichten einer Kultfigur* (Wiesbaden: Harrassowitz Verlag in Kommission, 2017), pp. 306–309; Ulrike Gleixner, 'Die lesende Fürstin: Büchersammlungen als lebenslange Bildungspraxis', in Juliana Jacobi etc. (eds.), *Vormoderne Bildungsgänge. Selbst-und Fremdbeschreibung in der Frühen Neuzeit* (Köln: Böhlau, 2010), pp. 207–224.

12    On the problem of 'female' sources for library history, see Susie West, 'Rare Books and Rare Women: Gender and Private Libraries 1660–1830', in Evelyn Kerslake and Nickianne Moody (eds.), *Gendering Library History* (Liverpool: John Moores University, 2000), pp. 179–195, 180.

13    West, 'Rare Books', p. 188.

FIGURE 15.1    Bookplate of Elisabeth Sophie Marie
© HERZOG AUGUST BIBLIOTHEK WOLFENBÜTTEL

Furthermore, she meticulously documented the Bible collection. She had a catalogue printed in 1752, which recorded all the Bibles sorted by language, of which approximately 30 copies have survived in German libraries until today.[14] In addition, the HAB archives hold an amended copy of the catalogue, which depicts the growth of the collection after 1752.[15] While the textual content of the catalogue is central to understanding the Duchess' collecting practises, the chosen imagery also reveals a lot about the collector. The frontispiece of the catalogue (Fig. 15.2) shows a portrait of the Duchess enthroned above her library room. Below, a putto raises a portrait of Martin Luther, apparently bringing it to her side. The illustration shows a remarkable self-confidence on the part of the Duchess, but is also part of a political strategy; despite the many conversions in the House of Brunswick-Wolfenbüttel, Elisabeth takes a stand and secures her family's position among the most important Protestant dynasties in the Holy Roman Empire.[16] Using book illustrations as a mode of empowerment was not a new strategy in the eighteenth century, the relation-ship between 'female images and female book ownership and their political import in these works' has been well researched.[17] However, the frontispiece is also remarkable in a second aspect; it prominently shows the 'Bücher-Saal', the 'book room' of the Duchess. Although presented in an idealised form, it never-theless shows how Elisabeth claims the library as her own space, confirming that library rooms were more than 'sites of male agency only'.[18]

Parallel to the catalogues, the *historical-critical news* on the Duchesses' Bible collection was published from 1753 onwards.[19] In this book series, Elisabeth's court preacher Georg Ludolph Otto Knoch (1705–1783) recorded detailed

---

14    Georg Ludolph Otto Knoch, *Bibliotheca Biblica. Das ist Verzeichnis der Bibel-Sammlung, welche die durchlauchtigste Fürstin und Frau Elisabeth Sophia Maria erst verwittwete Herzogin zu Braunschweig und Lüneburg [...] in mancherley Sprachen, absonderlich der teutschen durch D. Mart. Luthern, gesammlet u. in dero Bücher-Schatz auf dem grauen Hofe, der christlichen Kirche zum Besten aufgestellet hat* (Braunschweig: 1752).

15    Wolfenbüttel, Herzog August Bibliothek, BA I, 633, *Katalog der Bibelsammlung Elisabeth Sophia Marias* (1752). Online <http://diglib.hab.de/mss/ba-1-633/start.htm> (accessed 29 September 2021).

16    See Gleixner, 'Lutherbildnisse'. On the role of books for dynastic women, see Jill Bepler, 'Traditions of reading, writing and collecting: books in the lives of dynastic women in early modern Germany', in Elisabeth Wåghäll Nivre (ed.), *(Re)Contextualizing literary and cultural history* (Stockholm: Stockholm University, 2013), pp. 223–52.

17    Cynthia J. Brown, *The Queen's Library: Image-Making at the Court of Anne of Brittany, 1477–1514* (Philadelphia: University of Pennsylvania Press, 2010), p. 10.

18    West, 'Rare Books', p. 185.

19    Georg Ludolph Otto Knoch, *Historisch-critische Nachrichten von der braunschweigischen Bibelsammlung* (10 vols., Wolfenbüttel: Meißner, 1749–1750).

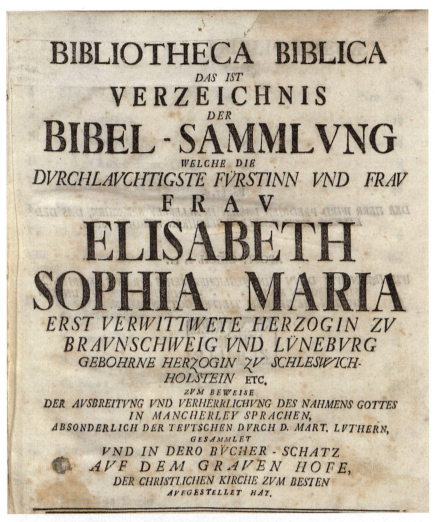

BIBLIOTHECA BIBLICA
*DAS IST*
VERZEICHNIS
*DER*
BIBEL - SAMMLVNG
*WELCHE DIE*
*DVRCHLAVCHTIGSTE FVRSTINN VND FRAV*
*FRAV*
ELISABETH
SOPHIA MARIA
*ERST VERWITTWETE HERZOGIN ZV*
*BRAVNSCHWEIG VND LVNEBVRG*
*GEBOHRNE HERZOGIN ZV SCHLESWICH-*
*HOLSTEIN* ETC.
*ZVM BEWEISE*
*DER AVSBREITVNG VND VERHERRLICHVNG DES NAHMENS GOTTES*
*IN MANCHERLEY SPRACHEN,*
*ABSONDERLICH DER TEVTSCHEN DVRCH D. MART. LVTHERN,*
*GESAMMLET*
*VND IN DERO BVCHER - SCHATZ*
*AVF DEM GRAVEN HOFE,*
*DER CHRISTLICHEN KIRCHE ZVM BESTEN*
*AVFGESTELLET HAT.*

FIGURE 15.2    Frontispiece of Knoch, Bibliotheca Biblica
© HERZOG AUGUST BIBLIOTHEK WOLFENBÜTTEL

information on selected Bibles.[20] For every chosen copy, Knoch would give an overview of the current state of research and describe the condition of the volume as well as special features in great detail. In some cases, information on the copy's provenance and even prices or other value indicators were added. That allows us to conclude earlier collection information and retrace

---

20    On Knoch, see Heimo Reinitzer, *Biblia deutsch. Luthers Bibelübersetzung und ihre Tradition* (Wolfenbüttel: Herzog August Bibliothek, 1983), pp. 313–315.

the object's path before coming to Wolfenbüttel. The publication clearly shows how important it was to Elisabeth Sophie Marie to disseminate her collection and promote it as a unique phenomenon. Further evidence of these efforts is the guest book she created to record all her visitors. It contains names, dates, and in many cases, sayings and biblical passages with which the guests immortalised themselves.[21] This little guest book, clad in velvet, demonstrates the popularity of Elizabeth's collections, establishing these holdings as a popular attraction for visitors to Brunswick. At the same time, it shows again how her collections were a central part of her image cultivation as a pious and learned woman. With the guest book, she asserted ownership and demonstrated generosity by sharing her treasures with others.

From this perspective, it is not surprising that she wanted to determine what the new home of her books should look like towards the end of her life. The Duchess, who at the time of donation was 80 years old, did not want to leave the details to the executors of her will, but instead made sure that the Bibles got their rightful place herself. Her decisiveness in gifting the collection only under specific conditions hints at a great independence and female agency. Additionally, Elisabeth's various initiatives for documenting and preserving the collection show that she cared for her books and that they were part of her everyday life as a widow. She was interested in the active shaping of a library that served not only the purpose of self-representation but, also, her scholarly interests. So far, Elisabeth's extraordinary book ownership has primarily been interpreted as a demonstration of piety by the Lutheran 'Landesmutter' and a status symbol.[22] Heino Reinitzer even claimed that 'Duchess Elisabeth Sophie Marie was a less learned than a pious woman', without providing any evidence to support his argument.[23] Of course, the collection was an important part of the widow's self-fashioning as a devout Christian, but the donation to the Wolfenbüttel library and Elisabeth's insistence on the public availability of the collection paint a more nuanced picture. The dowager Duchess perceived her collection as a service to scholars. The catalogues and the historical-critical news, indicates that, even early on, this concern for beneficial usage permeated

---

21    Wolfenbüttel, Herzog August Bibliothek, Cod. Guelf. 125.25a Extrav, *Stammbuch der Herzogin Elisabeth Sophie Marie von Braunschweig*. Online <http://diglib.hab.de/mss/125 -25a-extrav/start.htm> (accessed 29 September 2021).

22    See Gleixner, 'Lutherbildnisse'. On the political and religious role of princesses as 'mothers of the territory', see Jill Bepler, 'Die Fürstin als Betsäule. Anleitung und Praxis der Erbauung am Hof', *Morgen-Glantz. Zeitschrift der Christian-Knorr-von-Rosenroth-Gesellschaft*, 12 (2002), pp. 249–264.

23    See Reinitzer, *Biblia deutsch*, p. 314: "Herzogin Elisabeth Sophie Marie war eine weniger gelehrte als fromme Frau."

her collection-building activities. These documents were created specifically to inform scholars of the treasures that could be found in Brunswick, and were likely to encourage the use of the collection for learned purposes. Both publications were auxiliary instruments for biblical scholars and were clearly written with their requirements in mind. The sheer size of the collection made it a scholar's paradise, and Elisabeth's efforts in building it were publicly acclaimed. In 1752, even the scholarly journal *Göttingische Zeitung von Gelehrten Sachen* praised the *Bibliotheca Biblica*, saying 'that until now the whole world has not seen the like of it'.[24]

Scholars gladly took up the offer to work with the holdings. A series of dedications suggests that scholars used the collection to engage in publishing, and some works are explicitly based on Elisabeth's book collection. The dedications cannot be read only as evidence of patron-client relationships; they are also testimonials of the scholarly value of the collection and Elisabeth's efforts to promote it.[25] One example of a publication that was prepared with the help of Elisabeth's collection is Johann Karl Koken's (1715–1773) new German Bible edition from 1750, for which the editor collated the different Bible texts that he could find in her collection.[26] David Clément (1701–1760) published a rare book catalogue based in parts on Elisabeth's collection.[27] Most prominently, Elisabeth supported the famous church historian Johann Lorenz von Mosheim (1693–1755). She financed his education in Lübeck, and she promoted his appointment as professor of theology to Helmstedt.[28]

---

24 See *Göttingische Zeitung von gelehrten Sachen*, 1752, p. 99: "Wohl niemahlen haben wir in unsern Blättern eines Bücher=Verzeichnisses Erwähnung gethan, von welchem wir, ohne zu erröthen, hätten sagen können, daß es seines gleichen nicht habe. Alleine, da wir diese kostbare und ansehmende Bibel=Sammlung anzeigen, so dürffen wir wohl sagen, daß bis iezo noch in der ganzen Welt ihres gleichen nicht gesehen worden seye."

25 On the epistemic value of dedications to women, see Nieves Baranda Leturio, 'Women's reading habits: book dedications to female patrons in early modern Spain' in Rosilie Hernández and Anne J. Cruz (eds.), *Women's Literacy in Early Modern Spain and the New World* (London: Taylor & Francis Group, 2011), pp. 19–39 <http://ebookcentral.pro quest.com/lib/unilu-ebooks/detail.action?docID=4414814.>.

26 Johann Karl Koken (ed.), *Biblia, Das ist: Die ganze Heilige Schrift Altes und Neues Testament* (Hildesheim: Christoph Johann Hieronymus Hartz, 1750).

27 David Clément, *Bibliotheque Curieuse Historique Et Critique, Ou Catalogue Raisonné De Livres Dificiles A Trouver* (Göttingen: Schmid, 1750).

28 Angelika Alwast and Jendris Alwast, 'Johann Lorenz Mosheim', *Biographisches Lexikon für Schleswig-Holstein und Lübeck*, 10 (Neumünster: Wachholtz 1994), pp. 258–263. On Mosheim and his theological positions, see Martin Mulsow (ed.), *Johann Lorenz Mosheim (1693–1755). Theologie im Spannungsfeld von Philosophie, Philologie und Geschichte* (Wiesbaden: Harrassowitz, 1997). On female patrons see Helen Smith, *"Grossly Material*

Moreover, Elisabeth Sophie Marie was an author of two theological treatises herself.[29] Indeed, Elisabeth stands in a tradition with lay people, and especially women, who used Bible reading as a starting point for a non-professional writing culture.[30] In her first book, written in 1714, the Duchess compared Lutheran and Catholic dogmas, based on an edition of the Council of Trent, published by Domenico Farri in 1595.[31] The book consists of a German translation of each dogma as postulated by the Catholic Church and a juxtaposition of the text to the Lutheran doctrine, which, following Luther's idea of the 'sola scriptura', she derived from selected Bible passages. She finished every article with a personal prayer. Her second work was published in 1750.[32] It follows the logic of her first publication; she translated a version of the Catholic confession of faith—in this case, a *Confessio Romano-Catholica* used in the conversion of Hungarian Protestants—and discusses the arguments article by article, refuting them from her Protestant perspective.[33] She addressed her work to the Jesuit Franz Seedorf, who in 1747 published a series of letters explaining how he convinced Frederick Michael, Count Palatine of Zweibrücken (1724–1767), to convert to Catholicism.[34] She saw it as her task to critically question the arguments and contrast them with the Word of God. Furthermore, she considered

---

Things": Women and Book Production in Early Modern England (Oxford University Press, 2012) pp. 53–86.

29  Molekamp, *Women and the Bible*, p. 221.

30  See Narveson, *Bible Readers*.

31  Elisabeth Sophie Marie von Braunschweig-Lüneburg, *Kurtzer Auszug etlicher zwischen den Catholiken und Lutheranern streitigen Glaubens-Lehren aus des Concilii zu Trient und der Göttl. Schrifft eigenen Worten, wie auch dem hiebey gefügten päbstl. Glaubens-Bekändtniß und Religions-Eyde treulich gefasset* (Wolfenbüttel: 1714). The work exists in at least two more editions from 1720 and 1747 respectively. Elisabeth Sophie Marie probably based her translation on Domenico Farri (ed.), *Concilium tridentinum sub Paulo III, Iulio III, et Pio IIII Pont. Max. celebratum: accessere Pij IIII & v bullae, quaedam decreta explicantes & sacrae scripturae loci in margine: nunc demum nouis figuris exornatum & à mendis quibus scatebat typographorum incuria vindicatum: cum Indice librorum prohibitorum, à deputatione ipsius Concilij confecto* (Venice: Farri, 1595).

32  Elisabeth Sophie Marie von Braunschweig-Lüneburg, *Eine deutlichere Erläuterung der Glaubens-Lehren, so in den zwölf Briefen des Jesuiten Seedorffs enthalten, nach dem Glaubens-Bekänntniß, welches die Protestanten in Ungarn, bey ihrem Uebertritt zur Röm. Kirche schweren müssen* (Braunschweig: Meyer, 1750).

33  This 'Confessio Romano-Catholica in Hungaria Evangelicis publice praescripta & proposita' is printed in *Acta historico-ecclesiastica: oder gesammlete Nachrichten von der neuesten Kirchen-Geschichten*, 3 (Weimar: Siegmund Heinrich Hoffmann, 1738), pp. 21–25.

34  Franz Seedorf, *Lettres sur divers points de controverse, contenant les principaux motifs qui ont déterminé le Duc Frédéric des Deux Ponts à se réunir à la S. Eglise Catholique* (Liège: Kints, 1747). These letters provoked a series of reactions in the following years, see most prominently Christoph Matthäus Pfaff, *Beantwortung der zwölf Briefe des Hn. P. Seedorfs* (Tübingen: Osiander, 1750).

it her duty to explain the contents to her fellow Christians so that they could make informed judgements and 'examine everything and keep what is best'.[35] Most interestingly, Elisabeth states that it is an essential part of the Protestant confessions to read Catholic books and compare them to the Word of God, by which she meant the text of the Luther Bible.[36] If we look at her collection, we see that she indeed collected German Bible translations from other confessions. While the German Luther translations are clearly in the majority with 294 editions, she still owned sixteen German Catholic Bibles from the time after the Reformation and forty Bibles by Reformed Protestants.[37] Comparing different versions of the Word of God was an essential practice of her faith, and we can consider her Bible collection, and library, an important instrument in her exercise of religion.

Even though both her publications have been classified as polemic pamphlets, they do not show apparent signs of pugnacity. In her texts, Elisabeth Sophie Marie does not verbally attack Catholics, nor does she classify them as heretics. On the contrary, one could even argue that she made continuous efforts to gain a better understanding of the opposing viewpoints and propose solutions to bridge the gap. The publications show, without a doubt, to what extent Elisabeth was an expert in the Holy Scriptures and how she considered this expertise the only instrument towards God's truth. We can assume then, that she was the most fervent user of her collection. In the end, this raises questions concerning her scholarly ambitions and the nature of her theological position, which is more complex than the label of 'pious Lutheran' suggests.

Although we know that Elisabeth's collection was at the core of her own learning and knowledge production and also inspired other scholars, we know very little about how the books actually came into her possession. It is unclear how the Dowager Duchess financed her collections, but she must have spent large parts of her available income on books and she continuously acquired Bibles at auctions. In 1743, she bought the whole collection of Johann Georg Palm, a Lutheran theologian from Hamburg.[38] In some cases, we know that the Duchess specifically aimed for high-value objects. She would buy rare pieces,

---

35 See Braunschweig-Lüneburg, *Erläuterung*, p. 5: "Prüfet alles und das Beste behaltet, denn die wahre Religion muß nicht wieder Gottes Ehre, Wahrheit, Weißheit, Heiligkeit, Gerechtigkeit, Barmherzigkeit und Allmacht streiten, wohl aber uns den Trost geben, daß wenn wir nach der uns von Gott gegebenen Vorschrift, davon wir nichts abnoch hinzuthun dürffen, unsern Glauben und Leben durch des heiligen Geistes Beystand richten, wir unserer durch Christentum erworbenen Kindschaft und Seligkeit, gewiß versichert seyn, und am Ende unsere Seelen mit Freuden in Abrahams Schooß legen können."

36 Braunschweig-Lüneburg, *Erläuterung*, p. 4.

37 See Knoch, *Bibliotheca Biblica*, pp. 86–142.

38 On the different provenances of her acquisitions see Reinitzer, *Biblia deutsch*, p. 314.

and had a particular focus on special characteristics that made her books unique. A close look at the Bibles reveals that she owned books containing inscriptions by Martin Luther and Philipp Melanchthon. Though the direct means by which she acquired these books remains a gap in the research, the collection itself implies Elisabeth was very well aware of the value of the books she bought and of the added value she created by assembling some very rare pieces. In any case, her collection had such a high value that her dower could not have sufficed for the large sums she paid. We know that she owned allodial land, which she managed very successfully.[39] That meant that she could dispose of the generated income autonomously and independently. Furthermore, she had the right of alienation, meaning that she could decide to sell or transfer her property at her own will. Future research will be able to show how her landowner and administrator's activities enabled her to build the collection.

Beyond the very tangible financial value, the Bibles can be considered capital in another way; Elisabeth's wish to be remembered as the collection owner was not the result of vanity. The fact that she insisted on her portrait and an inscription is to be understood as a way to ensure her *memoria*. In a poem she wrote, she clearly stated that the Word of God was her most valuable treasure.[40] By establishing that the collection remained a unit and marked with her portrait, she ensured that she would not be forgotten. Like others, who endowed a chapel for their salvation, she donated her Bibles for this purpose. The Bibles can thus be understood as an earthly investment for Elisabeth Sophie Marie's heavenly future. When the Dowager Duchess gifted the collection to the Wolfenbüttel library, she not only made a materially precious donation but also put her salvation into the librarian's hands.

## 3     The History of the Herzog August Library: Making Women (In)Visible

While inheritance of princely private libraries after the death of the owners was common practice, the donation of such a valuable collection of books was an absolute exception. Only very few donations made by women before

---

39      Christof Römer, 'Das Zeitalter des Hochabsolutismus (1635–1735)', in Horst-Rüdiger Jarck and Gerhard Schildt (eds.), *Die Braunschweigische Landesgeschichte. Jahrtausendrückblick einer Region* (Braunschweig: Appelhans, 2000), p. 561.

40      "Wer Gottes theure Wort sich hier zum Schatz erwählt, der kann nicht reicher seyn; er find't drin was ihm fehlt [...] Hier findt ich Schatz' darnach die Diebe niemals graben, Die allzeit meine sind, auch noch im Tod mich laben." Knoch, *Nachrichten*, VIIf.

their death are recorded for the Early Modern period in Germany.[41] The fact that Elisabeth Sophie Marie's donation had few precedents shows even more clearly that this was a well-considered step. She wanted the memory of her name to be associated with the collection for all eternity.

A look at the history of the Herzog August Library shows that the Duchesses' wishes concerning her books were not respected for long. Even though Elisabeth prepared everything so that she and her collection would not be forgotten, few people today know of the origins of the thousands of books that can still be found scattered in the HAB's stacks. The fading of the memory started with the non-biblical collection, which came to Wolfenbüttel shortly after Elisabeth's death. Even though the books were supposed to be kept separately, they were soon integrated into the rest of the collection, forming part of today's 'Mittlere Aufstellung'.[42] This process is partially documented; the library archives contain a handwritten catalogue of her library from 1768, intended to record the non-biblical collection.[43] However, the librarian Karl Johann Anton von Cichin (1723–1793) was stopped in the middle of his cataloguing work, and the information value remains limited. Only folio and quarto formats are recorded; the more substantial rest of the library is missing. According to Cichin's statement, soon after cataloguing began, the decision was made to classify the books in the overall holdings, so there was no longer any need for separate recording.

Therefore, we deal with a collection that no longer exists in its original context and has only been handed down to us in fragmentary written form. This was the fate of almost all the private collections that entered the Wolfenbüttel library in the seventeenth and eighteenth centuries.[44] We do not know to what

41 For example Elisabeth Juliane von Braunschweig-Wolfenbüttel (1634–1704) and Sophie Eleanore Gräfin zu Stolberg-Stolberg. See Dagmar Jank, *Bibliotheken von Frauen. Ein Lexikon.* (Wiesbaden: Harrassowitz, 2019), pp. 39, 210.

42 For one of the more comprehensive books on the history of the HAB, see Mechthild Raabe, *Leser und Lektüre vom 17. zum 19. Jahrhundert: die Ausleihbücher der Herzog August Bibliothek Wolfenbüttel 1664–1806* (8 vols., Munich: Saur, 1989–1998). A new library history is currently being prepared in the context of the HAB's 450th anniversary, which includes a history of the holdings and a detailed description of the 'Mittlere Aufstellung' by Hartmut Beyer.

43 Wolfenbüttel, Herzog August Bibliothek, BA I, 634, *Standortkatalog der Bibliotheken der Herzogin Elisabeth Sophia Maria sowie der Prinzen Wilhelm Adolf und Ludwig Ernst* (1768). Online <http://diglib.hab.de/mss/ba-1-634/start.htm> (accessed 29 September 2021).

44 On the so-called "Fürstenbibliotheken" in Wolfenbüttel, see Werner Arnold, 'Wolfenbüttel, Herzog August Bibliothek, Fürstenbibliotheken des 17. und 18. Jahrhunderts', in Bernhard Fabian (ed.), *Handbuch der historischen Buchbestände in Deutschland*, 2/2 (Hildesheim: Olms Neue Medien, 1998), pp. 211–213. On private Ducal libraries in general, see Werner Arnold, 'Identität durch Bücher: Fürstenbibliotheken in der Frühen Neuzeit', *Wolfenbütteler Notizen zur Buchgeschichte*, 36 (2011), pp. 91–108; Jill Bepler and Helga Meise (eds.),

extent the original private libraries are still at the HAB and how many volumes were lost over time, when they were sold as duplicates, for example. As for the Bible collection, we can confirm that it is physically there almost in its entirety; yet it remains practically invisible to visitors and users. Unlike Elisabeth Sophie Marie's wishes concerning the collection, her Bibles were simply integrated into the general Bible collection, even though they are the core of these outstanding stocks. Furthermore, four copies of the printed catalogue as well as three copies of the historical-critical news on the collection are available in the HAB, waiting to be explored by researchers. But only in recent years has interest in Elisabeth's legacy increased.

The general disintegration happened in the nineteenth century, at the same time when the original library of Duke Augustus was receiving increased attention. The contributions of other family members, and especially women, were forgotten. In Otto Heinemann's history of the library from 1894, Elisabeth Sophie Marie's Bible collection does not even fill a whole page.[45] Thanks to new technologies, however, we now have the opportunity to investigate the many different collections that make up the HAB and counteract the variety of biases that have guided research in library and book history in the last century.[46] Various projects at the HAB have been involved with the digital reconstruction of the original collections. Starting from the historical catalogues, the holdings are searched for specific copies. Of particular relevance are, of course, provenance notes and bookplates. As far as the Bible collection is concerned, we can say with certainty that Elisabeth used her own bookplate for almost all the copies. Other Duchesses also used bookplates or *supralibros* very consistently to mark their possessions.[47] These devices enable us to identify previous owners and trace object biographies. In this way, personal relationships—such as donations or inheritances—can be reconstructed and acquisition processes can be traced. In Elisabeth Sophie Marie's case, the same previous owners repeatedly appear, clearly indicating that she purchased entire collections or at least 'book packages'.

---

     *Sammeln, Lesen, Übersetzen als höfische Praxis der Frühen Neuzeit. Die böhmische Bibliothek der Fürsten Eggenberg im Kontext der Fürsten-und Fürstinnenbibliotheken der Zeit* (Wiesbaden: Harrassowitz, 2010).

45    Otto von Heinemann, *Die Herzogliche Bibliothek zu Wolfenbüttel: ein Beitrag zur Geschichte deutscher Büchersammlungen*, (Wolfenbüttel: Zwissler, 1894), pp. 141–142.

46    On this topic, see Sarah Lindenbaum, 'Hiding in Plain Sight: How Electronic Records Can Lead Us to Early Modern Women Readers', in Knight etc. (eds.), *Women's Bookscapes*, pp. 193–213.

47    This is for example the case for Philippine Charlotte (1716–1801) and Antoinette Amalie (1696–1762) of Brunswick-Wolfenbüttel.

In addition to provenance entries, wear and other signs of use are highly significant, as they give us clues about reading behaviour. Particularly valuable in this context are also annotations, notes and comments that provide evidence of how books were read, which are often the only traces that we have left from 'less extraordinary readers', as Heidi Brayman Hackel phrased it.[48] It is these traces that give us insights into practices of reading but also into the relationship of collectors and their books, and the modes of appropriation used.[49] Some works previously owned by Elisabeth Sophie Marie contain information on the date of reading. Many of the books also have old shelf marks, which, on the one hand, help us clearly assign the books to a specific provenance, and on the other hand, are an indication of earlier collection contexts. Thanks to them, we can systematically reconstruct how the books were arranged initially. The ultimate goal is to record every single item in a specific collection and enrich it with the associated metadata to depict the sources and objects as completely as possible. That happens both on the general bibliographical level (i.e. titles, authors, places, etc.) as well as specifically related to the copy, such as old shelf marks, provenance entries, reading traces, notes. So far, the procedure has mainly been tested with libraries of male scholars, like Leonhard Christoph Sturm or Benedikt Bahnsen. But a project concerning women's libraries is still ongoing and the aim for the coming years is to fully reconstruct the collections of four eighteenth century Duchesses, among them Elisabeth's Bible collection as well as the non-biblical library.[50]

Although the autoptic examination of the books is laborious, the effort is worthwhile as we have collected a great deal of information. Each book becomes a small piece of the puzzle that helps us to better understand the phenomenon of princely private collections. And, especially in the case of the women's libraries, the digital showcase of the collections that entered the

---

48    Heidi Brayman Hackel, *Reading Material in Early Modern England: Print, Gender, and Literacy* (Cambridge: Cambridge University Press, 2009), p. 8.

49    A valuable study on female reading practices and marginalia is Julie Crawford, 'Reconsidering Early Modern Women's Reading, or, How Margaret Hoby Read Her de Mornay', *Huntington Library Quarterly*, 73, (2010), pp. 193–223. For further examples on the use and functions of marginalia, see Katherine Acheson (ed.), *Early Modern English Marginalia: Material Readings in Early Modern Culture* (New York, London: Routledge, 2018).

50    Library reconstructions of the HAB can be found at <https://bibliotheksrekonstruk tion.hab.de/> (accessed 06 November 2022). For further information, see Hartmut Beyer, Jörn Münkner, Timo Steyer and Katrin Schmidt, 'Bibliotheken im Buch: Die Erschließung von privaten Büchersammlungen der Frühneuzeit über Auktionskataloge', in Hannah Busch etc. (eds.), *Kodikologie und Paläographie im Digitalen Zeitalter*, 4 (Norderstedt: Books on Demand 2017), pp. 43–70.

Wolfenbüttel holdings helps make their contributions visible to what today is one of the most important research libraries for the history of the Middle Ages and Early Modern Europe worldwide.

## 4    Conclusion: Private Collections as Historical Sources

When combining gender and book history, we are confronted with a source bias that is often hard to overcome. However, the case study of Elisabeth Sophie Marie shows that taking a closer look can be extremely rewarding. The collection, which had almost disappeared from the HAB's collective memory, can teach us a great deal about the agency of female princely book collectors in the Holy Roman Empire. While the contents of Elisabeth's collection, with its focus on Bibles and other theological literature, might correspond to the supposed image of a 'typical' women's library of the early modern period at first glance, a deeper analysis reveals some particularities of the library. Of course, Elisabeth was a pious woman and the collection is the result of a quest for the True Word of God. Beyond this obvious realisation, the Duchess's practices suggest a particular involvement in church political affairs as well as a scholarly engagement as theological controversialist. For the English context, Femke Molekamp discovered that vernacular Bibles permitted women a 'interpretative and activist reading, leading to both literary creation and political activism.'[51] In the same way, Elisabeth used her Bibles as a demonstration of her literacy and quest for knowledge, turning her into a religious activist. In addition, the Duchess was also a patron for a series of scholars and was overall regarded as an important player in the field of biblical scholarship, not only because of her own expertise but also because she used her connections and money to compile a unique resource for scholars.

However, it is not only epistemic practices like reading and writing, or making the books available to scholars that tell us about Elisabeth's agency. It is also the materiality and value of the collection that give insights into the Duchesses standing. She was rich and independent enough to buy a large quantity of Bibles, which must have cost a fortune. Elisabeth was capable of making her own economic decisions, a capacity that is often underestimated when it comes to women. Her books thus marked both 'her economic and intellectual independence'.[52] Building up this kind of property was part of building a 'sense

---

51    Molekamp, *Women and the Bible*, p. 3.
52    Edith Snook, 'Elizabeth Isham's 'own Bookes': Property, Propriety, and the Self as Library', in Knight etc. (eds.), *Bookscapes*, pp. 80.

of self'.[53] This culminated into an ultimate self-representation when giving her collection away to the Wolfenbüttel library. By doing so, she thought to have secured herself the greatest benefit of all, eternal memoria—a simple wish that she probably shared with many.

In conclusion, I would like to underline that the primary aim of this case study is not to emphasise the exceptionality of the collection or the collector. Nor is the purpose to make claims about typical libraries of women, as it is simply not possible to make a valid statement about the general contents of Early Modern German collections at this time, with the real basis of comparison currently missing. Instead, this case study offers observations that will hopefully become part of a solid basis of data soon, finally allowing us to systematically compare collections. Only then will we be properly able to ask questions that go beyond established narratives, which are still too often centred around a supposedly 'male' default situation or generally gendered assumptions. Until then, we should primarily let the collections speak for themselves; they have a lot to tell.

---

53    Leah Knight etc., 'Introduction', in Knight etc. (eds.), *Bookscapes*, p. 11.

## PART 6

## *Crafting Identity: Religion and Gender*

∵

# CHAPTER 16

# Seditious Pamphlets 'Mid-wifed into the World': Gender and the Confederate Stationers' Clandestine Publishing Business in Restoration England

*Verônica Calsoni Lima*

In April 1668, Roger L'Estrange, the Surveyor of the Press, wrote a letter to inform Secretary Joseph Williamson about the seizure of a seditious broadside, *The Poor-Whores Petition*.[1] Spuriously signed by Madame Cresswell and Damaris Page, two brothel keepers, the text humbly claimed for the protection of the Countess of Castlemaine, Barbara Palmer. As she was one of the king's mistresses, the petitioners appealed to her 'great Experience' in their 'Trade' to ask for help 'to prevent Our Utter Ruine' and 'restore us to our former practice with Honour, Freedom and Safety'.[2] Referring to the recent attacks on brothels during the Bawdy House Riots, the satire expressed profound discontentment from nonconformists towards the moral and religious politics of the time. While the government was enforcing laws against dissenters, it was also ignoring violations concerning prostitution.[3] Thus, *The Poor-Whores Petition* aimed to expose the debauchery of the king's court, where the 'Venerial pleasures' from '*Rome & Venice*' seemed to be common.[4] While mocking the Countess of Castlemaine, who had recently converted to Catholicism, the satire implied that Charles II was morally, religiously, and politically corrupt.[5] Such a dangerous message had to be censored.

---

1   This research was funded by the São Paulo Research Foundation (FAPESP): grants #2017/06970-2 and #2018/03730-3. Public Record Office (PRO), State Papers (SP) 29/239/8. I want to thank Luís Filipe Silvério Lima, Carolina Vaz de Carvalho, and Jonathan Portela Dias for reading and commenting on the initial version of this chapter.
2   *The Poor-Whores Petition* (London, 1668), fl. 1.
3   Tim Harris, 'The Bawdy House Riots of 1668', *The Historical Journal*, 29, (1986), pp. 537–56.
4   *Poor-Whores Petition*, fl. 1.
5   Tim Harris, *London Crowds in the Reign of Charles II: Propaganda and Politics from the Restoration until the Exclusion Crisis* (Cambridge: Cambridge University Press, 1987); Richard Greaves, *Enemies under His Feet: Radicals and Nonconformists in Britain, 1664–1677* (Stanford: Stanford University Press, 1990); Julia Marciari Alexander and Catharine MacLeod (eds.), *Politics, Transgression, and Representation at the Court of Charles II* (New Haven: Yale University Press, 2007).

The task proved to be hard. L'Estrange's letter reported the censor's frustrated attempts to suppress the broadside and detain the web of its publishers and distributors. According to the correspondence, some hawkers, who were selling copies of *The Poor-Whores Petition*, confessed that the texts came from a carpenter in Blue Anchor Alley. On his turn, the carpenter informed that the broadsides were provided by Anna Brewster, the widow of a bookseller named Thomas. Upon examination, Anna's son declared that the papers had been delivered to the Brewsters' bookshop by a printer's wife, Joan Darby. Although her husband John was already in custody, L'Estrange stated that nothing had been found with him. Therefore, the broadside's suppression depended on the confessions of Anna Brewster and Joan Darby. Notwithstanding, the censor knew he would not have it from them, because they were 'taken to be a couple of y^e craftyest & most obstinate of y^e trade'.[6]

Besides the two women, authorities were suspicious of another female stationer, Elizabeth Calvert, and demanded a search of her house.[7] She was the widow of Giles Calvert, whose illicit and radical publications of sectarian and republican tracts were well known since the Civil Wars. Furthermore, Elizabeth had strong connections with Anna Brewster and Joan Darby. Giles Calvert was Thomas Brewster's former master. Also, Joan was first married to Simon Dover, a printer who had been punished for producing seditious pamphlets for Giles Calvert and Thomas Brewster in the early 1660s. Tried, fined, pilloried, and arrested for his infraction, Dover died in prison in 1664. His widow soon married John Darby. At about the same time, Anna Brewster and Elizabeth Calvert lost their husbands too. Thomas Brewster passed away while imprisoned in 1664. Giles Calvert had died a little earlier, in August 1663, after frequent periods of incarceration.[8]

Giles Calvert, Thomas Brewster, and Simon Dover were all arrested due to anti-royalist and dissent pamphlets published at the beginning of the Restoration. They seemed to have been involved in an underground network discovered and named by Roger L'Estrange.[9] These so called 'Confederate Stationers' included others too, such as Livewell Chapman, a Fifth Monarchist bookseller; John Twyn, a nonconformist printer; and Francis Smith, a Baptist preacher and bookseller. Together, they spread several prophetic-political texts against the Stuart family, the monarchical rule, and the established church.

---

6  PRO SP29/239/8.

7  PRO SP29/88/94.

8  *The Intelligencer*, 34 (London: Richard Hodgkinson, 1664); PRO SP44/16/115; Maureen Bell, 'Elizabeth Calvert and the "Confederates"', *Publishing History*, 32 (1992), pp. 5–49.

9  Roger L'Estrange, *Considerations and proposals in order to the regulation of the press* (London: A.C., 1663), p. 6.

Scholars have examined the Confederate Stationers' pamphlets, discussing how their clandestine publishing business expressed their millenarian and republican aspirations, but there are still rich grounds for research on their activities, especially regarding gender roles within the group.[10] Maureen Bell stressed the importance of the 'Confederate Women' to the maintenance of their seditious publications while men were absent. As the male Confederates were constantly imprisoned or hidden, the printing and distribution of their texts heavily depended on the stationers' wives as well.[11] Following Bell's pioneering study, this essay intends to complement it by analysing the work of the female Confederates. I do not intend to develop a comprehensive account of all their publications. Instead, I will focus on documents that provide us with the opportunity to perceive the processes and tactics employed in the production and distribution of their clandestine pamphlets. Though sometimes archival sources offer brief and circumstantial references to women, closer scrutiny can reveal glimpses of their activities in illegal trades. Throughout this chapter, I argue that the case of the Confederate Stationers cannot be understood without considering the importance of women's participation. Rather than being mere assistants to their husbands' businesses, the stationers' wives and widows were integral parts of the network.[12]

In fact, the success of the Confederates' publications was sometimes a clear reflection of female work. Censorship was efficient, and it contained male stationers several times, but as laws treated men and women differently, female

---

10   See, for example, Timothy Crist, 'Francis Smith and the Opposition Press in England, 1660–1688', PhD Thesis: University of Cambridge, 1977; John Hetet, 'A Literary Underground in Restoration England: Printers and Dissenters in the Context of Constraints, 1660–1689', PhD Thesis: University of Cambridge, 1987; Richard Greaves, *Deliver Us from Evil: The Radical Underground in Britain, 1660–1663* (Oxford: Oxford University Press, 1986); N.H. Keeble, *The Literary Culture of Nonconformity in Later Seventeenth Century England* (Leicester: Leicester University Press, 1987); Bell, 'Elizabeth Calvert'; Maureen Bell, '"Her Usual Practices": The Later Career of Elizabeth Calvert, 1664–75', *Publishing History*, 35 (1994), pp. 5–64; Melinda Zook, *Protestantism, Politics, and Women in Britain, 1660–1714* (Hampshire: Palgrave McMillan, 2013).

11   Bell, 'Elizabeth Calvert'; Bell, '"Her Usual Practices"'.

12   On female stationers, see, among others: Paula McDowell, *The Women of Grub Street: Press, Politics and Gender in the London Literary Marketplace, 1679–1730* (Oxford: Oxford University Press, 2007); Helen Smith, *'Grossly Material Things': Women and Book Production in Early Modern England* (Oxford: Oxford University Press, 2012); Cait Coker, 'Gendered Spheres: Theorizing Space in the English Printing House', *The Seventeenth Century* 33 (2017), pp. 323–36; Cait Coker, 'Pressed and Stitched: Empirical Bibliography and the Gendering of Books and Book History', *Huntington Library Quarterly* 84 (2021), pp. 167–75; Valerie Wayne (ed.), *Women's Labour and the History of the Book in Early Modern England* (London: The Arden Shakespeare, 2020).

printers and booksellers were hardly stopped. Women were more elusive due to their legal and social status in the early modern period. Though female activities in the public space were often limited, their exclusion as 'outsiders', as put by Barbara Todd, could also provide them opportunities to escape from restraints.[13] The Confederates' case exemplifies how illicit trades prospered because of the paradoxical ways society dealt with women. The rigid persecution against male Confederates made their female counterparts some of the main people in charge of the clandestine business. In the following pages, I intend to discuss how the Confederate Women managed to publish seditious texts even during periods of strict censorship in Restoration England.

## 1    The Confederate Stationers

Roger L'Estrange identified the seditious confederacy while aiming to achieve an office in the new government. Despite his intentions in presenting himself as a protector of the public order, there are reasons to believe anti-royalist stationers were indeed engaged in illicit activities against the Restoration settlement. While many printers and booksellers had welcomed the king, the Calverts, Brewsters, Chapmans, Dovers (later Darbys), and Smiths were constantly defying the authorities, risking financial losses and harsh punishments to publish seditious ideas.[14]

Following a trail of dissent literature published soon after Charles II's ascension, L'Estrange denounced the Confederates' business even before his appointment to the post of censor in August 1663. In fact, his designation might have resulted from his contributions to the discovery of illegal publications.[15] In 1661, L'Estrange reported the detection of a clandestine alliance between stationers while investigating 'a virulent pamphlet' recently issued, *A Phenix, or, the Solemn League and Covenant*, which praised the 1643 agreement signed between Scottish covenanters and English parliamentarians during the Civil Wars and justified Charles I's execution in 1649.[16]

---

13    Barbara Todd, 'Property and a Woman's Place in Restoration London', *Women's History Review* 19(2010), p. 182.

14    Hetet, 'A Literary Underground'.

15    Keeble, *The Literary Culture*; Anne Dunan-Page and Beth Lynch (eds.), *Roger L'Estrange and the Making of Restoration Culture* (London: Ashgate, 2008); Darrick N. Taylor, 'L'Estrange His Life: Public and Persona in the Life and Career of Sir Roger L'Estrange, 1616–1704', PhD Thesis: University of Kansas, 2011; Roger L'Estrange, *A modest plea both for the caveat, and the author of it* (London: Henry Brome, 1661), p. 3.

16    Ibid., p. 11; *A Phenix, or, The Solemn League and Covenant* (Edinburgh, 1661).

L'Estrange's private search led him to Thomas Creake's print shop, where he found sheets of *A Phenix* and another suspicious yet still unfinished pamphlet, *Mirabilis Annus, or The Year of Prodigies*. After reading a few sentences, L'Estrange decided to confiscate *Mirabilis Annus* for thinking it was the 'most impudent forgery ... to strike the People' against the king.[17] The pamphlet was an anonymous account of recent floods, comets, blazing starts, sudden deaths, and other unusual phenomena.[18] With an apocalyptic approach, the text argued that these events were shreds of evidence of God's actions towards the destruction of earthly and Anti-Christian powers—including Charles II's government—, and the ascension of the Millenium.[19]

Thomas Creake was arrested and examined before the Secretary of State on 29 June 1661. The printer confessed to having produced *A Phenix* upon the request of Livewell Chapman, Giles Calvert, and Thomas Brewster. The booksellers had also commissioned the issuing of 2,000 copies of *Mirabilis Annus*. Creake had finished part of the work and gave it to George Thresher, a bookbinder, who was supposed to stitch the papers. On the same 29 June, Calvert and Thresher were examined as well. Although Calvert denied the accusations, Thresher confirmed Creake's information. Calvert's apprentice, Mathias Walker, also declared that his master had sent copies of *A Phenix* to a former apprentice in Bristol, Richard Moone.[20] Following these first arrests, Chapman and Brewster rapidly fled from London.[21] In July, a warrant for Peter Cole, a printer and bookseller, was issued. In August, Francis Smith was sent to prison, where he remained until the spring of 1662.[22]

Despite these turbulent circumstances, *Mirabilis Annus* was successfully published sometime between July and October, circulating outside of London and arriving in other counties, such as Leicestershire, where a bookseller and bookbinder, Nathan Brooks, had dispersed it as well.[23] But if the authorities had diligently confiscated the sheets at Creake's house and detained the men connected to the seditious pamphlet, we may ask: how *Mirabilis Annus* was

---

17    L'Estrange, *A modest plea*, p. 11.
18    In December 1661, the independent preacher Henry Jessey was arrested on pretences of having authored the pamphlet. On his examination, Jessey confessed he was taking notes on prodigies. However, as there were no other proofs against him, the censors released him soon afterwards. George Cockayne was also considered as a possible author, but he was never detained for it. PRO SP29/43/236; SP29/45/49; SP44/5/59.
19    *Eniautos terastios, mirabilis annus, or The year of prodigies and wonders* (London, 1661).
20    PRO SP29/38/121, 122, 123, 124.
21    Bell, 'Elizabeth Calvert'.
22    PRO SP29/39/283; SP29/43/35.
23    The pamphlet's preface dates from 25 July 1661. *Mirabilis annus*; PRO SP29/43/12, 13, 14, 53, 54.

printed and dispersed? If most of the Confederate Stationers were restrained or fled, who managed to continue its production after L'Estrange's search? Part of the answer to these questions is in a warrant from 4 October 1661. It demanded the arrest of Elizabeth Calvert for publishing 'a treasonable & seditious book entitled Severale prodigies & apparitions seen in yᵉ heavens from August yᵉ 1ˢᵗ 1660 to yᵉ latter end of May 1661'.[24]

The extent of women's collaboration with the Confederates' trade was far larger than these lines might suggest. Elizabeth Calvert was hardly the only female stationer to contribute to *Mirabilis Annus*'s publication. Even though the records rarely mention wives of printers and booksellers, the male Confederates' absence indicates that the pamphlet's production was carried on by their female counterparts, who kept running the businesses.[25] The fact that there were no warrants to arrest Hannah Chapman, Anna Brewster, and Eleanor Smith does not mean they were excluded from the activities. Their omission reflected the nature of seventeenth-century laws. According to Barbara Kreps, a married woman (or a *femme covert*) 'had no legal identity independent of her husband's'.[26] The bond between husband and wife legally designated the couple as a single person. Consequently, a woman's infraction would be considered a male flaw in governing his wife, hence, he was the one to be punished. Usually, accountability was a consequence faced by *sole femmes*, such as spinsters or widows.[27]

Elizabeth Calvert was only arrested because, when authorities found her dispersing copies of *Mirabilis Annus*, her husband was away from London. As Giles had left the city soon after his release on 30 July 1661, his wife was treated as a *sole femme*.[28] Eleanor Smith would not be kept in custody if Francis Smith were already in jail. Conversely, the fact that Hannah Chapman and Anna Brewster were not detained is a sign of the authorities' lack of evidence against the two women. Besides, Barbara Hanawalt's studies showed that the justice systems 'treated women more leniently. Fewer women than men are arrested'.[29] Elizabeth Calvert's exceptional punishment confirmed the

24    PRO SP44/5/39.
25    Bell, 'Elizabeth Calvert'.
26    Barbara Kreps, 'The Paradox of Women: The Legal Position of Early Modern Wives and Thomas Dekker's "The Honest Whore"', *ELH*, 69(2002), p. 86.
27    Sara M. Butler, 'The Law as a Weapon in Marital Disputes: Evidence from the Late Medieval Court of Chancery, 1424–1529', *Journal of British Studies* 43(2004), pp. 291–316.
28    Bell, 'Elizabeth Calvert'.
29    Barbara Hanawalt, 'The Female Felon in Fourteenth-Century England', in Susan Mosher Stuard (ed.), *Women in Medieval Society* (Philadelphia: University of Pennsylvania Press, 1976), p. 128. For other studies on female imprisonment throughout history, see: Barbara Hanawalt and David Wallace (eds.), *Medieval Crime and Social Control* (Minneapolis:

rule. She was liable for exceeding the expectations regarding female behaviour, being caught while selling seditious papers during her husband's absence.[30] Therefore, the other Confederate Women were as engaged in *Mirabilis Annus's* publication as Elizabeth Calvert, but they were not spotted in action.[31]

The Confederate Women published *Mirabilis Annus* together. More importantly than simply continuing a work in progress, following directions from their husbands, the female stationers were completely aware of the strategies to publish illegal pamphlets. Thus, they had found alternatives to avoid censorship and issue *Mirabilis Annus*. Anonymity, fake imprints, and private presses were some of their clandestine resources. Sometimes they would also fragment the production process between separate printing houses, preventing the sheets to be with a single stationer. It has been proved that shared printing was a common feature of the early modern book trade, but seditious works resorted to it for distinct reasons.[32] Manuscripts could be divided between printers, who would simultaneously produce parts or editions of the same text. This practice diminished their financial and legal risks. If a printer were arrested, as happened to Thomas Creake, the text would be only partially lost. Publishers would also be safer from censorship since the fragmented work would be harder to track. Unaware of the entire content of *Mirabilis Annus*, Creake was not suspicious of it. The Confederates did not expect him to denounce the publication to the authorities. They could not foresee, though, Roger L'Estrange's search at Creake's print shop.[33]

As Thomas Creake explained in his testimonies, labour division was intentional in illegal trades. The Confederates had also employed the practice in 1660 while printing *The Speeches and Prayers of Some of the Late King's Judges* in

---

University of Minnesota Press, 1999); Mary Bosworth, 'Confining Femininity: A History of Gender, Power and Imprisonment', *Theoretical Criminology* 4(2000), pp. 265–84; Garthine Walker, *Crime, Gender and Social Order in Early Modern England* (Cambridge: Cambridge University Press, 2003).

30   PRO SP29/44/182.

31   PRO SP29/41/110; SP29/43/32.

32   Peter Blayney, 'The Prevalence of Shared Printing in the Early Seventeenth Century', *Papers of the Bibliographical Society of America*, 67 (1973), pp. 437–42; D.F. McKenzie, *Making Meaning: "Printers of the Mind" and Other Essays* (Boston: University of Massachusetts Press, 2002); David McKitterick, *Print, Manuscript and the Search for Order: 1450–1830* (London: Cambridge University Press, 2006).

33   Hetet, 'A Literary Underground'; Beth Lynch, 'Mr. Smirke and "Mr. Filth": A Bibliographic Case Study in Nonconformity Printing', *The Library* 1(2000), pp. 46–71; Stephen Bardle, *The Literary Underground in the 1660s: Andrew Marvell, George Wither, Ralph Wallis, and the World of Restoration Satire and Pamphleteering* (Oxford: Oxford University Press, 2012).

honour of the regicides. They resorted to it again when they had asked Creake to produce part of *Mirabilis Annus*. Simon Dover and other printers—probably Peter Cole (Dover's former master), Thomas Leach or John Twyn—might have continued the work. Sheets were later delivered to bookbinders, such as George Thresher, Nathan Brooks, and one Mr. Perry; and various booksellers.[34]

We know that both male and female Confederates divided their publications because this practice produced physical features. By comparing copies of their pamphlets, it is possible to notice variations in the spelling, decorations, and typefaces; errors in pagination; discontinuities between gatherings; and other characteristics that indicate both shared and frequently interrupted printing processes. Timothy Crist and Maureen Bell observed these issues. When examining *Mirabilis Annus*, both scholars acknowledged the existence of two editions, catalogued by Wing as E3127 and E3127A. Despite the equivalent content, there are differences both in length and composition. E3127 has sixty-four pages, arranged in the following collation formula: A-D$^4$ F-H$^4$ 2H-I$^4$. E3127A has eighty-eight pages, collated as $\pi^2$ A-M$^4$. E3127A also contains an engraved frontispiece, depicting twelve natural and supernatural phenomena described in *Mirabilis Annus*. Both editions were composed with similar Roman typefaces and minor decorations, such as capital letters and printers' flowers. They also employed Italics to emphasise sentences, quotations, and references.[35]

Crist and Bell suggested that Francis Smith made *Mirabilis Annus*'s first edition (E3127). According to the authors, the discontinuity between gatherings resulted from the work's interruption after Smith's imprisonment in August.[36] E3127A was attributed to Elizabeth Calvert as a second edition. She was only arrested in October and, presumably, had time for more polished work, also including a frontispiece in it.[37] *Mirabilis Annus*'s copies, however, show signs of variations that were missed by Crist and Bell. Besides the two editions identified in Wing's catalogue, there are remarkably diverse specimens. For example, Figures 16.1, 16.2, and 16.3 reproduce three different copies of the pamphlet held at the Bodleian Libraries. When compared, it is noticeable that none of the types, decorations, marginalia, and spacing coincide. All the three quires signed as B came from distinct printing presses. This is just one of the several cases of variations between and within the copies. *Mirabilis Annus*'s material

---

34    PRO SP29/68/240; SP29/92/16; SP29/38/121a; *An exact narrative of the tryal and condemnation of John Twyn ... with the tryals of Thomas Brewster, bookseller. Simon Dover, printer. Nathan Brooks, bookbinder* (London: Thomas Mabb for Henry Brome, 1664).

35    Crist, 'Francis Smith'; Bell, "'Her Usual Practices'".

36    PRO SP29/43/35.

37    Crist, 'Francis Smith'; Bell, 'Elizabeth Calvert'.

*Severall Prodigies and Apparitions seen in the
Heavens from* August *the* 1. 1660. *to the
latter end of* May, 1661.

### I.

 Everal persons who were reaping Wheat in a
Field about a quarter of a Mile from *Hertford*,
near six of the Clock in the Evening, *August* 1.
1660. espyed two Suns in the Firmament, the
One West, the Other more Northerly at some
distance each from other; they were as they
judged of equal height and bignesse, and beams did issue from
both, only that more Northerly shone not so bright as the other.
They continued in their view near half an hour, and then were
both overshadowed by a Cloud. This is Testifyed by honest
credible persons who were eye-witnesses.

*These* παςηλιοι, *as the Greeks call them, do naturally portend
much moysture and rainy weather.*

*But God ordains them (as some learned men conceive) to sig-
nifie several Judgements, as War, Famine, and Pestilence. Some
do affirm, they portend the * fall of great men from their power,
who rule with pride and disdain. They also signifie (as others
do conjecture) disturbances and innovations in matters of Religion.*

*There were two Suns seen in* England *at one time, shining at a
good distance from each other in the beginning of* Queen *Maries
raign: See* Bakers Chron. p. 346.

*Several Suns were seen near* Prague, *about the time of the
dreadful persecution which the* Protestants *sustained there from
the hands of the bloody* Papists. *See* Bohem. Hist. p. 335.

### II.

IN the same month was seen also at *Stratford Bow* near *London*, the likenesse of a great Ship in the Air, which by degrees
lessened till it came to be as small as a mans Arm, but kept its
form all the while, and at last disappeared. This is testifyed
by

B

*Two suns seen
near Hertford
Aug. 1. 1660.
Naturaliter
portendunt &
prænunciant
Pluviæ. Zanch
de operibus dei,
p. 348. Parheli-
us est magnum
pluviarum sig-
num. Her. Trist-
meg. l. 5. p. 473
Ex dei autem
ordinatione va-
ria ejus Judi-
cia, vel Bella,
vel Fames, &c.
Zanch. ibid.
Pucerus, lib.
Metorolog.
p. 340.
* As it happe-
ned Anno 1156.
2 Suns appeard
prognostica-
ting the death
of Tho. Becket
Arch B. of
Cant au insolet
proud Prelate
Lycost. p. 112.
The likenesse
of a ship seen
in the Air at
Stratford-bow
near London.*

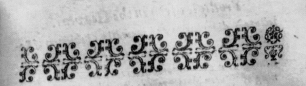

# Several Prodigies and Apparitions seen in the Heavens from August the 1. 1660. to the latter end of May, 1661.

### I.

Everal persons who were reaping Wheat in a Field about a quarter of a Mile from *Hertford*, near six of the Clock in the Evening, *August* 1. 1660. espyed two Suns in the Firmament, the One West, the Other more Northerly at some distance each from other; they were as they judged of equal height and bigneſſe, and beams did iſſue from both, only that more Northerly ſhone not ſo bright as the other. They continued in their view near half an hour, and then were both overſhadowed by a cloud. This is Teſtified by honeſt credible perſons who were eye-witneſſes.

Theſe παςήλιοι, as the Greeks call them, do naturally portend much moyſture and rainy weather.

But God ordaines them (as ſome learned men conceive) to ſignifie ſeverall Judgments, as War, Famine, and Peſtilence. Some do affirm, they portend the *fall of Great Men from their power, who rule with pride and diſdain. They alſo ſignifie (as others do conjecture)

B

Two Suns ſeen near *Hertford, Aug.* 1. 1660.
*Naturaliter portendunt & prænunciant Pluvias.* Zanch. de *operibus Dei,* p.348. *Parhelius eſt magnum pluviarum ſignum.* Her. Triſmeg. *l.* 5. p. 473. *Ex Dei autem ordinatione varia ejus Judicia, vel Bella, vel Fames,&c.*Zanc. *ibid.*
Pucerus, Lib. Metorolog. p. 340.
* As it happened Anno 1156. 2 Suns appear'd,prognoſticating the death of Tho.Becket Arch-B. of Cant. an inſolent proud Prelate. Lycoſt. p.412.

FIGURE 16.2    The Bodleian Libraries, University of Oxford, Tanner 225(3), p. 1

1

*Several* PRODIGIES *and* APPA-
RITIONS *seen in the Heavens, from*
Auguſt *the* 1. 1660. *to the Latter End of*
May, 1661.

## I.

SEveral Perſons who were reaping Wheat in a
Field about a quarter of a Mile from *Hert-*
*ford*, near ſix of the Clock in the Evening
*Auguſt* 1. 1660. eſpied two Suns in the
Firmament, the One Weſt, the Other Northerly at
ſome diſtance each from other; they were as they
judged of equall height and bigneſs, and beams did
iſſue from both onely that more Northerly ſhone not ſo
bright as the other. They continued in their view near
half an hour, and then were both overſhadowed
by a cloud. This is Teſtified by honeſt credible perſons who were eye-witneſſes.

*Two Suns ſeen*
*near Hertford,*
*Aug.* 1 1660.
*Naturaliter porten-*
*dunt & prænuntiant*
*Pluvias.* Zanch *de*
*operibus Dei.* p 348
*Parhelius eſt mag-*
*num pluviarū ſig-*
*num. Her.* Triſmeg,
*l.* 5. *p.*473.
*Ex Dei autem or-*
*dinatione varia*
*ejus Judicia, vel*
*Bella, vel Fames,*
&c. Zanc *ibid*
Pucerus, *Lib. Meto-*
*rolog* p. 340.
* As it happened
*Anno* 1156. 2 Suns
appear'd, prognoſti-
cating the death of
*Tho. Becket* Arch.
B of Cant an inſo-
lent proud Prelate,
Lycoſt. p. 412

    Theſe πα ηλιοι, *as the Greeks call them*, *do naturally*
*portend much moiſture and rainy weather.*
    But *God Ordaines them* ( *as ſome Learned men con-*
*ceive* ) *to ſignifie ſeveral Judgements*, *as War*, *Fa-*
*mine, and Peſtilence*. *Some do affirm, they portend the*
* *fall of Great Men from their power*, *who rule with*
*Pride and diſdain* *They alſo ſignifie* (*as others do con-*
B *jecture*)

aspects indicate that, at some point, the bookbinders merged gatherings from different print runs, as if a range of options were available to be combined during the collation and stitching of the pamphlets. Consequently, the distinction between editions and impressions of *Mirabilis Annus'* are hard to discern. E3127 and E3127A do not correspond to the variety of items resulting from the fragmented production processes employed by the Confederates.

*Mirabilis Annus's* variations exemplify the publishing strategies of the Confederate Stationers, confirming the complex and collective work developed by both male and female stationers. The hypothesis of Timothy Crist and Maureen Bell erases this feature. It is possible to highlight Francis Smith and Elizabeth Calvert prominent roles in commissioning, editing, organising, and distributing *Mirabilis Annus*, but they were hardly the sole producers of the text. Although they might have used private and clandestine presses, they were booksellers and not printers. Francis Smith and Elizabeth Calvert probably employed a range of printers to continue the work after Roger L'Estrange's interruption, managing the completion of the pamphlets' impression and distribution.

Regardless of the imprisonments and constraints, the Confederates' projects remained active due to women's efforts. Sequels of *Mirabilis Annus* appeared in 1662 when most of the male Confederates were still hiding or facing periods of incarceration. Thus, Elizabeth Calvert, Anna Brewster, Hannah Chapman, and Eleanor Smith were probably the main publishers of the two parts of *Mirabilis Annus Secundus*.[38] Attempting to avoid censorship, they tried a different editorial approach, though. *Mirabilis Annus'* first volume included parallels, explaining the meaning of each mysterious event reported in the text, guiding the readers to understand the incidents as prophetic signs of the imminent coming of Christ's Kingdom. But, as the two parts of *Mirabilis Annus Secundus* circulated after the Printing Act's promulgation, the Confederates decided to suppress the parallels. They justified the omission in the preface to the first part of *Mirabilis Annus Secundus*, stating that 'in the ears of many [the parallels] did trumpet out nothing less than *Sedition and Rebellion'*.[39]

*Mirabilis Annus Secundus'* final part maintained the anxious tone regarding press censorship. Its preface declared that the 'watchful eye that is continually upon the *Press'* had interfered in their production, causing delays and faults in

---

38    Maureen Bell, 'Hannah Allen and the Development of a Puritan Publishing Business, 1646–51', *Publishing History*, 26 (1989), pp. 5–66; Bell, 'Elizabeth Calvert'; Bell, '"Her Usual Practices"'.

39    *Mirabilis annus secundus, or, The second year of prodigies* (London, 1662), fl. 4.

the publications.[40] In fact, there were many disturbances in their trade. Giles Calvert had returned to London by March 1662, but he faced troubles again sometime afterwards.[41] His wife was also imprisoned in December 1662.[42] Thomas Brewster went to London briefly, however, he escaped from the authorities once more.[43] His whereabouts were discovered only in February 1663. He was in Bristol, 'in private lodgings, with two boxes of books'.[44] If one 'S. Dover' was Simon Dover, the State Papers suggest he was also examined in June 1662, but no further proceedings were taken.[45]

The Confederates expressed their recent sufferings in the prelude to the second part of *Mirabilis Annus Secundus*:

> Having at length, through the assistance of Providence, overcome the many interruptions which have attended the *Press*, we have (though much later than we promised, and indeed intended) at last Mid-wifed into the World a *Second Part* of this years *Prodigies*.[46]

Obviously, we cannot take this preambular statement at face value, since the Confederates were clearly aiming at the readers' benevolence. Nevertheless, it is quite interesting to notice that while doing it, they compared the efforts employed in publishing the pamphlet to midwifery labours.

Comparisons between human and textual reproduction were common in the early modern period. Metaphors characterised printed texts as children, whose imprints expressed paternity over them. Conversely, the printing press was depicted as a machine capable of delivering information. Although childbirth and midwifery were inscribed in a female sphere, those analogies did not restrict to gender roles. Both male and female stationers used them to refer to their work.[47] Therefore, it is not possible to confirm if the Confederate Women were alluding to their gender in this preface, even though the female stationers were probably ahead of the publication. Regardless of that, the metaphor is

---

40   *Mirabilis annus secundus: or, The second part of the second years prodigies* (London, 1662), p. 53v.

41   PRO SP44/9/77.

42   PRO SP44/9/131, 198; SP29/65/6.

43   L'Estrange, *Truth and loyalty*.

44   PRO SP29/68/9.

45   PRO SP29/56/266; SP29/88/94.

46   *The second part of the second years prodigies*, fl. 2.

47   Gerald MacLean, 'Literacy, Class, and Gender in Restoration England', *Text*, 7 (1994), pp. 307–35; Helen Smith, '"Print[Ing] Your Royal Father Off": Early Modern Female Stationers and the Gendering of the British Book Trades', *Text*, 15 (2003), pp. 163–186; Douglas A. Brooks (ed.), *Printing and Parenting in Early Modern England* (London: Routledge, 2017).

interesting for blurring the gender roles in this seditious work. Acting like midwives, both male and female Confederates had facilitated the birth of *Mirabilis Annus'* series.

The analogy also pictured the stationers' activities ambiguously. On one hand, the Confederates were midwives and not the actual parents of the text. If the miraculous events reported in the pamphlets came from God's actions, the publishers were sole mediators. God was the author. On the other hand, their work as midwives was particularly important in the context of persecution. If they were not willing to take the risks involved in the publication, God's words might have been ignored (or worse, censored by the government). In this sense, the Confederates projected themselves to their audience as true Christians engaged in amplifying the divine message in those challenging times.[48]

## 2      Midwives of Seditious Pamphlets

The publication of clandestine pamphlets was a dangerous undertaking that demanded the work of skilled 'midwives' to assure that texts could be delivered under complex conditions. Those abilities comprehended more than flawless publications. In fact, the Confederates' pamphlets were full of mistakes resulting from shared, rapid, and interrupted printing processes. They usually corrected faults in apologetic erratas. In these paratexts, the Confederates' rhetoric stressed their good intentions. Their pamphlets were defective because they had to endure persecution to provide the public with virtuous ideas. For instance, at the end of *Two Treatises* by Henry Vane, the Confederates explained that,

> Many other obscurities through the mistake of words, and misplacing of Points, have happened in the *Printing of this General Epistle*, by reason of the several *difficulties* that attended its *Publication:* It being twice taken in the *Press*, and *two Presses*, well furnished with *Materials*, taken away in the doing of it.[49]

---

48    Margreta De Grazia, 'Imprints: Shakespeare, Gutenberg, and Descartes', in Douglas A. Brooks (ed.), *Printing and Parenting on Early Modern England*, pp. 29–58.

49    Henry Vane, *Two treatises* (London, 1662), p. 98v.

Published in the middle of 1662, *Two Treatises* gathered writings from Vane's time in prison. He was convicted and executed for treason in June 1662 for his collaboration with the parliamentarian cause in the previous decades. His late works were issued posthumously by the Confederates. Combining republican aspirations and apocalyptic beliefs, his texts revealed, as stated by Ruth Mayers, 'that adversity only strengthened Vane's confidence in the cause, and his divine calling to encourage, guide, and awaken the saints by his testimony and example'.[50]

*Two Treatises* included *An Epistle General to the Mystical Body of Christ on Earth* and *The Face of Times*, which were also sold separately. Besides these works, the Confederates published other tracts honouring Vane's memory: *The Trial of Sir Henry Vane*; *The Substance of What Sir Henry Vane Intended to Have Spoken Upon the Scaffold*; and *The Life and Death of Sir Henry Vane*. Battling over Vane's public figure, these works refused to depict the deceased as a traitor, describing him as a martyr of the 'good old cause'.[51]

The Confederates aimed at transforming Vane's theatrical trial and condemnation into examples of faith in God and dedication to the public good. The authorities responded to these seditious intentions by conducting various searches. According to the investigations,

> Twinning printed the *generall Epistle* of Sir *Henry Vane*. ... Bruister managed the printing of Sir *H: Vane's triale, and life & death*. And ... Mrs Chapman, of yᵉ face of Times.[52]

Peter Bodvell provided most of this information. As an apprentice to Thomas Brewster, he lived at the bookseller's house and saw many of the illicit works happening there. He knew his master had republished *A Healing Question* by Henry Vane in 1660 and suspected of Brewster's connection with the later series of pamphlets on Vane. However, it is important to remember that the

---

50    Ruth Mayers, 'Vane, Sir Henry, the younger (1613–1662), politician and author', *Oxford Dictionary of National Biography*, 2004 <https://www.oxforddnb.com/view/10.1093/ref:odnb/9780198614128.001.0001/odnb-9780198614128-e-28086> (accessed 19 September 2021).

51    John Coffey, 'The Martyrdom of Sir Henry Vane the Younger: From Apocalyptic Witness to Heroic Whig', in Thomas S. Freeman and Thomas Mayer (eds.), *Martyrs and Martyrdom in England, c. 1400–1700* (Suffolk: Boydell Press, 2007), pp. 221–39.

52    PRO SP29/67/325.

bookseller was still hiding in Bristol by the time these tracts were circulating. Therefore, Bodvell's statement probably referred to Anna Brewster's activities.[53]

Bodvell also indicated Hannah Chapman's involvement. He might have seen her talking to Anna Brewster or visiting their masters' bookshop. And this reference is quite significant. It allows us to perceive the continual work of Hannah Chapman in the book trade. Though her name barely appears in official records during the Restoration, Hannah had been working as a bookseller for decades. She was born in a stationers' family; both her father and brother were booksellers. It is no surprise that she married a man, Benjamin Allen, from the trade in 1632. Fourteen years later, Benjamin died and left his belongings to Hannah. She ran the bookshop until 1651, developing a solid publishing business based on connections with sectarian communities. Then, she wedded Livewell Chapman, her former apprentice. Her name vanished from title pages and registers at the Stationers' Company afterwards, but she never quit her job. Her contacts both with dissenters and stationers were useful to Chapman, who would become the main publisher of Fifth Monarchists.[54] Furthermore, her husband's frequent arrests during the 1650s and 1660s did not result in interruptions in the bookshop's activities, hence Hannah was continuously involved in the businesses.[55] She was also briefly mentioned in a warrant from April 1660. There were successive attempts to detain Livewell Chapman between March and April for publishing *Plain English to His Excellencie the Lord General Monck*, an anti-Stuart text which depicted Charles I's execution as the 'most noble Act of Justice'.[56] As he did not appear before the authorities when first requested, his wife was summoned as well. He was arrested later, while she remained free.[57]

Both Hannah Chapman and Anna Brewster were used to the book trade and the seditious networks. If Bodvell was right, the women employed John Twyn as their printer. Despite being only mentioned as the producer of *The*

53  PRO SP29/62/58; SP29/68/240.

54  Bernard Capp, *The Fifth Monarchy Men: A Study in Seventeenth Century English Millenarianism* (London: Faber and Faber, 2008).

55  Bell, 'Hannah Allen'; Amos Tubb, 'Independent Presses: The Politics of Print in England During the Late 1640s', *The Seventeenth Century* 27(2012), pp. 287–312; Verônica Calsoni Lima, 'Impresso para ser vendido na Crown em Pope's Head Alley: Hannah Allen, Livewell Chapman e a disseminação de panfletos radicais religiosos durante a Revolução Inglesa (1646–1665)' (Master's Thesis: Universidade Federal de São Paulo, 2016).

56  *Plain English to His Excellencie the Lord General Monck* (London, 1660), p. 3.

57  Mary Anne Everett Green (ed.), *Calendar of State Papers Domestic: Interregnum, 1659–60* (London: Her Majesty's Stationery Office), p. 272.

*General Epistle*, Twyn certainly composed the other tracts on Vane as well. The pamphlets' *mise-en-page* was similar; they probably came from the same printing press. If that was the case, it suggests that Hannah Chapman and Anna Brewster trusted John Twyn, allowing him to execute several controversial jobs in a brief period. Maybe they relied on Twyn because he was a nonconformist as well. Or, perhaps, their confidence in him had pecuniary foundations. The printer was a poor widower, who faced difficulties raising his small children. Early modern English society provided aid to widows in poverty situations, but no similar care was offered to widowers.[58] Twyn was forced to accept illicit works (which were very profitable) to sustain his family. He would not risk losing his source of income by denouncing his employers.[59]

In fact, the poverty of printers was a subject of attention. Roger L'Estrange addressed it in his publications and suggestions for press control. As he ascended to the post of censor, he directed the matter, creating incentives for poor stationers to denounce illicit businesses. Informers would be safe from prison and gain monetary rewards. Through networks of intelligence and official powers, L'Estrange reinforced his persecution of clandestine and seditious publications, disturbing the Confederate Stationers on other occasions.[60]

Soon after his ascension, the censor harassed printers and booksellers, frequently searching their houses, and requiring details on other stationers. Throughout 1663, there were several arrests and examinations. Giles Calvert was in Newgate Prison in January. Thomas Leach and Peter Bodvell gave testimonies a couple of times. In February, Thomas Brewster was captured by Bristol's Lord Mayor, who also found out about the clandestine distribution network carried on by Richard Moone. Authorities detained Livewell Chapman in March, together with his landlord, Mr Leonard, who had allowed the bookseller to keep a private press in his lodgings. In June, Elizabeth Calvert was arrested, probably due to her husband's release for poor health conditions.[61]

More importantly, in October, the Surveyor of the Press discovered two valuable proofs against the Confederates. First, after receiving information that John Twyn was working at strange hours, L'Estrange decided to surprise the stationer in the middle of the night. The censor appeared at Twyn's house

---

58  *An exact narrative*; Sandra Cavallo and Lyndan Warner (eds.), *Widowhood in Medieval and Early Modern Europe* (London: Routledge, 2014).

59  Hetet, 'A Literary Underground'.

60  Taylor, 'L'Estrange His Life'; Dunan-Page and Lynch, *Roger L'Estrange and the Making of Restoration Culture*; Keeble, *The Literary Culture*; N.H. Keeble, *The Restoration: England in the 1660s* (Malden: Blackwell, 2002).

61  PRO SP29/67/2, 69, 325; SP29/49/36; SP29/68/9, 240; SP44/9/296; SP44/10/39; SP44/15/81.

while the printer was working on *A Treatise of the Execution of Justice*, a pamphlet accusing Charles II of tyranny and claiming his deposition. Twyn was immediately arrested.[62] Wet sheets, broken forms, and proofread pages were apprehended.[63]

Secondly, while inspecting Simon Dover's print shop, L'Estrange found copies of *The Panther-Prophesy*, a text predicting the fall of a tyrannical ruler, implying that Charles II would be defeated by Christ's Second Coming.[64] After his discovery, the censor compared a decorative piece from the pamphlet's title page to the types inside Dover's cases and concluded that *The Panther-Prophesy* was printed with those same materials.[65]

## 3      The 'Feminine Part of Every Rebellion'

The confiscated objects both from Dover's and Twyn's houses served as proof to build a case against the stationers.[66] Printers and booksellers were rarely tried in criminal courts. Book trade issues were solved within the Stationers' Company. Alternatively, authorities could imprison, charge, or apply other punishments to offenders without further judicial proceedings. But now the authorities had the opportunity to set important precedents to deal with seditious libels.[67] Besides sheets and types, the censors had the detailed statements of Thomas Creake and George Thresher regarding the operations of the Confederates' clandestine network. Consequently, Simon Dover, Nathan Brooks, Thomas Brewster, and John Twyn went to the Old Bailey in February 1664. Livewell Chapman, who was imprisoned, was excused from the proceedings, for being too ill.[68]

---

62    *A treatise of the execution of justice* (London, 1663).

63    *An exact narrative.*

64    Owen Lloyd, *The panther-prophesy, or, A premonition to all people, of sad calamities and miseries like to befal these islands* (London, 1662).

65    *An exact narrative.*

66    Subheading quoted from *An exact narrative*, p. 50.

67    Frederick Seaton Siebert, *Freedom of the Press in England, 1476–1776* (Urbana: University of Illinois Press, 1965); Philip Hamburger, 'The Development of the Law of Seditious Libel and the Control of the Press', *Stanford Law Review*, 37(1985), pp. 661–765; Jody Greene, *The Trouble with Ownership: Literary Property and Authorial Liability in England, 1660–1730* (Philadelphia: University of Pennsylvania Press, 2005); Cyndia Susan Clegg, *Press Censorship in Caroline England* (Cambridge: Cambridge University Press, 2010); Randy Robertson, *Censorship and Conflict in Seventeenth-Century England: The Subtle Art of Division* (Philadelphia: Pennsylvania State University Press, 2009).

68    PRO SP29/90/25.

All the female Confederates were excepted from the trial as well. There were incriminating proofs against them, but authorities considered it was more important to prosecute men since women hardly faced condemnations. As discussed by Barbara Hanawalt, even when courts judged cases against women, they were usually acquitted.[69] Female activity, thus, was only mentioned during the trial when it served to incriminate men. For example, L'Estrange's testimony informed the court that he had intercepted a letter from Simon Dover to his wife. In the correspondence, from February 1664, Simon asked Joan to arrange 'a safe and convenient Room to dry books in' and to delay an unknown publication until 'I am certain I shall be tryed'.[70] To the court, Joan's part in the seditious undertaking only stressed the printer's culpability. He was a flawed man, unable of guiding his wife to perform good actions. Simon then was responsible for Joan's crimes. It is no surprise then that he was convicted. Simon Dover and his fellows Thomas Brewster and Nathan Brooks were guilty of sedition and sentenced to be fined, pilloried, and imprisoned.[71]

Although Elizabeth Calvert was a widow by the time of the trial and no longer had coverture of her late husband, mentions of her activities only served to indict another male stationer, John Twyn. The printer confessed that Elizabeth Calvert was the commissioner of *A Treatise of the Execution of Justice*. The bookseller's maid, Elizabeth Evans, made the contacts with Twyn, providing him with the manuscript, receiving part of the printed sheets, and paying for the job. The authorities searched Elizabeth Calvert's house on the day after John Twyn's arrest, in October 1663, but the bookseller and her maid were missing. Instead, Elizabeth Calvert's son, Nathaniel, and her apprentice, Mathias Stevenson, were arrested. Returning home, possibly because Nathaniel got seriously sick, Elizabeth Calvert was detained in February 1664. She remained silent during her examination, but Twyn had assured the authorities that Elizabeth was responsible for the pamphlet's publication.[72] It did not matter, though; she was not accountable for *A Treatise of the Execution of Justice*. Unable to provide an author's name, John Twyn faced charges of treason himself. The proofread sheets apprehended by L'Estrange contained Twyn's handwritten corrections, demonstrating he had understood the text's content and worked to improve its presentation to the readers.[73] Consequently, Twyn was found guilty. He was hanged, drawn, and quartered in a violent public

---

69   Hanawalt, 'The Female Felon', p. 128.
70   *An exact narrative*, p. 62.
71   PRO SP44/15/226.
72   PRO SP44/15/200, 204, 220, 240; SP29/89/120; SP29/83/119, 120; SP29/81/81; *An exact narrative*.
73   Greene, *The Trouble with Ownership*.

spectacle. In their turn, Elizabeth Calvert and her maid stayed imprisoned until April. Calvert's release followed a petition to bury Nathaniel, her recently deceased son.[74]

The fact that the Confederate Women did not face the same punishments that their male counterparts do not mean they were completely excused. Elizabeth Calvert was kept a close prisoner for months. Furthermore, the families of the Calverts, Brewster, Dovers, Chapmans, and Smiths were considerably impoverished.[75] Nevertheless, women were far more evasive of the authorities' constrictions. While their gender invalidated their autonomy in various public spaces, it also protected them from getting harsher retribution. Paradoxically, they were allowed to perform a significant role in the publication of anti-royalist and dissent propaganda, while their husbands were condemned.

The case of the Confederate Women sheds light on a classical statement quoted by Sergeant Morton during the 1664 trials:

> Dispersing seditious Books is very near a kin to raising of Tumults, they are as like as Brother and Sister; Raising of Tumults is the more Masculine, and Printing and Dispersing Seditious books, is the Feminine part of every Rebellion.[76]

The excerpt came from Francis Bacon's *Essays*, who had read it in Virgil's *Aeneid*. According to the epic poem, the goddess Fame, sister of two violent giants, disturbed the cities by rapidly spreading the news regarding Dido and Aeneas' love encounter. In Bacon's interpretation, which Morton followed, seditious words were as dangerous as riots. Indeed, printing and dispersing seditious texts were *parts* of rebellions. Despite its strongness, male tumults were sometimes easier to detain than feminine dangerous words, whose slipperiness was capable of great damage.[77]

## 4      Wives and Widows

Despite their prominent role in the clandestine trade, the Confederate Women adopted a language of fragility. In their petitions, they often depicted

74    SP44/16/23; SP29/92/15, 16; *An exact narrative.*
75    Francis Smith, *An Account of the Injurious Proceedings of Sir George Jeffreys Knt* (London: Francis Smith, 1681), p. 19.
76    *An exact narrative*, p. 50.
77    Martin Dzelzainis, "'The Feminine Part of Every Rebellion": Francis Bacon on Sedition and Libel, and the Beginning of Ideology', *Huntington Library Quarterly* 69 (2006), pp. 139–52.

themselves as incompetent women. When asking for their husbands' release, they explained how much they relied on their men to run their businesses and provide for their families. As a widow, Elizabeth Calvert also enforced her duty as a devoted mother. When she was in prison, Elizabeth appealed to be free, so she could take care of her children. This rhetoric aimed at the authorities' mercy, but it did not reflect the characteristics of the female Confederates. They were skilled stationers, whose printing and trade abilities maintained them in the book trade even after the 1664 trials.[78]

After the exemplary punishment of the male Confederates, it might seem that Roger L'Estrange and the Restoration censorship had overthrown the clandestine network, however, seditious books and pamphlets continued to be issued against the government due to the work of stationers' wives and widows. Both Hannah and Livewell Chapman passed away in 1665, victims of the plague, but Elizabeth Calvert, Anna Brewster, and Joan Dover continued to publish illicit pamphlets throughout the decade.[79] Their work reflected both their financial necessities and their political and religious beliefs. Prohibited books were very profitable, providing financial gains to pay debts left by their late husbands.[80] At the same time, it is necessary to acknowledge that they were committed nonconformists.[81] Therefore, they reacted to the restrictive Restoration policies. The Acts of Conformity (1662) and Conventicles (1664) had disturbed their religious liberties, thence, their texts often defied Charles II's impositions.[82]

For example, in 1664, Joan Dover printed *The Jury-Man's Charged* by the Fifth Monarchist Richard Creaven; *England's Warning* by the Quaker John Swinton; and works by the Quaker Rebecca Travers.[83] As a result, warrants for her

---

78    See their petitions in: PRO SP29/43/76; SP29/83/16; SP44/15/236; SP29/85/62; SP29/90/25; SP44/16/1.

79    Lima, 'Impresso para ser vendido'.

80    Robert Darnton, *Édition et Sédition: L'univers de La Littérature Clandestine Au XVIIIe Siècle* (Paris: Gallimard, 1991).

81    Ian Green, *Print and Protestantism in Early Modern England* (Oxford: Oxford University Press, 2000).

82    Bell, 'Elizabeth Calvert'; Bell, '"Her Usual Practices"'; Keeble, *The Literary Culture*; Greaves, *Deliver Us from Evil*; Greaves, *Enemies under His Feet*; Harold Weber, *Paper Bullets: Print and Kingship under Charles II* (Lexington: University Press of Kentucky, 1996); Elizabeth Sauer, *'Paper-Contestations' and Textual Communities in England, 1640–1675* (Toronto: University of Toronto Press, 2005).

83    *The jury-man charged; or, A letter to a citizen of London* (London, 1664); John Swinton, *Englands warning: or A friendly admonition to the rulers thereof* (London, 1664); Rebecca Travers, *This is for all or any of those (by what name or title soever they be distinguished) that resist the spirit, and despise the grace that brings salvation* (London, 1664).

apprehension appeared on 2 May 1664. Authorities also demanded the arrests of her servant, John Gaines, and her husband. Although the date of Joan's second wedding is unknown, it seems that John Darby was already living with the widow by May 1664. As Simon Dover, John Darby was also an apprentice to Peter Cole. Freed in 1660, his name only started to appear on imprints from 1667. Thus, he was working at Joan Dover's print shop as a journeyman before their wedding. Interestingly, though, is the fact that despite Joan and John's union, pamphlets continued to carry Joan Dover's name from 1664 to 1666, suggesting that she was autonomous in the trade. Nevertheless, for the judicial system, John Darby rapidly assumed the new patriarchal position of the house. In June, L'Estrange seized unlicensed and seditious texts. The surname 'Dover' was not included in his list of houses to search, but 'Darby' was.[84]

Elizabeth Calvert never married again. Consequently, authorities had to name her in warrants. For that reason, there is a broader trail of her illegal businesses throughout the 1660s.[85] Investigations of her activities reveal the maintenance of her Confederate alliances. For instance, in 1667, Elizabeth Calvert was in trouble with the authorities due to the publication of *London's Flames*, an anti-Catholic piece attributing the catastrophic 1666 fire to a popish plot. Letters from Thomas Langton, Mayor of Bristol, informed the Secretary of State of the seizure of fifty copies of the seditious pamphlet.[86] The texts reached Bristol because Elizabeth Calvert had sent them to another bookseller's widow, Susannah Moone. Both women had known each other for a long time as Richard Moone was an apprentice to Giles Calvert between 1645 and 1652. The language employed in Elizabeth's letter to her 'Loving friend' suggests that she was often providing Susannah Moone with clandestine pamphlets.[87]

Besides the polemic around *London's Flames*, Elizabeth Calvert managed to publish other illegal texts with the help of her allies in the trade. As the first pages of this chapter had mentioned, the controversial *Poor-Whores Petition* was published and dispersed by Elizabeth Calvert, Joan and John Darby, and Anna Brewster. The broadside was probably printed in one or two private presses. In May 1668, Elizabeth was caught with an illegal press and dozens of type cases in a house belonging to a dissident, Elizabeth Poole, in Southwark.[88]

---

84　　PRO SP29/109/159; PRO SP44/16/115; PRO SP29/99/247.

85　　Bell, "'Her Usual Practices'".

86　　*Londons flames discovered by informations taken before the Committee* (London, 1667).

87　　PRO SP29/209/85.

88　　Mary Anne Everett Green (ed.), *Calendar of State Papers Domestic: Charles II, 1667–8* (London: Her Majesty's Stationery Office, 1893), p. 363; Stationers' Company, *Court Book D*, fl. 139v.

Meanwhile, Anna Brewster and the Darbys were sharing a clandestine press set at Blue Anchor Alley.[89]

The discovery of their illicit presses stresses the extent of women's agency in the seditious book trade. It makes it easier to infer that the female Confederates were not only performing tasks guided by their husbands during their inconvenient absences. Throughout the 1660s, these women were actively engaged in clandestine businesses, looking for alternatives to maintain publications under difficult circumstances. It is quite interesting to notice how they managed to resist and sustain illegal trades while the Restoration was enforcing press control.

Roger L'Estrange observed their impertinence when he addressed the Secretary of State in his letter from April 1668. The Confederate Women were some 'of $y^e$ craftyest & most obstinate of $y^e$ trade', and the censor realised that he had no proper means to detain them.[90] It is difficult to affirm that the Confederate Stationers consciously took advantage of gender issues to protect their clandestine businesses, but women played a fundamental part in the network's survival. Laws were flawed, and the Confederate Women found ways to explore spaces to act in the book trade, defying the constraints that authorities tried to implement.

---

89    PRO SP29/239/8, 10; SP44/28/2.
90    PRO SP29/239/8.

# CHAPTER 17

# Printing Prophecy before 1550: Fame, Piety, and Gender in Northern Europe

*Rabia Gregory*

The designs of early printed prayer manuals preserve attitudes about fame, gender, piety, and public perception of living saints between the 1450s and the 1520s.[1] Print-making technologies introduced new ways for European Christians to interact with and learn from religious teachers during the fifteenth century. One aspect of this phenomenon was the publication of vernacular devotional books authored by 'living saints,' local figures known for their piety and gifts of prophecy, that is, the ability to transmit God's revelations to their communities.[2] Prior to the 1450s, seekers of spiritual advice had to physically travel if they wished to speak with a respected preacher, monastic, or anchorite. Print technologies changed the gendered social roles of living saints by creating new possibilities for religious instruction in the fifteenth-and sixteenth centuries. Printing made it possible to disseminate the experience of consulting a living saint internationally and posthumously, creating a path to international fame, memorialisation, and, potentially, canonisation.[3] To evaluate the significance of gender on the publishing of prophetic books, this essay undertakes a comparative study of the illustrated vernacular books attributed to three spiritually gifted authors: anchorites St. Nikolaus of Flüe (1417–1487)

---

1 Due to travel restrictions during the Covid-19 pandemic, this study focuses primarily on digitised and microfilmed books and manuscripts. The bibliography includes static links to digitised manuscript and book facsimiles for early printed works when available. Unless otherwise indicated, all translations are my own.

2 I borrow the phrase 'living saints' from Gabriella Zarri's work. She defines 'living saints (Sante Vive)' as figures who were recognised for their holiness while alive, whether they have subsequently been canonised, Gabriella Zarri, *Le sante vive: Profezie di corte e devozione femminile tra '400 e '500* (Turin: Rosenberg & Sellier, 1990).

3 It is beyond the scope of this essay to consider why only one of these authors has been canonised. In addition to considerations such as whether one living saint conformed more closely to expectations of gendered piety than another, or post-Tridentine preference for male saints, other reasons may include the influence of Protestantism, decline of pilgrimage in some regions, as well as the relative importance of Nikolaus for Swiss national identity. For an overview of scholarship on gender and canonisation, see Rubin, Miri. 'Cults of saints', in Judith M. Bennett and Ruth Mazo Karras (eds.), *The Oxford Handbook of Women and Gender in Medieval Europe*, (Oxford: Oxford University Press, 2013), pp. 480–495.

© KONINKLIJKE BRILL BV, LEIDEN, 2025 | DOI:10.1163/9789004701656_018

and Bl. Bertha Jacobs (1426–1514) and the Clarissan nun Magdalena Beutler of Freiburg (1407–1458). These living saints each developed effective prayer techniques they shared with neighbours and pilgrims that would subsequently be adapted for both print and manuscript prayer books.[4] I propose that strategies introduced when adapting prayer techniques for printed books stripped away gendered aspects of devotion that determined paths for religious vocation, restricted access to sacred spaces, and which were typically present in devotional manuscripts. These changes include replacing gender-specific pronouns with inclusive wording and crafting visual representations of living saints that used gender-neutral visual cues to represent sanctity. Because these illustrations distilled key elements of an author's piety into easily recognizable visual symbols, they offer important evidence about the role of gender in constructing piety during the first decades of European printing.

Comparative studies can be an effective approach for identifying and analysing meaningful differences between seemingly similar subjects.[5] This chapter adopts a careful comparative approach to determine what, if any, role gender played in the publication of vernacular devotional books written by or attributed to living saints. I focus on how printers used woodcuts and textual narratives to adapt the physical experience of visiting a living saint for advice into a portable and international tool for learning to pray. A comparative study of the books attributed to three near-contemporary living saints affords the opportunity to consider the role of gender differences in relation to authorship and sanctity in the period. These books used images—aural, visual, verbal—to evoke piety and impart spiritual knowledge. By comparing design, format, paratext, and the relationships between manuscript and printed copies of prayers attributed to each living saint, I show that though gender shaped lived experiences of living saints, gendered representations of the performance of piety were not a significant factor in the design or marketing of early printed prayer books.

1        Gendered Piety in Paratext

Surviving books attributed to living saints preserve important clues about marketing, devotional culture, and gendered piety in Europe during the first

---

4  As Anneke Mulder-Bakker notes, during the twelfth through fourteenth centuries, anchoresses offered advice to visitors as part of their daily labour, Anneke Mulder-Bakker, *Lives of the Anchoresses: the rise of the Urban Recluse in Medieval Europe*. Translated by Myra Heerspink Scholz (Philadelphia: University of Pennsylvania Press, 2013), pp. 3–12.

5  Jonathan Z. Smith, *Imagining Religion: From Babylon to Jonestown*. (Chicago: University of Chicago Press, 1982), p. 26.

decades of printing. While a devotional manuscript's owner may have received spiritual guidance from a confessor or other local teacher who ensured that their practice was doctrinally sound, printed devotional manuals taught readers *how* to pray—describing the emotional experiences and visualisation processes of meditation and contemplation, in addition to providing the texts of effective prayers. They effectively combined the functions of spiritual instructor, devotional images, and prayers into a single volume. First produced in the German cities of Augsburg and Nuremberg in the late 1460s, likely by spiritual directors working in collaboration with women's religious communities, this new genre of book soon spread throughout German and Dutch-speaking regions of Europe. Printed prayer manuals transformed the individualised emotional and visionary experiences of historical figures to create recognizable brands of sanctity. These books recreated the experience of working with a spiritual teacher with prefatory woodcuts and textual narratives.

As Jonathan Green has documented, illustrations of visions in early printed books fulfilled both textual and paratextual functions by translating phrases into woodcuts, depicting real events and establishing authorial authority and sanctity.[6] Printers in the last quarter of the fifteenth century codified and legitimised previously unknown vernacular religious texts by taking idiosyncratic manuscript copies, illustrating them, and introducing them into new, standardised books.

Because the design of devotional books was relatively fixed, elements of paratext such as woodcuts and titles offer valuable data for comparative gender analysis. Our current concepts of 'book' and 'print' first took on their new (and now almost outdated) meanings in the fifteenth century as part of a reformulation of vocabulary created by printers transferring incipits and titles from manuscripts to printed books.[7] To adapt manuscript texts for the general reader, printers made several important innovations in both format and narrative text, including shifting gendered pronouns such as 'sister/daughter/

---

6  Jonathan Green, *Printing and Prophecy: Prognostication and Media Change 1450–1550*. (Ann Arbor: University of Michigan Press, 2012), pp. 86–8.

7  Sarah Werner, *Studying Early Printed Books, 1450–1850: A Practical Guide* (Chichester: Wiley Blackwell, 2019) pp. 64–6, 92–3; Laurie E. Maguire, *The Rhetoric of the Page* (Oxford: Oxford University Press, 2020); Martha W. Driver, 'There and Back Again: Manuscripts after Printing', in Corinne Saunders, Richard Marshall, Alexander R. Lawrie, and Lauren Atkinson (eds.), *Middle English Manuscripts and their Legacies: a volume in honour of Ian Doyle* (Leiden: Brill, 2021), pp. 155–188. A.I. Doyle, Elizabeth Rainey and D.B. Wilson, *Manuscript to Print: Tradition and Innovation in the Renaissance Book* (Durham: University of Durham Press, 1975); Douglas C. McMurtrie, *Miniature incunabula: some preliminary notes on small books printed during the fifteenth century* (Chicago: privately printed, 1929); Kristian Jensen (ed.), *Incunabula and their readers: printing, selling and using books in the fifteenth century* (London: British Library, 2003).

son/brother' to more universal language such as 'person' or all Christian persons, and even adding biographical information about authors that was rarely included in manuscripts, often condensing texts but also sometimes adding passages on other devotional subjects. Some printers also commissioned prefatory images and other original woodcuts. The use of prefatory woodcuts in early printed books dates to at least the 1470s. These images sometimes appeared before or after a title page or title wrapper, or preceded the first line of printed text.[8] While some prefatory woodcuts were custom-cut for a particular book, printers often repurposed blocks from other projects for a prefatory image. The earliest prefatory images were printed on a separate page from a book's title, but by the end of the fifteenth century, they were often integrated into a single page. Information about the publisher and publication date now found on modern title pages appeared instead in colophons in the earliest books. By the 1470s, printed prefatory images were often sold with stencilled colouring or quickly hand-coloured in shops. The title and prefatory image helped convey important information about a book's purpose and likely benefit. They also served as wrappers protecting the unbound pages.[9] Through their representation of living saints, as well as their choice of adjectives and pronouns, prefatory images and titles preserve important information about how printers marketed books attributed to living saints and embed gendered markers of difference, both gender difference, and the difference between a living saint and a pious Christian reader.

Author portraits, narrative elements, and publication histories reveal that despite significant differences in agency, autonomy, and personal freedom experienced by male and female living saints, a shared brand of sanctity shaped their representation as pious authors in printed prayer manuals. Though certain gendered elements, such as pronouns and visual markers like hairstyle and clothing differentiated male and female living saints, surviving books do not explicitly gender the performance of piety. I use gendered piety to describe the devotional acts and religious experiences, which might have

---

8 On prefatory woodcuts and the development of title pages see Laura Nuvoloni 'The Woodcut as Exemplar: Sources of Inspiration for the Decoration of a Venetian Incunabulum', *Transactions of the Cambridge Bibliographical Society*, 15 (2012), pp. 141–63; Margaret M. Smith, 'The End-title, the Early Title-page, and the Wrapper: Their inter-connections', *Transactions of the Cambridge Bibliographical Society*, 11 (1997), pp. 95–111; Sabine Griese, 'Layoutformen des Buchs im 15. Jahrhundert', in Christoph Reske and Wolfgang Schmitz (eds.), *Material Aspekte in der Inkunabelforschung* (Wiesbaden: Harrassowitz Verlag, 2017), pp. 9–42; Garold Cole, 'The Historical Development of the Title Page', *The Journal of Library History*, 6 (1971), pp. 303–16.

9 On the use of title pages and other front matter to market books see, Yves G. Vermeulen, *Tot Profijt En Genoegen: Motiveringen voor de Produktie van Nederlandstalige Gedrukte Teksten, 1477–1540* (Groningen: Wolters-Noordhoff/Forsten, 1986).

distinct cultural significations according to gender. This phrase challenges the assumptions that gender was a simple binary in the late Middle Ages, recognising that the performance of gender might differ according to social status, religious vocation, region, and context. The piety or transgression of actions like drinking pus, ascetic practices like flagellation, and somatic miracles such as lactation or reception of the stigmata depended on an individual's gender. There were different, often contradictory hermeneutics for recognising spiritual authority, and gender was only one component in determining an individuals' status as living saint.

Throughout this essay I use gendered piety to identify how the same action may have different values and meanings according to an individual's gender and to acknowledge that humans, as gendered beings, may understand and be understood through competing hermeneutics if they are operating within religious or secular spaces. In other words, the same action or characteristic might have a different meaning according to the gender of the individual as well as whether the action is undertaken as part of practising religion. Submitting to or resisting ecclesiastical authority, teaching, preaching, somatic experiences, asceticism, as well as the association of masculinity with authority, literacy, intellectual rather than emotional revelation, and femininity with submission, bodiliness, visual experiences, and vulnerability to demonic influences are all examples of how fifteenth-century society and twenty-first century scholars have understood the gendered mutability of Christian piety.[10] Idealised statements about gender roles from legal and theological treatises must be balanced with information from other sources, such as popular literature, legal cases, and material culture. Potential living saints were evaluated both for their performance of piety—conforming to the tropes and expectations of saintliness set out in hagiography—and the doctrinal soundness of their teachings and revelations.

Gendered aspects of piety which shaped daily life for living saints are less prevalent in printed devotional manuals than humility, and engagement with the public as a teacher. In extant printed manuals, prefatory woodcuts present key elements of a living saint's piety and supplement textual narratives describing authors teaching pilgrims, engaged in prayer, and receiving divine messages. Visual representations of living saints were so uniform that a woodcut designed to represent one living saint would often be repurposed

---

10    In recent years, feminist bibliographers have gone beyond identifying women printers, scribes, and authors to consider the implications of gender on the production of books (whether manuscript or print) more broadly. See especially Victoria E. Burke and Jonathan Gibson (eds.), *Women and Early Modern Manuscript Culture* (Aldershot: Ashgate, 2004) and Kate Ozment, 'Rationale for Feminist Bibliography', *Textual Cultures*, 13 (2020), pp. 149–78.

to represent other holy persons. Printed iconography prioritised the qualities of teaching and prayer over the identity markers of individual saints, likely to assist with marketing books. These simplified representations of living saints made clear at a single glance that a devotional text offered prayer techniques rather than, for instance, a saint's biography. Consequently, printed devotional manuals capture a distillation of qualities of piety that, regardless of an individual's gender, authorised a living saint as a spiritual instructor.

## 2      Living Saints and Their Books

Illustrated printed prayer books show that though gender shaped the forms of religious life a person might pursue, it did not limit who could teach prayer or attain salvation. All three of these saints are near contemporaries, and all three entered enclosure, became famous for offering spiritual advice to visitors, authored prayers that became popular internationally, were visited by pilgrims, and appeared in illustrated vernacular prayer manuals shortly after their deaths. Additionally, each was the subject of multiple editions of printed books in the fifteenth and sixteenth centuries. These books were issued by many publishers, and the earliest books in each case are small and illustrated with custom woodcuts. Known extant manuscripts attributed to these authors are not closely related to surviving printed books. Because of these similarities in manuscript and print editions of their work, it is possible to focus on the *differences* between Magdalena Beutler, Nikolaus of Flüe, and Bertha Jacobs to evaluate how gender contributed to the production of their books.

Magdalena Beutler, Nikolaus of Flüe, and Bertha Jacobs were near contemporaries who all willingly entered the enclosed religious life. As living saints, they each fulfilled similar cultural, religious, and economic roles, becoming famous for their prayers and spiritual advice. Though from approximately the same social status, they had different family backgrounds, educations, and religious experiences. Bertha Jacobs and Magdalena Beutler were literate and reportedly copied manuscripts recording their spiritual experiences, while Nikolaus of Flüe was illiterate and depended on hired scribes. Nikolaus and Magdalena experienced documented miracles (Magdalena received the stigmata, Nikolaus lived on nothing but the Eucharist for 19.5 years), while Bertha did not. Nikolaus was married and had several children while Magdalena and Bertha were not. Nikolaus undertook military service in his youth, while Magdalena and Bertha joined religious communities.

These differences originate in fifteenth-century gender norms. Young girls could not undertake military service but might learn to read in monastic communities. Men had more freedom to travel than women, to enter marriages or to leave them, and to meet with the public without supervision or enclosure. Male anchorites were permitted to live in rural locations as well as urban anchorholds, while women who dedicated themselves to a religious career, whether in isolation or community, were restricted to enclosure.[11] Magdalena von Freiburg, as she was sometimes known, entered the convent at the age of five with her widowed mother. A spiritually gifted child, she became a respected visionary and teacher. Though her miraculous death, resurrection, and reception of the stigmata were viewed with skepticism by reformers like Johannes Nider, Magdalena's community valued her spiritual teachings and preserved her manuscript texts. Nikolaus of Flüe, also known as Bruder Klaus, was a father, soldier, and pilgrim who retired from his family obligations to enter a hermitage in Ranft, Obwalden, in the canton of Unterwalden, where he lived on nothing but the Eucharistic host for nearly twenty years. Contemporary sources describe his work speaking with pilgrims, and he was mentioned by Felix Fabri, Johannes Trithemius, and Geiler von Keyserberg. He also appeared in Hartmann Schedel's Nuremberg Chronicle with a woodcut showing his gaunt face as an account of his miraculous fasting.[12] Nikolaus of Flüe was beatified in 1669 and canonised in 1947. Though illiterate, several prayers attributed to him survive in near-contemporary manuscripts, as well as legal documents pertaining to his family that were the work of hired scribes.

Bertha Jacobs, known as Sister Bertken, entered an anchorhold in Utrecht after several years enclosed in a Canoness house of the *Devotio Moderna*, where she wrote music for communal use. In her anchorhold, Bertha lived an austere life, always dressed modestly in a hairshirt, barefoot, and dedicated to daily prayer. Her work included writing and helping visitors with their spiritual concerns. While some of the earliest manuscripts attributed to her, which contain songs, may be linked to her time in communal life, Bertha Jacobs' published books are, or at least purport to be, the daily writing that was part of her religious vocation during her time as an anchorite. All the books discussed in this paper are small-format, portable, and hand-sized, most measuring less than 14 × 20 cm. All editions of Nicolaus' *Bruder Klaus* are quarto format with 10 woodcuts produced on 2–3 sheets of paper. The Geerard Leeu edition of Beutler's *Golden Litany* is slightly larger than the custom-cut woodcut measuring 8 × 5.3 cm; subsequent editions are all octavo format; the Huntington's copy measures roughly 18 × 14 cm after having been trimmed by a binder. The earliest book I examine is *Bruder Klaus*, sometimes referred to as *Pilgertraktat*. Most likely first produced in Augsburg, *Bruder Klaus* was issued in three known

---

11    Mulder-Bakker, *Lives of the Anchoresses*, p. 4.
12    Roland Gröbli, *Die Sehnsucht nach dem "einig Wesen": Leben und Lehre des Bruder Klaus von Flüe* (Zürich: NZN, 1995), p. 33.

editions before 1500.[13] *Bruder Klaus* adopts the narrative voice of a pilgrim who has visited Nikolaus of Flüe. Using a first-person 'Ich' voice, the anonymous pilgrim describes Nikolaus's appearance and setting and recounts their conversations.

*Bruder Klaus* uses a dialogue between pilgrim and anchorite to explain Nikolaus's prayer techniques. Through this conversation, readers share in the experience of conversing with Nikolaus and learn about the path to salvation through a spiritual wheel with spokes revealed to the hermit in a vision. Each of the surviving fifteenth-century editions of this book include woodcuts depicting Niklaus of Flüe's hermitage as well as the spiritual wheel and its meanings. The printed books are the first extant record of Nikolaus's visions or the wheel and spokes that would become part of his iconography and legacy.[14]

An updated version of the book was printed in at least two editions by Petrus Canisius in the last quarter of the sixteenth century. Both editions incorporate woodcuts from the life of Christ into their prayer sequences but do not include any representations of Nikolaus of Flüe. Extant fifteenth-century manuscripts related to Nikolaus are unillustrated prayer books that include a single short prayer, like Berlin, Staatsbibliothek, MGQ 636, a 1491 manuscript that includes the first known copy of *Das Nützest, Klausens gewonlich bet.* A representative example of how manuscript copies acknowledged the authorship of living saints is Karlsruhe, BLB, Cod St Georgen 41. Though more luxurious than most personal prayer books, with numerous miniatures and historiated initials, the manuscript contains no portraits of Nikolaus. The only explicit reference appears following a wonderfully detailed depiction of the Ecce Homo. The artist has taken great care to present luxurious textiles, landscape and architectural details, and a badly wounded Jesus. On the following page a rubricated title indicates 'bruder Klaus' was the source of a particular prayer on the pater noster that presumably would be used while contemplating this image (Fig. 17.1). The artist and owner had the talent and budget to have produced a depiction of Nikolaus or his visions had this been considered a priority for the book's design and use.

---

13     Niklaus of Flüe's hermitage was in Flüeli-Ranft, Unterwalden, and remains a pilgrimage site today. The three extant fifteenth century editions are: *Bruder Claus* (Augsburg: Peter Berger, c.1487) USTC 744053 <http://nbn-resolving.de/urn/resolver.pl?urn=urn:nbn:de:bvb:12-bsb00019163-5>; *Bruder Claus* (Nuremberg: Marx Ayrer, 1488) USTC 744054 <http://nbn-resolving.de/urn/resolver.pl?urn=urn:nbn:de:bvb:12-bsb00026459-4>; *Bruder Claus* (Nuremberg: Peter Wagner, c.1489–90) USTC 744055 <http://nbn-resolving.de/urn/resolver.pl?urn=urn:nbn:de:bvb:12-bsb00006092-8>.

14     For a discussion of how these early printed books relate to other fifteenth century manuscripts and artwork relating to Nikolaus von Flüe see Gröbli, *Sehnsucht*, p. 32.

FIGURE 17.1　　Gebetbuch, freigemachte Horen. Karlsruhe, BLB, Cod St Georgen 41

Though an unusually luxurious manuscript, it was typical for fifteenth-and sixteenth-century manuscripts preserving prayers of Nikolaus, Bertha, and Magdalena to indicate authorship with only the briefest rubricated reference. These manuscripts typically only contained a single prayer and lacked the biographical information in near-contemporary printed editions of the same texts.

While the first printed books linked to Nikolaus were produced near his hermitage, the first printed books linked to Magdalena Beutler would be published in translation in another country. They too used woodcuts and biographical narratives to emphasise the author's spiritual accomplishments. Illustrated books had been printed in southern Germany for several decades before the first illustrated books printed with moveable type were produced in the Low Countries. However, there are no known German editions of the *Golden Litany*, a collection of prayers attributed to Magdalena Beutler prior to her work being issued in Dutch.[15] The first edition of the *Golden Litany* was produced in Antwerp by Geerard Leeu, published 29 November 1492. Leeu's edition contained a single custom woodcut depicting Magdalena kneeling before the altar meditating before a crucifix (Fig. 17.2).

All known copies with title images show a female figure and a crucifixion, linked to Leeu's design. This may indicate that Leeu's strategies for marketing the book were integral to what made the *Golden Litany* a printed devotional book. A new edition, published in Delft in 1494 (by Snellaert), closely copied Leeu's woodcut and was printed on both the recto and verso of the title page. The other reprints were by Govaert Bac (1493, 1497) and Adriaen van Liesvelt (1494). Bac and Liesvelt also used woodcuts copied from Leeu's vernacular devotional books. A final edition by Henrick Lettersneider (1496–7) exists in a single imperfect copy missing the first page; it is unclear whether this edition had a prefatory woodcut.[16] That each illustrated edition included a prefatory

---

15    The *Golden Litany* was reportedly revealed to Magdalena in relation to her reception of the stigmata. This text survives in at least 88 manuscripts before 1500 (in German, Dutch, English, and Low German), six known print editions in Dutch and Low German before 1500 and numerous reprints into the 1800s. Though she died before Niklaus of Flüe and manuscript copies of her work were circulating in German-speaking regions, no surviving fifteenth-century German editions of this text are known. I discuss Magdalena's career and her acclaim as a teacher in Rabia Gregory, 'Thinking of Their Sisters: Authority and Authorship in Late Medieval Women's Religious Communities', *Journal of Medieval Religious Cultures*, 40 (2014), pp. 75–100. See also Willhelm Schleussner, 'Magdalena von Freiburg eine pseudomystische Erscheinung des späteren Mittelalters 1407–1458', *Der Katholik*, 87 (1907), pp. 15–32, and Karen Greenspan, '*Erklärung des Vaterunsers*: A Critical Edition of a Fifteenth-century Mystical Treatise by Magdalena Beutler of Freiburg', PhD Thesis (University of Massachusetts at Amherst, 1984).

16    Leeu's edition has been digitised by the British Library and I have used it for my translations and summaries: *Een Schoen mirakel vander openbaringhen der gulden letanien van der passion ons heeren* (Antwerp: Geerard Leeu, 29 Nov 1492) <http://access.bl.uk/item /viewer/ark:/81055/vdc_100110188956.0x000001> USTC 436163.
     I also examined the Huntington Library's copy of the Golden Litany (Govaert Bac, 1495) USTC 436199 several years ago. This copy is bound with two other late-fifteenth century illustrated vernacular devotional manuals in Dutch My discussion of the other editions is dependent on the reproductions of woodcuts and discussion of editions in Ina Kok, *Woodcuts in Incunabula Printed in the Low Countries* (Amsterdam: HES & De Graaf, 2013).

FIGURE 17.2    *Een Schoen mirakel vander openbaringhen der gulden letanien van der passion
ons heeren* (Antwerp: Gerard Leeu, 29 Nov 1492)
IMAGE COURTESY OF THE BRITISH LIBRARY, DIGITAL STORE IA.49852.
USTC 436163

woodcut showing a living saint in prayer, and that the opening lines of text link this scene to the moment Magdalena received the book's contents, is a significant aspect of how the book presented Magdalena's spiritual authority.

My final examples, Bertha Jacobs' *Boeck tracterende van desen puncten* (Sister Bertken's Book) and *Een boecken van dye passie ons liefs heren Jhesu Christi* (A Devout book on the Passion of Christ), also include prefatory images of a woman in prayer before a crucifix. These volumes were produced most immediately after the author's death, plausibly using a now-lost manuscript original reportedly discovered in Bertha's cell after her death in 1514.[17] *A Devout book on the Passion of Christ* (Fig. 17.3) and *Sister Bertken's Book* were Dutch prayer and songbooks published posthumously in 1516 and reissued at least three times before 1520.

FIGURE 17.3
*Een boecxken gemaket van suster bertken* (Antwerp: Michiel van Hoogstraten, 1535)

---

17   The following discussion of these texts and their illustrations depends on the critical introduction to the 1955 edition now digitised on dbnl.org: Suster Bertken van Utrecht, *Een boecxken gemaket ende bescreven van suster Bertken die LVII iaren besloten heeft ghesloten tot Utrecht in die buerkercke naar de eerste uitgave van Jan Berntsz Utrecht Opnieuw uitgegeven* edited by Catherina van de Graft (Zwolle: W.E.J. Tjeenk Willink, 1955), <https://dbnl.org/tekst/bert009ccva01_01/colofon.php>. The discussion of the discovery of the manuscripts is pp. 27–8, built from a transcription of an account in Latin and Dutch inscribed by the prior of the canons regular inscribed in a copy of the *legenda aurea* now in the library of the University of Utrecht. I have also consulted two digitised copies, the 1515 *Een boecxken gemaket van suster Bertken* <https://books.google.com/books?id=vItjAAAAcAAJ&num=6&pg=PP14#v=onepage&q&f=false> and Jan Severesen's 1518 edition <https://books.google.com/books?id=d-95ui3R-rMC&pg=PP1#v=onepage&q&f=false>.

Like *Bruder Klaus* and the *Golden Litany*, Sister Bertken's books were published with a prefatory woodcut depicting the author in prayer, and, like *Bruder Klaus*, they also included woodcuts showing scenes from the life of Christ and works of mercy. *Sister Bertken's Book* advertises its connection to the written words of the author and includes songs in addition to prayers. Some of her songs also survive in Dutch and Low German manuscript collections near-contemporary with these printed books, suggesting that these compositions were in circulation before her death. As their designs and contents reveal, publishers and consumers were less interested in what had really happened in a holy person's life than what they could teach their communities.

## 3     Gendered Piety in Author Portraits

The first page of each of the above books included an author portrait. Manuscript author portraits varied from rough pen drawings to luxurious illuminations. While some might be tucked into a flourished initial, most were larger full-or half-page compositions added to a manuscript by a trained artist. In printed books, prefatory images depicting a book's author were made using woodcuts, some of which were re-used from earlier projects or would subsequently illustrate future publications. They identified a book's contents, attracted the potential buyer, and helped the reader understand what experience or information the book might provide. They also may have operated as devotional images, providing a visual aid to prayer practices. The earliest author portraits of Klaus, Magdalena, and Bertha emphasise the physical acts of praying and teaching, demonstrate piety through modest dress, and present living saints as largely interchangeable holy persons, rather than highlighting the distinctive features of a particular individual's spiritual career. Although gendered differences such as hair length, attire, and location (exterior vs interior spaces) are present, these author portraits use the same gestures and details to indicate a living saint's performance of piety. Unlike contemporary hagiographies and other written sources, many of which definitively recognise gendered differences in the performance of piety, these printed author portraits uniformly emphasise each living saint's humility, asceticism, teaching of prayers, and divine encounters by presenting them as spiritual teachers.

*Bruder Klaus* opened with a prefatory author portrait, one of ten woodcuts designed for Peter Berger's first surviving edition. Max Ayer's 1488 and Peter Wagner's 1489–90 editions reproduce this visual program and also contain 10 woodcuts. Berger's 1487 imprint has an undecorated title page followed by a brief table of contents. The first woodcut in each extant edition is an author portrait of Nikolaus. In the 1487 edition, this author portrait is positioned

A Jch was Jnn meiner ellendung
vnd befuͦchet die ſtett dͦer genaden
vnd des ablas·Da kam ich vnd fand
ein menſchen des namen was bruͦder
Claus da ich in anfach da erfrewet
ſich mein hercz wann ich ſahe an im

die wunder gotes das er lebet on die natuͤrliche ſpeis
Jch grieſſet jn vnd er enpfieng mich liepleich vnd ich
ſprach lieber vater·Jch wolt geren mit euͦch reden jn
der liebe gotes ·wann triſtus hat geſprochen·wa ewz
zwen geſamelt ſein jn meinem namen ·So wil ich ſein
jn i␣er mitte ·Nun wolt ich gern das der herz vnnſer
mittel were ·Er ſprach nun ſag dar was waiſt du voͤ
der liebe gotes zuͦſageͤ·Jch ſprach mein vater das iſt

FIGURE 17.4     *Bruder Claus* (Augsburg, Peter Berger, 1487) USTC 744053, f. 2v

above the opening lines of the text. In each extant copy, the artist presented
Nikolaus seated in a contemplative pose outside his hermitage with his chapel
in the background (Fig. 17.4).

He is barefoot, with long hair and a beard and modest dress. The artist has
carefully emphasised Nikolaus's large eyes and gaunt cheeks as a visual representation of the miracle of surviving without eating. The text below the author

portrait opens with the account of a penitent who visited Nikolaus in Ranft. According to the accompanying text, his pilgrim's heart rejoiced upon seeing that Nikolaus lived without eating, much in the same way that the viewer might have reacted to the author portrait. The narrator goes on to recount a conversation between Klaus and his guest that captures the kind of dialogues that would have occurred when any individual visited a living saint.[18] After answering a series of questions regarding God's love and the role of the Virgin Mary, Klaus then describes his prayer techniques and a spiritual wheel representing godly wisdom he has received in a vision (Fig. 17.5). The wheel is divided with spokes into six segments around a central circle. In the very centre is a point representing the undivided Godhead. Three spokes emanating out from but not piercing that central sphere represent the three persons of the Trinity.

A second expanded wheel (Fig. 17.6) links the first wheel to the life of Jesus. The text then goes on to describe the works of mercy Christians should perform to attain salvation. As Roland Gröbli has documented, these printed books are the only surviving accounts of Nikolaus receiving visions and they introduced the wheel designs that became part of Nikolaus's standard iconography.[19]

The same visual program with the same visual references emphasising Nikolaus's piety were repeated in the newly cut woodcuts of the Ayer and Berger editions. They also positioned an author portrait above the pilgrim's narrative, linking the narrative of the pilgrim's reaction to Nikolaus's gaunt cheeks with the reader's viewing of the woodcut. The Nuremberg artists emphasise the isolated forest, highlighting geographical features visitors still see when they travel to the site: the stream running between hermitage and chapel and the slopes of the mountains. They position Nikolaus in a contemplative posture outside his cell, as if waiting for a visiting pilgrim and use open space in the foreground to invite the viewer/reader to step into the pilgrim's role. As Carolyn Walker Bynum's groundbreaking study of women's spirituality and religious symbols demonstrated, extended fasting and the miracle of inedia were both fundamental practises to women's spirituality in the later Middle Ages.[20] Bynum

---

18    Gröbli discusses visitors to the anchorhold and lists all identifiable visitors, Gröbli, *Sehnsucht*, pp. 145–6.

19    Gröbli, *Sehnsucht*, pp. 48–50.

20    Bynum briefly discusses Nikolaus in her study of the religious significance of food but views him as an outlier. She argued that that food is at the center of women's piety, while '[b]etween the early Middle Ages and the fifteenth century, when the illiterate Swiss hermit Nicholas of Flüe (d.1487) became famous for living twenty years on the eucharist alone, such stories are not told of men', Caroline Walker Bynum, *Holy Feast and Holy Fast: The Religious Significance of Food to Medieval Women* (Berkeley: University of California Press, 1986), p. 95.

Vnd er hůb an vnd ſprach zů mir Si
heſt du diſe figur· Alſo iſt das gőtli
che weſen·Jn dem mitteln punckten
das iſt die vngeteÿlt gotheÿt darin=
nen ſich alle heÿligen erfrewen Die
drei ſpiczen dÿe do geen in den pun=
ckten des inwendigen czirckels·das ſeind die drei per=
ſon vnd geent auß von der einigen gotheÿt·Vnd ha=
ben vmbegriffen den himel vnd darzů alle welt dÿe

FIGURE 17.5     *Bruder Claus* (Augsburg, Peter Berger, 1487) USTC 744053, f. 5r

FIGURE 17.6    *Bruder Claus* (Augsburg, Peter Berger, 1487) USTC 744053, f. 7v

and others have suggested Klaus's spirituality was feminised, though there is little explicitly gendered feminine in this narrative or the woodcut illustrations other than his fasting. Elements of this image are gendered male, such as the hair, modest habit, and Nikolaus's wilderness hermitage. These images are integral to this book's operation and design. They establish the character of 'Bruder Klaus' as a forest-dwelling hermit and teacher, and establish the relationship between the living saint, the pilgrim's narrative voice, and the reader. The geographic location and other details clearly evoke the hermitage and chapel near Ranft. In other words, *this* hermit is 'Bruder Klaus,' the well-known living saint, but he is performing a particular kind of piety unique to hermits: living in isolation, teaching pilgrims, and praying in a natural landscape. These early representations of 'Bruder Klaus' adapt gender-neutral generic qualities of a living saint (prayer, teaching, asceticism) to include elements specific to the text.

Distilling a saint's charismatic qualities to emphasise the most essential performance of Christian piety informs Geerard Leeu's author portrait depicting a pious Magdalena in prayer. The image was commissioned for the first print edition of the *Golden Litany* and is closely related to other depictions of female living saints as well as depictions of both male and female recipients of the stigmata. The artist presents Magdalena kneeling in a chapel (Fig. 17.2). The tiled flooring and the angle of the altar emphasise the perspectival lines of the stigmata shooting from the apparition of Jesus on the altar to Magdalena's hands, feet, and side. A small slit in Magdalena's otherwise perfectly modest habit shows the reception of the side wound and her hair is covered with a veil. A line animating the reception of the stigmata traces one of Christ's wounds on his feet to her left foot. The technique of presenting the stigmata as a series of lines tracing from the wounds of a resurrected Jesus to the penitent's bodies originates with the well-known depictions of Francis of Assisi. Though identification with Christ's wounds and reception of the stigmata became important for medieval women's spirituality, as a Clarissan, Magdalena's stigmata may be read as belonging to the Franciscan visual and religious tradition even if it is also more generally an aspect of female piety. Her eyes gaze at Jesus, her smile is gentle. The later design cut by Snellaert's woodcutter is less graceful, her face less precisely rendered, but it captures the details of the chapel and wounds in the same way. The opening lines of the *Golden Litany* describe Magdalena as 'a very holy devout woman'.[21] According to the opening narrative, she spends

---

21    'ee[n] seer heylige devote vrouwe gehieten Magdalena', *Een Schoen mirakel vanden open-baringhen der gulden letanie*, (Antwerp: Geraert Leeu, 1492).

each day and night dedicated to prayer exercises focusing on the sorrows and wounds of Jesus Christ. While praying, she asks for a more perfect prayer and a better understanding of the pain of the Crucifixion. She is greeted by a vision of Jesus's open wounds, and he delivers the text of the *Golden Litany* in a letter. Though her revelation and reception of the stigmata came under suspicion by Johannes Nider, as I have argued elsewhere, the widespread circulation of Magdalena's writing in both print and manuscript suggests that there were different gendered hermeneutics for establishing spiritual authority. Outside of the historical context of her religious community, Magdalena's teaching becomes authorised by revelatory experience and the efficacy of the prayer itself.[22]

As with manuscript copies of prayers attributed to Nikolaus of Flüe, manuscript copies of Magdalena's treatises are undecorated, indicating authorship, if it is stated at all, in rubricated titles. Though it is possible that these prayer books do not include information about Magdalena's life out of concerns about the legitimacy of her spiritual experiences, I believe it is more likely that creators of manuscripts selected Magdalena's prayers with full knowledge of her reputation and out of a conviction that her prayers were useful. The *Golden Litany* most often appeared in personalised manuscript prayer books following the Hours, often alongside indulgences and other prayers attributed to saints, popes, and other respected religious figures. They would have been used over an extended period of time, and likely with guidance from a spiritual director. These elements had to be recreated by printers through author portraits and prefatory narratives.

When considered alongside the extant manuscript tradition, the importance of the prefatory image for Leeu's edition becomes clearer. The printed books needed the additional narrative, authorship attribution, and author portrait to meet the needs of a generic reader. They also allowed the prayers to function in a way similar to what we know about daily devotion and the structures of support and education in late medieval religious communities, where oral instruction was an essential part of religious formation and books were often community property. It seems plausible that these extant manuscripts, most from Observant religious communities with high literacy rates, were originally part of larger libraries that included works describing Magdalena's life and miracles, perhaps even in manuscripts used for table reading. Familiarity with Magdalena's reputation in Clarissan communities would eliminate the need to establish her religious authority in personalised prayer books. When

---

22    Gregory, *Thinking of their Sisters*, pp. 88–91.

removed from this original context and transposed north to the Low Countries, Magdalena's prayers required paratext to establish her authority and guide their use.

Govaert Bac is the first known printer to use a different woodcut showing a generic pious woman for the prefatory image in an edition of Magdalena's *Golden Litany*. Rather than reproducing a representation of Magdalena receiving the stigmata in an enclosed space, Bac cut a new version of a depiction of a woman in secular dress kneeling before the Christ Child nailed to a tree (Fig. 17.7).

This woodcut closely follows one first used in another of Leeu's books, an illustrated narrative issued in 1488 with the title *Die gheestelike Kintsheyt Ihesu ghemoraliseert* [On the Moralised Spiritual Childhood of Jesus]. This woodcut appeared at the end of the text and illustrated an account of a Christian soul praying before the Christchild, who had been nailed to the tree by the seven virtues. Rather than representing the written narrative, Leeu's artist transposed the scene to a pastoral landscape, removing the striking iconography of Christ crucified by the Virtues. By using this image to introduce Magdalena's prayers, Bac removed all references to the historical Magdalena's spiritual authority. She was no longer a pious enclosed woman who received the stigmata, and instead became a generic soul or prayerful woman. The praying figure is gendered female with the elegant low-cut gown with loose flowing hair, suggesting sinfulness and sexual impropriety, in contrast to the modest habit and veil that marked Magdalena's female piety in earlier editions. Ina Kok proposed that Bac re-used this woodcut from a now-lost edition of *On the Moralised Spiritual Childhood of Jesus*, perhaps copying all thirty-seven original woodcuts.[23] I think it just as likely that he commissioned the woodcut for use in the *Golden Litany* as this is the only illustration from Leeu's *Spiritual Childhood* that Bac is known to have printed and he used it in two editions of the *Golden Litany*. While Leeu's author portrait for his edition of the *Golden Litany* emphasised Magdalena's spiritual authority as a living saint to authorise the text, Bac's prefatory image includes none of the visual symbols communicating Magdalena's unique spiritual reputation. Instead, the woodcut's design highlights the ways in which *this* praying woman is like the reader, a penitent soul who is devoted to Jesus. It shifts the focus of the text from an unattainable miracle (Magdalena's reception of the stigmata) to an attainable spiritual practice (praying as she did before the crucifix).

---

23    Kok, *Woodcuts in Incunabula*, vol 1, pp. 250–1.

FIGURE 17.7 *Die gulden litanie vander passien Christi* (Antwerpen, Govaert Bac, [1493–1495]) USTC 436199

Replacing author portraits with more generic depictions of the prayerful soul became more common during the sixteenth century. This substitution of the iconography of a living saint through an author portrait with a depiction of generic holy person can be seen in the sixteenth-century editions of Bertha Jacobsz's books and later editions of *Bruder Klaus*, which used passion images rather than the distinctive prayer wheel to illustrate his prayers. I focus here on her *A Devout Book on the Passion of Christ*, which was published with an author portrait in several early editions. Both of her published works also incorporated woodcuts depicting scenes from the passion of Christ. Unlike books produced decades earlier, the earliest copies of Bertha Jacobs' *Devout Book on the Passion of Christ* combine an author portrait with the book's title on a single page. In these woodcuts, Bertha kneels before Jesus in an interior space. Though not every edition included an author portrait, in those which did, Bertha is dressed modestly, and the bed of her cell is visible in the distance, reminding the viewer of the way that she has dedicated her life to constant prayer. Like Nikolaus and Magdalena, she is performing the role of a living saint through prayer, teaching, and humility. Bertha's role as a teacher and author is emphasised in the title above the author portrait: this book was made and written by Sister Bertken.[24] The full titles also clearly state Bertha's religious profession as an anchoress in Utrecht.

As with known copies of the writing of Magdalena and Nikolaus, near-contemporary manuscripts do not include Bertha's biography or a visual representation of her. For instance, Berlin Staatsbibl. Ms Germ Oct 190 153, dated to the end of the fifteenth century, includes a song written by Bertha with the incipit: 'This song was written by Sister Bertha, the Anchoress from Utrecht (Dit liedekijn heeft gemaect hairt suster die clusenarinne t utrecht).' Bertha is also represented as a generic living saint in some editions of her books and sometimes linked to representations of the Loving Soul. Printers also repurposed other generic representations of pious women to illustrate Bertha's books. The first edition by Berntsz, issued in Utrecht in 1515, re-uses a block from Hans Schaufelin's 1480 edition of Otto von Passau's *24 Elders*. Visually, the block is related to the iconography in Bac's edition of the *Golden Litany*, as it too presents the Loving Soul, in this case kneeling before the throne of God rather than a crucified Christchild. An even more literal example of excising a living saint's unique characteristics occurs in Jan Severszoon's editions of Bertha's book. Each edition re-used a woodcut originally depicting Catherine

---

24    The phrase *gemaket van suster bertken* is in the 1516 title, which is expanded to *gemaket ende bescrcreven* in the 1516 edition.

of Siena tormented by demons for Bertha's author portrait, from which the demons had been sliced away. The block was also used to represent Geertruid von Oosten in his 1517 *Divisiechroniek*. Severszoon's woman praying in front of an altar in modest attire is not an exact portrait of Catherine, Geertruit, *or* Bertken, but rather a stylised representation of a pious everywoman engaged in skillful prayer.[25] Without a distinctive author portrait, these books introduced Bertha through a textual biography and interspersed her prayers and lessons with devotional woodcuts. The shift from distinct author portraits to more general prefatory images may simply have been a pragmatic choice as printers often re-used blocks on hand when they could plausibly be linked to other narratives. As paratext replaced in-person conversation with a living saint, and then author portraits were replaced with repurposed woodcuts, the distinctive qualities of living saints were diminished.

Encountering the teaching of a living saint through a sixteenth-century printed book differed significantly from near-contemporary accounts from those who knew them best, and thus often obscured gendered aspects of an individual's piety. For instance, Bertha's confessor detailed her prayer life and daily work, emphasising her humility, modest dress, and chastity and using adjectives that highlighted the feminised aspects of her spirituality. Printed books condensed this career into a single image intended to only assert her piety and capture the physical space of her enclosure. Similarly, though contemporary records describe Nikolaus receiving visitors, inspiring sermons, and offering spiritual advice, the printed books downplayed his relative freedom, authority, and erased his family completely, these gendered elements of his life are absent from printed books. The historical Magdalena's experiences as a child oblate, the limits of enclosure, and accusations of false mystical experiences are also gendered elements of her religious career entirely absent from printed editions of her work. Instead, their author portraits emphasised the similarities between these figures that had made them living saints: co-suffering with Jesus, modest dress, contemplating a devotional image, and isolation in a sacred space. These visual signifiers of sanctity were available to Christians of any gender, and were well-suited to introducing prayers that would be useful for all Christian people.

---

25    *Een boecxken*, pp. 6–7.

## 4    Conclusion: Gender, Fame, and Piety

Early author portraits that opened printed prayer books offered prospective buyers visual proof of the efficacy of the prayers themselves: they show physical signs of the prayers working, whether through Magdalena's stigmata, Bertha's visions, or Nikolaus's inedia. These illustrations emphasised the importance of teaching as a form of spiritual labor, and provide a visual guide for the correct way to pray before the altar and contemplate the experience of being crucified with Christ. The performance of piety for each of these living saints follows the same general themes regardless of gender: isolation, penitence, the work of teaching, and the obligation to share with the community successful prayer techniques and spiritual revelations. By the end of the fifteenth century, printers had already started introducing generic woodcuts of holy individuals into the role of author portrait, as with Govaert Bac's edition of the *Golden Litany*. The gendered piety of an individual—such as Klaus's mountain hermitage, Bertha's urban anchorhold, or Magdalena's stigmata—were elided into forms of devotion that were less explicitly gendered, such as passion devotion.

Similarities in design and purpose between *Bruder Klaus, The Golden Litany* and *A Devout Book on the Passion of Christ* are representative of the new devotional books printed in Europe in the last decades of the fifteenth century. Such books were to be portable, illustrated, entertaining, and taught prayer techniques centered on devotion to Jesus rather than more gendered forms of piety. Each of these books—published after the deaths of their respective authors—represents both the fame of the authors and a way of understanding what piety *looked* like around 1500: a prayerful penitent contemplating Jesus on the Cross. That sixteenth-century editions of these books replaced the prayerful author portrait with depictions of Jesus reinforces the sense that the gendered and uniquely inimitable spiritual qualities of living saints were of secondary importance in the design of prefatory images and title pages for prayer books.

Although the laws and norms of late medieval Europe might determine which avenues of religious devotion a person could pursue, the same criteria for piety were used to promote the reputations of living saints. Each of the authors discussed here were famous in a modern sense: they were internationally known and respected. People talked about them, bought books about them, and traveled to see them. Whether they were locally supported or suspected of possible false teachings, the success of their books reveals a shared trajectory: renouncing the world, successful prayer practice that leads to revelations, which are taught to the community and eventually written down.

Teaching others to pray was an essential part of each living saint's professional labor. Making such lessons available in printed books would have been a natural extension of that social function. While hagiographers documented miraculous events and visions with care, a living saint's fame began with communal recognition of their exemplary piety through the active work of receiving guests and offering spiritual advice.

Women like Magdalena and Bertha could not live as hermits in the woods as Nikolaus did, while married parents like Nikolaus of Flüe could typically not be accepted into a monastic community as a full member, though many did live in monastic communities as third-order members. Bertha Jacobs was able to leave her canoness community, associated with the *Devotio Moderna*'s Windesheim chapter, to become an anchoress, but would not have been able to retire to a wilderness. Though child oblates like Magdalena sometimes were able to leave the community they had been placed into rather than making a monastic profession, it was rare. In addition to lacking the social skills to cope with a world outside the convent, child oblates generally would have had difficulty marrying or working. Many stayed within their communities as lay brothers or sisters if they did not take monastic vows. This may be why Magdalena Beutler did not leave the community she grew up in or seek to transfer to a different kind of enclosed life. Nikolaus's responsibilities as father and husband continued after leaving his family, as surviving information about visits from wife and children and his involvement in fulfilling legal obligations regarding property attest. After their deaths, perhaps because the authors could no longer be visited, the books became a kind of paper-made enclosure, displaying piety and acting as a mediator for religious education.

The printed editions of *Bruder Klaus*, the *Golden Litany*, and *A Devout Book on the Passion of Christ* downplay these gender-specific aspects of religious life in favor of gender-neutral characteristics of pious spiritual teachers guiding visitors to a more skillful prayer practice. This is typical for illustrated devotional books produced before 1550, many of which emphasised gender-neutral aspects of piety to market books to a wider potential audience. Their designs incorporated elements *both* of manuscript prayer books *and* of popular devotional practices (pilgrimage, visiting anchorholds, consulting with spiritual experts). Their title pages and woodcuts recognised that gender determined what forms of religious life a person might pursue, but did not restrict which readers might attain salvation. Collectively, illustrated vernacular prayer manuals were the product of a European religious culture that valued spiritual teachers who offered clear and replicable information about how to pray.

# CHAPTER 18

# Learning Your Papist ABCs: Gendered Instruction and Printed Books in Clandestine Catholic Schools in the Dutch Republic

*Elise Watson*

On 13 November 1699, a frustrated group of Reformed pastors and elders in North Brabant sent a printed complaint directly to the States General, the governing body of the Dutch Republic. This group was writing to protest what they called the recurrent and 'violent impudence of the papists'. They were particularly concerned about the scandal of multiple Catholic schools in their community, which they noted were 'constantly supplied with young beguines, giving great cause for superstition'.[1] While this complaint included many other details of this so-called papist impudence, it reserved its greatest vitriol for these schools and their female teachers.

Complaints from Reformed consistories, synods and secular councils about the presence of these schools and the women who taught in them were ubiquitous in this period.[2] Educating the next generation was a high priority for minority Catholics in the Dutch Republic, and the lay religious women who called themselves spiritual daughters (*geestelijke dochters*) were instrumental in this process. The educational programmes they ran, and the schools they established for girls, called *maagdenhuizen*, demanded enormous quantities of confessional print, particularly catechisms and schoolbooks. These women helped print these books and sell them in bookshops, in permanent stalls on the street, and door-to-door. For spiritual daughters, their gender played an essential role in their use and distribution of pedagogical books. It made them more susceptible to public criticism from Reformed authorities, who saw them as more easily corruptible and superstitious. However, the invisibility of their gender and ambiguity of their religious status also meant that this criticism

---

1   Noord-Hollands Archief (henceforth NHA), 279 Collectie van aanwinsten van het R.-K. Bisdom Haarlem, inv. 224.

2   Joke Spaans, 'Orphans and students: recruiting boys and girls for the Holland Mission', in Benjamin J. Kaplan, Judith Pollmann, Bob Moore and Henk van Nierop (eds.), *Catholic Communities in Protestant States: Britain and the Netherlands* (Manchester: Manchester University Press, 2009), pp. 183–99; Christine Kooi, *Calvinists and Catholics During Holland's Golden Age: Heretics and Idolaters* (Cambridge: Cambridge University Press, 2012), pp. 162–4.

### (1)

## Aen de Hoogh Mog. Heeren

*Staten Generael der Vereenighde Nederlanden*

*Requeste voor het Classis van Peel- en Kempelandt, Meyerye van 's Hertogenbosch.*

Eeft onderdanig te kennen het Classis van Peel-en Kempelandt, Meyerye van 's Hertogen-bosch, dat sy in April van den voorleden jare 1698. haer genoodtsaeckt hebben gevonden aen U Hoogh Mog. gantsch ootmoedigh by Requeste voor te dragen in wat voegen de stoutigheden der Papisten dagelyckx in de voorsz. Meyerye toenamen, directelyck strydende jegen U Hoog Mog. pieuse intentie, Placaten, en verscheyde Resolutien van tijdt tot tijdt geëmaneert en genomen, dat het U Hoogh Mog. wel gelieft heeft gehadt op de voorsz. Requeste by der selver Resolutie in dato den aghtsten April 1698. goedt te vinden en te verstaen, dat copye van de selve Requeste gesonden soude werden aen den Hoogh-schout, midtsgaders Quartier-schouten en andere Officieren van de Stadt en Meyerye van 's Hertogen-bosch, en deselve gelasten yeder inden haren haer te informeren op het geene in de voorsz. Requeste wierdt te kennen gegeven, en de Placaten en Reglementen van haer Hoogh Mog. op dat subject geëmaneert na behooren te doen executeren, en aen haer Hoogh Mog. te reseriberen wat by haer respectivelyck daer in sal wesen ondervonden en de gedaen; ende ingevolge van dien de Supplianten gehoopt hadden het selve, soo als behoorde, van een goedt effect soude sijn geweest, doch tot haer leetwesen sich nu wederom genoodtsaeckt vinden Uw Hoogh Mog. moylijck te vallen, en voor te dragen, dat de voorsz. Uw Hoogh Mog. Resolutie niet anders heeft geopereert, als dat men maer seer weynigh tijdt heeft konnen bespeuren dat de selve is geobserveert ende naegekomen geworden, en zedert de stoutigheden der Papisten in allen deelen niet alleen weder sijn geworden als te vooren, maer noch meerder en grooter aengewassen en toegenomen; namentlijck, in het plegen van haren gewaenden Godtsdienst, met het doen van openbare Bedevaerden, insonderheydt in het Dorp van Beeck, de Doncks-wyingh genaemt, daer in een groote meenighte vanMenschen en alderhande Paepen assisteeren, ende als dan in het openbaer met de soo genaemde Beelden van Heyligen hare afgoderyen en superstitien bedrijven; gelyck mede tot Oirs, daer St. Jans Hooft vertoont werdt, en op vele andere plaetsen meer; daer men sonder de minste schroom diergelycke afgoderyë publicq pleegt tot groote ergenisse van de Gereformeerden; wordende tot Oirschot alle jaren publicq de Mis gedaen in de open lucht; alomme, den dagh des Heeren met allerhande wulpsheden ontheylight, de geordende Klooster-Monnicken soo veel als oyt met volkomen liberteyt gevonden, die het Landt doorloopen, en haer beurs gemaeckt hebbende by de onnosele Ingesetenen, alles in haer Kloosters slepen, en oorsake zijn van veel twist, onluste en verwerringen, tot soo verre dat 'er meenighmael moorden en doodtslagen uyt voorkomen, soo als onlanghs omtrent het Dorp van Someren is voorgevallen, en ongetwijfelt aen Uw Hoogh Mog. sal bekent zijn; dervende selfs soo geordende als ongeordende Papen tot Romen proces voeren wie dat besitter van die en andere plaetsen onder het ressort van Uw Hoog Mog. gelegen sal wesen, zijnde tot Geldorp een Paepsche Voster, dewelcke aldaer door den Heer jegens wil en danck van den Officier wert gemainteneert, gelijck op meer andere plaetsen geschiedt; tot Best twee

Paepsche

*13 Nov:*

*1699.*

---

FIGURE 18.1  Printed complaint from the classis of Peel and Kempenland to the States General on the subject of 'papist impudence' (1699), NHA, 279, inv. 224

rarely translated into direct action. As a result, due to the assumptions made by men in positions of political and ecclesiastical power, spiritual daughters were remarkably effective teachers and book distributors in the Dutch Republic.

The unique position of these spiritual daughters in Dutch society has attracted the attention of gender historians for almost a century.[3] Spiritual daughters find their company in a group of many other women in the medieval and early modern periods who evaded the normative dichotomy of marriage or the cloister (*aut maritus aut murus*), either by joining established tertiary orders or living by their own informal rules of religious life.[4] Even if they wanted to, they were prohibited from becoming formally cloistered both by anti-Catholic ordinances within the Dutch Republic, and by the Catholic ecclesiastical missionary organisation, the Dutch Mission (*Missio Hollandica*). In spite of this, spiritual daughters forged paths for themselves as religious women who were also part of a marginalised religious group. They found confessors, to whom they made vows of chastity and obedience, and lived either on their own or in communities with other likeminded women. Marit Monteiro estimates that over 5,000 of these women lived and worked in the Dutch Republic throughout the seventeenth century.[5] They also went by many names: while their superiors generally called them spiritual virgins (*geestelijke maagden*), they were often referred to by Reformed authorities as *kloppen*. In most egodocuments that survive in their hands, they referred to themselves as spiritual daughters (*geestelijke dochters* or *filiae spirituales*). They interacted with books as printers, booksellers, and readers.[6]

---

3　The first notable study of these women was the doctoral thesis of Eugenia Thiessing, published as *Over klopjes en kwezels* (Utrecht: Dekker, 1935). For two more recent studies that summarise twentieth-century scholarship see Evelyne Verheggen, *Beelden voor passie en hartstocht. Bid-en devotieprenten in de Noordelijke Nederlanden, 17de en 18de eeuw* (Zutphen: Walburg Pers, 2006) and Joke Spaans' investigation of the community called De Hoek in Haarlem, *De Levens der Maechden. Het verhaal van een religieuze vrouwengemeenschap in de eerste helft van de zeventiende eeuw* (Hilversum: Verloren, 2012). The most foundational work is still Marit Monteiro, *Geestelijke maagden: leven tussen klooster en wereld in Noord-Nederland gedurende de zeventiende eeuw* (Hilversum: Verloren, 1996).

4　Susan E. Dinan, 'Female Religious Communities Beyond the Convent', in Allyson M. Poska, Jane Couchman and Katherine A. Melver (eds.), *The Ashgate Research Companion to Women and Gender in Early Modern Europe* (Farnham: Ashgate, 2013), p. 124.

5　Marit Monteiro, 'Power in Piety: Inspiration, Ambitions and Strategies of Spiritual Virgins in the Northern Netherlands during the Seventeenth Century', in Laurence Lux-Sterritt and Carmen M. Mangion (eds.), *Gender, Catholicism and Spirituality: Women and the Roman Catholic Church in Britain and Europe, 1200–1900* (Basingstoke: Palgrave Macmillan, 2010), p. 115.

6　The term *kloppen* has an unclear etymology, but potentially pejorative associations. For the most recent scholarship on the work of these women in the book trade see Elise Watson,

FIGURE 18.2    Engraved depiction of a spiritual daughter by Jacob de Man ca. 1680. Museum
Catharijneconvent, Utrecht, photo Ruben de Heer. OKM dp10040

## 1    Spiritual Daughters and Catholic Schools

The spiritual daughters lived in a Dutch Republic that was both fragmented and strengthened by religious division. Since 1581, Catholics had been banned from any sort of public religious practice by the States General of the United Provinces. However, the 1579 Union of Utrecht guaranteed religious freedom to Catholics and the right not to face persecution for private beliefs. Catholics persisted as a significant proportion of the population, carving out niches for themselves in society. In 1586, the States General banned Catholic schools and prohibited the use of any sort of 'papist' reading material in their curricula.[7] After the Synod of Dordrecht in 1618, different cities began to institute requirements for schoolmasters to affirm their adherence to the Reformed faith. Local synods were responsible for ensuring that schools were teaching Reformed curricula and shutting down any papist schools that had sprung up in the meantime. This was, predictably, difficult to enforce, and implementation was selective and uneven.[8]

Catholic schools endured in spite of these rules. Some parents in Holland sent their children to be educated in convents in the Generality Lands, majority Catholic lands governed directly by the States General after 1648.[9] However, in areas with large populations of Catholics such as Utrecht, confessional schools could exist with little interference. Catholic schools sometimes threatened the attendance rates of the local Reformed schools so severely that they were reported to the authorities in order to reduce competition.[10] These schools were usually run by a combination of priests and spiritual daughters. While few

---

'The Jesuitesses in the Bookshop: Catholic Lay Sisters' Participation in the Dutch Book Trade, 1650–1750', *Studies in Church History*, 57 (2021), pp. 163–184. See also Lienke Paulina Leuven, *De boekhandel te Amsterdam door katholieken gedreven tijdens de Republiek* (Epe: Hooiberg, 1951), p. 28; Paul Hoftijzer, 'Women in the early modern Dutch book trade', in Suzanna van Dijk, Lia van Gemert, and Sheila Ottway (eds.), *Writing the history of women's writing: toward an international approach* (Amsterdam: Royal Netherlands Academy of Arts and Sciences, 2001), pp. 211–22.

7    P.Th.F.M. Boekholt and E.P. de Booy, *Geschiedenis van de school in Nederland vanaf de middeleeuwen tot aan de huidige tijd* (Assen: Van Gorcum, 1987), pp. 18–9.

8    Boekholt and de Booy, *Geschiedenis van de school*, pp. 20, 26; Andrew Pettegree and Arthur der Weduwen, *The Bookshop of the World: Making and Trading Books in the Dutch Golden Age* (New Haven, CT: Yale University Press, 2019), p. 154; Kooi, *Calvinists and Catholics*, pp. 207–12.

9    Kooi, *Calvinists and Catholics*, p. 210.

10   Boekholt and de Booy, *Geschiedenis van de school*, p. 26; Willem Frijhoff, 'The confessions and the book in the Dutch Republic', in Heinz Schilling and Stefan Ehrenpreis (eds.), *Frühneuzeitliche Bildungsgeschichte der Reformierten in konfessionsvergleich-ender*

towns had enough Catholics to occupy their own distinctive area of the city, Delft had its own *Papenhoek*, 'papist's corner', centred around a house church and a school.[11] In order to educate their students in the faith, spiritual daughters required a large selection of printed confessional literature. This included simple ABC books, instructional songbooks, catechisms of every length, and Bible storybooks. In the seventeenth century, printing firms also started to produce cheap books aimed at children, usually broadsheets with simple woodcut illustrations. Educational books could be bought in bookshops, but were also advertised and sold by the schoolmasters themselves. The material used to produce these makes it clear that they were to be used until they fell apart.[12]

Spiritual daughters interacted with this didactic print in a variety of ways. Some, like the seventeenth-century spiritual daughter Hendrikje Cool, worked as sellers of Catholic educational books. Cool, part of an important Catholic printing family, sold Catholic books out of her family home on the Warmoesstraat in Amsterdam. Her probate inventory demonstrates a huge variety of printed pedagogical material that would have found its home in Catholic schools. Pedagogical print, mostly catechisms, makes up more than a quarter of her entire stock. These were also generally the least expensive books in her shop, rarely valued at more than one guilder each.[13] Other spiritual daughters sold books on the street in temporary or permanent book stalls, including catechisms and ABC books. Some even sold rosaries and devotional works door-to-door.[14] Spiritual daughters were also some of the most committed and enthusiastic teachers of Catholic children. In his report of 1658, one Carmelite missionary commended them for their exceptional dedication to imparting commitment to right doctrine in their students.[15] Parents would send their children significant distances to be taught by renowned spiritual

*Perspektive* (Berlin: Duncker & Humblot, 2007), p. 193; Pettegree and der Weduwen, *Bookshop of the World*, p. 154.

11  Kooi, *Calvinists and Catholics*, p. 180.

12  Monteiro, *Geestelijke maagden*, pp. 94–5; Annemarie van Toorn, Marijke Spies and Sietske Hoogerhuis, 'Christen Jeugd, leerd Konst en Deugd. De zeventiende eeuw', in Netty Heimeriks and Willem van Toorn (eds.), *De hele Bibelebontse berg: De geschiedenis van het kinderboek in Nederland & Vlaanderen van de middeleeuwen tot heden* (Amsterdam: Querido, 1990), pp. 109–11; Pettegree and der Weduwen, *Bookshop of the World*, pp. 159, 85.

13  Amsterdam City Archives, Archief van de Notarissen ter Standplaats Amsterdam (5075), Johannes Commelin (226), Minuutacten no. 5619, fols 542^r–66^r. For more on Cool as a bookseller see Elise Watson, 'The Jesuitesses in the Bookshop', pp. 163–84.

14  Hoftijzer, 'Women in the early modern Dutch book trade', p. 215; Leuven, *De Boekhandel te Amsterdam*, p. 42; Jeroen Salman, *Pedlars and the Popular Press: Itinerant Distribution Networks in England and the Netherlands 1600–1850* (Leiden: Brill, 2013), pp. 196–204.

15  Petrus a Matre Dei, *Clara Relatio missionis Hollandicae et provinciarum confoederatum ... anno 1658* (Rotterdam: Hendriksen, 1891), p. 94. Cited in Kooi, *Calvinists and Catholics*, pp. 208–9.

daughters. This sometimes even included Reformed parents and children.[16] The *maagdenhuis* in Amsterdam grew at such a rate that its rules had to be rewritten in 1685 to accommodate the flow of new students and ensure that the school had an appropriate level of male clerical oversight, adding four new priests as supervisors.[17] In their capacity as teachers, spiritual daughters would probably have worked as book distributors as well, as schoolteachers commonly wrote, published and sold educational books to their students themselves.[18]

## 2    Catholic and Protestant Conflict

This enthusiasm came at a cost, making schools the centre of local power struggles even within the Catholic Church. According to the diary of a contemporary witness, around 1649 Roeland de Pottere, a Jesuit priest in Delft, received an assignment to take charge of the local *maagdenhuis*.[19] The school, founded by Jesuit Lodewijk Makeblijde in 1626, had been under the supervision of two spiritual daughters. While one, Maria Bartolomeus, was the headmistress of the school, and had contributed essentially all of the funds required to build it, the property was in the name of the other, Anna Jans. Since Jans was known to be far less well off, this protected the school against demands for bribes or inquests by magistrates. Once de Pottere was appointed, Jans became tired of being used as a figurehead. She rejected de Pottere's authority, and protested against his appointment so vehemently that the school, in a time of increased persecution in Delft, had to be split in two. Jans claimed the best front rooms for her lessons, leaving de Pottere in the back. Though she was renowned for her teaching, so much so that students came from as far as Amsterdam to learn from her, Anna eventually left the school to move into the local beguinage. However, this caused some regrets from the sisters there: as one noted slyly, 'If I had known that Father De Pottere would be so happy to be rid of Anna Jans, we would not have gotten involved.'[20] Anna Jans demonstrates how spiritual daughters could weaponise their value in these gendered roles.

16    M.G. Spiertz, 'Priest and Layman in a Minority Church: The Roman Catholic Church in the Northern Netherlands 1592–1686', *Studies in Church History*, 26 (1989), p. 300.
17    NHA, 225 Oud-Katholiek Bisdom Haarlem, inv. 377.
18    Pettegree and der Weduwen, *Bookshop of the World*, pp. 151–2.
19    This account is reproduced in Paul Begheyn s.j., 'The pastoral journeys of the Dutch Jesuit Roeland de Pottere (1584–1675) in Delft and environs: An Eyewitness About the Years 1621–1662', *LIAS*, 35.1–2 (2008), pp. 186–208.
20    Begheyn, 'Roeland de Pottere', pp. 197–8.

Consistorial objections to spiritual daughters teaching in schools were frequent and numerous. Christine Kooi records these complaints across the consistories of Haarlem, Delft, Dordrecht and Amsterdam in the 1650s.[21] Printed grievances about the spiritual daughters were also prolific. Reformed consistories complained that spiritual daughters were aggressive with their catechising strategies, and were circulating too much Catholic literature. A series of edicts in the 1630s and 1640s by the States of Holland castigated them specifically, as well as their teaching of 'papist superstition'.[22] The Synod of Gelderland lamented in 1658 that '*kloppen* schools will cause papist impudence to awaken superstition'.[23] In the cities, especially in the more population-dense province of Holland, Reformed consistories protested the aggressive catechising strategies of local Catholics. In 1632, the classis of Gouda complained that spiritual daughters were creeping into the houses of their Reformed neighbours and preaching to them in their beds, reading them the Catholic catechism while they were powerless to object. The spiritual daughter Maritgen Wouters raised consistorial eyebrows when she welcomed her niece into the Amsterdam *maagdenhuis* against the will of the girl's Reformed mother.[24] The image of spiritual daughters as predators, filling the minds of children with dangerous heresy, was ever-present for Reformed ministers. Writing in the 1690s, Martin Wijbinga, a Reformed minister in Gelderland, reported on the 'papist impudence' taking place in the barony of Hedel. While the other papists were causing chaos in the town on feast days and Sundays, he wrote, the *kloppen* took this opportunity to corrupt the minds of local children and set them against their Reformed elders.[25]

Despite the intensity of these complaints, they never seemed to crystallise into action. For example, the printed complaint sent to the States General in 1699 mentioned in the introduction was the second such complaint from this group in a row, as the first had been completely ignored and no action had been taken.[26] The protestations of Reformed ministers and consistories rarely seemed to be heeded, and although decrees were passed and fines were levied

---

21   Kooi, *Calvinists and Catholics*, pp. 208–12.

22   Charles H. Parker, *Faith on the Margins: Catholics and Catholicism in the Dutch Golden Age* (Cambridge, MA: Harvard University Press, 2008), p. 142. See also Monteiro, *Geestelijke Maagden*, p. 89.

23   Gelders Archief (henceforth GA), 0336 Nederlandse Hervormde Kerk, Synode van Gelderland te Arnhem (henceforth NHK), no. 2, Article 10, 1658.

24   Spaans, 'Orphans and Students', p. 195.

25   GA, NHK, inv. 93, f. 1ʳ.

26   NHA, 279 Collectie van aanwinsten van het R.-K. Bisdom Haarlem, inv. 224.

against the spiritual daughters they seemed to have little to no impetus for actual enforcement.[27] Indeed, these printed and written complaints seemed to replace this implementation altogether. The relationship between gender and Catholicism, in particular women's perceived susceptibility to be unwitting and foolish tools of dangerous papist ideals, has long been characterised, especially in scholarship of English Catholicism. Reformed ministers and magistrates used print to depict this image of spiritual daughters both as sinister papists and irrational, easily deceived women.[28]

This lack of action by authorities meant that opponents of Dutch Catholics needed to take matters into their own hands. In fact, as the classis of Amsterdam wrote in a resolution to its ministers in 1639, they should 'preach against popery, disprove thoroughly its principal arguments, refute completely its circulated books, visit households often, and if possible, confront the priests or at least the papists'.[29] This confrontation was necessary, as little existed to stop these papist books from circulating. While booksellers could be seen as pedlars of dangerous ideas, sometimes even being compared to Jesuits for their aggressive persuasive strategies, they were generally regarded as businesspeople and left alone.[30] Well-respected printers and booksellers in Amsterdam like Joan Blaeu and Louis Elzevier printed and sold Catholic books with little hindrance or detriment.[31] Catholic printers rarely faced any censure at all for printing Catholic material, and in fact formed a flourishing part of the Dutch book trade, especially in Amsterdam.[32] The public criticism of spiritual daughters, therefore, were the only censure they received for their activities.

---

27  Parker, *Faith on the Margins*, p. 44.

28  Kooi, *Calvinists and Catholics*, pp. 162–4, 209. For a similar analysis of this phenomenon among Catholic women in England see Frances E. Dolan, *Whores of Babylon: Catholicism, Gender, and Seventeenth-Century Print Culture* (Ithaca, NY: Cornell University Press, 1999), especially ch. 1 '"Home-bred Enemies": Imagining Catholics', pp. 16–44.

29  Translated and cited in Kooi, *Calvinists and Catholics*, p. 78.

30  This comparison is made explicit in the polemical pamphlet *Favlse position ofte Valschen regel van practijcke der Paepscher Kramers ende Koop-lieden* (Middelburg, 1617) USTC 1011037, cited in Salman, *Pedlars and the Popular Press*, pp. 33–4.

31  For example see their printing of Jesuit books in Paul Begheyn, s.j., *Jesuit Books in the Dutch Republic and its Generality Lands, 1567–1773* (Leiden: Brill, 2014).

32  Ingrid Weekhout, *Boekencensuur in de Noordelijke Nederlanden. De vrijheid van de drukpers in de zeventiende eeuw* (Den Haag: Sdu Uitgevers, 1998), pp. 99–100; Pettegree and der Weduwen, *Bookshop of the World*, pp. 338–44.

## 3      Spiritual Daughters 'Going to Culemborg'?

The case of Culemborg exemplifies the active apostolate of the spiritual daughters firsthand. Though geographically a part of the province of Gelderland, this city was technically a *vrijstad* (free city), in which many regular Dutch laws did not apply. It garnered a reputation as being a den of criminals and thieves, so much so that the phrase 'going to Culemborg' became a euphemism for bankruptcy in Amsterdam. The flexibility of these regulations allowed the spiritual daughters to establish a school there, one that was prominent enough to attract the children of several noble families and even a few Reformed students.[33] However, the presence of this multiconfessional Catholic school run by religious women was too controversial for even a free city. In 1668, the Synod of South Holland recommended that the city pass more laws that constrained the activity of the '*cloppen* and the papists'.[34] In response, in a mandate of 1669 the lord of Culemborg banned the Bible, the catechism, and all Catholic teaching material from schools, in addition to outlawing the existence of Catholic schools entirely.[35] This decree was followed by a careful list identifying all the spiritual daughters in the area, numbering 69 in total. By 1670, the list had to continue onto a new sheet, as more women continued to join the unofficial order in defiance of these decrees. In 1679, nine years later, an updated memorandum offered a defeated change in tone. Spiritual daughters could continue to operate their schools: however, they had to integrated Reformed books into their curriculum. They were also allowed to maintain their religious status, as long as no new women were consecrated.[36] In 1685, three spiritual daughters verified before a notary in Culemborg that they were, indeed, still teaching the catechism to children.[37]

This startling change in Culemborg likely had several causes. First, the intervening period had seen the invasion of French armies in the Disaster Year of 1672, who devastated the city. While these soldiers did not always have positive relationships with their Dutch co-religionists, they still represented a threatening, heretical force to the Reformed and religious liberation to the Catholics.[38]

---

33      Jaap Geraerts, *Patrons of the Old Faith: The Catholic Nobility in Utrecht and Guelders, c. 1580–1702* (Leiden: Brill, 2018), p. 94.

34      GA, 0370 Heren en graven van Culemborg (henceforth Culemborg), inv. 3058, no. 2.

35      GA, Culemborg, inv. 3058, no. 1, f. 1ʳ.

36      GA, Culemborg, inv. 3058, no. 5.

37      Parker, *Faith on the Margins*, p. 142.

38      Angela Vanhaelen, 'Utrecht's Transformations: Claiming the Dom through Representation, Iconoclasm and Ritual', *De Zeventiende Eeuw*, 21.2 (2005), pp. 354–74; Bertrand Forclaz, '"Rather French than Subject to the Prince of Orange": The Conflicting Loyalties of the

FIGURE 18.3    List of spiritual daughters in Culemborg from 1669–70. GA 0370 inv. 3058 no. 5, 1ʳ⁻ᵛ

This devastation precluded any meaningful implementation of anti-Catholic censorship. However, even before 1672 spiritual daughters and teachers were continuing to rise steadily in number. This indicates that Reformed authorities in Culemborg had no to shut these schools down in the first place. Even under the most direct censure, a command to cease teaching using Catholic books, the spiritual daughters were able to persevere until this demand was reversed completely, requesting the inclusion of Reformed books in a Catholic curriculum.

## 4    Gender, Education and Print

The case of Culemborg illustrates the multifaceted tensions that surrounded spiritual daughters' work in schools and in the book trade. While spiritual daughters faced few limitations in selling catechisms on the street, their

Utrecht Catholics during the French Occupation (1672–73)', *Church History and Religious Culture*, 87 (2007), pp. 509–33.

presence in schools was a much greater concern, as evidenced by the lord of Culemborg's attempt to ban Catholic books from schools. However, even when spiritual daughters were castigated for their work as teachers, they rarely if ever faced actual censure for this work. In most cases, any sort of direct action was replaced by public criticism, whether that came in the form of printed polemic or simply written complaints from the local Reformed minister or consistory.

The gender of the spiritual daughters played strongly into this dynamic. While Jesuits and secular priests could be imprisoned, tortured or exiled for their clearly treasonous positions, spiritual daughters were afforded a greater sense of security and stability due to their gender. They were a threat and an annoyance, and seen as having been misled by Catholicism in a deeply gendered way, but were not viewed as being capable of the same sort of sedition as a priest. For example, in a published pamphlet Reformed minister Samuel Ampzing called the spiritual daughters in Haarlem 'a swarm of crawling ants ... in a dirty papist anthill', inconvenient but unthreatening.[39] Similarly, in their efficacious proselytising and bookselling spiritual daughters were not seen as a serious menace, able to be reprimanded by public criticism alone.

Spiritual daughters played essential roles in Dutch Catholic society as printers, booksellers and teachers. The schools they ran crucially supplied generations of Catholic children and converts with the catechesis they sought to sustain the faith. This allowed them to fulfil roles that the more visible priests were not able to occupy. As a result, they were exceptionally productive and efficacious in their use and distribution of Catholic print. The 'constant supply of young beguines' in North Brabant that invited so much complaint may have rightfully deserved the Reformed ire they attracted, for their remarkable success in sustaining the Catholic faith.

---

39    Samuel Ampzing, *Svppressie vande vermeynde vergaderinge der iesvwyteszen door Vrbanus VIII* (Haarlem, 1632) USTC 1026054, f. A2ᵛ.

# PART 7

## *Gendered Perception and Reality*

∴

# CHAPTER 19

# The Keys to the Forbidden Books: the Duchess of Almodóvar and Her Libraries

*Laura Guinot Ferri*

This chapter analyses the roles played by women in the strategies that families developed for the circulation and distribution of books.[1] The objective is to understand not only how inheritance between members of the high nobility was managed, a better known and more studied question, but also the specific forms in which female cultural practices were expressed. I would also like to underline the importance of family and emotional ties between women in the same family, and the relevance of these ties for younger women. All of this will make it possible to study how precisely this position as aristocratic women allowed them to enact agency through the process of decision-making on questions related to the legacy of tangible and intangible assets. Therefore, we understand this agency or capacity for action not as a transgression in their gender roles, but as the expression of the benefits and privileges as noblewomen.

This text will focus on the Hispanic Monarchy during the eighteenth century and specifically on María Joaquina Monserrat y Acuña, First Duchess of Almodóvar, and her niece Josefa Dominga Catalá, the future duchess of the same title. The inheritance of books received by Josefa at different moments of her life provides two major insights. On the one hand, it offers an ideal chance to explore the cultural universe in which the young woman lived, and on the other, a unique opportunity to examine the strategies of control developed by different institutions concerned with both the management of the family legacy and the dangers of inappropriate reading. In these cases, the participation of the Inquisition became a fundamental element of the procedure for regulating which works, *a priori*, should not be read, according to a more general discourse in Europe on the risks that could arise from reading inappropriate books.

Studies on private libraries have analysed reading habits, the management and the inheritance of books, the legacy of a specific individual or lineage,

---

1 This research has received funding from the European Research Council: CIRGEN, ERC Advanced Grant, Grant Agreement No. 787015.

and the circulation and reception of literary works and genres.[2] From this perspective, books become both objects that provide proof of the purchasing power of their owners, depending on their materials, finish or format, and also instruments used for the acquisition of specific knowledge, whether for academic purposes or pleasure. They are also objects that have a symbolic value as elements of social distinction for the family and for the individuals who own or have access to the library, thus contributing to the construction of their own identities. They represent, therefore, a legacy that is both tangible and intangible.[3] Generally, the inventories made before the imminent death of the owner, or at other times in the person's life due to other circumstances such as change of residence have been used to study these libraries in depth.[4] The problem, however, is that these documents provide a fixed image of a specific moment in the person's life, so they are the books that he or she actually owned in a specific year. We should pay attention to other possible acquisitions, and of books sold or lost during the owner's life.

It is also necessary to evaluate all the other possibilities of accessing the written word during the eighteenth century. I refer to the loans made by other individuals or institutions, and other 'literary' genres with a more volatile format, such as the periodical press or chapbooks. All this means that the study of a person's books does not necessarily tell us exactly what their reading habits were, although it can undoubtedly provide some guidance. Accordingly, I am more interested in investigating the composition of libraries and their circulation within aristocratic families over the years, and more specifically the role of women in this context as heirs and transmitters of that legacy. The sources available to this study, several inventories of books inherited by Josefa Dominga Catalá, allow us to move away from the idea of the library as a fixed photograph taken in a specific year, bringing dynamism to the study of the

---

2   On libraries and readers, the classic works are: Trevor Dadson, *Libros, lectores y lecturas. Estudios sobre bibliotecas particulares españolas del Siglo de Oro* (Madrid: ARCO/LIBROS, 1998), Roger Chartier, *Libros, lecturas y lectores en la Edad Moderna* (Madrid: Alianza Editorial, 1994), Guglielmo Cavallo and Roger Chartier (eds.), *A History of Reading in the West* (Massachusetts: University of Massachusetts Press, 2003), and Robert Darnton, 'First steps towards a History of Reading', *Australian Journal of French Studies*, 23 (1986), pp. 5–30.

3   Renata Ago, *Il Gusto delle cose: una storia degli oggetti nella Roma del Seicento* (Roma: Donzelli, 2006).

4   Many authors, such as the previously cited Trevor Dadson, have analysed book inventories. For the case of Spain see Inmaculada Arias de Saavedra, 'Los espacios de las bibliotecas en el Antiguo Régimen', in M. Birrial Salcedo (ed.), *La(s) casa(s) en la Edad Moderna* (Zaragoza: Institución Fernando el Católico, 2017), pp. 341–364; Natalia Maillard Álvarez and Manuel Francisco Fernández Chaves (coord.), *Bibliotecas de la Monarquía Hispánica en la primera globalización (siglos XVI–XVIII)* (Zaragoza: Prensas Universitarias de Zaragoza, 2021).

construction of family libraries. This perspective will focus mainly on one of these inventories, examining the role played by the Inquisition in the regulation of women's reading during the process of the transmission of the books.

Women's relationship with libraries has been more difficult to chart than men's, given that very few inventories have survived, most of which belonged to queens and noblewomen. Moreover, often certain family libraries appear under male ownership, when both men and women in that family could have made use of it. It is also necessary to take into account the higher illiteracy rates among women than among men.[5] In any case, both men and women inherited collections of books that had belonged to their families, a legacy that they could add to during their lives via the acquisition of new works. However, it was not always possible to conserve the library and in fact, books inherited were often valued to be sold at public auctions.[6] The owners' scope for action in this context could vary in accordance with several factors, one of which was the heir or heiress being underage. This was the case of Josefa Dominga Catalá, who inherited her first books at the age of 12 following the death of her grandmother. This library, inventoried and valued in 1776, was then managed by her legal tutor: her uncle Pedro Francisco Suárez de Góngora y Luján, Marquis of Almodóvar, who must have considered it more useful to sell most of the books and make investments that were financially beneficial for his niece. Therefore, Josefa was unable to enjoy this first inheritance freely, a circumstance that would change some years later.

In this process of transmission of books between family members, a fundamental role was played by the Inquisition, which within Catholic spheres was responsible for controlling the orthodoxy of people. Everything started from Rome, where the Sacred Congregation of the Index elaborated various Indexes of Prohibited Books during the early modern period, lists that included those

---

5  On women's libraries in Spain see Inmaculada Arias de Saavedra y Gloria Franco Rubio, 'Lecturas de mujeres, lecturas de reinas. La biblioteca de Bárbara de Braganza', in I. Arias de Saavedra (ed.), *Vida cotidiana en la España de la Ilustración* (Granada: EUG, 2012), pp. 505–549. About women, lineage, patrimony and books see Anne J. Cruz, 'Reading over men's shoulders: noblewomen's libraries and reading practices', in A.J. Cruz and R. Hernández (eds.), *Women's Literacy in Early Modern Spain and the New World* (Burlington: Ashgate, 2011), pp. 41–58. On books and family lineage see Edith Snook, 'Elizabeth Isham's "own books": Property, Propriety, and the Self as Library', in L. Knight, M. White and E. Sauer (eds.), *Women's Bookscapes in Early Modern Britain* (Michigan: University of Michigan Press, 2018), pp. 77–93.

6  On book auctions and catalogues, see Alicia C. Montoya and Rindert Jagersma, 'Marketing Maria Sibylla Merian, 1720–1800: Book Auctions, Gender and Reading Culture in the Dutch Republic', *Book History*, 21 (2018), pp. 56–88.

works and authors regarded as dangerous. After that, Catholic territories such as the Kingdom of Spain created their own Indexes through the Tribunal of the Holy Office of the Inquisition, which could vary from the instructions given from Rome.[7] I will use both terms, Inquisition and Holy Office, as synonyms to refer to the same institution based in Spanish territories. This censorship was intended to prevent any kind of attack on the Catholic faith and the circulation of ideas considered to be harmful. For this reason, this Holy Office had instructions to inspect bookshops, printing houses, and both public and private libraries. However, it was possible, and relatively normal, to apply for a special permit to read specific works. These were licences for the reading of prohibited books, granted to individuals in positions of privilege and also to institutions, as was the case for the *Real Academia Española de la Historia* (Royal Spanish Academy of History), for instance.[8] The death of an owner, or the transfer of assets from one residence to another, provided an ideal opportunity to seize these kinds of objects. At that moment, if there was no licence, those works that appeared in the Index were requisitioned. Meanwhile, if there was a licence or deference to the family affected, the inquisitors could study the conditions under which the heirs could keep some of those works, as shall be seen in more detail upon analysis of the Duchesses of Almodóvar's case.

Inquisitorial control also highlights the debate, widespread during the eighteenth century, over the dangers of reading in a society in which literacy and the reading public were increasing. In this context, the particular concern with regard to the growing number of women readers reveals both the perception of an increase in the female reading public and a specific gendered manifestation of the dangers of reading. The case of the Duchesses of Almodóvar shows the important role of aristocratic women as transmitters of knowledge and family assets, but also how the interpretation of some books as particularly dangerous was heavily influenced by the gender of the subject.

---

7   Jesús Martínez de Bujanda, *El índice de libros prohibidos y expurgados de la Inquisición española (1551–1819). Evolución y contenido* (Madrid: Biblioteca de Autores Cristianos, 2016).

8   On licences to read prohibited books see Juan Carlos Galende Díaz and Bárbara Santiago Medina, 'La atracción de lo prohibido: las licencias inquisitoriales para leer libros como tipología diplomática (siglo XVIII)', in *III Simpósio Internacional de Estudos Inquisitoriais: novas fronteiras* (Cachoeira-BA: Anais Eletrônicos: 2016). On inquisitorial control: Xenia von Tippelskirch, *Sotto controllo. Letture femminili in Italia nella prima età moderna* (Roma: Viella, 2011); Idalia García Aguilar, 'Before we are condemned: inquisitorial fears and private libraries of New Spain', in N. Maillard (ed.), *Books in the Catholic World during the Early Modern Period* (Leiden and Boston: Brill, 2014), pp. 171–189; On book censorship see Milena Sabato, 'Comparing book censorship: an Italian and European perspective (centuries XVI–XVIII)', *European Scientific Journal*, 10 (2014), pp. 53–58.

## 1    The Duchess of Almodóvar and 'Her' Books

Josefa Dominga Catalá, born in 1764, was a prominent aristocrat who lived between the late eighteenth and the early nineteenth centuries.[9] Her privileged position was the result of the combination of various elements: several ancestral lineages which merged in her person, the inheritances she received, such as titles, and lands or houses, as well as her active participation in the management and defence of her interests and properties. At the age of twelve, following the death of her grandmother, she entered the tutelage of her uncle the Marquis of Almodóvar, who had married María Joaquina Monserrat y Acuña in 1773. As Almodóvar had been appointed Spanish ambassador to the Portuguese court, the couple resided in Lisbon, where Josefa joined them in 1776. This was when the relationship between aunt, uncle and niece began to be forged. In particular, the relationship established between María Joaquina and Josefa was consolidated in subsequent years in London, where the Marquis and Marchioness served as ambassadors between 1778 and 1779. The Almodóvars had two children of their own who died shortly after birth, which perhaps served to strengthen the affectionate relationship between aunt and niece. In 1780, after various complications in London and a somewhat hasty return to Spain, they ended up living in Madrid.

The Marquis's career path was recognised with the granting of the title of Duke of Almodóvar, which made him a Grandee of Spain. From then onwards they all lived in Madrid, and the Duke would participate in the most important intellectual circles in the capital. He wrote the *Década epistolar sobre el estado de las letras en Francia* (Epistolary decade of the state of literature in France) in 1781, based on *Les trois siècles de la littérature françoise* by Sabatier de Castres, and years later the *Historia política de los establecimientos ultramarinos de las naciones europeas* (Political history of overseas establishments from European nations), based on the *Histoire philosophique et politique des établissemens et du commerce des européens dans les deux Indes*, written by the Abbé Raynal. He was also a member of the *Real Academia Española de la Historia* (Royal Spanish Academy of History), among other commitments. Meanwhile, his wife, the Duchess of Almodóvar, joined the recently created *Junta de Damas de Honor*

---

9    On the Duchess of Almodóvar see Irene Ballester Buigues, *La duquessa d'Almodóvar: vida d'una aristócrata valenciana a la fi del segle XVIII* (Xaló: Institut d'Estudis Comarcals de la Marina Alta, 2007); About her library there is more information in Irene Ballester Buigues, (ed.), *Dos-cents anys a l'ombra de la duquessa d'Almodóvar* (Valencia: Edicions 96, 2015), Laura Guinot Ferri, 'Mujeres en el tejido de redes de sociabilidad y la gestión de bibliotecas en el siglo XVIII: el entorno cultural e intelectual de las duquesas de Almodóvar', Arenal. Revista de Historia de las Mujeres, 29/2 (2022), pp. 419–445.

*y Mérito* (Women's Council of Honour and Merit), the women's section of the *Sociedad Económica de Amigos del País* (Economic Society of the Friends of the Country). The couple thus formed a marriage of highly educated individuals who moved in an extremely important culturally and socially enlightened circle at the end of the eighteenth century. This was the context surrounding the life of their niece, who in 1782 married Benito Osorio, Marquis of Mortara, a marriage arranged by both families. However, in 1789, when she was 25, they requested a marriage annulment, after which she never remarried. From that moment onwards, Josefa participated actively in the defence of her interests and property, which resulted in numerous lawsuits and saw her, along with her administrators, take personal responsibility for many of her duties as a member of different lineages. As she was now of legal age, and released from her marriage and her uncle's tutelage, she probably enjoyed a privileged situation and had greater freedom than other similar women who were dependent on their fathers, husbands or other male figures.

The Duke of Almodóvar died in 1794, having stipulated in his will that, in the absence of legitimate heirs following the death of his two children, his niece Josefa Dominga Catalá would inherit his entire estate.[10] However, according to the will, there should be a distribution between his wife, in the event that she were still alive when he died, as was the case, and his niece. More specifically, María Joaquina would maintain usufruct over most of those assets until her death, when they would pass directly to Josefa. This circumstance led to various agreements between aunt and niece, who must have been very close, as was especially proven by the case of the Duke's library. This was to be inherited by Josefa, who also openly expressed her interest in conserving the books, although it appears that she was unable to keep all of them. Probably, some had to be sold or given to others. Among the documentation collected on the occasion of the Duke's death and preserved in the *Duquesa de Almodóvar Fund* of the Archive of the Diputación de Valencia, a list of the books included in the Index of Prohibited Books that formed part of the Duke of Almodóvar's library has been located. However, a complete inventory of all the works that belonged to Pedro Francisco Suárez is not yet known. On the occasion of the Inquisition's intervention during the transfer of assets between family members, the forbidden books in his library were listed in a small inventory, possibly by order of María Joaquina.

---

10    Archivo Histórico de Protocolos de Madrid (AHPM), T. 18204, f. 637r–642r: Poder para testar otorgado, uno a favor del otro, por Pedro Francisco Suárez de Góngora, y su esposa, María de los Desamparados Acuña y Prado. AHPM, T. 18212, f. 411r–414r: Testamento de Pedro Francisco Suárez de Góngora.

Most interestingly, the management of these works shows the closeness of the relationship between Josefa and María Joaquina, and the young woman's clear desire to conserve most of her uncle's books, as well as María Joaquina's role as intermediary, acting to guarantee her niece's rights. All of this also demonstrates the active role of women in the control of their lineage's own legacy. In this case, this active role of both María Joaquina and Josefa shows a special concern for a collection with not only patrimonial but also cultural and intellectual significance. The Duke of Almodóvar had a library valued at 37,863 *reales*, a substantial book collection similar to other men in his same position.[11] It was the result of his various travels and his dedication as a man of letters and an official of the monarchy. The fact that he decided to bequeath the estate to his niece seems to indicate a desire to keep the library within the lineage, as she was also the heiress to the title of Duchess of Almodóvar, but it also suggests that Josefa possessed intellectual skills and interests that her uncle probably helped to cultivate. He had been responsible for her from the age of twelve, including her education, which surely resulted in an extremely well-educated and cultured woman. It is not surprising, then, that he wished for her to receive his spectacular collection, a wish that his wife María Joaquina also expressed in a letter that she wrote in 1796 to the chamber secretary of the Archbishop and Inquisitor of Toledo. It included the following request: her niece had to be able to keep the books, under the same conditions that she, Maria Joaquina, had been able to keep them.

> In accordance with Your Eminence's Decree of 13 October 1794, the original copy of which I include, I attach a list of the Prohibited Books found in my late husband's library, in order that Your Eminence might rule as he judges to be most fitting and appropriate in light of the conclusion of the testamentary proceedings according to which the Library passes into the hands of my niece the Duchess of Almodóvar, Marchioness of Quirra, who requests of Your Eminence continued custody of said books under the same terms and conditions as conceded to me by Your Eminence.[12]

The reply, however, was not particularly favourable, though neither was it completely negative. Josefa was not allowed to keep all the books in the library included in the Index, so an assessor, Joaquín Lorenzo de Villanueva, had to

---

11    Inmaculada Arias de Saavedra, 'Libros, lectores y bibliotecas privadas en la España del siglo XVIII', *Chronica Nova*, 35 (2009), pp. 15–61. The valuation of the Duke's library is included in Archivo General y Fotográfico de la Diputación de Valencia: Fondo Duquesa de Almodóvar. e 1.4, Sucesiones, Caja 13. Testamentos y Herencias. 1777–1814.

12    Archivo General y Fotográfico de la Diputación de Valencia: Fondo Duquesa de Almodóvar. e 1.4, Sucesiones, Caja 19.

visit the house in order to confiscate those that were inappropriate, but he could allow her to keep other, less harmful volumes at his discretion. Which he did, leaving 41 in their possession, whilst another 24 had to be sent to the Court of the Holy Office. The General Inquisitor Francisco Lorenzana informed María Joaquina to this effect, with words of particular significance, since they indicate a clear intention to keep those harmful books away from prying eyes. For that reason, only the duchesses could have access to the library, which they had to keep under lock and key:

> I received Your Excellency's letter of 31 August last with the list that accompanied it of the Prohibited Books that were found in the Library of your late husband, the Honourable Duke of Almodóvar, and having learned of their contents ... regarding them I must tell Your Excellency that since some of them are dreadful, and that even those that have a licence should not be read, and almost all those contained in the same List are bad, the situation does not allow me to acquiesce to Your Excellency's request that I allow your niece, (to whom the said library has been awarded) to continue in the custody of them in the same terms and under the same reservation that I granted it to Your Excellency: and so I have ordered with this day's date that the assessor Don Joaquín Lorenzo Villanueva ... goes to your house and explains with the greatest civility required that it is necessary that you or Her Excellency your niece hand over to the Holy Office the books on the list, except those that in the opinion of assessor Villanueva neither contained such pernicious maxims, nor could cause such serious damage. The latter works, exempt from the aforementioned commissioned and sound judgement, shall henceforth be safeguarded in the locked cabinet where they are currently located, the key to which Your Excellency or your niece Her Excellency the Duchess of Almodóvar shall have in their possession, to prevent any misplacement of said works or their being read by any person lacking the necessary Licence to do so.[13]

As can be seen from the Inquisitor's reply, and from María Joaquina's previous letter, it seems that the widowed Duchess of Almodóvar held special permission to keep all the books found in her late husband's library that were included in the Index. Although the evidence of this permission is not preserved nowadays, Pedro Francisco Suárez must have had a special licence for this type of work since, as Marcelin Defourneaux pointed out, many people who are known to have owned, read and translated French works, many of

---

13    Archivo General y Fotográfico de la Diputación de Valencia: Fondo Duquesa de Almodóvar. e 1.4, Sucesiones, Caja 19.

which were banned, do not appear in the Inquisitorial Register.[14] It is quite possible that the Duke of Almodóvar was one of those who had permission to read forbidden works. However, at the point when the library was to pass into the hands of his niece, a younger, and furthermore, 'divorced' woman, the attitude of the Inquisition seemed to be more cautious and careful. It should be remembered that at the time of her uncle's death, Josefa was 30 years old and had had her marriage to Benito Osorio annulled. The Inquisitor General's reasons for not allowing the transmission of all the books to the young woman could be diverse, although they are not entirely clear in the letter. They could keep those that did not contain 'such pernicious maxims' and would not cause 'such serious damage'.[15]

In other words, according to the Inquisition's interpretation, all these books were dangerous, but some were likely to cause less harm than others. For this reason, only licensed individuals had special permission to read or keep certain works, and in this case, these individuals were both Duchesses of Almodóvar. Only they would have the key to the cabinet in which the works were preserved, to prevent them from being lost or, more importantly, from being read by unlicensed persons. The Holy Office, then, seems to display here a concern not so much with gender as with class, since these curious glances could be those of the servants who also lived in the house or the people who visited it, who had to be protected from reading or accessing texts of a harmful nature. However, this treatment of banned books was not unusual, since Spanish academies and scientific societies were also given the same warning: they were allowed to have certain works as long as they were kept in a specific room and separated from other books. The key would only be held by the librarian and the director of the institution, in the same way that in this case, Josefa and María Joaquina became the guardians of this part of the library.[16]

This testimony of the works belonging to the Index of Prohibited Books provides an approximate idea of the interests that Pedro Francisco Suárez had, as well as the influence of his travels and career on the creation of his library. In fact, some of the books found in this inventory were those used by the Duke to write his *Década epistolar sobre el estado de las letras en Francia* (Epistolary decade of the state of literature in France), in which he evaluated the work

---

14  Marcelin Defourneaux, *Inquisición y censura de libros en la España del siglo XVIII* (Madrid: Taurus, 1973), p. 180. The author explains that, since 1776, someone who possessed a licence (many of them given in Rome but invalid in Spain) had to register it in the Holy Office, but many did not do it.

15  Archivo General y Fotográfico de la Diputación de Valencia: Fondo Duquesa de Almodóvar. e 1.4, Sucesiones, Caja 19.

16  On licences to academies and scientific societies see Defourneaux, *Inquisición y censura*, pp. 176–177.

TABLE 19.1   A selection of nine of the most significant and well known titles from the library
of the Duke of Almodóvar

| Author | Title |
|---|---|
| Gregorio Leti | *El ceremonial histórico y político, obra utilísima a todos los embajadores* (Political and historical ceremonial, useful work for ambassadors). Probably in Italian |
| William Robertson | *The History of America.* In English or in French |
| Samuel Puffendorf | *Introduction á la l'histoire générale et politique de l'univers.* (Introduction to the general and political history of the universe). Probably in French. |
| Hugo Grotius | *De jure belli et pacis.* (About law of war and peace). Probably in French |
| Abbé Raynal | *Histoire philosophique et politique des établissemens et du commerce des européens dans les deux Indes*[a] |
| Denis Diderot | Moral works |
| Jean François Marmontel | *Bélisaire* (French novel) |
| Erasmus of Rotterdam? | New Testament in Greek |
| Several authors | *The Encyclopaedia* (all the volumes) |

a   This book, in fact, was the original version of the *Historia política de los establecimientos ultra-marinos de las naciones europeas* (Political history of overseas establishments from European nations), that Almodóvar published in Spain between 1784 and 1790 under the pseudonym of Eduardo Malo de Luque. Apparently, he was denounced to the Inquisition because of this work, but the process did not succeed, Defourneaux, *Inquisición y censura,* pp. 202–203.

of French authors for the Spanish audience.[17] Likewise, the choice made by the inquisitorial assessor also provides an insight into the Inquisition's criteria for choosing some texts and discarding others. A selection of the works and authors for which permission to read was granted, albeit limited, can be seen in Table 19.1. The date of publication has not been included, as it is not in the original source either, so we cannot be sure which edition the Duke had.

In general, although the inventory lists the abridged titles in Spanish, most of these works were in French, though the Duke also owned some in Italian, Spanish and English. The interests displayed by this collection were fundamentally oriented towards political history and law, a reflection of Almodóvar's desire to be well informed on these subjects in order to perform his duties as an ambassador, as a servant of the monarchy and as an intellectual. The Duke

17    Ibid., pp. 186–189.

must have acquired many of these works during his diplomatic travels, especially during his stay in London between 1778 and 1779 and on his return journey to Spain, when, according to the sources, he passed through Paris before settling in Madrid in 1780.

According to the assessor's criteria, these books, despite their potential danger and their inclusion in the Index, could be retained by both duchesses under lock and key. Both women were, therefore, able to have access to these works, although it is not known if they ever actually read them. María Joaquina was indeed fluent in Italian and French, as confirmed by the British ambassador to Spain, Thomas Robinson.[18] Josefa had probably learnt the same languages during her travels with her aunt and uncle, so the possibility of reading the books in other languages perhaps would not present a problem. In any case, the collection opened the doors to the thought of authors such as Diderot or Puffendorf, as well as to the great project of the Enlightenment, the *Encyclopaedia*. However, they were not so lucky with other books, which, according to the criteria of the assessor Villanueva and the Holy Office in general, were completely forbidden and dangerous. Again, here we can see a selection of these works in Table 19.2. The date of publication has not been included here either for the same reasons stated above.

TABLE 19.2 A selection of some of the titles included in the library of the Duke of Almodóvar that were forbbiden to the duchesses

| Author | Title |
| --- | --- |
| Casiodoro de Reina | Spanish translation of the Bible |
| Cipriano de Valera | Spanish translation of the Bible |
| No author | Ferrara Bible (translation into Judeo-Spanish) |
| Pierre Bayle | *Dictionnaire historique et critique* |
| Antonio Enríquez Gómez | *Sansón Nazareno. Poema heroico.* (Samson. Heroic poem). |
| Paolo Sarpi | *La Historia del Concilio de Trento* (The History of the Council of Trent) |
| Pietro Aretino | Comedies in Italian |
| Alexandre Xavier Panel | *La Sabiduría y la Locura en el Púlpito de las Monjas* (Wisdom and Madness on Nun's Pulpit) |

18    Baron Grantham Thomas Robinson, British ambassador in Spain in 1778, explained this to his brother Frederick Robinson when the Almodovars were going to move from Madrid to London to start their period as Spanish ambassadors. Bedfordhsire and Luton Archives: L 30/15/54/43. Letter from Thomas Robinson to Frederick Robinson, May 1778.

TABLE 19.2   A selection of some of the titles included in the library of the Duke (*cont.*)

| Author | Title |
| --- | --- |
| Boccaccio | *Decameron* |
| Marguerite de Navarre | *Heptameron* |
| No author | *Les amours de Henri IV, Roi de France: avec ses lettres galantes à la duchesse de Beaufort et à la marquise de Verneuil* (The loves of Henry IV, king of France: with his gallant letters to the duchess of Beaufort and the marchioness of Verneuil) |
| Voltaire and Rousseau | Several works |

In this case, there are some translations of the Bible, all of them originally from the sixteenth century, although it is not clear which editions the Duke had. The first authorised translation of the Bible into Spanish, after other versions were banned, would not be published until 1793. Likewise, the duchesses also had to dispose of other texts with stories from the Bible in Spanish, some comedies, burlesque works, tales and works of a gallant nature. And, of course, most of the works of Voltaire and Rousseau. Therefore, the criteria for prohibition, in this case, seem to be mainly religious texts of an unorthodox nature, works of a literary nature such as comedies, short stories and other tales, and authors considered dangerous because of their philosophical or moral ideas.

The contrast between authorised works and the requisitioned books raises a debate about the motives of the Holy Office's assessor in making this selection. Did the special circumstance that two women would be the recipients of the collection influence his decision? Did the social class factor play an important role in keeping the books from the gaze of others? On the one hand, there is an initial selection that separates the books that can be kept from the books that must be sent to the Inquisition office. Here, along with other factors, a gender component probably comes into play, which suggests that these two women should not read certain literary works, religious works and books by certain authors considered to be particularly harmful. On the other hand, other reasons also seem to have been considered, which determine that the texts approved for both duchesses remain dangerous for unlicensed persons, in this case probably the staff of the duke's household, who should not even have access to this part of the library. Social status, therefore, is also an important factor to take into account, and aristocratic women agreed with this perception too. An example is the case of the Spanish Countess of Lalaing, who translated the work of Madame de Lambert from French. The Inquisition, however, did not authorise this publication, explaining that it could cause religious doubts to women, but the Countess, Cayetana de la Cerda, answered that it was not addressed to 'calceteras y lavanderas' (hosiers and laundresses). She had, therefore, an elitist perception of her readership, probably educated noblewomen.[19]

In the case studied here, it is particularly important to consider the influence of a certain gendered construction of reading on its criteria for banning some of the works. This case took place within an extant and lively eighteenth-century debate on the dangers of reading, which highlighted the contrast between the construction of the image of the woman reader and the actual reading possibilities for women.

## 2    Gender, Books and the Dangers of Reading

The inquisitorial control was directed towards the reading of those works that could be harmful to the Catholic faith due to their heretical or problematic maxims. But the regulation of reading by the Inquisition must also be understood in the eighteenth century as part of a transnational concern of the civil and ecclesiastical authorities for the literacy and education of the population, and for the benefits or dangers of reading.[20] Throughout the century, the number of readers progressively increased, or at least the perception of the existence of a wider and more varied readership than that of previous periods did. In fact, this is how it is represented in art, since the increase in literacy and the practice of reading led 'this activity to be framed as an object worthy of being represented'.[21] For this reason, these images of men and women reading served to consecrate reading as a common, everyday practice, without limits of sex, age or class.[22] Accordingly, the identification of a new type of sentimental reading became very significant with the perception of a 'new' kind of audience on the rise, the feminine.[23] Iconographic representations of female

19    Mónica Bolufer, 'Una ética de la excelencia: Cayetana de la Cerda y la circulación de Madame de Lambert en España', *Cuadernos de Historia Moderna*, 40 (2015), pp. 241–264.

20    Patrizia Delpiano, *Il governo della lettura. Chiesa e libri nell'Italia del Settecento* (Bolonia: Il Mulino, 2007), p. 35.

21    Tiziana Plebani, 'La rivoluzione della lettura e la rivoluzione dell'immagine della lettura', in L. Braida e S. Tatti (eds.), *Il libro. Editoria e pratiche di lettura nel Settecento* (Roma: Edizioni di Storia e Letteratura, 2016), p. 5.

22    Plebani, 'La rivoluzione', p. 6.

23    On women and reading see Jacqueline Pearson, *Women's Reading in Britain: 1750–1835. A dangerous recreation* (Cambridge: Cambridge University Press, 1999); Isabelle Brouard-Arens (dir.), *Lectrices d'Ancien Régime* (Rennes: Presses universitaires de Rennes, 2003); Maria Pia Donato e Xenia von Tippelskirch, «Il tanto leggere mi fa doler la testa».

readers multiplied during the eighteenth century, many of them surrounded by a halo of sensuality, privacy and intimacy.[24] In the same way, authors also imagined their ideal readers, to whom they addressed their works, thus constructing a certain perception of the public. This phenomenon was particularly pronounced in the periodical press, which increasingly appealed to a female readership with its opinion articles, letters, poetry and short stories.[25]

However, this was all despite the fact that the growth of literacy in Europe remained limited and uneven, and illiteracy rates remained high, especially in rural areas, among the working classes, and among women.[26] There exists, therefore, a contrast between the constructed image and everyday reality. Real women readers did not grow as much during the eighteenth century, and are also harder to find in the sources. As Jacqueline Pearson stated: 'Women readers are paradoxically both the most visible in the literature and the most invisible in the historical record'.[27] The study of libraries seeks to answer some of these questions, but always bearing in mind that indications of actual reading drawn from the study of inventories should be treated with great caution. It has already been observed that possession did not mean reading, as in the case of Josefa Dominga Catalá's inherited library, but the presence of certain books available and within the reach of these aristocrats gives an idea of the potential cultural and intellectual universe to which many noble or bourgeois women could have access precisely through inheritance or the use of libraries belonging to their families.

These potential readings seem particularly interesting in this specific case for two main reasons. Firstly, María Joaquina and Josefa expressly stated their wish to keep the books in a letter to the Inquisitor General. And, secondly, the Holy Office accepted this request and intervened to select which of the works that were, in principle, forbidden, could be kept and guarded. This is even despite the fact that both the Inquisition and other institutions continued to control the reading of lay people, especially women, who were represented

Appunti sulle lettrici alla soglia del pubblico', in B. Borello, *Pubblico e pubblici di antico regime* (Pisa: Pacini Editore, 2009), pp. 1–20.

24    Chartier, *Libros, lecturas*, pp. 160–161.

25    Mónica Bolufer, '*Espectadores* y lectoras: representaciones e influencia del público femenino en la prensa del siglo XVIII', *Cuadernos de Estudio del Siglo XVIII*, 5 (1995), pp. 23–57.

26    On women's education in Spain see Inmaculada Arias de Saavedra, 'Lectura y bibliotecas de mujeres en la España del siglo XVIII. Una aproximación', *Cuadernos de Ilustración y Romanticismo*, 23 (2017), pp. 57–82.

27    Pearson, *Women's Reading*, p. 12.

as weaker and more susceptible to influence and sentiment.[28] As in previous centuries, there was a suspicion of the negative influence reading could have on souls.[29] Literature excited fantasy and allowed the imagination to run wild, which could lead to confusion between reality and fiction.[30] According to the misogynistic thinking of the time, excessive imagination could also lead to lasciviousness, especially for women. For this reason, certain literary genres were recommended for women and others were especially condemned, such as novels, which were on the rise in the eighteenth century.[31] This can be seen in the case analysed here with the example of *Les amours de Henri IV*, completely forbidden for the duchesses. In fact, criticisms of women's reading were taking on very clear sexual connotations, which were accentuated in the eighteenth century, as reflected in the art, where solitary reading by women is often perceived as an act linked to pleasure and far removed from virtue.[32] As an example, in the following image this relationship between female reading and the sensual can be appreciated (Fig. 19.1). The scene depicts a relaxed, dreamy woman in a somewhat erotic position after reading a book that she has let fall from her right hand.

This strongly sensual character of books led the Inquisition to take a special interest in literary works with regard to women's reading from the sixteenth century onwards.[33] Besides, it was also common to consider the female audience as a simple, less capable, and infantilised audience.[34] It was the negative version of the association between a female public and a lay, non-specialist audience, which was also used for other purposes by authors, publishers and printers seeking to broaden their readership, in this case, to write, publish or

---

28    Catherine M. Jaffe, 'Doña Leonora's Library: Women's Reading from The Spectator (1711) to the Semanario de Salamanca (1795)', in C.M. Jaffe and E. Franklin Lewis (eds.), *Eve's Enlightenment: Women's Experience in Spain and Spanish America 1626–1839* (Baton Rouge: Louisiana State University Press, 2009), p. 188. There were different levels of control, such as the rules imposed by editorial corporations, privileges given to certain publishers, or the preventive examination of texts by political authorities; Sabato, 'Comparing book censorship', pp. 56–57.

29    Tippelskirch, *Sotto controllo*, p. 156.

30    Delpiano, *Il governo della lettura*, p. 55.

31    Mónica Bolufer, 'Poisonous plants or schools of virtue? The second 'rise' of the novel in eighteenth-century Spain', in J. Mander (ed.), *Remapping the rise of the European novel* (Oxford: Voltaire Foundation, 2007), pp. 199–214.

32    Pearson, *Women's Reading*, p. 8.

33    Tippelskirch, *Sotto controllo*, p. 118.

34    Delpiano, *Il governo della lettura*, p. 178; Pearson, *Women's Reading*, p. 18.

FIGURE 19.1    *Le midi.* Emmanuel Jean Nepomucène de Ghendt after Pierre-Antoine
Baudouin. *c.*1765. National Gallery of Art, Washington

sell works aimed 'at ladies' that were in fact intended for a general audience.[35]
In short, there was a very powerful transnational discourse which, with its

35    This category has been very well analysed in History of Science by authors such as Paula
      Findlen, 'Becoming a Scientist: Gender and Knowledge in Eighteenth-Century Italy',
      *Science in Context*, 16 (2003), pp. 59–87.

specific manifestations in each territory, considered that women's reading should be especially supervised. Although they should not be completely ignorant, they did not need to be overly informed either.[36]

In the same vein, in the case of the Duchess of Almodóvar, we can see an intervention by the Inquisition which seems to have wanted to regulate women's reading in the process of transferring the patrimonial property of the Duke of Almodóvar to his niece. Thus, the assessor Villanueva argued that certain texts on history, political history, civil law or works such as the *Encyclopaedia*, most of which were French, were not so dangerous as to be completely withdrawn from two well-educated, enlightened women. Deference to such an important aristocratic family weighed heavily in this decision. However, the consideration of certain books as particularly dangerous for women seems to have influenced the selection, since a number of works were denied to them, including collections of short stories, works of literature and translations of the Bible into the vernacular language. As well as being particularly concerned about the effects of works of fiction on the female imagination, the Inquisition seems to have been especially worried about women's access, even that of educated women, to translations of biblical texts into vernacular languages, a concern that was heightened in the case of common audiences.[37]

All this not only helps to understand the Inquisition's idea of the dangers of reading for women and its efforts to regulate it, but also allows us to reflect on women's access to reading. People of notable social standing such as Josefa Dominga and María Joaquina had the opportunity to surround themselves with an environment particularly conducive to their education, learning and intellectual development, in this case through the figure and legacy of Pedro Francisco Suárez, Duke of Almodóvar, uncle and husband of these two women. This situation, together with the absence of other heirs, meant that Josefa could be the recipient of an impressive library built up over the years by the Duke during his travels around Europe. María Joaquina's intervention in this context to ensure that her niece could keep the banned books in the library highlights the intellectual and patrimonial value of the entire collection, and shows the strategies that could be developed by women who, like them, had to deal with the management of enormous estates over which they did not always have full decision-making capacity, but did have the power to intervene.

Josefa herself, who as a child in 1776 had not been able to keep the library in her grandmother's house in Valencia, as heiress of the lineage, was able to make her own decisions as an adult after the death of her uncle the Duke in 1794. In this study I have analysed how she dealt with the inheritance of this library,

---

36    Pearson, *Women's Reading*, p. 49.
37    Tippelskirch, *Sotto controllo*, p. 126.

part of an immense heritage spread throughout the Hispanic Monarchy, which she managed for years. Sometime later she again showed this capacity to take the initiative when faced with a new inheritance of books in 1800. On this date, she received an inheritance from her uncle Joaquín Antonio de Castellví, Count of Carlet. From this relative, her mother's cousin who had no other heirs, she obtained numerous assets, including a library of 706 works and a whole set of instruments for physics experiments.[38] The Count of Carlet was an enlightened intellectual with a great love for science, who also made numerous trips around Europe. The result of these experiences was this collection of books and scientific material that he decided to bequeath to his niece, for whom a whole world of knowledge was opened up to explore. Josefa decided to sell all the physics machines, mostly to the University of Valencia, the city where they both lived in 1800. However, she does not seem to have done the same with the books, of which no document of sale has been preserved. The result of all these inheritances accumulated throughout her lifetime must, therefore, have been an enormous library which we do not know if she kept forever, given that no post-mortem inventory of her books has been located, but which undoubtedly represents a potential universe of readings on history, law, travel, literature and science, among many other subjects.

## 3    Conclusions

The documents related to the libraries inherited by Josefa Dominga Catalá, Duchess of Almodóvar, are a great source to deepen into women's relationship with books and family patrimony during the Enlightenment. Her capacity for action and the active role of her aunt, the widowed Duchess María Joaquina Monserrat, in this processing of transferring assets demonstrates how aristocratic women were able to intervene directly in questions of legacy and patrimony. The case also offers new possibilities to understand women's access to reading, and the importance of gender and status in the circulation of books.

The study of this particular family serves to highlight, firstly, women's legal ability to enact agency in the processes and strategies for the transmission of family assets, especially in the absence of 'other' male heirs. In this respect, it is an activity particular to lineages as prominent and relevant as that of the Almodóvars, families who had to manage very large estates where both purchasing power and social prestige were at stake. For this reason, we must understand these asset management strategies as a common and necessary

---

38    Archivo General y Fotográfico de la Diputación de Valencia: Fondo Duquesa de Almodóvar. e 1.4, Sucesiones, Caja 19.

aristocratic practice, but which also, in the case of women, gave them access to a greater capacity for movement and action than society expected of them. It should be added that it was not only social rank that influenced women's capacity for agency, since marital status and reaching the age of majority were also factors to be taken into account. As we have seen, widowhood or 'divorce', i.e. the absence of a male partner, often gave women greater freedom and allowed them to be the masters of their own lives, which in fact, makes them more visible in historical sources.

Secondly, the management of inheritance has allowed us to delve deeper into the relationship between women and books during the eighteenth century. The privileged position of aristocrats such as the Duchesses of Almodóvar meant that many of these women had access to a wide range of reading material, mostly through their family libraries or those of their husbands' families. The problem lies once again in the sources, since many of these collections appear under the ownership of a male or a lineage, so we do not know who really had access to these works, although we suspect that many women made use of the libraries of their fathers, brothers, uncles or husbands, especially on privileged circles. It is therefore essential to take into account not only a component of gender but also of social rank when analysing the possibilities of women's access to reading. The study of the inheritance process of one of these collections has allowed us to understand the ways and strategies that women developed to appropriate the books, as well as the patrimonial and intellectual interests behind this action.

Thirdly, it is important to appreciate that status also influenced the actions of the Inquisition. The example studied shows that the institution may have been relatively more permissive in the case of individuals of high social standing and with relevant social ties. This respect for status, however, could not obscure the fact that the recipients of the books were two women, so it can be understood that wariness towards the female sex was also common in the case of women of privileged social position. And this brings me to one of the most relevant ideas: the importance of a gendered component in inquisitorial control and censorship as part of a transnational debate about what women should or should not read in the eighteenth century.

### Acknowledgement

This chapter has been published in Open Access thanks to funding from the European Research Council under the European Union's Horizon 2020 research and innovation programme (Project CIRGEN, ERC Grant Agreement No. 787015).

# CHAPTER 20

# Lace, Letters, and the Calligraphic Manuscripts of Esther Inglis

*Georgianna Ziegler*

In 1599, Franco-Scottish calligrapher Esther Inglis finished an elaborate gift manuscript for Queen Elizabeth I.[1] Encased in a red velvet binding embroidered with the Tudor rose, the manuscript contains 150 Psalms in French in a great variety of handwriting styles, including some that look as though they are stitched to the page. The gift accompanied a letter from King James VI of Scotland, and apparently was well-received by the Queen.[2] We will return to this manuscript in greater detail, but the combination of letters and needlework was not unusual, although in this particular object it occurs as a tour-de-force.

Much excellent work by scholars such as Ann Jones, Peter Stallybrass, and Susan Frye has been done on the relationship between writing and sewing, but little specific attention has been focused on lace and embroidery in particular and their resonances with the art of calligraphy, and it this intersection that I examine here. Jones and Stallybrass are especially interested in the ways in which Englishwomen used their needlework to interact with the public world, while creating many objects for domestic use from bed hangings, cushions, and mirror frames to pieces of clothing and samplers. They show how much of this work incorporated images and ideas as well as actual texts from pattern and emblem books and Biblical and political engravings.[3] In her book *Pens and Needles: Women's Textualities in Early Modern England*, Susan Frye enlarges upon this topic, focusing on the interplay between subject (the women sewing and writing) and object (their creations), and the formation of meaning in the

---

1   I am deeply grateful to Dr. Jamie Reid Baxter for reading an earlier version of this manuscript and for generously providing background material from his own research.

2   The Queen's reception of the manuscript is described in a letter by Inglis's husband, Bartilmo Kello, reproduced in A.H. Scott-Elliot and Elspeth Yeo, 'Calligraphic Manuscripts of Esther Inglis (1571–1624): A Catalogue', *PBSA*, 84:1 (March 1990), p. 35. For this manuscript in the context of Elizabethan gift-giving, see Lisa M. Klein, 'Your Humble Handmaid: Elizabethan Gifts of Needlework', *Renaissance Quarterly*, 50:2 (1997), pp. 474–475.

3   Ann Rosalind Jones and Peter Stallybrass, *Renaissance Clothing and the Materials of Memory* (Cambridge: Cambridge University Press, 2000), pp. 134–171.

interface between the two.[4] I am interested in comparing the many similarities between calligraphic and needlework practices, and the relationship between their tools and methods, by exploring instructional manuals published for each craft. These 'how-to' books were similar to commonplacing or scrapbooking, in that they involved collecting and organising disparate items, specifically patterns—many of which would have begun life as hand-drawn—into printed books. The books were then used by their owners to create non-print objects again, such as manuscripts and pieces of lace or embroidery. Further, while calligraphy has often been considered an art acquired by men and embroidery a craft pursued by women, this essay will complicate that dichotomy by demonstrating that the skills of both handwriting and embroidery were considered 'art', and that both were practised—and taught—by men as well as women. The second part of this essay will focus on the work of Esther Inglis as a case study to show how one woman, trained in the skills of these manuals, created her own manuscripts, many with embroidered bindings, combining design and text from often male-authored printed books into new and intimate handmade creations.

The earliest manuals with designs for writing or lace and embroidery appeared around the same time in the 1520s and 30s, sometimes even under the same auspices, as the presses were set up to print sheets of woodcuts or later, engravings. Giovanni Antonio Tagliente was one of the first, publishing both kinds of manuals in Venice. Tagliente was a professional calligrapher, but also a publisher of books on reading and arithmetic.[5] His 1524 writing manual focusing on chancery italic script was printed more than twenty times up until 1560. Addressed to the discriminating reader, it promised to present the rules, proportion, and modes of writing letters to satisfy 'the various appetites of men'.[6] The book combines pages of woodcut examples along with a running 'how-to' text, including a famous illustration of the tools of calligraphy (Fig. 20.1).

---

4   Susan Frye, *Pens and Needles: Women's Textualities in Early Modern England* (Philadelphia: University of Pennsylvania Press, 2010).

5   Stanley Morison, *Early Italian Writing Books*, ed. Nicolas Barker (London: British Library, 1990), p. 64; Anne Jacobson Schutte, 'Teaching Adults to Read in Sixteenth-Century Venice: Giovanni Antonio Tagliente's *Libro Maistrevole*', *Sixteenth Century Journal*, 17 (1986), pp. 3–16. For a survey of copyrights on writing and embroidery manuals, see Christopher Whitcombe, *Copyright in the Renaissance: prints and the privilegio in Sixteenth Century Venice and Rome* (Boston: Brill, 2004), chapter 12. For a review of the history of calligraphy before Inglis, see Nicolas Barker, *Esther Inglis's Les Proverbes de Salomon* (London: The Roxburghe Club, 2012), pp. 1–28.

6   Schutte, 'Teaching Adults', p. 6. Giovanni Antonio Tagliente, *Lo presente libro insegna la vera arte delo excellente scrivere ...* (Venezia, 1524), USTC 857981.

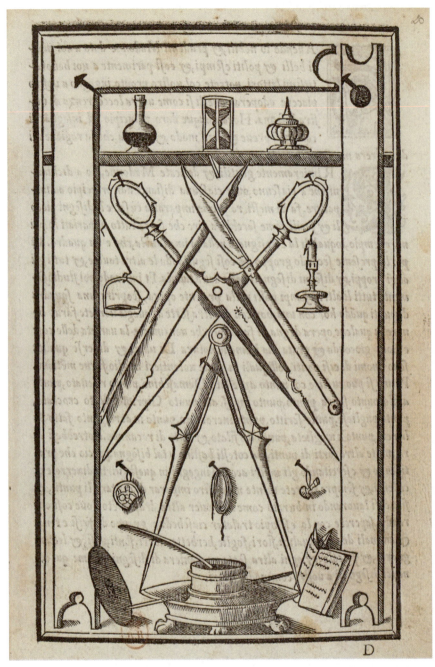

FIGURE 20.1     Tools for calligraphy in Tagliente's writing manual from 1524, *Lo presente libro insegna la vera arte delo excellente scrivere* (Venezia, s.n., 1524) USTC 857981

His sewing and design manual, titled *Opera Nuova*, was first published in 1527.[7] Rather than dedicating it to a particular woman, he directed it 'to any noble and illustrious women', as well as other moderate and chaste readers, but he also advertised that it would be 'of great utility to any artist'. He advocated the same learning process of working in stages from the easier to the more difficult, for both handwriting and embroidery. Among the many designs presented in his embroidery book, he listed 'antique majuscule letters, and the French, and many other sorts of designs and letters to be able to sew and embroider ...'.[8] Indeed, Tagliente used several plates from his writing book in his sewing book, notably an alphabet page and the one showing tools of the trade. And just as he set out different styles of handwriting, so too he described a large variety of stitches.

The reproduction in both books of the woodcut showing tools of the trade is a reminder of the similarity in materials.[9] The primary tools were pen and ink for calligraphers and needles and thread for lacemakers and embroiderers. The latter might also use bobbins, frames or pillows, depending on the type of needlework. Both writing and lace-making or embroidery called for pens and ink to draw letters or patterns; both might use a compass or rule to mark out the page or measure squares or circles for patterns; both used scissors. Calligraphy and needlework both depended on the copying of patterns until the person became highly enough skilled to create their own. Lady Grace Mildmay noted in her diary that she had achieved that satisfaction: 'every day I spent some time in works of my own invention without sample of drawing or pattern before me, for carpet or cushion work'. This skill, she acknowledged, 'God wrought in me'.[10] Those learning handwriting copied the models directly from the book (or sometimes *in* the book). Those engaged in lace making or embroidery might use a pounce to transfer the design in the book to a piece of cloth or parchment, or they might measure out a grid from the book and copy the design.

Finally, both calligraphy and needlework employed paper and parchment. Indeed, parchment often became an integral part of the lace. It might be used

---

7 Giovanni Tagliente, *Opera nuova che insegna alle donne a cusire ...* (Venezia, 1527), USTC 857984.

8 'lettere antique maiuscole, & le francesche, & molte altre sorti de disegni & lettere per poter cuscire, et racammare ...', Tagliente, *Opera nuova*, sig. [Aiiv].

9 Randall A. Rosenfeld, 'Using illustration of tools from sixteenth-century writing manuals', *Gazette du Livre Médiéval*, 33 (1998), pp. 42–43 cautions about how to read such tools.

10 Thus, like Inglis, she recognises her talent as coming from God. Lady Grace Mildmay, 'Autobiography', in Linda Pollock (ed.) *With Faith and Physic: the Life of a Tudor Gentlewoman ...* (London: Collins and Brown, 1993), p. 26.

as a pattern on which lace was worked in a 'buttonhole stitch'; or as the base for cushion lace, where the parchment pattern was pricked by pins fastening it to a cushion and the lace was worked on the pins; or in a 'card stitch' where thin strips of parchment were wrapped with thread, often metallic, creating a three-dimensional quality to the design.[11] Even in their very materiality, then, lacework and calligraphy incorporated components of each other.

Pietro Paolo Tozzi's lace book *Ghirlanda* is dedicated to Sister Maria Ginevra Machiavelli in Bologna. The book combines alphabets with borders of lace designs, advertised on the title page as 'beautiful letters, wise sayings, new laces'.[12] Notably, the wise sayings are written within lace border patterns, just as calligraphic manuals often used sententiae as models for handwriting, providing moral instruction for all learners. Tozzi published a number of illustrated books, including Sebastiano Zanella's manual on chancery hand.[13] He seems to have intended the *Ghirlanda* as a general 'how-to' book, since it also includes instructions on keeping daily expense accounts. Though this information can be used by anyone, the dedication to a nun and the title advertising a 'Garland ... picked from the most famous gardens of Italy', suggest that the book was directed to a female audience. While the metaphor of works as a bouquet of flowers was often used for collections of sententiae, prayers, or poetry (see Isabella Whitney's *A sweet nosgay, or pleasant posye*, 1573), it was also found in the titles of Italian needlework books, advertising their offerings as a garden (*Giardineto novo di Punti*, Venice, 1551), flowers (*Fiori di Ricami*, Bologna, 1591 and Siena 1603), or fruits (*I Frutti opera nuova*, Venice, 1564), attractive marketing devices for female purchasers.[14]

Tozzi's book is merely a late example among a whole group of lace and embroidery books that included letters as some element of the design. Indeed, examining early samplers with alphabets, Bianca Calibresi argues 'that needlework [should] be understood as a Renaissance writing technology in its own right'.[15] Plates with letters are found in Giovanni Vavassore (*Corona di racammi*, Venice, after 1530); *La fleur des patrons de lingerie* (c.1515–33); *A neawe treatys:*

---

11    'punto a reticella' and 'punto di cartella', Mrs. Bury Palliser, *History of Lace*, rev. M. Jourdain and Alice Dryden (1911; rpt. New York: Dover, 1984), pp. 50, 32, 36–37.

12    'Belle Lettere/ Dove Sententie/ Novi Merli' (Padova, [1604]) USTC 4038061.

13    Sebastiano Zanella, *Novo modo di scrivere* (Padova, Pietro Paolo Tozzi, 1605) USTC 4036774.

14    Wendy Wall points out how these sorts of terms highlight the collective aspect of miscellanies, which is what these embroidery books are, The *Imprint of Gender* (Ithaca: Cornell University Press, 1993), p. 103. Whitney, *Sweet Nosgay* (London, 1573), USTC 516754; the others are not letterpress and therefore not in the USTC.

15    Bianca Calibresi, '"you sow, Ile read": Letters and Literacies in Early Modern Samplers', in Heidi Hackel and Catherine E. Kelly (eds.), *Reading Women* (Philadelphia: University of Pennsylvania Press, 2008), p. 81.

*as co[n]cernynge the excellency of the nedle* (Antwerp, Vorsterman, *c.*1530–40s); and books by Domenico da Sera (*Le livre de lingerie*, Paris, 1584), and Giovanni Ostaus (*La Vera Perfettione del Disegno*, Venice, 1567, 1584).[16] Vavassore, in fact, instructed women 'to write with the needle', as a way for them to practise their letters.[17] The books by Vavassore and Ostaus were directed to 'women and young girls' in general, or in the case of Ostaus, to Lucretia Cantarini Priula, a Venetian noblewoman. Dominico da Sera unusually directed his book to both male and female readers, thus leading us to consider the larger topic of how lace and calligraphic manuals were gendered.

The pen and the needle invite metonymical comparison: one represents masculine learning, the other female handiwork. This contrast is set forth clearly in Ludovico Dolce's *Dialogue on the Instruction of Women* (1547) where his character Dorothea says, 'to tell the truth, knowing how to sew for women is equivalent to knowing how to write for men'.[18] And it is also true that most of the authors of both kinds of books were men and that the stated or implied audience for writing books was primarily male, while that for lace books was female. And yet—there are enough exceptions on both sides to complicate this facile distinction.[19]

To begin with, women as well as men were involved in the design and printing of both kinds of books. In addition to the male authors of writing books we have noted, Marie Pavie, a French woman, published a series of engraved handwriting specimens around 1600, while Maria Strick in the Netherlands published four writing manuals and ran a school.[20] Furthermore, men such as Sera, Tozzi, and Vavassori were joined in publishing lace designs by Elisabetta Catanea Parasole and Lucretia Romana in Italy, as well as Rosina Fuerst in Germany. The *Nüe Modelbuch* (Zurich, 1561) was directed to daughters and 'other laceworkers', and seems to have been the combined work of a male printer with a female designer, 'R.M.', thus illustrating Helen Smith's proposal

16   *Corona*, USTC 802547: La *fleur*, USTC 29671; *A neawe treatys*, USTC 437461; Sera, *Le livre de lingerie*, USTC 21222; and Ostaus, *La vera perfettione del disegno* ..., USTC 845601.

17   Fremke Speelberg, *Fashion & Virtue: Textile Patterns and the Print Revolution 1520–1620* (New York: Metropolitan Museum of Art, 2016), p. 28.

18   Quoted in Patricia Fortini Brown, *Private Lives in Renaissance Venice* (New Haven: Yale University Press, 2004), p. 113.

19   See Jones and Stallybrass, *Renaissance Clothing*, p. 144. Frye discusses why this dichotomy continued to hold in modern critical discourse, even when it was outdated, Frye, *Pens and Needles*, p. 25.

20   See Robert Williams, 'A Moon to Their Sun: Writing Mistresses of the Sixteenth and Seventeenth Centuries', *Fine Print*, 2.2 (1985), pp. 88–98; Ton Croiset van Uchelen, 'Maria Strick, Schoolmistress and Calligrapher in Early Seventeenth-Century Holland', *Quaerendo*, 39 (2009), pp. 83–132.

that we think of early modern books 'not as male-or female-authored but as the interface at which numerous agents coincide, in complex and varied ways'.[21]

The books themselves might be gender neutral or directed towards one sex or the other. The 1584 lace book by Dominico da Sera mentioned above is one of the most even-handed in its presentation. In it, Sera tells his readers that he has travelled widely in Europe and has gathered and edited eighty patterns, 'for the use & singular profit of many, men as well as women'.[22] He appended to his letter a *Balade* which further explained that he composed 'this very useful book' for everyone, 'especially those who are talented' and who wanted to 'understand well the arts of handwork', and his refrain is '[t]o all people who work with the needle'.[23] Sera's title is also gender-neutral, *The new book of lingerie*, as opposed to the titles of many Italian needlework books with female-loaded terms such as 'the triumph of virtue', or 'the crown [or precious gem] of noble and virtuous women'. In northern Europe, including Paris where Sera was published, or German-speaking countries and England, pattern books tended to have more sober, neutral titles such as those of Federico de Vinciolo, an Italian published in France, England, and Germany: *New and Singular Patternes & Workes of Linnen*.[24] One reason for the difference in title may have been that more women *and* men were involved in lacemaking and embroidery in northern Europe, while the appeal in Italy was to private women of leisure, and the women in their households.[25] The 1591 English edition of Vinciolo's book was dedicated by the publisher Adrian Poyntz to a woman from the merchant class, Mistress Susan Saltonstall, wife of a London alderman. As Wendy Wall has observed, 'the text's "packaging", ... speaks to the specific conditions by which meaning was and is transmitted,' and '"gender" was itself a crucial and formative ... category' in this packaging.[26]

The authors of several needlework books boasted that they offered patterns from different countries. Cesare Vecellio reminded his reader that he had

---

21    R.M. *Nüw modelbuch* ... (Zürich: Christoph Froschauer, 1561), USTC 678765. See Speelberg, *Fashion and Virtue*, p. 39; Helen Smith, *'Grossly Material Things'* (Oxford: University Press, 2012), p. 4.

22    '& est pour l'vtilité & singulier profit de plusieurs, tant hommes que femmes ...', Sera, *Lingerie* ..., sig. [2r].

23    Sera, *Lingerie*, sig. [2v].

24    *Les Singuliers et nouveaux pourtraicts et ouvrages de Lingerie* (Paris, 1587); French editions, USTC 47354; English edition, USTC 517254; German editions, Strasbourg, 1592, USTC 677123.

25    See Vecellio's dedication to Sig. Viena Vendramina Nani where he mentions the virtuous young women from the city whom she trains in her household (quoted in Palliser, *History of Lace*, p. 485).

26    Wendy Wall, *Imprint of Gender*, pp. 5, 7 fn 14.

already published a book on costumes of the world, and he set his lace patterns in the context of 'the modern practice of all of Europe'.[27] Lucretia Romana advertised 'ornaments of singular beauty that can be found in all Europe' in her Venetian pattern book of 1600, and John Taylor in his well-known poem 'Praise of the Needle' outdid almost everyone by claiming to have gathered patterns not only from Europe, but from Muscovy, Poland, China, Mexico and the West Indies.[28] These are obviously sales pitches, but they also suggest an educational purpose—that by learning these stitches, women and men will be in touch with the best that the wider world has to offer. Jones and Stallybrass have written about Englishwomen that 'if needlework demonstrates [their] capacities, it does so by absorbing Middle Eastern, Far Eastern and New World designs, and by empowering the needlewoman to represent anything in the world,' but the same was certainly true for male embroiderers.[29]

Though many lace and embroidery pattern books cling to the notion that working with the needle is something women ought to be doing, there is some sense that the work is not only beautiful, but useful and necessary, as one Venetian book puts it.[30] The manuals repeat that mastering these ever more complex designs is not only a way to conquer boredom, but 'to learn much', according to the sonnet in a 1587 French manual.[31] Another French poem in a 1605 manual dedicated to Marie de Medici went further, laying out a meta-physical context for lace as an 'art composed by number and by measure'. It compared a finished band of lace to a beautiful picture of the heavens, wherein each open place represents a sign—the middle, the degrees of the celestial sphere and the squares, virtues.[32] Turning from lace to letters, we remember that handwriting is also an art of measure. Tagliente, for example, taught by rule and proportion, and Pierre Le Bé, in an introductory poem to his 1601 book of Roman letters, said that the reader can find in it divers characters with the

---

27    Cesare Vecellio, *Corona delle Nobili et Virtuose Donne, libro primo* (Venice, 1591), sig. A2r, USTC 862178.

28    Lucretia Romana [and Elisabetta Parasole Catanea], *Ornamento nobile per ogni gentil matrona* (Venice, 1600), secondary title page, *Ornamento Delle Donne, Di singolar bellezza, che in tutta Europa si offerua*, sig. Ar. BNF copy, 1620 ed, USTC 4041672; John Taylor, *The Needles Excellency* (London, 1631), sig. [A4r], USTC 3015203.

29    Jones and Stallybrass, *Renaissance Clothing*, p. 137.

30    *Opera nova di recami intitolata il monte ...* (Venice: Sessa, 15??), The title page advertises: 'Opera non meu bella che utile, & necessaria', USTC 763811.

31    Federico Vinciolo, *Les singuliers et nouveaux pourtraicts ... de Lingerie* (Paris, 1587), sig. Aiiiir.

32    See 'Discours du Lacis', in Matthias Mignerak, *La pratique de l'aiguille industrieuse* (Paris, 1605), sigs. Aiiir–[Aiiiv], USTC 6015542.

symmetry and art of perfecting them, in true form, width and height.[33] Le Bé dedicated another set of letters to Marie de Bragelogne, offering them as patterns for various kinds of needlework.[34]

Le Bé's appeal to a broader audience of men and women was not unique among handwriting books. Two early German books by Wolfgang Fugger and Johann Neudorffer were directed 'to the good and use of all', and to everyone who 'with special benefit, may learn and understand the correct basis for writing well'.[35] In England, Francis Clement's book *The Petie Schole* (1587), intended for the middle class, indicated that tailors, weavers and seamstresses can now read and suggests children learn from them.[36] The book combines reading with learning to write and patterns for Secretary hand. Class factors here in a somewhat different way than it does with needlework. The latter was a skill that could be learned and practised at all social levels, from male and female workers making lace or embroidering for a living, to noble women and their ladies providing decorative work for their homes and dress. Complex designs could be achieved by any skilled worker whether artisan or amateur.

With writing however, learning and practising more complex hands would fall to those with a special talent such as calligraphers, or to those with the leisure to pursue this skill beyond the basic levels. This was especially true for women who could only learn the finer points of writing if they had time for such pursuits, if their families could afford a writing-master, or if it was a remunerative skill passed down in a family, in the case of Esther Inglis from mother to daughter. We know that Queen Elizabeth was trained by Roger Ascham, and that John Davies of Hereford taught a number of women including Elizabeth Cary, Elizabeth Dutton, Anne Tracy, and Elizabeth Baskerville.[37] There were at least three writing manuals dedicated to women, all from the upper classes: Jean de Beau-Chesne's 1593 *Key of Writing* (*La Clef de l'Escriture*) to his pupils, Mary, Elizabeth and Alathea Talbot, daughters of the Earl of Shrewsbury;

---

33    Pierre Le Bé, *Bele Prérie où chacun peut voir les lettres* ... (Paris, 1601) fol. [3], USTC 6000013.

34    Dedication and set of letters bound with the Paris, 1601 edition of Le Bé's book at the Bibliothèque National. The first sets of letters are dedicated to 'Monsieur le Grand-Lieutenant General au Bailliage, de la Ville de Sainct Denis'.

35    Wolfgang Fugger, *Ein Nutzlich und wolgegrundt formular* (Nürnberg, 1553), UTSC 645375; Johann Neudörffer the Younger, *Kurtze Fürweisung* (manuscript, Nürnberg, 1578), Newberry Library Wing MS ZW 547.N391; items 25 and 44 in Kathryn A. Atkins, *Masters of the Italic Letter* (Boston: David Godine, 1988).

36    Francis Clement, *The Petie Schole with an English Orthographie, wherin by rules ... is taught a method to enable both a childe to reade perfectly ... & also the unperfect to write English aright* (London, Thomas Vautrollier, 1587), p. 9, USTC 510693.

37    Henry Woudhuysen, *Sir Philip Sidney and the Circulation of Manuscripts 1558–1640* (Oxford: Clarendon Press, 1996), p. 38.

Lucas Materot's 1608 writing book to Marguerite de Valois, wife of Henri IV; and a manuscript writing manual by Beau-Chesne, custom-made for Princess Elizabeth, daughter of James VI and I.[38] Materot even designated certain styles of writing as especially appropriate for women, with 'letters easy for women to imitate'.[39] In the Netherlands there were girls' schools in which writing was taught. One of these was run by Maria Strick (1577–1625), who was praised as 'first among schoolmistresses in the use of pens, as well as in the French language, Arithmetic, and all kinds of Handwork useful to girls', thus linking writing and sewing once again.[40]

## 1    Esther Inglis, Designer with Needle and Pen

Strick's contemporary, Esther Inglis, came from a Huguenot family who had settled in Scotland. She learned the art of calligraphy from her mother Marie Presot, and it is likely that in her early years she helped with the teaching of handwriting at the French School run by her father in Edinburgh.[41] Unlike Strick, however, Inglis developed her career not as an educator but as a professional creator of calligraphically beautiful and physically tiny books. Around 1596, she married Bartilmo Kello, who seems to have taken charge of official foreign correspondence from Scotland, and later served as a Protestant minister. He is known to have also served in some clandestine operations for James VI with the court of Elizabeth I and the wider European Protestant network.[42] Inglis

---

38    Beau-Chesne, *La Clef* (London, 1593), STC 6445.3; Lucas Materot, *Les Oeuvres ... où l'on comprendra facilement la manière de bien et proprement escrire* (Avignon: J. Bramereau, 1608), USTC 6810795; Newberry Library Wing MS ZW 639 .B382.

39    'lettre facile à imiter pour les femmes', Materot, *Les Oeuvres*, fols. 49r, 50r. Lodovico Curione's *La Notomia delle Cancellaresche corsive* (Rome, 1588) includes a plate of secretary labelled 'lettre qui escrivent les dames de France'. See Heather Wolfe, 'Women's Handwriting', in Laura Lunger Knoppers (ed.), *The Cambridge Companion to Early Modern Women's Writing* (Cambridge: Cambridge University Press, 2009), p. 33.

40    Croiset van Uchelen, 'Maria Strick', p. 107.

41    Sara Gweneth Ross, 'Esther Inglis: Linguist, Calligrapher, Miniaturist, and Christian Humanist', in Julie D. Campbell and Ann R. Larsen (eds.), *Early Modern Women and Transnational Communities of Letters* (Farnham, England: Ashgate, 2009), p. 160.

42    Though a document exists appointing him as 'Clerk of all Passports', it was never signed and may have been written as a job proposal by Kello himself, see David Laing, 'Notes Relating to Mrs Esther (Langlois or) Inglis ...', *Proceedings of the Society of Antiquaries of Scotland*, 6 (Edinburgh: Neill, 1868), p. 288; Tricia Bracher, 'Esther Inglis and the English Succession Crisis of 1599', in James Daybell (ed.), *Women and Politics in Early Modern England* (Aldershot, Hamp., England: Ashgate, 2004), pp. 136–137; and Barker, *Les Proverbes*, pp. 41–44.

probably helped write out fair copies of the foreign correspondence, and she certainly created a number of miniature books for presentation to English and Scottish members of the courts of Elizabeth I and King James, as well as prominent supporters of the Protestant cause in Europe.[43]

Her skills with pen and needle were praised in several poems by distinguished male contemporaries, which she reproduced in many of her manuscripts.[44] In particular, Robert Rollock and John Johnston commended her skills with both instruments. Rollock wrote: 'Her needle vies with her pen/ Esther's skill vanquishes both—no prize for a winner'.[45] Johnston's epigram is worth citing in full:

> On Esther Inglis, a Most Rare Woman
> Neither is the labour slight, nor the glory inconsiderable.
> Everything is extraordinary: and what great grace lies in the smallest things?
> Make and compose numberless lines of verse, shapely designs and letters.
> All these she delivers, even outdoes with her needle, art and poetry—
> Such that Nature, might have mourned herself conquered by a mortal hand,
> Were it not that she knew these things to be the extraordinary gifts of the great God.[46]

For Johnston, it was Inglis's combined skills with writing, needlework and poetry that made her a worthy match with Nature, not a competitor, since Inglis's skills like the workings of Nature were divinely given.

---

43  For up-to-date lists of her known manuscripts, their locations and dedicatees, see Georgianna Ziegler, 'Esther Inglis: Calligrapher, Artist, Embroiderer, Writer' at <https://estheringlis.com>.

44  On the importance of Andrew Melville, John Johnston and Robert Rollock as members of a humanist circle including Inglis see Jamie Reid Baxter, 'Esther Inglis: A Franco-Scottish Jacobean Writer and her *Octonaries Upon The Vanitie And Inconstancie of the World*', SSL, 48.2 (2022), pp. 72–78; and Sarah Gweneth Ross, 'Esther Inglis Linguist', pp. 173–75.

45  'Cum penna sed certat acus: at vincit utramque/ Estherae probitas: praemia nulla tamen', translation a slight variation on that found in Barker, *Les Proverbes*, p. 28, n. 21.

46  Translation by William Poole and Jamie Reid Baxter via personal email to the author, 5 April 2021. The Latin reads: '"In Estheram Anglam rarissimam foeminam"/ Nec labor in tenui, tenuis nec gloria. rara/ Omnia: et in minimis gratia quanta subest?/ Finge, face innumeros numeros formasque notasque,/ Haec dat vel superat omnia acu, arte, lyrâ./ Mortali quod victa manu Natura doleret, / Ni sciat haec magni munera rara Dei./IOHANNES IONSTONVS'. Found in Christ Church MS 180 (1599) as well as others.

At least sixty-one of Inglis's manuscripts survive, in addition to a letter to James VI & I and an inscription in an album amicorum.[47] The earliest extant manuscript was made when she was about sixteen and serves as a copybook, displaying her mastery of five styles of writing, including *lettera rognosa* done with a broken line that looks like sewing stitches.[48] It was typical of calligraphic manuals to produce morally uplifting texts for their practitioners to copy. Here Inglis used translations of Psalms 2 and 94, with a few verses on each page, first in French and then in Latin. The pages are all framed with double-ruled lines which she likely made herself, and three pages at the back summarise five of the alphabets she used. Already thinking of herself as a professional, she ended her little book with the calligrapher's motto, 'Not the pen itself but the skill [in using it]'. This and the Latin verses by her father commending her skill, she was to re-use several times until 1606.[49] Like some printed calligraphic manuals, this little volume also shows signs of having been used as a copy book, perhaps by a child learning to write; folios 14ᵛ–15ʳ show wobbly S's and an H.

Another of her early calligraphic display books probably dates from the late 1580s to the early 1590s. It contains quotations from *Psalms* and *Proverbs* in English, but now written in forty different hands instead of just five. On every page but one (fol. 49), the verses are written between two alphabets at the top and bottom, a format familiar in standard calligraphic manuals. In February 1605, Inglis presented the book to seventeen-year-old Susan de Vere shortly after she married Philip Herbert, favourite of King James and soon-to-be Earl of Montgomery. In the dedication added at that time, Inglis called her work 'flovris ... collected of Dame FLORAS blossomes', hoping Lady Susan will accept it 'becaus it is the work of a woman of one, desyrous to serue and honour your L[adyship]'.[50] As we have seen with needlework books, calling it a collection of flowers was a marketing device directed towards a female audience, but Inglis also saw the appeal for her female dedicatees. Continuing with the garden motif, she referred to her work as 'a few grapes of hir collection' in a 1606 manuscript for Elizabeth, Lady Erskine.[51]

Two other early manuscripts whose design shows direct influence from calligraphic manuals are her 1591 *Discovrs de la Foy*, dedicated to Queen Elizabeth,

47   Esther Inglis, ALS to James VI and I, NLS, Adv. MS.33.1.6, vol. 20, no. 21; Album amicorum of George Craig, 1604, EUL, MS La.III.525, fol. 8r.

48   BL Sloane MS 987, fol. 24r.

49   'Nil penna sed usus', translation suggested by Dr. Alasdair A. MacDonald, personal email to the author, 28 July 2021. Scott-Elliot and Yeo, 'Calligraphic Manuscripts', p. 13.

50   Harvard, Houghton Library, MS Typ 428.1, fol. [1r].

51   Esther Inglis, 'A New Yeeres guift', Newberry Library Wing MS miniature ZW 645.K29.

and the 1592 *Livret traittant de la Grandeur de Dieu*, with no dedication.[52] Both are small oblong books whose text is written out between ruled margins, 'in diverse kinds of letters' as she said to the Queen.[53] Both books include samples of *tagliata* and *rognota* scripts that look like embroidery stitches. There is no other decoration on the pages, but eventually this style would evolve into her oblong-shaped coloured manuscripts where the text—often from *Psalms*, *Proverbs*, or the moralistic *Quatrains* and *Octonaires* by the Sieur de Pybrac and Antoine de la Roche Chandieu, respectively—is illuminated above with flowers, birds, frogs or insects, thus creating a kind of hybrid between a calligraphic and an embroidery manual. Thanks to Anneke Bakker, we now know that Inglis consulted at least two sources for her flower paintings which would have been used by embroiderers and lacemakers as well. One is the *Florae Deae* (c.1590, attributed to Adriaen Collaert), and the other is a set of printed engravings made specifically for embroiderers, *Fiori Naturali per Ricami d'ogni sorte* (c.1600).[54] Inglis's own work inspired others, not only to write in her manuscripts, as we saw earlier, but to imitate embroidery. One of her coloured volumes now in the National Records of Scotland contains actual pieces of silk embroidery cut out and pasted in by a later, probably nineteenth-century owner.[55]

There is never a sense in Inglis's dedications that she was co-opting a man's skill by setting herself up as a calligrapher. Indeed, the example of her own mother was at hand, and as we saw, in addition to her father who might be accused of partiality, her talent was fully appreciated by her male humanist colleagues. The cross-gendering of certain skill sets was part of the culture. After all, the chief embroiderer serving the Scottish royal household was a

---

52   *Discovrs*, Huntington Library MS HM 26068 and *Livret*, University of Edinburgh MS La.III.440. The text of the latter is from a work by Pierre du Val, Bishop of Sées; the source for the text of *Discovrs* has never been identified and has been credited to Inglis herself by Jamie Reid-Baxter, 'Esther Inglis's *Discours de la foy* and her *"pourtraict de la RELIGION CHRESTIENNE"*, gifted to Elizabeth Tudor on 1 January 1591', *Journal of the Edinburgh Bibliographical Society*, 17 (2022), pp. 63–94.

53   'en diuerses sortes de lettres', *Discours*, fol. [7v].

54   Bakker notes that the *Florae Deae* engravings are mostly copied directly from Collaert's *Florilegium* (Antwerp, c.1590), USTC 406864, but in reverse, Bakker, 'Dame Flora', pp. 55–57, 71, n. 9. It's possible that Inglis used the *Florilegium* instead of the rare set of engravings of the *Florae*, and pricked the images so that she could transfer them in reverse to her own pages.

55   Inglis, *Octonaires* by Antoine de la Roche Chandieu, presented to Ludovic Stuart, 2nd Duke of Lennox, as a New Year's gift in 1607. Deposited at NRS by the family of Sir John Clerk of Penicuik, NRS MS GD18/4508.

man, William Beaton.[56] While Inglis did use the humility topos to present her work, noting that her 'boldness' (hardiesse) was 'more than feminine' in her dedication of a 1605 manuscript to Thomas Hayes (subsequently Lord Mayor of London), what has not been noted is that the term 'hardiesse' or 'hardiment', was also used by male authors of handwriting and embroidery manuals.[57] Beau-Chesne in dedicating his *Tresor d'Escriture* to François de Mandelot, Governor of Lyon, writes: 'I have made so bold to present it to you'.[58] Likewise, in dedicating *Les Secondes Oevvres, et Svbtiles Inventions de Lingerie* (1594) to Catherine de Bourbon, Vinciolo said that because she helped keep virtue and the arts alive, he had taken his book 'hardimen' from the press to present to her.[59] 'To make bold' for both men was a humility stance from author to patron, as it was with Inglis. However, Inglis's dedication became even more daring due to her gender, which she usually excused by suggesting it was a boldness not appropriate for women, while embodying it in the very act of making the presentation. In at least three manuscripts, she presented herself as banishing 'feminine fear', and having the spirit of the queen of Amazons.[60] She did not consider her calligraphic skill itself as unwomanly, but the presentation of her work to those socially superior.

In her dedications, Inglis also called attention to the variety of letters and designs she could create, thus highlighting her talent, as many male calligraphers did. Writing to Sir Thomas Hayes (*c.*1606) she noted: 'I think I've traced as many sorts of characters and flowers as anyone else'; to Catherine de Parthenay, Vicomtesse de Rohan (1601), 'the variety of handwriting of which I think I have traced as many sorts as anyone else of this time'.[61] We have seen that the creators of needlework manuals frequently highlighted the variety of patterns they can offer, but calligraphers did the same. Jehan de Beau-Chesne in the dedication to his *Tresor* noted that he was ornamenting his work with 'divers alphabets of letters which have never yet been brought to light by any

---

56    Amy L. Juhala, 'Shifts and Continuities in the Scottish Royal Court, 1580–1603', in David Parkinson (ed.) *James VI and I, Literature and Scotland* (Leuven: Peeters, 2013), p. 23.

57    'la hardiesse plus que feminine de vous presenter', fol. 2r. Newberry Wing MS ZW645.K292.

58    'J'ay prins la hardiesse de le vous presenter', Beau-Chesne, *Le Tresor d'Escriture* (Lyon, 1580), sig. *4. USTC 13202.

59    'Voila l'occasion (excellente Princesse)/ Pour laquelle hardiment i'ay tiré de la presse/ Ce liure de reseaux pour vous le presenter'. Frederico Vinciolo, *Les Secondes Oeuvres et Subtiles Inventions* (Paris, 1594), sig. [Aiiiv], USTC 47666 (1595 ed.).

60    Folger MS V.a.93; NLS MS 24908; BL Royal MS 17.D.XVI.

61    'ie pense trace d'autant de façons de characteres et fleurs qu'aucun autre', Newberry Wing MS ZW645.K292; 'la varieté de l'escriture de laquelle ... ie pense avoir tracé autant de façons diverses qu'aucun autre de ce temps', NYPL Spencer Coll. MS 8. Inglis also invented at least two scripts. See Barker, *Les Proverbes*, pp. 70–71.

other writer before me'.[62] In his dedication of *Nouveaux Pourtraicts de Point Coupé* (1598) to 'Dames et Damoiselles', the publisher Jacques Foillet acknowledged that, 'especially as diversity contents the spirit, I want to offer you many kinds of Works'. To him and to others, embroidery was a way of keeping women interested so they would not get bored: 'take pleasure in my work', he continued, 'and by that chase away ennui'.[63]

While the calligraphers and embroidery instructors saw practical benefits for their audiences, Inglis looked for a less tangible but more uplifting benefit for the souls of her dedicatees. I have written elsewhere of the importance of the hand for Inglis; that she saw the handmade quality of her work as a divine gift, but also as creating something of value for the recipient.[64] In her mind, the curiosity and beauty of her creations in script and paint should raise the minds of her audience to think of spiritual things. Her dedication in 1602 of texts from *Ecclesiastes* and *Jeremiah* to Archibald Campbell, Seventh Earl of Argyll was only one of the places where she made this intention very clear. She asked him to accept 'this little Book written by my hand in several sorts of characters, so that the variety of handwriting pleasing the eyes, the spirit will similarly be raised towards the great Creator'.[65]

In addition to the power of her manuscripts themselves to bring spiritual enlightenment to their recipients, Inglis always acknowledged her own skills as coming from God. Accompanying many of her self-portraits is the motto 'From the Eternal, goodness,/ From myself, evil or nothing', underlining her Protestant belief that all goodness is God's, not what she can achieve herself.[66] In six of her manuscripts, including the 1599 one for Queen Elizabeth to be discussed below, Inglis added her own 'Prière a Dieu'. It opens by saying:

---

62    'diuers alphabets de lettres qui n'ont encores esté mises en lumiere, par aucun escriuain deuant moy', Beau-Chesne, *Tresor*, sig. *4.

63    'd'aultant que la diuersité co[n]tente les esprits, i'ay bien voulu vous representer maintes sortes d'Ouurages'; 'prendre plaisir à ce mien labeur, & par iceluy chasser paresse', Foillet, *Nouveaux Pourtraicts* (Montbeliard, 1598), sigs. Aiir, Aiiir, USTC 48678.

64    Georgianna Ziegler, "'Hand-Ma[i]de Books": The Manuscripts of Esther Inglis, Early-Modern Precursors of the Artists' Book', in Peter Beal and Margaret J. M. Ezell (eds.) *English Manuscript Studies 1100–1700*, vol. 9, *Writings by Early Modern Women* (London: The British Library, 2000), pp. 73–87.

65    'ce petit Liuret escrit de ma main en plusieurs sortes de caracteres, afin que la varieté de l'escriture delectant la veuë, l'esprit soit pareillement esleué envers le grand Createur ...', NLS MS 20498 [fol. 2v].

66    'De l'Eternel le bien,/ De moy, le mal ou rien'. This 'ultra-Calvinist "motto" [comes] from a book of sacred sonnets published at London in 1573 by another Huguenot refugee, the poet-pastor Marin Le Saulx', see Jamie Reid-Baxter, "'Glore of thy sex, and miracle to men" Esther Inglis and Scottish Jacobean Culture', *iScot Magazine*, February/March 2019.

O Lord to thine honour And by thy grace also,
I made this little book, ...
Assure, open, lift up, enlighten and gyde
My heart, my eye, my foot, my spirit and also my hand.[67]

Beau-Chesne made a similar gesture in the dedication of his *Clef de l'escriture* to the Talbot girls, where he wrote that he had been 'moued by many honorable and of the better sort, to bring to light that knowledge which God by his goodnesse hath liberally imparted vnto me'.[68] Such a stance is distinctly Protestant, and reveals Beau-Chesne's background as similar to that of Inglis and her family—religious refugees from France who settled in Britain. Given the fact that Beau-Chesne was dwelling in London when the Langlois family arrived, and had just had the first calligraphic manual in England (1571) published by another Huguenot, Thomas Vautrollier, it is highly likely that he would have met Inglis's family and especially her calligraphically talented mother, Marie Presot.[69] Although, as is well-known, Calvin himself had mixed feelings about the arts, at heart he recognised that these were among the gifts of God, and that it behooved any individual—which in the church would include men and women—to accept their gift and to recognise that it came from God.[70]

---

67    Translation by Jamie Reid Baxter. The original poem reads:
         Seigneur a ton honneur, et par ta grace aussi
         I'ai parfait ce Liure, ainsi Seigneur ains  i
         Pour ne faire oncques rien, au monde que ne duise
         Ton sainct Esprit tousiours en ce sentier humain
         Asseure, ouure, redresse, illumine, conduise,
         Mon coeur, mon oeil, mon pied, mon esprit, et ma main.
         (Christ Church College MS 180, (p. [155])

68    Beau-Chesne, *Clef*, sig. [*iiv].

69    Robert Williams noted that Marie Presot 'may have known' Jean de Beau-Chesne, but does not draw out these further connections. Williams, 'A Moon', p. 90.
         Vautrollier published the kinds of books, including Beau-Chesne's manual, that Nicholas Langlois would have needed when he set up his French School in Edinburgh, and indeed, both men had ties with the court of James VI: Vautrollier in supplying books to the tutor of the young king (1578–1581), and Langlois, around the same time, receiving a pension from the King for his school (1581). On Vautrollier, see John Corbett, 'The Prentise and the Printer: James VI and Thomas Vautrollier', in Kevin J. McGinley and Nicola Royan (eds.), *The Apparelling of Truth: Literature and Literary Culture in the Reign of James VI* (Newcastle-upon-Tyne: Cambridge Scholars Publishing, 2010), pp. 80–93. For Langlois' pension see *Register of the Privy Seal of Scotland*, VIII, no. 591, p. 98.

70    'But forasmuch as carving and painting are the giftes of God, I require that they both be purely and lawfully used. God gave them to us "for his glorie"'. John Calvin, *Institution of Christian Religion*, trans. Thomas Norton (London, 1599), Bk.1, chap. 2. 11 sig. [D5v], USTC 513899.

From her earliest self-portraits, Inglis presented herself as a skilled pen-woman with some of the tools of the trade that we saw used in the illustration to Tagliente's writing and lace books. Borrowing the depiction of a woman writer from an engraved portrait by Pierre Woeiriot of Georgette de Montenay found in editions of her *Emblemes Chrestiennes*, Inglis depicted herself with pen in hand and inkwell at the ready, along with a copy book in front of her. These are found in the eight stunning black-and-white manuscripts of 1599 to 1602. Beginning with her colour portraits around 1606–07, she presented herself entirely as a calligrapher, discarding the lute and music from Montenay's portrait and adding more tools of her art: a brush, and finally a rule and calipers in her last great black-and-white self-portrait of 1624, a presentation to Prince Charles.[71] Musical instruments were traditionally a way for women artists to show that they had 'ladylike' accomplishments, but Inglis was assured enough to depict herself as an artist of pen and brush.[72]

It is likely that Inglis made most of the embroidered bindings found on sixteen of her extant volumes.[73] Her skills as an embroiderer were well-known, and it would have been expensive to outsource such work. On the other hand, the cost of materials was not inconsequential, especially the gold or silver-wrapped threads used on a number of her bindings, and the seed pearls on bindings for Queen Elizabeth (1599), Prince Maurice of Nassau (1599), Prince Henry (1608 and 1609), and Prince Charles (two in 1624).[74] It is possible that friends with Scottish or English court connections may have helped supply some of the rich materials needed for these royal bindings, and some of the more complex later bindings were likely outsourced to a professional embroiderer who could have been a man or woman.[75] Designs used on her embroidered bindings include

71    Georgette de Montenay, *Cent Emblemes Chrestiennes* (Lyons, 1584), USTC 12640, probably the edition used by Inglis. Esther Inglis, *Emblemes Chrestiens*, 1624, BL Royal MS 17.D.XVI.

72    See Georgianna Ziegler, 'Portraits of a Lady: the Self-presentation of Esther Inglis, Protestant Limner', *Renaissance Quarterly*, 76 (2023), pp. 565–67, 580.

73    See Barker, *Les Proverbes*, p. 29.

74    Christ Church Oxford MS 180; Folger Library MS V.a.93; Folger Library MS V.a.94 and Private Library, Norfolk; British Library Royal MS 17.D.XVI, and Wormsley Library, BM 1850.

75    A wardrobe account from Elizabeth I shows seed pearls at 1 pence each in 1566–69. In 1600 two hundred pearls would be worth about £1.62 (given inflation) which was the equivalent of about 20-days' work of a skilled tradesman, see Janet Arnold, *Queen Elizabeth's Wardrobe Unlock'd* (Leeds: Maney, 1988), p. 25. My calculations are based on the Inflation Calculator from the Bank of England <https://www.bankofengland.co.uk/monetary-policy/inflation/inflation-calculator>, and the National Archives Currency Converter <https://www.nationalarchives.gov.uk/currency-converter/#currency-result>. Describing the Hardwick Hall embroideries, Santina M. Levey notes 'the high cost of

the Prince of Wales feathers, as well as a Tudor rose, phoenix, ship, fish, flowers in pots, and twisting vine borders. The latter six types could have been found in embroidery manuals or emblem books. Indeed, potted flowers are a recurring motif, found as early as 1530 in Vavassori's *Essemplario di lavori* and later in the manuscript pattern books of Lunardo Fero (1559) and Thomas Trevillion (1608).[76] Bands of twisting leafy vines were also staples in lace and embroidery manuals, what Santina Levey calls 'linked foliate S-shapes ... an international Renaissance style'.[77]

In concluding this investigation of the relationship between the work of Esther Inglis and the traditions of calligraphic and needlework manuals, I want to focus on one of the early black-and-white manuscripts, *Le Livre des Psaumes*, made for Queen Elizabeth in 1599.[78] Here Inglis combined techniques of calligraphy with needlework, highlighting her skills of writing and embroidery and her exquisite sense of design as she brought together many sources to create a tour-de-force gift fit for a queen. She even asked the queen to keep it in 'some retired corner of your cabinet' as a precious object.[79]

The red velvet binding features a crowned Tudor rose on front and back, embroidered in silver-gilt thread and surrounded by a green-leafy wreath, all within a border of vines, leaves and flowers, highlighted with silver-gilt thread and pearls (Fig. 20.2).

Inglis carried this design through to the title page, where the crowned rose sits atop an elaborate architectural border copied from a 1589 edition of *De gli Automati* (Fig. 20.3), then to the penultimate page of the manuscript, where another crowned Tudor rose decorated with 'pearls' (as on the binding) rests between a heraldic lion and dragon, all drawn in pen and ink (Fig. 20.4).[80] The lion and dragon in turn echo the royal coat of arms at the beginning of the book, elaborately drawn on the verso of the title page (Fig. 20.5). Inglis may have copied the arms from the title page to the Geneva Bible in English, printed by Christopher Barker.[81] The allegorical figures of Mercy and Justice may again

---

metal threads meant that they were used sparingly ...', Santina M. Levey, *Elizabethan Treasures: the Hardwick Hall Textiles* (London: The National Trust, 1998), pp. 63–64.

76   Lunardo Fero, Manuscript of embroidery designs (Venice, 1559), V&A no. E.1940-1909; Thomas Trevillion, Manuscript miscellany (England, 1608), Folger MS V.b.232.

77   Levey, *Elizabethan Treasures*, p. 63.

78   Oxford, Christ Church College MS 180.

79   'quelque coing retiré de vostre cabinet'. Inglis asks this of her dedicatees in several of her manuscripts. Similarly, the publisher of Vinciolo's 1594 pattern book hopes that Catherine de Bourbon will find a place for it 'en vostre Cabinet' (Aiijr).

80   Hero Alexandrinus, *De Gli Automati* (Venice: Girolamo Porto, 1589), USTC 835654.

81   *The Holy Bible* ... (London: Christopher Barker, 1584), USTC 510082.

FIGURE 20.2     Embroidered cover of *Le Livre des Pseaumes*, 1599. Christ Church Oxford,
MS 180

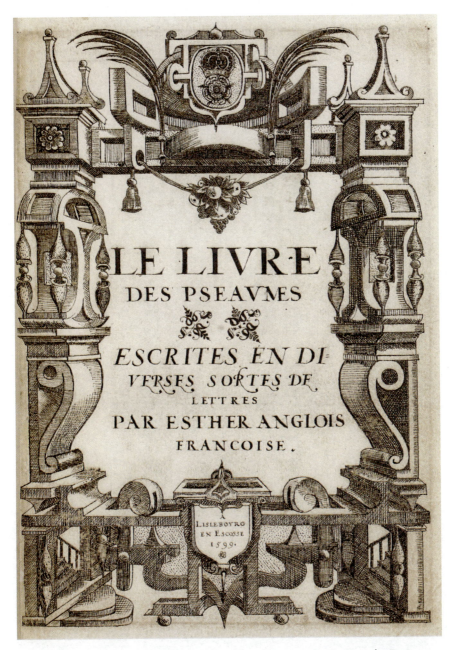

FIGURE 20.3    Copy by Inglis of title page of *De gli Automati* in *Le Livre des Pseaumes*.
Christ Church Oxford, MS 180

FIGURE 20.4 Penultimate page of *Le Livre des Pseaumes*, 1599. Christ Church Oxford, MS 180

FIGURE 20.5     Verso of the title page of *Le Livre des Pseaumes*, 1599. Christ Church Oxford, MS 180

have been inspired by title pages to earlier editions of Barker's Geneva Bible.[82] Thus in re-imagining the decorative title pages made by male printers, Inglis created a wholly new object, encased in the Queen's devices.

Inglis's dedication to the Queen (Fig. 20.6) is headed with an elaborate ornament of thistles, pansies and other flowers possibly taken from the 1588 Geneva Bible, but also found in a 1586 mathematical manuscript by Scottish calligrapher John Geddy as the top of his decorative title page frame. It is possible that Inglis knew that manuscript since she used several other designs from it in this book for the Queen.[83] Her entire volume contains decorative bands, separating blocks of text; she could have copied these from printers' ornaments, but also from an embroidery manual, where such band designs were prominent. The use of these ornaments along with a variety of handwriting styles set in a beaded border give some of the pages the look of a sampler (Fig. 20.7). The technique of creating a sampler—and as we saw, composing the calligraphic and lace manuals themselves—is similar to commonplacing; that is, 'the ordering of fragments according to thematic consistencies'.[84] In Inglis's case, her 'fragments' came from a variety of calligraphic and printed sources and were carefully chosen to create a new harmonious whole encasing the Psalms, much as the women of the mixed-gendered community Little Gidding created their cut-and-paste Biblical Harmonies a few years later.[85]

Esther Inglis was the product of a highly cultured, humanistic, Protestant, multilingual society in sixteenth-century Edinburgh that drew heavily on Continental books and ideas.[86] Among these would have been the age-old dis-

---

82    While Inglis follows the text of the Psalms from the French Geneva Bible (1588), the figures on the coat-of-arms page are most similar to those on the title pages to Barker's English editions. See for example, *The Holy Bible* ... (London: Christopher Barker, 1578), USTC 508635.

83    The 1588 Geneva Bible as a source is identified by Scott-Elliott and Yeo, 'Calligraphic Manuscripts', p. 34. The association with Geddy's manuscript (University of St. Andrews Library MS QA33.G4), was noted by Jamie Reid Baxter in a talk to the Edinburgh Bibliographical Society, 18 Feb. 2021, kindly shared with the author. Inglis may well have known Geddy.

84    Adam Smyth, 'Commonplace Culture: A List of Sixteen Traits', in Anne Lawrence-Mathers and Phillipa Hardman (eds.) *Women and Writing, c.1340–c.1650* (York: York Medieval Press, 2010), p. 98.

85    On Little Gidding and gender, see Whitney Trettien, *Cut/Copy/Paste: Fragments from the History of Bookwork* (Minneapolis: University of Minnesota Press, 2021), Chapter 1. <https://manifold.umn.edu/read/cut-copy-paste/section/315b46da-208c-4e3b-ac62-4107 a636ba80#ch01>.

86    As Margaret Lane Ford writes, 'Scots were well aware of what was available in print on the Continent and had the means to be supplied with it, whether through the extensive Scots networks abroad or through a book-trade at home' Margaret Lane Ford, 'Importation

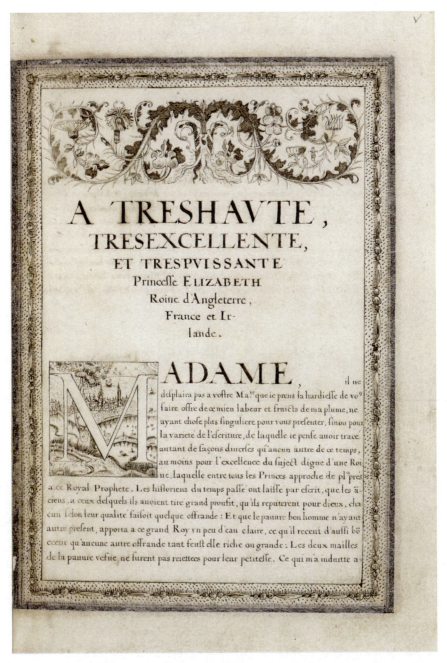

FIGURE 20.6    Inglis's dedication to Queen Elizabeth I in *Le Livre des Pseaumes*, 1599.
Christ Church Oxford, MS 180

FIGURE 20.7    Example of Inglis's decorative bands separating text blocks in *Le Livre des Pseaumes*, 1599. Christ Church Oxford, MS 180

cussion of imitation versus invention, taught in conjunction with rhetoric and applied to poetry. As James VI wrote in his treatise 'Of Scottis Poesie', 'Inuention, is ane of the cheif vertewis in a Poete', but it has to come from Nature; 'For airt is onely bot ane help and a remembraunce to Nature'.[87] In his verses praising Inglis, Andrew Melville wrote of her hand, emulating nature, creating 'living symbols, breathing tokens of heaven', but it was her mind, directing the hand, which 'surpasses all wonderful things'.[88] In other words, it was her God-given invention which made anew the sources on which she draws. According to early modern concepts of gender, Melville was thus implicitly suggesting that Inglis used her imagination and creativity, traits that were usually gendered masculine. The fact that her *sex* was female did not in this case preclude her taking on these masculine attributes, since gender was based on contrasting notions such as spirit versus flesh, or mind versus matter, but not on sex. Thus men and women could, and did practise the skills of writing and sewing, as we have seen throughout this investigation.[89]

Esther Inglis created her remarkable manuscripts by imitating texts and designs which she ordered in new ways. Although she was praised for her skill with the pen and the needle, I suggest that in much of her creative work the two instruments become one, simultaneously expressing the arts of needle-work through penmanship. As her friend Robert Rollock wrote: 'Her needle vies with her pen: Esther's skill vanquishes both', and that skill is her invention, a divine gift as she understands it.

---

of Printed books into England and Scotland', in Lotte Hellinga and J.B. Trapp (eds.), *The Cambridge History of the Book in Britain*, vol. III, 1400–1557 (Cambridge: Cambridge University Press, 1999), p. 201.

87    James VI, *The Essayes of A Prentise, in the Divine Art of Poesie* (Edinburgh: Thomas Vautrollier, 1584), sigs. [Miiv]–Miiir, USTC 510023. See also Rocío G. Sumillera, *Invention: The Language of English Renaissance Poetics* (MHRA, 2019) <https://doi.org/10.2307/j .ctv16kkz9p>.

88    'Signa creans animata, polum spirantia signa: ... mira omnia vincit/ Mens manui moderans, dum manus urget opus', Christ Church MS 180, fol. [viiv]. Translation from Bridging the Continental Divide: <https://www.dps.gla.ac.uk/electronic-resource/display /?pid=d2_MelA_047&aid=MelA>.

89    On early understandings of gender, see Claire Colebrook, 'Gender before Modernity', in *Gender* (London: Palgrave Macmillan, 2004), Chapter 1.

# CHAPTER 21

# Rare Books and Rarer Personalities: Belle da Costa Greene, Wilfrid Michael Voynich, and Stylised Gender Performance in the Rare Book Trade, c.1890–1930

*Natalia Fantetti*

The idea of gender as an action, or rather, a series of them, is not new. From Simone de Beauvoir's commonly cited maxim that 'one is not born, but rather, becomes a woman' to the landmark essays discussing gender and performativity by Judith Butler, gender is now regularly viewed as a doing of some kind.[1] We play with tropes and signals that create femininity and masculinity, situating ourselves along the spectrum of gender as we make our way through the world. Of course, the terms 'femininity' and 'masculinity' are in themselves multi-dimensional and resist being interpreted in a single way. This requires us to make the next logical leap to pluralise our thinking into femininities and masculinities, and in doing so, to consider the particular ways in which these identities may be constituted. It is not enough, however, to simply be cognisant of these theoretical performative pluralities, but to utilise these ideas in order to parse apart the actions and constructed identities of historical individuals. The rare book trade in the first half of the twentieth century offers us two prime examples where such analysis is incredibly fruitful: Belle da Costa Greene (1879–1950) and Wilfrid Michael Voynich (1865–1930). It initially may seem odd to compare and contrast published accounts of these two people considering that they did not have the same experiences or opportunities. One

---

1  The research for this article has been undertaken as part of the CULTIVATE MSS project, which has received funding from the European Research Council (ERC) under the European Union's Horizon 2020 research and innovation programme (Grant agreement No. 817988). This essay was written during the global COVID-19 pandemic, which has restricted my access to libraries and archives. The title is a play on E. Millicent Sowerby's memoir of her time in the trade, one section of which is dedicated to her time working with Voynich. Simone de Beauvoir, *The Second Sex*, trans. Constance Borde and Sheila Malovany-Chevallier (London: Vintage Books, 2011), p. 293; Judith Butler has returned to ideas about gender and performativity in several essays, but those found in her landmark book *Gender Trouble: Feminism and the Subversion of Identity* (New York: Routledge, 1990) are particularly helpful.

was a woman of colour, the other was a white man; one was an employee of a grand institution, the other was the owner of their own business. And yet I would argue that it is worth setting them side by side as they are the individuals that exemplify the use of gendered performativity in the construction of their public personalities in the field and time in which they operated.

It is perhaps unsurprising that accounts of a trade in literature would contain dramatic characters, strong personalities, and eccentric dispositions. Published narratives written in hindsight by those who were there and newspaper articles that told of events as they happened needed to populate their stories with memorable figures, in order to keep them interesting. As such, it is necessary to separate our two subjects from what was reported about them, in order to explore the ways in which they managed expectations and perceptions to navigate the book trade. Wanting to make an impact, and doing so by projecting a larger-than-life personality, is certainly not unusual within the rare book trade, or elsewhere. What sets Greene and Voynich apart, however, is that in creating these public images, they actively utilised very specific ideas of femininity and masculinity that played into recognisable, contemporary gender stereotypes, and encouraged such representations of themselves by their contemporaries. Therefore, a critical exploration of how they constructed their public selves in relation to gender ideas and ideals is necessary to understand their reputations and legacies within the trade.

## 1      Belle da Costa Greene

By the time she was a key figure in the rare book world, Greene was already no stranger to constructing a public-facing identity, as before any ideas of gender performativity came into play, Greene had already reinvented herself along the lines of race. She was born Belle Marion Greener in 1879 to Genevieve Fleet and Richard Theodore Greener, the first black graduate of Harvard College, an African American rights activist, and later dean of Howard Law School.[2] Her mother's family were equally, if not more prominent, in the African American community, having been 'part of a stable community of free people of colour in

---

2  Katherine Reynolds Chaddock, *Uncompromising Activist: Richard Greener, First Black Graduate of Harvard College* (Baltimore: Johns Hopkins University Press, 2017), p. 1; 'Richard Theodore Greener', *Britannica Online* <https://www.britannica.com/biography/Richard -Theodore-Greener> (accessed 22 July 2022).

Georgetown and then Washington, D.C., for most of the nineteenth century'.[3] Eventually their relationship soured, and after the disappointments of living in the post-Reconstruction South and Genevieve's increasing 'enjoyment of the New York white world', Richard moved out of the family home in 1897.[4]

Her father's desertion of the family marked a point of reinvention for the rest of the Greeners, for by 1900, Belle, her mother, and her four siblings were officially documented as white.[5] Adopting the surname Greene, the family disguised their African American ancestry by claiming a Portuguese connection that manifested itself with the insertion of 'da Costa' into their names. The newly minted Greenes would cut all ties with their pasts, keeping to white circles and neighbourhoods, in order to keep up the appearances that their new identities demanded. Despite the rumours surrounding her ethnicity during her lifetime, Greene ostensibly succeeded in obscuring her roots, and it was not until 1999 that the historian Jean Strouse officially revealed Greene's relationship to Richard Greener, and thus, the truth of her racial background.[6] In passing as white she gained access to privileges that would have eluded her as a woman of colour, including working in the library at Princeton, which as Stefan M. Bradley notes, did not allow African American students to attend 'in earnest until the middle of the twentieth century' (despite being a northern town and an elite university, it 'was as segregated as any place below the Mason-Dixon Line for much of its history').[7] One wonders what her turn of the century employers would have thought had they known that one of their librarians was a woman of colour. And yet it was at Princeton that she met Junius Spencer Morgan, a professional connection that would prove to be a pivotal moment in Greene's career.[8]

In 1905, following a meeting facilitated by Junius, Greene was hired as the personal librarian to the extraordinarily wealthy J. Pierpont Morgan, for nearly twice what she was earning at Princeton.[9] Not content to remain in the

3   Heidi Ardizzone, *An Illuminated Life: Belle da Costa Greene's Journey from Prejudice to Privilege* (New York: W.W. Norton & Company, 2007), p. 27.

4   Reynolds Chaddock, *Uncompromising Activist*, p. 126.

5   Ardizzone, *An Illuminated Life*, pp. 52–53.

6   Ardizzone, *An Illuminated Life*, pp. 54–55; Alexandra Lapierre, *Belle Greene* (New York: Europa Editions, 2022), p. 489.

7   Stefan M. Bradley, 'The Southern-Most Ivy: Princeton University from Jim Crow Admissions to Anti-Apartheid Protests', *American Studies*, 51 (Fall/Winter 2010), p. 109.

8   Joanna Scutts, 'The Mysterious Woman Behind J.P. Morgan's Library', *TIME* (17 May 2016) <https://time.com/4336930/the-mysterious-woman-behind-j-p-morgans-library/> (accessed 21 September 2021).

9   Jean Strouse, *Morgan: American Financier* (London: The Harvill Press, 1999), p. 509.

library quietly attending the manuscripts, she often stood in for Morgan in the auction room and quickly garnered respect amongst those in the trade.[10] After Morgan's death in 1913, esteemed scholars and bookdealers such as Hercules Read and Jacques Seligmann 'were in constant contact with Greene', and despite Morgan's son (J. Pierpont Morgan Jr., known as Jack) supposedly being in charge of his father's affairs, 'their warm and supporting letters show that they considered Belle rather than Jack as the person who had inherited the responsibility of the collection'.[11] Greene continued to work in a personal capacity for Jack Morgan for several years, eventually becoming Director of the Pierpont Morgan Library once it was incorporated as a public entity in 1924. She would hold this position until her retirement in 1948.[12]

Whilst Greene had nearly always presented an image of someone not to be trifled with, as well as a sense of elegant hauteur, her femininity increasingly became formidable, with her reputation changing over time from that of a spirited, fashionable woman to one of the great names in the book trade. The bookdealer H.P. Kraus recalled of his first meeting with the 'strong-willed, not easily charmed, [...] elder stateswoman of American rare book librarians' in the 1940s that 'her manner befitted her station: regal, aloof. I trembled'.[13] Considering that she apparently began her association with the brusque and bullish Morgan 'quaking with fear and shaking like an aspen', by the end of her career she had seemingly supplanted him as the terroriser-in-chief to young book dealers at the helm of the Morgan Library.[14] Though it was not her name hanging above the door, she had become synonymous with the library itself, with Lawrence C. Wroth writing in a tribute to her as part of a 1949 retrospective exhibition held in her honour that '[s]he could not conceive of herself apart from the institution she served'.[15]

Greene was perceived as a singular figure in her own time, with Voynich himself highlighting her exceptionalism during an interview in 1912 with E. Millicent Sowerby (who later became his employee). According to Sowerby's

---

10    Scutts, 'The Mysterious Woman'.

11    Flaminia Gennari-Santori, '"This Feminine Scholar": Belle da Costa Greene and the Shaping of J.P. Morgan's Legacy', *Visual Resources*, 33 (2017), p. 191.

12    Scutts, 'The Mysterious Woman'.

13    H.P. Kraus, *A Rare Book Saga: The Autobiography of H.P. Kraus* (New York: G.P. Putnam's Sons, 1978), p. 87.

14    'Education: Belle of the Books', *TIME* (April 11 1949) <http://content.time.com/time/mag azine/article/0,9171,800100,00.html> (accessed 10 August 2021).

15    Lawrence C. Wroth, 'A Tribute to the Library and its first Director' in *The First Quarter Century of the Pierpont Morgan Library: A Retrospective Exhibition in Honor of Belle Da Costa Greene* (New York: The Spiral Press, 1949), p. 28.

retelling, Voynich held up Greene as the only woman who had been successful in the rare book trade, stating that,

> she was [the] most remarkable woman in the United States of America, Miss Belle Da Costa Greene of Mr. Morgan's libraries in New York. No other woman could do what she had done; she was unique.[16]

In some respects, Voynich was not exaggerating here. Just a year before this interview at the Hoe Sale, whilst she was not the only professional woman present (the *New York Times* also mentioned the bookdealer Madame Théophile Belin in its coverage), Greene was the only one who could deal at the very top of the market.[17] The second-most expensive book sold (at $42,800) went to the Pierpont Morgan Library.[18]

Greene was not only unusual in being both a woman and a big spender in the auction room; those who encountered her commented on her distinctive appearance too, as striking hats and furs were part of Greene's usual work wardrobe. Her sartorial credentials are evidenced in a sketch by Paul Helleu of 1913, as Helleu was known for his portraits of elegant women, with 'his sitters always finely attired, often in striking hats, gloves, furs, muffs, and counting amongst the loveliest socialites of the time', as John S. Grioni notes (Fig. 21.1).[19]

With her penchant for jewels and fine clothes, hers was a hyper-feminine presence in the auction room, leading *The New York Times* to write that she 'bore no earthly resemblance to the traditional bookworm so far as appearance went'.[20] Certainly, there would not have been many who would have attended an after-dinner auction session in a 'sweeping gown of watered silk' as Greene reportedly did one evening during the Hoe sale.[21] The impact of her glamourous clothes was augmented by the use of heavy perfume, so that one could

---

16    E. Millicent Sowerby, *Rare people and rare books* (London: Constable and Company Ltd., 1967), p. 4.

17    "'J.P. Morgan's Librarian says High Book Prices are Harmful': Miss Belle De Costa Green Thinks the Amounts Paid for Many of the Volumes of the Hoe Collection Are Ridiculous", *The New York Times* (30 April 1911), p. 13.

18    'Morgan pays $42,800 for Book at Hoe Sale: Competitive Bidding to the Last for "Le Morte D'Arthur,", Printed by Caxton', *The New York Times* (2 May 1911), p. 1.

19    John S. Grioni, 'Helleu's Nudes' in *Konsthistorik tidskrift/Journal of Art History*, 62 (1993), p. 221.

20    'J.P. Morgan's Librarian says High Book Prices are Harmful', p. 13.

21    Wesley Towner and Stephen Varble, *The Elegant Auctioneers* (New York: Hill & Wang, 1970), p. 276.

FIGURE 21.1    Paul Helleu, *Portrait of Belle da Costa Greene*, 1913, The Morgan Library &
Museum
IMAGE IN THE PUBLIC DOMAIN

not fail to notice her, or her feminine presence, when she entered the room.[22]
Traditional bookworm or not, she had a career in rare books spanning over four
decades, becoming a well-respected expert on rare books and manuscripts in
the process. Her stylised femininity allowed her to make an impression from

22    Cass Canfield, *The Incredible Pierpont Morgan* (London: Hamish Hamilton, 1974), p. 152.

the outset in the male-dominated top end of the market and she parlayed this notoriety into establishing a powerful reputation within the trade.

## 2      Wilfrid Michael Voynich

Voynich was also a figure whose appearance and activities attracted comment. Born in 1864 in Lithuania to Polish parents, Voynich went on to study both law and chemistry.[23] At university he got involved with the Polish nationalist movement, which resulted in his arrest, an eighteen-month incarceration in the Warsaw Citadel, and being sentenced without trial to exile in Siberia for five years—from which he made a daring escape. According to Arnold Hunt, Voynich was 'not averse to playing up the glamour and mystery surrounding his revolutionary past' in later years, to the extent that in certain company he would 'point dramatically to the wounds he had received in the course of those adventures'.[24] The culmination of his Siberian prison break brought him to London in 1890, and to the woman who would become his wife, then Ethel Lilian Boole.[25] She shared Voynich's revolutionary sympathies, and for a time, they both collaborated with a group of Russian exiles to oppose and expose tsarist oppression. As their involvement with the group wound down, Ethel, now also Voynich, took up her writing career in earnest (in which she would become very successful) and Wilfrid Voynich turned to bookselling.[26]

Voynich entered the antiquarian book trade about 1897, with his business operations extending to offices with varying degrees of success in London, Paris, Florence, Warsaw, and New York.[27] We do not know exactly how long each of his continental ventures lasted, though his long standing employee Herbert Garland stated that the Florentine and Parisian bookshops were opened in 1908 and 1912 respectively.[28] According to the company letterhead, the Warsaw branch was opened by November 1910.[29] They must have been doing reasonably well in the first half of the 1910s given that all three

---

23      Arnold Hunt, 'Voynich the Buyer', in Raymond Clemens (ed.), *The Voynich Manuscript* (New Haven: Yale University Press, 2016), p. 11.

24      Ibid., p. 12.

25      Gerry Kennedy, *The Booles and The Hintons: Two dynasties that helped shape the modern world* (Cork: Atrium, 2016), p. 158.

26      Ibid., p. 14.

27      Herbert Garland, 'Some Famous English Bookshops III: Notes on the Firm of W.M. Voynich', *New Library World*, 34 (1932), pp. 225–228; James Clegg (ed.), *Clegg's International Directory of Booksellers* (Rochdale: Aldine Press, 1914) p. 323.

28      Garland, 'Some Famous English Bookshops', pp. 226–227.

29      W.M. Voynich, Letter to H.H. Furness, 11.11.1910, University of Pennsylvania Special Collections, Ms. Coll. 1356, Box 10 Folder 4.

establishmentswerestilllistedinthe1914editionof*Clegg'sInternationalDirectory of Booksellers*.[30] This is as much as I have been able to ascertain. However it is clear that Voynich began to use New York as his primary base from 1916 whilst still making book-hunting trips across to Europe, and towards the end of that decade and in the early 1920s, was conducting a brisk business. Although the remaining offices in New York and London were not in the best financial state at his death in 1930, his reputation was such that even those in the next generation of book dealers held him in great esteem, with H.P. Kraus writing that '[a]ll I can say is that he rose like a meteor in the antiquarian sky and his catalogues testify to his abilities'.[31]

Despite being described by Sowerby as simultaneously having 'the head and shoulders of a great Norwegian god' and being 'the greatest international rare-book dealer of his time', contemporary photographs do not show him to have been all that different visually from his colleagues in the trade in the way that Greene was.[32] In the photograph taken in his Soho Square office in London, and published in *The Tatler* in 1904, Voynich appears to be the embodiment of the traditional rare bookseller (Fig. 21.2).

Dressed smartly, though conventionally, he does not meet the camera's gaze but rather intently studies what is perhaps a scholarly volume, due to its two columns and size. He has his papers set up haphazardly around him and wears glasses, the well known hallmark of the studious man. Whilst a feature in *The Tatler* suggests a certain degree of celebrity, there is little else that would indicate this man was some kind of larger-than-life personality. There must have been something else in his manner, charisma or public image that made others perceive him as an unusual figure in the rare book trade in the first half of the twentieth century. By the time the bookseller Giuseppe Orioli had met him, Voynich was perhaps no longer a physically imposing presence, being 'a bent kind of creature and getting on for sixty'.[33] Yet the young Orioli seems to have been in awe of the elder bookseller, as Voynich tells him of the manuscripts and incunabula found in his earlier book hunting expeditions, claiming '[w]hat I have discovered in Italy is altogether unbelievable!'.[34] This depiction of Voynich as a book man who actively sought out and 'discovered' rare books from libraries and monasteries as one might discover buried treasure, would

---

30    Clegg, *Clegg's International Directory of Booksellers*, pp. 288, 316, 323.

31    Kraus, *A Rare Book Saga*, p. 219.

32    Sowerby, *Rare People*, pp. 3, 8.

33    Giuseppe Orioli, *Adventures of a Bookseller* (London: Chatto & Windus, 1938), p. 76.

34    Ibid., p. 77.

MR. VOYNICH AMONG HIS BOOKS IN SOHO SQUARE

FIGURE 21.2     Wilfrid Voynich, Photograph reproduced in *The Tatler* 1904
                CHRONICLE/ALAMY STOCK PHOTO

certainly have differentiated him from his contemporaries, whose time was largely spent in the auction rooms of London.

Neither those involved in the trade nor the newspapers were much in the habit of describing booksellers as gods or intrepid explorers, preferring to draw their analogies from the realm of great military leaders, as with Bernard Quaritch, who was likened at his death in 1899 to Napoleon and Wellington.[35] In the case of Quaritch, the argument could be made that as a market leader it is not a stretch to compare him to a great wartime leader. But why the styling of Voynich as some hyper-masculine, god-like adventurer by others? I would argue that, as with Greene, their peers were picking up and running with the public personalities that they both wished to promote and encourage, and that such personalities were the result of an exploitation of a specific kind of femininity or masculinity.

---

35     'A Great Bookseller's Career: The Late Mr. Bernard Quaritch', *The Westminster Gazette* (19 December 1899), p. 8.

## 3      Gender in the Rare Book Trade

By locating Greene and Voynich in their historical context, we can perhaps begin to understand the reasoning behind their choice to navigate the rare book world in such a stylised, gendered fashion. Though their contemporaries (like Sowerby and Orioli) no doubt aided in the flourishing of such personae, the key issue here is that instead of simply being subject to existing social structures, both of our protagonists actively used and relied on these gendered standards to create their distinct public images. And having something distinct about you could prove to be good for business, especially given the period in which they were operating. The proliferation of newspapers and print in the nineteenth century led to the newspapers of the twentieth century's increasing focus on impressive and unusual persons. The papers were interested in selling, and sensationalism sold. Whilst sensationalism can of course refer to gruesome crimes, Jack Breslin reminds us that '[s]ensationalism also includes sex, scandals, disasters (human and natural) and celebrity gossip, as well as unusual persons and unexpected events'.[36] It is this idea of unusual persons that we should keep in mind when thinking about Greene and Voynich, who both traded on their notoriety, albeit in different ways.

Greene and Voynich had very different opinions of, and relationships with, the press. Though she was known to speak her mind in company, Greene was not enthusiastic about talking to journalists. As a result, she often ended up being more talked about than anything else, with particular attention being paid to her image as a seemingly anomalous feminine figure amongst the rare books. For example, after Greene had been working for Morgan for several years, the *Chicago Tribune* ran an article in 1912 with the headline "The Cleverest Girl I Know', Says J. Pierpont Morgan', complete with a photograph of Greene; an illustration of a small-waisted young lady in clothes more likely seen in the pages of Vogue, arranging books on a shelf. It is worth considering that the 'girl' in question here was then thirty-two, which, by the standards of the time, was past the normal age of an ingenue figure that the title would like to portray. Moreover, the sub-headline claims that '[s]he knows more about books than any other American', and the reader is told that she is,

---

36      Jack Breslin, 'Naughty Seeds of Sensationalism: Gossip and Celebrity in 19th-Century Reporting', in David B. Sachsman and David W. Bulla (eds.), *Sensationalism: Murder, Mayhem, Mudslinging, Scandals, and Disasters in 19th-Century Reporting* (Oxon: Routledge, 2017), p. 115.

chic, vivacious, and interesting ... She wears her hair long and does not wear glasses, runs to Europe on secret missions, and is the terror of continental collectors' agents.[37]

In doing so, the writer presents Greene as something akin to the Mata Hari of the rare book world. Notably, the only quote from Greene herself is a few sentences at the very end of the article on Morgan's collecting habits; the rest of the article is the raptures of Morgan and the journalist.

Greene did occasionally speak out on book-related matters, as in a *New York Times* article, in which she gave 'a rare, lengthy interview' to decry the high prices at the Hoe Sale, or in a more personal interview given in her own home (in other words, her territory) to the same paper in 1912.[38] Greene preferred to make her presence felt in person, where she had greater control. To Greene, the journalist and the unknown reader at the other end of the process were unreliable mediators that could distort the image she wished to portray. For whilst she was undoubtedly confident in her overt femininity, and the way it could knock her competitors off kilter in the auction room, she did not appreciate being characterised as 'half actress and half college girl' by the press.[39] Her biographer Heidi Ardizzone believes that this was not the only reason that Greene shunned media attention. Having changed her name from Belle Marion Greener in order to pass and live as white, she could not afford to have her name and image widely disseminated beyond New York: 'Hiding in full view was a clever disguise. But it was also risky, and Belle tried to contain the publication of her name as much as possible'.[40] Thus, the media represented a potentially dangerous mediator to the image of Belle Greene that she was trying to maintain.

Voynich, in contrast, had no such qualms about the press, and sought instead to market himself as much as his books. He gave interviews more freely, even from the early years of his business in London, such as one in 1904 to *The Tatler*, which announced him as 'A Man who Digs Up Buried Books', conjuring up notions of a somewhat bookish, yet intrepid, adventurer. In the same article, the reader is told both of his being 'extremely delicate in appearance,

37    '"The Cleverest Girl I Know", Says J. Pierpont Morgan', *Chicago Tribune* (11 August 1912),
       p. 46.

38    Ardizzone, p. 244. For the 1912 interview see 'Spending J.P. Morgan's Money for Rare Books:
       That is One of the Pleasant Duties of the Librarian of the Financier, Miss Belle Green, who
       at 26 has Won Fame by her Intimate Knowledge of Valuable Tomes', *The New York Times*
       (12 April 1912), p. 1.

39    Ardizzone, *An Illuminated Life*, p. 246.

40    Ibid.

the paleness of his face intensified by the loose dark hair above it' to bolster his heroic credentials, and of his daring escape from a Siberian prison after being arrested and incarcerated for his 'participation in a Polish national movement'.[41] It is worth noting that the photograph that ran alongside this description is the one included earlier in this essay; a photograph which, as previously mentioned, hews closer to the image of a conventional-looking bookseller than a political radical and prison escapee. This dissonance between text and image is suggestive of the gap between presentation and perception that Voynich sought to exploit. In this example, his pale face and dark hair take on a romantic air when cast alongside ideas of revolution and imprisonment.

A similarly early article from the other side of the Atlantic likewise recounts his Siberian exploits, but also mentions the frequently told, yet somewhat improbable origins of his bookselling business starting with 'a capital of something less than a sovereign'.[42] Though this story plays into a neat trajectory of the penniless revolutionary who gradually builds up his fortunes, the truth is probably less triumphantly masculine, a point which I will return to later. Both the tales of the half-crown and the Siberian prison break illustrate, however, the kind of masculine traits that Voynich wished to play up: audacious, revolutionary (if tinged with a little romanticism), adventuring, and most of all, successful. Like Greene, therefore, Voynich may also have been presenting some stories in order to obscure some points about his origins and spotlight others.

Despite being noted for their singularity or exoticism, it must be highlighted that both Greene and Voynich were playing to certain, gendered types that already existed in the socio-cultural consciousness of the time. As Judith Butler writes, '[t]he choice to assume a certain type of body, to live or wear one's body a certain way, implies a world of already established corporeal styles'.[43] We might think of Greene's couture dresses, furs, and jewels as being an extension of her corporeality and as being suggestive of a pre-established kind of femininity, for she was not the only woman who dressed in this way at this time. The difference is that she did so purposefully in an environment that was predominantly male and had associations of the staid and academic kind. This pointed use of gender stereotypes that were associated with a different social sphere suggests that Greene was manipulating societal and professional expectations to suit her own ends. Her oft-quoted retort that '[j]ust

---

41  'Concerning a Great Bookseller whose Wife Writes Good Books', *The Tatler*, No. 125 (25 May 1904), p. 309.

42  'What and Who? What are the New Books; Who Write and Publish Them?', *The Buffalo Commercial* (18 April 1902), p. 7.

43  Judith Butler, 'Variations on Sex and Gender: Beauvoir, Wittig, Foucault' in Sara Salih (ed.), *The Judith Butler Reader* (Massachusetts: Blackwell Publishing, 2004), p. 26.

because I am a librarian does not mean I have to dress like one' demonstrates a rejection of what was perhaps expected of her as a *librarian*, but not as a woman of her time moving in certain social circles.[44] It suited her to be seen by those in the trade as something of an anomaly, for it meant she could court attention as she wished. Of course, the media could, and did, distort this image into one of airheaded girlishness when really they were dealing with a knowledgeable scholar. Thus, her dislike of such outlets is understandable, but what also comes to light is that she wanted her particular style of femininity to be received in a certain way.

On the other hand, Voynich was happier to let the media conjecture and contradict itself. For that worked in his favour when it came to his brand of masculinity, which again, was a specific stereotype. The way in which Voynich established his stylised version of gender was not as outwardly visible and corporeal as Greene's, with his clothes and outward appearance coinciding with those of other men of his age and station within the trade. Rather, it was his tales of revolutionary escapades and his adventuring way of conducting bookselling business by going directly to the monasteries and libraries in Europe, which were recounted to contemporaries such as Orioli, and regurgitated time and again in the press that set him apart as a particular kind of man.[45]

Voynich took some of his books on an exhibition tour to the United States in 1914–1915 to drum up interest and sales, and explore whether he could take his business there. On route he courted the local press, and the fantastical parts of his story appeared in the papers. Although one *Kansas City Times* reporter remarked that '[h]e likes to talk about his books; about himself he will not speak, except in the briefest way', Voynich's version of 'brief' might actually have been a lot more that he cared to admit, or else was calculated to create mystery, and thus interest.[46] From Baltimore to Buffalo (where the *Enquirer* recorded his being 'outlawed in the land of the czar' before any mention of rare books), we see how this romanticised, yet decidedly masculine, adventuring persona was cultivated by the press, and given how often the same beats of his biography were repeated, I would argue, was surely promoted by the man himself.[47]

---

44    Strouse, *Morgan*, p. 510.

45    In his autobiography, Orioli claims meeting Voynich was what got him into bookselling. He recounts Voynich telling him of a story in which he duped some monks into trading their manuscripts and incunabula for what he calls "a cartload of modern trash in exchange", Orioli, *Adventures*, p. 77.

46    'Books Worth 8 Million: European Bibliophile Brings His Collection to America', *The Kansas City Times* (12 November 1915), p. 9.

47    See '2,000,000 Women Coming', *The Baltimore Sun* (24 March 1915), p. 3; 'Has Valuable Art Collection', *The Buffalo Enquirer* (9 December 1915), p. 6.

In the news coverage and press that related specifically to Ethel Voynich, and which therefore did not have Voynich as an intermediary to get his story across, the response to these parts of her husband's life and personality was far more varied. For example, soon after the release of her 1902 novel, *Jack Raymond*, she recounted an experience to a reporter, which culminated in Voynich defying a Russian spy that had ordered them to hand over papers, which 'would have endangered the lives and liberty of a score of men and women in Russia'.[48] However, a mere two years later she seems at pains to downplay his political past, with a journalist writing that '[a]ccording to her own confession, her life has been singularly free from startling incidents, and there is nothing that distresses and annoys her more' than the 'assertions freely and frequently made, that her husband's history is brimful [sic] of tragic accidents'.[49] Although it is unknown if all of Voynich's fantastical tales were true, there is certainly enough evidence to prove that at least some of it was, and so it is intriguing that Ethel Voynich chose to portray her husband this way, especially so soon after publicly casting him in such a different light. Perhaps she felt that it did not serve her at that moment to be seen as 'the wife of' a revolutionary type, as it might have been an obstacle to her being viewed as a writer on her own terms, though ultimately, this assumption may merely be conjecture. In any case, what is definitely apparent is that whilst the situation may have been more unclear for her, Voynich stood to gain from his relationship with Ethel.

## 4    Power Couples

Though relatively forgotten now in the English-speaking world, despite her 1897 novel *The Gadfly* remaining 'the best-selling novel by an Irish writer, beyond even James Joyce's *Ulysses*' (as of 2019), Ethel Voynich was something of a literary celebrity and political radical in her time.[50] From Voynich's perspective then, the idea of the mysterious bookseller and the famous writer would be quite the power couple, and, as well as his revolutionary exploits, Ethel Voynich and her career were similarly alluded to often in articles about him.[51] Likewise, Greene and Morgan were often mentioned if not in the same breath, then at least the same article as each other, and so they too may be seen

---

48    'The Nobleman and The Spy', *The Arizona Republic* (21 December 1902), p. 11.

49    'Mrs. Voynich's Third Novel', *The Courier-Journal* (3 July 1904), p. 28.

50    Stanley Weintraub, 'Bernard Shaw's Unproduced Melodrama: *The Gadfly, or The Son of the Cardinal*', *English Literature in Transition, 1880–1920*, 62 (2019), p. 528.

51    For example, 'Concerning a Great Bookseller whose Wife Writes Good Books', *The Tatler*, No. 125 (25 May 1904), p. 309.

as a power couple of sorts. Occupying halves of these partnerships impacted their versions of gender.

It is difficult to quantify the working relationship between Greene and Morgan, and just how much sway each had over the other, not least because it was, as Ardizzone suggests, 'not specifically romantic or sexual', but still 'far more than professional'.[52] Nonetheless, from Greene's nervous first encounter with Morgan, they seemed to have developed into a dynamic duo; he was the gruff, moneyed collector and she was the bright young thing who became a major guiding force in his collecting, particularly of rare books and manuscripts. In her biography of Morgan, Jean Strouse highlights the following line from one of Greene's letters; 'JP is so well trained now', she boasted to Berenson early in 1911, 'that he *rarely* ever buys a book or manuscript without consulting me'.[53] Greene's fondness for occasional hyperbole aside, we can at least identify Morgan as the financial partner in this relationship, with Greene more involved with the rare books themselves.

More unusually, the role occupied by Ethel Voynich was also that of financial backer. Although the papers (and hence, we assume, her husband) pedalled the story of the loaned half-crown as the beginning of the business, a closer look at the chronology tells a different story. As was stated earlier, Voynich began selling antiquarian books about 1897. In June of that year, Ethel published her novel *The Gadfly*, and it became an immediate success. As Gerry Kennedy writes, '[t]he public took to it fulsomely: it was published eight times in four years and by 1920 had reached eighteen editions'.[54] In the meantime, Voynich was able to acquire the sort of stock that has led even modern scholars, such as Hunt, to describe the 1898 sales catalogue as 'positively miraculous', especially considering the little experience Voynich had in the trade at this point.[55] The question that remains is how did he finance the procurement of such fine rare books to sell? It is highly suggestive that the business was launched just as there was an influx of cash into the household. Therefore, Kennedy's proposition that 'Ethel may have invested money from royalties from *The Gadfly*' in order to cover the cost of the books and manuscripts seems far more probable than a miraculously multiplying half-crown borrowed from

52    Ardizzone, *An Illuminated Life*, p. 147.

53    Quoted in Strouse, *Morgan*, p. 656.

54    Kennedy, *The Booles and The Hintons*, p. 221.

55    Arnold Hunt, 'Foreign Dealers in the English Trade' in Giles Mandelbrote (ed.), *Out of Print and Into Profit: A History of the Rare & Secondhand Book Trade in Britain in the 20th Century* (London: The British Library and Oak Knoll Press, 2006), p. 248.

the Russian revolutionary, Sergey Stepniak.[56] Given the fact that these origins have been obscured both in press accounts and in memoirs of those who knew the Voyniches, it suggests that both contemporaneously and subsequently, it was apparently unacceptable for the woman to be the financially supportive partner within a couple.[57] For if that were not the case, then why would it be necessary to replace a perfectly reasonable explanation with a situation in which another man steps in to help the hero of our story to go, if not from rags to riches, then at least to moderate financial success?

The personae that both Greene and Voynich chose to portray doubtless have a part to play in how these partnerships were perceived. To use the above example, it would not have done Voynich's decidedly masculine persona any good to have it known to the wider public that it was actually his wife's money that set him up with his business. Being seen as a successful businessman was part of being a successful bookseller, whereas being thought of as a great novelist did not depend as much on brisk business and financial prosperity. Trading on her name and fame as a novelist appears to have been justifiable however, as Ethel Voynich's literary career and substantial success in that regard continued to feature regularly in contemporary press coverage about Voynich.[58] Just as Ethel could offer her husband access to new people and opportunities due to her fame, so too could Morgan's name open doors to both industry types and New York high society for Greene. Being attached to Morgan did not only mean coming into the rare book world already as a serious player due to his money and kudos earned off the back of his previous purchases, but entry into the kinds of social circles that would have been closed off to most women of colour at this time. The symbiotic, dual nature of this relationship should not be underestimated as Greene's hyper femininity in a man's world was likely rendered more socially acceptable by virtue of playing off against Morgan's brusque masculinity, while his fearsome reputation was injected with a shot of glamour due to his unusual lady librarian. In that sense, they could be seen as opposite, yet complementary, personalities.

---

56    Kennedy, *The Booles and The Hintons*, p. 222.

57    The Stepniak story is also the one recounted by Sowerby, though she too expresses doubt over its veracity, Sowerby, *Rare people*, p. 9.

58    All of the newspaper articles cited in this paper regarding Voynich mention his wife, with *The Tatler* one including her in the title as the 'Wife [who] Writes Good Books': 'Concerning a Great Bookseller'.

## 5      Conclusion

Both Greene and Voynich loomed large in their field in the early part of the twentieth century; the numerous accounts by their contemporaries and newspaper articles could not suggest otherwise. By different means and for different reasons, they achieved a level of celebrity that was reserved for few of their peers. And yet, the trajectories of their careers and consequent 'afterlives' have not been simple. During her lifetime, Greene was hailed as an integral part of the Pierpont Morgan Library, but later fell into obscurity. Only three decades had elapsed since her death when, an introductory note to a volume of essays published in 1981 highlighted the lives and work of female interpreters of the visual arts, and the volume's editor, Claire Richter Sherman, cited the 'lack of sufficient or accessible biographical materials' prevented the completion of an essay on Greene, despite her being a 'likely subject'.[59] This remained the case until the publication of Jean Strouse's landmark biography of J. Pierpont Morgan in 1999, when details about her life, career, and identity finally came to light. At present, Greene is having something of a critical and cultural renaissance, not only being the subject for a planned major exhibition at the Morgan Library in 2024, but also serving as the inspiration for two separate historical fiction novels.[60]

Despite the triumphant book-buying expeditions and multiple bookstores of his younger years, Voynich died leaving a business that had shrunk to the locations in London and New York and that existed on a month-by-month basis. The manuscript that is now known by his name remained unsold at his death, as it continued to be for many years, only finding its eventual home at Yale University in 1969 by way of the bookseller H.P. Kraus.[61] Nevertheless, scholars have not forgotten his earlier professional successes, with Arnold Hunt

---

59      Clare Richter Sherman, 'Introductory Note', in Claire Richter Sherman with Adele M. Holcomb (eds.), *Women as Interpreters of the Visual Arts, 1820–1979* (Connecticut: Greenwood Press, 1981), p. xx.

60      The two novels are: Marie Benedict and Victoria Christopher Murray, *The Personal Librarian* (New York: Berkley, 2021) and Alexandra Lapierre, *Belle Greene*, Tina Kover (trans.), (New York: Europa Editions, 2022). The second was originally written in French and published in 2021. For information about the exhibition, see <https://www.themorgan.org/belle-greene/exhibition> (accessed 25 July 2022).

61      In brief: Ethel Voynich inherited the manuscript and tried to sell it over the next thirty years, unsuccessfully, with Anne Nill, Wilfrid Voynich's long-time assistant in the New York office. It then passed to Nill after Ethel's death, who sold it to Kraus in 1961. See Raymond Clemens, 'The World's Most Mysterious Manuscript', in Raymond Clemens (ed.), *The Voynich Manuscript* (New Haven: Yale University Press, 2016), pp. 53–54.

describing him as 'one of the most remarkable characters ever to have passed through the antiquarian booktrade'.[62] It is perhaps worth noting that Voynich's legacy has not followed the distinct 'loss and recovery' path that Greene's has, staying more within the scholarly conversation over the years likely due, at least in part, to the fame of the Voynich manuscript and ultimately the fact that he was a man with his *own* name on the door, rather than working for somebody else as Greene had done. I do not think it is a coincidence that renewed interest in Greene, both from critical quarters and the general public, has occurred at a time when rediscovering stories of women aligns with the cultural zeitgeist.

To return briefly to Hunt's description of Voynich, the deployment of the word 'character' is useful to us when looking at Greene and Voynich. For they meticulously constructed and assumed particular roles when stepping out onto the public stage in order to be received in certain ways and negotiate the rare book world in the early part of the twentieth century. However, this careful calibration of their public-facing images owes a great debt to conceptualisations of gender and the manipulation of gender-based, societal expectations, and as such, gender becomes a crucial element to understanding the personae they constructed. The faces they presented to the public were not simply drawn out of thin air, but responded to and reflected societal norms and expectations. Both Greene and Voynich were playing to gendered stereotypes that already existed within the contemporary public consciousness, whether it was found in the glamourous sketches of *Vogue* or in the adventure stories of *The Boy's Own Paper*. The ultimate difference is that they decided to transfer these associations into a space, the world of rare books, in which such stereotypes were seen as uncommon and, thus, could use this notoriety as a springboard for contending with the trade. In doing so, they undoubtedly left an indelible mark on the rare book world.

---

62    Hunt, 'Foreign Dealers in the English Trade', p. 247.

# CHAPTER 22

# Neither Radical nor Domestic: Women of the Bindery Local No. 125 of San Francisco 1902–1917

*Susan McElrath*

The rich collection of materials on the Bindery Women's Local Union No. 125 at the Labor Archives and Research Center at San Francisco State University offers a rare opportunity to study an all-female union on the west coast of the United States not connected to the garment or textile industries. These records preserve evidence of members' views on organised labour and the role union membership played in their lives. Recovering the authentic voices of working women often has proved elusive due to the dearth of sources, and at first glance, these records preserve only limited information on the beliefs and perspectives of most members. The lack of detail in the minute book of the local and scant official correspondence is an obstacle for researchers seeking to understand individual motivations. However, the records do provide an invaluable list of members' names, which form the basis for developing a group profile.[1] By using data from the United States Census from 1900 through 1920, it is possible to compare members of Local 125 to other women bookbinders and women workers more generally. This data, combined with references to the union and its members in local newspapers and labour journals, opens a window on these women's collective story and illustrates the impact of location and occupation on the union and its members.

The picture that emerges from an examination of the collective lives of these bookbinders is of young women making decisions about how to navigate two different worlds. One was a traditional one where family ties often had a profound influence on their choices regarding employment and union membership. But these union members also were experiencing a new dynamic where union membership was part of their identity as wage earners in a world formerly the exclusive realm of men. The women of Local 125 often did not act

---

1  This roster is comprised of 887 union members who were listed either in the membership ledger or mentioned in the minutes, as well as a list of officers and members who served on committees and in other roles such as shop stewards. I found 282 of the women (32% of the roster) listed in the United States Census with the occupation bookbinder, with an additional fifty-six women listed with no occupation, being at school, or some other employment raising the total to 38% of the roster.

© KONINKLIJKE BRILL BV, LEIDEN, 2025 | DOI:10.1163/9789004701656_023

as staunch unionists, much to the frustration of their elected leaders. Likewise, the males at the top of the international union were ambivalent about the female presence in their organisation, which led to openly sexist expressions. By moving beyond a purely domestic sphere, the women bookbinders of San Francisco started a process, however unconsciously, of reimagining their status as actors in a wage economy. Union membership facilitated their desire to maximise earnings, and as such, participating in union activities was an important stage for the gradual emergence of women in establishing their economic and personal independence.

San Francisco was fertile ground for the participation of women in labour unions at the turn of the twentieth century.[2] It was a time when unskilled factory workers and workers in the service industries were organising into new unions.[3] San Francisco's population in 1900 was mostly composed of foreign-born (40.1%) or first-generation immigrants (30.4%).[4] The residents were one-third Irish and one-sixth German, while there were relatively few immigrants from Southern or Eastern Europe.[5] Nationwide, 50% of working women were immigrants or daughters of immigrants, but the majority of San Francisco's working women were first generation natives.[6] They outnumbered immigrants and women with native parentage.[7]

By almost any rubric, San Francisco was a pro-labour city. The city was home to a wide variety of unions including the Cooks' Association of the Pacific Coast, the International Seamen's Union of America, the Musicians' Mutual Protective Union, and the San Francisco Waitresses' Union. Most of the industrial union locals in San Francisco had fewer than 500 members in a city that consisted primarily of small-scale light manufacturing.[8] These locals generally coordinated their activities with and received support from the Labor Council of San Francisco. There also were several trades councils organised around specific trades or industries.

---

2   Robert Edward Lee Knight, *Industrial Relations in San Francisco Bay Area 1900–1918* (California: University of California Press, 1960), p. 100.

3   Ibid.

4   Rebecca J. Mead, 'Trade-Unionism and Political Activity Among San Francisco Wage-Earning Women, 1900–1922', (MA Thesis: San Francisco State University, 1991), p. 22.

5   Ibid., p. 25.

6   Alice Kessler-Harris, *Out to Work: A History of Wage-Earning Women in the United States*, (New York: Oxford University Press, 1982), p. 153.

7   Mead, 'Trade-Unionism and Political Activity', p. 25.

8   Knight, *Industrial Relations in San Francisco Bay Area*, p. 100.

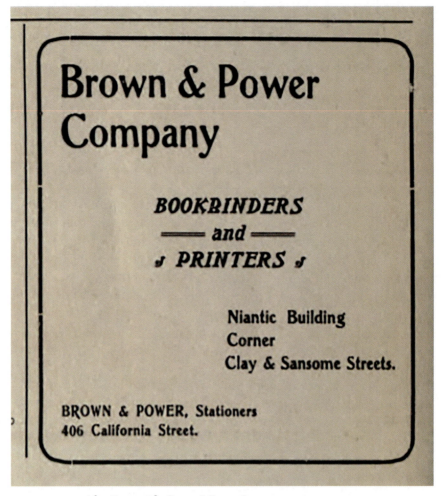

FIGURE 22.1    Advertisement for Brown & Power Company, 1902

Bookbinding was an industrial process, with workers operating a variety of equipment and machines. Women in this industry performed tasks requiring dexterity and attention to detail, such as collating and press feeding. The women worked in a variety of businesses including binderies, blank book manufacturers, lithographers, and printers.[9] The established wage in San Francisco

9   Bindery Women's Union, Local 125: Minutes 1906–1917, Bookbinders and Bindery Women's Union, Local 31–125 Records, Box 1, Volume 6, Labor Archives and Research Center, San Francisco State University, (Hereafter cited as Minutes), List of Shop Stewards, 1907.

in 1902 was seven dollars a week for a journeywoman bookbinder, although most of these women worked nine hours days for six dollars a week.[10]

This pro-union environment, combined with support from the International Brotherhood of Bookbinders, facilitated the entry of women into the ranks of organised labour. The nature of bindery work, both skilled and unskilled, and the high level of unionisation made bindery jobs desirable for women and their families. Unionisation brought direct advantages including higher wages and financial support in the aftermath of the 1906 San Francisco earthquake and fire. A demographic analysis of members shows that economic benefits were a prime factor in how members valued union membership. Most of the union's members were single, lived with family and contributed their wages to the family. Many of these families had multiple children working in the industry, which suggests that the women and their families saw binderies as offering good, safe jobs. Since many of these siblings also joined the union, they also saw value in union membership. For the women workers in these families, unionisation raised their profile within the bookbinding trades and forced male co-workers to listen to and respond to their concerns. Their collective voice gave them power to seek improvements and the authority to negotiate with their employers, which led to material gains.

By 1900, over half of all American bookbinders were female. The largest all female union in the International Brotherhood of Bookbinders in 1912 was Local 43 in New York City with 1,600 members. According to Mary Van Kleeck's 1913 study of women bookbinders in New York, forty out of 200 shops in Manhattan were organised.[11] San Francisco followed a different model. The women bookbinders were 'virtually 100 percent organised'.[12] This stood in contrast to the national norm, where only 1.5% of women workers were unionised in 1910.[13] Even in San Francisco where the rate was significantly higher, only 7.6% of working women were members of trade unions.[14] Bookbinding was an exception, and it was this supportive context that fostered the growth and development of Local 125.

The Bindery Women's Local Union No. 125 was organised in September 1902 as an auxiliary of Bookbinders Local Union No. 31 with the full support of the Allied Printing Trades Council of San Francisco. It had 100 charter members. The

---

10    'Local Union No. 125, San Francisco, Cal'., *International Bookbinder*, 11 (1910), p. 31, <https://babel.hathitrust.org/cgi/pt?id=nyp.33433010712226&view=1up&seq=1>.

11    Mary Van Kleeck, *Women in the Bookbinding Trade* (New York: Survey Associates, Inc., 1913), p. 190.

12    Mead, 'Trade-Unionism and Political Activity', p. 73.

13    Kessler-Harris, *Out to Work*, p. 152.

14    Mead, 'Trade-Unionism and Political Activity', p. 38.

union drafted its charter and adopted bylaws in November 1902. Membership in the union grew rapidly in its first year. It averaged 267 members between 1902 and 1913 with its peak membership of 290 members in 1913.

Local 125's first and most successful strike lasted four weeks in June 1903. According to the *San Francisco Chronicle*, the strike crippled 'a large number of shops, including several of the larger manufactories of blank books'.[15] The journeymen bookbinders joined the bindery women on strike in mid-June after enduring what the newspaper reported as 'three weeks of enforced idleness owing to the strike of the women which tied up every shop in this city'.[16] When the union members settled the strike, they had achieved all their goals including regulating the apprentice system, establishing eight and a half hours as the workday, and setting the minimum wage at eight dollars per week for journeywomen. In January 1906, both locals, No. 31 and 125 demanded an eight-hour workday. After several conferences, the employer's association agreed to this change, but asked that it not go into effect until July 1, 1906.

The San Francisco earthquake and fire on April 18, 1906, had a devastating impact on the printing industry. The fire destroyed every bindery and printing office in the city of San Francisco. In a report to the International Brotherhood of Bookbinders, locals 31 and 125, who had been meeting together for six months after the fire, stated that most firms re-established their binderies in the city by the end of July 1906. The union remained vigilant and supportive in the aftermath offering financial and employment assistance. The newspaper of the international union reported that

> some will have better homes, better and more machinery and healthier locations. Very few of the places will be near the old Printers' Row, as it was called, but they will be scattered all over town.[17]

Despite the disruption of a natural disaster, the eight-hour day went into effect July 1, 1906, on schedule.

---

15    'Bindery Women Out On Strike: Numerous Shops Tied Up—Salesladies and Milliners Plan Two Entertainments', *San Francisco Chronicle*, 02 June 1903 <https://www.proquest.com/historical-newspapers/bindery-women-out-on-strike/docview/573315129/se-2?accountid=14496>.

16    'Binders Strike Out of Sympathy: Conference Barren of Result Forced Journeymen into Continued Idleness', *San Francisco Chronicle*, 21 June 1903 <https://www.proquest.com/historical-newspapers/binders-strike-out-sympathy/docview/573331537/se-2?accountid=14496>.

17    'Local Unions 31 and 125, San Francisco, Cal.—Second Letter', *International Bookbinder*, 7 (1906), p. 243 <https://babel.hathitrust.org/cgi/pt?id=mdp.39015077902271&view=1up&seq=1&skin=2021>.

According to a 1913 study of women trade unions in San Francisco by Lillian Matthews, work 'was extremely plentiful' after the fire.[18] The printing and binding shops 'ran night and day in order to fill the immense demands they had to meet'.[19] The employers offered bonuses to the workers on the midnight until eight am shift. Matthews described the two kinds of shops that appeared after the fire. Large ones with modern equipment that were 'airy and well-lighted' and small one-room establishments at the rear of a stationery store or a small printing office with one employee doing pamphlet work.[20] The new machinery led to changes such as the elimination of hand folding at many of the larger shops. According to Matthews, employment in the large shops was regular and two-thirds of the members worked in the same shop until they left the workforce. The other third worked irregularly and shifted from one shop to another.[21] Matthews attributed the formation of the union as the catalyst for the women to assess their working conditions, which led to the realisation that their wages had steadily decreased in the previous three years. Unionisation had stopped this downward trend.[22]

In April 1917, declining attendance and financial concerns forced the union to amalgamate with the Bookbinders Union Local 31. Though they remained two distinct organisations, the amalgamated union had a common set of officers. The Bindery Women sought and won a fixed proportion of offices and delegate positions for themselves.[23] The vote to merge was eighty-nine in favour and twenty-five against, suggesting there was continuing interest by some members in maintaining their own union.[24] The opposition to the merger also points to concerns about the relationship between the members of Local 125 with Local 31. Though their fellow unionists were supportive, they sent mixed messages. While the men spoke about 'our cause,' they also used demeaning language to describe the women. How did the women feel when the men called them 'a little wonder' or stated that one of the members had 'the walk of a real soldier?'[25] This language suggests there was friction between

---

18    Lillian R. Matthews, *Women in Trade Unions in San Francisco* (Berkeley: University of California Press, 1913), p. 42.
19    Ibid.
20    Ibid., p. 45.
21    Ibid., p. 46.
22    Ibid.
23    Louise Ploeger, 'Trade Unionism among the Women of San Francisco 1920' (MA Thesis: University of California, Berkeley, 1920); Mead, 'Trade-Unionism and Political Activity'.
24    Minutes, 20 April 1917.
25    *International Bookbinder*, 6 (1905), p. 171 <https://babel.hathitrust.org/cgi/pt?id=nyp.3 3433010712176&view=1up&seq=1&skin=2021>; 'Local Union No. 31, San Francisco, Cal', *International Bookbinder*, 7 (1906), p. 276. <https://babel.hathitrust.org/cgi/pt?id=mdp

the two unions. One must also ask if the printing trades in San Francisco and the International Bookbinders Union were truly progressive in attitude to their female members or if their support was based more on self-interest to avoid competition.[26] Despite its emphasis on establishing women only locals, the International Brotherhood of Bookbinders did not nominate and elect its first women officers until 1906. At its convention in Denver in 1914, the women delegates made a demand for a larger share of official honours and claimed they were entitled to four members of the executive committee, instead of two out of the nine, as they represented nearly half of the total membership.[27] Though the union did not increase the number of women officers, it reduced the number of male representatives on the executive committee, so the percentage increased to 33%, a number that remained less than women's actual percentage of the membership. This reluctance to expand women's leadership roles suggests men regarded women as economic competitors but not equals in the organisation. Leaders were supportive of keeping women's wages high but did not want to cede significant control of the union. In addition, the language reveals a lack of respect for the women as advocates and activists.

If men were ambivalent about women in the union movement, the members of Local 125 also were unsure about their identity as unionists. The minutes show a lack of interest in social and political issues other than minimum wage legislation from both the rank and file and the officers. Labour and suffrage activists Maud Younger and Lillian Coffin spoke to Local 125 about women's suffrage. They encouraged endorsement of the cause, but there were no follow up activities recorded in the minutes.[28] Ella Wunderlich, one of the officers, reported at the October 1908 meeting that she received a call from Mrs. French, the wife of the former president of the typographical union, asking her to get involved in women's suffrage. She declined this request, stating that she was too busy. Ella Wunderlich also 'was of the opinion that most of the girls considered it a joke', highlighting the insignificance of this issue to the membership. According to the minutes, 'all seemed to be of the opinion that if the women did vote they would vote more intelligently than the men'. Thus, women bookbinders felt capable of voting but did not see its relevance to their immediate concerns.[29] Likewise, the Anti-Prohibition League invited

---

.39015077902271&view=1up&seq=1&skin=2021>; 'Local Union No. 31, San Francisco, Cal'. *International Bookbinder*, 8 (1907), p. 299, <https://babel.hathitrust.org/cgi/pt?id=nyp.334 33010712192&view=1up&seq=1&skin=2021>.

26    Mead, 'Trade-Unionism and Political Activity', p. 70.

27    'Bookbinders' Convention', *Labor Clarion* 13 (19 June 1914), p. 16.

28    Minutes, 12 April 1908.

29    Ibid., 9 October 1908.

the union to send delegates to their meetings, but the union's minutes do not record any action in response even though many San Francisco labour organisations actively campaigned against prohibition.[30] The one issue that got the leadership's attention was California Assembly Bill 1251, which established a commission to determine minimum wages for women. The union sent two delegates to the state capitol, Sacramento, in March 1913 to testify in opposition to the bill. It passed despite unanimous opposition from San Francisco's labour unions, who feared its overall downward pressure on wages.[31] Many of the union member's families relied on their income, thus the political issues of interest were those having a direct economic impact.

While the binders in Local 125 seemed uninterested in social causes they perceived to be peripheral to the issues of wages and working hours, union membership did provide one additional benefit. After-hours social events hosted by the union offered safe entertainment and a respite from the drudgery of the long work day. But these seemingly innocuous gatherings also allowed the women to interact outside of their traditional realms. This socialisation as union members became a small but significant aspect of their identities as women in the early 20th century.

The formation of a new identity based on union membership was not a seamless transition, and the members of Local 125 held differing opinions about the value of their union membership. Though there were quite a few active members, many attended meetings irregularly and fell behind with their dues' payments. For example, 14% had their memberships suspended and reinstated in the union's first four years. Concerns about attendance and delinquency in paying dues featured heavily in the minutes by 1907. The union adopted a new plan for collecting dues in September 1915 due to budgetary issues.[32] By 1916, Local 125 was in arrears in its dues to the International Brotherhood of Bookbinders.[33] Their financial situation was one of the main issues that led to the amalgamation with the male bookbinder's union. During this period, the union also addressed concerns about rule violations and established fines and

---

30     Ibid., 4 April 1916.

31     'Loyal to Darrow', *San Francisco Call*, 22 March 1913, California Digital Newspaper Collection <https://cdnc.ucr.edu/>; 'San Francisco Labor Bodies Opposed to Passage of Bill Fixing Lowest Salaries', *Sacramento Daily Union*, 26 March 1913, California Digital Newspaper Collection <https://cdnc.ucr.edu/>. The first set of rates went into effect for cannery workers in 1916.

32     Minutes, 20 August 1915; Ibid., 17 September 1915.

33     'Does your local union pay its per capita tax promptly?' *International Bookbinder*, 16 (1915), p. 315, <https://babel.hathitrust.org/cgi/pt?id=mdp.39015077902354&view=1up&s eq=7&skin=2021>.

expulsion procedures. The struggle to maintain an active membership points to the uneven evolution of women toward true economic independence. They valued higher wages, but perhaps did not yet appreciate the importance of collective action in preserving their gains.[34]

In order to better understand the motivations of these women unionists, one must look to sources beyond the official records of the local. Matching names from the membership ledger to data from the United States Census and San Francisco city directories facilitates the creation of a collective portrait of the union. This data shows some pronounced trends. The members of the Bindery Women's Local 125 of San Francisco were predominantly single, between the ages of sixteen and twenty-five (Fig. 22.2), and were born in California to foreign-born parents. Most of their parents were from Ireland. There were forty-two sets of sisters and twenty-five members had brothers working in the printing industry. Most worked for a minimum of three to four years. They lived with their parents and gave their wages to their families. Twenty-nine percent lived in mother headed households. These mothers were mainly widows who relied on their children's income.

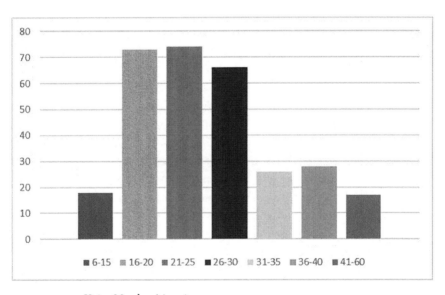

FIGURE 22.2    Union Members' Ages in 1910

---

34    Minutes, 9 April 1913. First mention in minutes (10 July 1912), 'any girl who has been reported as working over eight hours should be tried by the executive committee and if found guilty' fined five dollars for first violation and expelled at second.

In contrast to the profile of the rank and file, the officers of the union tended to be older and were more likely to have foreign-born parents. Though a higher percentage of the officers lived on their own, they overwhelmingly still lived with their parents. Fifteen percent of the officers were over twenty-five when they formed the union. The women who served on committees were slightly younger but still somewhat older than the general membership. One-third were over the age of twenty-five. A representative example of an active member is Frankie Conroy. Her father was from Ireland. Her mother was born in the United States to Irish parents. Frankie was seventeen in 1900, and she had four siblings two of whom were working.[35] As the officers and more active members tended to be older, the union's leadership was more stable than its membership and therefore spoke with greater authority at the bargaining table.

A vital source to understand better how women bindery workers in San Francisco differed from women bookbinders in other cities and other working women in San Francisco is Mary Van Kleeck's 1913 study of bookbinders in Manhattan, New York.[36] Twenty-six percent of all women bookbinders in the United States worked in New York City. The next largest contingent was in Chicago with 10%. San Francisco was number ten on the list at 1.4%.[37] In New York, 90% of the bookbinders were born in the United States. Twenty-nine percent had native-born parents.[38] Similarly, in San Francisco, 93% of the bookbinders were born in the United States and 32% had native-born parents.[39] Over half of the foreign-born parents were from Ireland with the next largest group from Germany (Fig. 22.3). A few examples from the roster include Minnie Goan whose parents were from Ireland and sisters Sophie and Gertie Finke whose parents were from Germany.[40]

Van Kleeck looked at the longevity of women bookbinders and discovered that 17% had worked less than one year, 46% one to three years, and 36% five years or more.[41] Assuming that union membership roughly correlated with employment in the bindery industry, 20% of the members listed on rolls of Local 125 in 1902 withdrew within one to three years. The remainder were on

35    Frankie Conroy. Year: 1900; Census Place: San Francisco, San Francisco, California; Page: 11; Enumeration District: 0040; FHL microfilm: 1240101.

36    Van Kleeck, *Women in the Bookbinding Trade*.

37    Ibid., p. 31.

38    Ibid., p. 36.

39    Information compiled from Ancestry.com. 1900–1920 United States Federal Census.

40    Minnie A Goan. Year: 1900; Census Place: San Francisco, San Francisco, California; Page: 2; Enumeration District: 0043; FHL microfilm: 1240101; Sophie Finke. Year: 1910; Census Place: San Francisco Assembly District 39, San Francisco, California; Roll: T624_100; Page: 10A; Enumeration District: 0213; FHL microfilm: 1374113.

41    Van Kleeck, *Women in the Bookbinding Trade*, p. 98.

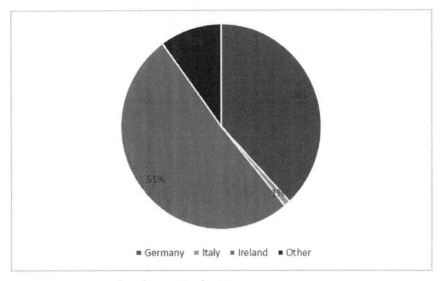

FIGURE 22.3    Nationality of Union Members' Parents

rolls for at least three to four years.[42] Based on these findings, women bookbinders in San Francisco worked longer. According to Alice Kessler-Harris,
30.6% of female bookbinders lived in families headed by a mother and in more
than a third of these families, mothers as well as daughters worked for wages.[43]
In comparison to the working women in general in the United States, the
number of mother headed households in San Francisco was similar (29%) but
there was a much lower percentage of working mothers. Sixty-nine percent of
the San Francisco mothers with bookbinder daughters were not working. The
mothers who worked had a variety of occupations including boarding/lodging
house keeper, nurse, janitress at a public school, and grocer. Eighty-four percent were widows and over half had more than four children living at home.
Thirty-five percent had a son living at home. With multiple children earning an
income, it was possible for these women to stay home to care for their younger
children.

Using this data, we can compare the Bindery Women to other women workers in the early years of the twentieth century and to the working women
of San Francisco. According to Kessler-Harris, 87% of working women were

---

42    Bindery Women's Union, Local 125: Membership Ledger 1902–1905, Bookbinders and
      Bindery Women's Union, Local 31–125 Records, Box 1, Volume 5, Labor Archives and
      Research Center, San Francisco State University.
43    Kessler-Harris, *Out to Work*, pp. 122–3.

unmarried in 1900 with nearly half under age twenty-five.[44] The San Francisco bindery workers were more heavily single and younger than the national work force. Ninety-six percent of the union members listed in the 1900 census were single and 85% of them were under the age of twenty-five. Leslie Woodcock Tentler stated that 21.2% of the 'female non-agricultural workforce' were married in 1920.[45] Only 10% of the San Francisco bindery workers were married in 1910. In addition, two were divorced and two were widows. According to Rebecca J. Mead, 54.8% of the population of women wage earners in San Francisco 'fit the pattern of auxiliary earners in male-headed households, and most of these women were sisters and daughters rather than wives'.[46] The Bindery Women matched this profile. Fifty-nine percent of the bindery workers lived in male-headed households. Three quarters lived with their father or brother.

Nationwide, 50% of working women were immigrants or daughters of immigrants.[47] The majority of San Francisco's working women were first generation natives.[48] The Bindery Women fit this profile perfectly with 93% born in the United States compared to 7% foreign born. Of the 93%, 71% are first generation and 29% have native-born parents.[49] By 1900, 54.8% of the working women in San Francisco lived with their families and 45.2% lived on their own (Fig. 22.4).[50] The Bindery Women differed in that 93% lived with a family member in 1900. Even by 1910, there were still only 15% living on their own either as head of the household or as a lodger or boarder.

According to Tentler, 'working-class girls often insisted on employment in a store or factory where friends worked, and they frequently sought work only in the immediate neighbourhood'.[51] What the census showed was that the bookbinders followed their sisters and brothers into the workplace. There were forty-two sets of sisters on the union roster. They were mostly pairs but there were a few instances with more including the Masi Sisters. The three eldest, Grace (twenty-one), Lottie (nineteen) and Hazel (seventeen), worked as stitchers and table hands. Their youngest sister, Violet, joined the union in 1914 when

44    Ibid., p. 153.
45    Leslie Woodcock Tentler, *Wage-Earning Women: Industrial Work and Family in the United States, 1900–1930*, (New York: Oxford University Press, 1979), p. 59.
46    Mead, 'Trade-Unionism and Political Activity', p. 9.
47    Kessler-Harris, *Out to Work*, p. 153.
48    Mead, 'Trade-Unionism and Political Activity', p. 25.
49    Ibid.
50    Ibid., p. 12.
51    Tentler, *Wage Earning Women*, p. 105.

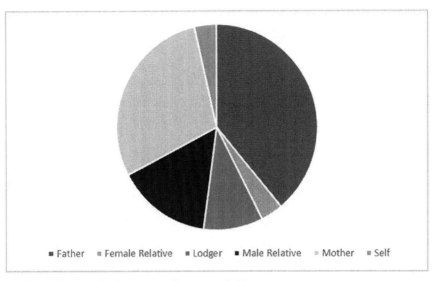

FIGURE 22.4     Heads of Union Members' Households

she was sixteen.[52] Twenty-five of the bookbinders had a brother employed in the printing trades.

In addition to the United States Census, newspapers can provide useful information about the union and its members' activities. Of particular interest are the insights about members' participation in other organisations. The San Francisco Bindery Women sent delegates to several other labour organisations including the Allied Printing Trades Council of San Francisco, the International Brotherhood of Bookbinders, and the San Francisco Labor Council. Members of the Bindery Women held a variety of positions in these organisations including Vice President. They served on committees on appeals, a charter revision convention, and Labor Day programming. In addition, they joined the Women's Union Label League and the Label Section of the San Francisco Labor Council. Several officers were members of the Companions of the Forest, a social and benevolent organization, which was associated with the Ancient Order of Foresters. Others participated in the Improved Order of the Red Men, the California Anti–White Slavery League, and the City Beautiful Convention in 1913. This activism stands in contrast to the struggle to maintain a stable membership and is evidence of the union leadership's interest in advocating for the working people of San Francisco. It also demonstrates

52     Grace G Masi. Year: 1910; Census Place: San Francisco Assembly District 34, San Francisco, California; Roll: T624_97; Page: 3B; Enumeration District: 0096; FHL microfilm: 1374110.

their appreciation for the role of labour unions in the lives of all workers in San Francisco both union and non-union.

The members of Local 125 showed little interest in social and political issues such as prohibition and women's suffrage but were vocal advocates for worker's rights. The issues most important to them concerned wages and work hours. While it may not surprise us that such bread-and-butter issues were paramount for women, some of whom lived in female-led households, this focus on the issues with direct impact on their lives also suggests a striving for economic self-sufficiency. One important implication of the union's success in shortening the workday is the impact on these women's lives. It is an example of young women establishing a separate sphere of personal space where they exerted more control over how they spent their time outside of the bindery. Women's history scholars have noted the move away from lives solely devoted to economic subsistence as a key turning point for women seeking to claim greater agency in the conduct of their lives.[53]

The union provided a collective voice for these women, and through union membership, the women bookbinders of San Francisco emerged from the shadows of anonymity. The support of the International Brotherhood of Bookbinders and the powerful labour unions in the city fostered the growth of the union and its members. By gaining the power to advocate for themselves these women achieved both material and more intangible improvements in their lives. Increased wages and shorter working hours were benefits they could directly attribute to participation in the labour movement. But whether they fully understood it, the bookbinders had also made a psychological leap toward self-sufficiency.

The women of Local 125 acted collectively in pursuit of their economic self-interest. Many of these women followed the path of employment in book-binding and union membership established by male relatives, but despite their ambivalence about the union, its members discovered the power of collective action. The experience of a successful strike for higher wages and negotiations for a shorter working day did not just have a material impact on their lives. The union was the vehicle for these women to assess their status and pursue strat-egies for making improvements. The women bookbinders of San Francisco included elected leaders whose interests modelled the evolution of women's views on the importance of union membership. These women actively sought leadership roles and promoted the concerns of the rank and file both in nego-tiations with employers and within the international union. They did not

53    Kathy Peiss, *Cheap Amusements: Working Women and Leisure in Turn-of-the-Century New York.* (Philadelphia: Temple University Press, 1986).

hesitate to testify against measures they felt would harm women workers such as the state minimum wage bill. Through their actions, they demonstrated a willingness to advocate and press for more control over their working conditions and lives. Despite members' delinquency in paying dues and lack of interest in union activities, the fact that the membership levels were steady throughout this period suggests that they recognised the value of collective action and the need to push for change in both the workplace and the union.

The women bookbinders of Local 125 offered a glimpse into their collective futures in October 1908 when a report of a union meeting noted that the members 'seemed to be of the opinion that if the women did vote they would vote more intelligently than the men'.[54] This sense that they could operate successfully in a world formerly dominated by men suggests that they were beginning to regard themselves as independent agents of their own destinies. Their perspective was not feminist or even proto-feminist, but as union members they discovered the power of collective action to improve their lives. Because they were among the first women in their families to experience this, it was a significant step forward.

---

54     Minutes, 9 October 1908.

# PART 8

## *Towards Inclusive Histories*

∵

# CHAPTER 23

# Women, Wills, and the Early London Book Trade (1557–1666)

*Kirk Melnikoff*

Bolstered by research into early modern domestic economies and the history of the book, Maureen Bell, Paula McDowell, Helen Smith, and, most recently, Valerie Wayne, among others, have helped us to recognise the extent to which women—as printers, booksellers, bookbinders, publishers, and wholesalers—made essential contributions to the early English book trade.[1] Research of this kind, however, has so far been significantly hampered by a dearth of documentary evidence as bookwomen only sporadically appear either in Stationers' Company documents or in book imprints. For the past few years, the newly assembled Book Trade Probate (BTP) team has been gathering and transcribing wills, probate licences, administrations, sentences, and inventories for a two-part project on early modern book-trade probate.[2] The first stage will conclude with publication of the print volume *Playbook Wills, 1529–1690* (University of Manchester Press, 2025), while the second will culminate in an exhaustive, searchable online database of transcribed book-trade probate material. So far, we have located more than five hundred London book-trade wills dating from 1557 to 1666, from the incorporation of the Stationers' Company to the Great Fire of London. Women figure significantly in these documents. They not only are invoked regularly as legatees, executrixes, overseers, and witnesses, but they also appear in eighty-eight wills as testators, mostly widows.[3]

---

1  I am indebted both to Peter W.M. Blayney and Lucy Munro for their help in locating some of the wills recorded here. Maureen Bell, 'Women in the English book trade 1557–1700', *Leipziger Jahrbuch zur Buchgeschichte*, 6 (1996), pp. 13–46; Paula McDowell, *The Women of Grub Street: press, politics, and gender in the London literary marketplace, 1678–1730* (Oxford: Oxford University Press, 1998); Helen Smith, *'Grossly Material Things': Women and book production in early modern England* (Oxford: Oxford University Press, 2012); Valerie Wayne (ed.), *Women's labor and the history of the book in early modern England* (London: Bloomsbury, 2020).

2  The Book Trade Probate team consists of me, Aaron Pratt, Breanne Weber, Mouli Chaudhuri, Sarah Whichello, and Katie Holly.

3  It was exceedingly unusual for a book-trade widow not to be named executrix of her dead husband's estate. Of the husbands whose wills we have located, only John Norton, John

Like those of men, early modern women's wills can reveal home towns, residences, church parishes, and burial locations. They also can identify in their bequests family members (immediate and extended, living and dead), close friends, business associates (and the larger networks in which they operated), household servants, and apprentices (past and present). Bequests can be extensive, gifting not just money, leases, and property but an array of household items, and as such, they can provide fascinating catalogs of a woman's cherished possessions. Jane Costerdine, for example, in 1654 left four pieces of jewelry to family and friends: to her sister-in-law Susanna Pagitt she left 'a ring ... having fiue stones in itt, and one lost out'; to her cousin John Pagitt 'a little Ring with a stone in itt'; to her cousin Thomas Pagitt 'a little Ring which is enamelled with white, and a little stone in it'; and to her neighbor 'M$^r$ Crane a little Ring with this motto (what wee decreed is now agreed)'.[4] Jacomine Langford willed her 'husbandes best suite and cloake and Hatt and His best stockinges and garters'.[5] Anne Humble gifted all of the needlework cushions and bedding 'Done and wrought' by her daughters.[6] Jane Brookbank gave a cousin 'her husbandes best suit and Cloake with a Gold Ring made vp in a Truelouers knott'.[7] Jane Jaggard gave 'all [her] bookes in the closett in her chamber'.[8]

Wills also can give us a sense—admittedly a rough one—of the size of a woman's assets at the time of her death.[9] The six monetary bequests in Jane Costerdine's 1654 will together amount only to thirty pounds, ten shillings. By comparison, in her 1618 will Elizabeth Oliffe dictated bequests to her family and friends amounting to around 320 pounds, including five shillings 'to the man that shall make my grave'.[10] Even more impressive were the property bequests in the extensive 1638 will of Elizabeth Adams. To her children,

---

Sudbury, and William Crawley did not make their wives executrixes. (Richard Garford outlived his wife Priscilla.) See Appendix.

4    Public Records Office (PRO), PROB 11/297/45. Will quotations come either from original wills or register copies. Transcriptions are diplomatic. Years are rendered in the New Style dating system. Names have been regularised.

5    PRO, PROB 11/181/261.

6    PRO, PROB 11/194/187.

7    London Metropolitan Archives (LMA), DL/C/B/005/MS09172/52, no.137

8    LMA, DL/AL/C/003/MS09052/006, no.170.

9    Early modern wills offer incomplete accounts of testators' estates. Not only were the values of property and amounts of debt not included but total assets could be outweighed—sometimes significantly—by debts, thus nullifying a will's bequests. See Amy Louise Erickson, *Women and property in early modern England* (New York: Routledge, 1993), pp. 32–33.

10    LMA, DL/C/B/005/MS09172/30, no.35.

grandchildren, and their spouses, she gifted considerable land and tenement holdings in Hertfordshire along with yearly rents coming from freehold lands in the same county. With these, she also dictated that a further one hundred pounds be spent on her funeral.

Evidence of book-trade work can also be found in women's wills. In some cases, book-trade women single out business subordinates, suggesting perhaps a working relationship. More than a dozen left legacies to apprentices working under their supervision, while a few more singled out journeymen for bequests. Alice Badger, Anne Boler, Margaret Kembe, Joyce Macham, Joan Man, Katherine Vincent, and Joan Wolfe all gifted rights-to-copy to their heirs.[11] Those that Joyce Macham transferred to her son Samuel in 1627 were all established during the tenure of her bookseller husband Samuel Macham.[12] Katherine Vincent even went so far to name the four titles licensed by her husband that she was gifting to her son George: 'Fower Coppies vizt one called the posie of godlie prayers an other called the Euerrie dayes sacrifice the third the misery of inforced marriage, and the other called the Oliffe leafe'.[13] Anne Boler, on the other hand, left the rights-to-copy of her bookseller husband James to her eldest son of the same name, while '[a]ll and euerie such Coppies of bookes as [she had] bought since [her] said Husbandes death' were gifted to her youngest son Thomas.[14]

A few widows even refer to the tools or products of their trade, others to their larger businesses. Isabella Everest and Anne Lownes each left all their 'wares' to a female family member, a sister and daughter respectively.[15] Anne Boler, Susanna Crawley, Dorothy (Jaggard Downes) Fawne, Joyce French, Jacomine Langford, and Katherine Sudbury all bequeathed bibles.[16] Susanna Crawley left a 'booke of Doctor Pessons vppon the now Covenant' and Maric

---

11   In early modern England after 1557, 'rights-to-copy' were conferred by the Stationers' Company, not by the state. Before and after this time, a 'privilege' to print a title or an entire class of titles could also be granted by a monarch. Authorial copyright did not exist. See Peter W.M. Blayney, 'The Publication of Playbooks', John D. Cox and David Scott Kastan (eds.), *A new history of early English drama* (New York: Columbia University Press), pp. 398–400.

12   For Joyce Macham's work as a publisher after her husband's death, see Alan Farmer, 'Widow publishers in London, 1540–1640', in Valerie Wayne (ed.), *Women's labor and the history of the book in early modern England* (London: Bloomsbury, 2020), pp. 56–7.

13   LMA, DL/C/B/004/MS09171/023/227v.

14   PRO, PROB 11/176/126.

15   LMA, DL/AL/C/003/MS09052/007, no.155, PROB 11/148/625.

16   Crawley specifically left her 'greate Bible with silver Clapses' (PRO, PROB 11/311/358) and Langford both her own and her 'husband[es] bible' (PRO, PROB 11/181/261).

Brewer gave 'a booke of Docto$^r$ Halls workes'.[17] In 1574 Joan Wolfe left to her son and son-in-law 'all the presses letters furniture Coppies and other necessaries Instrumentes and tooles being with in my prynting howse or belonging vnto the same for concerning or belonging to the arte of prynting And also all the bookes whatsoeuer being in my shoppe; my saide dwelling howse or ells wheare'.[18] Anne Cooke followed suit in 1598, gifting to her son Henry 'all the ymplement[es] that belongeth to the Shop[p]e and to the trade'.[19] In 1641, Sarah Fairbeard similarly directed that her 'executors ... indeavour to obtaine from the Cittie of London and Companie of Mercers a Newe Lease of my newe Shopp at the Royall Exchange in London, in the name and for the vse of my said Neece'.[20] Two decades later in 1659, Jane Bell left 'vnto [her] said daughter Elizabeth the summe of ffiue pounds more to be paid by my Executor out of [her] printing house'.[21]

Even while some of these women like Margaret Hodgetts and Elizabeth Bellamy apparently chose to leave the book trade shortly after they were widowed, a number of them appear to have carried on for years with their work as publishers, booksellers, binders, distributors, and printers.[22] The printer William Wilson even dictated in his 1665 will that his wife Mary continue running his printing house after his death. In attempting to account for a widow's activity (i.e. its course and kind), we should keep in mind that it was in large part dependent upon her financial situation after her husband's estate went through probate. In London and towns across England, it had long been customary to break up a husband's land, leases, and personal property or 'chattel' (i.e. his money, trade implements and merchandise, personal effects, and

---

17    PRO, PROB 11/311/358, LMA, DL/C/B/005/MS09172/49, no.32. Crawley's bequest is *The new covenant* (1629), a collection of sermons by Anglican clergyman John Preston. These were originally delivered at Lincoln's Inn. Brewer's 'booke', *The works of Joseph Hall B[ishop] of Exeter*, was first published in the mid 1630s.

18    PRO, PROB 11/56/386.

19    PRO, PROB 11/91/477.

20    PRO, PROB 11/191/367.

21    PRO, PROB 11/296/336.

22    Margaret Hodgetts transferred four rights-to-copy to Robert Allott in early 1626, months after her husband John died, Edward Arber, (ed.), *A transcript of the registers of the Company of Stationers of London, 1554–1640 A.D.*, vol. IV (London: 1875–1894), p. 418. While the fishmonger Edward (Tapp Hurlock) Bellamy left one third of his estate to his wife Elizabeth in 1656, he chose to leave his book business (bookshop, book holdings, and rights-to-copy) to his daughter Mary (wife of the bookseller George Hurlock).

household items) after his death.[23] If a husband's debts were significant, his widow often could only rest assured of retaining what was called her 'chamber' (i.e. her linen, jewels, clothing, bed, hangings, and chests).[24] In London, ecclesiastical law dictated that one third of the value of a husband's leases and personal property—after debts were settled—should go to his widow, one third to his children, and one third to family, friends, and associates in separate bequests.[25] If he died intestate (i.e. not having left a will), one third went to his widow, the other two thirds to his children. One important consequence of this system was that many book-trade widows found themselves with significantly reduced means to carry on the family business once their late husband's estate was settled. In her survey of around 455 English wills from the early modern period in which the widow served as executrix, Amy Louise Erickson found that in 97 cases the widow ended up either in debt or with nothing when all was said and done.[26] This figure does not include the many widows who must have emerged from the process with substantially fewer assets. A widow's decision not to continue working in the book trade, in other words, likely had more to do with simple economics than with anything else. When the draper-turned-stationer Richard Brookbank died in 1643, the probate licence associated with him listed the value of his estate at around thirty-nine pounds. As he and his wife Jane had no children, his monetary bequests were limited to friends and relatives, ten shillings in total. Like many testators before him, he also dictated that all of his debts be 'truely paide' before the remainder be given to his spouse.[27] When Jane died two years later, her estate was valued at twelve pounds, possibly so reduced because of her husband's previous debts.

As suggestive as the wills of book-trade women can be, this probate material has so far been mostly ignored. Just one of the probate documents that Strickland Gibson reproduces in his 1907 *Abstracts from the Wills and*

---

23    While the freehold and copyhold property that a woman brought to a marriage was legally held by her husband, it was put under her control upon his death, Erickson, *Women and property*, p. 25.

24    Allowable funeral expenses were also deducted before the estate was divided. See Peter W.M. Blayney, *The Stationers' Company and the printers of London, 1501–1557*, vol. 1 (Cambridge: Cambridge University Press, 2013), p. 84.

25    The freehold and copyhold property that a husband both brought to and acquired during a marriage could usually either be distributed by bequests in his will or, if he died intestate or did not include such dictates in his will, conferred along the lines of the English system of primogeniture according to manorial and borough custom, Erickson, *Women and property*, pp. 26–27.

26    Ibid., p. 174.

27    LMA, DL/C/B/005/MS09172/50, no.33.

*Testamentary Documents of Binders, Printers, and Stationers of Oxford, from 1493 to 1638* comes from a woman (Anne Herks), while George J. Gray and William Mortlock Palmer include material from just two widows (Magdalen Graves and Margaret Pilgrim) among the forty-seven sets of probate documents in their *Abstracts from the Wills and Testamentary Documents of Printers, Binders, and Stationers of Cambridge, from 1504 to 1699* published eight years later. In his 1904 *Abstracts from the Wills of English Printers and Stationers: From 1492 to 1630*, Henry R. Plomer included partial transcriptions of the wills of Lucy Reynes (proved in 1549), Elizabeth Toye (proved in 1565), and Joan Wolfe (proved in 1574). In the volume's introduction, he makes it clear that his main purpose in including this material was to 'supplement the information given in the wills of their husbands', even while admitting that Joan Wolfe's will is 'an interesting and valuable record'.[28] A comparison of Plomer's abstracts with the wills themselves reveals his capricious method. Plomer promises that his abstracts include bequests, but in actuality they provide only partial lists of these legacies.[29] In his Reynes and Wolfe abstracts, women legatees are often cut, as are a number of sums and objects.

The earliest London women's wills the BTP project has so far identified that were left before the incorporation of the Stationers' Company in 1557 come from Joan Hebson and Anne Taverner. John Hebson had served as the Stationers' warden before naming his wife joint executor of his estate and dying in 1502. Within a year, Joan Hebson would finalise her own will, dictating sales of tenements in Eastcheap and in Barking and leaving money to a priest to sing and pray for her own soul and the souls of her two husbands. Anne Taverner's relatively extensive will was witnessed on 3 December 1537 and proved nine days later. Anne married the bookbinder John Taverner sometime in the late fifteenth or early sixteenth century, and she ran his rented Paternoster Row shop after his death in 1531.[30] John plied his trade as a binder, retailer, and textwriter (i.e. a writer and copyist of non-legal manuscript texts) during his long career, and by the 1520s he would come to be one of the wealthiest stationers in London and a respected citizen.[31] In Anne's will, the lion's share of the bequests are given to her daughter Margaret and her husband the stationer-haberdasher William Bull, and to her stationer son Nicholas and his

---

28    Henry R. Plomer, *Abstracts from the wills of English printers and stationers: from 1492 to 1630* (London: The Bibliographical Society, 1904), p. iii.
29    Plomer, *Abstracts*, p. ii.
30    See Blayney, *Stationers' Company*, vol. I, p. 472.
31    Ibid., p. 209.

wife Mary. To the former pair, she left most of her 'owne propre goodes', including a goblet with 'a Castle in the Bottome and a foote of syluer', three furred
gowns, a 'bedstede hanginge and all other thinges therto belonging', and two
chestes one grete and one other small'. To the latter, she left the 'Residew of all
my goodes not bequethed my Dettes and this my legaces paied'.[32] The Bulls
would run the Paternoster Row business after 1537, and as such it is possible
that the implements of her scribal textwriting and bookbinding business were
passed onto the Bulls in Anne's two chestes.[33]

At the end of the period considered here is the will of Dorothy (Jaggard
Downes) Fawne that was witnessed in Hackney on 15 September 1666, just
two weeks after the Great Fire had gutted much of London.[34] Dorothy enjoyed
close connections with three prominent seventeenth-century stationer families before she married the widower bookseller Luke Fawne in the late 1650s or
early 1660s: the Weavers, the Jaggards, and the Downeses.[35] She was the daughter of the bookseller Edmond Weaver, and she was almost certainly the Dorothy
who married the printer Isaac Jaggard in the 1610s or 1620s. Among other things,
the Jaggards were key members of the syndicate that published Shakespeare's
First Folio in 1623. After Isaac's death in the spring of 1627, Dorothy would
continue working at her Barbican printing house for a short time until she
appears to have sold the business to the brothers Thomas and Richard Cotes.[36]
By 1638, she had married Thomas Downes, joining his long standing bookselling business in St. Paul's Churchyard.[37] In her will, Dorothy left bequests to
the Stationers' Company, to former Fawne apprentices Jonathan Robinson

---

32    PRO, PROB 11/27/170.

33    See C. Paul Christianson, 'The Stationers of Paternoster Row, 1534–1557', *Papers of the
      Bibliographical Society of America*, 87 (1993), p. 84.

34    Luke Fawne died in March, 1666, and his lengthy will was proved shortly thereafter on
      March 26th. In it, Fawne left hundreds of pounds in legacies to his family and friends as
      well as the residue of his estate to his wife. For more on the Fawnes, see H.A. Shield, 'Links
      with Shakespeare IV', *Notes and Queries*, 194.25 (1949), pp. 536–537.

35    Edmund Weaver and his sons Gabriel, Thomas, and Edmund were all booksellers.
      Edmund senior was originally freed as a Draper before being transferred to the Stationers'
      Company in 1600, Arber, *transcript*, vol. II p. 725. Thomas Downes, his son Thomas, and
      his brother Bartholomew were booksellers as well.

36    Arber, *transcript*, vol. IV p. 182. With the exception of twenty pounds to his brother
      Thomas and five pounds to the poor, Isaac left his wife 'All the rest of my goodes and
      chattles money and debts whatsoeuer', LMA, DL/AL/C/003/MS09052/007, no.29. He also
      made her his sole executrix. Within weeks of Isaac's death in 1627, Dorothy published
      Lancelot Andrewes's *Seven sermons on the wonderful combat between Christ and Satan*.

37    Thomas Downes named Dorothy his executrix and left her the residue of his estate after
      his debts had been satisfied and his legacies (amounting to 140 pounds) had been paid.

and Brabazon Aylmer, to Jane Greene (possibly the widow of Charles Greene who had apprenticed with Dorothy's father), and to the bookseller Anthony Dowse who she calls a 'welbeloued ffreind'. She left her 'great Bible lyeing in the Parlour' to another of her close friends, Robert Welden.

In early modern England, unmarried women could elect to leave a will if they were twelve-years-old or older. In the early 1580s, Anne Hill, the unmarried daughter of the deceased printer William Hill, was working as a servant in the household of Humphrey Winnington. In September, 1582, the 21-year-old Anne finalised a will in which she distributed a twenty-pound legacy from her father as well as a one-hundred-mark 'obligacon' due to her from the draper Richard Smith.[38] Though most of the women connected to the book trade were either a wife, a widow, or, like Anne Hill, a daughter, some who worked in a printing house or bookshop did so as an unmarried and unrelated servant. Little evidence of these women exist. Most of what we do know comes from burial entries in parish registers and court proceedings. We do, however, have at least one will from a female servant who worked in the early English book trade. In May 1565, Margaret Dourman left her estate ('goodes cattells Iewells debtes and houshold stuffe') to the barber surgeon Richard West along with ten shillings to 'poore folke at the day of [her] buryall'.[39] When she drew up her will, Dourman was employed by the London bookseller Roger Ireland, possibly at the Holy Ghost in St. Paul's Churchyard.[40] Ireland was an original member of the Stationers' Company, and he had risen in the company's administrative ranks to an assistant in the 1560s and then to a warden around the time of Dourman's death. Working for Ireland was probably anything but mundane. In the early 1550s, he seems to have acquired his own London tennis court and was around the same time accused of running an illegal gambling operation.[41]

Married women were not legally qualified to leave a will because they were understood to be under the protection of their husbands (i.e. 'covert baron'

---

His largest legacy of one hundred pounds went to John Weaver, orphan son of Dorothy's brother Edmund whom she and Thomas had taken in.

38    LMA, DL/C/B/005/MS09172/011D, no.115. William Hill died in 1564. For more on his short career, see Blayney, *Stationers' Company*, vol. II, pp. 617–620. The Richard Smith referenced here might be the draper bookseller who apprenticed first with Thomas Pettit and then with John Wight. For more on the interesting career of Smith, see Kirk Melnikoff, *Elizabethan publishing, and makings of literary culture* (Toronto: University of Toronto Press, 2018), pp. 99–136.

39    LMA, DL/C/0359/001/76r.

40    Roger Ireland's only imprint, a 1569 almanack, advertises Ireland's bookshop at the sign of the Holy Ghost.

41    Blayney, *Stationers' Company*, vol. II p. 895.

in the common-law terminology of the day). There were exceptions to this. A wife could negotiate freedom of testation (i.e. power to leave a will) as part of her marriage contract; she could also be given permission to leave a will by her husband.[42] Of the book-trade wills from women that we have so far found, four were left by wives with living husbands. Joan (Morton) Patchet in 1561 and Jane Constable in 1631 each left a will which cites the permission of her husband.[43] After the deaths of her first and second husbands, Margaret Morrall married the London bookseller Henry Danson in 1608.[44] Margaret's will records that she had been granted permission to 'at any tyme make or cause to be made any writing vnder my hand and Seale wherein or whereby I might and may give and dispose of three hundred powndes of lawfull money of England'.[45] It then dictates that the three hundred pounds be divided equally between her eldest son Robert Wood and his fiancée Margaret Coates, John Morrall, and Aminadab Morrall. These were her only bequests.[46] At some point in the middle decades of the seventeenth century, Priscilla Garford received a seven-hundred pound legacy from her mother. Later on, she may have negotiated a freedom of testation at her marriage.[47] Whatever the terms of existence, her 1665 will dictates that this legacy be passed onto her husband Richard Garford.

Remarriage was a complicated proposition for many a book-trade widow. If she chose to marry a non-stationer, she had to relinquish her rights-to-copy and her shares in Stationers' Company stock. Cuthbert Burby's widow Elizabeth, for example, married the gentleman Humphrey Turner at St Michael, Cornhill on 17 October 1609. Stationers' Company policies explain why she transferred all of her rights-to-copy to the booksellers William Welby and Nicholas Bourne on 16 October, and why her shares of Stationers' Company stock were re-assigned

---

42    E.A.J. Honigmann and Susan Brock, eds., *Playhouse wills, 1558–1642: an edition of wills by Shakespeare and his contemporaries in the London theatre* (Manchester: Manchester University Press, 1993), p. 12.

43    Jane Constable's father was the London butcher Christopher Child who died in 1625, naming his wife Joan and Jane executors in his will. In her will, Jane asked her husband to act as executor of her father's estate after her death.

44    Margaret first married the London saddler Eachey Wood at some point in the final two decades of the sixteenth century. After the death of Wood, she then married the London merchant tailor William Morrall in 1593.

45    PRO, PROB 11/146/468.

46    Margaret's will was proved two years later in September, 1625. Henry Danson died sometime after 1627.

47    Priscilla Garford's parents were John and Margaret Foot. Her brother was the wealthy London grocer Thomas Foot who was elected Lord Mayor of London in 1649.

to four bookmen on 21 October.[48] Even if a widow elected to remarry a stationer, it was sometimes the case that she faced financial consequences as
a result of dictates in her deceased husband's will. In 1570, Stephen Kevall
insisted in his will that if his wife Jane remarry that she pay five separate legacies amounting to over eighty-two pounds. Similarly, in his 1603 will, the bookseller Henry Hooke directed that if his wife Alice remarry 'that before the day
of the Solemination of her maryage she enter into sufficient bond to give vnto
eyther of my two sonnes samuell & nathanaell Hook twentie pund A pice'.[49]
Neither Jane Kevall nor Alice Hooke ended up remarrying.

In 1665, with the bookseller John Grove and the stationer apprentice
Nicholas Hooper standing by as witnesses, Joan Mead affixed her seal to each
of her will's three manuscript pages. She also signed each of these with her own
full name. Mead's ability to write was not exceptional. A number of women
who worked in the early modern book trade were literate. As Helen Smith has
documented, widows frequently penned notes in the Stationers' Company
register in transferring rights-to-copy, and they also wrote letters to company
leaders in order officially to resign yeoman, apprentice, and livery shares in the
company's stock.[50] Like Joan Mead's does, wills can provide evidence of the
extent of literacy among book-trade women. Around 33% of the eighty-eight
wills (i.e. twenty-eight) that we have found include women's signatures, either
an original signature, or, if a register copy, evidence of an original. Over half
(i.e. forty-seven) of these wills contain marks instead of signatures. By comparison, around 10% of husbands' wills are marked, and 70% have signatures.

While we should be careful about what we conclude from this signature
evidence, it is at least possible that these twenty-eight widows were fully literate, adept in both reading and writing.[51] As such, they would have not only
been able to pen administrative notes and missives, they also would have been
able to write out customer receipts and keep business records (i.e. account
books, day books, and the like). If publishing was a part of their business, they
would have been able to read, correct, even copy edit as well. Nineteen of the
women who left wills in the period we are considering are advertised in at least
one imprint as publisher. A further three more widows (i.e. Dorothy [Jaggard
Downes] Fawne, Elizabeth Toye, and Alice Wolfe) published titles without

---

48   See Arber, *transcript*, vol. III, pp. 419–421; Jackson, *Records*, p. 38.
49   LMA, DL/AL/C/003/MS09052/001D, no.113.
50   Smith, '*Grossly Material Things*', pp. 91–92.
51   For pitfalls in assessing literacy through signature evidence, see Roger Chartier, 'The prac-
     tical impact of writing', in Roger Chartier (ed.), *A history of private life, volume 3: Passions
     of the Renaissance* (Cambridge: Harvard University Press, 1989), pp. 111–159.

putting their own name in an imprint. Of these twenty-two publishing widows, ten signed their wills (Elizabeth Adams, Elizabeth [Tapp Hurlock] Bellamy, Anne Boler, Lucretia East, Sarah Fairbeard, Dorothy [Jaggard Downes] Fawne, Mercy Meighen, Elizabeth [White Burby] Turner, Katherine Vincent, and Joan Wolfe), and nine left their marks (Jane Bell, Joan Broome, Susan Islipp, Joyce [Norton] Law, Joyce Macham, Elizabeth Overton, Elizabeth Toye, Sarah White, and Alice Wolfe). Of the former group, Elizabeth Adams, Anne Boler, Dorothy (Jaggard Downes) Fawne, Elizabeth (White Burby) Turner, and Mercy Meighen each published new titles after her husband's death. Of the latter, only Joan Broome did so. While Broome represents an important exception, literacy may have had something to do with the extent to which widow publishers were, to use Alan Farmer's terminology, 'entrepreneurial'.[52]

Many book-trade women's wills include bequests of specific items. The strong majority of these are either articles of clothing, textiles associated with eating and sleeping (napkins, pillow cases, sheets, etc.), furniture, jewellery, kitchenware, or expensive tableware (goblets, salts, tankards, etc.). In a number of cases, such bequests are extensive, providing an inventory of sorts of the kinds of things a widow would have surrounded herself with before, during, and after her marriage. For example, Mary Bishop, wife of the bookseller George Bishop, left her cousin Mary Walker 'Twoe boales pcell guilt, a guilt sault, twoe guilt pottes one Douzen of spones my great Chest w^th Drawers, my Wayneskott Chest ... my Walnuttree bedsted, Two Nedleworke Chaires, one Chaire of peartree in the hall, one Cipres Chest in the Wainskott Chamber, The Court Cubbord in my Chamber, and my little Tabell in the hall'.[53] With recurring articles of clothing like petticoats, girdles, and coats and objects like bowls, pots, silverware, chests, bedframes, chairs, cupboards, and tables, there are, however, more unique bequests. To the books already mentioned should be added Joanne Waye's 'blacke gowne whiche was [her] morninge gowne at the buriall of [her] husband ... garded with velvett', Joan Wolfe's 'neste of Goblet[es] of siluer parcell gilte with a cover being marked vppon the couer w^th an R and an I engraphen', Elizabeth's Toye's 'Couerlet of Imagerie', Elizabeth Oliffe's 'paynted Clothe & hanginge', and Elizabeth (Bankworth) Blount's beaver hat.[54] The wills of book-trade widowers that we have transcribed rarely contain significant numbers of object bequests, nor do they contain the same kind. In these, widowers usually distribute their goods as bulk legacies.

---

52   Farmer, 'Widow publishers', pp. 54–57.
53   PRO, PROB 11/122/203.
54   PRO, PROB 11/68/367; PRO, PROB 11/56/386; PRO, PROB 11/48/210; LMA, DL/C/B/005/MS09172/030, no.35.

If they do leave objects, these are usually items of clothing. Such contrasting bequests could be taken to be a result of the different roles that book-trade men and women played in what were more often than not domestic operations. Even while wives and widows were tasked with running or helping to run the first-floor printing houses, bookshop(s), or book stall(s) of the family businesses, they at the same time were also responsible for overseeing the everyday affairs of the household having to do with cleaning and cooking.

As Helen Smith pointed out a decade ago, for early modern women,

> sex is unlikely to have been the most significant category of identity. ... Early modern subjectivity was formed in relation to external rather than interior commitments and identifications. Women like Anne Griffin, Joan Orwin, and Elizabeth Toye identified themselves as members of the community of stationers, as well as, at various points, wives, mothers, widows, and members of political and religious communities.[55]

Women's wills suggest that, at least as far as book-trade funerary practices were organized, the orientation of these commitments and identifications may have been shifting. In the 1570s, a number of widows singled out disenfranchised women as a supporting cast for their funerals. In her 1577 will, Jane Kevall bequeathed twelve gowns of cloth at 'sixe shillinge eight pence the yarde' to eight poor women so that they could accompany her corpse to burial.[56] Nine years later, Joan Jugge gifted 'eighte pore women dwellinge within the saide parishe of Christ churche eight black gownes of five shilling[es] the yarde', and Mary Bishop in 1613 left 'vnto Three skoore poore women, And to so many poore Women more as I shall happen to be yeares ould aboue Threescore, att the tyme of my Decease, To every of them A black Cloth gowne of Eight shillinges a yeard, And also a lockeram smock of Sixteene pence an Ell att the least'.[57] Later charitable bequests are not only less often given to bolster participation in funerary rituals, they are also often directed towards company widows. In 1616, Alice (Waterson Coldock) Bing singled out stationers' widows for twelve charitable bequests, and two decades later Anne Boler gave 'fortie shilling[es] in money to be distributed to amongst eight poore widowes of the

---

55    Smith, '*Grossly Material Things*', p. 90.
56    PRO, PROB 11/63/346.
57    PRO, PROB 11/72/698; PRO, PROB 11/122/203.

said Company of Stationers equallie parte & parte like'.[58] It may be that these later wills speak to a burgeoning company identity among book-trade widows after the sixteenth century.[59]

The observations offered here are tentative. All of them need to be tested against an exhaustive collection of early modern book-trade probate material from both women and men. Over the coming years, the Book Trade Probate project will undoubtedly unearth more wills, and these may modify the impressions conjured here. Even then, conclusions about the activities of book-trade women drawn from probate material will need to be weighed against other evidence from the period. Only around 15% of the book-trade wills that we have so far identified come from women, meaning that such probate evidence will likely be partial at best. Moreover, only around 20% of eligible adults left wills in the early seventeenth century, and those that did often had significant estates to pass on.[60] For every will that we have from the likes of Margaret Dourman, in other words, there are dozens of wills from successful bookwomen like Joan Wolfe, Elizabeth Adams, and Anne Boler.

Still, no other set of resources documenting women connected with the early-modern English book trade provides anywhere near the quantity and quality of evidence as wills. Many of those surveyed here—from both husbands and wives—confirm what sixteenth- and seventeenth-century book imprints and Stationers' Company records vaguely attest: that a significant number of widows continued to work in the trade after the death of their husbands, even as England's probate laws and customs made this sometimes a difficult proposition. Suggested as well is the high probability that these women had been essential partners in these businesses while their husbands were still living. Women's wills conjure too tantalising images of the lives led by bookwomen as wives, daughters, widows, even maidservants. Until we readily acknowledge that these lives intersected in significant ways with foundational books like Calvin's *Institutes of the Christian Religion*, the Geneva Bible, Gerard's *Herbal*, and the First Folio, our understanding of early modern English culture will necessarily be incomplete.

---

58    PRO, PROB 11/176/126.

59    Farmer has recently identified a network of book-trade widow publishers in London in the 1630s, one that included Anne Boler, 'Widow publishers', pp. 57–61.

60    Honigmann and Brock, *Playhouse wills*, p. 11. See also Erickson, *Women and property*, pp. 32–33.

## Appendix: Women's English Book-Trade Wills (1557–1666)

| Name (%: widow publisher) (*: listed in Bell) | signed / marked / ncptv (@: sick) | Will Witnessed | Will Proved | Executor(s) (full names given for women) |
|---|---|---|---|---|
| Joan (Morton) Patchet | –@ | 1561 | 1561 (ComCL) | J.Wilford (son-in-law) |
| Margaret Dourman | – | 1565 | 1565 (PCC) | R.West |
| Elizabeth Toye%* | marked | 1565 | 1565 (CCL) | H.Toye (son) |
| Margery Lobley | – | 1567 | 1567 (ComCL) | T.Lobley and L.Lloyd |
| Joan Wolfe%* | signed@ | 1574 | 1574 (PCC) | R.Wolfe (son), J.Hun (son-in-law) |
| Jane Kevall | signed | 1576 | 1581 (PCC) | Alice Woodcock (cousin) |
| Joanne Waye | signed | 1581 | 1584 (PCC) | Elizabeth Poultney (daughter), H.Poultney (son-in-law) |
| Anne Hill | signed@ | 1582 | 1584 (ComCL) | W.Hill (youngest brother) |
| Joan Jugge%* | – | 1588 | 1588 (PCC) | Susan Norcott, Joanne Crayford (daughters) |
| Anne (Dewyxsell) Nichols | marked@ | 1591 | 1591 (ComCL) | W.Phillips |
| Alice Judson | marked | 1592 | 1592 (ComCL) | R.Judson, T.Judson (sons) |
| Joanne (Johnson) Tyas | marked | 1593 | 1593 (PCC) | C.Barnett (father) R.Curwin |
| Anne Cooke | –@ | 1598 | 1598 (PCC) | W.Cooke (son) |

| erseer(s) ll names given women) | Witness(es) (full names given for women) | Husband(s) (#: widow named executrix of will) | Husband(s) Will(s) Witnessed |
|---|---|---|---|
| ᴉe | M.Lingley, O.Gladell, J.Pavier, T.Cotwell | Edward Morton, Richard Patchet | N/A, N/A |
| ᴉe | R.Oker, J.Vicares | – | – |
| ʃoodall (brother), ᴉwood | R.Jugge, J.Cooke, T.Bedford, A.Bande | Robert Toye# | 1556 |
| ᴉe | H.Flycke, W.Korke | Michael Lobley# | 1567 |
| ᴇvenson, ᴉrrison ᴉ-in-laws) | R.Henton, G.Cawood, R.Colvis | Reynard Wolfe# | 1574 |
| ʃoodcock ᴉsin), T.Hall | J.Peyto, R.Savage, T.Walker | Stephen Kevall# | 1576 |
| ʃright, J.Gunneld ᴇnds) | W.Dent, R.Holte, H.West, T.Atkinson | Richard Waye# | 1577 |
| ʃinnington | Dorothy Wynnington, A.Paget, T.Felton, Joane Neale, T.Frier | – | – |
| ʃatkins (son-in- ), N.Gibbons ᴉsin) | R.Watkins, F.Coldock, T.Robinson, R.Wright | Richard Jugge# | 1577 |
| ᴉe | J.Whitney, J.Snowe, J.Williamson | Thomas Dewyxsell#, Thomas Nichols | 1566, N/A |
| ᴉolsick | Joan Sparrow, Alice Westmoreland | John Judson# | 1589 |
| ᴉe | J.Fletcher, R.Curwen | Henry Johnson#, Thomas Tyas# | 1588, 1591 |
| ᴉooke ᴇther-in-law) | A.Field | William Cooke# | 1597 |

(*cont.*)

| Name (%: widow publisher) (*: listed in Bell) | signed / marked / ncptv (@: sick) | Will Witnessed | Will Proved | Executor(s) (full names given for women) |
|---|---|---|---|---|
| Joan Broome%* | marked@ | 1601 | 1601 (PCC) | T.Man, Sybil Grantam (niece) |
| Alice Hooke | marked | 1603 | 1603 (AL) | N.Hooke (son) |
| Margery Cooke | marked@ | 1608 | 1608 (PCSP) | T.Cooke (son), L.Lisle (son-in-law) |
| Joyce French | marked@ | 1608 | 1609 (PCSP) | Joan Baynes (cousin) |
| Mary Bishop | signed@ | 1613 | 1613 (PCC) | G.Cawood (cousin) |
| Joan Baynes | marked@ | 1614 | 1614 (PCSP) | W.Baynes (brother), O.Minstowe |
| Anne Chappell | marked@ | 1614 | 1614 (ComCL) | J.Bentley (friend) |
| Jane Yardley* | marked | 1614 | 1615 (ComCL) | T.Yardley (son) |
| Sara White%* | marked@ | 1615 | 1615 (PCC) | E.White (son) |
| Alice (Waterson Coldock) Bing* | marked@ | 1616 | 1616 (PCC) | Joanne Bright (daughter) |
| Anne Hatfield | marked@ | 1617 | 1617 (PCC) | W.Wilmot (cousin) |
| Elizabeth Oliffe* | marked@ | 1617 | 1617 (AL) | T.Oliffe (son) |
| Katherine Vincent%* | signed | 1618 | 1618 (ComCL) | R.Bowen (brother) |
| Alice Wolfe%* | marked | 1618 | 1618 (PCC) | J.Daniell (son-in-law) |

| erseer(s) ll names given women) | Witness(es) (full names given for women) | Husband(s) (#: widow named executrix of will) | Husband(s) Will(s) Witnessed |
|---|---|---|---|
| /right | H.Lownes, T.Man, W.Tewe, Susan Trare | William Broome | N/A |
| helton, W.Kinge | B.Greenhill, Isabel Southwell, Catherine Shelton | Henry Hooke | N/A |
| orton | J.Norton, H.Dyson | Toby Cooke | N/A |
| ie | T.Hatchbery, R.Baynes, H.Daughty | Peter French# | 1584 |
| spley, L.Stringer nd) | E.White, W.Aspley, W.Harsnett, J.Browne | George Bishop# | 1610 |
| ie | E.Farye, Alice Deacken, Elizabeth Warden | Robert Baynes# | 1613 |
| ie | J.Hutchins, Anne Hill | Thomas Chappell# | 1606 |
| lynce, N.Allan nds) | G.Blynce, T.Lillue, R.Waylett | Richard Yardley# | 1593 |
| awson, W.Smyth, lde, W.Need nds) | R.Parker, R.Glover | Edward White# | 1612 |
| eake, E.Blount nds) | N.Kempe, E.Weaver, W.Barrett, J.Gibbons | Richard Waterson, Francis Coldock#, Isaac Bing# | N/A, 1603, 1604 |
| teman (friend), riffin (servant) | R.Berrowe, T.Addis, R.Hartley | Arnold Hatfield# | 1612 |
| ardener (friend), lgeway, F.Snell, ckman | T.Stanbanke, W.Henley, A.Hudson, | Richard Oliffe | N/A |
| e | R.Cooke, P.Hughes, Sir J.Cooper | George Vincent# | 1618 |
| niell (son-in-law) | Anne Trotter, N.Commerford, Katherine Haward, Elizabeth Trotter | John Wolfe | N/A |

(*cont.*)

| Name (%: widow publisher) (*: listed in Bell) | signed / marked / ncptv (@: sick) | Will Witnessed | Will Proved | Executor(s) (full names given for women) |
|---|---|---|---|---|
| Katherine Hudson | marked@ | 1618 | 1618 (ComCL) | R.Hudson (son) |
| Anne Snowden* | ncptv@ | 1619 | 1619 (ComCL) | – |
| Anne Harrison* | marked@ | 1621 | 1621 (PCC) | J.Harrison (son) |
| Anne Hooper | marked@ | 1621 | 1621 (PCC) | T.Ansten (cousin R.Constable |
| Margaret (Wood Morrall) Danson | marked | 1623 | 1625 (PCC) | R.Wood (son [1st marriage)]) |
| Agnes Standish* | signed@ | 1623 | 1623 (PCC) | T.Colchester (brother) |
| Margaret Edmondes | ncptv@ | 1624 | 1624 (PCC) | J.Edmondes (grandson) |
| Katherine Collins | signed@ | 1625 | 1625 (AL) | A.Collins (son) |
| Anne Hyde | ncptv@ | 1625 | 1625 (AL) | S.Chappell (brother) |
| Jane Jaggard | signed@ | 1625 | 1625 (AL) | M.Bowles (son-in-law) |
| Anne Lownes | marked@ | 1625 | 1626 (PCC) | Anne Lownes (daughter) |
| Elizabeth Snodham* | signed | 1625 | 1626 (PCC) | Elizabeth Turner (daughter) |

| erseer(s) ll names given women) | Witness(es) (full names given for women) | Husband(s) (#: widow named executrix of will) | Husband(s) Will(s) Witnessed |
|---|---|---|---|
| eake (friend),?. rpe (cousin) | R.Yorke, J.Sharpe, R.Rothwell | Richard Hudson# | 1600 |
| owe, W.Hudson | Alice Shawe, T.Bishop, R.Shawe, Mary Wharton | Lionel Snowden# | 1616 |
| Iale (son-in-law) | T.Griffin, E.Blackman, S.Speede | John Harrison# | 1616 |
| ield (cousin), Cooke, ymcottes, T.Berrie | N/A | Humphrey Hooper# | 1613 |
| oates, J.Andrews ends) | N/A | Eachey Wood, William Morrall, Henry Danson | N/A, N/A, N/A |
| illy, T.Hooper ends) | W.Tilly, R.Morgan, T.Hutchins, R.Hutchins | John Standish# | 1613 |
| ie | J.Eaton, R.Waynman, 'other credible witnesses' | William Edmondes# | 1597 |
| lipp, T.Purfoot others) | N/A | Richard Collins# | 1613 |
| ie | Sara Cookson, Elizabeth Mitton, Marie Calcott, Margarett Brogden, Sara Taylor | John Hyde# | 1624 |
| ans, H.Corrington ends) | J.Jaggard, A.Woodfall, Alice Heywood, Anne Sodburne, R.Glover | William Jaggard# | 1623 |
| ie | G.Cole, E.Blount, W.Cole, E.Brewster | Matthew Lownes# | 1625 |
| Ieaver, W.Stansby ends) | J.Owtred, Sir W.Agard, Jane Mercer | Thomas Snodham# | 1625 |

*(cont.)*

| Name (%: widow publisher) (*: listed in Bell) | signed / marked / ncptv (@: sick) | Will Witnessed | Will Proved | Executor(s) (full names given for women) |
|---|---|---|---|---|
| Anne Bradwood | marked@ | 1626 | 1626 (PCC) | Elizabeth Hodesden (daughter) |
| Isabel Combes | signed@ | 1626 | 1626 (ComCL) | R.Boyce (cousin) |
| Joyce Macham%* | marked@ | 1627 | 1627 (ComCL) | S.Macham (son) |
| Lucretia East%* | signed | 1628 | 1629 (PCC) | E.Weaver (friend) |
| Isabella Everest | marked@ | 1629 | 1629 (AL) | Elizabeth Foster |
| Elizabeth (White Burby) Turner%* | signed@ | 1630 | 1630 (PCC) | E.Burby (son) |
| Jane Constable | signed@ | 1631 | 1631 (PCC) | R.Constable (husband) |
| Margaret Burre | signed | 1632 | 1638 (PCC) | T.Bevand (kinsman) |
| Margaret Hodgetts* | marked@ | 1634 | 1634 (PCC) | L.Blomeley (son-in-law) |
| Antoinetta Draper | marked@ | 1635 | 1635 (AL) | J.Sands (friend) |
| Judith Taylor* | marked@ | 1635 | 1635 (ComCL) | E.Banbury (friend) |
| Anne Boler%* | signed@ | 1637 | 1638 (PCC) | R.Barrett, R.Marmyon (sons-in-law) |
| Elizabeth Adams%* | signed@ | 1638 | 1638 (PCSP) | Elizabeth Lucks (daughter), W.Mongre (son-in-law) |

| erseer(s) ll names given women) | Witness(es) (full names given for women) | Husband(s) (#: widow named executrix of will) | Husband(s) Will(s) Witnessed |
|---|---|---|---|
| aylor (son-in- ·), T.Day | D.Stevens, G.Tayler, T.Daie | Melchisidec Bradwood# | 1618 |
| Ham, E.Masters ighbors and nds) | Margery Hinton, Mary Ham, J.Swannsey | John Combes# | 1623 |
| Vaterson (friend) | S.Waterson, F.Wnson, R.Dickon | Samuel Macham# | 1625 |
| ne | T.Gerard, J.Clifford, A.Hill, B.Hill, T.Bartram W.Nayler | Thomas East# | 1608 |
| ne | T.Abbott, R. Williamson | Stephen Everest# | 1628 |
| Mason, Middleton n-in-law) | Providence Moore, W.Agard, Susan Catur, G.Allestry | Andrew White, Cuthbert Burby#, Humphrey Turner | N/A, 1607, N/A |
| ne | J.Hatt, C.Barker, F.Constable, Alice Constable | Robert Constable# | 1635 |
| Middleton other), R.Sproston usin) | J.Naylor, J.Ellys | Walter Burre# | 1622 |
| ne | W.Fermey, R.Richardson | John Hodgetts# | 1625 |
| spar (friend) | [C.Dach], J.Maine, L.[] | Thomas Draper | N/A |
| ne | T.Harbart, J.Perrie | Richard Taylor | N/A |
| utchins (cousin), ownes (friend), ephens (friend) | Anne Griffin, J.Grew, J.Hayne | James Boler# | 1635 |
| ne | W.Frithe, A.Hebb | Thomas Adams# | 1620 |

(*cont.*)

| Name (%: widow publisher) (*: listed in Bell) | signed / marked / ncptv (@: sick) | Will Witnessed | Will Proved | Executor(s) (full names given for women) |
| --- | --- | --- | --- | --- |
| Jacomine Langford | signed | 1639 | 1639 (PCC) | M.Sparkes (father) |
| Marie Brewer | signed | 1640 | 1641 (ComCL) | E.Barton (sister) |
| Anne Bird | signed@ | 1641 | 1641 (PCC) | E.Dawkins (brother) |
| Elizabeth Blundell | marked@ | 1641 | 1641 (AL) | T.Evens (servant) |
| Sarah Fairbeard%* | signed | 1641 | 1643 (PCC) | Dorothy Sanders (niece), rector & churchwardens of St Mildred |
| Katherine Sudbury | signed@ | 1641 | 1643 (PCC) | Katherine Wigna (kinswoman) |
| Dorothy Cooke | – | 1642 | 1642 (ComCL) | N/A |
| Joyce Norton%* | marked | 1643 | 1643 (ComCL) | ?.Duckett, E.Washington (son-in-laws) |
| Alice Young | marked@ | 1643 | 1643 (ComCL) | J.Young (son) |
| Mary Ward* | ncptv@ | 1644 | 1644 (ComCL) | G.Mannering (brother) |
| Jane Brookbank | marked@ | 1645 | 1645 (ComCL) | Marie Nicholson (sister) |
| Anne Humble | marked@ | 1645 | 1645 (PCC) | W.Humble and T.Humble (sons) |
| Elizabeth (Bankworth) Blount* | marked@ | 1647 | ? (PCC) | Phillipp Bankworth (daughter) |

| erseer(s) ll names given women) | Witness(es) (full names given for women) | Husband(s) (#: widow named executrix of will) | Husband(s) Will(s) Witnessed |
|---|---|---|---|
| 1e | H.Baskerville, R.Miles, Anne Peters | Bernard Langford# | 1639 |
| 1e | T.Bradshaw, W.Norett, A.Breces, T.Dutton | Hugh Brewer# | 1632 |
| rewster, hornton (friends) | J.Ward, W.Burton, E.Wheston, R.Wilkes | Robert Bird# | 1641 |
| 1e | J.Phillips, Ellen Evans, H.Arnold | Edward Blundell | N/A |
| 1e | J.Alport, Elizabeth Alport, J.Parry | George Fairbeard | N/A |
| Iurleston, mpson (friends) | A.Brimskell, J.Beresford, R.Earle | John Sudbury | 1621 |
| ae | R.Bowyer, R.Stevens | Josias Cooke# | 1642 |
| ale (son-in-law) | O.Hickes, G.Nightengale | John Norton | 1613 |
| 1e | A.Colston, T.Downs, T. Jagger, R.Wood | Robert Young | N/A |
| ae | E.Thirkins, Margerie Parker, Maryanne Harstead | Samuel Ward# | 1636 |
| yce (friend) | T.Wynne, J.Palmer | Richard Brookbank# | 1643 |
| ae | W.Bow, E.Trussell, H.Williamson, F.Shepard | George Humble# | 1645 |
| ae | E.Tekinge, T.Osborne, E.Steevens | Richard Bankworth#, Edward Blount | 1614, N/A |

(*cont.*)

| Name (%: widow publisher) (*: listed in Bell) | signed / marked / ncptv (@: sick) | Will Witnessed | Will Proved | Executor(s) (full names given for women) |
|---|---|---|---|---|
| Alice Constable | ncptv@ | 1647 | 1647 (CCW) | N/A |
| Joan Bloome | marked@ | 1648 | 1648 (PCC) | Katherine Mason |
| Anna Cole | signed@ | 1648 | 1649 (PCC) | S.Franklin and Marcy Franklin (cousins) |
| Joan Man%* | ncptv@ | 1651 | 1651 (PCC) | J.Holden (son-in-law) |
| Susan Islipp%* | marked | 1653 | 1661 (PCC) | W.Hunt |
| Mercy Meighen%* | signed@ | 1653 | 1654 (PCC) | G.Bedell, T.Collin (son-in-law) |
| Jane Costerdine | marked | 1654 | 1660 (PCC) | R.Pagitt (grandso and godson) |
| Alice Badger | marked@ | 1655 | 1655 (PCC) | G.Badger (son) |
| Katherine Perry* | marked@ | 1657 | 1658 (PCC) | J.Leeson, M.Bark (neighbors) |
| Elizabeth Randall | marked@ | 1658 | 1658 (PCC) | W.Flower, Elizabeth Flower (cousins) |
| Jane Bell%* | marked@ | 1659 | 1659 (PCC) | H.Bell (son) |
| Elizabeth Hancock | marked@ | 1659 | 1659 (PCC) | Mary Hall (niece |
| Elizabeth Overton%* | marked@ | 1659 | 1659 (PCC) | N.Overton (son) |

| erseer(s) ll names given women) | Witness(es) (full names given for women) | Husband(s) (#: widow named executrix of will) | Husband(s) Will(s) Witnessed |
|---|---|---|---|
| ne | W.Heath, B.D., J.Benson. | Francis Constable | N/A |
| Bundocke, T.Cable | J.Fuller, Anne Burten, R.Bundocke | John Bloome# | 1642 |
| ne | R.Howe, J.Goodridge, T.Meade, Ellen Meade, Ellen Watkins | George Cole# | 1637 |
| ne | F.Locke, F.Miles | Paul Man | N/A |
| ne | W.Tibbes, J.Penry | Adam Islipp# | 1639 |
| ne | J.Marton, J.Bettiscombe, Sybill Seares | Richard Meighen | N/A |
| ne | A.Burt, T.Barrett | Mathew Costerdine# | 1650 |
| ne | F.Collins, A.Kettlebey, W.George, T.Collinwood | Richard Badger# | 1641 |
| ne | W.Millisman, J.Pridemore | William Perry | N/A |
| ne | W.Tibbs, G.Copping, J.Walsingham, E.Metcalfe | James Randall# | 1643 |
| ne | T.Bowyer, Elizabeth Godshall, Anne Moore, Alice Jones, R.Screven | Moses Bell# | 1649 |
| ne | T.Shadwell, J.Tooler | Edward Hancock# | 1655 |
| Pape (friend) | W.Pape, D.Strong, R.Saterthwaite | Henry Overton# | 1646 |

(*cont.*)

| Name (%: widow publisher) (*: listed in Bell) | signed / marked / ncptv (@: sick) | Will Witnessed | Will Proved | Executor(s) (full names given for women) |
|---|---|---|---|---|
| Elizabeth (Tapp Hurlock) Bellamy%* | signed@ | 1661 | 1661 (PCC) | R.Bellamy (son) |
| Susanna Crawley | signed | 1663 | 1663 (PCC) | J.Ferne (cousin) |
| Margaret Falkner* | marked@ | 1663 | 1664 (PCC) | Margaret Hobson |
| Elizabeth Hinson | marked@ | 1663 | 1665 (PCC) | J.Hinson (son) |
| Margaret Kembe | marked | 1663 | 1665 (PCC) | Sarah Feake (daughter) |
| Priscilla Garford | marked@ | 1665 | 1666 (AL) | R.Garford (husband) |
| Joan Mead | signed@ | 1665 | 1666 (PCC) | Mary Torshell (daughter) |
| Alice (Norton) Warren%* | – | 1665 | 1665 (PCC) | J.Norton (son) |
| Mary (Okes) Wilson | marked@ | 1665 | 1665 (PCC) | T.Paxton, T.Bland (cousins) |
| Dorothy (Jaggard Downes) Fawne%* | signed | 1666 | 1666 (PCC) | J.Weaver |

(AL=Archdeaconry of London/ ComCL=Commissary Court of London/ CCL=Consistory Court of London/ CCW = Consistory Court of the Royal Peculiar of the Dean and Chapter of Westminster/PCC=Prerogative Court of Canterbury/PCSP=Peculiar Court of St Paul's)

| erseer(s) ll names given women) | Witness(es) (full names given for women) | Husband(s) (#: widow named executrix of will) | Husband(s) Will(s) Witnessed |
|---|---|---|---|
| ne | J.Peters, Anne Taylor, H.Horne, Sarah Kent[ley] | John Tapp#, Joseph Hurlock#, Edward Bellamy# | 1631, 1633, 1656 |
| ne | J.Wall, J.Wynch | William Crawley | 1648 |
| ne | A.Butcher, E.Copleston, W.Surfett | Francis Falkner# | 1650 |
| ne | T.Porter, B.Pickering | John Hinson# | 1653 |
| wer (friend), Valler (cousin),?. lls | W.Bodd, H.Willoughby, Joanne Church | Andrew Kembe | N/A |
| ne | N/A | Richard Garford | 1672 |
| 1apman n-in-law) | J.Grove, N.Hooper, J.Man | Robert Mead# | 1658 |
| ne | Mary Soloman, J.Norton (son), J.Brent | John Norton, Thomas Warren | N/A, N/A |
| ne | R.Spooner, G.Steele | John Okes#, William Wilson# | 1644, 1665 |
| Velden, A.Dowse ends) | J.Masson, J.Crouchley | Isaac Jaggard#, Thomas Downes#, Luke Fawne# | 1627, 1658, 1666 |

# CHAPTER 24

# 'Come Buy This Book of Me': Commodifying Difference in the Marketing of British Books, 1750–1830

*Kandice Sharren and Kate Ozment*

In 1750, *The Maiden's Prize, or, The Batchelor's Puzzle* was published in London with a curious attribution. The author is identified as

> Mrs. Anne Ward, a beautiful young Lady of Five Hundred Pounds a Year. Who vows never to Marry any Man but him who resolves the following Questions. She likewise promises the ingenious Married Man an Hundred Guineas for his Trouble.[1]

Later in the text, Ward is identified as sixteen years old and the book includes a woodcut of a youthful woman with long, curly hair in a flowered gown. Humorous and clever authorial personae were not uncommon, but Ward's is interesting for the specificity with which it asks the reader to imagine the author's imagined body, linked to an explicit age (sixteen), appearance (beautiful), intellectual capacity (witty), socioeconomic situation (£500 a year), and marital status (single). While this book was almost certainly a fictionalised jest rather than a woman promising, in print, to marry whoever solved her riddles, the authorial persona is notable as an exaggerated example of a significant trend in Britain and Ireland where the marginal social position of women authors was marketed as a commodity by the authors themselves and their publishers. *The Maiden's Prize* seems designed to elicit interest through an affective bond based on novelty and humour, but these bonds were employed differently for books attributed to authors of less secure economic status and with less normative bodies. Rather than humour, these books' marketing relied on an emotive response of sympathy to encourage the viewer to transition from spectator to consumer.

This chapter explores this latter category as a notable subset within what has been a rigorous discussion of women's authorship in Britain and Ireland from 1750–1830. Scholarship on women's authorship has been attuned to the

---

1 Ann Ward, 'The Maiden's prize, or, The batchelor's puzzle', *The Women's Print History Project*, title ID 1698 (2019), accessed 16 May 2021.

intersection of gender and class, and we broaden this to include an analy-sis animated by the work of intersectionality. 'Intersectionality' was coined by Kimberlé Crenshaw to describe overlapping systems of oppression. She argued that analyses of oppression that consider race *or* gender rather than race *and* gender do not capture the experience of women of colour.[2] This foundational idea has been expanded to include broader aspects of identity, as Jason Farr notes in his book on representations of sexuality and disability in the eighteenth century, but similarly to Farr, we are resistant to employing this term when discussing white women.[3] This chapter discusses at least one Black woman, Phillis Wheatley, but since our dataset consists of largely white women when authorship is known, we see our analysis as indebted to inter-sectionality more than directly employing it. We are informed by the field's attention to how oppression is influenced by multiple discourses of power, and we use this to develop a methodology that considers how language describing age, race, ability, and class are used on title pages. A distant reading approach allows us to locate patterns of identity-based language attached to authorial personae. Switching to close reading, we examine how identity is constructed and performed in particular texts and how this language invokes a certain kind of voice, body, intellect, and experience in the figure of an author seeking a public audience.

We argue that these authorship lines use identity-based language to inspire bonds of sympathy, ranging from kinship to a hierarchical power dynamic, between a deliberately crafted non-normative authorial personae and an imag-ined reader who fits what Audre Lorde calls the 'mythical norm'. Lorde argues that the norm of white, male, heteronormative, not a child but still youthful, able-bodied, and wealthy is the myth against which everyone psychologi-cally measures themselves, and against which they measure everyone else.[4] The 'myth' in mythical norm emphasises that the concept is constructed, not rooted in essentialist understandings of identities or bodies, but nevertheless creates powerful epistemological categories that shape access to agency, politi-cal power, and safety. Lorde addresses a twentieth-century American ideal

---

2   Kimberlé Crenshaw, 'Demarginalizing the Intersection of Race and Sex: A Black Feminist Critique of Antidiscrimination Doctrine, Feminist Theory and Antiracist Politics', *University of Chicago Legal Forum*, 1 (1989), pp. 139–167.

3   Jason Farr, *Novel Bodies: Disability and Sexuality in Eighteenth-Century British Literature* (New Brunswick, NJ: Bucknell University Press, 2019). Farr cites Nikol G. Alexander-Floyd as one of the scholars calling attention to the '(neo)colonization' of intersectionality (qtd on page 10), and we add to this Trust Kupupika's apt analysis of necessity of couching this methodology in Black feminist thinking in 'Shaping Our Freedom Dreams: Reclaiming Intersectionality Through Black Feminist Legal Theory', *Virginia Law Review*, 107 (2021), pp. 27–47.

4   Audre Lorde, 'Age, Race, Class and Sex: Women Redefining Difference', in *Sister Outsider: Essays and Speeches by Audre Lorde* (Berkeley, CA: Crossing Press, 1984), pp. 110–123, at 116.

that is translatable to late eighteenth and early nineteenth century British and Irish literary production in some respects, although there are important differences: for authors trying to lay claim to cultural authority, advanced age could be a boon rather than a hinderance, and queerness was largely unspoken and understood through actions rather than a marker of identity.[5]

In the books we examine, authors' gender, race, and social standing determine whether or not they appear as marginal in book marketing. For example, the most recognisable literary authors included figures such as Samuel Johnson, Alexander Pope, and Lord Byron, all white educated men in Britain. Despite each author's deviations from the period's mythical norm (all were disabled, Pope was Catholic, and Byron was queer), the marketing of their books, during their lifetimes and afterward, does not emphasise marginal aspects of their identities. By contrast, the authorship lines we consider present personae that deviate from the mythical norm through a combination of gender, race, class, and other factors. We observe that when femininity is present as a deviation from the masculine norm, authors are more likely to be presented as commodities to be textually consumed by an imagined normative audience through the exchange of sympathy. For personae that perform smaller deviations from the mythical norm, sympathy can be engaged through novelty or kinship, as with Ward. For less normative personae, such as Wheatley, the affective response of sympathy is generated by descriptions of authors' bodies, abilities, and lived experiences rooted in a hierarchical relationship between author and consumer. The author is positioned as the supplicant asking for anything from forgiving reviews to financial aid to a recognition of her shared humanity. We conclude that deviations from the mythical imagined as a consumable in marketing strategies code and re-encode beliefs about the intellectual capabilities of marginalised groups participating in literary authorship.

## 1      Part One: Distant Reading Authorship Language

The period on which we focus, from 1750–1830 in mostly Great Britain and Ireland, has been of much interest for scholars of women's authorship and print. The Industrial Revolution changed printing technology dramatically for the first time since the invention of the common press. New methods for making paper and the iron platen press combined with increasing literacy rates to put more books in the hands of more readers. As more books circulated, publishers had to find new ways of rendering the increasingly ubiquitous objects

---

5  For an overview, see Eve Kosofsky Sedgwick, *Between Men: English Literature and Male Homosocial Desire*, (New York, NY: Columbia University Press, 1985).

as individualised, and they relied on authorial identity as one method of differentiation. While selling authorial personae was not new to this period, changes in the scale of the marketplace and legal structures that redefined authors as producers of intellectual property contributed to a culture that fetishised the author.[6]

Authorial identity usually manifests as authorial personae, which were constructed to fill the author-function with identity-based language. It was not expected for the author-function to reference a specific person; anonymous and pseudonymous authorship were common, and as Robert J. Griffin argues, authorship lines linked books to imagined bodies, other books, literary traditions, or even affective states of being.[7] Generalised and vague attributions including 'by a lady' gestured to an identity without signing the book, and it is estimated around 11% of novels in this period carried a version of this attribution.[8] In cases when an author is named, or onymous publication, authorship lines and other paratextual materials often construct a narrative that references authors' biographical lives to elicit a specific response from a reader. This version of the author presented in marketing language is not synonymous with the 'real' author, but instead uses the language of identity and the signifier of a name to render them legible as subjects to readers while obscuring their origins as constructions.[9] Readers are invited into a relationship with the persona designed to elicit an affective response that will lead to purchase of the book.

---

6   Catherine Ingrassia, *Authorship, Commerce, and Gender in Early Eighteenth-Century England: A Culture of Paper Credit*, (Cambridge: Cambridge University Press, 1998), Mark Rose, *Authors and Owners: The Invention of Copyright*, (Boston: Harvard University Press, 1993), and Jerome J. McGann, *The Romantic Ideology: A Critical Investigation*, (Chicago: The University of Chicago Press, 1983).

7   Robert J. Griffin, 'Introduction', in Robert J. Griffin (ed), *The Faces of Anonymity: Anonymous and Pseudonymous Publication from the Sixteenth to the Twentieth Century* (New York: Palgrave Macmillan, 2003), pp. 1–17. The use of anonymity and pseudonymity varied by genre: James Raven and Peter Garside identify that around 72% of fiction published from 1770–1799 was published without attribution, a number that decreased to just under half from 1800–1829, whereas Paula Feldman notes that 'during the period 1770–1835, women *rarely* published books of verse anonymously' and those who did would often attach their name to a subsequent edition or publication. See Peter Garside, 'Historical Introduction: The English Novel in the Romantic Era', in Rainer Schöwerling and Peter Garside (eds), *The English Novel 1770–1829: A Bibliographical Survey of Prose Fiction Published in the British Isles*, vol. II (Oxford: Oxford University Press, 2000), pp. 13–103, at 66. See Paula R. Feldman, 'Women Poets and Anonymity in the Romantic Era', *New Literary History*, 33 (Spring 2002) pp. 279–89, at 279.

8   James Raven, 'Historical Introduction: The Novel Comes of Age', in Antonia Forster and James Raven (eds), *The English Novel 1770–1829: A Bibliographical Survey of Prose Fiction Published in the British Isles*, vol. I (Oxford: Oxford University Press, 2000) pp. 13–121, at 42–43. Our thanks to David Mazella for locating this citation.

9   This passage is indebted to Roland Barthes, *Mythologies*, Richard Howard and Annette Lavers (trans), (New York: Hill and Wang, 2012).

We build on this existing research to consider feminised authorship constructed through additional axes of identity: age, race, ability, and class.[10] We use the *Women's Print History Project* (*WPHP*) to create a dataset of examples of how feminised authorship is referenced on title pages. The *WPHP* is a bibliography that attempts to provide researched records of all printed books tied to women's production from 1750–1830, mostly in Great Britain and Ireland.[11] It pulls from bibliographic records for printed books in this period such as the *English Short Title Catalogue, Orlando Project*, the *Jackson Bibliography of Romantic Poetry*, and James Raven and Peter Garside's *The English Novel*. As Figure 24.1 shows, the *WPHP* logs authorship of books in a few ways, two of which are notable for our study: a transcription of the authorship line on the title page record (in the Signed Author field) and a researched field that locates biographical details of authors or editors (the Contributors field).

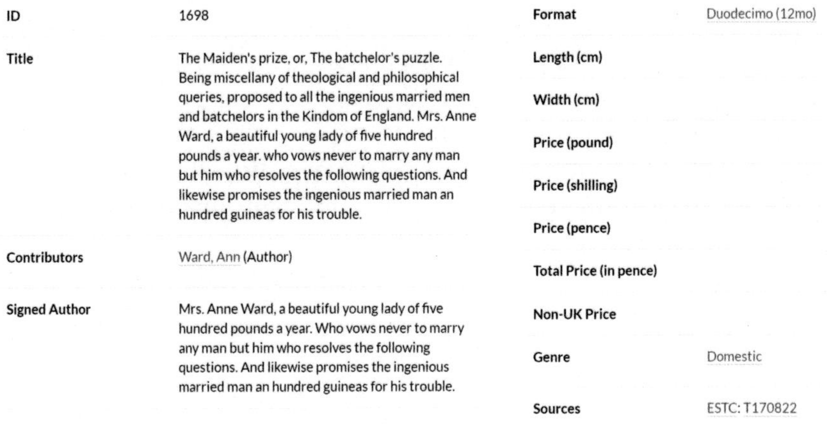

| ID | 1698 | Format | Duodecimo (12mo) |
|---|---|---|---|
| Title | The Maiden's prize, or, The batchelor's puzzle. Being miscellany of theological and philosophical queries, proposed to all the ingenious married men and batchelors in the Kindom of England. Mrs. Anne Ward, a beautiful young lady of five hundred pounds a year. who vows never to marry any man but him who resolves the following questions. And likewise promises the ingenious married man an hundred guineas for his trouble. | Length (cm) | |
| | | Width (cm) | |
| | | Price (pound) | |
| | | Price (shilling) | |
| | | Price (pence) | |
| Contributors | Ward, Ann (Author) | Total Price (in pence) | |
| Signed Author | Mrs. Anne Ward, a beautiful young lady of five hundred pounds a year. Who vows never to marry any man but him who resolves the following questions. And likewise promises the ingenious married man an hundred guineas for his trouble. | Non-UK Price | |
| | | Genre | Domestic |
| | | Sources | ESTC: T170822 |

FIGURE 24.1     A screenshot of the title record for Ann Ward's *The Maiden's Prize*, accessed 15 May 2021

---

10     'Lady' is a classed term, but it is not linked to a concrete status by this period, see Jennie Batchelor, 'Anon, Pseud and "By a Lady": The Spectre of Anonymity in Women's Literary History', in Jennie Batchelor and Gillian Dow (eds), *Women's Writing, 1660–1830: Feminisms and Futures*, (New York, NY: Palgrave Macmillan, 2016) pp. 79–96 and Margaret J. M. Ezell, '"By a Lady": The Mask of the Feminine in Restoration, Early Eighteenth-Century Print Culture', in Robert J. Griffin (ed), *The Faces of Anonymity: Anonymous and Pseudonymous Publication from the Sixteenth to the Twentieth Century* (New York: Palgrave Macmillan, 2003) pp. 63–79.

11     For the construction and functions of the *WPHP*, see Kandice Sharren et al, 'Gendering Digital Bibliography with the *Women's Print History Project*', *Eighteenth-Century Studies* 54 (2021) pp. 887–908.

We use the Signed Author field for distant reading because we are interested in all titles that mark themselves as coming from a feminised authorial hand.[12] In the close reading phase, we consider the Contributors field as context for the textual performance of authorship, as it connects books to biographical lives where possible.

To build the dataset, we used 38 search terms for feminised and classed markers of identity in the Signed Author field. These are a mixture of generic references like 'woman' and 'female', relational language like 'sister' and 'aunt', and honorifics ranging from 'Mrs' to 'countess' and 'queen'. Results for these search terms returned a total of 6,588 records, which we examined in Microsoft Excel to remove records that fell outside our parameters. We removed records that referenced subsequent editions as they frequently repeated authorship from the first edition and we are more interested in broad trends. Secondly, we removed records that were false returns when previous titles with feminised language were referenced, which we see in titles such as Charlotte Lennox's *Henrietta* (1758), where the Signed Author field reads 'By the author of The female Quixote' and the title returned for 'female'.[13] Table 24.1 details the original and cleaned returns for the 38 search terms.

TABLE 24.1    A table showing the 38 search terms, arranged alphabetically. Data shows original numbers and the numbers after we removed subsequent editions and false returns. Data was pulled on 20 August 2021

| Search term | Raw return | Cleaned return | Search term | Raw return | Cleaned return |
| --- | --- | --- | --- | --- | --- |
| Abbess | 1 | 1 | Mamma | 1 | 0 |
| Aunt | 36 | 9 | Marchioness | 12 | 4 |
| Author | 2029 | 1192 | Mater | 0 | 0 |
| Authoress | 139 | 98 | Matron | 3 | 0 |
| Baroness | 4 | 3 | Miss | 544 | 313 |
| Child | 47 | 1 | Mistress | 7 | 2 |
| Countess | 41 | 26 | Mlle | 1 | 1 |
| Dame | 3 | 3 | Mme | 11 | 8 |

---

12    An important note is that the *WPHP* enables this research because it fully transcribes all author information, which is often truncated in the *ESTC* and other bibliographies that have origins as printed documents. This was a space-saving technique for printed enumerative bibliographies, since space was money.

13    Charlotte Lennox, 'Henrietta. By the author of The Female Quixote. In two volumes', *The Women's Print History Project*, title ID 2432 (2019), accessed 16 May 2021.

TABLE 24.1     A table showing the 38 search terms, arranged alphabetically (*cont.*)

| Search term | Raw return | Cleaned return | Search term | Raw return | Cleaned return |
|---|---|---|---|---|---|
| Daughter | 116 | 42 | Mother | 126 | 31 |
| Duchess | 13 | 7 | Mrs | 2090 | 1030 |
| Empress | 0 | 0 | Niece | 2 | 1 |
| Female | 46 | 9 | Princess | 1 | 1 |
| Girl | 53 | 5 | Queen | 8 | 1 |
| Lady | 857 | 522 | Sister | 11 | 7 |
| Madam | 20 | 9 | Tsarina | 0 | 0 |
| Madame | 151 | 85 | Viscountess | 0 | 0 |
| Mademoiselle | 7 | 7 | Widow | 94 | 16 |
| Maid | 18 | 5 | Wife | 47 | 13 |
| Mama | 1 | 0 | Woman | 48 | 16 |

TABLE 24.2     A table showing the construction of our three datasets. Datasets 2 and 3 will be used for the following analysis. Data was pulled on 20 August 2021

| Dataset | Organizing principles | Record count |
|---|---|---|
| Dataset One (D1) | Raw Return of 38 Search Terms | 6,588 |
| Dataset Two (D2) | Removed False Returns and Subsequent Editions from D1 | 3,486 |
| Dataset Three (D3) | Removed Duplicate Title IDs from D2 | 2,945 |

The cleaned records were labelled Dataset 2 and used to explore individual search terms. We prepared a third dataset where we combined all records from Dataset 2 and removed duplicate title IDs for titles with multiple feminised names in the signed author field. Ward's *The Maiden's Prize* is one such example, as it returned for both 'lady' and 'Mrs'. Dataset 3 is used to talk about the genre breakdown that follows. Table 24.2 shows the counts for all three datasets.

It is important to note the limitations of this process and how it shapes the conclusions we make about feminised authorship. First, we only searched for feminised honorifics and language, not feminised names. Our process did not return *Miscellanies in Prose and Verse* (1750) by Mary Jones, as the author or the

TABLE 24.3    A genre breakdown of Dataset 3, using the taxonomy of the *WPHP*. For an overview of how the database logs genre, see Project Methodology at womensprinthistoryproject.com.

| Genre | # of titles | % of whole | Genre | # of titles | % of whole |
|---|---|---|---|---|---|
| Biography | 31 | 1.1% | Letters | 53 | 1.8% |
| Catalogue | 6 | 0.2% | Memoirs | 36 | 1.2% |
| Domestic | 50 | 1.7% | Miscellany | 17 | 0.6% |
| Drama | 113 | 3.8% | Music | 15 | 0.5% |
| Education | 27 | 0.9% | Poetry (all) | 520 | 17.7% |
| Essays | 26 | 0.9% | Political Writing | 32 | 1.1% |
| Fiction (all) | 1254 | 42.6% | Religion/Biblical | 62 | 2.1% |
| History | 13 | 0.4% | Science | 22 | 0.7% |
| Juvenile | 575 | 19.5% | Travel | 75 | 2.5% |
| Legal | 1 | 0.0% | Works | 20 | 0.7% |

publishers did not use a feminised honorific for the authorship line.[14] However, this book can be understood as reflective of feminised authorship because 'Mary' is a common woman's name in this period. We made this choice due to practicality, as we will likely never be able to think of every feminine name to search for individually, and this would have resulted in a mass of duplicate records as it was common for names to have an honorific, which our dataset includes. Secondly, the *WPHP* is not comprehensive and somewhat replicates genre biases as it pulls from existing bibliographic records that favour novels and poetry. We are wary of saying anything definitive about genre trends, but Table 24.3 includes a breakdown of the data by genre for reference.

## 2     Part Two: Close Reading Case Studies of Youth and Gender

Constructing this larger dataset allowed us to identify a cluster of records that perform difference with identity-based language. While existing scholarship prepared us to locate authorial personae, we found that they were in a one-sided dialogue with an equally fictionalised reader. While more readers than before were women, children, and the working classes, authorship lines

---

14    Mary Jones, 'Miscellanies in prose and verse. By Mary Jones', *The Women's Print History Project*, title ID 6174 (2019) accessed 14 May 2021.

still seem to define readership in terms of those with the most power: those who fit Lorde's mythical norm.[15] To create an affective bond between authors whose books performed difference and an imagined normative audience, authorship lines use techniques from sentimental fiction.

Throughout the second half of the eighteenth century, the nature of sympathy was widely debated, especially the question of whether it was an instinctive sentimental response produced by the 'mirror-like' quality of the mind, which 'reflect each other's emotions', or the result of rational assessment, in which sympathy is generated by an individual's 'consideration of what he himself would feel if he was reduced to the same unhappy situation, and, what perhaps is impossible, was at the same time able to regard it with his present reason and judgment'.[16] In fiction, textual strategies for producing sympathy of either mode often highlighted its pleasurable capacity, in which the reader was positioned as uniquely 'discriminating', and 'the exceptional connoisseur of commendable sympathies'.[17] These dynamics of sympathy are frequently unequal, relying on an observer and the observed; Lorri G. Nandrea argues that it relies on an understanding of difference between the subject and the object where the viewer has power over the victim.[18] Nandrea explains, 'The paradigmatic sympathetic exchange is rooted in another's pain; it seems to require a wounded victim' and 'The pleasure of the onlooker … thus carries both masochistic and sadistic implications'.[19]

The nature and stakes of the victim's suffering can vary widely, from social embarrassment to life-(and virtue-)threatening scenarios. Deidre Lynch pinpoints Frances Burney's *Evelina, or The History of a Young Lady's Entrance into the World* (1778) as a genre-defining work that sets up a dynamic in which readers

---

15    Martyn Lyons, 'New Readers in the Nineteenth Century: Women, Children, Workers', in Guglielmo Cavallo and Roger Chartier (eds), *A History of Reading in the West*, Lydia G. Cochrane (trans) (Amherst: University of Massachusetts Press, 1999) pp. 313–344.

16    David Hume, *A Treatise of Human Nature: Being an attempt to introduce the experimental method of reasoning into moral subjects* (Kitchener, ON: Batoche, 1999) p. 252; Adam Smith, *The Theory of Moral Sentiments*, Patrick Hanley (ed.) (New York: Penguin Classics, 2009) p. 17.

17    Deidre Shauna Lynch, *The Economy of Character: Novels, Market Culture, and the Business of Inner Meaning* (Chicago: Chicago University Press, 1999), p. 152; John Mullan, *Sentiment and Sociability: The Language of Feeling in the Eighteenth Century* (Oxford: Oxford University Press, 1990), p. 14.

18    Lorri G. Nandrea, *Misfit Forms: Paths Not Taken by the British Novel* (New York: Fordham University Press, 2015).

19    Nandrea, *Misfit Forms*, pp. 52–53.

share a space of sensibility with the heroine, [and] quickly learn to dis-
credit as mere appearance the appearances that the supporting characters see when they look at her.[20]

Here, the stakes are relatively low; while Evelina at various points in the
novel fears losing the affections of a deserving gentleman, she is rarely in
life-threatening danger. By contrast, a sentimental novel like Henry Mackenzie's
*Man of Feeling* (1771) includes sketches of impoverished farmers and sex workers, whose circumstances are presented in pitiable terms. Britain and Ireland's
social structures were based on patriarchy, racialised colonialism, ableism, and
classism, these stories make visible that a lack of access to power structures
could be identifiable as worthy of sympathy by readers who consumed this distress through the safe distance of spectatorship. At the same time, such sympathy was often limited to those whose behaviour was legible and acceptable to
those who held power within these structures.[21]

Authorship lines in our dataset follow the same beats of sentimental fiction where readers as spectators are invited into a bond with the author as
victim, and personae consequently perform distress or victimhood to activate
the bonds of sympathy. In the context of a patriarchal society and a reviewing
culture that was often harsh in its condemnation of women's writing, feminised authorship was always a risky proposition. Whether presenting authors
as innocent young ladies entering the world of print or impoverished and
disabled labouring-class women, many of the titles in our dataset emphasise
authors' vulnerability. Such descriptions of authorship issue an invitation to
readers to approach the author's production on sympathetic and forgiving
terms, creating a dynamic similar to the one Lynch describes between reader
and heroine. However, even if the customer feels a kinship with the author,
what Nandrea articulates as *sentimentality* as opposed to sympathy, the nature
of capitalism still renders their engagement with the book as consumption of
the author's precarity or pain.

Distant reading made visible the degrees to which marketing language
on title pages with feminised authorship responded to an interest in authorial personae's subject positions by invoking various kinds of sympathy and
interest from an imagined reader. A common strategy involves describing the
author's youth, which evokes associations of vulnerability and innocence. This

---

20     Lynch, *Economy of Character*, pp. 152.
21     For a full discussion of the limits of sympathy in Romantic-era fiction, see Kandice
      Sharren, 'The Texture of Sympathy: Narrating Sympathetic Failure in Frances Burney's
      *Camilla* and *The Wanderer*', *European Romantic Review*, 28 (2017) pp. 701–727.

strategy is explicitly engaged in conjunction with gender and class on an interesting subset in the dataset, seventy-eight total records of poetry and novels, which are genres often linked to youthful and female readers in the period.[22] We define 'gestures to youth' as using works like 'young' and 'girl' or listing an age under twenty, but exclude words like 'Miss', as it has mixed connotations.[23] Even within this restricted definition, there is ambiguity in how youth is characterised. 'Young' is used to indicate anything from 'a young lady of distinction, eleven years of age' to 'Elizabeth Wast [sic], a young woman, sometimes mustress [sic] of the trades hospital in Edinburgh' to 'Mrs. Anne Ward, a beautiful young lady of five hundred pounds a year'.[24] Here, 'young' includes a child, an adult servant, and a woman of marriageable age. While youth as a marketing tactic is not consistent in its definitions, there are two distinct trends in how youth is presented to the imagined audience: as a commodification of innocence presented as kinship, and as a trigger for an affective response of sympathy meant to inspire pity.

First, we consider kinship. Youth is used to commodify innocence in paradoxical ways in our dataset. Much of the literature and juvenile education materials of this period, which overlaps with Romanticism, engaged in debates about the 'natural goodness' of humanity that was spoiled by engagements with society. Childhood was the 'age of innocence' and therefore goodness, perhaps typified by Jean-Jacques Rousseau's *Émile* (1763 in English).[25] Youth

---

22   See Jacqueline Pearson, *Women's Reading in Britain, 1750–1835: A Dangerous Recreation* (Cambridge: Cambridge University Press, 2005).

23   *Miss*, the second most common honorific in the dataset with 544 individual records, both is and is not a marker of youth, as it usually indicates a woman's unmarried status. *Miss* potentially infantilizes the women attached to it, even when it refers to women like Jane Porter, who used the identifier on her title pages well into her sixties. The effect is compounded by the inconsistent use of *Miss* for older unmarried women; well-respected single women such as Elizabeth Carter and Hannah More were referred to, in private and in print, as Mrs. Carter and Mrs. More. Depending on its framing, *Miss* can be used to indicate either a woman's youth and innocence, a perhaps lamentable lack of experience, or the absence of these qualities through a recent marriage; these complex associations mean that we have excluded it from our discussion of youth in this paper.

24   Caroline Elizabeth Sarah Norton, 'The Dandies' Rout', *The Women's Print History Project*, title ID 103 (2019); Elisabeth Wast, 'The most remarkable passages in the life and spiritual experiences of Elizabeth Wast, A Young Woman, Sometime Mustress of the Trades Hospital in Edinburgh, Most particularly, her Spiritual Experiences in attending Sacramental Occasions, and Praying Societies', *The Women's Print History Project*, title ID 3158 (2019); Ward, title ID 1698. All accessed 16 May 2021.

25   For an overview of attitudes about childhood and children's literature, see M.O. Grenby, *The Child Reader, 1700–1840* (Cambridge: Cambridge University Press, 2011) and James Holt McGavran (ed.), *Romanticism and Children's Literature in Nineteenth-Century England* (Athens: University of Georgia Press, 2009).

on title pages could be used to affirm a point of view as innocent and marked with natural feminine sentimentality when the author was white, British, and feminised, which we see reflected in books marked as 'by a young lady': *A Search After Happiness: A Pastoral* (1773); *A Sentimental Tour through Newcastle* (1794); and *Poetical Effusions* (1824).[26] In these examples, 'lady' seems to be used generically, although it gestures to gentility especially when compared to how 'girl' is used below. The combination of youth and femininity in these attributions positions figures who were characterised in essentialist terms as more sentimental. Since sentiment was valued for young people and women, the marketing centres the dominant ideology in the hopes that readers will find resonance and kinship with their own values.

Similarly, we see a tactic with youth deployed as a defensive technique or to frame the reception of the text. Four records emphasise this publication is a 'first' for the author with language such as: 'first attempt by a young lady', 'By a young lady, her first literary attempt', and 'Being the first literary production of a young lady'.[27] All of the titles are fiction. This technique couples gender with age as inexperience, which could be used to soften a critical response to the text, to fetishise a youthful perspective in a period that valued child-hood, or to motivate the reader to buy the book based on a sentimental desire to support a new author. We cannot overlook the erotics of this technique, however. White women's virginity was commodified with a specific emphasis placed on inexperience as the safeguard of feminine virtue.[28] Since feminine commercial authorship had been linked to prostitution of the mind, similar to prostitution of the body, for a century, it is possible that part of the appeal of this language was the pleasure of experiencing a woman's 'first time'.[29] The use of 'lady' is intended to invoke genteel respectability, but conversely it might

---

26    Hannah More, 'A search after happiness: a pastoral', *The Women's Print History Project*, title ID 4208 (2019); Jane Harvey, 'A sentimental tour through Newcastle', *The Women's Print History Project*, title ID 4821 (2019); and Unknown, 'Poetical Effusions', *The Women's Print History Project*, title ID 11683 (2019). All accessed 16 May 2021.

27    Unknown, 'Lumley-House: a novel', *The Women's Print History Project*, title ID 5551 (2019); Mrs. Barnby, 'The rock; or Alfred and Anna. A Scottish tale', *The Women's Print History Project*, 2019, title ID 6946 (2010); and Martha Hugill, 'St. Bernard's priory. An old English tale; being the first literary production of a young lady', *The Women's Print History Project*, title ID 7043 (2019). All accessed 16 May 2021.

28    As with all prevailing beliefs, this was debated as it was reinforced. The most famous cri-tique of feminine virtue being attached to feminine inexperience is Mary Wollstonecraft's *Vindications of the Rights of Women* (1792).

29    See Bradford K. Mudge, *The Whore's Story: Women, Pornography, and the British Novel, 1684–1830* (Oxford: Oxford University Press, 2000) and Janet Todd, *The Sign of Angellica: Women, Writing and Fiction 1660–1800* (New York: Columbia University Press, 1989).

work to heighten the pleasure of reading, since a higher-class woman's virginity was more socially valuable. In any case, the commodification of youthful innocence places the author in supplication to the reader but in a way that invokes the dominant ideology of valuing the natural innocence of children and the virginal innocence of white women.

As the second pattern for how the language of youth is used with authorial personae, we identified records where the power dynamic between the persona and imagined reader is much wider and rendered in a more dramatic hierarchy with the reader and consumer holding the most power. These books use a unique descriptor on the title pages: 'girl'. Only three records use 'girl', which carries different connotations from the ubiquitous gentility of 'young lady'. First is the anonymous author of *Feelings of the Heart; or, the Letters of a Country Girl*, which uses the same romanticisation of youth and pastoral innocence as the examples above.[30] The authorship line, 'written by herself, and addressed to a lady of quality' is ambiguous, describing the narrator of a work of fiction rather than the specific historical individual that wrote the work. However, the other titles demand closer scrutiny as they invoke authorial personae that are further removed from the mythical norm compared to the anonymous country girl, and the relationship between the imagined audience and the authorial personae is positioned through hierarchical sympathy rather than sentimentality.

One record uses 'girl' in relation to Phillis Wheatley in her 1770 elegy on the death of George Whitefield, signed, 'By Phillis, a Servant Girl of 17 Years of Age, belonging to Mr. J. Wheatley, of Boston;—And has been but 9 Years in this Country from Africa'.[31] The WPHP contains reprints of this poem with titles that vary so widely we initially did not recognise them as subsequent editions; three are published in the United States and use the language 'servant girl', and three are published in Great Britain and use the language 'Negro girl'.[32] The others vary in authorship but largely omit Wheatley in favour of Whitefield and the dedicatee, Selina Hastings the Countess of Huntingdon. In the United States, the authorship line notes that Wheatley was enslaved by John Wheatley,

---

30    Unknown, 'The feelings of the heart; or, the history of a country girl. Written by herself, and addressed to a lady of quality. In two volumes', *The Women's Print History Project*, title ID 3911 (2019) accessed 28 Sept. 2021.

31    Phillis Wheatley, 'An Elegiac Poem, on the Death of that celebrated Divine, and eminent Servant of Jesus Christ, the late Reverend, and pious George Whitefield', *The Women's Print History Project*, title ID 14253 (2019) accessed 16 May 2021.

32    'Wheatley, Phillis' *The Women's Print History Project*, person ID 3814 (2010) Accessed 23 Sept. 2021. The Wheatley editions are still being updated, and numbers may vary from our analysis, dated above.

signalled with the language 'belonging', and was kidnapped from Africa, which would indicate to readers that she was an enslaved Black woman. The 'but' before nine years is meant to draw attention to her remarkable poetic skill as an English language learner. In Great Britain, the publishers, Wheatley, or her friends altered the language to indicate her race rather than her homeland but still drawing attention to her enslaved status: 'by Phillis, a Negro Girl, Seventeen Years of age, Belonging to Mr. J. Wheatley of Boston'.[33]

Although Wheatley's 1773 collection *Poems on Various Subjects, Religious and Moral* did not use 'girl' on its title page, the same language plays out in its paratextual materials. The title page describes the author as, 'Phillis Wheatley, Negro Servant to Mr. John Wheatley, of Boston, in New England', attempting to soften the language of belonging to one of service.[34] The dehumanising publication process to which Wheatley was subjected are detailed in the address 'To the Publick', where a council of men attest to her authorship, saying,

> We ... do assure the World, that the Poems specified in the following Pages, were (as we verily believe) written by Phillis, a young Negro Girl, who was but a few Years since, brought an uncultivated Barbarian from Africa.[35]

This passage has been read and re-read in literature on Wheatley, but we revisit it within this context to consider how the recurrence of the word 'girl', emphasised as 'young' and linked to her race alongside the colonial and imperialist dismissal of her culture, stands in so stark a contrast to the other examples of youthful authorship in the dataset. The previous examples seem to use youth as a disarming tactic that evokes kinship, but the 'young ladies' were not put to a judge to prove their intellectual abilities. In contrast, the persona constructed for Wheatley's books is invested in coupling racialised girlhood with extreme vulnerability. This is not to say that Wheatley was not vulnerable; she was a Black woman in a system designed to give her no legal subjectivity, and there are no more precarious positions than that. This is to say that the version of

---

33    Phillis Wheatley and Ebenezer Pemberton, 'Heaven the Residence of the Saints, A Sermon. Occasioned by the sudden and much lamented Death of the Rev. George Whitefield, A.M., Chaplain to the right Honourable the Countess of Huntingdon [sic]. Delivered at the Thursday lecture at Boston, in America, Oct 11, 1770. By Ebenezer Pemberton, D.D. Paster [sic] of a Church in Boston. To which is added an Elegiac Poem on his Death, by Phillis, a Negro Girl, Seventeen Years of age, Belonging to Mr. J. Wheatley of Boston', *The Women's Print History Project*, title ID 15548 (2019) accessed 23 Sept. 2021.

34    Phillis Wheatley, *Poems on various subjects, religious and moral* (London: A. Bell, 1773).

35    Wheatley, *Poems on various subjects*, n.p.

this reality that is translated to the authorial persona, with what it includes and how it includes it, is a construction designed to elicit a specific response from an imagined normative reader.

The construction of this persona is based on a hierarchy in which the reader acts as the spectator of Wheatley's social death: there are no clearly articulated benefits to the author while her precarity is emphasised with more detail than most authors receive with onymous publication.[36] Through extensive biographical references, the persona invites readers to imagine they are seeing the 'authentic' Wheatley in these materials, rendered as a pitiable object to be consumed. Wheatley-as-persona is created by relying on the knowledge that Wheatley-as-empirical-body also exists, and her identity was a curiosity as she was one of the earliest Black and feminised literary voices to publish in English, and 1770–1773 was the height of her transatlantic career.[37] The level of biographical detail included with the persona is comparable to Anne Ward, but while Ward seems to be gesturing playfully to the status of a woman with a modest fortune as a 'prize', Wheatley's example has higher stakes and less space to articulate what its goals are. The persona is never allowed to directly state that the purpose of the volume was to earn the author's freedom, although that seems to have been the case. Instead, the books' marketing and paratext are all white voices, the 'white envelope'.[38] As Jennifer Rene Young argues, Wheatley's books were published by white women patrons who used them to promote Christian conversion and the abolition of slavery.[39] Similarly to the white women who used the abolitionist movement to claim their own space in political discourse, the women who helped produce the book dehumanise the author with the repeated use of 'girl': it is always a word said *about* her, not

36    For more on slavery as "social death" see Orlando Patterson, *Slavery and Social Death: A Comparative Study, With a New Preface* (Cambridge: Harvard University Press, 2018).

37    Jennifer Rene Young, 'Marketing a Sable Muse: Phillis Wheatley and the Antebellum Press', in John C. Shields and Eric D. Lamore (eds.), *New Essays on Phillis Wheatley* (Knoxville: The University of Tennessee Press, 2011) pp. 209–245.

38    John Sekora, 'Black Message/White Envelope: Genre, Authenticity, and Authority in the Antebellum Slave Narrative', *Callaloo*, 32 (1987) pp. 482–515. Sekora's piece analyzes the fraught nature of trying to locate an "authentic" voice in heavily mediated texts, and we do not see this discussion as engaging in a search for authenticity in response. Rather, we are locating how the marketing functions in contrast to the content of the poetry. For more on the unknowability of the archive of enslavement, see Simon Gikandi, 'Rethinking the Archive of Enslavement', *Early American Literature*, 50 (2015), pp. 81–102 and for specifics about the challenges for Black women, Saidiya Hartman, 'Venus in Two Acts', *Small Axe*, 12 (2008), pp. 1–14.

39    Young, 'Marketing a Sable Muse', p. 211.

one she uses herself.[40] Since the intention was to motivate readers to purchase her book but there is no clearly articulated intention that she will get any of the profits or her freedom from the purchase, capitalism renders the reader as a consumer who can alleviate their discomfort with systemic inequality by supporting an individual with vague transfer of money.

Yet, readers who did purchase the book would find much more in the poems, where the white-crafted persona of Wheatley gives way, more so, to the poet. Rhetoric within the poems asserts her right to publish, intimate knowledge of poetic style, and, to the reading public, her status as human. Wheatley's knowledge of poetic form and authors such as Shakespeare and Milton is well documented, and she speaks the language of power as it would have been recognised by British audiences.[41] They also explore, as Tara Bynum lays out, creative and imaginative texts that have nothing to do with 'the burdens of [Wheatley's] Black womanhood'.[42] Bynum's work centres the joy and humanity of Wheatley's letters and life; she was a human who brushed her teeth and had friends and a family. The marketing of Wheatley's books may flatten Wheatley-the-empirical-body to Wheatley-as-persona for capitalist consumption, but the text resists this easy categorisation of the author and her work for the reader willing to look.

The final instance of 'girl' is *The Blind Poem*, printed in Dublin in 1789. While it is different from Wheatley's positionality, it similarly makes visible fractures of the relationship between the marketed persona and the humanity within the text. The title page proclaims that the poem was 'Written by a Girl, born Blind and now in her eighteenth year,' and several pages in, we find it is

> Dedicated to The World, by the Authoress, Mary Byrne, of Wicklow. Price 3s. 3d. or such Greater Price as the Affluent choose to bestow on Poverty.[43]

The by-line not only conveys information about the author's name, age, birthplace, and physical body but turns these details into a demand for payment

---

40 Lilla Marie Crisafulli, 'Women and Abolitionism: Hannah More's and Ann Yearsley's Poetry of Freedom', in Cora Kaplan and John Oldfield (eds), *Imagining Transatlantic Slavery* (London: Palgrave Macmillan, 2010) pp. 110–124.

41 See James Edward Ford III, 'The Difficult Miracle: Reading Phillis Wheatley against the Master's Discourse', CR: *The New Centennial Review*, 18 (2018) pp. 181–224.

42 Tara Bynum, 'Phillis Wheatley on Friendship', *Legacy*, 31 (2014) pp. 42–51.

43 Mary Byrne, *The blind poem. Written by a girl, born blind, and now in her eighteenth year. Dedicated to the world, by the authoress, Mary Byrne, of Wicklow. Price 3s. 3d. or such greater price as the affluent choose to bestow on poverty* (Dublin: Bartholomew Corcoran, 1789).

from prospective readers, who are framed as affluent in contrast to the author's poverty. The author's gender, youth, and blindness take precedence over her individual identity; we do not learn her name until the dedication, when she names herself as 'Mary Byrne, of Wicklow'. The other paratexts of *The Blind Poem* provide further biographical information about its author: the preface, seemingly written by an editor, describes her as

> the Daughter of a labouring Man near the Town of Wicklow, whose Genius was first discovered, at the Age of twelve years, by a Gentleman, then Priest in the Parish.[44]

The title page and the preface construct a disability- and class-based narrative about 'a Blind girl at the age of eighteen years' with a remarkable talent. This resonates with the novelty and curiosity invoked in the titles that characterised the text as a first production, but here the differentiating factor is that the audience should find it surprising or appealing that a disabled young author has considerable poetic talent. The preface continues in this vein:

> The offering her Compositions to the Public was the Idea of a Lady, who on accidentally hearing her repeat a Few of her Lines ... thought an Arrangement of the Whole might be productive of some pecuniary Advantages, which her situation so much needed.[45]

By highlighting her youth, her lower-class status, and her disability, the title page and preface craft a sympathetic narrative that invites a wealthy audience to support her by way of her poetry.

In contrast to Wheatley's book where the author is not allowed a direct address to the audience, Byrne's book affords the author space to frame her own reception and complicate the seemingly straightforward sympathetic appeal and commodification of disability in the authorship line. The preface is followed by a lengthier dedication, authored by Byrne, that creates an entirely different tone of arch knowingness. Rather than presenting herself as pitiable object, she comments on the norms of print, which demand 'a Dedication ... address'd to a Great Friend' and notes her hope that 'Curiosity will lead the crowd to buy a Poem, written by a Blind girl at the age of eighteen years'.[46]

---

44    Ibid., p. iii.
45    Ibid., p. iii.
46    Ibid., pp. iv–v.

This dedication concludes with a short poem, which draws even more explicit attention to the effects of Byrne's paratextual strategies:

> I'll hold a pound you've pass'd my Preface by,
> Which pray turn back and read—I'll tell you why,
> 'Twill Pity claim where Censure should be giv'n
> And Pity is an Attribute of Heav'n.
> Here then we'll pause by way of Episode,
> (      )
> Well now you've read it, do you think it good?
> For nothing you will say———save only this,
> To screen the Errors of the Poetess;
> —The very Purpose she intends to gain,
> For many think her foolish or insane,
> And if such Hint has met the Reader's Ear,
> The Preface makes the matter plain and clear,
> But you're impatient to go on I find,
> Pray then proceed I wish you a fair Wind.[47]

When she frames the Preface as an attempt to elicit 'Pity' instead of 'Censure' from the reader, Byrne demonstrates her awareness that the identity-based language attached to her persona will shape its reception. Similarly to Wheatley, the persona relies on the existence of an empirical body to pull biographical details and render the persona as a proxy for the author's subjectivity. Byrne's book invites readers into a self-conscious engagement with the persona as constructed by the paratexts surrounding the poem. By first acknowledging that readers have likely skipped the prefatory material, and then appending a poem that instructs them to flip back and read it, Byrne reframes the pitiable tale and request for pecuniary aid as a *literary* strategy that will induce readers to overlook 'the Errors of the Poetess'.

This strategy is further complicated by the text itself. A mock epic, *The Blind Poem* presents itself as self-consciously literary, invoking Jonathan Swift and Alexander Pope to construct a religious argument that sets Byrne's literal blindness against the blindness of those who place value on their observation of the material world over the wisdom of her Catholic religion. At various points in the poem, she takes aim at Deists and Unitarians, who, 'Call *Logicks, Metaphysicks* to their Aid, / Or through the Labyrinth of Reason wade'

---

47    Ibid., p. v.

in a futile attempt to understand God through rational means.[48] As Edward Larrissy notes, blindness in the Romantic period presented a complex set of epistemological problems in response to enlightenment philosophy's emphasis on phenomenology:

> the problem of those born blind is especially urgent for empiricist philosophers such as Locke, who note only show the mature complexity of mental life as built up from early sensory experience, but in doing so have resort primarily, as we have seen, to the sense of sight.[49]

As a result, by the Romantic period blindness and the figure of the blind bard did not emphasise a 'kind of exchange—outer for inner vision' so much as 'an exchange of visual immediacy for the associative and musical power of words'.[50] In Byrne's publication, both possibilities are at play: Byrne characterises the ability to perceive the material world as a barrier to religious truth, or 'inner vision', but the preface's narrative of the priest who discovered Byrne's 'Genius'—and the virtuosic quality of the poem itself—suggests the exchange of sight for an enhanced linguistic facility. Thus, although the paratextual material seems to demand the potential buyer's sympathy and one-sided patronage, the poem itself invokes a logic of exchange: sight for insight, sight for poetic ability, three shillings and threepence for moral and religious instruction. As with Wheatley, while the marketing alone seems to limit the possibility for humanity due to its reliance on a hierarchical power structure, the text within resists this flattening and creates space for the author's voice to complicate their own persona.

Although she is the only author in the dataset to combine youth and blindness, Byrne is not the only author to indicate blindness in the Signed Author field. There are two other titles: 'The Lamentation of Sarah Bursnell, composed by herself, a blind woman' (c.1792), a broadside poem, and *The extraordinary life and Christian experience of Margaret Davidson, (as dictated by herself) Who was a poor, blind woman among the People called Methodists, but rich towards God, and illuminated with the light of life* (1782), a spiritual autobiography supplemented by poetry.[51] The strategies employed in these titles exemplify the

48    Ibid., p. 12.
49    Edward Larrissy, *The Blind and Blindness in Literature of the Romantic Period* (Edinburgh: Edinburgh University Press, 2007) pp. 21.
50    Larrissy, *Blind and Blindness*, pp. 27.
51    Sarah Busnell, 'The lamentation of Sarah Bursnell, composed by herself, a blind woman', *The Women's Print History Project*, title ID 7544 (2019); and Margaret Davidson and Edward Smyth, 'The extraordinary life and Christian experience of Margaret Davidson, (as

tension between blindness as a source of pity and blindness as an opportunity for heightened sensitivity to both language and religion. Like Byrne's, both authors' works are religious in nature and make use of some similar strategies; Bursnell's poem describes how '[a]t the age of twenty-two [she] lost [her] precious sight' and contains an appeal for pecuniary aid, calling upon the reader to '[c]ome buy this book of me'.[52] The preface to Davidson's autobiography describes how her encounter with Methodism led her to '[discover] such a brightness of understanding, and such uncommon fluency of speech, as excited the admiration of all that knew her'.[53] But while Bursnell's poem is a fairly straightforward broadside ballad telling a pitiable tale, Davidson uses many of the same rhetorical flourishes as Byrne. Although Methodist rather than Catholic, the similarities between Byrne and Davidson are striking: the preface to Davidson's work creates a persona where Davidson is 'sprung ... from the lowest dregs of the people', noting that, 'Deprived of sight in her infancy, she had not the least advantage from education'.[54] Byrne's facility with language led her to be instructed in eighteenth-century poetic conventions, while Davidson's provided her with the opportunity to take on her own spiritual authority:

> She was not only taught *the truth as it is in Jesus*, but was enabled also to teach it to others, in so forcible and convincing a manner, that, to my own knowledge, several have been *turned from the error of their ways*, thro' the instrumentality of her fervent prayers, and lively exhortations.[55]

The relative simplicity of Bursnell's self-representation in contrast to the lengthier description of Davidson and Byrne, on both the title page and in the preface, suggest that despite the complex associations with blindness during the Romantic period, the authors and their publishers anticipated that the default response to a blind woman or girl would be pity, and that anything else required more framing.

---

dictated by herself) Who was a poor, blind woman among the People called Methodists, but rich towards God, and illuminated with the light of life. To which are added, some of her letters and hymns. By the Rev. Edward Smyth', *The Women's Print History Project*, title ID 5711 (2019) both accessed 28 Sept. 2021.

52    Sarah Bursnell, *The Lamentation of Sarah Bursnell, composed by herself, a blind woman* (Worcester: James Grundy, *c.*1792), lines 9 and 43.

53    Margaret Davidson, *The extraordinary life and Christian experience of Margaret Davidson, (as dictated by herself) Who was a poor, blind woman among the People called Methodists, but rich towards God, and illuminated with the light of life. To which are added, some of her letters and hymns* (Dublin: Bennett Dugdale, 1782) pp. 2.

54    Ibid., p. 2.

55    Ibid., p. 2. Emphasis in original.

In this context, the description of Byrne on the title page and the accompanying price information—'Price 3s. 3d. or such Greater Price as the Affluent choose to bestow on Poverty'—take on a parodic quality even while they denote a genuine financial need, indicating Byrne's uneasiness with the commodification of self within the book, and especially of her blindness. However, the defensiveness implied by this comic deflection also highlights Byrne's vulnerability beyond the persona: as the daughter of a labouring-class man unable to work because of her disability, Byrne's position is precarious and dependent upon the patronage of the priest who discovered her talent, the lady who urged publication, and the buyers of her book. Unlike the 'young ladies' whose literary efforts are presented in the language of innocence and accomplishment, Byrne's position is more resonant with, though not the same as, what motivates Wheatley's publication; as 'a Girl, born Blind and now in her eighteenth year', her appearance in print a necessity of her social and economic situation. Both Wheatley and Byrne's books evoke novelty in their marketing—Byrne self-consciously and Wheatley through paratext that seems surprised at its author's abilities—but as both authors are writing with subjectivities that differ from the mythical norm in several degrees, novelty is rendered as urgency rather than an appeal to interest or kinship.

The complex interactions of disability, class, and commodified authorship are also visible in Susannah Harrison's *Songs in the Night* (1780).[56] Harrison's *Songs* is a book of hymns that Bridget Keegan describes as 'one of the best-selling collections written by a labouring class poet in the late eighteenth century'.[57] First published anonymously, the title page characterises Harrison as 'a young woman under deep afflictions.' Although Harrison's authorship was revealed via an acrostic poem at the beginning of the second edition, which altered its by-line to 'a young woman under heavy afflictions', her name did not appear on the title page until a 1799 edition printed in Edinburgh, fifteen years after Harrison's death in 1784.[58] The book's persona seems to have used similar techniques to previous examples in that it relied on aspects of the author's biography to render it legible as a proxy for the author's subjectivity. But rather

---

56    The digitised first edition in *Eighteenth-Century Collections Online* contains a frontispiece with a silhouette labelled "Susannah Harrison, Author of Songs in the Night." However, given that Harrison prefaced the second edition with an acrostic poem that identified her by name apparently for the first time, we believe that this frontispiece was likely bound into the book later.

57    Bridget Keegan, 'Mysticisms and Mystifications: The Demands of Laboring-Class Religious Poetry', *Criticism* 47.4 (2005), p. 471.

58    This description was used for all subsequent editions, including American reprints, see 'Harrison, Susannah', *The Women's Print History Project*, person ID 2478 (2019) accessed 20 Aug. 2021.

than a specific disability or status as enslaved, the persona's references to 'deep' or 'heavy' afflictions remain ambiguous. In the preface, the editor John Conder writes,

> Her Father dying when she was young, and leaving a large family unprovided for, she went out to Service at sixteen Years of Age; in which Station she continued till *August,* 1772; when Disorders seized her, which ever since have baffled the Power of Medicine and the Skill of Physicians.[59]

He continues by outlining how Harrison taught herself to read and write, reassuring readers, 'If there should be any Profit arise from the Sale thereof, it will be faithfully applied to the Author's use', a comment that is counterbalanced by his emphasis on how Harrison's wish to publish was not guided by the need for money, but the result of her belief that 'she was actually in dying circumstances'.[60]

Like the deployment of difference for previous authorial personae, in Harrison's book 'affliction' and 'disorder' spur the sympathetic imaginations of readers, who are invited to aid the ailing author. However, unlike other authors whose poems and narratives incorporate biographical details or references, Harrison's poetic strategy matches the one outlined by the editor in the preface when he notes that the poems 'might, under the Blessing of the Most High, be of some Use to others, more especially to the Sons and Daughters of Affliction'.[61] At times, the poems contain oblique references to an illness: the opening poem in the volume contains the line, 'This Year, perhaps, may be my last!'[62] However, despite occasional references such as this to the author's health or sense of her own mortality, the poems themselves remain general religious meditations on topics including evening, fast days, and significant biblical passages. The generality of the poems mirrors the undefined nature of the persona's afflictions, meaning that the reader is not only invited to sympathise with its particular circumstances, but also to potentially identify with the circumstances and emotions described in her poems. While this may seem to suggest that Harrison's book resists commodifying her subject position, the popularity of *Songs in the Night* indicates that it was, in fact, a very successful

---

59    Susannah Harrison, *Songs in the night; by a young woman under deep afflictions* (London: Robert Hawes, Thomas Vallance, and Alexander Hogg: 1780) p. iii.

60    Ibid., pp. iii–iv.

61    Ibid., p. iv.

62    Ibid., p. 8.

commodity. It continued to be reprinted for over forty years, appearing in at least fifteen editions in Britain and America between 1780 and 1823.[63]

*Songs in the Night*'s successful negotiation of concrete, particular circumstances and identity alongside generally applicable poems foregrounds how the commodification of authors in our dataset is not necessarily about representing them as individuals, but about ways of categorising them or making their subjects legible within a defined taxonomy of identity. While Wheatley's youth, race, and status as enslaved, or Byrne, Bursnell, Davidson and Harrison's disabilities stand out as relatively unique features of their identities within the context of eighteenth-century authorship, their title pages capture larger categories as well. Words like 'girl' and 'woman' stand in contrast to 'lady' as implicit indications that these authors belong to more precarious social and economic situations.

The tension between general identity categories and individual lived experience in how Wheatley, Byrne and Harrison are represented on their title pages and in their paratexts is a signifier of their marginalised positions. Unlike the more normative 'ladies' who published in the period, these authors' identities required explanation, often mediated through prefatory material authored by wealthier patrons and mentors. Their non-normative status and the qualifiers used to describe their authorship presented a marketing opportunity, which sought to engage readers' interest and sympathies by framing them as exceptional. While this may have been done for the 'benefit' of the authors, we can see how sexism, ageism, racism, classism, and ableism creep into the marketing of books that commodify marginalised identity as a sales tactic, even though the authors may have received financial or other remunerations in return.

From this study, we conclude that an approach to gendered authorship informed by intersectional theory makes visible that gender is one aspect of a wider commodification of power and marginality, self and other, in dialogue. The close-reading analysis used around 2.5% of the records in our dataset, and from these records alone we can see to the extent to which a class- and gender-based analysis of feminised authorship has been able neither to capture fully the multifaceted ways that the language of feminised identity appears on title pages in this period, nor how it functions as a reflection of power structures in ways independent of yet in conversation with the texts within and the biographical authors. Historical studies have been slower to adopt multi-axis frameworks for analysing gendered authorial production due

63    'Harrison, Susannah', *The Women's Print History Project*, person ID 2478 (2019) accessed 29 Sept. 2021.

to the challenges of even finding basic information about women in the historical record. With the development of digital projects like the *WPHP* that provide more data about how books were marketed, we can nuance our recovery narrative of women's authorship to include more about the interplay between gendered texts and gendered marketing.

Secondly, this analysis emphasises the importance of understanding books as products of businesses and publishers who meaningfully shape how they were received and circulated. Each record in the dataset represents hundreds, if not thousands, of physical books circulating in Europe, North America, and beyond, and author descriptions are not just reflections of cultural beliefs, but a key site of how beliefs about intellectual capabilities and literary production are coded and re-encoded. Marketing language relies on stereotypes to shape how feminised authors appear in print, almost always in a form of supplication, and this reinforces that a performance of distress is a required part of commercial artistic expression if a creator differentiates from the mythical norm. Consuming non-normative identities through the safety of spectatorship and a power hierarchy, similar to what bell hooks calls 'eating the Other', is still present in contemporary publishing.[64] For example, the #OwnVoices movement, which pushes for books representing marginalised groups to be written by authors who belong to those groups, commodifies authorial identity that departs from the 'mythical norm' in ways that are similar to the eighteenth- and nineteenth-century books we have considered in this paper. While this study has focused on the specific ways publishers and authors used author lines to market books, further work is needed to explore the historical conditions that led to this form of marketing and consumption of identity in the eighteenth century. Considering books as products as much as artistic expression allows us to potentially connect these disparate data points.

---

64    bell hooks, 'Eating the Other: Desire and Resistance', *Black Looks: Race and Representation* (Boston: South End Press, 1992), pp. 21–39.

# CHAPTER 25

# Affective Bibliography: Three Queer Approaches to Print

*Malcolm Noble*

Print was, and is, critical to the emergence and functioning of queer cultures. As Christopher Bram put it, '[t]he gay revolution began as a literary revolution'.[1] In this chapter, I argue for the need for queer bibliography, by which I mean new ways of handling and interrogating queer materials queerly from a print historical perspective. I then contextualise this with reference to queer methods, feminist bibliography and the place of affect in queer pedagogy, before presenting three methods for affective bibliography.[2] Whilst much of my attention here is focused on the classroom, it has clear application to research too; in radical pedagogic terms I seek to collapse this division. Certainly, there is clear scope to develop a queer bibliography along similar lines to the feminist and Black liberation bibliographies which are producing urgent, powerful, and radical ways of interpreting print.[3]

---

1    I am grateful to attendees for helpful responses during the conference, and to Benjamin Poore and Sarah Pyke for generous comments on an early draft. The editors, Jessica Farrell-Jobst and Elise Watson gave extremely patient and helpful advice. Christopher Bram, *Eminent Outlaws: The Gay Writers Who Changed America* (New York: Hachette, 2012), p. 1, quoted in David K. Johnson, *Buying Gay: How Physique Entrepreneurs Sparked a Movement* (New York: Columbia University Press, 2019), pp. 56–57.

2    Affect theory describes the nonrepresentational encounters humans have beyond conscious knowing, not empirically seen or felt but that we both enact and experience being enacted upon us. See Gregory J. Seigworth and Melissa Gregg, 'An Inventory of Shimmers', in Gregory J. Seigworth and Melissa Gregg (eds.), *The Affect Theory Reader* (Durham: Duke University Press, 2010), pp. 1–25. Queer affect has proven to be a particularly essential branch of affect studies; most famously see Sarah Ahmed, *Queer Phenomenology: Orientations, Objects, Others* (Durham: Duke University Press, 2006).

3    For example, see Sarah Werner, 'Working Toward a Feminist Printing History', *Printing History*, 27/28 (2020), pp. 11–25, and Kate Ozment, 'Rationale for Feminist Bibliography', *Textual Cultures*, 13 (2020), pp. 149–178. On Black bibliography, see Derrick R. Spires, 'On Liberation Bibliography: The 2021 BSA Annual Meeting Keynote', *The Papers of the Bibliographical Society of America*, 116 (2022), pp. 1–20 <https://doi.org/10.1086/718342>. In addition to a scholarly literature, in 2021, the Rare Book School offered courses on Black bibliography: 'Why Black Bibliography Matters', *Rare Book School* <https://rarebookschool .org/courses/general/why-black-bibliography-matters-6-hours/> (accessed 10 September 2021); 'African American Print Cultures in the Nineteenth-Century United States', *Rare Book*

Just as feminist bibliography seeks to apply feminist theory and methods to bibliography and book history, so queer bibliography approaches material books and texts in queer ways.[4] The relationship between gender and sexuality as social categories means that these queer methods will have broader application including for feminist bibliography and those answering questions of gender and print. The literature on feminist bibliography is considerably more developed, and for me a very clear and direct inspiration, particularly the work of Sarah Werner and Kate Ozment. Queer bibliography has much to offer feminist bibliography. For examples, disrupting normative notions of the book around sexuality serves to complicate understandings of the book as 'a gendered object'.[5] Queering the book as an object makes space for feminist analysis. Destabilising hierarchies and textual data likewise support feminist book projects of recovery such as the work done by Cait Coker and Ozment, amongst others.[6] There is not space here to sketch out fully queer bibliography or its potential to contribute to feminist book history, but the two projects have clearly in common the decentring of straight white cisgendered male perspectives on the book as a material object.

If a definition of queer is a contradiction, I turn to Heather Love to assemble a working one: 'queer studies defines itself as a critical field that questions stable categories of identity', noting that queer and transgender studies have in common 'dissident methodologies'.[7] This seems the diametric opposite of the underpinning logic of bibliographical practice, largely predicated as it is on interrogating material texts to ascribe various fixed categories with technical precision. In this chapter, *queer* is used in several ways: in terms of disruptive kinds of approaches and methods, and of materials relating to or of particular interest to sexual and gender minorities—Love's 'nonnormative desires and sexual practices'.[8] Both of these are explicitly set against the (hetero)sexist, ableist, racist patriarchy as it manifests in traditional bibliography.

*School* <https://rarebookschool.org/courses/history/african-american-print-cultures-in-the-nineteenth-century-united-states/> (accessed 10 September 2021).

4  A nuanced discussion of this is given by Ozment, 'Rationale for Feminist Bibliography', p. 151.

5  Leslie Howsam, 'In My View: Women and Book History', SHARP *News*, 7 (1998), p. 1.

6  Cait Coker and Kate Ozment, 'Building the Women in Book History Bibliography, or Digital Enumerative Bibliography as Preservation of Feminist Labor', *Digital Humanities Quarterly*, 13 (2019); Ozment, 'Rationale for Feminist Bibliography', p. 151.

7  Heather Love, 'Queer', TSQ: *Transgender Studies Quarterly*, 1 (2014), p. 172.

8  Love, 'Queer', p. 172.

1        The Need for Queer Bibliography

Repeatedly, it is print that catalyses the finding of non-normative sexual and gender identities. As Susannah Radstone puts it, '[w]here there is no readily available wider community, or where access to a wider movement is restricted, novels frequently move centre stage, becoming crucial reference points'.[9] Jeffrey Escoffier reflects that 'I read my way through the literature on homosexuality'.[10] Alison Hennegan recounts using 'a pricking of my thumbs, a capacity which led me, unfailingly and time and time again to choose the 'right' book for me, however unlikely its disguise.' This was a process, she explains, of picking up on codes, 'a particular publisher's colophon, in chapter headings, in an author's photograph or coded biographical note, in the identity of a series editor, in the cumulative effect of a writer's previous publications listed in the front'.[11] Amy Gall remembers sitting in her father's closet, reading a 'battered copy of *Letters to Penthouse* ... that made the backs of my knees sweat'.[12] In handling material received thus, the bibliographer needs some kind of heightened sensibility. Eve Kosofsky Sedgwick's foundational work is predicated in part on readings which 'attend to performative aspects of texts ... as sites of definitional creation, violence, and rupture'.[13] As we explore the intensity and significance of the relationship between reader and texts, there is a need to understand every nuance. Just as 'in the vicinity of the closet, even what *counts* as a speech act is problematised on a perfectly routine basis', so too bibliographic features become amplified, taking on heightened importance.[14] It is for this reason that we need queer bibliography: a kind of sensitivity to recover experiences and understand the meaning and function material texts had to and for their readers. Reading in this way has a gendered aspect, whether in regards to non-normative gender identities as part of the queer literary experience, or in the ways in which traditional binaries affect access to and interaction with literature.

9       Susannah Radstone, 'Introduction: Sweet Dreams and the Perverse Imagination', in Susannah Radstone (ed.), *Sweet Dreams: Sexuality, Gender and Popular Fiction* (London: Lawrence & Wishart, 1988), p. 10.

10      Jeffrey Escoffier, *American Homo: Community and Perversity* (London: Verso, 2018), pp. 80, 82, 87.

11      Alison Hennegan, 'On Becoming a Lesbian Reader', in Radstone, *Sweet Dreams*, pp. 166–7.

12      Amy Gall, 'Out There: The Lesbian in Literature', in Elizabeth McNeil et al (eds.), *Mapping Queer Space(s) of Praxis and Pedagogy* (Cham: Springer International Publishing, 2018), p. 127.

13      Eve Kosofsky Sedgwick, *Epistemology of the Closet* (Berkeley: University of California Press, 2008), p. 3.

14      Sedgwick, *Epistemology of the Closet*, p. 3.

There is need for queer bibliography outside the Anglophone Atlantic sphere. Recently, a flurry of scholarly activity on queer culture in late-Soviet Poland has focused on the role of print in building community, fostering political activism, and in providing individuals with information. As the Iron Curtain became increasingly threadbare, translations of works by authors such as Jean Genet and James Baldwin were of great importance to emerging communities, as were local queer publications.[15] Łukasz Szulc argues that two magazines, *Filo* and *Etap*, were of crucial importance: 'the history of the magazines [is] inseparable from the history of homosexual activism in the country'.[16] At about the same time in India, the homophobic onslaught in the media also triggered 'the establishment of queer publications such as *Bombay Dost* by Ashok Row Kavin, in 1990, which ushered [a] queer revolution in queer media, followed quickly by other magazines and ezines'.[17] These discussions have come from media and communications perspectives, leaving much scope for queer bibliography.

For print historians, queer bibliography is necessary for three reasons. First, there is an intellectual imperative for bibliographers and print historians to be able to handle the material before them thoroughly, in order to read all the coding and nuances of what is before them. Such an approach has the potential to enrich deeply book history. Second, there is a moral imperative in terms of the classroom particularly. A 2015 NUS report found that LGBT students were dissatisfied when asked the extent to which LGB or trans* 'experiences and history [are] reflected in my curriculum'.[18] The challenge presented by this report is to address not only the content of our curricula but also pedagogy. Queer pedagogies can help, especially around ideas of refiguring classroom spaces as places in which questioning is encouraged.[19] The interrogation of objects

15    On permeability and translated texts, see Tomasz Basiuk, 'One's Younger Self in Personal Testimony and Literary Translation', in Jędrzej Burszta and Tomasz Basiuk (eds.), *Queers in State Socialism: Cruising 1970s Poland* (London: Routledge, 2021), pp. 23–5; on local queer print see Błażej Warkocki, '"Transgression Has Become a Fact": A Gothic Genealogy of Queerness in the People's Republic of Poland', in Burszta and Basiuk, *Queers in State Socialism*, pp. 33–44.

16    Łukasz Szulc, *Transnational Homosexuals in Communist Poland: Cross-Border Flows in Gay and Lesbian Magazines* (Cham: Palgrave Macmillan, 2018), p. 11.

17    Rohit K. Dasgupta, 'Online Romeos and Gay-Dia: Exploring Queer Spaces in Digital India', in McNeil, *Queer Space(s) of Praxis and Pedagogy*, p. 187.

18    NUS, *Education Beyond the Straight and Narrow—LGBT Students' Experiences in Higher Education* (London: NUS, 2015), p. 37. The results presented were complex, but on a scale of 1–10, no group exceeded 4.8/10 in satisfaction.

19    María Laura Gutiérrez, 'The Pedagogy of/in Images. Notes on Lesbian Desire and Knowing How to Fuck', in Moira Pérez and Gracia Trujillo-Barbadillo (eds.), *Queer Epistemologies*

sits at the centre of what I am proposing. Third, it serves to add complexity to the understandings of gender in relation to print—to the way in which print and print work was and is gendered, and the role of gender in print. In short, queer bibliography has much to contribute: of being able to read these physical objects bibliographically, with care, and with nuance.

## 2      Queer Methods

An emerging body of literature considers queer methods by finding methods that align with queer theory, including (auto)ethnography and other social-scientific methods.[20] A useful starting point to contemplate queer methods comes from Amin Ghaziani and Matt Brim's challenging of categories, imploring readers to: 'reject unchanging categories'; 'reject impermeable categories' and 'reject dualisms'.[21] Ghaziani and Brim are not necessarily writing about descriptive bibliography, although their critique of current epistemological practices, based on unchanging and impermeable categories is something which applies to many bibliographic methods. Questions such as: 'what kind of binding?', 'what kind of paper?' are fundamental to traditional bibliography. Kate Ozment argues bibliography followed contemporary preoccupations during the emergence of the field so that '[t]his narrowed identity creates a discourse where standards are universally applied that in reality are neither prepared nor equipped to analy[s]e the experiences of historical subjects, books, and texts that fall outside a distinct set of parameters'.[22] In other words, the preoccupations of much traditional book history reflect those of rich, white, Victorian, straight men. Undoing and destabilising categories and

_in Education: Luso-Hispanic Dialogues and Shared Horizons_ (London: Palgrave Macmillan, 2020), p. 86; Kat Rands, Jess McDonald, and Lauren Clapp, 'Landscaping Classrooms toward Queer Utopias', in Angela Jones (ed.), _A Critical Inquiry into Queer Utopias_ (New York: Palgrave Macmillan, 2013), pp. 150, 153.

20    Kath Browne and Catherine J. Nash, 'Queer Methods and Methodologies: An Introduction', in Kath Browne and Catherine J. Nash (eds.), _Queer Methods and Methodologies: Intersecting Queer Theories and Social Science Research_ (London: Routledge, 2016), p. 1; Heather Love, '"How the Other Half Thinks": An Introduction to the Volume', in Amin Ghaziani and Matt Brim (eds.), _Imagining Queer Methods_ (New York: New York University Press, 2019), p. 29. See also discussions in other essays in these collections.

21    Amin Ghaziani and Matt Brim, 'Queer Methods: Four Provocations for an Emerging Field', in Ghaziani and Brim, _Imagining Queer Methods_, pp. 8–13; I set aside the fourth element of rejecting interest group politics for the purposes of this discussion.

22    Ozment, 'Rationale for feminist bibliography', p. 150.

classification are a core concern of many queer approaches, given that queer itself does not 'adhere to stable classificatory systems'.[23]

The failure of conventional classifications to accommodate queer print material is highlighted by two quite different works. Melissa Adler has unpicked the epistemological operations of the Library of Congress catalogue, and the challenges of working with such a system, which obscures through the use of medical and scientific categories and languages, resulting in a kind of 'biblio-cide' as material is unfindable. Beyond the catalogue and on the shelves, the fundamental issue is that print 'cannot be in more than once place at once'.[24] Berhard Cella and Orlando Pesatore's *Queer Publishing: a family tree* presents a useful example of queer methodology for print material, predicated on play-fulness with the term family tree, as it 'makes no claims to being complete or to presenting a canon or an essential queer library'. By considering two Viennese collections, they trace 'the creation of identities and images relat-ing to queer lifestyles' in the very broadest terms, the only criterion for inclu-sion being 'the medium of publishing—regardless of print runs and channels of distribution'.[25] The family tree, perhaps the most heteronormative form of knowledge, is deliberately usurped here, as the *verboten* and the explicit are placed alongside mainstream materials, assembled in groups, but not hierar-chies or lineages in any conventional sense. The end result is, of course, all the more useful for this approach.

As queer studies emerged, so too did critiques around whether their empiri-cal grounding was sufficient. Lisa Duggan's seminal 1995 essay suggested queer studies have led to the 'progressive impoverishment of the empirical, historical grounding for textual analyses', due to concentration of what was then 'les-bian/gay studies' in 'fields devoted to textual analysis—primarily literary and media studies based in the twentieth century'. This led to a call for historians to engage with queer theory and ground and challenge it historically.[26] Duggan also suggests that '[q]ueer studies must recognize the importance of empiri-cally grounded work in history, anthropology and social and political theory'.[27] These questions have not been entirely resolved and Rachel Corbman, in her

23    Ghaziani and Brim, 'Queer Methods', pp. 3–5.

24    Melissa Adler, *Cruising the Library: Perversities in the Organization of Knowledge* (New York: Fordham University Press, 2017), pp. 36–37, 49, 110, 124.

25    Berhard Cella and Orlando Pescatore, *Queer Publishing: A Family Tree* (Vienna: Salon für Kunstbuch, 2019), unpaginated.

26    Lisa Duggan, 'The Discipline Problem: Queer Theory Meets Lesbian and Gay History', *GLQ: A Journal of Lesbian and Gay Studies*, 2 (1995), pp. 179–91 reprinted in *Sex Wars* (London: Routledge, 2006), p. 187; see also discussion in Love, 'How the Other Half Thinks', p. 31.

27    Duggan, 'Discipline Problem', p. 195.

reconsideration of Duggan's essay '[d]oes queer studies have an anti-empirical problem?', even encourages the consideration made by fields other than queer theory alone to the development of queer studies.[28] This does, however, point to a space in which queer bibliography could make a contribution, with relevance to textual studies, but which offers methods which are at once empirical and queer.

## 3       Feminist Bibliography

Sarah Werner's response to the challenge of doing book history and bibliography in a way that achieves feminist praxis is to address this starting in the classroom. Accessibility is the explicit motivation for her 2019 *Studying Early Printed Books*, her '"baby Gaskell"', a beginner's level exploration of how the handpress worked and why bibliographic knowledge is a useful tool for understanding book history'.[29] Gaskell's text, one of the standard works on the handpress is not easy for many students, even at the postgraduate level, or rather, it requires considerable effort before it will yield the richness of the bibliographical approach. Typically presented as 'the classic manual on bibliography'.[30] In contrast, Werner's book is subtitled 'a practical guide', and is deliberately written for the broadest range of students, and I have been happy to recommend it on reading lists as the initial text for students, with Gaskell for more detailed reference.[31] Werner's classroom praxis is inspiring and replicable:

> We can shift from modeling expertise as bibliographers to modeling questioning, and in so doing, we can bring in newcomers to our work and expand the types of work that bibliography does. For me, one of the key elements of being a feminist is ensuring everyone has access and the tools needed to succeed.[32]

28      Rachel Corbman, 'Does Queer Studies Have an Anti-Empiricism Problem?', GLQ: A Journal of Lesbian and Gay Studies, 25 (2019), pp. 57–62.

29      Werner, 'Working Toward a Feminist Printing History', p. 11.

30      Philip Gaskell, *New Introduction to Bibliography: The Classic Manual of Bibliography* (New Castle: Oak Knoll Press, 2002).

31      Sarah Werner, *Studying Early Printed Books, 1450–1800: A Practical Guide* (Hoboken: Wiley, 2019).

32      Sarah Werner, 'Notes on Feminist Bibliography', *Wynken de Worde*, 2020 <https://sarahwerner.net/blog/2020/03/notes-on-feminist-bibliography/> (accessed 17 May 2021).

The idea of asking questions, of democratising access to knowledge, and indeed challenging what counts as knowledge, resonates profoundly from an adult education perspective. This corresponds, too, to what David M. Halperin identifies as the original motivation of queer theory: 'an impulse to transform what could count as knowledge, as well as by a determination to transform the practices by knowledge functioned within the institution of the university'.[33] I build on Werner's thought for my development of a queer approach to bibliography, by encouraging questioning, devalorising rigid categories, and embracing a more emotional response.

## 4    Affect and Pedagogy

The Affective Turn has come to be of considerable importance to queer theory and, increasingly, queer pedagogy.[34] There is clear scope to apply this to print material. The kind of affective pedagogic capacity that Anna Hickey-Moody argues art can have is 'the aptitude to change a body's limits. Art can re-adjust what a person is or is not able to feel, understand, produce and connect'.[35] Maggie MacLure seeks 'research practices that would be capable of engaging the materiality of language itself—its material force and its entanglements in bodies and matter'.[36] For Kathleen Stewart, affects 'don't lend themselves to a perfect, three-tiered parallelism between analytic subject, concept, and world'.[37] Much of the literature offers much more heavily theoretical positions than I take here, and for the purposes of this chapter a broad view of affect is taken, as occupying the space between sensation, feel, and the cognitive process of this into emotions.[38] Kadji Amin goes as far as to suggest that queer is

---

33    David M. Halperin, 'The Normalization of Queer Theory', *Journal of Homosexuality*, 45 (2003), pp. 339–43.

34    See for example the considerable range of studies cited by Alyssa D. Niccolini, 'Affect', in Nelson M. Rodriguez etc (eds.), *Critical Concepts in Queer Studies and Education* (New York: Palgrave Macmillan, 2016), pp. 5–6).

35    Anna Hickey Moody, 'Affect as Method: Feelings, Aesthetics and Affective Pedagogy', in Rebecca Coleman and Jessica Ringrose (eds.), *Deleuze and Research Methodologies* (Edinburgh: Edinburgh University Press, 2013), p. 88.

36    Maggie MacLure, 'Researching without Representation? Language and Materiality in Post-Qualitative Methodology', *International Journal of Qualitative Studies in Education*, 26 (2013), p. 658.

37    Kathleen Stewart, *Ordinary Affects* (Durham, NC: Duke University Press, 2007), p. 4.

38    A useful summary of theoretical positions on affect can be found in Karen Simecek, 'Affect Theory', *The Year's Work in Critical and Cultural Theory*, 28 (2020), pp. 414–433. See also, Claire Armon-Jones, *Varieties of Affect* (New York: Harvester Wheatsheaf, 1991); Ruth

also affective, '[t]he method that orients what may be felicitously named *queer* is, I propose, fundamentally *affective*: it is a matter of sensing some resonance between one's object of study and the inchoate cluster of feelings that inhabit and animate the term *queer*.'[39]

Whilst considering the role of erotic noir in informal sex education in a high school in the United States, Alyssa Niccolini unpacks a moment when a student is caught reading *Purple Panties*, 'a collection of lesbian erotica', during a class. Niccolini explores the complex set of affects—the 'entanglements of pleasure, excitement, arousal, disgust, shame and even wild eruptions of laughter'—which arise from this and their pedagogic implications.[40] Whilst writing from an educational perspective, Niccolini offers grist to the bibliographic mill, in the questions she poses: '[h]ow might attention to the excitability and unpredictability inherent when 'bodies' interact, such as the contact between students and teachers and academic and erotic/a texts, offer new lines of inquiry for research in sexualities education?'[41] Print is by nature affective, and if our reading of it is affective, so should our bibliography be; it offers a particular serendipity in terms of queer material.

## 5 Three Approaches to Affective Bibliography

*This is no book,*
*Who touches this, touches a man,*
*(Is it night? Are we here alone?)*
*It is I you hold, and who holds you,*
*I spring from the pages into your arms—decease calls me forth.*
　　　WALT WHITMAN, 'So Long!', *Leaves of Grass*

I want to outline a more fluid, messy, emotional approach to bibliography. This is not suitable only for queer material, but it is an approach that is

　　　Leys, *The Ascent of Affect: Genealogy and Critique* (Chicago: The University of Chicago Press, 2017).
39　Kadji Amin, 'Haunted by the 1990s: Queer Theory's Affective Histories', in Ghaziani and Brim (eds.), *Imagining Queer Methods* (New York: New York University Press, 2019), p. 277.
40　Alyssa D. Niccolini, 'Straight Talk and Thick Desire in Erotica Noir: Reworking the Textures of Sex Education in and out of the Classroom', *Sex Education*, 13, supplement 1 (2013), p. S8.
41　Niccolini, 'Straight Talk and Thick Desire', p. S12.

fundamentally queer. I present three approaches to what I am calling affective bibliography, each centred on a present participle: handling, bounding, and reading.

## 6      Answering Walt Whitman: Handling Books

Firstly, we might turn towards print objects and offer more emotional and more generous, speculative description, focused on touch. It seems absurd to suggest a more object-oriented approach to bibliography, given this is ostensibly what the thing is. However, it is worth reflecting. Bibliography is a tactile art, and we should place an emphasis on *handling*: by holding and looking, we make knowledge, and as such, anywhere that print material is handled is an epistemological site. In classrooms we can conduct an enquiry together as students ask questions and respond to objects. Print is generally, if not always, literally *handled*; there is a manual quality to the bibliographer's work. Yet, students in a special collections room are unlikely to be encouraged to touch. This situation has been further exacerbated by the Covid-19 pandemic, which has seen much access being restricted to digital surrogates, raising serious questions about the resulting epistemological consequences. Whilst the convenience of remote access to texts may well be preferable to non-bibliographers, it seriously constrains the student of books as material objects. Outside the rare book room, there is plenty of scope for inexpensive and easily replaceable books to handled roughly. Handling in this rarefied atmosphere seems to encourage a hyper-awareness of the danger of even the gentlest touch of hands as they manipulate paper or vellum. These moments can be remarkably intimate and tender—we might well hold our breath as we gently turn a page.

When Walter Benjamin unpacks his library, his talk is about touch: '[a]s he holds them in his hands, he seems to be seeing through them into their distant past as though inspired': in the hands of an old collector 'the acquisition of an old book is its rebirth'.[42] The kind of touch Walt Whitman suggested enables a connection between authors and readers. His parenthetical questions '(Is it night? Are we here alone?)' remind us that where and when a text is read matters. It seems a reasonable assertion that queer texts are more likely to have been read privately rather than on a commuter train. The plurality of selves with Whitman is underscored by these questions, as the dialogue with a book and its author highlight the complexity of being alone with a book.

---

42    Walter Benjamin, 'Unpacking My Library: A Talk about Book Collecting', in Hannah Arendt (ed.), *Illuminations*, trans. by Harry Zorn (London: Bodley Head, 2015), p. 62.

To focus on touch, it helps to close your eyes. Ian Gadd suggests blindfolding a student volunteer and inviting comment on a contemporary book.[43] However, accumulate a class set of airline masks if you can—befriend a frequent flyer if necessary. Perhaps present each student with a harlequin romance, or a book from a selection of any which are to hand. Students will immediately grasp the richness of approaching books without (necessarily) reading the words on the pages. The sheer richness of what can be garnered through touch is extraordinary. They might guess if it is poetry, cookery, or a novel; so the group will literally grasp the potential of bibliography and book history.

Books are designed to be touched, to be 'manipulated with fingers', argues Gillian Silverman, and like '[a]ll touched objects, function briefly as prosthetics'.[44] Beyond mere touch, we might consider texture in the way Eve Kosofsky Sedgwick does, after Renu Bora: 'other senses beyond the visual and haptic are involved in the perception of texture, as when we hear the brush-brush of corduroy trousers or the crunch of extra-crispy chicken'.[45] Moreover, we might hear different types of paper, binding, as books are touched, handled, read. This announces if the paper is cheap, or expensive; if it is high enough glossy quality to carry colour, or if it is mundane office printing paper folded in half to make an inexpensive zine. Does the spine squeak to announce the book's newness, or silently submit to lying open from repeated use? Might it possibly even crack, inducing a nervous tension in special collections? This all requires manipulation, and for this kind of teaching, we need books which can be handled quite roughly.

## 7       Leaky and Absorbent: Bounding Books

An affective bibliography also raises the question of where and how we bound books—not in the sense of protective bindings, but in the sense of defining its physical extent: what properly counts as part of any given book? Textual and literary approaches can help us determine where a book physically begins. Stephanie Ann Frampton, reflecting on George Poulet, suggests that 'the book

43      Ian Gadd, 'From Printing Type to Blackboard™: Teaching the History of the Early Modern Book to Literary Undergraduates in a "New" UK University', in Ann R. Hawkins (ed.), *Teaching Bibliography, Textual Criticism, and Book History* (London: Pickering & Chatto, 2006), p. 65.

44      Gillian Silverman, 'Touch', in Matthew Rubery and Leah Price (eds.), *Further Reading* (Oxford: Oxford University Press, 2020), p. 191.

45      Eve Kosofsky Sedgwick, *Touching Feeling: Affect, Pedagogy, Performativity* (Durham: Duke University Press, 2003), p. 15.

is always an unfinished object ... until it finds a reader'.[46] In a way Gérard Genette's pivotal work on paratexts offers a literary approach expanding books to include what Jeremy Smith summarises as 'mediating phenomena'.[47] Genette's French title was *Seuils* (thresholds).[48] Just as these questions were posed of a text, we might ask too where the threshold of a book lies.

Just as Genette looked around texts, we might take a broader view of books or other printed matter. In a sense, books are 'leaky' and 'absorbent'. Where, exactly, is a printed text bounded? They can shed their clothing—dust jackets are often discarded; what about promotional stickers 'signed by the author' or '£5 off'? library labels? book-marks? book-plates? marginalia? train tickets? boarding passes whose thermal print is all but faded? request slips? stray hairs? inscriptions—by the author, by the owner, by the gift-giver, by the annotating reader? what about foxing?[49] These are things invaluable for all sorts of bibliography and provenance research, but the more we compile this list, the more it seems that the bounding of the book is blurred, as it becomes less clear where and when a readers' fingers actually start touching a book. When readers touch early printed books rebound in the nineteenth century, the bibliographer concerned with bindings might not even engage with any part of the original book. Therefore, Whitman's suggestion that his readers are not touching a book is further complicated.

Jhumpa Lahiri's essay on her relationship with book-covers as an author offers a view which is both bibliographical and emotional. For authors, '[a] cover only appears when the book is finished'. For her, there is a conflict between the joy of completion and 'a disconnect, a disequilibrium'. It is at once 'superficial' but also 'essential, vital'.[50] This serves to break down the idea that there was a single date when a book began to be, even if there were only ever one printing of one state. If these are jackets rather than covers, then it becomes clothing which can be shed by readers or by institutions. Jackets are arguably the least-stable aspect of a book in certain ways: they may be removed to fit more works on the shelf, for ease of operation in a lending library, or

---

46   Stephanie Ann Frampton, 'In the Library', in Alexandra Gillespie and Deidre Lynch (eds.), *The Unfinished Book* (Oxford: Oxford University Press, 2021), p. 219.

47   Jeremy J. Smith, 'Foreword', in Hannah C. Tweed and Diane G. Scott (eds.), *Medical Paratexts from Medieval to Modern: Dissecting the Page* (Cham: Palgrave Macmillan, 2019), p. v.

48   Gérard Genette, *Paratexts: Thresholds of Interpretation* trans. by Jane E. Lewin (Cambridge: Cambridge University Press, 1997), p. 2.

49   On foxing, see Joshua Calhoun, 'Book Microbiomes', in Alexandra Gillespie and Deidre Lynch (eds.), *The Unfinished Book* (Oxford: Oxford University Press, 2021), pp. 460–73.

50   Jhumpa Lahiri, *The Clothing of Books* (London: Bloomsbury, 2017), pp. 13, 16, 18.

because they become worn over time. Readers might discard for aesthetic reasons or preferences, or deploy prophylactic coverings to preserve covers. As Gill Partington puts it '[i]t is stamped with the book's title and in that sense belongs to it, yet it remains a separate and separable entity'. As such, it is perhaps unsurprising that they have been relatively neglected by bibliographers. Through this lens, 'the jacket begins to operate less like a paratext and more as what Jacques Derrida calls a "supplement" which "adds in order to replace"'.[51] The protective and marketing roles of jackets rendered them ephemeral for some readers and collectors. In summary, jackets and covers serve to confuse the bounding of books.

All these affective elements must be interpreted together. Genette considered paratexts cumulatively, that they must be understood in combination: '[t]he paratext, then, is empirically made up of a heterogeneous group of practices and discourses of all kinds and dating from all periods which I federate under the term 'paratext' in the name of a common interest, or a convergence of effects'.[52] In this sense the affective responses must be considered together as well as individually. The complexity, instability, and particularity of any copy is stressed. Not only is a text unfinished, but an affective approach admits of ambiguity as to where the physical object actually finishes. One way to tackle this in a classroom would be to encourage students to narrate their own responses, in writing or audio or aloud. At the same time, we all might acknowledge, the pleasure and thrill of this labour.[53] In a sense, the task is to answer back Whitman, to acknowledge in whose hands the text is handled, where, and when.

## 8      New Old Readings

The third dimension of affective bibliography I offer here encourages the development of different practises of reading. Sometimes these might be particular to a certain perspective or format of print. In a sense, the discussion of readings is more textual, but there is a physical element to this too. Hennegan, as a young lesbian reader, filtered out the bits she did not want in a text:

---

51    Gill Partington, 'Dust Jackets', in Adam Smyth and Dennis Duncan (ed.), *Book Parts* (Oxford: Oxford University Press, 2019), pp. 13, 21–22.

52    Genette, *Paratexts*, p. 2 n3.

53    It hardly seems necessary to offer a justification for the pleasure of bibliography, but the discussion in G. Gabrielle Starr and Amy M. Belfi, 'Pleasure', in Rubery and Price, *Further Reading*, pp. 282–92 offers this, whilst focused on reading including the aesthetic pleasures associated with it.

'I had to find a way of reading *round* those elements I rejected whilst discovering a means of reading my way *to* the ones I needed', 'reading in a way which forced character, theme and plot to yield every last scrap of knowledge and perception'.[54] These relate to accommodations made to the text by both those producing material to enable them to enter (relatively) mainstream marketplaces, but also the way readers learned to parse material, so destabilising the book further.

In order to evade censors, gay and lesbian pulp fiction in the 1960s would see homosexual characters meet unpleasant endings: death, redemption by heterosexual marriage. Stephanie Foote argues readers would 'stop reading before the last chapter in order to avoid the undesirable ending'.[55] The books take on a different physical shape in the hands of queer readers, as they become used to ignoring the last portion; perhaps not unlike the majority of readers ignoring the endnotes or bibliography at the back of non-fiction title. These books could be judged by their covers, as visual clues gave away the contents. Pamela Roberston Wojcik explains how:

> titillating garish paperback covers with men in tight T-shirts exchanging lurid glances, women in lingerie posing provocatively in duos, or three people in queerly triangulated relationships, set in various seedy locales—prisons, bars, and cheap apartments—with adjectives like 'twilight,' 'strange,' 'odd,' 'forbidden,' 'unnatural,' 'bizarre,' 'tormented,' and 'secret,' [serve] to describe the characters and actions within.[56]

'Pulp' did not originally demarcate genre, rather production: 'smaller pages and with smaller type, thus permitting them to circulate more easily as pocket books and through mail-order catalogues', facilitating material production, distribution, and consumption, outside the mainstream US booktrade.[57] James Gifford offers advice to contemporary readers considering reading gay pulp:

---

54   Hennegan, 'On Becoming a Lesbian Reader', p. 169.

55   Referenced in Drewey Wayne Gunn and Jaime Harker, 'Introduction', in Drewey Wayne Gunn and Jaime Harker (eds.), *1960s Gay Pulp Fiction: The Misplaced Heritage* (Amherst: University of Massachusetts Press, 2013), p. 19; Stephanie Foote, 'Deviant Classics: Pulps and the Making of Lesbian Print Culture', *Signs*, 31, 1 (2005), pp. 169–90; see also, on an earlier context, Javier Samper Vendrell, *The Seduction of Youth: Print Culture and Homosexual Rights in the Weimar Republic* (Toronto: University of Toronto Press, 2020), p. 71.

56   Pamela Robertson Wojcik, '"Menus for Men ... or What Have You": Consuming Gay Male Culture in Lou Rand Hogan's "The Gay Detective" and "The Gay Cookbook"', in Gunn and Harker, *1960s Gay Pulp Fiction*, p. 120.

57   Wojcik, '"Menus for Men ... or What have You"', p. 121.

approaching with an open mind, understand it as a product of its time which may speak to modern readers still, that they might 'command a hefty price', and perhaps most excitingly, 'enjoy the freedom that this pulp represents and sends down the decades to you'.[58] There is a moment for connexion with these previous readers. The survival, the freedom, and the cost, all relate to the production, circulation, and consumption of this material. We can feel this, as pages crumble because they are acidic and cheap and were never intended to have long lives ahead of them. Indeed, as Drewey Wayne Gunn and Jaime Harker note, for these as for other queer material their very survival is against the odds—'save for the bravest or those in like-minded city neighbourhoods, they hid [queer pulp] away or destroyed them'.[59] Material that has survived in this particular way is worthy of respect, but an acknowledgment of this should feed into affective bibliography.

Reading strategies may offer the intersectional approaches which are urgently needed.[60] Matt Brim's pedagogic approach uses John Keene's *Counternarratives* (2015) so 'addressing the systemic failure to teach [B]lack queer reading practices'. This is a literary approach predicated on bibliography, as bibliographic and paratextual features are combined to challenge students. Titles and sub-titles are arranged in ways which defamiliarise and force students to interpret differently: 'longer titles stretched wide across the top of the page, the table of contents forms the shape of a cross', so the *mise-en-page* must explicitly form part of their reading. Typography and even maps, which are reproduced too small to read, disorienting readers and serving as 'tools of defamiliarization'. As a result of which 'it is necessary to grapple with the context of that disorientation and its pedagogical implications'.[61]

From this disorientation, a wide range of questions are raised with students, including:

> How do I read this book? What kind of book is this? What have I been reading? *How* have I been reading it? What does it mean to read as I have been reading? And what explains the informed illiteracy—or the ignorances created by dominant knowledge practices—at the intersection of

---

58      James J. Gifford, 'Proem: How to Read Gay Pulp Fiction', in Gunn and Harker, *1960s Gay Pulp Fiction*, p. 41.

59      Gunn and Harker, 'Introduction', p. 7.

60      On the urgent need for this, see Roderick A. Ferguson, *One-Dimensional Queer* (Medford: Polity, 2019).

61      Matt Brim, '*Counternarratives*: A Black Queer Reader', in Ghaziani and Brim, *Imagining Queer Methods*, pp. 144, 146–7.

[B]lack queer human that makes a [B]lack queer reader necessary in the first place?[62]

The book thus becomes a tool against orientation. It becomes a queer object of disorientation in the way that Sara Ahmed posits: '[w]hen we experience disorientation, we might notice orientation as something we do not have', and so ask '[w]hat does it mean to be orientated?'[63] In the classroom we can use print objects to disorientate, orientate, and in turn, interrogate why they tell us what they tell us, and how they make us feel.

## 9      Conclusion

Thus far, bibliography has largely failed to develop useful strategies for handling queer materials or handling materials queerly. In this short chapter, I have offered some tentative arguments for queer ways for handling print material in order to understand the meaning of queer print to queer readers. I have also offered three methods which focus on books in hands, to consider: the emotional nature and labour of handling print, the difficulty of bounding books, and the contingent ways in which we read books—historically, socially, geographically, and otherwise. In this chapter I have assembled some queer bibliographic methods to offer affective ways attuned to the needs of queer materials and of queer readers. But affective methods have broader implications beyond questions of non-normative sexuality and gender. Questions such as 'how are we orientated to, and disorientated by, print materials?', apply to all aspects of print history. Affective responses to print material have clear implications for gender, given that the book itself is 'a gendered object', and reading is often a gendered activity.[64] My emphasis here may have been on queer cadences, resonances, and nuances, but all readers have some kind of emotional response to what is placed in their hands. For example, David McKitterick's discussion of the cutting up of devotional images, of how to understand early printing as 'only a partial mechanisation of manuscript practice', and the ambiguity, complexity and instability of early print seems to lend itself to these kinds of methods.[65] Fundamentally, bibliographers ought

---

62    Brim, '*Counternarratives*: A Black Queer Reader', p. 150.
63    Sara Ahmed, *Queer Phenomenology: Orientations, Objects, Others* (Durham, NC: Duke University Press, 2006), pp. 5–6.
64    Howsam, 'In My View: Women and Book History', p. 1.
65    David McKitterick, *Print, Manuscript and the Search for Order: 1450–1830* (Cambridge: Cambridge University Press, 2003), *passim*, but especially pp. 57–8, 63, 87, 97, 100, 215–6.

to attempt to recover these emotional experiences to really understand how print was received and what it meant to readers.

What we must do, in part, is take up Roger Chartier's task of 'identify[ing] the specific mechanisms that distinguish the various communities of readers and traditions of reading'.[66] Bibliography has much potential to those studying queer print culture. In many ways, the major imperatives of book history remain unchanged. Robert Darnton's communications circuits and simple questions: '[h]ow do books come into being? [h]ow do they reach readers? [w]hat do readers make of them?', sit at the heart of queer bibliography, but given that much queer material circulates outside mainstream channels, the answers to these questions may well prove to be outside the capacity of traditional bibliographic practices.[67] Feminist and Black liberational bibliographers offer work which can serve as mirror and model for a queer bibliography. Given the crucial role for print in mediating queer culture and identities, the need for a queer bibliography is clear, and is an urgent task for those working on queer print.

Queering bibliographic methods has important ramifications for those concerned with print and gender. The normative frameworks in which the book and bookwork are gendered are related to those which define and regulate sexuality; exploring the relationship between print and sexuality serves to improve our understanding of gender and the book. I have not discussed at all the importance of print to trans culture, but this is of undoubted importance, and has had some scholarly attention.[68] Few would deny the liberatory power of books and print—it is the implicit assumption underpinning bibliography, book history, and textual analysis. We can increasingly talk of transformative bibliography. When placed alongside Black and feminist bibliographic methods, practices, and traditions, queer bibliography can help make visible the material meanings of text against normative structures, with crucial implications not least for gender. Undoubtedly, these transformative approaches to bibliography will be at their most powerful when mustered intersectionally.

---

66    Cited in Katherine Acheson, 'Visual Form and Reading Communities: The Example of Early Modern Broadside Elegies', in Mary Hammond (ed.), *The Edinburgh History of Reading: Early Readers* (Edinburgh: Edinburgh University Press, 2020), p. 156.

67    Robert Darnton, '"What is the History of Books?" Revisited', *Modern Intellectual History*, 4, 3 (2007), p.495.

68    For example, see: Lisa Z. Sigel, 'Trans Culture and the Circulation of Ideas', in *The Edinburgh History of Reading: Subversive Readers* (Edinburgh: Edinburgh University Press, 2020), pp. 184–206.

# Index